GLOBAL ISSUES

CQ Press, an imprint of SAGE, is the leading publisher of books, periodicals, and electronic products on American government and international affairs. CQ Press consistently ranks among the top commercial publishers in terms of quality, as evidenced by the numerous awards its products have won over the years. CQ Press owes its existence to Nelson Poynter, former publisher of the *St. Petersburg Times,* and his wife Henrietta, with whom he founded Congressional Quarterly in 1945. Poynter established CQ with the mission of promoting democracy through education and in 1975 founded the Modern Media Institute, renamed The Poynter Institute for Media Studies after his death. The Poynter Institute (*www.poynter.org*) is a nonprofit organization dedicated to training journalists and media leaders.

In 2008, CQ Press was acquired by SAGE, a leading international publisher of journals, books, and electronic media for academic, educational, and professional markets. Since 1965, SAGE has helped inform and educate a global community of scholars, practitioners, researchers, and students spanning a wide range of subject areas, including business, humanities, social sciences, and science, technology, and medicine. A privately owned corporation, SAGE has offices in Los Angeles, London, New Delhi, Singapore, and Melbourne, in addition to the Washington DC office of CQ Press.

GLOBAL ISSUES

SELECTIONS FROM CQ RESEARCHER

2016 EDITION

FOR INFORMATION:

CQ Press

An Imprint of SAGE Publications, Inc.

2455 Teller Road

Thousand Oaks, California 91320

E-mail: order@sagepub.com

SAGE Publications Ltd.

1 Oliver's Yard

55 City Road

London EC1Y 1SP

United Kingdom

SAGE Publications India Pvt. Ltd.

B 1/I 1 Mohan Cooperative Industrial Area

Mathura Road, New Delhi 110 044

India

SAGE Publications Asia-Pacific Pte. Ltd.

3 Church Street

#10-04 Samsung Hub

Singapore 049483

Printed in the United States of America

ISBN 978-1-5063-4362-4

Acquisitions Editor: Michael Kerns

Editorial Assistant: Zachary Hoskins

Production Editor: Kelly DeRosa

Typesetter: C&M Digitals (P) Ltd.

Proofreader: Laura Webb

Cover Designer: Michael Dubowe

Marketing Manager: Amy Whitaker

16 17 18 19 20 10 9 8 7 6 5 4 3 2 1

Contents

Annotated Contents

CONFLICT, SECURITY, AND TERRORISM
Central American Gangs

Young people fleeing Central America's so-called Northern Triangle countries—El Salvador, Guatemala, and Honduras—for the United States tell of life made unliveable by violent street gangs, stratospheric homicide rates, extortion threats and official corruption. The violence has washed over into the United States, where Barrio-18 and MS-13—rival gangs with roots in both Southern California and Central America—have committed murder and mayhem in Los Angeles and other American cities. Though Central American civil wars and state-sponsored death squads were major news in the 1980s and '90s, most Americans only became aware of the present crisis in 2014, when tens of thousands of young migrants—many of them children traveling alone—poured over the U.S. border, seeking asylum. The Obama administration is funding a preventive strategy aimed at curbing gang violence in Central America, a contrast to the enforcement-heavy "Iron Fist" approach used in the region, now widely questioned. Critics are skeptical about the new U.S. strategy, and few experts expect the crisis to ease anytime soon.

European Migration Crisis

Members of the European Union (EU) are feeling besieged by a rising tide of refugees fleeing conflict and migrants seeking economic opportunity. Many of the refugees, who are mainly from the Middle East, are crossing the Mediterranean on overloaded boats or traveling via treacherous land routes, often victimized by unscrupulous human traffickers. National leaders disagree on what to do, other than fortify Europe's borders. Refugee organizations say strengthened borders will just push migrants, who have been dying by the thousands, to try even more dangerous routes. Similar criticism has been aimed at the EU's decision to send navies to destroy smugglers' boats and at NATO's launch of naval patrols to intercept migrants trying to reach Greece. Some economists argue that Europe needs more migrants to bolster its aging workforce. However, polls show most Europeans want fewer immigrants amid worries about unemployment and terrorism. Violent conflicts far from Europe — primarily the Syrian civil war — are driving the current surge. That leads observers increasingly to argue that an international solution to the migration crisis is needed.

Terrorism in Africa

Parts of Africa have become battlefronts in the fight against terrorism by jihadists and other extremists. The breakdown of law and order in large parts of northern and western Africa, notably Libya and Mali, has allowed Islamic State (ISIS) and al Qaeda, two rival Islamic terrorist organizations, to capture pockets of territory and stage deadly attacks both on civilian and military targets.. Some jihadi groups want to impose strict Islamic law, which calls for floggings, stonings and executions of nonbelievers. To the south, another violent group, Boko Haram, has killed thousands in Nigeria — and kidnapped hundreds of girls — and aligned itself with ISIS. In Somalia, al Shabab, an affiliate of al Qaeda, has launched attacks in neighboring countries and at home and is trying to prevent Somalia from re-establishing a functioning government. The United States has responded with limited military interventions and is partnering with allies and regional blocs to try to halt the violence. Meanwhile, tens of thousands of Africans are fleeing to Europe to escape violence or poverty, contributing to a refugee crisis of epic proportions.

Assessing the Threat from al Qaeda

Since carrying out the Sept. 11, 2001, attacks on the United States, al Qaeda has become more decentralized, and some say stronger, with affiliates launching sectarian attacks in the Middle East, Somalia, Algeria and beyond. The ruthless Islamic State of Iraq and Greater Syria currently sweeping through Iraq, was a part of al Qaeda

until February 2014, when it was expelled for excessive brutality. In Yemen, President Obama has launched more than 90 drone strikes against an al Qaeda affiliate there, known as Al Qaeda in the Arabian Peninsula, considered the most serious direct threat to the United States. Meanwhile, al Qaeda's traditional leadership in Pakistan is weaker as a result of U.S. drone strikes that peaked there in 2010 and the killing of Osama bin Laden by Navy SEALS in 2011. Counterterrorism experts are divided over how to define the al Qaeda of today, whether it continues to pose a danger to the West and how the United States should respond.

Transnational Crime

Instant global communications and open trade routes have been a boon to businesspeople and consumers — as well as to international criminals. "Transnational organized crime"— in U.N. and U.S government parlance — has been expanding over the past two decades, some officials say, threatening to overwhelm the legitimate world economy. Criminals have raced ahead of law enforcement in adapting to globalization and modern technology, experts argue, citing booming ivory and drug smuggling, human trafficking, piracy, cyber-theft and counterfeiting of luxury goods. Others counter that transnational crime is not new but simply a modern form of an old crime — smuggling — and that new technology also enables law enforcement to better track down criminals, even across borders. Both sides agree, however, that modern technology enables hackers, pirates, smugglers and others to inflict widespread damage more quickly than in the past. The intersection between internationally minded criminals and terrorism is another worry, with terrorists turning to crime to finance their operations.

Resurgent Russia

Russia is growing more assertive on the global stage, having regained its economic strength following the 1991 breakup of the Soviet Union. It has been most active in its own region, where a tug-of-war has broken out between Russia and the European Union as each tries to draw the nations of Eastern Europe and the Caucasus into their orbit. Ukrainian President Viktor Yanukovych recently reneged on an EU trade deal, reportedly after pressure from Moscow, touching off violent pro-EU protests throughout Ukraine. Russia's efforts to maintain influence over the former Soviet republics have fed speculation that President Vladimir Putin wants to reconstitute the Soviet bloc, which Russian officials deny. Meanwhile, Russia's relations with the United States have deteriorated, although the two countries are cooperating on hot-button issues such as Iran's nuclear program and Syria's civil war. Russia's relations with China are relatively good, however, even though the Chinese have eclipsed Russia economically in recent years.

Robotic Warfare

More than 40 countries—including the United States, Great Britain, Russia and China—are developing a new generation of robotic weapons that can be programmed to seek out and destroy enemy targets without direct human control. The push for autonomous machines has raised a host of legal and ethical questions and sparked concerns that the Geneva Conventions—international rules of war that date back to the 1860s—may not be adequate to control robotic warfare. Military experts say autonomous weapons could save lives by keeping soldiers out of harm's way and by using pinpoint accuracy to avoid civilian deaths and other collateral damage. But opponents fear the emerging technology might trigger a new arms race and encourage leaders to use force rather than diplomacy. Meanwhile, the U.S. military is developing revolutionary ways to supply and protect soldiers, including Kevlar underwear, invisible camouflage and customizable 3D-printed food.

INTERNATIONAL POLITICAL ECONOMY
European Unrest

Europe has been unable to haul itself out of the doldrums wrought by the 2008-09 global financial crisis. In addition to economic stagnation and high joblessness rates, immigration from poorer to richer countries has led to social tensions, made worse by a new influx of refugees fleeing Syria, Iraq and Afghanistan. Meanwhile, after decades of dormancy, anti-Semitism appears to be on the rise again. The 28-member European Union has responded to the economic malaise by bolstering its fiscal authority, but that has provoked a backlash from critics who believe national governments—and not the EU—should set policy. In such a climate, far-right,

anti-immigrant, anti-EU and even neo-Nazi political parties have been gaining eyebrow-raising victories at the ballot box. At the same time, foreign-policy experts say Hungary, an EU member, is sliding toward authoritarianism, adding to fears that Europe is headed in a dangerous direction.

Restoring Ties with Cuba

President Obama is opening a new chapter in the long and turbulent history of U.S. relations with Cuba. In December 2014 he announced plans to ease U.S. trade and travel restrictions and proposed re-establishing full diplomatic relations with Cuba. Then, last April, he met with Cuban President Raúl Castro. With these moves, Obama cast aside five decades of U.S. policy designed to isolate the island nation, a communist state since shortly after Raúl's brother, Fidel, seized power in a 1959 revolution and made common cause with the Soviet Union. Cuba has welcomed Obama's new policy, but cautiously, expressing doubts, for instance, about giving U.S. diplomats free rein on the island. American supporters of Obama's actions argue that trade and other sanctions have failed to motivate Cuba to abandon its communist ideology and improve its human rights record. But critics say Obama is giving up leverage that he could have used to force political and economic change at a time when Cuba faces new economic uncertainties.

U.S. Global Engagement

As concern grows about Russia's intentions in Ukraine and the civil war in Syria continues unabated, the United States faces increasing pressure from hawks to intervene militarily —though not with boots on the ground. But in the wake of the long wars in Iraq and Afghanistan, most Americans oppose involving U.S. troops in military actions abroad. Mindful of the potential for escalation and intent on shifting resources to domestic needs, the Obama administration has been using diplomacy and economic sanctions rather than bullets to assert American power. It has refused military aid to Ukraine but imposed economic sanctions in an attempt to stem what many view as an effort by Russian President Vladimir Putin to bring Ukraine under Moscow's control. In 2013, President Obama stopped short of bombing Syria after it used chemical weapons, instead sending aid for refugees of the war. Some U.S. allies applaud the administration's restraint, but others want to see more American muscle.

HUMAN RIGHTS
Manipulating the Human Genome

New genetic technologies allow scientists to delete a mutant gene and insert a healthy one, which someday may enable doctors to banish disease genes. Used in embryos, gene editing has the potential to eliminate inherited diseases, such as cystic fibrosis. Until recently, the techniques have been used only on embryos from laboratory animals. Last April, however, stunned scientists accused Chinese researchers of crossing a strict ethical boundary by using the technology on human embryos—albeit nonviable ones. Some ethicists and scientists fear that if the new genetic engineering techniques are used to alter viable human embryos, scientists would then begin creating "designer babies." The Chinese experiment raised fears that the notorious eugenics movement of the early 20th century—aimed at creating a perfect "master race"—might re-emerge. Twenty-nine countries—but not the United States—prohibit genetic manipulation of human embryos, and ethicists and scientists are calling for a worldwide ban or moratorium until such procedures are better understood.

Free Speech at Risk

Governments around the globe have been weakening free-speech protections because of concerns about security or offending religious believers. After a phone-hacking scandal erupted in the British press and Muslims worldwide violently protested images in the Western media of the Prophet Muhammad, European nations enacted new restrictions on hate speech, and Britain began considering limiting press freedom. Autocratic regimes increasingly are jailing journalists and political dissidents or simply buying media companies to use them for propaganda and to negate criticism. Muslim countries are adopting and rigidly enforcing blasphemy laws, some of which carry the death penalty. Meanwhile, some governments are blocking or monitoring social media and cybertraffic, increasing the risk of arrest for those who freely express

their thoughts online, and several online media platforms are adopting new guidelines for users.

ENVIRONMENTAL ISSUES
Global Hunger

New agricultural technology has enabled global food supplies to outstrip population growth, driving down the number of hungry people around the world from just over 1 billion in 1992 to 842 million in 2014 — a 17 percent drop. But food shortages and undernourishment remain huge problems in developing countries. Hunger stems from weather-related disasters such as droughts and floods, as well as from war, poverty, overpopulation, poor farming practices, government corruption, difficulties transporting food to markets, climate change and waste. Hunger is severest in sub-Saharan Africa, where 25 percent of the population is undernourished. Developed countries and humanitarian organizations have become proficient at providing emergency relief and promoting higher-yield, environmentally friendly agricultural practices, but the outlook on global hunger remains murky. Experts expect an expanding global population and growing economic affluence in developing countries to increase the demand for food, even as climate change hampers the planet's ability to feed itself.

Global Population Growth

The world's population, now about 7.2 billion people, could rise to nearly 11 billion or more by 2100, according to some estimates, with nearly all the growth in developing countries. Agricultural specialists worry about how the planet would feed 4 billion more people, and environmentalists say humans already are consuming natural resources at unsustainable rates. Expanding populations also create social pressure, especially in fast-growing nations that cannot generate enough jobs for their citizens. In some regions, notably sub-Saharan Africa, population growth is slowing progress toward key development goals, such as expanding education and improving maternal and child health. To address these challenges, wealthy donors are stepping up efforts to provide family planning to all who want it, and many advocates are calling for greater focus on women's rights, including the right to decide whether and when to have children. But the Catholic Church and other conservative groups say global population policy is too focused on birth control and instead should emphasize valuing and protecting life and raising people out of poverty.

Emerging Infectious Diseases

From the deadly Ebola outbreak in West Africa to a mysterious new illness that killed a Kansas farmer in summer 2014, emerging infectious diseases—illnesses never seen before or that reappear in new places or with new severity—threaten people around the world. About five new infections emerge in humans each year, typically three crossing over from animals. Many new kinds of infections also strike wild and domestic animals. Fifty years ago many medical scientists believed widespread use of antibiotics and vaccines would all but eliminate infectious disease. But factors such as environmental change, population growth, poverty and globalization are spurring new, often deadly, infections. Disease scientists urge policymakers to pay much more attention to animal health and to boost funding for public-health agencies here and abroad, but many conservatives say more money is not

the answer. Meanwhile, scientists are gaining new insights into the genetic makeup of disease-causing microbes, giving them hope of discovering more ways to prevent or fight infections.

Protecting the Oceans

Oceans cover more than 70 percent of Earth's surface and are essential for human life. They supply much of the world's food and oxygen. Today, however, many parts of the world's oceans are overfished and polluted. Climate change is altering marine ecology, and rising water temperatures are severely harming shellfish, coral reefs and other resources. Excess nutrients from land-based sources such as wastewater and fertilizer have created hundreds of ocean "dead zones," huge areas depleted of oxygen, where little or no sea life can survive. In the Gulf of Mexico, scientists are still assessing the effects on marine life stemming from the massive 2010 *Deepwater Horizon* oil spill. Ocean exploration has fired human imagination for centuries, and scientists are still finding new life forms, many of which could yield new medicines and other valuable products. But experts warn that without better protection, ocean water quality, fish stocks and marine habitats will suffer long-lasting damage.

Preface

In this pivotal era of international policymaking, scholars, students, practitioners and journalists seek answers to such critical questions as: Is economic stagnation in Europe fomenting extremism? Can easing sanctions with Cuba spur democracy? Is an unstoppable global pandemic possible? Students must first understand the facts and contexts of these and other global issues if they are to analyze and articulate well-reasoned positions.

The 2016 edition of *Global Issues* provides comprehensive and unbiased coverage of today's most pressing global problems. This edition is a compilation of 16 recent reports from *CQ Researcher*, a weekly policy brief that unpacks difficult concepts and provides balanced coverage of competing perspectives. Each article analyzes past, present and possible political maneuvering, is designed to promote in-depth discussion and further research and helps readers formulate their own positions on crucial international issues.

This collection is organized into four subject areas that span a range of important international policy concerns: conflict, security, and terrorism; international political economy; religious and human rights; and environmental issues. Ten of these reports are new to this edition.

Global Issues is a valuable supplement for courses on world affairs in political science, geography, economics and sociology. Citizens, journalists and business and government leaders also turn to it to become better informed on key issues, actors and policy positions.

CQ RESEARCHER

CQ Researcher was founded in 1923 as *Editorial Research Reports* and was sold primarily to newspapers as a research tool. The magazine was renamed and redesigned in 1991 as *CQ Researcher*. Today, students are its primary audience. While still used by hundreds of journalists and newspapers, many of which reprint portions of the reports, *Researcher's* main subscribers are now high school, college and public libraries. In 2002, *Researcher* won the American Bar Association's coveted Silver Gavel Award for magazine excellence for a series of nine reports on civil liberties and other legal issues.

Researcher writers—all highly experienced journalists—sometimes compare the experience of writing a *Researcher* report to drafting a college term paper. Indeed, there are many similarities. Each report is as long as many term papers—about 11,000 words—and is written by one person without any significant outside help. One of the key differences is that the writers interview leading experts, scholars and government officials for each issue.

Like students, writers begin the creative process by choosing a topic. Working with *Researcher's* editors, the writer identifies a controversial subject that has important public policy implications. After a topic is selected, the writer embarks on one to two weeks of intense research. Newspaper and magazine articles are clipped or downloaded, books are ordered and information is gathered from a wide variety of sources, including interest groups, universities and the government. Once the writers are well informed, they develop a detailed outline and begin the interview process. Each report requires a minimum of ten to fifteen interviews with academics, officials, lobbyists and people working in the field. Only after all interviews are completed does the writing begin.

CHAPTER FORMAT

Each issue of *CQ Researcher*, and therefore each selection in this book, is structured in the same way. A selection begins with an introductory overview, which is briefly explored in greater detail in the rest of the report.

The second section chronicles the most important and current debates in the field. It is structured around a number of key issues questions, such as "Can free speech survive government repression?" and "Can gang violence in Central America be stopped?" This section is the core of each selection. The questions raised are often highly controversial and usually the object of much argument among scholars and practitioners. Hence, the answers

provided are never conclusive, but rather detail the range of opinion within the field.

Following those issue questions is the "Background" section, which provides a history of the issue being examined. This retrospective includes important legislative and executive actions and court decisions to inform readers on how current policy evolved.

Next, the "Current Situation" section examines important contemporary policy issues, legislation under consideration and action being taken. Each selection ends with an "Outlook" section that gives a sense of what new regulations, court rulings and possible policy initiatives might be put into place in the next five to ten years.

Each report contains features that augment the main text: sidebars that examine issues related to the topic, a pro/con debate by two outside experts, a chronology of key dates and events and an annotated bibliography that details the major sources used by the writer.

ACKNOWLEDGMENTS

We wish to thank many people for helping to make this collection a reality. Thomas J. Billitteri, managing editor of *CQ Researcher*, gave us his enthusiastic support and cooperation as we developed this edition. He and his talented editors and writers have amassed a first-class collection of *Researcher* articles, and we are fortunate to have access to this rich cache. We also thankfully acknowledge the advice and feedback from current readers and are gratified by their satisfaction with the book.

Some readers may be learning about *CQ Researcher* for the first time. We expect that many readers will want regular access to this excellent weekly research tool. For subscription information or a no-obligation free trial of *Researcher*, please contact CQ Press at www.cqpress.com or toll-free at 1-866-4CQ-PRESS (1-866-427-7737).

We hope that you will be pleased by the 2016 edition of *Global Issues*. We welcome your feedback and suggestions for future editions. Please direct comments to Michael Kerns, Acquisitions Editor for American Government, Public Administration, and Public Policy, CQ Press, an imprint of SAGE, 2600 Virginia Avenue, NW, Suite 600, Washington, DC 20037; or send e-mail to Michael.Kerns@sagepub.com.

—*The Editors of CQ Press*

Contributors

Jill U. Adams writes a health column for *The Washington Post* and reports on health, biomedical research and environmental issues for magazines such as *Audubon*, *Scientific American* and *Science*. She holds a Ph.D. in pharmacology from Emory University.

Brian Beary, a freelance Irish journalist based in Washington, specializes in European Union (EU) affairs and is the U.S. correspondent for the daily newspaper, *Europolitics*. Originally from Dublin, he worked in Brussels from 1999-2006, completing internships in the EU Commission and European Parliament, and reporting on justice and home affairs policy for *Europolitics*. Beary also writes for the Washington-based European Institute. His recent reports for *CQ Researcher* include "Emerging Central Asia." He also wrote the 2011 CQ Press book, *Separatist Movements, A Global Reference*.

Marcia Clemmitt is a veteran social-policy reporter who previously served as editor in chief of *Medicine & Health* and staff writer for *The Scientist*. She has also been a high school math and physics teacher. She holds a liberal arts and sciences degree from St. John's College, Annapolis, and a master's degree in English from Georgetown University. Her recent *CQ Researcher* reports include "Sugar Controversies" and "Traumatic Brain Injury."

Sarah Glazer is a London-based freelancer who contributes regularly to *CQ Researcher*. Her articles on health, education and social-policy issues also have appeared in *The New York Times* and *The Washington Post*. Her recent *CQ Researcher* reports include "Free Speech on Campus" and "Prisoners and Mental Illness." She graduated from the University of Chicago with a B.A. in American history.

Alan Greenblatt covers foreign affairs for National Public Radio. He was previously a staff writer at *Governing* magazine and *CQ Weekly*, where he won the National Press Club's Sandy Hume Award for political journalism. He graduated from San Francisco State University in 1986 and received a master's degree in English literature from the University of Virginia in 1988. For the *CQ Researcher*, he wrote "Confronting Warming," "Future of the GOP" and "Immigration Debate." His recent *CQ Global Researcher* reports include "Rewriting History" and "International Adoption."

Peter Katel is a *CQ Researcher* contributing writer who previously reported on Haiti and Latin America for *Time* and *Newsweek* and covered the Southwest for newspapers in New Mexico. He has received several journalism awards, including the Bartolomé Mitre Award for coverage of drug trafficking, from the Inter-American Press Association. He holds an A.B. in university studies from the University of New Mexico. His recent reports include "Mexico's Future" and "3D Printing."

Barbara Mantel is a freelance writer in New York City. She was a 2012 Kiplinger Fellow and has won several journalism awards, including the National Press Club's Best Consumer Journalism Award and the Front Page Award from the Newswomen's Club of New York for her Nov. 1, 2009, *CQ Global Researcher* report "Terrorism and the Internet." She holds a B.A. in history and economics from the University of Virginia and an M.A. in economics from Northwestern University.

Daniel McGlynn is a California-based freelance journalist who covers science and the environment. His work has appeared in *The New York Times Magazine*, *Earth Island Journal*, *Bay Citizen*, and other publications. He holds a master's degree in journalism from the University of California, Berkeley. His recent *CQ Researcher* reports include "Digital Currency."

Tom Price is a Washington-based freelance journalist and a contributing writer for *CQ Researcher*. Previously, he was a correspondent in the Cox Newspapers Washington Bureau and chief politics writer for the *Dayton Daily News* and *The* (Dayton) *Journal Herald*. He is author or coauthor of five books including, with former U.S. Rep. Tony Hall (D-Ohio), *Changing the Face of Hunger: One Man's Story of How Liberals, Conservatives, Democrats, Republicans and People of Faith Are Joining Forces to Help the Hungry, the Poor and the Oppressed.*

Jennifer Weeks is a Massachusetts freelance writer who specializes in the environment, science, and health. She has written for *The Washington Post*, *Audubon*, *Popular Mechanics* and other magazines and previously was a policy analyst, congressional staffer and lobbyist. She has an A.B. degree from Williams College and master's degrees from the University of North Carolina and Harvard. Her recent *CQ Researcher* reports include "Regulating Toxic Chemicals" and "Future of the Arctic."

Global Issues,
2016 Edition

1

Central American Gangs

Peter Katel

Former Guatemalan President Alfonso Portillo was extradited in 2013 to the United States, where he was sentenced to nearly six years in prison after pleading guilty to money laundering. Central American officials say they are committed to fighting corruption, which many say contributes to lawlessness. In recent years, the U.S. government has spent about $100 million annually on drug interdiction, policing and anti-corruption programs in the region.

From *CQ Researcher*,
January 30, 2015.

After-school youth centers in El Salvador and Honduras were built — with U.S. money — as havens from violent street crime. But when Elizabeth G. Kennedy, an American doctoral candidate studying Central American gangs, visited one just outside of the Honduran capital of Tegucigalpa last year, gang graffiti scrawled on the inside walls took her aback. "To me," she recalls, "that means it was not a safe place."

Kennedy focuses on the region's Northern Triangle — El Salvador, Guatemala and Honduras. Material isn't lacking. Honduras has the world's highest murder rate, with 90.4 homicides per 100,000 population in 2012. El Salvador and Guatemala had rates of 41 and about 40 per 100,000, respectively. By comparison, the U.S. rate was 4.7.[1]

Though U.S. and Northern Triangle crime rates seem to show civilizations that are worlds apart, Central America and the United States are linked by a host of ties besides geographical proximity. Much of the killing is committed by street gangs originally established in Los Angeles. The region is also home to organized crime syndicates smuggling drugs north to the United States. And it saw heavy U.S. involvement in Cold War days, particularly in savage conflicts in the 1980s and early '90s that claimed hundreds of thousands of lives.

But until last summer the crime explosion that followed those late-20th-century civil wars drew little U.S. attention. However, in an exodus that peaked last June, more than 100,000 young people, including those in mother-and-toddler family groups, made their way from violence-plagued Central America to the U.S.-Mexico

1

border in 2013-14, pleading for asylum from criminals and governments that didn't protect them.[2]

"The whole system in El Salvador is corrupt," says a 19-year-old asylum-seeker who recently crossed the border. He asked not to be named for fear of jeopardizing relatives still in Central America. "The gang owned my neighbourhood."

Like others who have fled, he speaks of a society in which anyone with any assets or advantages — a relative abroad, a roadside snack stand, a store — must pay extortion demands or face death. Extortion also thrives in Guatemala and in Honduras, where bus and taxi drivers are frequent targets.[3]

Last year's tide of children seeking protection — about half of them unaccompanied — prompted several months of politically charged debate in the United States over border security and U.S. policy and aid programs in the Triangle countries.

Central America "has always been viewed as part of an area vital to [U.S.] national security," says Eric L. Olson,

Crime Spurs Exodus of Young

More than 100,000 young people, including unaccompanied youths and toddlers with their mothers, have crossed the U.S.-Mexico border over the past two years. Since the early 1980s, violence in Mexico, El Salvador, Guatemala and Honduras has contributed to a steady flow of immigrants into Arizona, New Mexico, Texas and California.

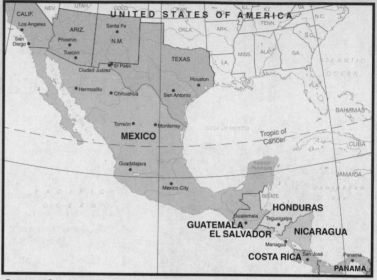

Source: "Southwest Border Unaccompanied Alien Children," U.S. Customs and Border Protection, undated, http://tinyurl.com/p3xm4sx

associate director of the Latin America Program at the Woodrow Wilson International Center for Scholars in Washington, a congressionally funded think tank. "And for lack of a better word, there is a humanitarian, moral component, when tens of thousands of children are showing up at the border fleeing something — to my mind fleeing violence and economic disaster and failing governments."

Many are also reuniting with their families. Half of El Salvador's 6.1 million people have relatives abroad, nearly all in the United States, where there are more than 3 million Central Americans, primarily from the Triangle countries.[4]

Family ties began linking Central America and the United States in the 1980s, when thousands of Salvadorans and Guatemalans fled civil wars and massacres. The refugees, many of whom eventually received temporary residence or asylum because of the violence in their home countries, headed primarily to Los Angeles. At the time, the United States, through its intelligence

agencies and military, was deeply involved in stemming what it saw as moves in its backyard instigated or inspired by the Soviet Union's regional ally Cuba.[5]

Many teenagers in the immigration wave, seeking protection in violent Los Angeles neighborhoods, joined existing street gangs, such as the 18th Street Gang (often called Barrio-18). Others started their own Central American outfit, Mara Salvatrucha, usually referred to as "MS-13."*[6]

Facing few job opportunities, many youths found gangs irresistible. "If a big part of your young people are increasingly attracted to the gangs as a way to advance themselves, these people cannot simply be seen as

---

* "Mara" is Spanish slang for gang; "salva" is short for Salvador; and "trucha" (trout) is Salvadoran slang for a smart person. "13" may refer to 'M,' the 13th letter of the alphabet, a mark of respect for the Mexican Mafia, a long-running LA-based gang.

demons," says José Luis Sanz, editor in chief of *El Faro* (*Lighthouse*), a Salvadoran news and analysis website.

Eventually, thousands of immigrant gang members ended up in prison for breaking U.S. laws. Then when Congress toughened immigration statutes, many were deported to birth countries they barely knew.[7]

By the early 2000s, gang rivalry had become the leading social and political issue in the Northern Triangle, after hundreds of killings between Barrio-18 and MS-13, along with murders of those who resisted extortion demands. But with exceptions — such as a mass killing of 28 bus passengers in San Pedro Sula, Honduras, in 2004 — the individual homicides attracted little attention outside the region.[8]

In recent decades U.S. drug enforcement agencies have focused on the Triangle as a trans-shipment point for South American cocaine heading for the United States, and — in the case of Guatemala — as an opium-poppy growing center. By 2012, the U.S. government was spending about $100 million a year on drug interdiction, policing and anti-corruption programs in Central America.[9]

Emphasizing large-scale interdiction instead of community-level crime has been "a problem in our security cooperation with these countries," says Ralph Espach, Latin American Affairs Program director at the Center for Naval Analyses, a federally funded think tank for the Navy and Marine Corps. "For years, and still today, we spend a lot of money so that police and military forces get better at interdicting drugs, but that does nothing to address the day-to-day concerns of citizens."

However, under the Obama administration, the U.S. government has been adding projects designed to improve public safety and create more opportunities for young people at risk of joining gangs.[10] Funding for the Central America Regional Security Initiative (CARSI) rose from $60 million in fiscal 2008 to $161.5 million in fiscal 2014, with more than half of it going to the Triangle.[11]

However, because the region's socioeconomic picture is so bleak, some analysts say doing away with the gangs will require deep socioeconomic changes by the leaders of the Triangle countries. Guatemala's income inequality is among the world's worst, with the richest 10 percent of the population accounting for 47 percent of national income. Half of Guatemalan children are chronically malnourished — the highest rate in Latin America — and about 30 percent of the population was

hungry in 2012, up 80 percent in 20 years. El Salvador's poverty rate declined from 47 percent to 41 percent between 2010 and 2013, but the country's basic socioeconomic conditions remained static. And Honduras' poverty rate is the region's highest, at more than 67 percent, with the richest 10 percent of the population receiving 43 percent of all income in 2010.[12]

Economic growth is hampered by lack of foreign investment due to fears about rampant crime. Roberta S. Jacobson, assistant secretary of State for the Western Hemisphere, told Congress late last year that the Obama administration's economic strategy for the region — dubbed the "prosperity agenda" — was designed to ensure that economic growth benefited more than "the well-connected few." Otherwise, she said, "extreme violence, severe economic inequality and social exclusion, and widespread corruption and poverty" would continue to afflict Central America, pushing its people to the United States.[13]

However, some of the blame for lack of growth in the region rests with the local leaders, Rep. Thomas Carper, D-Del., then-chairman of the Senate Homeland Security Committee, said at a July hearing. "We have a responsibility certainly to provide leadership as a nation," he said. "But, frankly, these countries need some leadership of their own."[14]

The new U.S.-backed community-level anti-crime projects have reduced murder, extortion and other crimes and increased citizens' perception of security, according to a survey of 29,000 respondents conducted by Vanderbilt University researchers over three years in 127 neighborhoods in the Triangle and Panama. Congressional critics of the Obama administration have argued that the assessment was inadequate because it did not evaluate individual programs.[15]

Researchers at the Wilson Center endorsed the Vanderbilt study but argued that "elevated levels of corruption" in the Triangle countries remain a major obstacle to improving public safety. "Penetration of the state by criminal groups means impunity for crime is extraordinarily high (95 percent or more), and disincentives to criminal activity are almost nonexistent," Olson and researcher Kathryn Moffat concluded.[16]

Meanwhile, the poor neighborhoods where most Central Americans live suffer their own form of criminal penetration. These areas are where gangs draw their

Honduras Has World's Highest Murder Rate

More than 90 homicides occurred in Honduras per 100,000 residents in 2012, the world's highest murder rate. El Salvador posted 41 homicides per 100,000 people, and Guatemala 39.9. Nicaragua, by comparison, has held its murder rate to around 13 homicides per 100,000 people since 2006 — nearly three times the U.S. rate.

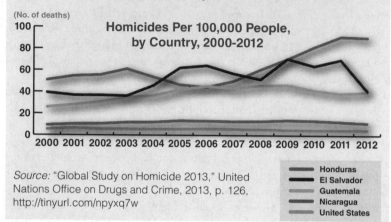

(No. of deaths)

Homicides Per 100,000 People, by Country, 2000-2012

Legend:
- Honduras
- El Salvador
- Guatemala
- Nicaragua
- United States

Source: "Global Study on Homicide 2013," United Nations Office on Drugs and Crime, 2013, p. 126, http://tinyurl.com/npyxq7w

recruits and extortion revenue, and their impact is measured in lives lost.

In the three Northern Triangle youth centers that Kennedy visited, she says, "All of them had a memorial wall with the names of murdered kids. One year-old center already had five names on the wall."

As U.S. and Central American officials, anti-crime activists and youth advocates continue trying to stem violence in the Northern Triangle, here are some of the questions they are contemplating:

Are the Northern Triangle countries in danger of being taken over by criminals?

The gangs that make life so dangerous in El Salvador, Guatemala and Honduras explain only part of the fear that criminals could end up exerting unfettered control over government.

Street gangs may control life at street level, especially in El Salvador, but in Guatemala and Honduras far bigger players have their hands on some of the levers of government, experts say. "You see a lot of infiltration of organized crime and traffickers, particularly at the municipal level in El Salvador, Guatemala and Honduras — [in the form of] money that goes into electoral races and

restrictions placed on local governments and local police forces, from which you can infer the influence of organized crime groups," says Michael E. Allison, a Central American specialist and chairman of the political science department at the University of Scranton in Scranton, Pa. He says that rather than completely taking over a Triangle government, "infiltrating the state is a more realistic strategy."

However, Olson of the Wilson Center's Latin America program sees the danger of complete criminal takeover as real. "It's not so much that it's a possible outcome," he says. "It's more, 'Is it a likely outcome?' It has to be held out as a real challenge."

High-level corruption is also an issue for U.S. security aid programs. U.S. law enforcement agencies working in the region overlook corruption within the police and military units that they work with, contrary to stated U.S. anti-corruption goals, according to the nonpartisan Congressional Research Service (CRS). "The U.S. government may be sending mixed messages to Central American governments," said a CRS report, "undermining its long-term goals."[17]

Examples of official corruption are plentiful in the region. In 2007 the U.N.-supported International Commission Against Impunity in Guatemala was formed because of fears that armed groups, including drug syndicates, were overtaking government institutions. In 2012 the commission named 18 judges who had issued questionable rulings on behalf of drug cartels. Then, in 2013, former Guatemalan President Alfonso Portillo was extradited to the United States, where he was sentenced to nearly six years in prison after pleading guilty in federal court in New York to charges of laundering millions of dollars in bribes from the government of Taiwan, paid to obtain Guatemalan diplomatic recognition. Last year, the director of Guatemala's prison system and his top aides were arrested for allegedly participating in a criminal organization run from a penitentiary.[18]

In addition, former Salvadoran president Francisco Flores (1999-2004) has been held under house arrest since last year on charges of embezzling $15 million in relief donations following a 2001 earthquake; ex-national police chief Erwin Sperisen of Guatemala is now serving a life term in Switzerland (where he had fled, as a dual citizen) for the deaths of seven prison inmates; and Mario Zelaya, head of the Honduran Institute of Social Security in 2010-2014, was arrested last year for overpaying companies owned by associates by about $200 million; he was found to have $7 million in personal assets.[19]

According to the Woodrow Wilson International Center for Scholars, Guatemala has been better at fighting corruption than Honduras, where it is "endemic" in the security and court systems. Internal police documents disclosed by a Honduran newspaper last year named nearly 200 officers allegedly involved in drug trafficking and other criminal activities.[20]

In El Salvador, which isn't on the major north-south drug-smuggling corridors, major organized-crime groups are considered less of a factor than in the other two Triangle countries. Nevertheless, Salvadoran investigative journalist Héctor Silva Ávalos wrote last year that the country's post-civil war national police force included top members implicated in human rights abuses during the conflict. However, with one exception, allegations or formal charges of aiding drug traffickers or gang members and of committing torture and attempted homicide have not been followed up. The "infiltration," Avalos concluded, was shaping the government's anti-crime strategy.[21]

Crime is highly diversified in the region, ranging from the international smuggling of cocaine, heroin, gems and expensive hardwoods to petty, street-level drug sales and extortion. These high- and low-level criminal activities demand different responses, as has occurred in Mexico. "But Mexico is a larger country and has a much bigger human infrastructure; in Central America you're talking about much smaller governments with much lower capacity to resist," Olson says.

Sonja Wolf, a German political scientist and drug policy specialist at one of Mexico's leading think tanks, the Centro de Investigación y Docencia Económicas (CIDE), is more optimistic. "If you are thinking of a 'failed state,' where nothing at all is working because corruption has essentially overwhelmed the state, that is not happening in Central America," she says. Governments

in the three countries "are trying in different ways, some more successfully than others, to tackle crime. And there is increasing awareness at a regional and international level that there is a problem."

The scarcity of solid data on criminal activity complicates any response to different forms of crime, the University of Scranton's Allison says. "We don't have very good statistics to know what is specifically gang-related, what is drug trafficking-related, what is ordinary crime," he says. "They all exist."

José Miguel Cruz, a political science professor at Florida International University in Miami, suggests that criminal takeover is well under way. "In my opinion, some of these countries for many years have already been taken over by criminal organizations," he says. He points to "the extent of corruption in Guatemala and Honduras, problems of violence, the penetration of organized crime even at the highest levels of government."

A native of El Salvador, Cruz adds that corruption and penetration do not touch all officials. "But it's very hard to say these are clean governments," he says. "If you have a corrupted government and a government penetrated by criminal organizations, you cannot expect they will be successful and efficient in combating crime at other levels."

Can negotiations curb criminal activity?

About 10 years after the spread of gangs, all three Northern Triangle governments responded with harsh strategies known as *Mano Dura* (iron fist) — a label the Salvadoran government officially adopted.

In 2003, El Salvador, under the conservative ARENA (Nationalist Republican Alliance) party, was the first country to adopt that strategy. It involved police-military sweeps through gang-controlled neighborhoods and the arrest and imprisonment of anyone whose appearance — including tattoos — indicated possible gang membership.[22]

In El Salvador, at least, the strategy backfired. The homicide rate increased from 56 per 100,000 population in 2003 to 65 per 100,000 in 2004 — the world's second-highest. In addition, imprisoned gang members used their time behind bars to devise new strategies — including adopting an inconspicuous appearance, with no visible tattoos.[23]

In 2011, the Salvadoran government — headed by a president whose political party grew out of the left-wing guerrilla force that fought in the country's civil war — helped broker a truce between the MS-13 and Barrio-18 gangs. From 2012, when it took effect, through mid-2013, homicides declined from about 14 a day to approximately five. The deal called for gangs to turn in all weapons and quit recruiting children, pledges they did not fully keep.[24]

But the government minister who helped arrange the peace agreement was dismissed in 2013, and his replacement opposed the truce. And the 2014 arrest of a Spanish priest who was a key truce negotiator cast the entire deal into disrepute. The Rev. Antonio Rodriguez was accused of smuggling drugs, cash, cell phones and phone chips to gang members in two prisons. He pleaded guilty to the phone charge, received a sentence of two years' probation and was allowed to return to Spain.[25]

The truce idea resurfaced last year with the installation of a new president who also had served in the former guerrilla force. But President Salvador Sánchez Cerén firmly closed the door on that option in late January, announcing that the government "is not negotiating and will not negotiate with gangs." San Salvador's archbishop issued a similar statement. The announcements followed news that gangs had declared a ceasefire and were seeking talks with the government. But the previous truce had been discredited by the time Sánchez Cerén took office, after hidden mass graves of more than 100 bodies were found in 2012 and 2013, casting doubt on whether the initial homicide decline attributed to the truce was genuine, or whether some gang members had hidden bodies to conceal continued killings.[26]

In Honduras, a Catholic Church-brokered gang truce in 2013 also saw negative initial results — an increase in homicides in the first four weeks of the ceasefire. Homicides may have fallen since then, but President Juan Orlando Hernández, inaugurated last year, claimed that his *Mano Dura* strategy — not the truce — was the reason.[27]

For those who reject a hard-line strategy on moral or practical grounds, truces might seem to be an obvious alternative. The problem, says Wolf of Mexico's CIDE think tank, is that the Salvadoran attempt at peacemaking, the most serious one so far, did not seem to have been well thought out.

"It looks like the gang truce was not really a truce between gangs but a strategy promoted by the government," she says. "It is not quite clear to what extent the gang members were interested in a truce. The government made some promises about what it would do in return for decreases in violence but never followed up on those promises."[28]

However, many people object to negotiating with criminals. The Wilson center's Olson notes, however, that the more popular *Mano Dura* strategy hasn't worked either. There was a tendency, "to criminalize entire neighborhoods," he says, "which leads to prison overcrowding — well over 300 percent beyond capacity in El Salvador."

A deeper question, Olson says, centers on a split between emotional support for a hard-line policy, on the one hand, and a police tendency toward brutal and unfocused repression. "It feels good to think that the police are out there getting the bad guys," he says. "But when you realize the way this plays itself out in communities, it's not such a positive experience."

Nevertheless, public opinion runs strongly against negotiations with gangs, says Kennedy, the American researcher, who lived in El Salvador in 2013-14 and studied violence and gangs on a Fulbright fellowship. "Citizens have no confidence in gang truces," she says, noting that extortion and disappearances — probable homicides linked to gangs — increased during the Salvadoran truce. "I did think that the truce was the right direction to go, but no one in the Northern Triangle supports that approach."

Sanz, the editor of *El Faro*, says the Salvadoran and Honduran governments are incapable of an enforcement-first strategy. "A direct confrontation to retake territory, maintain territorial control and then initiate government programs of other kinds seems to me unachievable," he says.

More than that, he says, government and society have a responsibility to start talking to gang members. "You have to take into account that most of them are young and are looking for a way to make a life," he says. "They are intelligent young people and respond to positive signs as well as negative ones."

Did the United States cause Central America's crime problem?

During the Cold War, events led to extensive U.S. political and military-advisory activity in the Northern

Triangle, including U.S.-supported counterinsurgency campaigns in Guatemala and El Salvador during devastating civil wars. And Honduras was the base for U.S.-backed fighters trying to topple a left-wing government in Nicaragua. Protection of U.S. security interests in Central America during that period had consequences that continue to affect the region.

"No country suffers more from the weapons and gangs left over from the war than El Salvador," President Clinton said during a 1999 visit to that country. In an oblique reference to the U.S. role in the war, he said, "Civil war and repression claimed tens of thousands of lives and cast many thousands more into exile . . . [during] a time which provoked in the United States bitter divisions about our role in your region."[29]

Clinton's successors have not spoken about the 1980s conflicts. But in announcing his administration's new community-based initiative, President Obama on a 2011 trip to El Salvador effectively shifted from concentrating on big drug cartels to what he called "a new effort against gangs . . . including the social and economic forces that drive young people toward criminality."[30]

The Congressional Research Service noted last year that in fiscal 1993-2007, aid related to law enforcement and economic development in the Triangle totaled about $450 million a year. It later increased to a total of $804 million in 2008-2014, in annual amounts that rose from $60 million to $161.5 million. But that was dwarfed by the $1.3 billion a year in U.S. military and economic aid that the United States sent to anti-communist forces and governments in the Northern Triangle during the 1979-1992 era of conflict.[31]

Some experts contend that the government dysfunction that has enabled Central American crime to take hold grows out of the Cold War era of heavy U.S. involvement in the region. "We made policy decisions that put short-term prioritization of winning battles against insurgents and people we considered communists over the

Youths Cite Violence as a Key Reason for Fleeing

More than four-fifths of unaccompanied youths leaving Northern Triangle countries since October 2011 said they came to the United States to join family members or pursue new opportunities, but many also cited violence as a prime reason for fleeing.

Why Children Say They Left Home Countries*

(Percentage)

* Data based on a study of 404 children

Source: Calculated from "Children on the Run," United Nations High Commissioner for Refugees, March 2014, pp. 7-11, http://tinyurl.com/newlw48

- Societal Violence
- Domestic Abuse
- Economic Deprivation/ Social Exclusion
- Join Family/Opportunities in U.S.

long-term stability of those countries," says Espach of the Center for Naval Analyses. "They are now living the results."

Nevertheless, he concedes that pointing the finger at past U.S. actions can enable Central American politicians to evade their own responsibilities, implying "that we should somehow solve these problems by giving more money."

Congress has shown some caution about aid to corrupt or abusive governments. In fiscal 2008, 15 percent of $60 million in Central America aid was conditioned on State Department certification of advances in human rights. And in fiscal 2012 and 2013, 20 percent of some aid to the Honduran police and military was withheld pending State Department certification of protection of civil liberties and human rights. After a 2013 department report found that rights were still seriously threatened, the Honduras withholding rate was raised to 35 percent. (Border security funding and anti-corruption and human rights training were exempted.)[32]

The Obama administration's shift beyond a strategy dedicated almost entirely to limiting the flow of drugs through the region is a welcome change, some experts say, because it focuses on funding programs to stop the crime and corruption that affect ordinary citizens. "In the categories of making the justice systems work better, doing community policing, trying to find community-level civil society organizations that work, job creation — these categories are right on," says Adam Isacson, a senior associate at the Washington Office on Latin America, a liberal think tank. But, he adds, "The real concern is the extent to which the governing elites of the countries are sharing these priorities."

Others note that the community-level crime that affects most Central Americans grew out of the migration prompted by the civil wars of the 1980s. The gangs that terrorize large swaths of the Triangle began in Los Angeles and were transplanted to Central America when their members were deported. "People come over the border and become involved in gangs in California, and the United States just throws them back," says Deborah T. Levenson, a Guatemala specialist and history professor at Boston College. "It led to the crime dynamic in Central America," she says, citing U.S. participation in the Central American civil wars. "The United States creates international problems and doesn't look for international solutions."

Yet some prominent Central Americans argue that the Triangle's governing business class does not accept enough responsibility for the region'sproblems. "Don't let the Central American elites, who have never paid taxes, off the hook this time," Kevin Casas-Zamora, vice president of Costa Rica in 2006-2007, told the U.S. Senate Caucus on International Narcotics Control in 2011. He noted that the average tax burden in Central America, 15.8 percent of gross domestic product (GDP), was below the Latin American average of 16.9 percent, and less than half the 34.8 percent average for industrialized nations.[33]

"It is Central America's misfortune that the countries that face the most serious threats from organized crime — Guatemala and Honduras — are those where economic elites are more reluctant to changing their ways," Casas-Zamora testified. "Such resistance has roots in their perceived success in vanquishing past political challenges, as much as in the increasing intertwining of their business activities with those of organized crime."

Isacson says that when U.S. officials do press Triangle officials on corruption, "That is not what Central American elites are interested in."

Cruz of Florida International University agrees that Central American governments should be held accountable, but he points out that U.S. aid programs have been strengthening them. The United States has "been sending aid to these governments with the hope that just by training them and giving them courses on human rights, that will change something on the ground," he says.

The recent U.S. strategic shift is a step in the right direction, Cruz says, but not enough of one. "In the last four or five years they have changed a little bit and are focusing on [crime] prevention and community-building," he says. "But in my opinion that has come too late."

BACKGROUND
United Fruit

U.S. political and economic involvement in Central America goes back to the 19th century, when American traders first began exporting bananas — then virtually unknown in the United States — from Caribbean islands and the Central American mainland.[34]

In 1954, the major U.S. banana exporter, United Fruit Co. (predecessor of Chiquita Brands of Cincinnati), played a major role in a CIA-backed coup in Guatemala that toppled the country's second democratically elected president. Jacobo Arbenz's ouster began the modern era of political violence and social disruption in Central America because it hardened positions among conservative elites fearing social revolt and left-wing activists who despaired of moderate reforms. Arbenz, who was inaugurated in 1951, had been moving to require the sale of unused land in vast estates. The policy alarmed United Fruit, Guatemala's biggest employer and owner of the country's only Atlantic port, Puerto Barrios, and virtually all of the country's railroads.[35]

The coup, which the CIA now acknowledges having directed, installed a military strongman and ushered in decades of ruthless military suppression of dissent.[36]

By 1970, a small Marxist guerrilla force had taken root in the rural highlands, and opposition to the government had begun growing in urban areas, where government-connected death squads "disappeared" 43 persons every five days, on average. Overall, the army and other government or government-sponsored militias killed 200,000 from 1962 to 1996, more than 80 percent of them Mayan Indians, who were viewed by the military as actual or potential guerrillas or sympathizers.[37]

Salvadoran Civil War

As the conflict deepened in Guatemala, tensions were building in El Salvador, a tiny coffee-, sugar- and cotton-producing country dominated by landowning families closely tied to the military.

The 1960s and '70s saw rising political and social conflict, which had last exploded in 1932 during a savagely repressed communist-led rural insurgency. An increasingly radical, left-wing, rural movement in the '60s prompted the government to establish a repressive paramilitary force that targeted peasants.[38]

Meanwhile, armed Marxist-Leninist groups were launching surprise attacks on government buildings in towns and cities.[39] Roman Catholic activists also helped build support for radical social change.

By the end of the '70s, the ruling class and its military allies were shooting at demonstrators and had formed "death squads" that kidnapped and killed left-wing activists.[40]

The ruthlessness led Archbishop Oscar Romero in San Salvador to protest. In an open letter to President Jimmy Carter in 1980, he urged the United States to stop aiding the Salvadoran military. The armed forces, he wrote, were involved in "injustice and repression."[41]

On March 23, 1980, Romero delivered a homily directed at security forces: "I implore, you, I beg you, I order you in the name of God: Stop the repression!" The next day, a sniper in a death squad commanded by a former Salvadoran army major shot Romero as he celebrated Mass at a hospital chapel in San Salvador.[42]

The assassination triggered a full-scale civil war, with the military fighting a guerrilla force led by the leading left-wing organization, the Farabundo Martí National Liberation Front (FMLN). The insurgents were inspired by the 1979 overthrow of Nicaraguan dictator Anastasio Somoza — supported by the United States until shortly before he was toppled — in a revolution led by the Cuban-supported Sandinista movement.*[43]

El Salvador's civil war cost an estimated 75,000 lives and was marked by episodes of horrific brutality, most of them committed by government forces.[44] Among the most notorious incidents were:

- The rapes and killings (only months after Romero's slaying) of four U.S. Roman Catholic churchwomen by troops who considered the women guerrilla sympathizers;
- A 1981 massacre of at least 700 men, women and children by a military counterinsurgency unit in and around the hamlet of El Mozote;
- FMLN summary executions of village mayors and other perceived enemies; and
- The military's 1989 slaying of six leading Jesuit priest scholars, their housekeeper and her daughter during a major FMLN offensive.[45]

The United States played a major role in the Salvadoran war, especially after Ronald Reagan became president in 1981. Washington's political establishment considered U.S. financial support and training of the Salvadoran military critical in preventing communism from spreading in Central America. Congress voted in 1982 to condition the aid on biannual certification of Salvadoran government human rights and pro-democracy programs.[46]

In Guatemala, the Carter administration had cut off military aid in 1977 because of human rights violations, part of Carter's foreign policy push to encourage respect for human rights.[47] But as Guatemala's counterinsurgency peaked in the 1980s, the Reagan administration restored some of the aid, and the CIA was paying the Guatemalan military brass. The sum of these U.S. actions is what led to Clinton's 1999 apology.[48]

As the U.S.-supported Guatemalan counterinsurgency was at its height, the Reagan administration actively backed a counterinsurgency in nearby Nicaragua. The "Contras" (counter-revolutionary militia) were fighting the leftist Sandinista government headed by Daniel Ortega. The Contras, who included former Nicaraguan army members, were based largely in Honduras and undertook their first attack in Nicaragua in 1982. Concern over Washington's role in the conflict led Congress later that year to prohibit U.S. funding of the Contras if it was aimed at toppling the Sandinista government.[49]

Honduras, the major Contra base, felt repercussions from the U.S. support of the anti-Sandinista force. Citing documentary evidence and interviews with some of those

---

* Marti, the leader of the failed 1932 Salvadoran insurgency, had been executed by the government. The Sandinistas took their name from Augusto Sandino, a Nicaraguan nationalist who led a guerrilla war against the U.S. occupation of Nicaragua from 1927 until 1934, when he was killed in an ambush.

involved, *The Baltimore Sun* reported in 1995 that the CIA had trained and aided a secret Honduran army unit that seized, tortured and killed hundreds of Hondurans suspected of left-wing activity in the 1980s. One American official from that era said later, however, that torturing and killing "was not the policy of the United States."[50]

Men who took part in the conflicts now are presidents of two Triangle countries: El Salvador's Salvador Sánchez Cerén was a commander in the FMLN guerrilla force. In Guatemala, Oscar Pérez Molina is a retired general who served in a highland region where some massacres occurred, but he has denied any role in the atrocities.[51]

"For the United States, it is important that I state clearly," President Clinton said in his 1999 visit to Guatemala, "that support for military forces or intelligence units which engage in violent and widespread repression . . . was wrong, and the United States must not repeat that mistake."[52]

In a more indirect gesture, President Obama visited the tomb of Archbishop Romero during a 2011 visit to El Salvador, although he did not make a statement. For (now-deceased) Robert White, who was U.S. ambassador to El Salvador when Romero was killed, Obama's gesture amounted to "a declaration that the United States is no longer identified with oligarchic governments."[53]

L.A. Gangland

The Central American wars affected several U.S. cities, notably Los Angeles. From 1980 to 1990, the number of Salvadoran immigrants entering the United States skyrocketed from 94,000 to 465,000, the majority to the Los Angeles area. An estimated 245,000 Guatemalans headed to the United States as well, many also settling in Los Angeles.[54]

Pico Union, the poor L.A. district that became the center of Salvadoran and Guatemalan immigrant life, already was home to Mexican-American street gangs, which had formed in the 1930s as protection from racist attacks.[55] Inevitably, many of the young Central American newcomers, also driven by a need to protect themselves, gravitated to the Mexican-American gangs.

For unknown reasons, Barrio-18 and MS-13 became fierce enemies, and quickly known to police. Thousands of gang members ended up in U.S. jails and prisons.

Then, events in their homelands led to radical changes in the conditions that had sent their families fleeing to the United States. In El Salvador, a 1992 peace accord ended the civil war.[56] The Guatemalan civil war ended in late 1996, when government and revolutionary forces signed an agreement that called for disbanding guerrilla forces, cutting the army by one-third, documenting past human rights abuses and strengthening civilian power.[57]

As in El Salvador, the Guatemalan peace accord included amnesty for crimes committed as part of the war. But the Guatemalan amnesty was less sweeping than its Salvadoran counterpart. Former President Efraín Ríos Montt was on trial for his possible role in the killing of more than 1,700 members of indigenous communities; he also faced charges in the rapes and tortures committed in connection with 15 massacres in 1982-83. He was convicted in 2013, won a dismissal on appeal and was put on trial again, but proceedings have been suspended.[58]

As El Salvador and Guatemala were beginning to rebound from their civil wars, Hurricane Mitch struck the Northern Triangle especially hard in 1998. Honduras suffered the most, with more than 7,000 killed and over 8,000 missing. After the storm, the number of Hondurans caught trying to cross the U.S. border jumped from 10,600 in fiscal 1998 to 18,800 in fiscal 1999. By 2010, the Honduran immigrant population in the United States had reached 523,000, partly due to the granting of a post-hurricane Temporary Protected Status (TPS), which provides short-term legal status and work authorization for immigrants fleeing natural disasters and conflict.[59]

As with earlier-arriving Salvadorans and Guatemalans, some uprooted young Hondurans gravitated to the Central American gangs.

Deporting Crime

A few years earlier, the Salvadoran peace accord and peace talks in Guatemala had caused a change in U.S. policy toward people abandoning those countries.

In the mid-'90s, the Clinton administration stopped protecting such refugees from deportation. The coming of peace, the administration reasoned, meant that those who had fled the violence could go home safely.[60]

Separately, the Los Angeles Police Department concluded after a major street riot in 1992 that Mara Salvatrucha (MS-13) members were major players in the looting and violence. Police and prosecutors, as part of a national crime crackdown, zeroed in on the then little-known gang and sent many members to prison.[61]

CHRONOLOGY

1951-1975 *CIA-organized Guatemala coup opens new era of political violence in Central America.*

1951 Newly elected Guatemalan President Jacobo Arbenz starts land reforms that alarm U.S.-based United Fruit Co.

1954 After intense lobbying by United Fruit, President Dwight D. Eisenhower orders CIA to organize coup against Arbenz; it succeeds.

1959 Cuban revolution leads to Communist government that supports revolutionary movements in the region.

1970 Government-backed death squads in Guatemala begin "disappearing" suspected subversives.

1979-1986 *Nicaragua's Sandinista revolution intensifies conflicts between left-wing guerrillas and repressive government, prompting U.S. support for the anti-Sandinista Contras.*

1979 Sandinista revolutionaries topple long-time U.S.-allied dictator in Nicaragua.

1980 Salvadoran death squad assassinates Archbishop Oscar Romero sparking war between government and leftist guerrillas.

1981 Salvadoran military kills more than 700, including children, in El Mozote and nearby communities; FMLN guerrillas execute Salvadoran mayors, other opponents.

1982 Congress ties U.S. aid to El Salvador to human rights and pro-democracy progress. . . . U.S.-backed Nicaraguan Contras attack Sandinista government.

1986 President Ronald Reagan advocates renewing aid to Contras on grounds that Sandinista victory would threaten Central America and prompt refugee exodus to United States.

1990-2003 *Central American refugee exodus to U.S. includes young people who join gangs and are then deported.*

1990 Number of Salvadoran and Guatemalan refugees in United States reaches 709,000; in the Los Angeles area,

some join Barrio-18 gang, others form Mara Salvatrucha (MS-13).

1992 Salvadoran government and FMLN guerrillas sign peace treaty.

1995 Illegal Immigration Reform and Immigrant Responsibility Act sets stage for more deportation of noncitizens convicted of crimes.

1996 Treaty between Guatemalan government and guerrillas ends civil conflict.

2003 United States deports more than 20,000 Central Americans for criminal and immigration law violations. . . . Conservative Salvadoran government adopts *Mano Dura* ("iron fist") strategy against gangs; Guatemala and Honduras take similar approaches.

2004-Present *Rising crime tied to gang expansion grows in importance as political issue in region.*

2004 Conservative candidate wins El Salvador presidency, adopts super *Mano Dura* strategy.

2009 Honduran military topples left-leaning president.

2012 Northern Central America registers stratospheric homicide rates, with Honduras worst in the world at 90.4 per 100,000. . . . U.S. arrests 80,000 Northern Triangle immigrants trying to enter the United States, double the previous year's total. . . . Salvadoran gangs sign peace accord.

2013 Conservative candidate wins Honduran presidential election, defeating wife of president ousted in 2009 coup. . . . Salvadoran minister who helped arrange gang truce is removed. . . . Honduran gang truce signed; early results unpromising.

2014 Number of unaccompanied Central American children detained at U.S.-Mexico border reaches 51,705; President Obama warns parents not to allow their children to flee. . . . Spanish priest who helped arrange Salvadoran gang truce is accused of smuggling goods to imprisoned gang members.

Nicaragua Escapes Grip of Gangs

Once-violent nation finds a way to keep disorder at bay.

The irony is hard to miss. A Central American country torn by armed conflict in the 1980s — and still ravaged by poverty and inequality — does not have a major gang or crime problem.

That country is Nicaragua, whose current president led a leftist government three decades ago that was reviled by the United States and condemned as a clear danger to the Americas.

Nicaragua would seem every bit as vulnerable to gang crime as its neighbors. The country's poverty rate of 58 percent is slightly higher than that of violence-wracked Guatemala (55 percent), and corruption remains a serious problem. Moreover, like Guatemala and El Salvador, Nicaragua was whipsawed by political violence in the past: In 1979 Sandinista revolutionaries overthrew a nearly 50-year-old dictatorship, only to face an armed insurrection from U.S.-backed Contra (counterrevolutionary) forces in the 1980s.[1]

Yet Nicaragua's most recent homicide statistics show a national rate of 11 killings per 100,000 in 2012 — about eight times lower than that of Honduras.[2]

Central Americans are well aware of the crime disparity between Nicaragua and countries in the zone of violence known as the Northern Triangle. The two major gangs that plague El Salvador, Guatemala and Honduras sound like far-away problems to Nicaraguans, even those in poor, vulnerable neighborhoods in Managua, Nicaragua's capital. "In this part of Central America the Mara Salvatrucha and Barrio-18 sound just as exotic as the Camorra [of Italy] or the Russian mafia," wrote reporter Roberto Valencia of *El Faro*, a Salvadoran news website, in 2011.[3]

Why is Nicaragua different? The consensus among those who know the region is that the Sandinistas can claim much, if not most, of the credit. "The revolution completely changed the dynamic of the state," says José Miguel Cruz, a political science professor from El Salvador at Florida International University. "The country's law enforcement institutions were born with a strong relationship with the community, in which the state apparatus — the police — would always know what was happening in the community."

In addition, says Michael L. Allison, chairman of the political science department at the University of Scranton and a Central America specialist, Nicaraguan political culture wasn't impregnated with mass violence to the same extent as the dictatorships in Guatemala and El Salvador. Although the Somoza regime, the Nicaraguan police state overthrown by the Sandinistas, remained in power using corruption, imprisonment, torture and killings, it didn't use massacres like its neighbors. "Nicaragua was always less violent," Allison says.

All told, Nicaragua under third-term President Daniel Ortega bears little resemblance to the security nightmare predicted by President Ronald Reagan 29 years ago. Reagan, citing the Sandinistas' close ideological and logistical connection to Cuba, the Soviet Union's only ally in the Americas, called Nicaragua a potential Soviet continental beachhead. "They will be in a position to threaten the Panama Canal, interdict our vital Caribbean sea lanes and, ultimately, move against Mexico," he said in a 1986 speech urging congressional approval of $100 million in aid to the counterrevolutionary forces known as the Contras.[4]

In that year — two years after Ortega was first elected president — Reagan also predicted that if the Sandinistas remained in power, "desperate Latin peoples by the millions would begin fleeing north into the cities of the southern United States or to wherever some hope of freedom remained."[5]

Four years later, the Sandinistas lost a presidential election to a U.S.-favored candidate. Then, in 2007, Ortega returned to power to head what critics call a one-party system dominated by his Sandinista National Liberation Front. But political tensions have not set off major violence or prompted a refugee wave to the United States (although Nicaraguans do flock to neighboring Costa Rica for better job opportunities).

In recent years, as tens of thousands of children and families from the Northern Triangle have appeared at the U.S. border with Mexico, the number of Nicaraguans each year didn't rise above two digits. Only 43 unaccompanied Nicaraguan children were found at the border in fiscal 2012. By last June, 99 percent of the children were coming from the Triangle and from Mexico.[6]

The United States did play a role in helping Nicaragua avoid the fate of its neighbors, some experts say. During the early-1990s transition from the first Sandinista period, officials in the Sandinista-created military and police, knowing the United States was keeping a close eye on them, realized that their futures depended on ensuring that these forces were nonpolitical and corruption-free.

"The Sandinistas agreed to a number of reforms that created a more professional and independent police force and army," says Eric L. Olson, associate director of the Latin America program at the Woodrow Wilson International Center for Scholars in Washington, a congressionally and privately funded think tank. "The army and police force are no longer part of the Sandinista system."

Cruz, however, says Nicaragua's security forces may now be slowly politicizing. In 2013, the police removed from the Social Security Institute a group of elderly demonstrators demanding payment of partial pensions. Last year, police violently broke up protests against land expropriations tied to a planned interoceanic canal.[7] And while low-level police corruption does exist, "the rings of criminals and hitmen that you find in the Guatemalan police," Cruz says, "you don't find that in Nicaragua."

In the Northern Triangle, by contrast, drug trafficking organizations "have penetrated portions of the police, treasury, customs, military, attorney general's offices, jails and court systems," wrote Steven Dudley, co-director of InSight Crime, a news website based in Medellín, Colombia, and Washington, D.C.[8]

One exception to Nicaragua's relative tranquility is the Mosquito Coast, an isolated region along the Caribbean that is divided into semiautonomous areas. In 2011, the most recent year for which figures are available, the homicide rate in the region was 43 per 100,000. Bordering Honduras, the Mosquito Coast has become a trans-shipment point for drugs sent north from Venezuela.[9]

But even if the trafficking has sparked an increase in homicides in the region, the Nicaraguan military draws respect from its U.S. counterparts for its work in tracking and stopping drug shipments. That's despite the Nicaraguan forces' origins in a revolutionary government that fought a U.S.-backed insurgency.

"You'll hear U.S. military people say that the Nicaraguans punch above their weight," says Ralph Espach, Latin American affairs program director at CNA Corp., a think tank specializing in security projects for the U.S. Department of Defense. "They may not care how it came about, historically."

— *Peter Katel*

President Daniel Ortega of Nicaragua, right, watches Miskito Indians living along the Mosquito Coast unload rice for the victims of Hurricane Felix in September 2007. The isolated region is a major drug trans-shipment center, but Nicaragua has not had the crime problems that plague the Northern Triangle countries.

MIGUEL ALVAREZ/AFP/Getty Images

[1] William A. Kandel, *et al.*, "Unaccompanied Alien Children: Potential Factors Contributing to Recent Immigration," Congressional Research Service, July 3, 2014, p. 9, http://tinyurl.com/nm5xvps.

[2] Marguerite Cawley, "Nicaragua Homicide Rate Drops to 11 per 100,000," *InSight Crime*, May 31, 2013, http://tinyurl.com/pvbv33u; "Global Study on Homicide," United Nations Office on Drugs and Crime, 2013, p. 24, http://tinyurl.com/npyxq7w; "Nicaragua," Transparency International, regularly updated, http://tinyurl.com/nno6fml.

[3] Quoted in Geoffrey Ramsey, "How Community Ties Kept 'Mara' Gangs Out of Nicaragua," *InSight Crime*, Nov. 9, 2011, http://tinyurl.com/qd4zs94.

[4] President Ronald Reagan, "Address to the Nation on the Situation in Nicaragua," March 16, 1986, President Reagan Archives, University of Texas, http://tinyurl.com/nnk75ox.

[5] *Ibid.*; "1984: Sandinistas claim election victory," BBC, undated, http://tinyurl.com/mrbmk2u.

[6] Tim Rogers, "Nicaragua Rewind: Ortega, Same as the Old Boss?" Pulitzer Center on Crisis Reporting, Dec. 12, 2012, http://tinyurl.com/kemng8v; Tim Merrill, ed., "The Chamorro Government," in *Nicaragua: A Country Study* (1993), http://tinyurl.com/lkx3989; "Unaccompanied Children (0-17) Apprehensions," U.S. Border Patrol, April 11, 2013, http://tinyurl.com/mrgwmc3; "Children in Danger: A Guide to the Humanitarian Challenge at the Border," Immigration Policy Center, July 10, 2014, http://tinyurl.com/p4249ff; Zach Dyer, "Nicaraguan migrants don't follow other Central Americans to US, choosing Costa Rica instead," *Tico Times*, Aug. 27, 2014, http://tinyurl.com/klmfwss.

[7] "Nicaragua" in "Freedom in the World 2014," Freedom House, undated, http://tinyurl.com/l3tn6z2; "Protests erupt in Nicaragua over interoceanic canal," *The Guardian*, Dec. 24, 2014, http://tinyurl.com/na8vkph.

[8] Steven S. Dudley, "Drug Trafficking Organizations in Central America: Transportistas Mexican Cartels, and Maras," in Cynthia Arnson and Eric L. Olson, eds., *Organized Crime in Central America: The Northern Triangle*, Woodrow Wilson International Center for Scholars, 2011, p. 34, http://tinyurl.com/k73g7vz.

[9] Hannah Stone, "Nicaragua Coast Becomes Gateway for Honduras Drug Flights," *InSight Crime*, April 20, 2013, http://tinyurl.com/knwhg5l.

Violence and Death
Stalk Latin America's Youth

"Everywhere here is dangerous. There is no security."

By the time he was 17, José says he had nowhere to turn. In school, at work, at home, the Mara Salvatrucha (MS-13) gang was trying to take over his life.

"I didn't want to be part of the gang," José, now a lanky 19-year-old, says of a *clika* — small unit — headed by a slightly older man with the street name "Scooby." "They forced me to do things I didn't want to do — like go to stores and demand money. I'd say, 'Scooby sent me, and you've got to give me $20.'"

If he had refused to cooperate? "They could beat me, they could kill me, they could kill someone from my family," he says.

José, not his real name, tells his story from his new home in New Mexico, where he arrived with his sister in 2012, rejoining their mother, who came eight years ago. After José's father's died in a traffic accident, his mother had to support José and his sister on El Salvador's $7.50-a-day minimum wage. When José, who is applying for asylum in the United States along with his sister, spoke at the offices of an immigrants' advocacy organization, he had just finished his high school classes for the day and was getting ready for his job in a Mexican restaurant.

His description of life in a working-class neighborhood in Olocuilta could not be independently verified. But his account was consistent with those of others who have fled

Central America's Northern Triangle countries — El Salvador, Guatemala and Honduras — as well as reports by journalists and academics. "Everywhere here is dangerous," 19-year-old Isais Sosa of Honduras told the *Los Angeles Times* in August. "There is no security. They kill people all the time. It's a sin to be young in Honduras."[1]

Statistics confirm the dangers facing Central America's young people. El Salvador has the world's highest homicide rate for people under age 20, and Guatemala is third. In those two nations, homicide is the leading cause of death for adolescent boys, according to the United Nations Children's Fund. Honduras, which has the world's highest overall homicide rate, had an adolescent and child homicide rate of 13 per 100,000 in 2012. El Salvador's rate was 42 per 100,000, and Guatemala's, 32 per 100,000.[2]

In a Washington, D.C., suburb, another young Salvadoran, 17-year-old Manuel, also not his real name, says gangs have sprung up in the Salvadoran countryside, in part because some city-bred gang members take refuge in rural areas. Manuel says after a week working in the fields, tending bean and corn crops for $10 a day, he would return to town, only to have half of his money seized.

Why not call the police? Manuel says he couldn't count on authorities' ability — or willingness — to protect him.

Congress, meanwhile, toughened federal immigration law. The Illegal Immigration Reform and Immigrant Responsibility Act of 1995 required deportation of non-citizens, including legal permanent residents (green card holders), who were convicted of felonies. Deportations of Central Americans, most for non-criminal immigration violations, tripled from about 8,000 in 1996 to some 24,000 in 2004. And in 2005-09, U.S. authorities arrested more than 2,500 suspected MS-13 members throughout the United States for a variety of offenses; many were deported.[62] Other gang members — or those believed to

be gang members — not convicted of felonies were deported for immigration law violations.[63]

The sudden influx of young gang members to countries they barely remembered not only deeply shocked the deportees but also horrified the Triangle nations, which used "iron-fist" tactics to crack down on the newcomers' activities.

In 2003, El Salvador was the first country to openly adopt the *Mano Dura* strategy.[64] The hard-line approach, which included locking up people because they looked like gang members, succeeded politically, at least initially.

Gangs, on the other hand, could be counted on to follow through on threats. "They told me they'd cut me to pieces, or endanger someone from my family," he says. "They had already killed someone from the same village, I think because he was from another gang."

Others who have lived in the Northern Triangle agree it's a waste of time to go to the authorities. A 17-year-old girl who left San Marcos, Guatemala, for Maryland in February says her grandmother advised against reporting kidnapping and death threats from a gang member who trailed the girl every time she stepped outside her home. "She told me they wouldn't do anything."

Student and restaurant cook José says anyone who reports a crime to the police is risking his life. "Some people in the authorities are involved with the gangs," he says. "You can go report a crime, but that same officer may go and tell the one who robbed you that so-and-so reported him, and then they'll retaliate against you."

The only way to steer clear of gangs is to never leave the house, young Central Americans say. But gang members even maintain a presence in schools. In José's high school in the Montelimar neighborhood of Olocuilta, the real authority rested with Mara Salvatrucha members who extorted money from students known to have relatives in the United States. The gang members don't do any schoolwork but demand to be treated as though they did, even including not getting held back a grade by the teachers. "If they're not passed into the next grade," he adds, "they threaten to kill the teachers.

To some Americans, the notion of large numbers of teachers who have no protection from schoolhouse gang members may sound implausible. But the dangers of teaching school are well documented in El Salvador. "It is deplorable that teaching has become a dangerous profession . . . targeted for murder, robbery or extortion," a retired teacher wrote to a news website in 2006. After 11 teachers were killed in 2011, 1,000 teachers requested transfers to other schools because of extortion demands. And as 2014 was coming to a close, a teachers union reported that 38 students and 10 teachers had been killed that year. Reasons weren't specified, although they may not have been considered necessary for the Salvadoran public. [3]

Refusing to bow to extortion — gangs call it "rent" — is only one way to get killed. José says in 2009 his uncle was shot to death in El Salvador's central market because his girlfriend was said to have been previously involved with a gang leader. "They shot him four times in the chest," he says.

José, who wants to be a chef, says he lost all hope for a normal life in his home country. "Life," he says, "has no value in El Salvador."

— Peter Katel

[1] Quoted in Cindy Carcamo, "In Honduras, U.S. deportees seek to journey north again," *Los Angeles Times*, Aug. 16, 2014, http://tinyurl.com/ll9bhrw.

[2] "Hidden in Plain Sight: A statistical analysis of violence against children," United Nations Children's Fund, September 2014, pp. 25-36, 40, 197, http://tinyurl.com/n584d23; "Global Study on Homicide," United Nations Office on Drugs and Crime, 2013, p. 24, http://tinyurl.com/npyxq7w.

[3] Miguel Martínez, "El acoso a los maestros," *El Faro*, Sept. 17, 2006, http://tinyurl.com/o5kzn75; Jaime López, "Mas de 1,000 maestros amenazados de muerte por extorsionistas," *elsalvador.com*, Aug. 16, 2011, http://tinyurl.com/lda8g5t; Ángela Castro-Liseth Alas, "Simeduco: 38 estudiantes y 10 maestros fueron asesinados en el 2014," *elsalvador.com*, Dec. 10, 2014, http://tinyurl.com/o7emry7.

Antonio Saca, the conservative ARENA (Nationalist Republican Alliance) Party candidate, won the 2004 presidential election. But that year, El Salvador's supreme court ruled the *Mano Dura* law unconstitutional because it presumed criminal activity without requiring proof. In response, Saca launched what he called the Super *Mano Dura* plan, which increased penalties for gang membership but extended some protections to minors charged with gang-related offenses.[65]

Despite negative results in El Salvador, the iron fist approach took hold throughout the Northern Triangle, with Honduras authorizing up to 12 years in prison for gang membership and Guatemala adopting *Mano Dura* in practice, although it never officially adapted the stiffer penalties.[66]

Meanwhile, in 2009, Honduras — whose heritage of military rule persisted in the national police force through the 1990s — suffered a major political failure. The military deposed and exiled President Manuel Zelaya, a left-leaning populist who had been trying to eliminate presidential term limits. Although Obama and regional leaders criticized the coup, they took no major steps to force Zelaya's return, and the United States recognized the election of a conservative president in late 2009. Another conservative won the 2013 election, defeating Zelaya's wife.[67]

By then, Honduras was home both to organized crime groups involved in drug smuggling and to thousands of Barrio-18 and MS-13 members, many of them among the more than 23,000 Hondurans deported from the United States in 2004-05. "Fragile public institutions, already poorly funded and improperly run, crumbled under the pressure of a swelling security epidemic," wrote Joanna Mateo, a human rights analyst with the Defense Department's Miami-based Southern Command.[68]

By 2012, Honduras had the world's highest recorded peacetime homicide rate: 90.4 per 100,000 population (the U.S. rate was 4.7). Meanwhile, El Salvador's murder rate dropped from a high of 70.9 in 2009 to 41.2 in 2012 (due to the now-dissolved gang truce), and Guatemala's fell to 39.9.[69]

That same year, U.S. border agents arrested 80,000 would-be immigrants from Northern Triangle countries — double the number arrested in 2011. About a third were from Honduras, a quarter from El Salvador and 40 percent from Guatemala.[70] The spike followed a steady increase in immigration from Central America's violence zone. By January 2011, 14 percent of all unauthorized immigrants in the United States — 1.5 million people — were from El Salvador, Guatemala and Honduras. Many had come as unaccompanied children, a trend that began in the early 2000s.[71]

In fiscal 2014, the number of unaccompanied children from the three Northern Triangle countries arrested at the Mexican border had soared to 51,705.[72] Another 61,000 Northern Triangle "family units" — small children with adults, usually their mothers — were also arrested at the border, compared with only 14,855 families, mostly from the Northern Triangle, arrested on the Southwest border the previous fiscal year.[73]

By June of 2014, the media and many politicians were describing the upsurge in Central Americans — especially the unaccompanied children — as a crisis. Obama even sent out a warning, via an ABC News interview: "Absolutely don't send your children unaccompanied, on trains or through a bunch of smugglers. Do not send your children to the borders. If they do make it, they'll get sent back. More importantly, they may not make it."[74]

CURRENT SITUATION
Asylum Applications

Responding to last summer's immigration spike, the Obama administration is allowing a small number of Northern Triangle minors to apply for asylum without leaving home.

The "in-country refugee/parole program," which began operating late last year, permits a parent who is legally in the United States to apply for a child to enter the United States because of a well-founded fear of persecution based on race, religion, nationality, political opinion or membership in a particular social group.[75] Under the "parole" option, an applicant may be admitted even if he or she doesn't meet the "persecution" criteria but is nonetheless found "at risk of harm."[76]

The program "provides those seeking asylum a 'right way' to come to our country, as opposed to crossing the border illegally," Vice President Joseph Biden said in November, in announcing the administration's move.[77]

But the program covers only a small number of people, immigrant defenders said. "Some of the most vulnerable kids have parents who don't have legal status in the U.S.," said Jennifer Podkul, senior program officer at the Women's Refugee Commission, a Washington-based advocacy organization.[78] The State Department acknowledged the program's limited scope, saying it would likely cover only "a relatively small number of children" in fiscal 2015, in part because the application process is lengthy. And no more than 4,000 refugees can be admitted to the United States from the entire Latin America/Caribbean region this year.[79]

House Western Hemisphere Subcommittee Chairman Matt Salmon, R-Ariz., argued at a hearing last November that the refugee program will not solve the Northern Triangle crisis. "The answer is not some mass exodus out of Central America," he said. "The answer is to solve the economic, the security problems."[80]

In a more broad-brush criticism, House Judiciary Committee Chairman Bob Goodlatte, R-Va., called the administration move "simply a government-sanctioned border surge."[81]

Nevertheless, the opening of the program coincided with the administration's expansion of detention space for adults arrested with small children at the Southwest border. Central Americans now make up the vast majority of that population.

Families are detained while the mothers press their claims for asylum. If they pass an initial "credible interview,"

Do U.S.-funded anti-gang programs in Central America work?

YES
Elizabeth Hogan
Acting assistant administrator,
Bureau for Latin America and the Caribbean,
U.S. Agency for International Development

From testimony before the House Subcommittee on the Western Hemisphere, Nov. 18, 2014

NO
U.S. Rep. Matt Salmon, R-Ariz.

From testimony before the House Subcommittee on the Western Hemisphere, Nov. 18, 2014

Through the Central America Regional Security Initiative, or CARSI, we are supporting crime- and violence-prevention programs that expand opportunities for youths living in high-crime neighborhoods and strengthening the institutions charged with administering justice and keeping people safe. USAID's [prevention] strategy revolves around smart targeting, both geographic and demographic, concentrating prevention efforts on high-risk youth and high-risk communities.

I am pleased to report that we have independent evidence that our programs are working. The final results from a rigorous four-year impact evaluation carried out by Vanderbilt University in El Salvador, Guatemala, Honduras and Panama show that as a direct result of USAID programs, reported crime is lower and citizens feel safer in the neighborhoods where we are working.

When compared to a 2010 baseline in these same target communities, the Vanderbilt evaluation found that in Guatemala, 60 percent fewer residents reported being aware of homicides; in Honduras, 57 percent fewer reported being aware of extortion; and in El Salvador, 36 percent fewer reported being aware of illegal drug sales in their neighborhoods. In short, where USAID works, people see their communities getting better.

While insecurity is cited as a primary driver for the migration of minors from the region, the lack of jobs and economic opportunity at home is also a critical factor. USAID's development programs also seek to improve educational opportunities and livelihoods for the poor and rural areas. These kind of economic development programs align with our crime-prevention programs to build a foundation for prosperity, and in so doing relieve the pressure on youth and their families to migrate north.

USAID continues to successfully utilize partnerships with the private sector to supplement and sustain our investments in Central America. We have leveraged approximately $40 million in private-sector resources to support at-risk youth. In Honduras, we've developed 41 partnerships with companies to strengthen key agricultural value chains [the moving of an agricultural product from farm to the consumer].

Despite the continued commitment of the region's governments and private entities, we recognize that our current levels of resources are insufficient to spur the kind of large-scale transformative change needed in the region. Additional funding would enable us to significantly scale successful programs in the communities in greatest need and fully implement the U.S. government's strategy for engagement with Central America, balancing the three interrelated objectives of prosperity, governance and security.

The U.S. taxpayer is very generous and wants to help the people of El Salvador, Guatemala and Honduras find a path to peace and prosperity in their respective countries. However, they also demand that we spend their hard-earned taxpayer money wisely and achieve measurable results.

We must acknowledge that previous programs in Central America have failed. Despite U.S. investments through CARSI [the Central America Regional Security Initiative], these countries continue to flail.

The high levels of gang violence and the lack of opportunity right here in our hemisphere not only affect the lives of millions in Central America but affect the United States, too. While the [Obama] administration has cited drops in the total number of children traveling north since June, the fact is that the conditions in El Salvador, Honduras and Guatemala continue to be very grave. . . .

I've consistently been supportive of U.S. efforts through CARSI to assist the region to build capacity to strengthen their respective police forces so they can . . . better confront the high levels of criminality brought on by gangs and drug trafficking organizations. Between 2005 and 2012, there was a 340 percent increase in murders of women and children in Honduras. While El Salvador maintains the world's highest rate of homicides against women and girls, Guatemala ranks third.

There is widespread mistrust of law enforcement and impunity rates as high as 95 percent. In addition to the need for stepping up capacity-building for law enforcement, all three of these Northern Triangle countries lack stable institutions and are plagued by corruption, so U.S. efforts to improve governance and democratic values are imperative.

In this time of tight budgets, are we evaluating each and every individual program that we fund, applying metrics and determining what works and what doesn't work? I am aware of the Vanderbilt study, a $3.5 million study to evaluate some of USAID's programs in the region. Unfortunately, the study does not provide us with project-by-project evaluations and cost-benefit analysis. . . .

Unfortunately, the Obama administration continues to incentivize the mass exodus of citizens from those countries by changing immigration policy by decree. The answer to problems plaguing the region is not to further incentivize citizens of El Salvador, Guatemala and Honduras to leave. Rather, we should double-down on serious efforts to empower people of the region to achieve lasting peace and prosperity in their countries.

John Moore/Getty Images

A youngster from El Salvador is among the immigrants arrested by the U.S. Border Patrol after crossing the Rio Grande from Mexico to McAllen, Texas, on Sept. 8, 2014. In the past two years, more than 100,000 young people from Central America — many traveling alone — have poured across the U.S. border. Their main reasons for leaving were to join family members in the United States, to pursue economic opportunities or to avoid gang violence.

they may be released on bond. At a temporary detention center in Artesia, N.M., which closed late last year, two-thirds of 1,200 mothers and children who had been held there were released on bond. The remaining families were deported.[82]

Meanwhile, the South Texas Family Residential Center in Dilley, southwest of San Antonio, has been enlarged from 480 to 2,400 beds. A similar facility in Karnes, southeast of San Antonio, can hold up to 532 adults and children. Private firms operate both centers.[83]

"We had a crisis, and we wanted to respond quickly," Bryan Cox, a spokesman for Immigration and Customs Enforcement, said last October.[84]

Calls for Reform

Last year's refugee crisis is forcing Central American governments to acknowledge that their efforts to improve their citizens' lives have fallen short.

Some of them even admit, in effect, that foreign observers have a point in their longtime criticism of Central American upper classes for resisting taxation.

Guatemalan Foreign Minister Luis Fernando Carrera Castro said at a Washington panel discussion in July that Guatemala's low taxes may sound like a dream to American conservatives. But, he added, "I believe our levels of taxation are so low that even the extremely conservative Americans will never support that."[85] In fact, Carrera said, if he were to endorse a U.S. tea-party-style position on taxation for Guatemala, "everybody would call me a communist."[86]

Carrera and his fellow foreign ministers from the Triangle who attended the panel session did not discuss the more sensitive issue of corruption. But behind closed doors, Vice President Biden suggested that after meeting with Central American presidents in June that at least some of them acknowledged improvement in that department was needed. "It was a private meeting, but I guarantee you that two of the countries' leaders said . . ., 'We're not cleaning up our institutions quickly enough,'" Biden said.[87]

Indeed, the depth of the Northern Triangle crisis has forced another attitude change as well, Biden said. "This was not a circumstance in which, like it used to be 15 years ago, where we'd sit in a meeting and it was all 'It's your fault, United States; we demand that you do the following.' There were no demands. There was an absolute recognition that there was a shared responsibility here."[88]

That might be because the refugee exodus resulted in international exposure of the violence in Central America. "We have law enforcement officers that are corrupt in too many cases," Rep. Thomas Carper, D-Del., then-chairman of the Senate Homeland Security Committee, said at a July hearing. "In too many cases, the judges are corrupt."[89]

Carper said he had challenged the Guatemalan president concerning cellphone calls made by penitentiary prisoners to organize criminal activities. The prison system has technology to block the calls but doesn't use it, he said. "They need to do their share as well," he said.

With corruption a well-recognized issue, Central American presidents have been trying to show resolve. In Honduras, President Hernández signed an agreement with Transparency International — a Berlin-based organization devoted to exposing and curbing corruption — that pledged his administration would open itself to citizen monitoring.[90]

Guatemalan President Molina said in December that his administration was committed to anti-corruption measures. Vice President Roxana Baldetti added, "We are aware that we are barely started on the work of putting corrupt officials in prison." She said that the government "will not hesitate to file charges."[91]

Salvadoran President Cerén was less specific on the subject in his inaugural speech last June. "We want an active citizenry . . . that demands that officials follow ethical principles," he said.[92]

OUTLOOK

'Not Optimistic'

There is only the most guarded optimism that progress can be made on the gang problem and institutional reform in the Northern Triangle over the next 10 years.

"There have been discussions, particularly after the humanitarian crisis of the unaccompanied children, of how to address the root causes of migration," says Adriana Beltrán, a senior associate at the Washington Office on Latin America. "There is an opportunity, but will the Central American governments step up to the plate and show the political will and commitment that is needed at their end?"

The Wilson Center's Olson agrees the decision rests with the powerful sectors of Central American societies. "Signs of hope" will remain weak, he says, "unless the elites and civil society decide they have to save their nations. That is what it will fundamentally take — some real commitment to profound reform."

But "projections are made on the basis of the current situation," says Wolf of Mexico's CIDE think tank "At the moment, looking at how things have been going in the past two decades, I am not optimistic."

What hope there is, she says, rests with "individuals and groups who want to see change and who keep up their struggles with a stronger fight against corruption and a continuation of institutional reforms."

Diana M. Orcés, a Vanderbilt University political science professor who co-wrote the assessment of U.S.-funded aid programs in Central America, says 10 years is too short a time for the Triangle countries to emerge from crisis. "The situation right now is getting worse," she says, although it would help, she adds, if effective gang truces could be devised. "That would be a perfect scenario to suppress violence."

Sanz of *El Faro* argues that a genuine resolution of the crisis depends on providing a real future for youths who see gang membership as their only hope.

"The young people are not stupid," he says. For now, "even the prospect of a solution, so that young people in the three countries would see that they have a chance to build lives," is utopian.

In today's conditions, he adds, "finishing school does not guarantee you control over your own life." Gang membership will continue to be the only alternative, he says, "as long as no other option makes sense."

NOTES

1. "Global Study on Homicide," U.N. Office on Drugs and Crime, 2013, pp. 24, 126, http://tinyurl.com/npyxq7w.

2. "Total Unaccompanied Alien Children Apprehensions by Month," U.S. Border Patrol, undated, http://tinyurl.com/pgckyo4; "Southwest Border Unaccompanied Children," U.S. Customs and Border Protection, undated, http://tinyurl.com/p3xm4sx.

3. Thomas Bruneau, Lucía Dammert, Elizabeth Skinner, eds., *Maras: Gang Violence and Security in Central America* (2011), Introduction (Kindle edition, no page numbers); Marlon Bishop, "Hello, I'm Calling From 'La Mafia,' " *Planet Money*, NPR, Dec. 18, 2014, http://tinyurl.com/ngp9p4w.

4. Manuel Orozco and Julia Yansura, "Understanding Central American Migration," *Inter-American Dialogue*, August 2014, p. 13, http://tinyurl.com/kb8n5md; Sierra Stoney and Jeanne Batalova, "Central American Immigrants in the United States," Migration Policy Institute, March 18, 2013, http://tinyurl.com/nvjsotc.

5. Sonja Wolf, "Mara Salvatrucha: The Most Dangerous Street Gang in the Americas?" University of Miami, 2012, http://tinyurl.com/odr2vzj; Susan Gzesh, "Central Americans and Asylum Policy in the Reagan Era," Migration Policy Institute, April 1, 2006, http://tinyurl.com/pbj4gfc.

6. Deborah T. Levenson, *Adios Niño: The Gangs of Guatemala City and the Politics of Death* (2013), pp. 3-4, 41; Marco Lara Klahr, *Hoy te toca la muerte: El imperio de las Maras visto desde dentro* (2006), pp. 98-99.

7. Ana Arana, "How the Street Gangs Took Central America," *Foreign Affairs*, May-June, 2005, http://tinyurl.com/oy6u355.

8. Ginger Thompson, "Gunmen Kill 28 on Bus in Honduras; Street Gangs Blamed," *The New York Times*, Dec. 25, 2004, http://tinyurl.com/q3cetku.

9. Michael Shifter, "Countering Criminal Violence in Central America," Council on Foreign Relations, pp. viii, 17-18, http://tinyurl.com/jwowb3d.

10. Eric L. Olson, ed., "Crime and Violence in Central America's Northern Triangle," Woodrow Wilson International Center for Scholars, 2015, p. 3, http://tinyurl.com/ov5jr5n; "Fact Sheet: Emergency Supplemental Request to Address the Increase in Child and Adult Migration from Central America," The White House, July 8, 2014, http://tinyurl.com/nf8erut; "Text of the Emergency Supplemental Appropriations Act, 2014," July 31, 2014, GovTrack, http://tinyurl.com/mrgnzuu.

11. Peter J. Meyer and Clare Ribando Seelke, "Central America Regional Security Initiative: Background and Policy Issues for Congress," Congressional Research Service, May 6, 2014, pp. 22-23, http://tinyurl.com/ndtszrs.

12. See the following Congressional Research Service reports: Peter J. Meyer, "Honduras-U.S. Relations," July 24, 2013, p. 17, http://tinyurl.com/c3vcovu; Clare Ribando Seelke, "El Salvador: Background and U.S. Relations," June 26, 2014, p. 8, http://tinyurl.com/kxt2kq5; Maureen Taft-Morales, "Guatemala: Political, Security and Socio-Economic Conditions and U.S. Relations," Aug. 7, 2014, p. 13, http://tinyurl.com/lvlemg9.

13. Roberta S. Jacobson, "Testimony Before the Subcommittee on Western Hemisphere Affairs," House of Representatives, Nov. 18, 2014, http://tinyurl.com/llzwmnt.

14. "Hearing of the Senate Homeland Security and Governmental Affairs Committee: 'Challenges at the Border . . .,'" transcript, Federal News Service, July 9, 2014.

15. Susan Berk-Seligson, *et al.*, "Impact Evaluation of USAID's Community-Based Crime and Violence Prevention Approach in Central America," Vanderbilt University, 2014, http://tinyurl.com/phfakd2.

16. Olson, *op. cit.*, p. 2.

17. Meyer and Seelke, *op. cit.*, p. 32.

18. Geoffrey Ramsey, "CICIG Names 18 'Judges of Impunity' in Guatemala," *InSight Crime*, Dec. 4, 2012, http://tinyurl.com/n8zu3pr; Marc Lacey, "Drug Gangs Use Violence to Sway Guatemala Vote," *The New York Times*, Aug. 4, 2007, http://tinyurl.com/kbpyvvf; "International Commission against Impunity in Guatemala," Department of Political Affairs, United Nations, undated, http://tinyurl.com/krl5atm; Benjamin Weiser, "Ex-President of Guatemala Faces Judge in Manhattan," *The New York Times*, May 28, 2013, http://tinyurl.com/lfd2sbg; "Former President of Guatemala, Alfonso Portillo, Pleads Guilty . . .," U.S. Attorney's Office, Southern District of New York, March 18, 2014, http://tinyurl.com/n7koj9x; Benjamin Weiser, "Guatemala: Ex-President Sentenced," *The New York Times*, May 22, 2014, http://tinyurl.com/kb8y9h4; Mirte Postema, "CICIG Investigation Could Be a Game-Change for Guatemala," *Americas Quarterly* blog, Sept. 9, 2014, http://tinyurl.com/ms4nzat.

19. Nelson Renteria, "Former El Salvador president wanted for corruption given house arrest," Reuters, Sept. 5, 2014, http://tinyurl.com/lfyu37p; "Guatemala ex-police chief jailed for life by Swiss court," BBC, June 6, 2014, http://tinyurl.com/l9qk5qr; Gustavo Palencia, "Honduras arrests ex-social security chief in $200 million graft bust," Reuters, Sept. 9, 2014, http://tinyurl.com/nzk8kve.

20. Aaron Korthuis, "CARSI in Honduras: Isolated Successes and Limited Impact," in Olson, *op. cit.*, p. 165.

21. Héctor Silva Ávalos, "Corruption in El Salvador: Politicians, Police, and Transportistas," *InSight Crime*, March 2014, pp. 2, 6-7, http://tinyurl.com/p74j753.

22. Sonja Wolf, "Mano Dura: Gang Suppression in El Salvador," *Sustainable Security*, March 1, 2011, http://tinyurl.com/p2hgzrt; Hannah Stone, "The Iron Fist Returns to El Salvador," *InSight Crime*, Feb. 2, 2012, http://tinyurl.com/naej9l6; Steven Dudley, "How 'Mano Dura' is Strengthening Gangs," *InSight Crime*, Nov. 21, 2010, http://tinyurl.com/o8yap8q.

23. *Ibid.*, Dudley; "Transnational Organized Crime in Central America: A Threat Assessment," U.N. Office on Drugs and Crime, 2012, p. 16, http://tinyurl.com/8d9tcq4.

24. Clara Ribando Seelke, "Gangs in Central America," *Congressional Research Service*, Feb. 20, 2014, pp. 11-12, http://tinyurl.com/puy9nnr.

25. Seth Robbins, "How one Spanish priest went gangster in Central America," *Global Post*, Sept. 23, 2014, http://tinyurl.com/nauggfo; Marguerite Cawley, "El Salvador Arrests Priest Over Gang Negotiations," *InSight Crime*, Aug. 4, 2014, http://tinyurl.com/olttfgw.

26. Steven Dudley, "Mass Graves Burying the Truth about El Salvador Gang Truce," *InSight Crime*, Jan. 1, 2014, http://tinyurl.com/ngl9y9n; David Gagne, "El Salvador Squashes Talk of Dialogue With Gangs," *InSight Crime*, Nov. 6, 2014, http://tinyurl.com/oh2od5h. Quoted in, "El Salvador cierra las puertas a negociación con pandillas," The Associated Press (*El Nuevo Herald*), Jan. 26, 2015, http://tinyurl.com/n7f9kgc.

27. James Bargent, "Murders in Honduras Rising Despite Gang Truce," *InSight Crime*, Aug. 5, 2013, http://tinyurl.com/men9n56; Roger A. Carvajal, *Violence in Honduras: An analysis of the failure in public security and the state's response to criminality* (2014), p. 12; Marguerite Cawley, "What Is Behind Reported Homicide Drops in Honduras, Guatemala?" *InSight Crime*, July 16, 2014, http://tinyurl.com/mpj9yag.

28. Olson, *op. cit.*, p. 66.

29. "President Clinton, Remarks to the Legislative Assembly of El Salvador in San Salvador," March 10, 1999, The American Presidency Project, University of California, Santa Barbara, http://tinyurl.com/pcsbow2.

30. Quoted in Matt Spetalnick and Alister Bull, "Obama pledges $200 million to Central America drug fight," Reuters, March 22, 2011, www. reuters.com/article/2011/03/22/us-obama-latin america-idUS TRE72G6YT20110322; "Remarks by President Obama and President Funes of El Salvador . . .," The White House, March 22, 2011, www.whitehouse.gov/the-press-office/ 2011/03/22/remarks-president-obama-and-president-funes-el-salvador-joint-press-conf.

31. Meyer and Seelke, *op. cit.*, pp. 20-22.

32. *Ibid.*, pp. 24-26; "Honduras 2013 Human Rights Report, Executive Summary," State Department, undated, http://tinyurl.com/npws7a9.

33. Quoted in Jen Sokatch, "Central America's elites must fund their own state security, expert says," *The Christian Science Monitor*, June 9, 2011, http://tinyurl.com/3qmwu58; Kevin Casas-Zamora, written testimony, "U.S.-Central America Security Cooperation," U.S. Senate Caucus on International Narcotics Control, May 25, 2011, http://tinyurl.com/qzkpztu.

34. Stephen Schlesinger and Stephen Kinzer, *Bitter Fruit: The Untold Story of the American Coup in Guatemala* (1983), pp. 65-67.

35. *Ibid.*, pp. 38, 50, 53; "United Fruit Chronology," United Fruit Historical Society, 2001, http://tinyurl.com/7685kme.

36. "Guatemala," Central Intelligence Agency [documents], http://tinyurl.com/ogknc7x; Schlesinger and Kinzer, *op. cit.*, pp. 37-79.

37. Levenson, *op. cit.*, pp. 23, 26; "Guatemala, Memory of Silence," Commission for Historical Clarification, Conclusions and Recommendations, 1999, pp. 17, 20-22, 85-86, http://tinyurl. com/olesezf.

38. Richard A. Haggerty, "The 1970s: The Road to Revolt," in "A County Study: El Salvador," Library of Congress, 1988, http://tinyurl.com/ oj3yp4q; Jeffrey L. Gould and Aldo A. Lauria-Santiago, *To Rise in Darkness: Revolution, Repression, and Memory in El Salvador, 1920-1932* (2008), pp. 170-209.

39. *Ibid.*, both.

40. *Ibid.*, Haggerty.

41. Quoted in Kate Doyle and Emily Willard, " 'Learn from History,' 31st Anniversary of the Assassination of Archbishop Oscar Romero," National Security Archive, March 23, 2011, http://tinyurl.com/ky8npps; Juan de Onis, "U.S. Giving Salvador Combat Equipment," *The New York Times*, Jan. 19, 1981, http://tinyurl.com/ ojoegqb.

42. Quoted in *ibid.*; "Report of the UN Truth Commission on El Salvador," United Nations, March 29, 1993, pp. 127-135, http://tinyurl.com/ 3cw3hf. Nearly a year after Romero was killed, outgoing President Carter approved $5 million in military aid to El Salvador.

43. Mike Allison, "El Salvador's brutal civil war: What we still don't know," Al Jazeera, March 1, 2012, http://tinyurl.com/7hgb2gt.

44. "Justice & the Generals," PBS, undated, http://tinyurl.com/o2e8dgp.

45. "From Madness to Hope: The 12-year war in El Salvador, Report of the Commission on the Truth for El Salvador," United Nations Security Council, March 15, 1993, pp. 40, 44, 114-121, http://tinyurl.com/3cw3hf; Mark Danner, "The Truth of El Mozote," *The New Yorker*, Dec. 6, 1993, http://tinyurl.com/kltm2og; Raymond Bonner, "Bringing El Salvador Nun Killers to Justice," *The Daily Beast*, Nov. 9, 2014, http://tinyurl.com/nn3herr; "El Salvador country profile," BBC, Aug. 16, 2012, http:// tinyurl.com/nk3ggae.

46. Richard A. Haggerty, "The United States Takes a Hand," in "A Country Study . . .," *op. cit.*

47. See President Carter's May 22, 1977, foreign policy speech at http://tinyurl.com/p7tv8p9.

48. Quoted in Elisabeth Malkin, "Trial on Guatemalan Civil War Carnage Leaves Out U.S. Role," *The New York Times*, May 16, 2013, http://tinyurl.com/odwb6lr; Michael E. Allison, "U.S. involvement in the Guatemalan genocide," *Central American politics* (blog), May 17, 2013, http://tinyurl.com/pndte3r.

49. "Central America, 1981-1993," U.S. State Department, Office of the Historian, updated Oct. 31, 2013, http://tinyurl.com/q26ur65.

50. Gary Cohn and Ginger Thompson, "When a wave of torture and murder staggered a small U.S. ally, truth was a casualty," *The Baltimore Sun*, June 11, 1995, http://tinyurl. com/o3fobqv; "The Nicaraguan Conflict," in Tim Merrill, ed., *Honduras: A Country Study* (1995), Library of Congress, http://tinyurl.com/c6ybx7.

51. Malkin, *op. cit.*; Tracy Wilkinson, "Salvador Sanchez Ceren wins El Salvador's presidential election," *Los Angeles Times*, March 13, 2014, http://tinyurl.com/mas4hxl.

52. "President Clinton, Remarks in a Roundtable Discussion on Peace Efforts in Guatemala City," March 10, 1999, The American Presidency Project, University of California, Santa Barbara, http://tinyurl.com/kprl9yv; John M. Broder, "Clinton Offers His Apologies To Guatemala," *The New York Times*, March 11, 1999, http://tiny url.com/q2ykotw.

53. Quoted in Marcos Aleman, "Obama to visit human rights activist's tomb," The Associated Press (*The Washington Post*), March 18, 2011, http://tiny url.com/p6hs5to; Doyle and Willard, *op. cit.*

54. Aaron Terrazas, "Salvadoran Immigrants in the United States," Migration Policy Institute, Jan. 5, 2010, http://tinyurl.com/qyv3ycs; James Smith, "Guatemala: Economic Migrants Replace Political Refugees," Migration Policy Institute, April 1, 2006, http://tinyurl.com/pl8nj9t.

55. Levenson, *op. cit.*, pp. 40-41.

56. Tim Golden, "Accord Reached to Halt Civil War in El Salvador," *The New York Times*, Jan. 1, 1992, http://tinyurl.com/pjp6ky6.

57. Larry Rohter, "Guatemalans Formally End 36-Year Civil War, Central America's Longest and Deadliest," *The New York Times*, Dec. 30, 1996, http://tinyurl.com/lkfmzfn; Marcie Mersky, "Human Rights in Negotiating Peace Agreements: Guatemala," International Council on Human Rights Policy, 2005, http://tinyurl.com/ mbu2ypb; "Indigenous and Tribal Peoples — Guatemala," International Labour Organisation, undated, http://tinyurl.com/m34yk7d.

58. "Guatemalan Court Suspends Genocide Retrial of Former Dictator," International Justice Resource Center, Jan. 8, 2015, http://tinyurl. com/mb8rplk; Emi MacLean and Sophie Beaudoin, "Eighteen Months After Initial Conviction . . .," *International Justice Monitor*, Jan. 6, 2015, http://tinyurl.com/mj4q59h; Kathy Gilsinan, "The Master's Thesis That Just Delayed a Genocide Trial," *The Atlantic*, Jan. 6, 2015, http://tinyurl.com/kf8rgxg; Linda Cooper and James Hodge, "El Salvador struggles to come to terms with violent past," *National Catholic Reporter*, March 24, 2014, http://tinyurl.com/ n5vfzma.

59. Daniel Reichman, "Honduras: The Perils of Remittance Dependence and Clandestine Migration," Migration Policy Institute, April 11, 2013, http://tinyurl.com/kjlrn9f; "Honduras: Assessment of the Damage Caused by Hurricane Mitch in 1998," Economic Commission for Latin and the Caribbean, United Nations, April 14, 1999, http://tinyurl.com/lkohb9x; Madeline Messick and Claire Bergeron, "Temporary Protected Status in the United States . . . ," Migration Policy Institute,

July 2, 2014, http://tinyurl.com/ku5ez4b. TPS also was granted to Salvadorans who fled after a series of 2001 earthquakes that killed 1,100 people.

60. Pamela Constable, "Refugees in U.S. at Risk of Being Uprooted Again," *The Washington Post*, March 28, 1997, http://tinyurl.com/mgzxsvj.

61. Ana Arana, "How the Street Gangs Took Central America," *Foreign Affairs*, May-June, 2005, http://tinyurl.com/oy6u355.

62. Mary Helen Johnson, "National Policies and the Rise of Transnational Gangs," Migration Policy Institute, April 1, 2006, http://tinyurl. com/k2jk6u5; Seelke, *op. cit.*, "Gangs in Central America."

63. *Ibid.*, Seelke.

64. Wolf, *op. cit.*; Stone, *op. cit.*; Dudley, *op. cit.*, "How 'Mano Dura' is Strengthening Gangs."

65. Seelke, *op. cit.*, "Gangs in Central America;" Melissa Siskind, "Guilt by Association: Transnational Gangs and the Merits of a New Mano Dura," *The George Washington International Law Review*, p. 306, http://tinyurl.com/jwu6cv4.

66. "Youth Gangs in Central America: Issues in Human Rights, Effective Policing, and Prevention," Washington Office on Latin America, November 2006, http://tinyurl.com/khn9n28; Seelke, *op. cit.*, p. 9.

67. Elisabeth Malkin, "Honduran President Is Ousted in Coup," *The New York Times*, June 28, 2009, http://tinyurl.com/nr3ybl; Dana Frank, "In Honduras, a Mess Made in the U.S.," *The New York Times*, Jan. 26, 2012, http://tinyurl. com/83vnve6; "Honduras elections: ruling National party's candidate wins presidential race," *The Guardian*, Nov. 26, 2013, http://tinyurl.com/ kuox9jw; Joanna Mateo, "Street Gangs of Honduras," in Bruneau, Dammert, and Skinner, *op. cit.*

68. *Ibid.*, Mateo.

69. "Global Study on Homicide, 2013," *op. cit.*

70. Sebastian Rotella, "The New Border: Illegal Immigration's Shifting Frontier," *ProPublica*, Dec. 5, 2012, http://tinyurl.com/aclcgqs.

71. Sierra Stoney and Jeanne Batalova, "Central American Immigrants in the United States," Migration Policy Institute, March 18, 2013, http://tinyurl.com/l9v6hoq.

72. William A. Kandel, coordinator, *et al.*, "Unaccompanied Alien Children: Potential Factors Contributing to Recent Immigration," Congressional Research Service, July 3, 2014, pp. 2-3, http://tinyurl.com/nm5xvps; "Southwest Border Unaccompanied . . . ," *op. cit.*

73. *Ibid.*, "Southwest Border Unaccompanied . . ."

74. Quoted in Devin Dwyer, "Obama Warns Central Americans: 'Do Not Send Your Children to the Borders,' " ABC News, June 26, 2014, http://tinyurl.com/k42xnj2.

75. "Launch of In-Country-Refugee/Parole Program for Children in El Salvador, Guatemala and Honduras," State Department, Dec. 3, 2014, http://tinyurl.com/kuokwtb; Michael D. Shear, "Obama Approves Plan to Let Children in Central America Apply for Refugee Status," *The New York Times*, Sept. 30, 2014, http://tinyurl.com/qbwo4cd.

76. "In-Country Refugee/Parole Program for Minors . . ., Fact Sheet," State Department, Nov. 14, 2014, http://tinyurl.com/olvth9n.

77. Quoted in Angela Greiling Keane, "Biden Promises Refugee Status to Central American Minors," Bloomberg News, Nov. 14, 2014, http://tinyurl.com/l3hllpq.

78. Quoted in *ibid.*

79. "In-Country Refugee/Parole Program . . . ," *op. cit.*

80. "Western Hemisphere Subcommittee hearing on 'Unaccompanied Alien Children: Pressing the Administration for a Strategy,' " transcript, Federal News Service, Nov. 18, 2014.

81. Quoted in Keane, *op. cit.*

82. Lauren Villagran, "Two-thirds of Artesia detainees have been released," *Albuquerque Journal*, Dec. 22, 2014, http://tinyurl.com/n5sbxy2.

83. "ICE's new family detention center in Dilley, Texas to open in December," U.S. Immigration and Customs Enforcement, Nov. 18, 2014, http://tinyurl.com/l3mvoyw; John Burnett, "How Will A Small Town in Arizona Manage an ICE Facility in Texas?" NPR, Oct. 28, 2014, http://tinyurl.com/pmuqlyt; Jason Buch, "Critics frown at ICE jail contracts," *San Antonio Express-News*, Oct. 11, 2014, http://tinyurl.com/l7lr38f.

84. Quoted in *ibid.*, Buch.

85. "The Woodrow Wilson Center Holds a Discussion on Unaccompanied Immigrant Children," *CQ Transcriptions*, July 24, 2014.

86. *Ibid.*

87. "Remarks to the Press with Q&A by Vice President Joe Biden in Guatemala," transcript, The White House, June 20, 2014, http://tinyurl. com/mjf6x44.

88. *Ibid.*

89. "Hearing of the Senate Homeland Security and Governmental Affairs Committee: 'Challenges at the Border . . .,'" transcript, Federal News Service, July 9, 2014.

90. "Honduras Government, ASJ and Transparency International Sign Agreement for Transparency," Transparency International, Oct. 6, 2014, http://tinyurl.com/o8rq9fp.

91. Quoted in, "Presidente Pérez Molina afirma que país es pionero en gobierno electrónico contra corrupción," President of Guatemala, Dec. 4, 2014, http://tinyurl.com/ompzuuh.

92. Quoted in, "Sánchez Cerén: 'Continuaré con el compromiso de no más corrupción," *Telesur*, June 1, 2014, http://tinyurl.com/keyr5nc.

BIBLIOGRAPHY
Selected Sources
Books

Bruneau, Thomas C., Lucía Dammert and Elizabeth Skinner, eds., *Maras: Gang Violence and Security in Central America*, **University of Texas Press, 2011.**
Scholars, including some from Central America, and many affiliated with military think tanks, examine the region's two major gangs — their origins, how they operate and why they have flourished.

Klahr, Marco Lara, *Hoy Te Toca La Muerte: El Imperio de las Maras visto desde dentro (Today You Die: The Empire of the Maras Seen From Within)*, **Editorial Planeta Mexicana, 2006.**
A Mexican journalist interviews ex-gang members in Central America (in Spanish).

Levenson, Deborah T., *Adios Niño: The Gangs of Guatemala City and the Politics of Death*, **Duke University Press, 2013.**
A Guatemala specialist and history professor at Boston College traces the murderous culture of Guatemalan gangs to the country's history of savage repression.

Articles

Bishop, Marlon, "Hello, I'm Calling From 'La Mafia,'" Planet Money, NPR, Dec. 18, 2014, http://tinyurl .com/ ngp9p4w.
Extortion demands are part of everyday life in the Northern Triangle, as a U.S. radio reporter documents from Honduras.

Carcamo, Cindy, "In Honduras, U.S. deportees seek to journey north again," *Los Angeles Times*, **Aug. 16, 2014, http://tinyurl.com/ll9bhrw.**
Young people deported to Honduras tell a reporter they are desperate to flee again because they fear for their lives.

Dudley, Steven, "El Salvador Gangs and Security Forces Up the Ante in Post-Truce Battle," *InSight Crime*, **Oct. 22, 2014, http://tinyurl.com/ovt9p3d.**
The cofounder of a crime news and analysis website examines the collapse of a truce between Salvadoran gangs.

Frank, Dana, "Hopeless in Honduras? The Election and the Future of Tegucigalpa," *Foreign Affairs*, **Nov. 22, 2013, http://tinyurl.com/p8ahfp2.**
A historian from the University of California, Santa Cruz, holds the U.S.-backed Honduran government responsible for the worsening of public safety.

Leland, John, "Fleeing Violence in Honduras, a Teenage Boy Seeks Asylum in Brooklyn," *The New York Times*, **Dec. 5, 2014, http://tinyurl.com/ qf4e8x3.**
Young people who fled Honduras tell of murderous violence in their home country.

Quinones, Sam, "The End of Gangs: Cleaning Up Los Angeles," *Pacific Standard*, **Dec. 29, 2014, http://tiny url.com/ns8o2c5.**
A journalist recounts the Los Angeles Police Department's success in reducing the threat of gangs, whose methods were transplanted to Central America.

Reports and Studies

Berk-Seligson, Susan, et al., "Impact Evaluation of USAID's Community-Based Crime and Violence Prevention Approach in Central America: Regional Report for El Salvador, Guatemala, Honduras and Panama," Latin American Public Opinion Project, Vanderbilt University, October 2014, http://tinyurl .com/phfakd2.
A team of scholars concludes that a "prevention" approach to criminal violence in vulnerable neighborhoods is proving effective.

Carvajal, Roger, "Violence in Honduras: An Analysis of the Failure in Public Security and the State's Response to Criminality," Naval Postgraduate School, 2014, http://tiny url.com/qbdw25d.
In a master's thesis, an Army major analyzes governmental dysfunction and corruption that have fostered high-level organized crime in Honduras and allowed gangs to flourish.

Espach, Ralph, and Daniel Haering, "Border Insecurity in Central America's Northern Triangle," Woodrow Wilson International Center for Scholars, Migration Policy Institute, November 2012, http:// tinyurl.com/o9yud5k.
Weak border controls and corruption are among the factors that have opened the Northern Triangle to Mexican drug syndicates, two experts — one based in Guatemala — conclude.

Meyer, Peter J., and Clare Ribando Seelke, "Central America Regional Security Initiative: Background and Policy Issues for Congress," Congressional Research Service, May 6, 2014, http://tinyurl.com/nmhrlox.
Experts from Congress' nonpartisan research arm examine the Obama administration's Central America aid strategy, concluding that improving public safety demands long-term assistance.

Olson, Eric L., ed., "Crime and Violence in Central America's Northern Triangle," Woodrow Wilson International Center for Scholars, 2015, http:// tinyurl.com/kjnujrs.
A team of experts from a Washington think tank says corruption, elites' resistance to paying more taxes and the absence of job opportunities remain obstacles to effective U.S. aid programs in Central America.

FOR MORE INFORMATION

El Faro, Calle El Mirador, Pasaje 11, No. 138, Col. Escalón, San Salvador, El Salvador; 011-503-2208-6685; www.elfaro .net. Salvadoran news site partly financed by U.S. and European foundations; includes reports in Spanish on public safety developments.

InSight Crime, 4400 Massachusetts Ave., N.W., Washington, DC 20016; 202-885-1000; www.insight-crime.org/. News site based in Medellín, Colombia, and Washington; provides news and analyses of crime and public safety based on its own reporting and reports from Latin American media.

Inter-American Dialogue, 1211 Connecticut Ave., N.W., Washington, DC 20036; 202-822-9002; www.thedialogue .org/remittancesmigration. Centrist think tank whose studies of the remittance economy — money sent home by immigrants — include analyses of Central American migration and its effects.

Plaza Pública, Universidad Rafael Landivar Vista Hermosa III, Campus Central, Xona 16, casa Plaza Pública, Guatemala; 011-502-2426-2644; www.plazapublica.com.gt. In-depth news site financed by a major Guatemalan university and European and U.S. foundations; areas of coverage (in Spanish) include crime and corruption.

Washington Office on Latin America, 1666 Connecticut Ave., N.W., Washington, DC 20009; 202-797-2171; www .wola.org/program/central_america. Liberal think tank that runs a Central America program; reports and analyses focus on Latin American and U.S. programs.

Woodrow Wilson International Center for Scholars, Latin American Program, 1 Woodrow Wilson Plaza, 1300 Pennsylvania Ave., N.W., Washington, DC 20004; 202-691-4000; www.wilsoncenter.org/program/latin-american-program. Congressionally chartered research center that conducts detailed studies of Central American developments.

2

European Migration Crisis

Sarah Glazer

A protester clashes with a policeman during an anti-immigration demonstration in Prague, Czech Republic, on July 18, 2015. The flood of refugees into Europe has fueled the rise of anti-immigrant parties in Europe, notably in Denmark and Finland. European governments have vacillated between viewing the surge as a humanitarian disaster worthy of sympathy and an invasion that must be stopped. Terrorist attacks by Muslim extremists have boosted support for the nationalists. Many human rights advocates say Europeans' offers to take in refugees are inadequate.

Matej Divizna/Getty Images

From *CQ Researcher*,
July 31, 2015; updated February 2016.

Sixteen-year-old Said, a Somalian, was handed over to traffickers by his parents, who have eight other children, in hopes he could reach relatives in Norway. Armed smugglers at the Libyan border imprisoned Said for nine months while his parents raised the money for his journey, he told the Washington-based Save the Children advocacy group. Then the smugglers beat him to force him onto an overloaded fishing trawler headed for Italy.[1]

Said was one of only 28 survivors among the trawler's estimated 800 passengers when the boat sank on April 19, 2015, after hitting a rescue ship.[2] It was the deadliest incident ever recorded in the Mediterranean Sea.[3]

Migrants had paid between $700 and $7,000 for the crossing — with a place on the top deck carrying the highest price. For many, that meant the difference between life and death. The passengers below deck were locked inside with no means of escape, according to some survivors.[4]

Humanitarian groups are calling the Mediterranean migration route to Europe the world's deadliest, with more than 3,000 deaths in 2015 and 368 just in January of this year, more than four times the toll during the same month in 2015.[5] The flood of people seeking haven in Europe is part of a worldwide exodus that the United Nations calls the worst refugee crisis since World War II.[6]

Last year, more than 1 million refugees and migrants crossed the Mediterranean into Europe, a five-fold increase over arrivals in 2014, according to the United Nations High Commissioner for Refugees (UNHCR).

The four-year-old civil war in Syria has been the single biggest driver of the surge, according to UNHCR.[7] Syrians made up 41 percent of those crossing the Mediterranean in January, the largest group by country of origin, followed by Afghans and Iraqis.[8]

European governments have vacillated between viewing the refugee surge as a humanitarian disaster worthy of sympathy or an invasion that must be stopped. At a summit meeting in June 2015, the 28-member European Union (EU) could not agree on a mandatory allocation plan by which nations would have to take in 40,000 asylum-seekers* from Syria and Eritrea who had reached Greece and Italy after April 15.[9]

In a deal negotiated last September, a majority of EU member states agreed to resettle another 120,000 refugees from Italy and Greece, but by February of this year fewer than 600 had been placed. Another summit on the refugee crisis ended in disarray Feb. 19, with European leaders in conflict over the right solution and pursuing contradictory policies.[10]

The flow of people into Europe not only has raised questions about how to help refugees fleeing war or persecution; it also has raised the perennial question of how many migrants Europe needs for its economy. Debate rages in many places over migration's impact and whether migrants will boost the economy or harm it by taking jobs from natives, lowering wages and overloading social services and housing.

A string of terrorist attacks since 2001 has made Europeans nervous about immigrants from Muslim countries, a fear underlined after the lethal November 2015 attack in Paris by Islamic State militants killed 130. At least one of the assailants had posed as a Syrian refugee and as many as four of those connected to the attack had entered Europe along the migrant trail, according to news reports.[11]

The attack occurred in a city already traumatized by the January 2015 attack on the satirical magazine *Charlie Hebdo* and a kosher grocery store in Paris by gunmen linked to Islamic militant groups in Yemen. However, all three gunmen were French, born and raised in Paris.[12]

Popular anxiety has helped fuel the rise of anti-immigrant, far-right parties in Europe, from famously liberal Scandinavia to Germany, France and the Netherlands.[13] The Danish People's Party doubled its share of the vote from four years ago to become the nation's second-largest party in June 2015.[14]

The ongoing Syrian conflict has only intensified the crisis. In February, as Russian air strikes hit the Syrian city of Aleppo, sending civilians fleeing, tens of thousands of Syrian refugees were massed in the cold at the Turkish border, closed to them by the Turkish government. Turkey has already taken in some 2.5 million Syrian refugees, and Turkish President Recep Tayyip Erdogan has threatened to send millions of refugees to Europe. The European Union has agreed to give Turkey €3 billion ($3.3 billion) in exchange for stemming the tide of refugees to Europe. But as of early February, Erdogan complained that he had still not received the money and was reportedly negotiating for more concessions from the EU.[15]

Cold winter weather has not stemmed the flow; by mid-February more than 84,000 migrants had arrived by sea this year, and arrivals in Greece were about 20 times the numbers counted over the same period last year.[16]

The route of migration has shifted from the first half of last year, when attention was focused on the perilous Mediterranean crossing from Libya to Italy. In recent months, many more migrants have been trying to enter Europe by taking the much shorter journey across the Aegean Sea from Turkey to Greece. However, experts say smugglers have been taking advantage of the shorter journey to place migrants in even more flimsy boats. Of the 410 migrants reported dead or missing at sea this year by mid-February, the vast majority (320) met their death in the Aegean, according to Joel A. Millman, spokesman for the International Organization for Migration (IOM), which has been tracking the fatalities.

"What we are witnessing in the Aegean Sea is even more horrendous than what we experienced in the Mediterranean," said Christopher Catrambone, founder of the nonprofit Migrant Offshore Aid Station, which rescues refugees at sea. "Due to the shorter distances, smugglers take increased risks at the expense of the refugees, often giving them worthless lifejackets and inflatable boats that simply cannot reach shore."[17]

---

* An asylum-seeker is a person seeking safety from persecution or serious harm who is awaiting a decision on an application for refugee status under national and international law.

Crossings Surge in Mediterranean, Balkans

More than 220,000 migrants and refugees* — mainly from the Middle East and Africa — entered Europe by land or sea in the first six months of 2015, including about 145,000 who crossed the Mediterranean, according to Frontex, the European Union's border agency. About 79,000 others crossed by land and sea from Turkey to Greece, most continuing by land through former Yugoslavian countries such as Macedonia into Hungary — nearly a tenfold increase over 2014.**

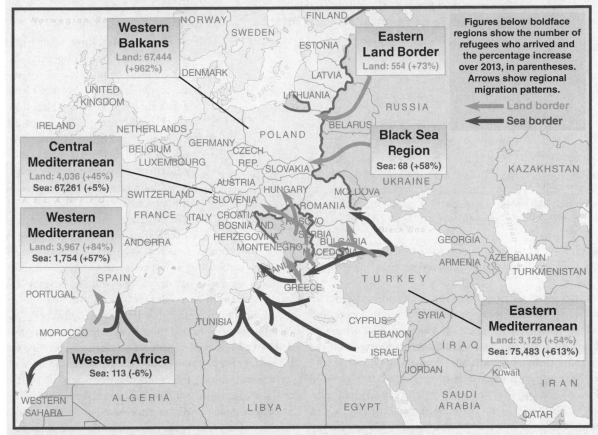

* The United Nations puts the total at 137,000.

** Figures for Western Africa, Western and Central Mediterranean (land only), Black Sea and Eastern Land Border near Poland are only through May 31, 2015.

Source: Data from Frontex, European Union, http://tinyurl.com/d299hvt

By the middle of last year, migration to Europe was already on a markedly accelerating trend along this route. On the sea route from Turkey, to Greece, the number of migrants detected crossing illegally increased 613 percent in the first six months of 2015 from the same period in 2014; the route from Greece through the Balkan countries of the former Yugoslavia saw a 962 percent increase, according to EU border agency Frontex. (*See map, above.*)[18]

Yet EU officials in Brussels emphasize that the 1 million migrants who arrived last year constitute only 2 percent of the continent's 500 million inhabitants and are a tiny number compared to the millions of Syrians

Refugee Deaths Rising in 2015

Almost 3,800 refugees and migrants died in 2015 while crossing the Mediterranean Sea. In April, 1,244 died in separate incidents when overloaded boats sank while traveling from Libya to Europe. As of February 14, 2016, 410 more were reported dead or missing this year, including 368 in January alone.

Refugee and Migrant Fatalities in the Mediterranean Sea, by Month, 2015 and 2016*

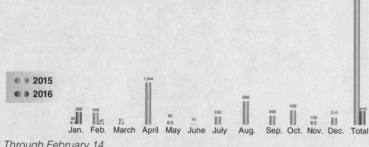

● 2015
● 2016

368 82	346 42	61	1,244	95	10	230	686	268	432	106	210	3,770 410
Jan.	Feb.	March	April	May	June	July	Aug.	Sep.	Oct.	Nov.	Dec.	Total

* Through February 14

Source: "Mediterranean Update," Missing Migrants Project, International Organization for Migration, February 16, 2016.

who have fled to Turkey, Lebanon and Jordan—the three countries where 90 percent of Syria's refugees have gone.[19]

It is "well within the European Union's means" to take in 1 million refugees displaced by the Syrian and other conflicts over the next few years, according to François Crépeau, the U.N. special rapporteur on the human rights of migrants.[20] Antonio Guterres, the U.N. high commissioner for refugees, has scolded Europe for taking in less than 4 percent of Syrian refugees. "Never was so little done by so many for so few. . . . Person for person, the wealthy EU is offering refuge to 1,000 times fewer Syrians than cash-strapped Lebanon," he wrote in 2014.[21]

Although international experts and diplomats at the U.N. may downplay the magnitude of the refugee problem for Europe, national leaders must answer to their constituents. Polls show that many Europeans want immigration to their country reduced, with majorities of 80 percent or more expressing that sentiment in the Mediterranean border nations of Italy and Greece, and more than half in the U.K. and France.[22]

Those who come principally to find work, often dubbed "economic migrants," account for close to half of

those crossing the sea, estimates Arezo Malakooti, director of migration research for Altai Consulting, a Paris-based consulting firm, and author of a study of Mediterranean migrants for the International Organization for Migration, an intergovernmental organization with 127 member states that works for humane migration.

"The real question is what to do with irregular [illegal] migrants who don't qualify for protection" as refugees, says Malakooti. "Most won't leave voluntarily when asked to. They have gone through great . . . dangers to get to Europe." Often they disappear to work in the black market, she says, where they are vulnerable to exploitation and are more likely to engage in criminal activity.

According to Human Rights Watch, while many migrants who come from countries such as Nigeria, Gambia, Senegal and Mali are seeking to improve their economic opportunities, some also may have endured human-rights violations and could have valid refugee claims.[23]

Pledging to strengthen borders has been Europe's typical response to unwanted migration. After the catastrophic sinking of Said's boat in April, the EU tripled spending for its border agency Frontex to conduct search-and-rescue operations involving migrant boats and stepped up patrols of Europe's external borders. In the summer of 2015, the EU began more closely monitoring migrant boats in the Mediterranean's international waters, the first phase of a controversial military strategy to break up human smuggling rings. On Oct. 7, 2015, the EU initiated the second phase of its military operation, involving search and seizure of smugglers' boats in international waters.[24] By February, it had seized 76 boats from illegal organizations and rescued over 9,000 people, it claimed.[25]

The migrant crisis has exposed divisions among the countries within Europe and especially within the Schengen area, a 26-country region that allows travelers to enter any of its member countries without showing a passport. Countries along the Schengen area's borders, such as Hungary and Greece, have been overwhelmed over the past year with migrants trying to reach other countries in Europe. Hungary's president announced plans in the summer of 2015 to build a 13-foot-high fence on its border with Serbia (which is outside the Schengen area), while France and Austria stepped up border patrols against refugees attempting to leave Italy.

By late January, more countries within the Schengen system had instituted temporary checks on borders to control the migrant influx— even famously generous Sweden, which in 2013 was the first country to offer permanent residence to all Syrians fleeing the civil war. Border controls were also in place in Austria, Germany, Denmark, Slovenia and Croatia. Ministers in those countries were pushing the EU to implement an emergency rule that would extend the controls for up to two years.[26]

EU officials have expressed fears that the erection of national frontiers could destroy the single market economy at the core of the European Union and its common currency, the euro. "Without Schengen . . . the euro has no point," said EU chief executive Jean-Claude Juncker.[27]

Some experts say tighter borders only push migrants to use riskier routes at extortionist prices. "We see smuggling networks getting stronger and stronger because the more you reinforce a border with patrols, the more [refugees] are in need of assistance from professional smugglers," and that creates a black market, says Ruben Andersson, an anthropologist at the London School of Economics and author of a 2014 book about illegal immigration to Europe, *Illegality, Inc.* "Smugglers are service providers," he says.

Despite heart-rending photographs of refugees crammed into unseaworthy or overcrowded boats, the single biggest entry point for migrants is much less dramatic — international airports. Most illegal immigrants arrive on a legal visa and then fail to leave, according to Frontex.[28]

Politicians such as British Prime Minister David Cameron say the key is to make it clear to these immigrants before they come that they will be found and sent home. Right now, most migrants believe that once they reach the Continent, they can easily slip across Europe's unguarded national borders and either apply for asylum in their country of choice or slip into the underground economy, says Demetrios Papademetriou, president of the Migration Policy Institute Europe, a think tank in Brussels.

To counter that, "you have to say, 'Guess what? We'll find you, we'll deport you; you will have lost thousands of dollars, and you will go back to the end of line,'" he says.

Like many other experts, Papademetriou believes Europe must streamline its asylum system to render decisions more quickly so that those who do not qualify for asylum can be immediately deported. It can take years for asylum-seekers to get a decision on their applications in both Germany, which takes one of the highest numbers of asylum-seekers in the EU, and in Britain, which takes far fewer.

Some experts say the root cause of the crisis can be traced to chaos in countries where Western governments have interfered militarily. In 2011, for example, a NATO bombing campaign helped rebels in Libya overthrow dictator Moammar Gadhafi.[29] "Who put the mess in the region if not the coalition that went to Iraq and then Libya?" asks historian Patrick Weil, an immigration expert at the University of Paris. He thinks a broader international agreement is needed so that other countries, including the United States and Canada, take in refugees.

Weil sees a second reason for getting the international community involved: "Europe is paralyzed because it's very difficult to change anything in the EU regulations — it takes many months of conversation." Moving beyond Europe, Weil says, holds the potential to finding a solution that is both international and effective.

As Europeans try to thrash out a plan for dealing with the immigration crisis, here are some of the questions being debated:

Does Europe need more immigrants?

The influx of refugees taking the sea route across the Mediterranean and the land route through the Balkans — the region encompassing the former Yugoslavia — has fanned Europeans' fears that the additional immigration will overwhelm schools, strain government services, compete with local workers for jobs and drive down wages.

In England, Nigel Farage, leader of the anti-immigration United Kingdom Independence Party (UKIP), proposed that immigrants be barred from a free education until they have lived in Britain for five years because of overcrowding in British schools.[30]

However, unlike Britain, which is undergoing something of a baby boom, much of Europe still suffers from low birth rates and an aging population. Europe as a whole has a fertility rate of 1.6 children per woman of childbearing age; the rate considered necessary to replace the existing population is 2.1.[31]

That means many countries will have to import workers who can contribute to their Social Security systems to support the growing number of elderly people on pensions, some experts say. Migration "could be the tonic that an aging continent needs" over the next few decades, said Philippe LeGrain, a former economic adviser to the president of the European Commission, the EU's politically independent executive arm, and a visiting senior fellow at the London School of Economics' European Institute.[32]

Immigration, he argues, is in Europe's self-interest because the Continent needs people to do jobs "that Europeans no longer want to do," such as picking fruit or caring for the aged —which he calls Europe's fastest-growing industry.

Moreover, the common perception that migrants are "job stealers" is a "harmful fantasy," said a recent report from the U.N. Special Rapporteur on the Human Rights of Migrants. A 14-year study into the effects of migration on 15 European countries showed that by performing manual labor, migrants from outside the EU pushed natives toward more highly skilled and better-paid jobs.[33]

Kanayo Nwanze, president of the Rome-based International Fund for Agricultural Development (IFAD), said in June that migrant workers are an "underappreciated" workforce that do not threaten European jobs. [34]

A report from IFAD shows that Europe's 50 million migrant workers spend most of their earnings locally. At the same time, European countries are among those that benefit the most from agricultural workers' remittances. For instance, portions of workers' earnings sent home to Moldova, in Eastern Europe, account for 22 percent of its GDP.[35]

European countries' demographic needs vary widely: Germany has an aging population and needs immigrants for its labor force.[36] By contrast, immigration has kept Britain's fertility rate close to the level needed to replace its population because foreign-born Britons tend to have more children than native-born Britons. On average, a woman born in Britain will have 1.8 children; among foreign-born women in Britain, the rate is 20 percent higher, or around 2.2 births per woman.[37]

In countries with double-digit unemployment rates — France, Spain, Italy — it's hard to make the case right now that workers need to be imported from outside. "Germany is looking for new foreign workers, [but] that is not at all the case in France," says immigration historian Weil. "The [political] pressure you have on the French government when you have 10 percent unemployment doesn't make it easy to make any decision to accept new immigrants." By contrast, Germany has the lowest unemployment rate of any EU country — 4.7 percent.[38]

Many studies show that immigrants' impact on wages is minimal, except for native-born workers in the bottom 15 to 20 percent of the income scale; their wages can be depressed by the presence of low-skilled immigrant laborers.[39]

"We know there's a major issue [at] the bottom of the labor market," says Sir David Metcalf, chair of Britain's Migration Advisory Committee, which advises Prime Minister Cameron on migration policy. At the bottom rungs of the ladder, wages for less-skilled British workers are undercut by low-skilled immigrants, who previously came from India and Africa and now come from EU countries in Eastern Europe such as Poland, he says. In addition, he says, the employers of unskilled migrant workers don't always comply with labor laws, which permits them to lower their labor costs.

Oxford University economist Paul Collier, while agreeing with other economists that effects on wages have been marginal so far, shifts the argument from an economic to a cultural one, in his 2013 book, *Exodus: Immigration and Multiculturalism in the 21st Century*, contending that "social effects are usually likely to trump economic effects." As evidence, he points to studies by Harvard political scientist Robert Putnam showing that the higher the concentration of immigrants in a community, the "less happy . . . the indigenous population."[40]

Collier's book argues that immigration can threaten the trust and the "mutual regard" that makes citizens willing to transfer their tax support to one another through a free health system like Britain's National Health Service or other European welfare programs.[41]

Yet surveys show that distrust of foreigners and hostility to immigrants is greatest in communities with few immigrants; diverse cities like London tend to be more accepting of foreigners, according to Eric Kaufmann, a professor of politics at Birkbeck College, University of London.

Londoners have benefited both culturally and economically from immigrants, says Jonathan Portes, principal research fellow at the National Institute of Economic and Social Research in London, and former chief economist for Labor Prime Minister Tony Blair, noting that London takes in over a third of Britain's migrants. "There is a reason London is by far the most successful, most dynamic but also one of most innovative and economically powerful cities in Europe. That's because we in London are by far the most open place to immigration from all parts of the world," he says.

Although the political debate is usually framed in terms of whether a nation should accept more or fewer migrants, it's also a question of whether the migrants bring the skills a society needs, notes economist Madeleine Sumption, director of the Migration Observatory, an independent research group at Oxford University. "Bringing in more people is less important than making sure that their skills are used properly, that people have an opportunity to get to jobs where they're paying higher taxes and addressing fiscal problems," she says, because immigrants in low-paid jobs won't be contributing much to government revenues and Social Security systems.

For example, Germany, which accepts the most immigrants in the EU, works with employers to place migrants in apprenticeship programs that will bring them up to the skill level needed.[42] The government also makes sure that "salaries will reflect people's qualifications and the actual job," says Papademetriou of Migration Policy Institute Europe, to ensure that employers do not underpay migrant workers and thereby displace highly paid German workers.

Immigrants can "cushion the blow" from an aging population in a country like Germany, but they can't entirely solve the problem, according to Reiner Klingholz, director of the Berlin Institute for Population and Development. After all, immigrants "get older too," he said.[43]

Dire predictions about Europe's shrinking labor force likely overstate the number of workers the Continent will need, Papademetriou points out, because technology and automation will probably eliminate many jobs in the future. For example, he cites a 2010 study for the European Council that predicted Europe will need as many as 100 million immigrants by 2030 to augment its declining labor force.[44]

"All this thinking in Europe is purely linear: It simply extrapolates on what we knew yesterday," he says, without taking into account the "dramatic ongoing technology revolution."

Are stronger border controls encouraging more smuggling of immigrants?

Most EU leaders say the union must make its external borders impenetrable to keep immigrants from coming to the Continent illegally. As Britain's Cameron told Parliament in May 2015, the EU needs to break "the link between setting off in a boat and achieving settlement in Europe."[45]

But anthropologist Andersson and other academic researchers disagree, and point to a paradox: When Europe tightens its external borders to discourage illegal immigration, more migrants try to come illegally.

Such a paradox has long been at work in Europe, they note. In preparation for joining the EU's passport-free Schengen Agreement in 1991, Spain began to impose new visa requirements for Moroccans, Tunisians and other African nationals. Spain also began patrolling its coastal border more vigilantly. Previously, many people from these countries crossed into Spain freely, often as seasonal workers, before returning to their home countries.[46]

"It's no coincidence" that a boat crisis by illegal immigrants followed fortified borders, Andersson says. During the early 2000s, scores of Africans drowned when their overloaded boats capsized en route to Spanish territory.

"Since the early days of the Schengen Agreement, we've seen this trend to ever riskier entry methods, more clandestine methods and stronger smuggling networks," he says. As Spain erected fences and rolled out patrols starting near the Strait of Gibraltar, he adds, "We see routes pushed to longer boat journeys toward the Spanish Canary Islands and now the central Mediterranean."

And illegal migration often increases in anticipation of future government crackdowns, according to Andersson. He says Spain's 2005 announcement of stronger measures to stop migrants from entering its North African enclaves of Melilla and Ceuta "spurred the largest-ever entry of migrants to these [places]."

Sea Crossings on Rise

More than one million refugees and migrants crossed the Mediterranean Sea from North Africa and the Middle East last year, compared to 216,000 in 2014. The number of people seeking haven in Europe has risen annually since 2012, and risen five-fold between 2014 and 2015.

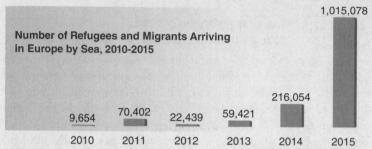

Number of Refugees and Migrants Arriving in Europe by Sea, 2010-2015

2010	2011	2012	2013	2014	2015
9,654	70,402	22,439	59,421	216,054	1,015,078

Source: "Refugees/Migrants Emergency Response - Mediterranean," United Nations High Commissioner for Refugees, data.unhcr.org/mediterranean/regional.php, accessed Feb. 22, 2016.

A report from the U.N.'s rapporteur on the human rights of migrants concludes that it is "impossible" to seal borders and that the recent growth in illegal migration is a "direct" effect of increasingly restrictive immigration policies that make it difficult for anyone from outside the EU to obtain a visa. The report urges the EU to provide more legal options, such as temporary work visas, which would allow multiple entries into Europe.[47]

In recent years, the report says, the region has deemed migration from outside the EU "undesirable" and has dramatically reduced legal migration opportunities, especially for low-skilled workers in domestic work, construction, farming and tourism.[48] "If you're from a poor nation," especially one in West Africa, Andersson says, "it's become so difficult to enter the EU that you have little option other than to get a fake passport to travel by air" or find some other illegal route.

The creation of a common external border goes back to the 1980s when five EU countries — West Germany, France, the Netherlands, Belgium and Luxembourg — decided they should abolish their internal borders to create a single market. They believed abolishing borders necessitated "compensatory measures," including strengthened external border controls and cooperation on immigration and asylum. In 1985, the five countries signed the Schengen Agreement establishing common rules regarding visas, checks at external borders and the right to asylum. The agreement was reached outside of the EU treaty structure but was incorporated in 1999 into the EU's body of common rights and obligations that is binding on all EU states, known as the "acquis." As a result, the borders dividing the 26 members of the Schengen area no longer required passports to cross, and typically booths once manned by border guards stood empty—at least until the latest migration crisis persuaded several member countries to reimpose border checks.[49]

As Andersson relates in his book, *Illegality, Inc.*, once countries like Spain joined the Schengen Agreement, they came under pressure from other EU countries to tighten visa restrictions on traditional migrants since they were now the area's only guarded frontier.

Frontex, which is charged with coordinating the Schengen area's external borders, was mainly concerned with replacing members' patchwork arrangements with a uniform system of border control, according to Frontex spokesperson Ewa Moncure. "It wasn't about strengthening borders but harmonizing requirements," she says of the obligations placed on new border countries joining the Schengen district. For example, if a country like Poland historically had no visa requirement for Ukrainians, she says, "when they joined Schengen they needed to add a visa for Ukraine."

The EU also encouraged border countries such as Spain to work out bilateral arrangements with transit countries like Libya and Morocco to prevent immigrants from leaving for Europe. Libyan leader Gadhafi famously warned that Europe would "turn black" unless the EU paid him 5 billion euros to block the arrival of illegal immigrants from Africa.[50]

But Andersson found that in the wake of these bilateral agreements, the arrest and detention of mainly African migrants just caused those migrants to try riskier routes: "Migrants who were out of money and suffering repression by security forces in Morocco took to the sea in tiny inflatable toy boats used in swimming pools by kids," he says.

Because of today's increasingly restrictive visas, some experts say, immigrants feel they must stay in the country where they've come to work because it will be impossible for them to re-enter legally if they leave.

"A large proportion just want to earn money, be educated and go back home," says Malakooti, author of the International Organization for Migration's recent report on Mediterranean migrants. "Promoting seasonal migration could be a positive response" to the crisis.

For asylum-seekers, it's almost a requirement to enter the EU illegally, because under current EU rules they have to be physically present in the desired country at the time of application to gain asylum. In fact, 90 percent of asylum-seekers in the EU are undocumented, because they usually have no legal way to enter Europe.[51]

Illegal entry is exacerbated by the so-called Dublin Regulation, which came into effect in 1997 and was accepted by all EU states in 2003. It requires asylum-seekers to seek asylum in the first country of the EU where they arrive. (The original goal was to prevent "asylum shopping," whereby an asylum-seeker rejected by one state makes multiple applications in other states.[52]) That means many arriving in Italy and Spain must slip over the border illegally if they want to seek asylum in Germany, Sweden or the U.K. — strong economies where they're more likely to find a job.

Increasingly, some migration experts and refugee groups are urging the EU to allow refugees to apply for asylum from outside the Continent. In March 2015, the European Commission for the first time floated the idea of setting up asylum processing centers in third countries, such as Egypt, Lebanon or Turkey, which often are migrant transit points.

On Nov. 29, 2015, the EU and Turkey struck a deal: Turkey would stem the flow of refugees to Europe and would offer work permits to Syrian refugees in exchange for €3 billion from the EU to help house and educate refugees. Marc Pierini, visiting scholar at Carnegie Europe said Turkey should consider allowing the determination of refugee status to take place on its territory and, together with the EU, create procedures for safe passage to Europe. However, by mid-February, Pierini and other observers conceded the agreement was far from delivering results and the Turkish government was demanding further concessions.[53]

The EU has also put pressure on Greece to do a better job of registering asylum seekers and weeding out those migrants that do not qualify for asylum. Greece has been accused of allowing thousands of migrants to quickly pass through the country rather than processing their applications for asylum.

On Jan. 27, EU officials told Greece it faced suspension from the Schengen zone unless it improved its handling of refugees within three months.[54]

Under threat of expulsion from the Schengen zone, Greece in mid-February moved swiftly to set up "hotspot" registration centers on five Aegean islands that had received over 800,000 migrants arriving by boat from Turkey last year. Greece promised four of the five centers would be up and running by the time of a Feb. 18 EU summit. But violent protests by residents on the Greek island of Kos delayed a fifth registration center there. Islanders objected that the center would interfere with tourism, the island's main industry.[55]

Ultimately, it comes down to having border controls credible enough to discourage illegal immigrants and their smugglers, some experts say. Papademetriou says it's possible to control the borders if EU countries make a concerted effort to go after smugglers and return immigrants who are in Europe illegally. "It's what you do *after* you rescue them that matters; that's what the smugglers and their cargo are looking at," he says.

Some humanitarian groups agree, at least partially. "To have a credible asylum system, you have to have a credible return system for those who don't meet the criteria for international protection," says Michael Diedring, secretary-general of the Brussels-based European Council on Refugees and Exiles, a coalition of 87 humanitarian groups.

Others say that efforts to help Mediterranean refugees stranded at sea have backfired by encouraging more people to make the dangerous crossing. Yet the number of illegal crossings and migrant deaths actually rose after Italy curtailed its rescue operations in 2014. Even before the April 2015 humanitarian disaster in the Mediterranean, 954 people had already died last year, compared with only 96 by the end of April 2014.[56] In 2015, more than 3,000 refugees died entering Mediterranean countries, most from drowning. However, this probably understates the total number of people who died trying to reach Europe last year as many other uncounted migrants perish crossing the Sahara Desert, according to the International Organization for Migration.[57]

Should Europe use military tactics to prevent human smuggling?

EU foreign and defense ministers backed a plan in May 2015 to use their countries' navies to intercept boats used to smuggle migrants across the Mediterranean and to destroy such boats before they leave Libyan waters.

On June 22, EU ministers announced they would begin the first phase of the military operations over the summer — using surveillance in international waters that could help them intercept smugglers.[58]

However, Germany insisted the EU get the U.N. Security Council's approval before seizing and destroying suspected vessels in either international waters or the territorial waters of Libya. An EU proposal said systematic efforts are needed "to identify, seize and destroy vessels and assets before they are used by smugglers."[59]

Germany said it would support armed action only if the EU had a U.N. mandate and Libya requested help; Russia was balking for similar reasons.[60] Because the EU does not have permission from either of the warring parties claiming to represent the Libyan government to enter its territorial waters, the surveillance operation cannot operate closer than 12 nautical miles off Libya.

Humanitarian groups concerned about civilian casualties opposed the military strategy. Often, fishing boats are sold to smugglers, making it hard to distinguish a boat's purpose. U.N. Secretary-General Ban Ki-moon said destroying the boats in Libyan harbors pre-emptively would threaten Libyan fishermen. "If you destroy all these boats that could be used to transport migrants then you may end up affecting the general economic capacity of those people," he said.[61]

The German news magazine *Der Spiegel* said military intervention could simply lead smugglers to charge higher prices to cross the Mediterranean; other experts warned smugglers might arm themselves.

"EU leaders are missing the point if they believe that once smugglers are arrested and boats are destroyed, people will no longer attempt to cross the Mediterranean," said the European Council on Refugees and Exiles. "Unintended consequences could include a shift to more dangerous alternatives, such as inflatable boats or smaller vessels carrying greater numbers."[62]

Malakooti, author of the recent report on Mediterranean migration, says the smuggling rings have become so numerous and decentralized that "if you target one link within a ring, the rest will regroup and continue operating."

However, Federica Mogherini, the EU's high representative for foreign affairs and security policy, has stressed "it is not only a humanitarian emergency but also a security crisis, since smuggling networks are linked to, and in some cases finance, terrorist activities, which contributes to instability in a region that is already unstable enough."[63]

Italian Prime Minister Matteo Renzi said his nation is already "at war" with human trafficking, and he urged the EU to help Italy fight it.[64] Between October 2013 and October 2014, Italy's navy intercepted smugglers' boats in an operation dubbed *Mare Nostrum* (Latin for "Our Sea"), which rescued more than 150,000 migrants and apprehended 330 suspected smugglers.[65] Italy ended the program in 2014 when other EU members, led by Britain, refused to contribute financial support because they believed the operation was encouraging migrants to cross the Mediterranean.[66]

A narrower operation run by Frontex replaced *Mare Nostrum*, with the border agency focusing on boats in distress only within 30 nautical miles of the Italian coast.[67]

On Oct. 7, 2015, the EU launched the second, more aggressive phase of its military operation against smugglers—boarding, inspecting and seizing smuggler boats in international waters off Libya. The new phase was dubbed Operation Sophia after a Somali baby born on a rescued boat in August. Since the EU obtained agreement for this operation from the internationally recognized Libyan government in eastern Libya's Tobruk, Russia dropped its long-standing opposition to the plan.

On Oct. 9, 2015, the UN Security Council passed a resolution giving the green light to this second phase of European military action. Many European leaders were hopeful they could step up action even further to seize boats within Libya's territorial waters; however the Libyan government was unwilling to give permission for this, and such a move would require another Security Council resolution.[68]

Some experts agree the EU should take stronger action. Col. Richard Kemp, former commander of British forces in Afghanistan, says the EU's current strategy of rescuing migrants at sea is "completely wrong" because it just encourages more migration. "We should be taking military action on the shores of North Africa to stop them coming," he says. As a model, he points to Australia's successful naval operation to push back migrant boats from Indonesia, which the Australian government says has reduced the migrant flow to a trickle.[69]

EU officials have also pointed to the international community's success in controlling piracy off the coast of Somalia, an operation known as Atalanta, which received the U.N. Security Council's blessing.[70] However, Peter Sutherland, the U.N. special envoy on migration and a former EU commissioner, said the comparison is not apt: "The calculus in the Mediterranean is far more complicated, with innocent refugees, including many children, in the line of fire between smugglers and any potential military operations."[71]

Whether the EU's seizure of boats in the Mediterranean has succeeded in deterring human smugglers or migrants remains an open question. By early February, Operation Sophia's commanders said it had seized 76 boats from illegal operations, led to the arrest of 46 people for suspected human trafficking and helped save more than 9,000 lives.[72]

However, by the time Operation Sophia kicked off in October 2015, the flow of migrants was already shifting away from Libyan ports to routes embarking from Turkey and the land route through the Balkans. Nevertheless, in December, Operation Sophia's commander, rear admiral Enrico Credendino claimed some of the credit for that shift. "For smugglers it is not possible to go into international waters. They know we are there," the admiral said.[73]

Migrants who were rescued by the USS Bataan on June 6, 2014, while trying to cross the Mediterranean await transfer to authorities from Malta. While many migrants are seeking to improve their economic opportunities, some also may have endured human rights violations and could have valid asylum claims.

In February, NATO defense ministers meeting in Brussels decided to deploy warships to stop smugglers bringing migrants from Turkey to Greece. Defense Secretary Ash Carter said, "There is now a criminal syndicate that is exploiting these poor people and this is an organized smuggling operation. Targeting that is the way that the greatest effect can be had."

However, like the EU military plan initiated over the summer, the move was greeted with skepticism from military analysts as air strikes over Aleppo were driving tens of thousands of Syrians from their homes toward the Turkish border. "[It is] hard to see how NATO's involvement could actually decrease the flow of migrants, especially as the intensifying conflict in Syria is pushing more refugees towards Turkey," said Wolfango Piccoli of Teneo Intelligence. "At best it may help to counter some of the worst aspects of human trafficking."[74]

BACKGROUND
Colonial Roots

Modern immigration to Europe began in the late 19th century as a result of Europe's colonial and trading activities, and colonialism helps explain where ethnic groups settled and whether they were accepted in their new countries.

CHRONOLOGY

1830-1858 *Immigrants from Europe's colonies provide new source of labor for the Continent.*

1830 France conquers Algeria, leading to arrival of Algerians, Moroccans and Tunisians in France.

1858 India officially becomes a British colony as British crown takes control from East India Company.

1954-1980s *Europe encourages immigration to rebuild post-World War II economy until a recession hits in the 1970s.*

1954 West Germany begins recruiting temporary foreign workers from Italy and Spain; in 1961, it signs an agreement with Turkey to import "guest workers" for two-year periods.

1973 West Germany discontinues guest-worker program.

1974 France and the Netherlands introduce "immigration stop" policies during 1970s recession, but immigration throughout European Union (EU) keeps rising because of family reunification and reluctance of guest workers to leave.

1977 France offers to pay immigrants to leave — with little success.

1985 Five member states of the European Economic Community sign a treaty allowing free movement among those nations by gradually abolishing border checks; 26 EU countries now belong to passport-free Schengen area.

1996-2000s *Terrorist attacks fuel European fears of migrants, especially those from Muslim countries.*

1996 Radical Algerian group explodes bombs on Paris subways and trains. . . . Al Qaeda calls on Muslims to kill Americans and their allies.

2000 Germany makes it easier for Turkish guest workers and their children to become citizens.

Sept. 11, 2001 Al Qaeda flies hijacked jetliners into the World Trade Center and Pentagon, killing nearly 3,000.

2004 EU Free Movement directive extends the right of EU citizens to look for a job anywhere within the Union; 10 Eastern European nations, including Poland and Hungary, join the EU, and thousands of Eastern Europeans move to Western Europe to work.

2005 London transit bombings kill 52. . . . Hundreds of African migrants storm the fence dividing the Spanish enclave of Melilla from Morocco; at least six die.

2006 Spain closes its land border to Melilla; 550 migrants drown trying to reach the Spanish Canary Islands.

2010-Present *Arab Spring uprisings lead to turmoil throughout the Middle East and a surge of refugees in Europe.*

2010 Anti-government protests and uprisings known as the Arab Spring begin in Tunisia. . . . Anti-immigration parties make unprecedented electoral gains in Europe. . . . Conservative David Cameron is elected British prime minister after promising to limit immigration; his government places caps on immigration from outside the EU.

2011 Syrian exodus begins as that nation's civil war intensifies. . . . Libya becomes a hub for smuggling refugees after rebels overthrow Moammar Gadhafi's government and chaos follows.

2013 Drowning of 360 migrants trying to reach the island of Lampedusa, Italy, spurs Italian government to launch Mare Nostrum search-and-rescue operation.

2014 Italy ends Mare Nostrum after Britain says it encourages migrants to come to Europe. . . . Immigration skyrockets to record levels.

2015 In April, more than 700 refugees drown when a Mediterranean boat heading to Italy from Libya sinks. . . . In May, the EU proposes using member countries' militaries to stop migrant smugglers; in June it launches the surveillance phase. . . . Hungary announces it will build a fence on its border with Serbia. . . . In September, German Chancellor Angela Merkel declares open door policy for Syrian refugees . . . . Oct. 7, EU launches ships to seize smugglers' boats. . . .

Nov. 13, Islamic State militants kill 130 people in Paris. . . . Sweden introduces border controls. . . . New Year's Eve celebrations in Cologne, Germany, marred by assaults on hundreds of women by North African migrants . . . 2015 tally of migrants who died in the Mediterranean tops 3,000; more than 1 million cross illegally by land and sea by end of 2015.

2016 New Year's Eve attacks sharply reduce German popular support for migrants. . . . In January, Sweden announces it will deport up to 80,000 asylum-seekers; Finland 20,000. . . . By January, EU countries imposing temporary border controls within borderless Schengen area include Sweden, Denmark, Norway, Germany, Austria, Norway, Slovenia, Hungary and France. . . . In February, NATO launches naval patrols of human smugglers' boats. . . . At February EU summit, divided countries seek agreement on migrant crisis.

Many of the originating countries were Muslim, now a source of much political anxiety with regard to migration into Europe. By the late 1800s, France, Britain and the Netherlands had gained control over most of the world's Muslim territories: France conquered Algiers in 1830, eventually also taking control of Morocco and Tunisia, along with eight predominantly Muslim countries in West Africa. The British colonized Nigeria, with a large Muslim population in the North, and India, which included modern-day Pakistan and Bangladesh. The Dutch dominated trade in Southeast Asia, where today's Indonesia — the world's most populous Muslim nation — was once a Dutch colony.[75]

By the end of the 19th century, France was importing low-paid workers from Algeria and other African territories, while other European countries recruited workers from their colonies and territories.

Many Europeans also emigrated during this period to the United States. From 1845 to 1855, the British Isles "were witness to scenes as desperate as those now being enacted in the Mediterranean," when more than 2 million migrants from impoverished Ireland left for North America in overpacked cargo ships, many dying along the way, writes chronicler Philip Hoare.[76]

Europe did not become a major immigrant destination until the 1950s, when it needed workers to rebuild cities and economies ravaged by World War II. After the wartime deaths of hundreds of thousands of working-age men, the U.K. sought workers from the British Empire: Indians and Pakistanis came beginning in the 1950s, Bangladeshis in the 1970s. In the postwar economic boom, France, Germany and the Netherlands also recruited immigrants from their former colonies.

"Millions of North Africans, sub-Saharan Africans and Turks came to Europe between 1950 and 1975, and no one died and there was no smuggling," observed Crépeau, the U.N. special rapporteur. It was easy for migrants to obtain a tourist visa and convert it to a work visa; they could return home and then come back. Unlike today, "mobility was the name of the game," Crépeau said.[77]

Indeed, most European governments saw immigrant labor as temporary. West Germany, Belgium and Sweden initiated "guest-worker" programs, recruiting workers first from Italy and Spain and later from North Africa and the Middle East. The number of Turkish guest workers in Germany soared from 329,000 in 1960 to 2.6 million by 1973, the year the program was discontinued.[78]

However, many of those guest workers wanted to stay in West Germany. German corporations pressured the government to make the guest-worker contracts renewable and to allow workers' families to join them.

Immigration Limits

By the late 1960s and early '70s, Europe's industries were declining and the Continent's need for overseas manpower was dwindling. Textile mills in England and linen mills in France would soon become obsolete, creating unemployment among migrants and a growing anti-immigrant sentiment.

On April 20, 1968, two weeks after the assassination of the Rev. Dr. Martin Luther King Jr. triggered riots in U.S. cities, Conservative British Parliament member Enoch Powell warned that the U.K.'s rising immigration would lead to similar racial tension. Citing the poet

For Syrian Refugee, Britain Is a Mixed Blessing

After perilous journey, asylum-seeker faces new obstacles.

To subdue his fear of the sea crossing, Ahmad Albkadla, a 22-year-old Syrian college student, doped himself up with sleeping pills for a week-long trip across the Mediterranean with 70 other refugees in a boat built for 17. Each time the drugs wore off, he awoke to the screams of other passengers, terrified that the craft would sink.

Albkadla had paid a smuggler in Alexandria, Egypt, $9,000 in 2013 to get him to the Italian coast, aiming to join his two older brothers in England. He did not know that his odyssey would last almost a year, including long stays in detention, and cost him double that amount by the end, mostly to compensate other smugglers.

Albkadla described his harrowing journey in a coffee shop in London, where he has been awaiting action on his asylum application since August 2013. As an asylum-seeker, he is not permitted to work, so he is dependent on his oldest brother.

Since 2010, the rate at which Britain refuses visas to Syrians — for study, work or joining family — has doubled, according to statistics released by the U.K. government's Home Office, and it now rejects 60 percent of Syrian visa requests.[1]

This means that a Syrian refugee who wants to seek asylum in Britain often has no choice but to enter the country illegally, refugee groups say, since asylum-seekers must be physically present in the country to apply.

In March 2015, the government said it was clamping down on Syrians with transit visas to other countries "to prevent the potential for a significant influx of citizens and nationals of Syria" and to stop "abuse" by Syrians trying to claim asylum in the U.K., "with the associated heavy burden on public resources."[2]

Despite the fact that Syrian asylum applications in the European Union (EU) last year surged by almost 150 percent to 123,000, only 2,222 Syrians applied to the U.K.[3] In part, this reflects migrants' perceptions that Britain is less welcoming to asylum-seekers than elsewhere; Britain ranked fifth among EU countries in the number of asylum-seekers admitted in 2014 and 16th when adjusted for population.[4]

Refugees in Britain often have to wait years to get action on their asylum applications. At the end of 2014, almost 23,000 asylum applications received by the government since April 2006 were still awaiting a decision. The government attributed the delays to staff reductions resulting from an agency restructuring.[5]

Albkadla says if he had known that settling in Britain would prove so difficult, he would have "prepared to die in Syria" rather than come to a country that fails to live up to its ideals.

As an activist opposed to Syrian President Bashar Assad, Albkadla believed that leaving Syria was his only option. In 2012 he had been arrested, jailed and tortured for participating in demonstrations against Assad in Daraa, Albkadla's home province.

Daraa was the birthplace in 2011 of an uprising against the regime that became a civil war. Today, regime and rebel

Virgil, he said, "I seem to see the River Tiber foaming with much blood."[79]

When the 1973-77 global recession hit, many immigrants remained in their adopted countries even if they were unemployed, spurring European fears that immigrants would compete for jobs with natives and burden welfare programs. Between 1973 and 1975, many European governments instituted "immigration stop" policies to discourage labor migration.

Paradoxically, more immigrants came to Europe during the decades after the "stop" policies were instituted than in the preceding decades, largely because families or spouses joined the original immigrants, who had often migrated alone. By 2003, the number of North Africans arriving

forces are still battling for the region, and Albkadla's two sisters have endured daily bombings, he says.

It took a $1,500 bribe for Albkadla's family to get him released from jail. A summons to serve in the regime's military, together with his fear of being re-arrested, prompted Albkadla to flee Syria.

Albkadla wanted to settle in Egypt, but after failing to find a job there his oldest brother urged him to come to England. It was simple to find a smuggler in Alexandria to get him across the Mediterranean to Italy, but Italian border officials refused to let the boat land and sent it on to Greece.

Within a few days of arriving in Greece, Albkadla says he got caught up in a police roundup of Muslim men in connection with the rape of a Greek woman. Released after more than five months in jail, he made his way to Macedonia.

He entered the EU through Hungary, via Serbia. He continued through Austria and Italy to Calais, France, a popular jumping-off point for migrants attempting to cross the English Channel illegally to England.

After camping out in a forest for a month, Albkadla paid a smuggler $4,000 to hide him in the back of a vegetable truck; when the driver opened the rear doors of his truck upon reaching England, he was surprised to discover Albkadla and seven other migrants sitting on top of his vegetables. He called police. Albkadla spent another two months in detention before British authorities released him to his brother.

In contrast to Albkadla's arduous journey, Mohammed Ateek, 27, a Syrian graduate student, came to England on a student visa and received asylum in 2013 within four months of applying. Ateek had organized anti-Assad demonstrations in London and written articles criticizing the regime.

Like Albkadla, Ateek laments Britain's stance toward refugees, saying it is at odds with its history. Between January 2014 and July 2015, Britain had permitted entry to

Syrian refugees Mohammed Ateek, left, and Ahmad Albkadla took different paths to England: Albkadla paid a smuggler to help him cross the Mediterranean. Ateek came to London on a student visa.

only 187 of the thousands of Syrians vetted by the United Nations as genuine refugees needing resettlement — "a pathetic number," Ateek says. "It can host more."[6]

— Sarah Glazer

[1] Colin Yeo, "Refusal rate for Syrian visa applications increases yet further," Free Movement, March 12, 2015, http://tinyurl.com/ocnjbeq. Also see "Immigration Statistics, October to December 2014," table vi, vol. 2, U.K. Home Office, updated Feb. 26, 2015, http://tinyurl.com/qbb839t.

[2] "Statement of Changes in Immigration Rules," U.K. Home Office, March 16, 2015, http://tinyurl.com/ndfh44l.

[3] The latest figure released in March by the U.K. Home Office was 2,222; see "Immigration Statistics, January to March 2015," Home Office, http://tinyurl.com/otjkjlt.

[4] "Immigration Statistics, October to December, 2014, *op. cit.*, Section 11, "International Comparisons."

[5] *Ibid.*

[6] Matt Dathan, "David Cameron says Britain will accept just 'a few hundred' more Syrian refugees despite 4 million displaced by the war," *The Independent*, June 19, 2015, http://tinyurl.com/oofuy5u.

in France was triple the number before the government began restricting immigration.[80]

Since then, EU governments have tried repeatedly to discourage immigration. Some, like France, have even offered monetary incentives and continued welfare support to immigrants if they returned home. Most of the programs ended in failure.[81]

Terrorist Attacks

Acts of terrorism in the 1990s and early 2000s fueled fears that radical Islamists could be entering Europe from Muslim countries. Between 1995 and 1996, Algerians linked to militant groups exploded bombs on Paris subways and trains. The Sept. 11, 2001, attacks by al Qaeda on the World Trade Center and the Pentagon also changed how Europeans perceived their Muslim neighbors: A group of Muslims who attended a mosque in Hamburg, Germany, had planned the attacks against the United States.

In 2004 terrorists linked to al Qaeda attacked Madrid's commuter trains, and a radical Islamist murdered Dutch filmmaker Theo van Gogh, an outspoken critic of Islam. The following year, on July 7, four suicide bombers struck London's transit system, killing 52; all four terrorists were young Britons with links to hardline Islamist groups.

In 2004, the EU admitted 10 new countries — the Czech Republic, Estonia, Hungary, Latvia, Lithuania, Poland, Slovakia, Slovenia, Cyprus and Malta. Under EU rules, citizens of those countries were free to move to any member nation to work, and thousands of Eastern Europeans poured into Western Europe.

While the EU was opening its eastern border, Africans continued to risk their lives to enter Europe from the south. Once Spain joined the Schengen Agreement, its North African enclaves of Ceuta and Melilla became an EU land border on the Africa continent. With that new border came new Europe-bound migrants who were "bedraggled, poor [and] black" — "quite unlike" earlier migrants from Morocco, India and Spain, anthropologist Andersson wrote.[82]

In the autumn of 2005, hundreds of sub-Saharan migrants rushed over the 10-foot-high razor-wire fences separating Melilla from Morocco; at least six died. The following year, after authorities managed to close off that entry point to Spain, record numbers of migrants headed to Spain's Canary Islands by boat. By September 2006, 550 people had drowned while undertaking the risky 600-mile voyage. [83]

In 2010 anti-immigration parties made unprecedented electoral gains in Europe. In Sweden, the nationalist Democrats won enough votes to gain representation in the parliament for the first time. In the Netherlands, the coalition government agreed to demands from the anti-immigration Freedom Party to make it harder for immigrants' spouses to join them.

In Britain, Cameron was elected prime minister after promising to cut immigration from hundreds of thousands to "tens of thousands," and his government capped immigration from outside the EU.[84]

The Arab Spring movement, sparked by Tunisian protests in 2010, had enormous implications for Europe, prompting record numbers of refugees to leave their homes in the Middle East.[85] Libya's uprising against the Gadhafi regime began in 2011 after government forces opened fire on protesters. In March of that year, NATO authorized strikes on government targets; Gadhafi fled and was killed by rebels in August 2011. And in Syria, peaceful protests against the regime of President Assad in 2011 escalated into a civil war after a brutal government crackdown.

In October 2013, the drowning of more than 360 migrants, mostly Eritreans and Somalis, who were trying to reach the Italian island of Lampedusa from Libya spurred the Italian government to launch the *Mare Nostrum* search-and-rescue effort.[86] Italy ended that effort in 2014, when Britain and other EU countries refused to contribute. However, illegal immigration continued at record levels.

EU Response

At an EU summit on June 26, 2015, where national leaders argued into the early hours of the morning, members could agree only on weak measures to solve the migrant crisis. Italy and Greece wanted to relocate 40,000 Syrian and Eritrean asylum-seekers to other EU countries, but national leaders squabbled over where they should be sent, and the idea of mandatory quotas was abandoned.[87]

Instead, the EU hopes to get member countries to voluntarily agree over the next two years to take those refugees.[88] As of July 20, the EU said it had received pledges from member countries to take 32,256 of the 40,000 in Italy and Greece.[89]

European Council President Donald Tusk of Poland expressed his frustration with this approach. "I can understand those who want this voluntary mechanism, but they will only be credible if they give precise and significant pledges by the end of July at the latest, because solidarity without sacrifice is pure hypocrisy," he said.[90]

Under the agreement, another 20,000 people identified by the U.N. as refugees living outside their home countries would be resettled in EU countries.

"If you look at the numbers that need assistance, [the 60,000-refugee target is] shoveling sand against the sea with a teaspoon," Diedring of the European Council on Refugees and Exiles says.

The summit had less difficulty deciding on tough measures to evict migrants crossing illegally into the EU who don't qualify for protection as refugees. The EU agreed to strengthen Frontex to help frontline countries such as Italy and Greece return those migrants to their home countries. The agreement also promised to create "hotspots" — reception facilities in frontline EU states where determinations can be made quickly as to who qualifies for international protection.[91]

At the summit — overshadowed the same day by terrorist attacks in Tunisia, Kuwait and France — Tusk said EU heads of state would present a new security strategy to combat global terrorism, but that plan is not expected until June 2016.[92]

Disintegrating Consensus

Several EU countries have tried to stop illegal migration on their own by tightening borders — even if the refugees are within the 26-country, passport-free Schengen area — posing another political challenge for the EU. By mid-January, temporary six-month border controls had been imposed by Sweden, Denmark, Germany, Austria, Norway, Slovenia, Hungary and France.

Hungary, which has become a frontline country of entry for migrants taking the land route through Serbia and whose government is known for anti-immigration rhetoric, announced in June 2015 it was building a 13-foot-high, 110-mile fence along its border with Serbia.[93]

The same month, Hungary briefly suspended the Dublin regulation, the EU rule requiring that refugees seeking asylum have their claims processed in the first EU country where they arrive and that they be returned to that first-arrival country. Hungarian government officials said "the boat is full," with more than 60,000 migrants having entered Hungary by June 2014, and that the country had "exhausted the resources at its disposal."[94]

In Italy, Prime Minister Renzi has been calling for a change to the Dublin regulation.[95] Italy and Greece have been criticized for not fingerprinting and processing all arriving asylum-seekers, instead letting them slip over the border to other EU countries. The U.N. estimated that half of all refugees who pass through Greece and Balkan countries on their way to Hungary and Northern Europe do so without being registered by authorities.[96]

Over the summer, France and Austria instituted checks at their borders for migrants from Italy: France at the Italian coastal town of Ventimiglia, and Austria near the Italian town of Bolzano.[97]

As thousands of migrants were trying to make their way illegally to Britain from the French ferry port of Calais in June 2015, Prime Minister Cameron pledged to build a fence at the port.[98] Britain, which does not participate in the borderless Schengen area, has already negotiated an "opt-out" of any refugee resettlement scheme and has indicated it won't participate in any new EU refugee relocation program.

Over the summer,, Britain was assembling the 2.5-mile fence to protect trucks entering the Eurotunnel terminal from migrants hitchhiking clandestinely — part of a $16.6 million security package by the British government to try to stop migrant smuggling from Calais.[99]

The Calais crisis reached a new pitch in July 2015 as hundreds of migrants stormed the Eurotunnel train terminal in Calais in an attempt to board trains traveling under the English Channel to England. Some sources speculated migrants had shifted tactics to a mass attempt to use the tunnel because security had been strengthened at the entrance to the Calais-Dover ferry in June, where many migrants tried to get into trucks secretly or hang onto the underside for the channel crossing. British officials pledged an additional 7 million pounds ($11 million) for fencing and said they would cooperate with France to return migrants to their home countries, especially to West Africa. (By February, officials were discussing building a covered tunnel over the tracks' most exposed point in anticipation of further refugee incursions over the summer.[100]) UKIP leader Farage called for the British army to be deployed to strengthen border controls on the British side of the channel.[101]

A Sudanese man died at the train tunnel when he was hit by a truck. More than 140 migrants were believed to have reached the U.K. after the two-day effort; police turned most migrants back and bused them to the makeshift camps where they have been staying in Calais.[102]

Anti-Immigrant Backlash

Nationalist parties in Europe have gained support as the flow of immigrants has increased in some traditionally homogeneous countries such as Denmark and Finland.

In addition, the recent string of terrorist attacks, mostly by Muslim extremists, has boosted support for the nationalists. Italian police arrested Abdelmajid Touil, a Moroccan whom authorities said supplied arms for an attack on a museum in Tunisia in March 2015 that killed 21. The Islamic State claimed responsibility for the assault.

According to authorities, Touil had entered Italy on a migrant boat in February.[103]

In June 2015, the anti-immigration Danish People's Party became the nation's second strongest party. Still fresh was the memory of a Feb. 14 rampage by the son of Palestinian immigrants at a free-speech event outside a synagogue that killed two and wounded five.

In neighboring Finland, the far-right, anti-immigration Finns Party joined the multiparty coalition governing Finland for the first time.[104]

In France, the Netherlands and Austria, anti-immigrant parties have led recent national polls. In the wake of the lethal January 2015 attack on staffers at *Charlie Hebdo* magazine in Paris, several anti-immigrant parties stressed that Europe should be more worried about radical Islamists getting into the country, and several commentators said far-right parties stood to gain voters from the attack by two Paris-born Muslim extremists.[105]

A coalition of far-right anti-immigration parties from five countries announced in June 2015 they were forming a political bloc in the European Parliament to gain more political clout. The group, Europe of Nations and Freedoms, is headed by Marine Le Pen, leader of France's anti-immigration National Front party. It includes parties of similar leanings from Austria, the Netherlands, Italy and Belgium, most of which made gains in the 2014 European elections.[106]

Some of these parties have begun to wield power within their countries. Within Italy, governors of the prosperous northern regions of Lombardy and Veneto, strongholds of the anti-immigration Northern League party, refused to take any more migrants that have arrived on the southern coasts.[107]

In Britain, the anti-immigrant United Kingdom Independence Party (UKIP) received 13 percent of the popular vote in Britain's parliamentary elections in May 2015, but because its support was so scattered it won only one parliamentary seat. "They don't have local strongholds, so they can't reach the status of the largest party in any one constituency, but they are now the third force in English politics [after the Conservative and Labor parties] and they are the second-largest party" in almost 100 districts, says Kaufmann of Birkbeck College.

Kaufmann says UKIP's performance in the European parliamentary election is a better indicator of its popularity — it received 28 percent of the national vote and the largest number of seats of any British party.[108]

One measure of UKIP's ability to pressure the mainstream parties is Cameron's pledge to hold a referendum on whether Britain should leave the EU. UKIP, which supports a British exit from the EU, has objected to the EU requirement that Britain accept unlimited numbers of migrants from Eastern European member countries.

Cameron announced Feb. 20 that Britain would hold a referendum on June 23, 2016, on whether to stay in the EU, after he had spent two days of hard bargaining renegotiating the terms of the U.K.'s agreement with Brussels, away from "ever-closer union." Cameron declared he was satisfied with the new deal and would campaign for Britain to stay in the Union, saying, "I believe that Britain will be safer, stronger and better off in a reformed European Union."[109]

However, critics of Cameron's deal said it was "watered down" from his original demands. For instance, Cameron initially said he wanted to require immigrants from the EU to wait four years before they could claim welfare benefits, a move that was strongly opposed by Eastern European countries. Poland, which sends thousands of immigrants to work in Britain, objected that the requirement would violate the EU principles barring discrimination against workers from other EU countries.[110] In the final agreement hammered out with EU leaders Feb. 19, Cameron agreed that the four-year limitation would not be a total ban but should be phased-in, "from an initial complete exclusion" to "gradually increasing access to such benefits" to recognize the worker's connection to the British labor force, according a European Commission statement.[111]

CURRENT SITUATION
Fears of Migrants Intensify

Europeans' anxieties about terrorism and their cultural differences with migrants were heightened by two shocking events as 2015 drew to a close.

On Nov. 13, a terrorist attack on Paris by Islamic State militants—which killed 130 people at cafes, restaurants and a large concert hall—was traced to several men who had traveled the migrant route. All of the known perpetrators were reported to be EU citizens. However, several were on terrorist watch lists and had been able to re-enter Europe from Syria undetected by posing as migrants or taking advantage of the chaos at border crossings.[112]

Should Britain reduce the number of immigrants?

YES

David Goodhart
Author, The British Dream: Successes and Failures of Post-war Immigration; director, Demos Integration Hub, London

Written for *CQ Researcher*, July 2015

Economists are not very good at seeing complete human beings. They tend to view the world as a giant value-maximizing machine: Allegiances and obligations, a settled sense of place, national social contracts and other such things feature in their story mainly as frictions.

If Britain was just a labor market, it would make perfect sense to fill as many jobs as possible with the most talented people from around the world and to keep the people doing more routine work on their toes by bringing in people from poorer countries with stronger work ethics and lower wage expectations.

But Britain is NOT just a market; it is a society of millions of micro-communities and networks of people held together by complex ties of obligation and mutual dependence. When the immigration door is half-opened, as it was in 1997, many of those relationships are disrupted. (And an unprecedented number of people came after 1997. England's ethnic minority population trebled, from around 7 percent in the mid-1990s to more than 22 percent now.)

If Britain had become a much richer country and growth benefited all classes, then objections to immigration would have been left to a small xenophobic minority. But even economists who favor large-scale immigration admit that the net impact of migration on growth, wages and employment has been negligible for the existing population. Moreover, everyone agrees that to the extent there has been an effect, it has been regressive: somewhat beneficial for employers (bingo! we no longer have to train anyone) and somewhat disadvantageous for citizens facing downward pressure on wages and more competition for jobs and public services.

Nobody sensible on my side of the argument wants to stop immigration, but we do want to return it to the more moderate levels of the recent past. The current levels cause brain drain from poor countries that desperately need energetic people while producing little economic benefit to rich countries and considerable social disruption and ethnic segregation. It is a lose-lose situation. Above all, it is the settled will of about 80 percent of the U.K. population, including 62 percent of ethnic minority Britons born here, that immigration be reduced.

Britons are not against individual immigrants, most of whom work hard and contribute to society. But people of all classes, ethnicities and regions do not see how large-scale immigration benefits them or their country, and they rightly want it reduced.

NO

Jonathan Portes
Director, National Institute of Economic and Social Research, London

Written for *CQ Researcher*, July 2015

Four years after the British government set a target of reducing net migration to the "tens of thousands," the target is widely regarded as Prime Minister David Cameron's biggest broken promise, with net migration currently running at a near-record 300,000 per year. But the attempt to reduce immigration to the government's target drives a bizarre set of policies designed to reduce skilled migration from outside the European Union (EU) and, even more crazily, to reduce the numbers of foreign students at U.K. universities.

Indeed, just a few weeks ago, applications exceeded the government's quota for skilled-worker visas. The BBC reported that "as well as nurses, doctors and teachers other visas refused were applications to bring in accountants, solicitors and management consultants." The economic benefits — short or long term — to the U.K. of leaving these posts unfilled are difficult to see.

On the contrary, these restrictions, and even more so further ones proposed by Cameron, will reduce growth and make us poorer. There is an increasing body of evidence that suggests migration, especially skilled migration, does more than help fill short-term gaps in the labor market — it also enhances productivity over the longer term.

Of course, public concern in the U.K. about immigration is not primarily about skilled workers or foreign students but about low-skilled migration from within the EU. Here the trade-offs are harder and bound up with wider debates about the U.K.'s role in the EU. But there is still no evidence EU migrants take jobs from natives overall, and any downward impact on wages appears to be small. Young, unskilled workers are having a hard time in the U.K., as in much of the rest of Europe. But immigration is not the main or even a major cause of this problem, and hence reducing immigration can't and won't be the solution.

It's worth noting that anti-immigration sentiment is higher in areas where economic prospects are poorer and, not coincidentally, there are fewer immigrants; by contrast London, still the most popular destination for immigrants by far, is much more at ease with high migration. Reducing immigration won't help those areas that feel "left behind," but it will damage more successful regions and sectors of the economy.

Sadly, too many British politicians share the view that reducing immigration would both reduce social tensions and do little economic damage. The evidence suggests the reverse is true.

At New Year's Eve festivities in Cologne, Germany, attacks on hundreds of women by groups of young men were blamed on migrants, described mainly as North African. More than 600 women came forward describing men harassing, groping and stripping them of clothes and valuables near the Cologne train station. One rape was reported.

The Cologne events quickly fed into anti-immigrant feeling in Germany and turned many Germans, particularly right-wing parties, against German Chancellor Angela Merkel's policy of welcoming refugees—a policy that she had announced Sept. 4, 2015, as an open door for Syrian refugees.

In a survey, 61 percent of Germans said they had become less happy about welcoming refugees since the Cologne assaults and 63 percent said there were already too many asylum seekers.[113]

Conservative partners in Merkel's ruling coalition called for Germany to close its borders. Horst Seehofer, Bavaria's conservative premier and leader of the coalition's sister party the Christian Social Union, in February 2016, called Merkel's generous refugee policy "a reign of injustice" and said he was considering whether Bavaria should sue the government in constitutional court.[114]

Merkel had announced her open-door policy in September 2015 in response to the hundreds of Syrians trapped in Hungary at the time by the Dublin Regulation, which requires asylum seekers to seek asylum in the first EU country where they arrive. Many of those refugees wished to continue on to Germany, where the prospects of jobs looked much better. Merkel decided to suspend the Dublin Regulation to allow Syrian refugees to claim asylum in Germany even though it was not their first country of entry. Critics said such a decision should have been made by parliament, not Merkel.

Migrant arrivals into Germany accelerated rapidly after Merkel's September open-door policy, and by the end of the year official statistics had counted 1.1 million refugees. However, after the Cologne attacks, which police blamed largely on North Africans, Germany's immigration policy became less generous— at least to migrants from that region. Germany said it would declare Algeria, Morocco and Tunisia "safe countries of origin," meaning migrants from those countries would have little chance of winning asylum.[115]

Can Turkey Stem the Migrants?

However, despite pressure on Merkel by her conservative coalition partners and critics, she was standing firm

against closing the borders to refugees in mid-February 2016, as she headed to Brussels for an EU summit on the migration crisis.

Instead, Merkel was focusing on negotiating a deal with Turkey to stem the tide of refugees from that country into Europe, now that Turkey was their main portal to the continent. Aware that she could not count on broad European support for allocating refugees among EU countries, Merkel was aiming to relocate up to 250,000 refugees a year from Turkey to "a coalition of the willing" —11 EU countries that had agreed in principle to the scheme. An EU agreement last year to relocate 160,000 refugees from Italy and Greece to member countries on a quota basis was already foundering in mid-February 2016. Fewer than 600 people had been resettled.

However, by February, negotiations with the Turkish government were running into difficulty. Merkel said it would be "ridiculous" to take in migrants from Turkey unless the Turkish government did more to curb the number of migrants setting off from its shores to Greece. Turkish officials were insisting that the resettlement scheme should not be linked to these illegal migrant flows.[116]

Underscoring the importance of these negotiations, EU leaders said they would meet with Turkey three weeks after the Feb. 18 summit. Merkel called it "a priority" to implement the previously agreed deal under which Turkey would stem refugees to Europe in exchange for €3 billion ($3.3 billion) in aid. Noting the heightened urgency, she said, "We all know spring is coming and the number of refugees coming to us will rise again."[117]

Merkel was also reportedly anxious to head off a push by central European nations led by Poland to help close Macedonia's border with Greece to seal off migrants heading north into Europe. A few days before the summit four central European countries—Hungary, Poland, Slovakia and the Czech republic—vowed to shut down the Balkan route from Turkey and promised to resist Merkel's call for all EU countries to take a share of refugees.[118]

Greece's government protested against this proposal on the grounds that it would trap thousands of migrants within its borders.

A Less Welcoming Europe

Increasingly, countries known for welcoming refugees seem anxious to send a discouraging signal to would-be migrants. Sweden, famous for having offered residency to any Syrian refugee who reached its borders, declared in late January 2016, that it was rejecting 80,000 asylum applications—about half of all those it received in 2015—and expected to deport up to half of those rejected. Finland said it expected to expel 65 percent of its 2015 asylum seekers.[119]

By February, approximately half of the EU's citizens were no longer living in a borderless Europe, as more countries instituted 6-month border controls. Under pressure from EU ministers, the European Commission was considering suspending the travel-free Schengen zone for two years under an emergency procedure that allows suspension if the EU zone is endangered by "serious deficiencies" at its external border—as the EU has charged exist at Greece's border.[120]

As countries closed their borders, Manuel Vallis, the French prime minister, was among several European leaders calling the refugee crisis—with its accompanying security challenges—an existential threat to the unity of the European Union.[121]

With Europe increasingly jittery about terrorist threats from Islamic radicals, some feared a backlash against Muslims. In France, hundreds of French Muslims have been placed under house arrest under emergency powers declared by French President Francois Hollande after the terrorist attacks in Paris. Of 407 people put under house arrest since Nov. 14, 2015, under suspicion of terrorism, the government has admitted it was mistaken in at least 41 cases.[122]

Further divisions among EU countries arose as the EU summit on the migration crisis opened in Brussels Feb. 18, 2016 evidence of a breakdown in attempts to find a coordinated response to Europe's migration crisis. Austria announced it would cap the number of refugees who could apply for asylum to 80 a day. EU leaders condemned the move, calling it a breach of international law. Under the Geneva Convention, to which Austria is a signatory, countries are required to hear all applications by refugees seeking asylum. Austria also announced it would cap the number of migrants who said they wanted to pass through to other countries, usually Germany or Sweden, to 3,200 a day.[123]

Mark Rutte, the Dutch prime minister, warned that the result could be "the bunching up of great amounts of people in difficult circumstances in northern Greece" who wanted to reach northern Europe.

Austrian Chancellor Werner Faymann defied the EU criticism of Austria's policy, however, saying, "we will stick to it."[124]

British Prime Minister David Cameron entered the Feb. 18, 2016, Brussels summit pleading with EU leaders to satisfy his demands on curbing EU migrants' welfare benefits so that he could campaign for his country to remain in the European Union in an upcoming June referendum. Under pressure from Eurosceptics from his own party who were criticizing his deal as already "watered down," Cameron opened with the demand that Britain should be able to restrict for four years the benefits that the government pays to supplement an individual worker's wages. Cameron wanted to be able to apply that four-year limitation to EU workers newly arriving during a period of 13 years.

That demand was said to have enraged eastern and southern European leaders, who were pushing for a far more limited "emergency brake" of five years. The "emergency brake" would only be implemented if Britain's welfare system came under "exceptional" strain from immigration. Cameron compromised with an agreement that the limitation could only be applied to workers newly arriving over a period of seven years. Cameron has argued that reducing access to government benefits will deter migrants from EU countries, whom many Britons view as competing with them for jobs.[125]

However, before the emergency "brake" can be pulled, there are at least two hurdles: The European Parliament must agree to it, and British voters must vote to remain in the EU.

On Feb. 20, 2016, Cameron announced that he would campaign for Britain to stay in the EU and would schedule a referendum for June 23, 2016. That same day, six members of his cabinet announced that they would vote for Britain to exit the European Union—a position known as Brexit, and polls were showing a deeply divided Britain on the question of remaining in the EU.[126]

As for the other major issue on the summit's agenda—resolving the EU's refugee crisis, European leaders remained at odds with no new resolution reached. However, EU leaders seemed to agree that reaching an agreement with Turkey was key to controlling the influx of refugees, announcing an emergency summit with Turkey to be held March 6, 2016.

Syria—Elusive Key to Refugee Crisis

In the final analysis, most political leaders recognize that the bulk of the migrant flow to Europe has been driven largely by the ongoing conflict in Syria and the inability to patch up a peaceful resolution. In early February, 2016, peace talks between warring Syrian parties under the aegis of the United Nations broke down just as they had begun, when Russia launched 320 air attacks on northern Syria within a 48-hour period.[127]

As the bombing continued into mid-February, 2016, some western diplomats and politicians charged that Russia was deliberately bombing civilians to gain leverage on the world stage. Part of Russia's strategy was "to exacerbate the refugee crisis and use it as a weapon to divide the transatlantic alliance and undermine the European project," charged Sen. John McCain, R-Ariz., chairman of the Senate Armed Services Committee.[128]

The war in Syria has apparently "transformed from a civil war into a world war," the German weekly news magazine Der Spiegel claimed, pointing to the strong military involvement of Russia, and the more ambivalent involvement of the United States, as well as the terror attacks in Paris. As long as the Russian bombing campaign continued, it looked doubtful that peace talks could resume as planned.[129]

Considering that pessimistic outlook, Europe was bracing itself for many more refugees attempting to breach its borders as warmer weather arrives.

OUTLOOK

Moral Dilemma

In many ways, humanitarian organizations and leaders of EU countries continue to talk past one another: While humanitarians emphasize the plight of refugees and Europe's moral obligation to take in more of them, national leaders say they are trying to stem a seemingly never-ending invasion of people threatening to overburden their way of life.

The result may be that even more countries will lose patience with Brussels, predicts Papademetriou of the Migration Policy Institute Europe. Currently, Germany and Sweden take nearly half of all asylum-seekers in Europe, but even Germany is running out of housing for refugees in its cities and facing popular resentment

against them—resentment that intensified sharply after the New Year's Eve Cologne attacks.[130]

"If Germany is one of only two countries that is open to refugees, I do not believe that Germany will be open two years from now," Papademetriou says. Unless Europe can minimize the "centrifugal forces" of migration, he says, more countries will say, " 'We'll go our own way,' " whether it is Britain pulling out of the EU or Hungary refusing to follow the Dublin regulations.

While analysts like Weil of the University of Paris favor a more international approach that would involve the United States and other major nations, others are skeptical that Western leaders will attack the root causes of migration: people fleeing unstable countries due to war, persecution or poverty.

"It's almost like Nation-Building 101 has gone out the window since 9/11," says Sajjan Gohel, international security director for the Asia-Pacific Foundation, a London-based think tank that provides analysis on global security issues.

Countries like the United States and its European allies seem to have forgotten the importance of rebuilding nations' postwar governments and economic structures — the way they did in Europe and Japan after World War II, says Gohel, who teaches international history at the London School of Economics. He points to the lack of stable governments in countries such as Libya, where NATO bombing helped overthrow Gadhafi.

"Eliminating despots is important," he says. "But hand in hand there has to be a process to help the country stand up for itself."

For U.N. human rights official Crépeau, the choice remains a moral one — for both refugees and European countries that host them.

"The moral imperative is to save lives, so that's the first thing to do," Crépeau said in an interview in April 2015. "If we continue what we've done — especially in Europe — it's not going to get better." [131]

European countries need to do the right thing — the moral thing, he said, by treating the refugees compassionately. "Would we find acceptable that our sons and daughters be treated the same way if they were in the same circumstances?" he asked. "If we answer no, then we have the answer to our moral dilemma."[132]

Debate in Europe is likely to continue over whether immigrants take jobs from natives, and, ultimately, whether they harm a nation's social fabric. Indeed, some analysts say the cultural question may be as important as economic and political ones.

The lack of a common "emotional citizenship," argues British writer David Goodhart, could ultimately threaten the kinds of generous welfare states European citizens are willing to support with high taxes. It's possible to imagine Britain becoming "a less civil, ever more unequal and ethnically divided country — as harsh and violent as the United States," he writes in his book *The British Dream.*[133]

Saira Grant, legal and policy director of the Joint Council for the Welfare of Immigrants, a British nonprofit advocating just immigration policies, says, "Xenophobia arises when people feel that because of someone else they're suffering." Britons express "legitimate concern" when they say it's getting harder to get a doctor's appointment with the National Health Service, Grant says, and harder to get their children into the school of their choice because of rising numbers of immigrants.

But the solution, she says, is for the government to invest more in such services, not to blame the arrival of immigrants. As for the acceptance of people from foreign cultures, she says, "cultural change is something that takes time" for the host country, something that has already happened to some extent in Britain, she says. As one example Grant cited Britain's favorite national dish for the past decade, chicken tikka masala, an Indian curry recipe.

Paradoxically, opposition to immigration tends to be highest in communities with few migrants, probably because those residents have not had much contact with foreigners, according to Kaufmann of Birkbeck College. Opposition to immigration, Kaufmann says, is "not about jobs, houses and schools; it's more about this sense of the country not being familiar, cultural alienation and dissonance."

Rising hostility to migrants in places like Hungary worries immigrant communities and those from different cultural backgrounds. In a questionnaire sent out by Hungary's government, 80 percent of the public favored a tougher approach on immigration and 60 percent said immigration and terrorism were linked. Right-wing groups have already demonstrated against immigration in Budapest and were planning more demonstrations outside of refugee camps and along the Serbian border, *The New York Times* reported last summer.[134]

"Until now there has been little Islamophobia in Hungary," said Zoltan Bolek, president of the Hungarian Islamic Community, one of two associations representing 10,000 Muslims in a country of 10 million. "So we are surprised at what is happening."

NOTES

1. "Mediterranean migrants crisis: What happened on the sinking boat?" BBC News, April 23, 2015, http://tinyurl.com/paj6k4d.

2. Alessandra Bonomolo and Stephanie Kirchgaessner, "Migrant boat captain arrested as survivors of sinking reach Italy," *The Guardian*, April 21, 2015, http://tinyurl.com/lr9a5u8.

3. "IOM Hails Effort to Raise Migrant Death Ship off Libya's Coast," International Organization for Migration, June 30, 2015, https://www.iom.int/news/iom-hails-efforts-raise-migrant-death-ship-libyas-coast

4. "Mediterranean migrants crisis: What happened on the sinking boat?" *op. cit.*

5. IOM, Mediterranean Update, "Comparison of Monthly Mediterranean Fatalities," data updated Feb. 11, 2016, http://missingmigrants.iom.int/sites/default/files/Mediterranean_Update_12_February_2016.pdf.

6. Jan Egeland, "This is the worst refugee crisis since World War II," *The Huffington Post*, Nov. 15, 2014, http://tinyurl.com/o7xfbo9.

7. "Worldwide displacement hits all-time high as war and persecution increase," United Nations High Commissioner for Refugees, June 18, 2015, http://tinyurl.com/opn2v9c. Also see "Total number of Syrian refugees exceeds 4 million for first time," United Nations High Commissioner for Refugees, press release, July 9, 2015, http://tinyurl.com/pwhklgu.

8. UNHCR, "Refugees/Migrants Emergency Response Mediterranean," February 2016, http://data.unhcr.org/mediterranean/regional.php

9. "Migration Trends across the Mediterranean," Altai Consulting and IOM, June 2015, http://tinyurl.com/o7n3zmx.

10. Stefan Wagstyl, "EU leaders in disarray over refugee crisis," *Financial Times*, Feb. 20, 2016, https://next.ft.com/content/93881f40-d725-11e5-829b-8564e7528e54

11. Andrew Higgins, "Links to Paris Attack Roils Debate over Migrants in Hungary," *New York Times*, Dec. 17, 2015, http://www.nytimes.com/2015/12/18/world/europe/hungary-refugees-keleti-budapest.html.

    See also, Anton Troianovski and Marcus Walker, "Paris Terror Attacks Transform Debate over Europe's Migrant Crisis," *Wall Street Journal*, Nov. 16, 2015, http://www.wsj.com/articles/paris-terror-attacks-transform-debate-over-europes-migration-crisis-1447608944

12. Brian Rohan *et al.*, "Charlie Hebdo gunmen had Weapons Training in Yemen," The Associated Press, *TheWorldPost*, Jan. 12, 2015, http://tinyurl.com/p634wkc.

13. Nick Gutteridge, "Mapped," Dec. 26, 2015, Express, Dec. 26, 2015, http://www.express.co.uk/news/world/629022/EU-migration-crisis-far-right-parties-Europe-Germany-Sweden-France

14. Richard Milne, "Danish election hastens demise of Scandinavia's social democracy," *Financial Times*, June 21, 2015, http://tinyurl.com/oeexl8g.

15. Agence France-Presse, "Turkish president threatens to send millions of Syrians to EU," *The Guardian*, Feb. 12, 2016, http://www.theguardian.com/world/2016/feb/12/turkish-president-threatens-to-send-millions-of-syrian-refugees-to-eu

16. International Organization for Migration, "Mediterranean Migrant Arrivals Pass 84,000," Feb. 16, 2016, https://www.iom.int/news/mediterranean-migrant-arrivals-2016-pass-84000-deaths-reach-410

17. Mark Micaleff, "Aegean Smugglers Taking Greater Risks at Expense of Refugees," Migrant Report, Jan. 25, 2016, http://migrantreport.org/5384-2/

18. Totals for the first six months of 2015 had not been published by Frontex at press time. Source is Ewa Moncure, Frontex press office.

19. "More than 4 million Syrians have now fled persecution," United Nations High Commissioner for Refugees, July 9, 2015, http://tinyurl.com/pvadygy.

20. François Crépeau, "Banking on mobility over a generation," Report of the Special Rapporteur on the Human Rights of Migrants, United Nations Office of the High Commissioner for Refugees, May 8, 2015, p. 13, http://tinyurl.com/padfeos.

21. Antonio Guterres, "Europe must give Syrian refugees a home," *The Guardian*, July 22, 2014, http://tinyurl.com/k2h3tgj.

22. "Most support limiting immigration," Pew Research Center, May 12, 2014, http://tinyurl.com/nmsdslq.

23. "The Mediterranean Migration Crisis," Human Rights Watch, June 19, 2015, http://tinyurl.com/o4hvgod.

24. European Union, "European Union Naval Force—Mediterranean Operation Sophia," Feb. 1, 2016, http://www.eeas.europa.eu/csdp/missions-and-operations/eunavfor-med/pdf/factsheet_eunavfor_med_en.pdf

25. "First Mission Medals in Operation Sophia," Naval Today.com, Feb. 3, 2016, http://navaltoday.com/2016/02/03/first-mission-medals-in-operation-sophia/

26. Bruno Waterfield, "Europe to end passport-free travel as migrant crisis grows," *The Times*, Jan. 26, 2016, http://www.thetimes.co.uk/tto/news/world/europe/article4674529.ece

27. Reuters, "End of Europe?" Jan. 18, 2016, http://uk.reuters.com/article/us-europe-migrants-alarm-insight-idUKKCN0UW107

28. "Migratory Routes Map," Frontex, May 2015, http://tinyurl.com/qhryosj.

29. C. J. Chivers and Eric Schmitt, "In Strikes on Libya by NATO, an Unspoken Civilian Toll," *The New York Times*, Dec. 17, 2011.

30. Scott Campbell, "Over 20,000 'British children 'will miss out on chosen primary school' as immigration soars," *Express*, April 11, 2015, http://tinyurl.com/q8o464p.

31. "UN Population data 2010-2015," cited in Report of the Special Rapporteur on Human Rights of Migrants, June 16, 2015, p. 5, http://tinyurl.com/padfeos.

32. Philippe Legrain, "Open up Europe! Let Migrants in," *The New York Times*, May 6, 2015, http://tinyurl.com/pneglm8.

33. "Banking on mobility over a generation," *op. cit.*, p. 14.

34. Giulia Segreti, "UN defends role of migrant workers in Europe," *Financial Times*, June 15, 2015, http://tinyurl.com/px3ndhg. Also see, "Remittances from Europe top $109 Billion," International Fund for Agricultural Development, June 15, 2015, http://tinyurl.com/qx4fgpb.

35. Segreti, *ibid.*

36. David Charter and Rosemary Bennett, "Immigrants to ensure Britons outnumber Germans," *The Times*, June 2, 2015.

37. Steve Doughty, "Polish mothers have more children once they come to Britain," *Daily mail.com*, Feb. 4, 2014, http://tinyurl.com/p4f5zp5.

38. "Unemployment Statistics," Eurostat, May 2015, http://tinyurl.com/qz8lbqg.

39. Christian Dustmann *et al.*, "The effect of immigration along the distribution of wages," *Review of Economic Studies*, 2013, http://tinyurl.com/lv8ms2g.

40. Paul Collier, *Exodus: Immigration and Multiculturalism in the 21st Century* (2013), p. 4, p. 138.

41. *Ibid.*, pp. 61-62.

42. "Migration and migrant population statistics," Eurostat, May 2015, http://tinyurl.com/pwyyzh3.

43. Maximilian Popp, "Immigration to Germany: 'Better Qualified than the Domestic Population,'" *Der Spiegel*, June 5, 2014, http://tinyurl.com/q83cfyx.

44. "Project Europe 2030 on the Challenge of Demography," Population and Development Review, European Council, Sept. 28, 2010, p. 647, http://tinyurl.com/p8rjl4p.

45. Prime Minister David Cameron, Speech on Immigration, May 21, 2015, http://tinyurl.com/ltlfqff.

46. Hein de Haas, "Smuggling is a reaction to border controls not the cause of migration," *Hein de Haas* blog, Oct. 5, 2013, http://tinyurl.com/odcppyt.

47. "Sealing international borders is impossible, it only empowers smugglers — New expert report warns,"

U.N. Office of the High Commissioner for Human Rights, June 16, 2015, http://tinyurl.com/pmbzcjm. Also see "Banking on mobility over a generation," *op. cit.*, pp. 5-6.

48. *Ibid.*, pp. 4-5, pp. 11-12.

49. "History of CEAS," European Council on Refugees and Exiles, undated, accessed July 24, 2015, http://tinyurl.com/pcxftoo.

50. Nick Squires, "Gaddafi: Europe will 'turn black,' unless EU pays Libya £4bn a year," *The Telegraph*, Aug. 31, 2010, http://tinyurl.com/2vt4hx3.

51. "Humanitarian Visas: Option or Obligation?" European Parliament, 2014, p. 7, http://tinyurl.com/p8dv6mo.

52. "History of CEAS," *op. cit.*

53. Marc Pierini, "The EU-Turkey Refugee Deal Needs a Reset," Carnegie Europe, Feb. 16, 2016, http://carnegieeurope.eu/strategiceurope/?fa=62783

54. Jim Brundsden "EU threatens to impose Greek border controls," *Financial Times*, Jan. 27, 2016, https://next.ft.com/content/674647a6-c4f9-11e5-808f-8231cd71622e.

55. Reuters, "Greece says four of five migrant registration centers ready," Feb. 18, 2016, http://www.reuters.com/article/us-europe-migrants-greece-idUSKCN0VP0MF.

56. "For those in peril," *The Economist*, April 25, 2015, http://tinyurl.com/kl9zrkr.

57. "Mediterranean Migrants Arrive in Italy, Greece — More Deaths Reported," International Organization for Migration, July 14, 2015, http://tinyurl.com/qzlu45p.

58. "Council launches EU Naval operation to disrupt human smugglers and traffickers in the Mediterranean," European Council, June 22, 2015, http://tinyurl.com/pntevbs.

59. Horand Knaup *et al.*, "Risky Deterrence," *Der Spiegel*, May 12, 2015, http://tinyurl.com/oqsflvt.

60. *Ibid.*

61. James Politi and Duncan Robinson, "Ban Ki Moon attacks EU plans for strikes on Libyan smugglers' boats," *Financial Times*, April 28, 2015, http://tinyurl.com/npgoqey.

62. "EU targets traffickers but fails refugees," European Council on Refugees and Exiles, April 24, 2015, http://tinyurl.com/qdsshe3.

63. Federica Mogherini's remarks at U.N. Security Council, EU External Action, May 11, 2015, http://tinyurl.com/odmuez8.

64. "Mediterranean Migrants Crisis," BBC, April 22, 2015, http://tinyurl.com/p4pqkdg.

65. "For those in peril," *The Economist, op. cit.*

66. Theresa May, "EU is Putting Migrants at Risk," *The Times*, May 13, 2015, http://tinyurl.com/o58daen.

67. Deaths declined from a peak of 1,265 in April to 4 in June of this year. See "Mediterranean Update: Missing Migrants Project," International Organization for Migration, June 29, 2015, http://tinyurl.com/qcjszl5.

68. Mark Micallef, "UN Security Council Green-Lights EU's Mediterranean Anti-Smuggler Operation," Migrant Report, Oct. 9, 2015, http://migrantreport.org/exclusive-leaked-draft-of-un-security-council-resolution/.

69. Paul Farrell, "Could Australia's 'stop the boats' policy solve Europe's migrant crisis?" *The Guardian*, April 22, 2015, http://tinyurl.com/plmp9mz.

70. "Emergency EU summit proposes 'ten point plan' to deal with Mediterranean refugee crisis," Migrant Rights Network, April 21, 2015, http://tinyurl.com/p3pleds.

71. Andrew Rettman, "EU Mission could endanger refugees, UN warns," *EUobserver*, May 11, 2015, http://tinyurl.com/qjwxzzg.

72. "First Mission Medals in Operation," Naval Today.com, posted Feb. 3, 2016, http://navaltoday.com/2016/02/03/first-mission-medals-in-operation-sophia/.

73. Eszter Zalan, "EU Naval Operation Saved 5,700 Lives," euobserver, Dec. 2, 2015, https://euobserver.com/migration/131345.

74. Alex Barker, "Nato Sends warships to Aegean to aid people-smuggling crackdown," *Financial Times*, Feb. 11, 2015, https://next.ft.com/content/3385c2de-d0b6-11e5-986a-62c79fcbcead.

75. See Sarah Glazer, "Europe's Immigration Turmoil," *CQ Global Researcher*, December 2010, pp. 304-310.

76. Philip Hoare, "'The sea does not care,' " *The Guardian*, April 21, 2015, http://tinyurl.com/nqao35j.

77. Gabrielle Jackson, "UN's François Crépeau on the refugee crisis: Instead of resisting migration, let's reorganise it," *The Guardian*, April 22, 2015, http://tinyurl.com/o2jtam4.

78. Christopher Caldwell, *Reflections on the Revolution in Europe* (2010), p. 26.

79. *Ibid.*, pp. 4-5.

80. Esther Ben-David, "Europe's Shifting Immigration Dynamic," *Middle East Quarterly*, Spring 2009, pp. 15-24, http://tinyurl.com/c6mqud.

81. *Ibid.*

82. Ruben Andersson, *Illegality, Inc.: Clandestine Migration and the Business of Bordering Europe* (2014).

83. Dale Fuchs, "Canary islands fear disaster as number of migrants soars," *The Guardian*, Sept. 3, 2006, http://tinyurl.com/p6j2ufw.

84. Glazer, *op. cit.* Also see Rosa Prince, "David Cameron: Net immigration will be capped at tens of thousands," *The Telegraph*, Jan. 10, 2010, http://tinyurl.com/oyfpzht.

85. For background, see Kenneth Jost, "Unrest in the Arab World," *CQ Researcher*, Feb. 1, 2013, pp. 105-132; and Roland Flamini, "Turmoil in the Arab World," *CQ Researcher*, May 3, 2011, pp. 209-236.

86. "Council launches EU naval operation to disrupt human smugglers and traffickers in the Mediterranean," European Council, June 22, 2015, http://tinyurl.com/pntevbs.

87. "Migrant Crisis," BBC News, May 27, 2015, http://tinyurl.com/offbvn7.

88. Zoya Sheftalovich and Maia de la Baume, "A 'most difficult' EU summit," *Politico EU*, June 26, 2015, http://tinyurl.com/onpheqw.

89. "Remarks of Commissioner Avramopolous," European Commission, July 20, 2015, http://tinyurl.com/q57dwpl.

90. "Remarks on migration by President Tusk," Europa, June 25, 2015, http://tinyurl.com/ qxrdpgm.

91. "European Council Conclusions on Migration," Europa, June 26, 2015, http://tinyurl.com/gxrdpdm.

92. *Ibid.*

93. Hannah Roberts, "Hungary building 13-ft high 110-mile fence," *Daily Mail*, June 17, 2015, http://tinyurl.com/nwml8vo.

94. "Hungary: 'The Boat is full': Hungary suspends EU asylum rule, blaming influx of migrants," *The Guardian*, June 23, 2015, http://tinyurl.com/ oe34t9b.

95. James MacKenzie, "Italy's Renzi warns EU on refugees as neighbours block border crossings," Reuters, June 14, 2015, http://tinyurl.com/q68xp6q.

96. "An average of 1,000 refugees now arriving on Greek islands every day," U.N. High Commissioner for Refugees, July 10, 2015, http://tinyurl.com/ortfjzt.

97. MacKenzie, *op. cit.*

98. Michael Savage, "Britain sends a barrier to keep out Calais migrants," *The Times*, June 29, 2015, http://tinyurl.com/oa8q5qr.

99. Michael Stotherd and Catherine Bennett, "Calais migrants waiting for chance to escape 'jungle,' " *Financial Times*, July 24, 2015, http://tinyurl.com/ pm6wnlx.

100. Graeme Paton, "Channel Tunnel grows by 600 m," *The Times*, Feb. 19, 2016, http://www.thetimes .co.uk/tto/business/industries/transport/article 4694300.ece.

101. Nicholas Cecil and Peter Allen, "Calais Chaos," *Evening Standard online*, July 29, 2015, http:// tinyurl.com/o3vmsps.

102. *Ibid.*

103. Jean-Baptiste Chastand, "Italy arrests migrant who reached Europe by boat over Tunisia museum attack," *The Telegraph*, May 20, 2015, http://tinyurl .com/obu85hv.

104. Melissa Eddy, "Anti-immigrant Party Gains in Denmark Elections," *The New York Times*, June 18, 2015, http://tinyurl.com/ox9p2fm. For details on the Finns Party joining the governing coalition see,

"Far-right set to enter government coalition in Finland," *The Guardian*, May 19, 2015, http:// tinyurl.com/p2lt8mm.

105. Matthew Karnitschnig *et al.*, "Europe's Anti-immigrant Parties Stand to Gain Ground in Wake of Paris Attacks," *The Wall Street Journal*, Jan. 16, 2015, http://tinyurl.com/otdsonk. Also see, "A backlash swells in Europe after Charlie Hebdo attack," *The Wall Street Journal*, Jan. 8, 2015, http://tinyurl.com/qz4cj2g.

106. Raf Casert, "With France's National Front," *U.S. News & World Report*, The Associated Press, June 16, 2015, http://tinyurl.com/qfg9hex.

107. MacKenzie, *op. cit.*

108. Patrick Wintour and Nicholas Watt, "Ukip wins European elections with ease," *The Guardian*, May 25, 2014, http://tinyurl.com/ogxt2yq.

109. "We're out!" Mail Online, Feb. 20, 2016, http:// www.dailymail.co.uk/home/index.html

110. "Polish minister warns David Cameron that proposed migrant reforms will cross a red line," *The Independent*, Dec. 2, 2014, http://tinyurl.com/oflrowz.

111. European Commission, "A new settlement for the UK in the EU," Feb. 19, 2016, http://ec.europa .eu/news/2016/02/20160219_en.htm

112. Patrick J. McDonnell and Alexandra Zavis, "Slain Paris plotter's Europe ties facilitated travel from Syria," Nov. 19, 2015, http://www.latimes.com/ world/europe/la-fg-paris-attacks-mastermind-20151119-story.html

113. "Cologne's Aftershocks," *The Economist*, Jan. 16, 2016, http://www.economist.com/news/ europe/21688418-ultimate-victim-sexual-assaults-migrants-could-be-angela-merkels-liberal-refugee

114. "Is the Welcome Culture Legal?" *The Economist*, Feb. 13, 2016, http://www.economist.com/news/ europe/21692916-under-pressure-reverse-her-refu gee-policy-angela-merkel-faces-court-case-welcome

115. "Germany tightens refugee policy as Finland joins Sweden in deportations," *The Guardian*, Jan. 29, 2016, http://www.theguardian.com/world/2016/ jan/29/germany-tightens-borders-as-finland-joins-sweden-in-deporting-refugees

116. Duncan Robinson, "Germany and Turkey at odds on migrants," *Financial Times*, Feb. 17, 2016, https://next.ft.com/content/45072e46-d59b-11e5-8887-98e7feb46f27?_i_location=http%3A%2F%2Fwww.ft.com%2Fcms%2Fs%2F0%2F45072e46-d59b-11e5-8887-98e7feb46f27.html&_i_referer=&classification=conditional_standard&iab=barrier-app

117. Duncan Robinson, "EU says asylum move breaches Geneva Convention," Feb. 19, *Financial Times*, https://next.ft.com/content/a415ef60-d651-11e5-829b-8564e7528e54

118. "Balkans plan iron curtain to stop migrants," *The Times*, Feb. 16, 2016, http://www.thetimes.co.uk/tto/news/world/europe/article4691200.ece.

119. David Crouch, "Sweden sends sharp signal with plan to expel up to 80,000 asylum seekers," *The Guardian*, Jan. 28, 2016, http://www.theguardian.com/world/2016/jan/28/sweden-to-expel-up-to-80000-rejected-asylum-seekers

120. Alex Barker, "EU ministers eye temporary Schengen suspension," *Financial Times*, Dec. 3, 2015, https://next.ft.com/content/137322ca-999d-11e5-9228-87e603d47bdc

121. Larry Elliott,"Dutch PM says refugee crisis could shut down Europe's open borders for good," *The Guardian*, Jan. 21, 2016, http://www.theguardian.com/world/2016/jan/21/dutch-pm-says-refugee-crisis-could-shut-down-europes-open-borders-for-good

122. Alissa J. Rubin, "Muslims in France Say Emergency Powers Go Too Far," *New York Times*, Feb. 17, 2016, http://www.nytimes.com/2016/02/18/world/europe/frances-emergency-powers-spur-charges-of-overreach-from-muslims.html?hp&action=click&pgtype=Homepage&clickSource=story-heading&module=second-column-region&region=top-news&WT.nav=top-news&_r=0

123. Duncan Robinson, "EU says Austria asylum move breaches Geneva convention," *Financial Times*, Feb. 19, 2016, https://next.ft.com/content/a415ef60-d651-11e5-829b-8564e7528e54

124. David Charter, "Austria to ignore EU warning over asylum limit," *The Times*, Feb. 19, 2016, http://www.thetimes.co.uk/tto/news/world/europe/article4694334.ece

125. Francis Elliott, "This is your last chance, EU leaders tell Britain," *The Times*, Feb. 19, 2016, http://www.thetimes.co.uk/tto/news/politics/article4694382.ece

126. Stephen Castle, "British Prime Minister Announce E.U. Referendum Date," *New York Times*, Feb. 20, 2016, http://www.nytimes.com/2016/02/21/world/europe/british-prime-minister-announces-eu-referendum-date.html?hp&action=click&pgtype=Homepage&clickSource=story-heading&module=first-column-region&region=top-news&WT.nav=top-news.

127. Spiegel staff, "The War of Western Failures," *Der Spiegel*, Feb. 17, 2016, http://www.spiegel.de/international/world/the-siege-of-aleppo-is-an-emblem-of-western-failure-in-syria-a-1077140.html.

128. "Russia accused of 'weaponizing' Syria refugees," CNBC, Feb. 15, 2016, http://www.cnbc.com/2016/02/15/russia-accused-of-weaponising-syria-refugees-john-mccain.html

129. Spiegel staff, op. cit.

130. "UN asks EU to share Sweden's refugees," *The Local*, Feb. 3, 2015, http://tinyurl.com/nlez2w8. Also see, Anthony Faiola, "A global surge in refugees leaves Europe struggling to cope," *The Washington Post*, April 21, 2015, http://tinyurl.com/q3h7bo9.

131. Gabrielle Jackson, "UN's François Crépeau on the refugee crisis," *The Guardian*, April 22, 2015, http://tinyurl.com/o2jtam4.

132. *Ibid.*

133. David Goodhart, *The British Dream* (2014), http://tinyurl.com/nqdjlrw.

134. Lyman, *op. cit.*

BIBLIOGRAPHY

Selected Sources
Books

Andersson, Ruben, *Illegality, Inc.: Clandestine Migration and the Business of Bordering Europe*, University of California Press, 2014.

Through interviews with Africans attempting to migrate to Spain and the border guards who try to stop them, a London School of Economics anthropologist presents a vivid argument for the futility of border controls.

Collier, Paul, Exodus: *Immigration and Multiculturalism in the 21st Century*, **Oxford University Press, 2013.**
An Oxford University economist, while granting the economic benefits of migration, warns that opening the door to migrants in densely populated Europe will lead to "prolonged social problems" and could undermine mutual trust.

Harding, Jeremy, *Border Vigils*, **Verso, 2012.**
A journalist reports on clandestine migration in Europe and the growing reluctance of the European Union (EU) to take in migrants from other parts of the world.

Articles

"Europe's boat people: For those in peril," *The Economist*, **April 25, 2015, http://tinyurl.com/kl9zrkr.**
Europe's asylum system will be very hard to change, says this political analysis of EU proposals to deal with today's refugees and economic migrants.

Cumming-Bruce, Nick, "U.N., Warning of Migrant Crisis in Greece, Urges Europe to Act," *The New York Times*, **July 10, 2015, http://tinyurl.com/oxkdtsf.**
The U.N. says refugees are overwhelming Greece and Balkan countries and urges the rest of Europe to take in more of them.

Farrell, Paul, "Could Australia's 'stop the boats' policy solve Europe's migrant crisis?" *The Guardian*, **April 22, 2015, http://tinyurl.com/plmp9mz.**
Australia turned back migrants' boats but its get-tough policy may simply be diverting refugees to other places, including Europe, experts say.

Mananashvili, Sergo, "The Legal and Political Feasibility of EU's Planned 'War on Smuggling' in Libya," *EJIL: Talk!, blog of the European Journal of International Law*, **June 10, 2015, http://tinyurl .com/o2uqav3.**
A legal researcher at the European University Institute in Florence, which studies EU issues, lays out the legal and political obstacles to the EU's military strategy for stopping migrant smugglers.

Reports and Studies

"Banking on mobility over a generation," Report of the Special Rapporteur on the Human Rights of Migrants, François Crépeau, United Nations Office of the High Commissioner for Refugees, June 16, 2015, http://tinyurl.com/ok8hgmm.
Arguing that sealing Europe's borders is impossible and only empowers smugglers, Crépeau, the U.N. special rapporteur on migrants' rights, urges the European Union to open more legal routes to migration.

"The Mediterranean Migration Crisis," Human Rights Watch, June 25, 2015, http://tinyurl.com/o4hvgod.
Human rights abuses are driving risky sea migration, and EU attempts to prevent the crossings are "likely to fail," says the rights group.

"Migration Trends Across the Mediterranean," Altai Consulting and International Organization for Migration, June 2015, http://tinyurl.com/nqjw6vl.
This report, based on interviews with 187 migrants, finds the "push" factors of war and instability have been more important than Europe's rescue mission at sea as the impetus for the recent surge of migrants across the Mediterranean.

"Most support limiting immigration," Chapter 3 in "A Fragile Rebound for EU Image on Eve of European Parliament Elections," Pew Research Center, May 12, 2014, http://tinyurl.com/nmsdslq.
Majorities in Greece, Italy, France and Britain want stricter immigration limits, polls by this nonpartisan think tank find.

"The Sea Route to Europe," U.N. High Commissioner for Refugees, July 1, 2015, http://tinyurl .com/poaqgp3.
The U.N.'s refugee agency says the majority of migrants crossing the Mediterranean are fleeing war or persecution.

Coleman, David, and Stuart Basten, "The Death of the West: An Alternative View," *Population Studies*, April 26, 2015 (online), pp. s107-s118, http://tinyurl .com/ooexnft.
Demographic researchers from Oxford University dispute predictions that an aging Europe will need much more immigration, saying delayed pension ages and

ongoing immigration already are solving the problem of a declining labor force.

Dustmann, Christian, Tommaso Frattini and Ian P. Preston, "The effect of immigration along the **distribution of wages,"** *Review of Economic Studies,* **2013, http://tinyurl.com/lv8ms2g.**
This widely cited study found migration does not drive down wages except at the lowest end of the wage scale.

For More Information

European Council on Refugees and Exiles, Rue Royale 146, 1st Floor, 1000 Brussels, Belgium; +32 (0)2 234 3800; www.ecre.org. European alliance of 87 nongovernmental organizations that protects and advances the rights of refugees.

Frontex, Plac Europejski 6, 00-844 Warsaw, Poland; + 48 22 205 95 00; http://frontex.europa.eu. EU agency that coordinates management of EU external borders.

International Organization for Migration, 17, Route des Morillons, CH-1211 Geneva 19, Switzerland; +41.22.717. 9111; www.iom.int. Tracks migrant flows and deaths in the Mediterranean.

Migration Policy Institute, 1400 16th St., N.W., Suite 300, Washington, DC 20036; 202-266-1940; www.migration

policy.org. Nonpartisan think tank that analyzes the movement of people worldwide.

Migration Watch UK, PO Box 765, Guildford GU2 4XN, United Kingdom; +44 207 340 6079; www.migra tionwatchuk.org. Think tank that advocates reduced immigration levels to Britain.

National Institute of Economic and Social Research, 2 Dean Trench St., Smith Square London, SW1P 3HE United Kingdom; +44 207 222 7665; http://niesr.ac.uk. Research organization that has found benefits from migration.

United Nations High Commissioner for Refugees, Case Postale 2500 CH-1211 Genève 2 Dépôt, Switzerland; +41 22 739 8111; www.unhcr.org/cgi-bin/texis/vtx/home. U.N. agency that leads action to protect refugees worldwide.

3

Terrorism in Africa

Brian Beary

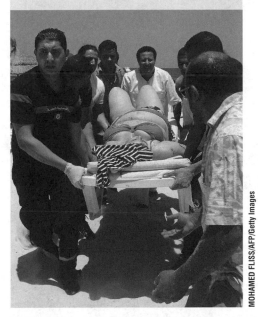

MOHAMED FLISS/AFP/Getty Images

Medics carry a wounded tourist to safety after a gunman killed 38 Western European vacationers in Tunisia on June 26, 2015. The Islamic State, a jihadist organization also known as ISIS and ISIL, claimed responsibility. "In recent weeks we've seen deadly [ISIL] attacks in Tunisia, Kuwait, and Egypt's Sinai Peninsula," President Obama said on July 6. "We see a growing ISIL presence in Libya and attempts to establish footholds across North Africa, the Middle East, the Caucasus, and Southeast Asia."

From *CQ Researcher*,
July 10, 2015; updated February 2016.

As vacationers sunned themselves on a hotel beach in the Tunisian resort town of Sousse on June 26, 2015, a man dressed as a tourist — a Kalashnikov assault rifle concealed under a furled beach umbrella — suddenly opened fire. For half an hour he ran from the beach to the pool to the hotel lobby, killing at least 38 people, including 30 Britons, before he was shot by police.

It was the worst terrorist attack in recent history in the North African country and the second within three months. The Islamic State — a Sunni Muslim-dominated jihadist organization also known as ISIS and ISIL — claimed responsibility.[1]

The same day in East Africa, the Islamic terrorist group al Shabab ("The Youth") attacked a military base and killed at least 30 Burundian soldiers. They were part of a pan-African effort to defeat the group, which has been expanding operations with deadly attacks on civilians in neighboring countries. In Egypt, scores were killed in early July in clashes between the Egyptian military and Sinai Province, an Islamic terrorist group that in November 2014 pledged allegiance to ISIS. The same week several hundred were killed in Nigeria as Boko Haram, a self-described ISIS affiliate that has been terrorizing villages and towns in northeastern Nigeria, launched new attacks to mark the Muslim holy month of Ramadan.[2]

Across parts of northern and eastern Africa, Islamic extremists — some with designs on the West — are murdering innocent civilians, trying to wrest power from weak or divided governments and control large pockets of territory.

Extremists Expand in Africa

Extremist groups in Africa have launched violent campaigns in recent years in northern, central and eastern Africa. Some experts say jihadists have expanded their influence in the Sahel — the semi-arid region below the Sahara Desert stretching from Senegal to the Red Sea — with funding from wealthy individuals in the Middle East.

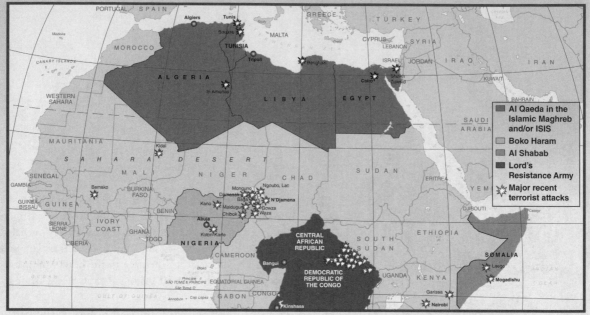

Source: Compiled by *CQ Researcher*/Brian Beary

Since the 2011 Arab Spring uprisings toppled authoritarian leaders in Tunisia, Libya and Egypt, jihadists have exploited weakened governments, posing a major security challenge not only for the African continent but also for Western nations struggling to contain terrorism throughout the Middle East and beyond. [3]

In fact, ISIS-inspired attacks targeted people in France and Yemen on the same day as the Somalia and Tunisia attacks, which coincided with the start of Ramadan. Near the French city of Lyon, a Muslim worker of North African descent decapitated his boss and tried to blow up an American-owned gas plant. And in Kuwait a suicide bomber blew himself up at a Shiite mosque, killing 27. [4]

"ISIL and its ideology also obviously pose a grave threat beyond the [Syria and Iraq] region," said President Obama on July 6. "In recent weeks we've seen deadly attacks in Tunisia, Kuwait and Egypt's Sinai Peninsula. We see a growing ISIL presence in Libya and attempts to establish footholds across North Africa, the Middle East, the Caucasus, and Southeast Asia." [5]

The United States has responded to northern and eastern Africa's "corridor of instability" by taking a "small footprint approach," with limited military interventions that do not involve boots on the ground, said Amanda Dory, deputy assistant secretary of Defense for African affairs. Instead, it is partnering with France and the United Kingdom (U.K.), along with new regional blocs such as the Sahel G5 — set up in 2014 by Mauritania, Mali, Niger, Chad and Burkina Faso to strengthen cooperation on development and security issues. "Going it alone is not a sustainable or viable solution," Dory said. [6]

When Sunni Muslim terrorist groups take over a region they usually impose strict Islamic law — or sharia — which calls for, among other things, floggings, stonings and executions of Shiite Muslims, Christians who refuse to convert to Islam and moderate Sunni Muslims who do not follow the group's strict interpretation of Islam.[7] Tens of thousands of Africans are fleeing the continent — some to escape the terrorist violence and some in search of a better life — contributing to a refugee and migrant crisis of epic proportions.

Besides ISIS and al Shabab, other major terrorist groups now entrenched in northern, eastern and central Africa include:

- *Al Qaeda in the Islamic Maghreb (AQIM)*, an affiliate of the Pakistan-based terrorist group that attacked the United States on Sept. 11, 2001, mostly operating in Algeria and Libya.[8] It emerged in the 2000s in Algeria, which became a hotbed of jihadism in the 1990s after the military banned the Islamist political party (FIS, or Front Islamique Salut), which had won parliamentary elections.[9]

- *Boko Haram*, which, loosely interpreted, means "Western education is a sin." The jihadist group is based in Nigeria's Muslim-dominated northeastern region. It kidnaps, rapes, kills children and burns down villages. The group has been particularly deadly since 2014, conducting cross-border strikes into neighboring Chad, Niger and Cameroon. In fall 2014 it was estimated the group has killed 13,000 people.[10]

- *Lord's Resistance Army (LRA)*, which claims to be a Christian fundamentalist group, has been terrorizing civilians in Central Africa for more than three decades. Spawned by the Ugandan civil war in the 1980s, the group is notorious for brutal rampages that have displaced 2 million people and resulted in the abduction of 60,000-100,000 children forced to become soldiers or slaves.[11] Pushed out of Uganda in the early 2000s, the group is now hiding in remote parts of the Central African Republic and Democratic Republic of Congo.[12]

While al Shabab recently has focused on killing Christians, Boko Haram attacks both Christians and Muslims. The Islamic State's trademark is its high-profile, ritualized beheadings, such as its murder of 21 Coptic Christians on a Libyan beach in February 2015, notes Tiffany Lynch, a senior policy analyst at the United States

A Somali soldier guards the site in Mogadishu, the capital, where the jihadist group al Shabab launched a suicide attack against a military intelligence training base on June 21. Three Shabab militants and a Somali intelligence official were killed. An affiliate of al Qaeda, Shabab seeks to replace Somalia's weak government with a caliphate, or Islamic state. In addition to attacks at home, the group has mounted large-scale raids in Kenya, Uganda and Djibouti.

Mohamed Abdiwahab/AFP/Getty Images

Commission on International Religious Freedom, an independent commission created by the U.S. government to defend freedom of religion abroad. Lynch has spent time in Nigeria and Kenya studying Boko Haram and al Shabab.[13]

The terrorist threat is most acute in Libya, where a schism in the political leadership last summer led to the creation of rival governments. The anti-Islamist Dignity coalition is based in Tobruk in eastern Libya while the Islamist — but not jihadist — Dawn coalition is based in the capital Tripoli.

Recently, terrorist groups have bolstered ties with one another: In 2012, al Shabab formally affiliated with al Qaeda, and Boko Haram in March 2015 declared itself aligned with ISIS. However, Tina Kaidanow, the U.S. Department of State's counterterrorism coordinator, told a June 19, 2015, press briefing that because some groups are "self-affiliating" with the Islamic State "it's a little hard to assess" how close the operational links are among them. Nevertheless, Boko Haram and ISIS share "a penchant for the use of brutal tactics, which include stonings, indiscriminate mass-casualty attacks and systematic oppression of women and girls, including enslavement, torture and rape."

While al Qaeda and the Islamic State embrace anti-Western, global jihad ideologies, important differences separate them, according to Thomas Joscelyn, a senior fellow at the Foundation for Defense of Democracies, a Washington think tank. Wherever it gains control, the Islamic State declares a caliphate — regionwide government organized around Islamic law as set out by the Prophet Muhammad in the seventh century. Al Qaeda's strategy, on the other hand, "is far more clandestine," Joscelyn explained, allowing affiliates, such as Ansar Al Sharia in North Africa and al Shabab, to keep their local names. "The extent of [al Qaeda's] international network is consistently underestimated," whereas ISIS' international presence "has been overestimated," he wrote.[14]

But the Islamic State "is a much more dangerous enemy" than al Qaeda, mostly because of its focus on building a caliphate in areas it controls, said Fran Townsend, a counterterrorism adviser to President George W. Bush in the early 2000s and now president of the Counter Extremism Project, a New York-based nongovernmental organization. "This is a really terrible thing, [which] creates a sense of urgency."[15]

"In contrast to the liberation movements of the 1980s, today's jihadist groups are not principally seeking to capture government power in their capitals," according to the German Institute for International and Security Affairs, a Berlin-based think tank. "For many jihadists the nation-state model has been superseded by a transnational perspective where national frontiers are increasingly irrelevant."[16] Jihadi groups in Africa seek to establish either a regionwide caliphate or separate, smaller Islamic theocracies.

The terror groups compete with one another for recruits, noted Vanda Felbab-Brown, a senior fellow at the Brookings Institution think tank in Washington who specializes in international and internal conflict and who recently returned from Somalia. What young fighter seeking to fight for Islam would want to go to the dusty, difficult terrain of Somalia, or to a place where chunks of territory have already been captured, she asked, highlighting how there are also tensions between al Shabab and the Islamic State.[17]

African terror groups get some of their funds — up to $200 million in recent years — from ransoms extracted from European governments for the safe return of their abducted citizens.[18] In 2009, the Swiss government paid about $12.4 million in ransom for the release of Swiss and German nationals kidnapped in Mali.[19]

Some terrorists clearly see more value in keeping their foreign hostages alive and extorting ransoms from their families or home governments than in executing them or allowing them to die. Since 2008 only 15 percent of al Qaeda's hostages captured in Africa and the Middle East have been killed, according to a *New York Times* investigation.[20] The U.K. and the United States, which refuse to pay ransoms, have pleaded with other governments to also refrain, arguing that such payments only encourage more kidnappings and fund terrorist operations.

The new wave of terrorism is playing out on a continent already plagued by pockets of violence elsewhere. In the Central African Republic, for instance, a power struggle between Christians and Muslims has caused tens of thousands of the country's Muslim minority to flee for their lives, taking refuge in neighboring Chad and Cameroon.[21] And a vicious civil war broke out in South Sudan after it became Africa's newest independent nation in July 2011. Caused by a leadership power struggle, the war has left up to 5 million people without enough food and has been particularly deadly for children. "The details of the worsening violence against children are unspeakable," UNICEF Director Anthony Lake said in June.[22]

As African and Western governments respond to intensifying security challenges, here are some of the key questions being posed:

Is African terrorism a significant threat to the West?

While the surge in terrorism has destabilized large parts of northern and eastern Africa, it is less clear how much of a direct threat it poses to the United States or other Western countries.

Joscelyn from the Foundation for Defense of Democracies pointed out that documents seized by the United States in 2011 during the raid on Qaeda leader Osama bin Laden's compound in Pakistan show that he ordered the organization's branches in Africa to select recruits capable of striking inside the United States. In addition, Joscelyn contended, al Qaeda and the Islamic State threaten Western interests "everywhere their jihadists fight."[23]

Besides an infamous 2012 attack on the U.S. consulate in Benghazi, Libya, armed Islamists in Libya also have attacked the embassies in Tripoli of Algeria, Morocco, Iran, South Korea and Spain, he pointed out.[24] And in neighboring Tunisia in March 2015, ISIS attacked the Bardo National Museum in the capital, Tunis, killing more than 20 people, mostly Western tourists.[25]

As for attacks by African terrorist groups inside Western countries, "There is a risk, but it is often overstated by Western security agencies." However, says E.J. Hogendoorn, deputy director of the Africa Program at the International Crisis Group, a nongovernmental organization that seeks to resolve conflict, "isolated individuals could engage in terrorist attacks in Europe and North America."

In terms of direct threats, the U.S. government is most concerned about al Shabab, the Defense Department's Dory said, but it is looking very closely at the Islamic State in Libya because "its proximity to Europe is a significant concern." As for Boko Haram's recent announcement that it is affiliating with the Islamic State, she said "we are still evaluating" the significance of this.[26]

Some Western countries have experienced so-called lone wolf attacks by followers of the Islamic State or al Qaeda, such as those on the Canadian parliament in Ottawa in October 2015 and on a cafe in Sydney, Australia, in December 2015.[27] But the State Department's Kaidanow said "it was difficult to assess whether these attacks were directed or inspired by ISIL or al Qaeda and its affiliates." Both groups encourage attacks by individual supporters in Western countries because their own operatives have difficulty traveling to the West due to terrorist no-fly lists, she said.

"The threat of lone wolves or small cells of terrorists is complex," Obama said on July 6. "It's harder to detect and harder to prevent. It's one of the most difficult challenges that we face."

In Somalia, Hogendoorn points out, al Shabab retains its potency despite strong European Union (EU) and U.S. support for the 22,000-strong multinational military force (AMISOM) created to respond to attacks on the government of Somalia and neighboring countries. The force is nominally led by the 54-country African Union, created in 2001 to promote stability on the continent.

Michael O'Hanlon, a senior fellow in national security and defense policy at the Brookings Institution, contended that Somalia badly needs the outside help. Their army is "a work in progress" — poorly paid, unpopular with the local population and made up of members from different clans, he said.[28]

The success of the Islamic State and al Qaeda has encouraged some Westerners to join them. The chaos in Libya is making it a favored destination for foreign militants, rivaling Iraq and Syria, where more than 22,000 would-be fighters from 100 nations, including 180 Americans, have traveled, Homeland Security Secretary Jeh Johnson told a U.N. ministerial meeting on foreign terrorist fighters in May 2015. He is most concerned that these fighters will "circumvent border security and security at airports," he said. He is working with foreign governments to enhance passenger screening "at certain overseas airports with direct flights to the United States," he said.[29]

Mattia Toaldo, a policy fellow at the European Council on Foreign Relations, an international think tank, agreed that ISIS has great potential to expand into Libya. However, he cautioned against paying too much attention to all armed Islamist groups in Libya, because some of them have mostly local grievances. His analysis is not shared by the Defense Department's Dory, who is concerned by how close Libya is to Europe. According to Toaldo, "we should be concerned about the [prolongation] of the civil war in Libya." Al Shabab in Somalia also is "still locally focused," said Felbab-Brown at Brookings, despite its attacks in neighboring Kenya.

Anouar Boukhars, a nonresident scholar in the Middle East program at the Carnegie Endowment for International Peace, a think tank in Washington with research centers around the world dedicated to advancing the cause of global peace, said Nigeria's Boko Haram "is still a local phenomenon . . . driven by local grievances." There has not been much coordination yet between Boko Haram and al Qaeda in the neighboring Maghreb region, he added.[30]

Toaldo said most recent terrorist attacks on European soil have been carried out by European nationals.[31] In January 2015, Islamic terrorists attacked the satirical magazine *Charlie Hebdo* and a kosher grocery store in Paris, killing 16 people. The terrorists, who were killed by police, were French-born but of Algerian and Senegalese descent and had ties to armed jihadists. One had received training from al Qaeda in Yemen.[32]

"What happened in France is just a sign of things to come," said Aref Ali Nayed, Libya's ambassador to the

United Arab Emirates. "It makes no sense to do this in compartments. You cannot have a consortium that is bombing ISIS in Syria and Iraq and not doing so in Libya." Since last summer, President Obama has authorized limited airstrikes against the Islamic State in Iraq and Syria and recently in Libya. However, he has said he has no plans to send U.S. troops to Libya.[33]

The Lord's Resistance Army (LRA) has "not targeted Americans or American interests" and is "not capable of overthrowing an allied government," according to a recent article in *Foreign Affairs*. The United States has sporadically deployed small-scale troop contingents to help governments fight the LRA, with mixed results.[34]

Is an Islamic caliphate likely in Africa?

Recent evidence shows that Islamic terror groups are making progress toward their goal of establishing caliphates in Africa — if not a regionwide one then separate states where sharia is imposed.

Al Shabab has established some of the structures that constitute a caliphate in areas it controls in Somalia, according to the International Crisis Group. It raises money from local citizens by collecting *zakat* and *sadaqa*, traditional Islamic forms of voluntary and obligatory alms and charity. The group also provides certain public services, such as digging irrigation canals and building mosques and Islamic schools — activities that have generated some local goodwill. It also has conducted public stonings and amputations in areas it controls.[35]

In Libya, the Islamic State has made major gains, according to Libyan Ambassador Nayed. "We are seeing an exponential growth of [ISIS]," he said. "Libya, because of its resources, has become the ATM machine, the gas station and the airport for [ISIS]. There is an unfortunate state of denial about all of this, and that is the most dangerous thing."[36]

According to *The Washington Post*, the social media propaganda and official statements of the Islamic State, which on June 29, 2014, declared a caliphate in Iraq and Syria, now state that the group plans to expand its caliphate to Libya "and to use Libya as a base of operations for further attacks."[37]

"There is real concern in Libya and the Sahel," says Hogendoorn, from the International Crisis Group, referring

Abubakar Shekau, third from left, heads the Nigerian Islamic extremist group Boko Haram, which kidnaps, rapes, kills children and burns down villages. Self-described as an affiliate of the Islamic State, the jihadist group has murdered some 13,000 civilians in Nigeria and nearby Chad, Cameroon and Niger.

to the semi-arid lands south of the Sahara Desert stretching from Senegal on the west coast of Africa to the Red Sea in the east. Jihadists in the region have stronger links to oil-rich Arab nations such as Saudi Arabia, where some wealthy individuals support them, he says.

However, according to Townsend of the Counter Extremism Project, since al Qaeda sponsored attacks inside Saudi Arabia in 2003, Saudi authorities have made a major effort to eradicate Islamist terrorism. The Saudis' level of cooperation with Americans is so extensive that they "rival our relationship with the British intelligence services," she said. For instance, the Saudis were key in helping the United States foil a 2009 al Qaeda plot to blow up a plane by placing a bomb in a printer cartridge in the cargo hold, she pointed out.[38]

Hogendoorn doubts that either Boko Haram or al Shabab can create a "durable" state, because they would need "significant financial resources." Imposing local taxes and engaging in illicit activities such as smuggling may sustain them temporarily, he says, but Western governments will continue to deploy military assets against them, preventing them from becoming too entrenched.

Terrorist Groups in Africa

The Islamic State recently expanded from the Middle East to North Africa, about 200 miles from the European coast. Three other Muslim fundamentalist groups are trying to establish Islamic enclaves, or caliphates, in Africa based on Muslim law, or sharia.

Group	Number of Fighters	Operating Countries
Al Qaeda in the Islamic Maghreb (AQIM)	About 1,000	Algeria, Chad, Libya, Mali, Mauritania and Tunisia
Based in Sahara Desert and Sahel regions. Group aims to rid North Africa of Western influence, overthrow current governments and implement fundamentalist, sharia-based rule. Members use assassinations, suicide bombings, kidnappings and executions to raise money and spread influence.		
Al Shabab	7,000-9,000	Djibouti, Kenya, Somalia and Uganda
Al Qaeda affiliate that aims to establish a fundamentalist state in Somalia and targets Christians. Transnational African security campaign weakened group in the early 2010s, but it has re-emerged in recent years, launching large-scale attacks in Kenya, Uganda and Djibouti.		
Boko Haram	About 9,000	Cameroon, Chad, Niger and Nigeria
Jihadist group based in northeastern Nigeria that has killed at least 13,000 people and displaced 1.5 million since 2009. Fighters target Christians and Muslims and have launched large-scale kidnappings and mass killings and have crossed into neighboring countries. Leadership announced affiliation with Islamic State in March 2015.		
Islamic State (also known as ISIS and ISIL)	N/A	Egypt, Libya, Algeria, Tunisia
Split from al Qaeda in Iraq in 2014 and aims to establish a caliphate to rule over the world's Muslims. Members spread message through extreme violence and well-produced videos and social media showing beheadings of Christian and Western hostages.		
Lord's Resistance Army (LRA)	Hundreds	Central African Republic, Democratic Republic of Congo
Claiming to be a Christian fundamentalist group, the LRA attacks civilians and has kidnapped up to 100,000 children to use as soldiers. Leader Joseph Kony founded the group in 1987 after the Ugandan civil war. Under pressure from the Ugandan military, aided by the United States, membership declined from thousands to hundreds since the late 1990s, but fighters continue to terrorize Central Africa.		

Sources: Council on Foreign Relations group profiles; Al Shabab figure estimates from "Who are Somalia's al-Shabab?" BBC, April 3, 2015, http://tinyurl.com/klml38f; Boko Haram membership estimate from Farouk Chothia, "Who are Nigeria's Boko Haram Islamists?" BBC, May 4, 2015, http://tinyurl.com/l8ka4tm; Lord's Resistance Army information from Alexis Arieff and Lauren Ploch, "The Lord's Resistance Army: The U.S. Response," Congressional Research Service, May 15, 2014, http:// tinyurl.com/pf2ml45; Max Fisher, "The Bizarre and Horrifying Story of the Lord's Resistance Army," *The Atlantic,* Oct. 17, 2011, http://tinyurl.com/o98o88d

According to Lynch, of the United States Commission on International Religious Freedom, Boko Haram is showing signs of wanting to be part of a broader, regional caliphate movement. "The Boko Haram leader has spoken warmly and fondly" of the Islamic State, Lynch says, referring to statements of affiliation he made in March and April. A Boko Haram leader has trained in Somalia with al Shabab, and a few Boko Haram fighters have gone to northern Mali to help al Qaeda, she says.

After a coup in Mali in 2012, foreign al Qaeda fighters forged an alliance with the local separatist Tuareg tribe and quickly gained control of a 250,000-square-mile area of northern Mali. Alarmed by the situation, France sent troops to Mali — a former French colony — in early 2013 and defeated the Tuareg-al Qaeda forces within months. Al Qaeda and the Tuareg parted ways, and many of the al Qaeda operatives dispersed and regrouped in neighboring Algeria and Libya.

The Tuaregs predate al Qaeda by centuries, said Georg Klute, a professor of African anthropology at the University of Bayreuth in Germany. In the early 1800s they waged jihad against their colonial overlords and again during World War I. The tribe claims to be descended from the first Islamic Army to capture North Africa in the seventh century.[39]

Wahabbism, an ultra-conservative strain of Islam, has been on the rise in Mali in recent years, shaking the country's "tradition of religious tolerance," according to Carnegie's Boukhars. Klute attributed the rise of radicalism to the country being "both too big and too small." It is too small to face the challenges posed by globalization, he said, but too big to cope with its ethnic and religious diversity.[40]

Are Western actions the main cause of terrorism in Africa?

Jihadi groups often cite the West's actions as justification for their violence. For instance, when ISIS beheaded the Coptic Christians on a Libyan beach in February 2015, the lead executioner said the killings were in retaliation for the 2011 death in Pakistan of al Qaeda founder Osama bin Laden at the hands of U.S. special forces.[41] Likewise, al Qaeda, in declaring war on the West in 1998, cited the presence of U.S. troops in Saudi Arabia — a sacred place for Muslims because it is the birthplace of the Prophet Muhammad.

Some experts say terrorists attract recruits because of both domestic and foreign-motivated resentments. "[It] goes back to both Middle Eastern Islamism and the way Islamists were suppressed by Middle Eastern dictators and felt humiliated by foreign occupiers," said Mustafa Akyol, a fellow at the German Marshall Fund of the United States, a nongovernmental organization that promotes transatlantic relations.

In Egypt, for instance, after Franco-British rule ended in 1952, Egypt's first major political leader was the militantly secular Gamal Abdel Nasser. His rise to power caused Islamic fundamentalist groups, such as Takfir Wal-Hijra, to develop and gain adherents.[42]

Similarly, the recent anti-Islamist crackdown by Egypt's new leaders — who launched a coup in 2013 and imprisoned and tortured members of the democratically elected conservative Muslim Brotherhood — has stirred a backlash by Egyptian Islamists.[43] In the Sinai Peninsula, attacks by the terrorist group Ansar Bayt al-Maqdis (AMB) against the Egyptian army have intensified in recent months. Last November AMB declared its allegiance to ISIS and changed its name to Sinai Province.[44]

In Libya, Islamists are acting out of fear that the government will repress them like the new military-led regime in Egypt has done, says Abdul Rahman Al Ageli, co-founder of the Libyan Youth Forum and a nonresident fellow at the Washington-based Atlantic Council think tank.

"Libya was not screwed up by the West," said Toaldo of the European Council on Foreign Relations. "It was screwed up by the [Gadhafi] dictatorship" that ruled the country from 1969 to 2011, when a popular uprising, assisted by NATO, toppled and murdered him. The post-Gadhafi Libyan leadership then made "crucial mistakes," he said.[45]

Townsend of the Counter Extremism Project blamed the rise of Islamic State in North Africa on the West, specifically on NATO, which she said failed to follow through after helping to topple Gadhafi in 2011. "I was slack-jawed," she said, by the failure of NATO to take the necessary follow-up steps. The new Libyan government did not get the security assistance and institution-building support it needed, she said, because attention was diverted to Syria and Iraq, which have become the core base and breeding ground of Islamist terrorism.

In addition, she said, the United States has failed to develop an effective counter-narrative in response to highly professional Islamic State propaganda. "Beheading videos are not protected by First Amendment rights," she said, referring to how ISIS widely disseminates videos of its mass executions, both to terrorize and to attract new recruits. The government should take a lead in denying the Islamic State a public space, and private companies should assist them, she argued.

The International Crisis Group's Hogendoorn says colonial transgressions are not the primary cause of today's unrest, noting "not all post-colonial states suffer from Islamist terrorism." But he contends that "the West exacerbates the problem by intervening in a ham-fisted way," citing Somalia as an illustration. When al Shabab established sharia-based law and order, "this raised alarm bells in the West, and Ethiopia intervened, with the implicit approval of the U.S.," he says. That fueled local support for al Shabab and resentment of the West, he says.

In Nigeria, the human rights organization Amnesty International has attributed Boko Haram's campaign of terror more to socio-economic problems in northern Nigeria than to Western actions, namely high youth unemployment, drug addiction, religious tensions, a culture of impunity by the ruling political elite and the government's failure to provide public services.[46]

Carnegie's Boukhars said the Nigerian military's brutal clampdown on Boko Haram in 2009 turned it into an extremely violent organization. Boko Haram "was not a terrorist group when it started," he said. In addition, he pointed out, in the 1990s economic belt-tightening imposed in many African countries by the International Monetary Fund was hard on the population and generated ill will toward the West. By contrast, Islamic institutions from conservative Arab countries in the Middle East have given aid to the poor in Africa.[47]

Boko Haram's violence is "a revolt against bad governance, corruption, lack of the rule of law," said the U.S. Commission on International Religious Freedom's Lynch. In such contexts, says Hogendoorn, some, generally less-educated people conclude that "if only our leaders were good Muslims and applied sharia law these problems would be solved."

BACKGROUND

Early Roots

Contemporary jihadist ideology takes its inspiration from the early centuries of Islam, when the Muslim world expanded from its birthplace in modern-day Saudi Arabia in the seventh century to encompass large swaths of the globe. At its zenith in the 1200s, various Muslim empires or states — called caliphates — stretched from Spain in Western Europe to Morocco in Western Africa and across the northern half of Africa, and across the Middle East to Indonesia and the southern Philippines in Southeast Asia.[48]

Saudi-born Muhammad Ibn Abd-al-Wahhab (1703-92), who accused the Ottoman Empire of corrupting Islam by practices such as worshiping at the graves of early leaders of the Muslim faith, founded the ultra-conservative Wahhabi strand of Islamic thought, which stresses the religion's monotheistic nature. Wahabbism spread from Saudi Arabia into parts of Africa.

In Muslim-dominated northern Nigeria, Usman Dan Fodio (1754-1817), who opposed the mixing of local animist religious traditions with Islam, launched a reform movement to rid Islam of outside influences. After leading a successful uprising against a local ruler, he became the political and religious leader of a new caliphate based in the city of Sokoto in northern Nigeria. The state was led by a sultan and governed according to Islamic principles, including revering the study of Islamic thought and abolishing hereditary leadership succession.

In the early 20th century, the caliphate ceased to exist after the British took control of the region. The British had established their dominion in Christian-dominated southern Nigeria around 1860.[49]

The discovery of oil in southern Nigeria in 1956 set the stage for a rise in sectarian tensions. Oil wealth predominantly benefited the country's Christian-dominated south, leaving the majority-Muslim population in the north struggling to develop that region's economy. After gaining independence from the U.K. in 1960, Nigeria became a federal state, in which most political power was supposed to devolve to the 36 state governments. However, after military coups in the late 1960s power was concentrated in the federal government, which remained dominated by the military for decades.

Many of the ruling generals were Muslim, which somewhat mitigated north-south tensions in the 1980s and '90s. But the military leadership was responsible for wide-scale human-rights abuses during this period, fomenting anti-government sentiment. When Nigeria transitioned to democracy in 1999, southern Christians gained political power, again increasing sectarian tensions. In 2002-03, 12 northern states introduced sharia law.[50]

In Egypt, Egyptian school teacher Hasan al Banna (1906-49) established the Muslim Brotherhood in 1928, aiming to restore Islamic rule in Egypt, controlled by the British since the early 1900s. Al Banna's movement later expanded to other Arab countries and Sudan.[51]

CHRONOLOGY

1920s-1980s *Jihadist groups emerge as religious tensions rise.*

1928 Egyptian schoolteacher Hasan al-Banna (1906-49) establishes the Muslim Brotherhood with the goal of re-Islamizing the Muslim world.

1956 Oil is discovered in Christian-dominated southern Nigeria, raising tensions between Muslims and Christians.

1979 Soviet Union invades Afghanistan to repress an anti-communist uprising, drawing thousands of militant Islamists, including from Africa, to the country to try to repel the Soviets. Afghanistan becomes a stronghold for al Qaeda, which spawns offshoots in eastern and northern Africa.

1986 As the civil war in Uganda winds down, spirit-medium Alice Auma establishes the Holy Spirit Mobile Forces, which eventually becomes the Lord's Resistance Army (LRA), a terrorist group that professes a fundamentalist Christian ideology.

1990s-2000 *Jihadists target the West.*

1991 Algerian authorities react to a parliamentary election victory by the Islamist FIS (Front Islamique du Salut) party by clamping down on all Islamist activity; civil war ensues. . . . Socialist-led Somali government collapses, plunging the country into chaos and providing fertile ground for the growth of militant Islamist groups.

1992 Al Qaeda leader Osama bin Laden moves to Sudan at invitation of the Islamist government. He plots anti-Western attacks, but relations with Sudanese authorities sour, and bin Laden is expelled; he returns to Afghanistan in 1996.

1998 Al Qaeda declares war on the West. . . . Al Qaeda operatives bomb U.S. embassies in Dar es Salaam, Tanzania, and Nairobi, Kenya, killing 224 and injuring 4,500.

1999 Nigeria begins transitioning from military rule to democracy, which worsens Christian-Muslim tensions because of Christians' growing political strength.

2001-Present *Increasingly aggressive Islamists capture territories in northern Africa.*

2001 Qaeda-led attacks in the United States on Sept. 11 kill nearly 3,000 civilians, destroy the World Trade Center and damage the Pentagon.

2002 Several states in northern Nigeria introduce Islamic law. . . . Muslim cleric Mohamed Yusuf establishes Boko Haram.

2011 Arab Spring uprisings across northern Africa loosen governments' grip on their territories, a boon for armed Islamist groups.

2012 Al Shabab formally affiliates with al Qaeda. . . . On Sept. 11, Islamist terrorists attack the U.S. consulate in Benghazi, Libya, killing four U.S. citizens, including the American ambassador.

2013 Al Qaeda-linked terrorists storm a gas plant at In Amenas, Algeria, and take hostages, leading to a gunfight with authorities in which 37 workers are killed. . . . Egyptian military forcibly removes the democratically elected Muslim Brotherhood from power in response to fears it was making the country too Islamic. . . . Four Shabab gunmen target Westerners and non-Muslims at the Westgate shopping mall in Nairobi, Kenya, killing at least 67 people.

2014 Boko Haram kidnaps 276 girls from a Nigerian school; the group later kills more than 600 people in Gwoza. . . . Shabab leader Ahmed Abdi Godane dies in U.S. drone strike in Somalia.

2015 Shabab gunmen kill 142 students and six police officers at Kenya's Garissa University (April 2). . . . Islamic State releases video showing its members beheading Ethiopian Christians in Libya (April 19). . . . Nigeria's presidency peacefully passes from a Christian to a Muslim (May 29). . . . U.S. airstrike in Libya kills Mokhtar Belmokhtar, a senior al Qaeda operative who led the 2013 assault on the In Amenas gas plant. . . . ISIS gunman kills 38 Western tourists in Tunisia (June 26). . . . Scores killed in clashes between ISIS-affiliated terrorists and Egyptian military (July 1). . . . In northeastern Nigeria, Boko Haram gunmen kill nearly 100 Muslims praying in a mosque (July 2). ISIS plants bomb on Russian commercial plane in Egypt, causing it to crash, killing all 224 passengers (Oct. 31). . . . In Paris, ISIS-affiliated Belgian and French nationals of Algerian and Moroccan parentage kill 130 civilians in bombings and shooting spree (Nov. 13). . . . Qaeda-affiliated gunmen storm hotel in Mali's capital, Bamako, killing 21 (Nov. 20).

2016 Qaeda operatives kidnap Swiss nun from her home in Timbuktu, Mali, and accuse her of converting Muslims to Christianity (Jan. 8) . . . Shabab gunmen kill 150 Kenyan peacekeeping troops in a raid on their

base in Gedo region, Somalia. . . . Al Qaeda-led attack on hotel and restaurant in Ougadougou, the capital of Burkina Faso, kills 29 (Jan. 15). . . . Lord's Resistance Army commander Dominic Ongwen answers war crimes charges at International Criminal Court in The Hague (Jan. 21). . . . Boko Haram militants kill 86 people in assault on Dalori village in northeastern Nigeria, including burning alive children (Jan. 30). . . . Egypt's Court of Appeals orders retrial of 149 Muslim Brotherhood activists sentenced to death on charges stemming from clashes with police in summer 2013 (Feb. 3).

Sayyid Qutb, an Egyptian scholar who had studied in the United States in the 1940s, became one of the Brotherhood's leading thinkers. He condemned Christianity and Judaism as decadent religions and urged establishment of an Islamic state. He was executed by Egypt in 1966 for allegedly plotting the assassination of President Nasser.[52]

In Sudan, a north-south sectarian divide similar to Nigeria's sowed the seeds of conflict. Sudan gained independence in 1956 after a century of joint British and Egyptian rule. But Sudan then became embroiled in decades-long civil wars that pitted the Muslim north against the Christian south. The south ultimately seceded in 2011.

Muslims dominated the Sudanese government in Khartoum, the capital, which became increasingly Islamist in the 1990s. The government sparked tensions with the West when it invited al Qaeda leader bin Laden to base himself there in the mid-1990s. In 1998, after al Qaeda operatives bombed the U.S. embassies in Kenya and Tanzania, the United States retaliated against Khartoum for harboring bin Laden by bombing a Khartoum pharmaceutical factory it claimed was producing chemical weapons. The Sudanese government angrily denied the allegation, and the episode soured the country's relations with the West.[53]

In northern Africa, colonial rule ended shortly after World War II. Libya gained independence from Italy in 1951, Egypt from the U.K. in 1952, Tunisia and Morocco from France in 1956, Mali and Niger from France in 1960 and Algeria from France in 1962. The new rulers

were nationalist, authoritarian and anti-Islamist, which fueled a rise in Islamic militancy.[54]

Algeria became an early hotbed of jihadism. The Islamist FIS (Front Islamique du Salut) party emerged in the mid-1980s from protests over the poorly performing Algerian economy, which was suffering from falling global prices for oil and gas, a mainstay of Algerian exports.[55]

After FIS won the first round of parliamentary elections in 1991, Algeria's military canceled the rest of the vote, banned the FIS and violently repressed its supporters. An ensuing civil war lasted until the late 1990s.

The Algerian unrest encouraged Tunisia's authoritarian leader, Zine el-Abidine Ben Ali, to ban Islamist activity in the 1990s. Some Tunisian Islamists turned to militant preachers and organizations in Gulf Arab states for leadership.[56] Throughout the decade, oil-rich Saudis established charities and built mosques and Islamic schools in northern Africa, many of which promoted fundamentalist Wahabbism.[57]

Al Qaeda's Rise

Al Qaeda developed in the 1980s from a movement led by religiously motivated Arab fighters who went to majority-Muslim Afghanistan to repel the "infidel" Soviets, who had invaded in 1979. Provided weapons covertly by the United States, the fighters — called mujahideen — succeeded in forcing out the Soviets in the late 1980s.

Bin Laden, a wealthy Saudi who had gone to Afghanistan to fight the Soviets, established al Qaeda ("the base") there in 1988. After moving his operations

African Migration to Europe Explodes

Refugees seek to escape violence, poverty.

A series of tragic drownings in the Mediterranean this year, caused by the capsizing of flimsy, overcrowded boats smuggling migrants, has shone a spotlight on a refugee problem that has reached epic proportions.

More than 1,800 people have drowned trying to cross the Mediterranean in the first half of 2015, including at least 800 who died in a single incident in April when a vessel piloted by smugglers slammed into a Portuguese container ship off the coast of Libya.[1] The surge of trans-Libya migration stems from the demise of state control in Libya, which has allowed smugglers to profit from human trafficking.

Libya has more than 350,000 internally displaced persons, along with 28,000 refugees and 9,000 asylum-seekers from other countries, according to the U.N. High Commissioner for Refugees (UNHCR). It is ill-equipped to handle them, with no legislation or procedures for receiving asylum claims.[2]

Human smuggling is nothing new for Libya, noted Fiona Mangan, an expert on smuggling trends and senior program officer at the Center for Governance, Law and Society at the United States Institute of Peace, a congressionally funded nonpartisan institution in Washington. Libya's longtime leader, Moammar Gadhafi, tolerated it to an extent, even proclaiming that "the black market is the people's market." A popular uprising in 2011, which NATO supported with airstrikes, toppled Gadhafi and he was later killed by militants. Smuggling of all commodities, including migrants, then mushroomed, she said.[3]

Sabha, a city in southwestern Libya, is now a major smuggling hub for Algeria and Niger, Mangan said. Al Kufrah in southeastern Libya, which borders Chad, Sudan and Egypt, is another. The port city of Zuwarah, west of the capital Tripoli and close to the Libya-Tunisia border, is another important departure point for Mediterranean crossings.

Since last summer, Libya has had rival governments: the anti-Islamist Dignity coalition based in Tobruk in the east and the Islamist — but non-jihadist — Dawn administration in Tripoli. In addition, the Islamic State "is inserting itself as a third force," said Frederic Wehrey, senior associate in the Middle East program at the Carnegie Endowment for International Peace, a think tank based in Washington with research centers around the world dedicated to advancing the cause of global peace.[4]

So far, there is no evidence that the jihadist Islamic State has taken over the migrant smuggling networks, said Wehrey. Underemployed local tribes such as the Tuaregs are more likely to involve themselves in smuggling, said Mangan, because smuggling provides a livelihood in a country where state institutions no longer function.

Some nationalities, such as Eritreans, are escaping repressive political regimes. The Eritrean government has

to Khartoum in 1991, bin Laden was forced out of Sudan in 1996 after he failed to help the country develop. He moved back to Afghanistan, where he was welcomed by the Taliban, an ultra-conservative Islamic movement from southern Afghanistan that had gained dominance among the country's warring factions and taken over the government. Also in the mid-1990s, Ayman al-Zawahri — an Egyptian surgeon who had founded his own movement, Egyptian Islamic Jihad — merged his group with bin Laden's.[58]

In 1998, al Qaeda declared war on the United States and its allies and announced that both civilians and the military were targets. In the first official anti-U.S. Qaeda attack, the group bombed the U.S. embassies in Nairobi, Kenya, and Dar es Salaam, Tanzania, on Aug. 7, 1998, killing 224 people and injuring 4,500.[59] The Nairobi bombing caused a four-story building next to the embassy to collapse.[60]

Two years later, on Oct. 12, 2000, two al Qaeda suicide attackers rammed an explosives-laden boat into the Navy destroyer *U.S.S. Cole* in the Port of Aden, Yemen, killing 17 U.S. sailors.[61]

Al Qaeda's Sept. 11, 2001, attacks in the United States, which killed nearly 3,000 people, made it the most notorious terror group in the world. It began to morph into a global franchise in subsequent years, with other militant Islamist groups adopting its name to gain greater recognition

one of the worst human-rights records in the world. Others, such as Gambians in West Africa, are fleeing poverty and lack of economic opportunity at home. "I know what the risks are. I know it's very hard," said Susso, a Gambian preparing to travel to Europe via Libya who asked that only his last name be used. Smugglers had left one of his cousins to die in the Libyan desert, and another had drowned at sea.[5]

Between January and March 2015, the European Union (EU) received more than 160,000 asylum claims, according to the UNHCR.[6] While Africans made up a significant slice of those claims, refugees escaping conflict in Afghanistan, Iraq and Syria represent the largest share. Alarmed by the influxes, EU foreign ministers decided on June 22 to deploy a military mission to stop the smuggling. The arsenal includes five warships, two submarines, three maritime patrol aircraft, two drones and three helicopters. At least 10 EU countries are contributing military assets.[7]

Phase one involves gathering information on the smugglers' "business model" via remote monitoring of the Libyan coast. The ministers also authorized a mission to seize and destroy smuggler ships — when they are not filled with migrants — but are seeking approval from the U.N. Security Council before launching that phase.

While the EU hopes such actions will deter the smugglers, Mangan stresses that conditions in Libya will continue to encourage them. With smuggling in all commodities, including migrants, remaining a lucrative and growing business, there is little incentive for the diverse armed groups in Libya to lay down their weapons and restore state order, she said.

— *Brian Beary*

Migrants whose boat overturned on June 10 as they fled terrorist violence in Libya arrive in the Tunisian town of Ben Guerdane after their rescue by Tunisia's coast guard and navy.

[1] "UN: Mediterranean sinking is worst ever with more than 800 dead," Fox News, The Associated Press, April 21, 2015, http://tinyurl.com/nn8lc8v.

[2] "2015 UNHCR Subregional Operations Profile — North Africa," United Nations High Commissioner for Refugees, undated, www.unhcr.org.

[3] Mangan's comments were made at conference entitled "The Fragile Sahel: Transnational Threats and Sustainable Solutions," Carnegie Endowment for International Peace, June 24, 2015.

[4] Wehrey's comments were made at *ibid*.

[5] *Ibid*.

[6] United Nations High Commissioner for Refugees, Statistics and Operational Data, http://tinyurl.com/34wntoj.

[7] Loreline Merelle, "Green light for EUNAVFOR Med," *Europolitics*, June 22, 2015.

and recruitment power. The group moved its headquarters from Afghanistan to Pakistan after the U.S.-led invasion of Afghanistan in 2001 toppled the Taliban.

Al Qaeda's most prominent affiliate in Africa is AQIM, based in Algeria — the first African group to adopt the al Qaeda brand.

Somalia's Chaos

In colonial times, Somalia was divided into areas ruled by the British, French and Italians. In 1960 an independent Somalia was formed from the British and Italian colonies, while the French colony later became Djibouti.

In 1991 Somalia's socialist government, led by 1969 coup leader Siad Barre, collapsed. The country descended into civil war, anarchy and famine.

In 1993, the U.S. deployed troops to lead a United Nations force sent to provide humanitarian and peacekeeping aid. But the United States refocused its military mission to pursue a Somali warlord, Muhammad Farah Aideed, whom it believed was thwarting efforts to restore peace and unity to the country. On Oct. 3 the United States dropped 120 elite soldiers into the capital Mogadishu, assigned to abduct some of Aideed's top lieutenants.

African Christians Face Terror, Persecution

Terrorists "want to reignite a religious war."

On April 2, four members of the Islamic terror group al Shabab burst onto the campus at Garissa University in Kenya, killing 142 students and six police officers.

The attackers tested the students' knowledge of Islam, killing those who failed. They shot or slit the throats of some, beheaded others and tricked female students into emerging from hiding by telling them the Koran banned the killing of women.[1] A Shabab statement two days later said the attack was in retaliation for Kenya contributing troops to an international military force fighting al Shabab in Somalia and for "unspeakable atrocities" committed by Kenyan soldiers against Muslims in East Africa.[2]

A rise in terrorism and religious extremism in northern and eastern Africa has led to increased attacks on Christians. Just this year in Libya the Islamic State has targeted Christians in three high-profile attacks: beheading Coptic Christians on a beach in February, executing a group of Ethiopian Christians in April and abducting 88 Eritrean Christians in June.[3]

Christians also face deadly persecution in northeastern Nigeria, where the Islamic terror group, Boko Haram, has burned villages, raped women and girls, kidnapped people, conscripted children into their ranks and slit the throats of Christians and Muslims it deems to have been corrupted.[4]

Boko Haram and its ilk have a chillingly simple goal, says Tiffany Lynch, a senior policy analyst at the United States Commission on International Religious Freedom, an independent commission created by the U.S. government to defend freedom of religion abroad, who spent time in Africa studying these groups: "They want to reignite a religious war."

Egypt is another danger zone for Christians, although the threat there stems more from fellow Egyptians than from global jihadists. For 30 years, Egypt's authoritarian leader, Hosni Mubarak, largely was able to keep a lid on violence targeting the nation's 8-million-strong Coptic Christian minority, whose religion dates to the time of Jesus.

After Mubarak was toppled during the 2011 Arab Spring movement, Islamic extremists — including Islamists such as the Muslim Brotherhood and the Salafis, followers of the ultra-conservative Saudi-based Wahhabism — began attacking Coptic Christians.[5]

One of the worst attacks occurred in May 2011, when hundreds of Salafists targeted three Coptic churches in the Imbaba neighborhood of Cairo. Fifteen people were killed and 232 injured.[6] Egypt's National Council for Human Rights, a government agency, blamed the Salafis for "the intensification of extremist religious interpretations that propose rearranging Egyptian society to exclude Christians." The Muslim Brotherhood and conservative Salafis were working together to "empty Egypt of

In an ensuing battle with local militias, two U.S. Blackhawk helicopters were shot down, 18 U.S. soldiers — and hundreds of Somali civilians — were killed. Images of the soldiers' naked bodies being dragged through the streets were relayed around the world. The United States withdrew its troops, and two years later the United Nations, having failed to restore order, discontinued its mission.[62]

Many years later it emerged that in the months before the battle with U.S. troops bin Laden had sent al Qaeda operatives to Somalia to help train Aideed's militias.[63] The episode harmed America's reputation among Somalis and made the United States reluctant to intervene militarily in internal conflicts.

For the next decade, Somalia was engulfed in clan warfare, with no functioning central government. Al Shabab came to prominence in 2005, aiming to establish a caliphate with Islamic ministers, regional administrators and courts. It earned respect — and recruits — among some Somalis for helping to fight the Ethiopians, who invaded Somalia in 2006 after the civil war threatened to spill over into Ethiopia.[64]

From 2004-12, Somalia was led by an internationally recognized Transitional Federal Government, but it was never able to defeat al Shabab, despite help from the United States and the African Union, which deployed a peacekeeping mission (AMISOM) to Somalia. In July 2010, al Shabab

Christians and make it an Islamic state," said Wagih Yacoub, a Coptic human-rights activist.[7]

The situation worsened in 2012 after the Muslim Brotherhood was voted into power and the Salafist al Nour party gained a significant number of seats in the legislature. But a military coup overthrew the Brotherhood in July 2013 after sectarian violence began to destabilize the country.[8]

Since then, Brotherhood supporters have turned on the Copts, claiming they helped the military junta. In March, for example, Muslims attacked Coptic homes to stop a church from being built in the village of El Galaa. After the Christians refused to cave in to Muslim demands that their church have no dome, cross, tower or bell and be accessible only via a side street, Muslims attacked their homes and looted their shops.[9]

The ousting of the Islamists from power has lessened, but not eradicated, the threat to Christians. However, Copts have been reassured by expressions of solidarity by General Abdel Fattah al-Sisi, the leader of the 2013 coup and now president of the country, and by his decision to order immediate air strikes against the Islamic State in Libya after the mass beheadings of Coptic Christians there in February.

But Dwight Bashir, deputy director of policy and research at the religious freedom commission, says the situation remains tenuous, because the Copts must "rely on the favor of a single individual," the Egyptian president. Often, he said, police do not conduct adequate investigations of attacks on Coptic Christians "due to fear of retribution against them by violent extremists."[10]

The surge in anti-Christian activity in Africa mirrors what is happening in the Middle East, particularly in Iraq and Syria, where ancient Christian churches — many of which predate Islam — have been destroyed or taken over by the Islamic State, and Christians have been driven from the country.[11]

— *Brian Beary*

[1] "An Atrocity in Kenya: Could things gets worse?" *The Economist*, April 11, 2015, http://tinyurl.com/ndlqflsf.

[2] "Somalia's Shebab warn Kenyan public of 'long, gruesome war,' " AFP, in *Times Live*, April 4, 2015, http://tinyurl.com/o7wjtm9.

[3] "ISIS captures 88 Eritrean Christians in Libya, US official confirms," Fox News, June 9, 2015, http://tinyurl.com/qzp9zjb.

[4] "Boko Haram at a glance," Amnesty International, April 13, 2015, http://tinyurl.com/on4lp8l.

[5] For background, see Kenneth Jost, "Unrest in the Arab World," *CQ Researcher*, Feb. 1, 2013, pp. 105-132; and Roland Flamini, "Turmoil in the Arab World," *CQ Researcher*, May 3, 2011, pp. 209-236.

[6] Alison Matheson, "Fears of 'Grave Future' for Egypt's Christians," *The Christian Post*, May 12, 2011, http://tinyurl.com/ona648j.

[7] *Ibid.*

[8] See Kirsten Powers, "The Muslim Brotherhood's War on Coptic Christians," *The Daily Beast*, Aug. 22, 2013, http://tinyurl.com/mlzwsrk.

[9] Written testimony of Samuel Tadros, Senior Fellow, Hudson Institute's Center for Religious Freedom, to United States House of Representatives, Committee on Foreign Affairs, Subcommittee on the Middle East and North Africa, hearing entitled "Egypt Two Years After Morsi: Part 1," http://www.hudson.org/research/11312-egypt-two-years-after-morsi-part-1

[10] Dwight Bashir, "Egypt's Sisi: Reformer or Strongman?" Atlantic Council, May 21, 2015, http://tinyurl.com/morc5tn.

[11] Jane Corbin, "Could Christianity be driven from Middle East?" BBC News, April 15, 2015, http://tinyurl.com/qy9uycf.

lashed out at Uganda for having contributed troops to AMISOM: three Shabab suicide bombers killed more than 60 people as they watched the World Cup soccer match in two locations in Kampala, Uganda's capital city.[65]

In February 2012, Shabab leader Ahmed Abdi Godane announced the group had joined al Qaeda, which had begun voicing support for al Shabab after the 2006 Ethiopian invasion caused al Shabab's ranks to swell. Some Shabab leaders criticized Godane for his harsh leadership style and for having strengthened the group's ties to al Qaeda, but he quickly repressed dissent, killing two of his main critics and consolidating his authority.[66] Godane was killed in a U.S. drone strike on Sept. 1, 2014.[67]

In recent years al Shabab has continued to lash out at its neighbors for supporting AMISOM. In September 2013, four Shabab gunmen killed at least 67 people at the Westgate shopping mall in Nairobi, Kenya. The attackers allowed Muslims to escape unharmed and targeted Westerners and local citizens.[68] Shabab said the attack was revenge for Kenya having sent troops to AMISOM.

On April 2, 2015, four Shabab gunmen slaughtered 142 students and six police officers at Garissa University, a girls' campus in Kenya. According to reports, the killers particularly targeted Christians and non-Muslims. Kenyan president Uhuru Kenyatta responded by bombing two Shabab camps in Somalia.[69]

Lord's Resistance Army

The origins of the Lord's Resistance Army (LRA) are the strangest of all the African terrorist groups. In 1986, Yoweri Museveni took power following a civil war in Uganda. Alice Auma, a spirit-medium and former fish peddler who came from northern Uganda and disliked the new leadership that came from the south, mounted an insurgency against the notoriously brutal new regime.

Claiming she had become infused with the spirit of an Italian army officer she had met at a nature reserve, Auma said her mission was to purify her native lands through combat. She assembled the 18,000-strong Holy Spirit Mobile Forces, which she instructed to cover themselves in shea nut oil to make them bullet-proof.[70] The insurgency was defeated by government troops in 1987, and Auma fled to Kenya, where she died in a refugee camp in 2007. Auma's remaining followers were quickly recruited by Joseph Kony, a young commander who claimed he was possessed by Auma's spirit and who shared Auma's aim to establish a Christian theocracy in Uganda.

Since then Kony has maintained a tight grip over the LRA, gaining notoriety for his cruelty — the torture and killing of civilians, destruction of villages and enslavement of children.[71]

"Once you're part of the system, it is not easy to escape," said John Otto Baptist, a former LRA member who was 12 years old when abducted by the group and forced to fight. "You accept that is your life, to keep killing and being a soldier."[72]

By the mid-2000s, the Ugandan army, assisted by the United States, had pushed the LRA out of Uganda. The group retreated to southern Sudan but was driven out and has since fled to the Central African Republic and the Democratic Republic of Congo.[73] At press time, Kony has eluded capture despite deployment of U.S. combat troops in 2008 and in 2011 with a "kill or capture" mission. The LRA continues to abduct and kill but on a smaller scale.[74]

Boko Haram

Boko Haram was established in 2002 in northeastern Nigeria by Islamist cleric Mohammed Yusuf. "Yusuf was an Islamic scholar who rejected secular authority in Nigeria and railed against the corruption of Nigeria's political elite," according to Amnesty International.[75] Boko Haram has targeted Christian civilians as well as Islamic scholars

STUART PRICE/AFP/Getty Images

Lord's Resistance Army leader Joseph Kony has gained notoriety for the Ugandan group's torture and killing of civilians, destruction of villages and enslavement of children. Kony has eluded capture despite deployment of U.S. forces in 2008 and 2011. The group been pushed out of Uganda and is much diminished, but it continues to terrorize Central Africa.

and clerics it deems are not strictly adhering to their interpretation of the fundamental Islamic texts.[76]

After police shot at Boko Haram members during a funeral procession in June 2009, more than 800 died in clashes between Boko Haram and Nigerian security forces.[77] Yusuf was then arrested and killed in police custody on July 30, 2009, but no one was held accountable for his death.[78]

Yusef's successor, Abubakar Shekau, announced that the group aimed to create an Islamic state in northern Nigeria. Boko Haram morphed into a violent terrorist group beginning in 2012, causing Nigeria's president to declare states of emergency in three states in northeastern Nigeria.

The group's attacks in northern Nigeria increased sharply in 2014. In February the group hacked or burned to death 59 boys at a secondary school as they slept in their beds, claiming that it was a sin for the boys to get a "Western education." In April, it kidnapped 276 girls at a secondary school in the town of Chibok, in northeastern Nigeria, sparking a global #bringbackourgirls campaign on social media.[79] In August 2014, the group killed at least 600 people in Gwoza, and in January 2015 it went on a killing spree across Nigeria that left hundreds of civilians dead.[80]

In early 2015, Nigerian security forces pushed Boko Haram out of the main urban centers and into remote areas, where it continued to raid towns and villages.

Arab Spring

The 2011 toppling of Gadhafi in Libya, and to a lesser extent the fleeing of Tunisian leader Ben Ali the same year, gave a boost to Islamist terrorists. Well-armed Malian Tuareg mercenaries who had been employed by Gadhafi returned home and mounted the separatist uprising in northern Mali in 2012, joined by AQIM.

However, France's intervention in January 2013 to defeat the Tuareg-al Qaeda alliance provoked an attack by AQIM on a gas plant at In Amenas in neighboring Algeria. Some 650 workers were taken hostage, and 37 were killed in an ensuing battle between the militants and the Algerian military.[81] In September 2014, Algerian Islamists claiming allegiance to Islamic State beheaded a French tourist, saying it was in revenge for U.S. airstrikes on ISIS in Iraq.[82]

In Libya, a local Islamist group, Ansar al-Sharia, attacked the U.S. consulate and CIA compound in Benghazi on Sept. 11, 2012, killing U.S. Ambassador Christopher Stevens and three other Americans.

In Tunisia, the 2011 election of a moderate Islamist party, Ennahda, led to an initial easing of restrictions on fundamentalist Islam. But the government changed course and began clamping down in September 2012 after Islamists stormed the U.S. embassy in Tunis.[83]

In 2014 ISIS began to rival, and in some cases eclipse AQIM, as the dominant jihadist movement in Africa. ISIS' popularity was largely due to its success in capturing large swaths of territory in Iraq and Syria. In addition, its mass killings of Christians and "non-pure" Muslims gained further attention.[84]

Egypt and the United Arab Emirates responded by carrying out airstrikes against Islamists in Libya, an emerging ISIS stronghold, thanks in part to two rival civil governments having emerged in summer 2014.[85]

CURRENT SITUATION
Magnet for Terrorists

Libya remains the biggest concern in Africa as a magnet for terrorists. The U.N. is mediating talks between Libya's two rival governments, trying to reunify the country as a first step toward restoring order. Libya's economy is struggling to stay afloat as the instability, which includes sabotage attacks on facilities and worker strikes, makes it difficult to produce and sell oil, its primary income source.[86]

The European Union and United States are supporting the reunification process from the sidelines, mindful that if Libya remains a failed state, it could become a staging post for Islamic terror attacks on the West. On June 14, a U.S. airstrike in Libya killed a senior al Qaeda operative, Mokhtar Belmokhtar, an Algerian-born national who led the deadly assault on the In Amenas gas plant.[87]

Meanwhile, Islamists in Libya have been defecting from AQIM to the Islamic State. Youth Forum's Ageli says ISIS in Libya is now led mainly by non-Libyans, while 95 percent of its adherents are "brainwashed youth." The Islamic State is strongest in coastal Libya, while AQIM's stronghold is in southwest Libya, where it engages in smuggling and kidnappings of foreigners for ransom.[88]

The Islamic State has continued to conduct mass executions. Besides the executions of the Egyptian Christians in February, the group disseminated a video on April 20 showing two groups of Ethiopian Christians being executed in Libya, one on a beach and the other at a location in southern Libya. The narrator said "our battle is a battle between faith and blasphemy, between truth and falsehood, until there is no more polytheism — and obedience becomes Allah's in its entirety."[89]

In neighboring Egypt, the anti-Islamist government has been cracking down on extremist activity. In May, it handed down death sentences to ousted former Muslim Brotherhood President Mohamed Morsi and more than 100 other Muslim Brotherhood followers.[90] An appeals court on June 16 upheld the sentence.[91]

Nigerian Election

In Nigeria, Boko Haram is continuing its terrorist attacks on civilians, in an insurgency that has crossed regional borders.

In June the group carried out revenge attacks in Chad and Niger, countries that had joined the Nigerian military in February in its counteroffensive, which had pushed Boko Haram out of most of the towns it occupied. At least 33 died in suicide bombings in Chad, and attacks on villages in Niger killed at least 40.[92] The conflict has displaced thousands of civilians, and refugee camps have sprung up.

Muhammadu Buhari, a Muslim, was sworn in as president on May 29 after defeating Goodluck Jonathan, a Christian, in March. Jonathan had been heavily criticized for having allowed the Boko Haram-led violence to escalate so badly.

Is an Islamic caliphate a viable threat to Africa?

YES
Joshua Meservey
Policy analyst, Allison Center for Foreign and National Security Policy, The Heritage Foundation

Written for *CQ Researcher*, June 2015

A radical Islamic caliphate certainly could be formed in Africa. In fact, it briefly happened last year when the terrorist organization Boko Haram announced it had set up an Islamic state in swathes of northern Nigeria. Later, however, the group declared allegiance to the Islamic State in Iraq and Syria (ISIS) and lost control of most of its occupied territory to a multinational military offensive. So now that caliphate exists in little more than name only.

Despite the heartening decline of Boko Haram, conditions elsewhere in Africa are conducive for another terrorist organization to form a radical Islamic caliphate. Boko Haram and ISIS both metastasized in contexts of weak government control: The Nigerian government has historically struggled to extend its authority in northern Nigeria where Boko Haram got its start, while ISIS' rise was enabled by a civil war ripping Syria apart and a feckless Iraqi government.

Africa, unfortunately, is home to a number of countries whose governments only weakly control significant portions of their territory. This, coupled with the proliferation of Islamic terrorist organizations in the Sahel, suggests we will see another Islamic caliphate on the continent.

Radical caliphates have so far been short-lived in Africa, but they do not need to exist long to pose a deadly threat. At one point Boko Haram had subjugated an area the size of West Virginia. It has killed an estimated 22,000 people since 2011, while destabilizing the entire region. At its zenith, the terrorist group al Shabab controlled nearly all of southern Somalia and most of the capital city Mogadishu. While never a formal caliphate, al Shabab was a de facto one, and its ruinous policies led to the deaths of more than a quarter of a million Somalis during a famine in 2011-2012.

Several areas in Africa require close attention, lest ISIS or a similar group succeeds in carving out a new state. Libya has descended into chaos as various warring factions slice up the country — and ISIS already has an affiliate there. In the vast Sahel region, northern Mali is again being destabilized by a variety of terrorist organizations as well as separatist groups, and the government lacks the capacity to bring it under control.

Other examples could be cited, but suffice to say that the threat of another Islamic caliphate being established somewhere on the Africa continent is all too real.

NO
John Voll
Professor Emeritus of Islamic History, Center for Muslim-Christian Understanding, Georgetown University

Written for *CQ Researcher*, June 2015

The proclamation of an Islamic caliphate has seldom been a major threat in sub-Saharan Africa. The most common feature of groups in the Sahel and the Horn of Africa that represent significant challenges to political order is the emergence of militant groups able to mobilize under-employed young men. These militias gain control of territory, terrorize inhabitants and create major refugee problems. They are the product of the disintegration of old-style social institutions at a time when modern weaponry is easily accessible.

In fact, caliphate-supporting militants play a minor role in groups representing threats in the Sahel/Horn region. Two of the most important involve non-Muslim militias. The Lord's Resistance Army began as the militia of an Acholi religious movement in Uganda and became a terror band threatening three Central African states. In newly independent South Sudan, well-armed ethnic militias are destroying the country.

Several conflicts do involve Muslim militias. In Darfur in Sudan, youth gangs, organized to oppose non-Arab peoples, became the notorious Janjaweed — well-armed bands terrorizing the population. In the Central African Republic, Christian and Muslim militias have created chaos. In Ethiopia, Muslim Somalis in the Ogaden liberation movement have opposed the central government. In these movements, there was little call for establishing a caliphate.

Three movements might indicate the viability of a caliphate as a threat, but on closer examination, they do not. In Somalia, the Shabab have ties to al Qaeda. They started as a militia associated with Islamic courts attempting to bring stability during the civil war, but a caliphate is not part of their program. Similarly, in West Africa, jihadi groups joined with Tuareg ethnic separatists in 2012 and controlled much of northern Mali for a time. They called for an extremist interpretation of sharia, or Islamic law, but not for a caliphate.

Boko Haram in Nigeria is the only group in Africa proclaiming an Islamic caliphate. It has roots in West African Muslim reformist activism, and its founder did not try to establish a caliphate.

The strength of Boko Haram, like that of Shabab and the Malian movement, comes from its militia, not its ideology. In a region where the median age ranges between 15 and 20, the most "viable" threats are well-armed gangs of young men. Some militias, like Boko Haram, adopt militant ideologies, but others, like those in South Sudan, are brutal expressions of ethnic identities. In these contexts, an Islamic caliphate, or even an extremist Islamist program, is not a significant threat.

President Obama's special assistant for African affairs, Grant Harris, said the United States remained concerned by Boko Haram's continued kidnapping of children and by abuses committed by Nigeria's military in its counteroffensive.[93]

According to Lynch, of the U.S. Commission on International Religious Freedom, while Christians so far have not carried out revenge killings against Muslims for the Boko Haram attacks, "there is growing distrust between Christian and Muslim communities," she says. "Some Christians claim Muslim clerics do not do enough to stop the violence. But if Muslim clerics do speak up, they get attacked by Boko Haram and their mosques are bombed."

Shabab Threat

On May 5, John Kerry became the first U.S. secretary of State to visit Somalia. Due to the continuing insecurity there, Kerry never left the airport at Mogadishu; instead, the Somali president and prime minister met him there. "I visited Somalia today because your country is turning around," said Kerry. The United States has not had an embassy in Somalia since 1991 and has given no indication when it might reopen one.[94]

On July 7, a Shabab attack on a quarry in Kenya near the border with Somalia killed at least 14 workers.[95]

Brookings' Felbab-Brown said security in Somalia during her recent visit was "more difficult" than in previous visits but still "remarkably better" than in 2008-09. Al Shabab has less territory than before but still controls many roads, and the number of Shabab attacks is on the rise, she said. The Somali government is very weak, and AMISOM is doing little to rebuild roads or bridges, she said.[96]

AMISOM is still operational in Somalia, with its biggest troop contingents from Ethiopia and Kenya, making those countries prime targets for Shabab attacks. Exacerbating the problem, the troops often treat Somalis in a heavy-handed manner, Felbab-Brown said.[97]

In Central Africa, efforts to defeat the Lord's Resistance Army are making steady progress. In January, captured commander Dominic Ongwen appeared at the International Criminal Court in The Hague on charges of enslavement, murder and pillage. U.S. Special Forces captured him during one of their numerous missions to kill or apprehend LRA leader Kony.[98]

Meanwhile, the international community is coalescing around a kidnapping policy of not paying ransom to terrorists. Following a meeting of 28 anti-ISIS coalition partners in Jeddah, Saudi Arabia, on May 7, participants adopted a joint declaration rejecting "the payment or facilitation of ransoms."[99]

OUTLOOK
'Unprecedented Commitment'

Counter-terrorism coordinator Kaidenow has said the terrorist threat in Africa and the Middle East is evolving quickly: "We cannot predict with precision what the landscape will look like one decade or even really a year from now."[100]

For the terror threat to diminish in Libya, she said, "what really needs to happen [is] a political process that will lead ultimately to the formation of a unity government," but there is little sign of a breakthrough on that front for now. As for the threat of Islamic terrorism, she said, it "is not something [the United States] can do ourselves" without help from regional governments.

Countries such as Saudi Arabia and the United Arab Emirates have made "an unprecedented commitment" to fight Islamic terrorism, said Townsend, of the Countering Extremism Project. The United States should give those countries counterterrorism training and logistical support, she added.

Because ISIS and other terrorist groups increasingly rely on U.S. social media outlets like Facebook, Twitter and YouTube to convey messages and recruit, the Obama administration recently started discussions with Silicon Valley on cutting off this oxygen source for the terrorists. And draft legislation is advancing in the Senate requiring, for the first time, social media companies to report suspected terrorism messages to federal law-enforcement authorities.[101]

In September, during a General Assembly meeting in New York City, heads of state also will hold what the United Nations is calling a summit on countering violent extremism worldwide.

The West's longstanding mantra has been that installing democracies in this part of the world is the best formula for future peace and prosperity. But Toaldo from the European Council on Foreign Relations warns the West to avoid thinking that simply holding elections will prevent the spread of terrorism in Africa. "I am not sure that counting ballots instead of bullets is a good idea," he said, citing Iraq as a cautionary tale.[102]

In the early 2000s, the United States oversaw free elections in Iraq that resulted in a Shiite Muslim-led government. Once in power, the government had no incentive to include minorities, such as the Sunnis. A decade on, Iraq is on the verge of collapse, and the Islamic State controls much of the country.

"Jihadism in Libya is a long-term challenge and by far the greatest of its kind in North Africa," said the German Institute for International and Security Affairs (SWP), a Berlin-based think tank, which urged Western governments not to pick sides among the two governments vying for control of Libya. Doing so, it warned, would only cause the benefiting side to use the support to crush its rival, which then would push the losing side into a tactical alliance with other armed Islamists.[103]

SWP also points to a societal issue in northern Africa that it believes is contributing to Islamist militancy. While the average marriage age keeps increasing due to economic hardship, premarital sex is taboo in these deeply conservative societies. "The frustration produced by these developments often leads not only to attempts to flee to Europe or escape in drug consumption or petty crime, but also a turn to extremist religious positions," it says.[104]

In a policy briefing paper, the International Crisis Group predicted that al Shabab will most likely remain a significant force for the foreseeable future. "Its armed units will retreat into smaller, remote and rural enclaves [and] groups of well-trained individuals will continue to carry out assassinations and terrorist attacks in urban areas, including increasingly in neighboring countries, especially Kenya," the paper said. "The long connection between al Shabab's current leadership and al Qaeda is likely to strengthen."[105]

In Central Africa, the hunt for LRA leader Kony will continue, as will ICC attempts to arrest and put LRA commanders on trial. The "underlying problem . . . [is] . . . the region's poor governance," noted *Foreign Affairs* magazine. Once the LRA gets chased out of one country, it quickly finds a safe haven in another.[106] But the group's agenda has always been a local one, and it has no known links to other terror groups, so it poses no threat to the United States and its allies.

In Nigeria, the concentration of oil resources in the south is likely to continue to exacerbate Christian-Muslim tensions and make it more difficult to eradicate religiously motivated violence. "Nigeria now occupies top places in two important terrorism indexes, with the number of deaths greater than in Syria or Pakistan," the SWP pointed out.[107]

If the Nigerian military cannot improve its dismal human rights record, it will stoke the flames of future violence. According to former U.S. Ambassador to Nigeria Princeton Lyman, it will be a big challenge for Nigeria's newly elected President Buhari to reform the military in the middle of a conflict with Boko Haram. "He has to shake up the leadership — but in a way that it doesn't collapse," Lyman said.[108]

The International Crisis Group's Hogendoorn believes that the West needs a change of emphasis in how it responds. Rather than just sending military missions or support to the affected countries, "it would be better for us to engage with the authorities in these countries," he argues, by encouraging better governance and reduced corruption.

EPILOGUE

The trajectory of terrorism in Africa continued along a similar path in the second half of 2015 and early 2016, with ISIS, al Qaeda and groups affiliated to these networks staging attacks in Egypt, Libya Mali, Nigeria, Somalia and — for the first time — Burkina Faso. The countries and regions targeted by the terrorists invariably had weak or divided governments who were struggling to control their borders and territories. Many of them are receiving help from neighboring countries and from Western governments, notably France and the United States, which is a further motivator for the terrorists in staging attacks.

Speaking about the terrorist activity in northern and western Africa, the U.S. State Department's Coordinator for Counter-Terrorism, Tina Kaidanow, said "Most of the branches are made up of pre-existing terrorist networks." She added: "We are watching closely" to see if these groups broaden their goals from local to global and are able to secure more financing on the back of their affiliations with the al Qaeda and ISIS brands. Kaidanow said that al Qaeda and ISIS were competing with one another for dominance. She pinpointed Libya as a country of concern as ISIS continues to grow there, due in part to the failure of the internationally-brokered negotiations to reunify the government.[109]

A Libyan military official said in February 2016 that armed forces loyal to the Libyan government amounted to around 1,400, less than half of the estimated strength of ISIS.[110] With the Western-led coalition continuing to increase the number of airstrikes targeting ISIS-controlled territories Iraq and Syria, some ISIS operatives are moving to Libya for refuge as the anti-ISIS airstrikes have yet to target Libya.[111]

On September 30, 2015, Russia began mounting airstrikes in Syria, claiming that it wanted to join the Western-led anti-jihadist military campaign. But this move was controversial, however, as the United States alleged that Russia was directing its airstrikes more at Sunni Arab militias fighting the forces of Syria's President Bashar al-Assad, than at jihadist operatives such as ISIS.[112] Russia is a longtime ally of Assad. The Russian intervention triggered a revenge attack from ISIS. On October 31, a Russian commercial plane carrying tourists from Egypt back home to Russia crashed when a bomb thought to have been smuggled on the plane by an ISIS operative exploded shortly after takeoff, killing all 224 aboard.[113]

The Belgian and French national ISIS supporters who carried out bombings and shootings in Paris on November 13 that killed 130 people were of Algerian and Moroccan parentage. Prior to the attacks, they were trained and radicalized in ISIS-held territories in Syria.[114]

In northern Africa, a Qaeda-affiliated terrorist group, al Mourabitoun, killed 20 people in Bamako, the capital of Mali, on November 20, in a hostage situation at the Radisson Blu hotel. On January 15, 2016, the same group was responsible for staging an attack on a hotel and restaurant in Burkino Faso in West Africa that killed 29 people.[115] On January 8, 2016 Al Qaeda in the Islamic Maghreb – or AQIM, a branch of al Qaeda – kidnapped a Swiss nun living in the historic city of Timbuktu in Mali. Claiming that she had been converting local Muslims to Christianity, the group later released a video of her in captivity wearing traditional Islamic dress.[116]

In Somalia, Qaeda-affiliated al Shabab continued to stage assaults on civilian and military targets, although failed to regain control of Somalia, which has a functioning but fragile government supported by African Union (AU) troops and Western governments.[117] On January 15, 2016, about 150 Kenyan troops, stationed in Somalia as part of the AU peacekeeping force, were killed in a Shabab raid on their barracks.[118] On January 21, five Shabab gunmen opened fire on civilians at a beachfront restaurant in the Somali capital Mogadishu, killing at least 17 people.[119]

While the new government in Nigeria consolidated control over regions previously held by Boko Haram, the terrorist group responded by mounting ambush-style attacks in towns and villages. On January 30, an assault in Dalori in northeastern Nigeria, for instance, resulted in 86 deaths, with children reportedly burned alive.[120] On February 9, three Boko Haram-affiliated girls masquerading as refugees blew themselves up upon entering the Dikwe refugee camp in northeastern Nigeria, killing 58 people.[121]

Meanwhile, the flow of refugees and economic migrants escaping war, instability and economic hardship in various African countries including Gambia, Ghana, Mali, Nigeria and Senegal continued towards Europe. A commonly-taken route for the migrants was through Niger, Libya and the Mediterranean Sea.[122] However, as the conflicts escalated in Iraq and Syria, with ISIS fighting to hold onto territories it seized in 2014, migration levels from Africa were eclipsed by a mass exodus from Syria, with around a million Syrians pouring into Europe in the final months of 2015.[123]

Most terrorist attacks in Africa continue to be mounted by Islamic militants. However, Joseph Kony, leader of the Lord's Resistance Army, a terrorist group that espouses a fundamentalist Christian ideology, remains at large, along with his estimated 120 remaining followers. They are thought to be hiding out in the Democratic Republic of Congo. In January 2016, the trial continued of one of Kony's top commanders, Dominic Ongwen, at the International Criminal Court in The Hague.[124]

NOTES

1. "Tunisia attack on Sousse beach 'kills 39,' " BBC News, June 27, 2015, http://tinyurl.com/poxb34r.

2. Ed Adamcyzk, "Attack on Somalia base kills at least 30," *United Press International*, June 26, 2015, http://tinyurl.com/nznkzox. Also see Guido Steinberg and Annette Weber (eds.), "Jihadism in

Africa," German Institute for International and Security Affairs, June 2015, http://tinyurl.com/pvc3om9. See also Erin Cunningham and Loveday Morris, "Militants launch major assault in Egypt's Sinai," *The Washington Post*, July 1, 2015, http://tinyurl.com/o9unmto; and Bukar Hussain and Aminu Abubakar, "Around 100 killed in 'Boko Haram' attack in NE Nigeria: witnesses," Agence France-Presse, July 2, 2015, http://tinyurl.com/oy9qlxg.

3. For background, see Kenneth Jost, "Unrest in the Arab World," *CQ Researcher*, Feb. 1, 2013, pp. 105-132; and Roland Flamini, "Turmoil in the Arab World," *CQ Researcher*, May 3, 2011, pp. 209-236.

4. Greg Botelho, "Terror attacks on 3 continents; ISIS claims responsibility in Tunisia, Kuwait," CNN, June 27, 2015, http://tinyurl.com/nzeggcr.

5. "Remarks by the President on Progress in the Fight Against ISIL," White House, July 6, 2015, http://tinyurl.com/nhj2ace.

6. Comments made at event entitled "The Fragile Sahel: Transnational Threats and Sustainable Solutions," Carnegie Endowment for International Peace, June 24, 2015. Also see "African nations form G5 to work on Sahel security, development," Reuters, Feb. 16, 2014, http://tinyurl.com/nwd823g.

7. "Nigeria: 'Our job is to shoot, slaughter and kill': Boko Haram's reign of terror in north east Nigeria," Amnesty International, April 13, 2015, http://tinyurl.com/okm9hjz.

8. For background, see Barbara Mantel, "Assessing the Threat from al Qaeda," *CQ Researcher*, June 27, 2014, pp. 553-576.

9. Steinberg and Weber, *op. cit.*

10. "Nigeria: 'Our job is to shoot, slaughter and kill' . . . ," *op. cit.* Also see "40 dead after Boko Haram attacks villages in Niger, official says," FOX News, The Associated Press, June 18, 2015, http://tinyurl.com/p4g3rk2. "Have over 13,000 people been killed in Nigeria's insurgency? The claim is broadly correct," Africa Check, Oct. 14, 2014, http://tinyurl.com/o7al39n.

11. Rick Gladstone, "Former Lord's Resistance Army Commander Appears at War Crimes Court," *The New York Times*, Jan. 26, 2015, http://tinyurl.com/om2ncpl.

12. Nicole Crowder, "A parent, a home, a leg — former child soldiers of the LRA tell 'what I lost' during years of captivity," *The Washington Post*, May 20, 2015, http://tinyurl.com/pynycvy.

13. David D. Kirkpatrick and Rukmini Callimachi, "Islamic State Video Shows Beheadings of Egyptian Christians in Libya," *The New York Times*, Feb. 15, 2015, http://tinyurl.com/na88xa6.

14. Thomas Joscelyn, "Terrorism in Africa: The Imminent Threat to the United States," *Long War Journal*, April 29, 2015, http://tinyurl.com/nbbqwl2.

15. "Smart Women, Smart Power: Fighting Terrorism in the Age of ISIS," Center for Strategic and International Studies, June 18, 2015, http://tinyurl.com/o95a7y9.

16. Steinberg and Weber, *op. cit.*

17. "Counterterrorism and state-building in Somalia: Progress or more of the same," Brookings Institution, May 21, 2015, http://tinyurl.com/orflgag.

18. "David Rohde Details Taliban Kidnapping in 'A Rope And A Prayer,' " National Public Radio, June 25, 2015, http://tinyurl.com/normha6.

19. Rukmini Callimachi, "Paying Ransoms, Europe Bankrolls Qaeda Terror," *The New York Times*, July 29, 2014, http://tinyurl.com/k8xa8az.

20. *Ibid.*

21. Sudarsan Raghavan, "Tens of thousands of Muslims flee Christian militias in Central African Republic," *The Washington Post*, Feb. 7, 2014, https://www.washingtonpost.com/world/africa/tens-of-thousands-of-muslims-flee-christian-militias-in-central-african-republic/2014/02/07/5a1adbb2-9032-11e3-84e1-27626c5ef5fb_story.html

22. Mark Santora, "As South Sudan Crisis Worsens, 'There Is No More Country,' " *The New York Times*, June 22, 2015, http://tinyurl.com/pltgnb4.

23. Joscelyn, *op. cit.*

24. *Ibid.*

25. Paul Cruikshank, "In Tunisia, terror attack undercuts Arab Spring's best prospect," CNN, March 19, 2015, http://tinyurl.com/q3a6zke.

26. Comments made at "The Fragile Sahel: Transnational Threats and Sustainable Solutions," *op. cit.*

27. Jason Hanna and Dana Ford, "Sources: Ottawa gunman had ties to jihadists," CNN, Oct. 23, 2014, http://tinyurl.com/ndr4dvf. See also Michelle Innis, "Sydney Hostage Siege Ends With Gunman and 2 Captives Dead as Police Storm Café," *The New York Times*, Dec. 15, 2014, http://tinyurl.com/pqee5zw.

28. "Counterterrorism and state-building in Somalia: Progress or more of the same," *op. cit.*

29. "Remarks by Secretary of Homeland Security Jeh Charles Johnson at the United Nations Interior Ministerial Security Council Briefing on Countering Foreign Terrorist Fighters — As Delivered," U.S. Department of Homeland Security, May 29, 2015, http://tinyurl.com/p3ou2pk.

30. "The Fragile Sahel: Transnational Threats and Sustainable Solutions," *op. cit.*

31. "Crisis in Libya: European and Libyan Views," panel discussion, Atlantic Council, May 20, 2015.

32. "2015 Paris Terror Attacks Fast Facts," CNN, Jan. 21, 2015, http://tinyurl.com/pgcqjzd.

33. Josh Rogin, "Daesh is making Libya part of their caliphate," *The Washington Post*, Feb. 4, 2015, http://tinyurl.com/o2b5nq6.

34. Mareike Schomerus, Tim Allen, and Koen Vlassenroot, "Obama Takes on the LRA," *Foreign Affairs*, Nov. 15, 2011, http://tinyurl.com/onexv4y. See also "Remarks by the President," *op. cit.*

35. "Somali: Al-Shabab: It Will Be a Long War," Policy Briefing No. 99, International Crisis Group, June 26, 2014, http://tinyurl.com/ozjue4h. Also see "Somali al-Shabab court 'stones teenager to death,'" BBC News, Oct. 22, 2014, http://tinyurl.com/pzeta9o.

36. Rogin, *op. cit.*

37. *Ibid.*

38. Press briefing for release of 2014 country reports on terrorism, June 19, 2015.

39. "The Fragile Sahel: Transnational Threats and Sustainable Solutions," *op. cit.*

40. *Ibid.*

41. Kirkpatrick and Callimachi, *op. cit.*

42. Mustafa Akyol, "Islam and the Liberal Order," German Marshall Fund of the United States, April 2015, pp. 36-53, http://tinyurl.com/nvdsdlx.

43. "Crisis in Libya: European and Libyan Views," *op. cit.*

44. Ola Noureldin, "Isis in the Sinai: Islamic State offshoot wins hearts and minds as Egypt's crackdown backfires," *International Business Times*, June 1, 2015, http://tinyurl.com/ndmhf8v.

45. "Crisis in Libya: European and Libyan Views," *op. cit.*

46. "Nigeria: 'Our job is to shoot, slaughter and kill' . . . ," *op. cit.*

47. "The Fragile Sahel: Transnational Threats and Sustainable Solutions," *op. cit.*

48. Bruce Livesy, "The Salafist Movement" PBS Frontline, Jan. 25, 2005, http://tinyurl.com/68xpm.

49. Steinberg and Weber, *op. cit.*

50. *Ibid.*

51. For background, see Brian Beary, "Religious Fundamentalism," *CQ Global Researcher*, Feb. 1, 2009, pp. 27-58.

52. Livesy, *op. cit.*

53. "U.S. missiles pound targets in Afghanistan, Sudan," CNN, Aug. 20, 1998, http://tinyurl.com/owhsqv3.

54. Steinberg and Weber, *op. cit.*

55. *Ibid.*

56. *Ibid.*

57. Beary, *op. cit.*

58. Livesy, *op. cit.*

59. For background, see Barbara Mantel, "Assessing the Threat from Al Qaeda," *CQ Researcher*, June 27, 2014, pp. 553-576.

60. William Claiborne, "Bombs Explode at 2 U.S. Embassies in Africa; Scores Dead," *The Washington Post*, Aug. 8, 1998, http://tinyurl.com/po2vg9m.

61. "USS Cole Bombing Fast Facts," CNN Library, Oct. 8, 2014, http://tinyurl.com/oagd6rs.

62. Mark Bowden, "A defining battle," *Philadelphia Inquirer*, Nov. 16, 1997, http://tinyurl.com/3uno8zg.

63. James Gordon Meek, "'Black Hawk Down' Anniversary: Al Qaeda's Hidden Hand," ABC News, Oct. 4, 2013, http://tinyurl.com/puw69cf.

64. For background, see Jason McLure, "The Troubled Horn of Africa," *CQ Researcher*, June 2009, pp. 149-176.

65. Ben Hancock, "Uganda bombing: Al Shabab suicide bombers attack during World Cup final," *The Christian Science Monitor*, July 12, 2010, http://tinyurl.com/nghl3po.

66. "Backgrounder — Al-Shabab," Council on Foreign Relations, http://tinyurl.com/qeb6smd. Also see "Somali: Al-Shabab: It Will Be a Long War," *op. cit.*

67. Raf Sanchez, "US confirms death of al-Shabaab leader in drone strike," *The Telegraph*, Sept. 5, 2014, http://tinyurl.com/pd4wglz.

68. Daniel Howden, "Terror in Westgate mall: the full story of the attacks that devastated Kenya," *The Guardian*, Oct. 4, 2013, http://tinyurl.com/p4xc3ab.

69. "An Atrocity in Kenya: Could things gets worse?" *The Economist*, April 11, 2015, http://tinyurl.com/ndhqfhf.

70. Max Fisher, "The Bizarre and Horrifying Story of the Lord's Resistance Army," *The Atlantic*, Oct. 17, 2011, http://tinyurl.com/ogpqj4f.

71. *Ibid.*

72. Crowder, *op. cit.*

73. Fisher, *op. cit.*

74. Mareike Schomerus, Tim Allen and Koen Vlassenroot, "Obama Takes on the LRA," *Foreign Affairs*, Nov. 15, 2011, http://tinyurl.com/onexv4y.

75. Mantel, *op. cit.*

76. "Nigeria: 'Our job is to shoot, slaughter and kill' . . . ," *op. cit.*

77. *Ibid.*

78. *Ibid.*

79. Mantel, *op. cit.*

80. "Nigeria: 'Our job is to shoot, slaughter and kill,' " *op. cit.*, http://tinyurl.com/ou6d52h.

81. "Jihad in Africa: The danger in the desert," *The Economist*, Jan. 26, 2013, http://tinyurl.com/p8fvp7f.

82. Rukmini Callimachi, "French Hostage in Algeria Is Beheaded in Video Released by Militants," *The New York Times*, Sept. 24, 2014, http://tinyurl.com/np6ptnu.

83. Steinberg and Weber, *op. cit.*

84. Akyol, *op. cit.*

85. Kim Sengupta, "Mediterranean migrant crisis: 'If Europe thinks bombing boats will stop smuggling, it will not. We will defend ourselves,' says Tripoli PM," *The Independent* (U.K.), May 28, 2015, http://tinyurl.com/pfdqnbg.

86. Anjli Raval, "Libya struggles to raise oil output," *Financial Times*, June 16, 2015, http://tinyurl.com/ozckw6h.

87. Tim Lister, "Mokhtar Belmokhtar: Al Qaeda figure was a legend among jihadists," CNN, June 14, 2015, http://tinyurl.com/o8tktpq.

88. "Crisis in Libya: European and Libyan Views," *op. cit.*

89. Eliott C. McLaughlin, "ISIS executes more Christians in Libya," CNN News, April 20, 2015, http://tinyurl.com/po6l5gd.

90. Dwight Bashir, "Egypt's Sisi: Reformer or Strongman?" Atlantic Council, May 21, 2015, http://tinyurl.com/morc5tn.

91. Kristen McTighe, "Ex-Egyptian president Morsi's death sentence upheld," *USA Today*, June 16, 2015, http://tinyurl.com/qb539rg.

92. "40 dead after Boko Haram attacks villages in Niger, official says," *op. cit.*

93. "Nigeria in transition: Prospects and challenges for the new government," Brookings Institution, June 8, 2015.

94. Rick Gladstone, "John Kerry Makes Unannounced Visit to Somalia," *The New York Times*, May 5, 2015, http://tinyurl.com/ot5juz4.

95. "Kenya: Al-Shabab kills quarry workers in Mandera gun attack," BBC News, July 7, 2015, http://tinyurl.com/oluvkpa.

96. "Counterterrorism and state-building in Somalia: Progress or more of the same," *op. cit.*

97. *Ibid.*

98. Gladstone, "Former Lord's Resistance Army Commander Appears at War Crimes Court," *op. cit.*

99. "Counter-ISIL Finance Group Kidnapping for Ransom Communiqué," U.S. Department of State, May 13, 2015, http://tinyurl.com/oc6xvqu.

100. Press briefing, U.S. State Department, June 19, 2015, www.state.gov/r/pa/prs/ps/2015/06/244030.htm.

101. "Press Briefing by Press Secretary Josh Earnest, 7/6/2015," White House, July 6, 2015, http://tinyurl.com/ox4prgy. Rhonda Schwartz and Brian Ross, "Officials: Facebook, Twitter Not Reporting ISIS Messages," ABC News, July 1, 2015, http://tinyurl.com/pdbsjv2.

102. "Crisis in Libya: European and Libyan Views," *op. cit.*

103. Steinberg and Weber, *op. cit.*

104. *Ibid.*

105. "Somali Al-Shabab: It Will Be a Long War," *op. cit.*

106. Schomerus, Allen and Vlassenroot, *op. cit.*

107. Steinberg and Weber, *op. cit.*

108. "Nigeria in transition: Prospects and challenges for the new government," *op. cit.*

109. Comments made at presentation entitled "A conversation on U.S. counterterrorism policy" at Center for Strategic and International Studies, Washington DC, Feb. 3, 2016, http://csis.org/event/countering-spread-isil-and-other-threats.

110. Gabriel Gatehouse, "Top IS commanders 'taking refuge' in Libya," BBC News, Feb. 3, 2016, http://www.bbc.com/news/world-africa-35486158.

111. Max Hofmann, "Opinion: Next anti-'IS' front will be Libya," Deutsche Welle, Feb. 2, 2016, http://www.dw.com/en/opinion-next-anti-is-front-will-be-libya/a-19021301.

112. Ed Payne, Barbara Starr and Susannah Cullinane, "Russia launches first airstrikes in Syria," CNN, Sept. 30, 2015, http://www.cnn.com/2015/09/30/politics/russia-syria-airstrikes-isis/index.html.

113. "Exclusive: EgyptAir mechanic suspected in Russian plane crash" Reuters, Jan. 29, 2016, http://www.reuters.com/article/us-egypt-crash-suspects-idUSKCN0V712V.

114. "The Paris attacks: What we know now," USA Today, Nov. 19, 2015, http://www.usatoday.com/story/news/2015/11/16/paris-attacks-what-we-know-now/75857842.

115. Faith Karimi and Sandra Betsis, "Burkina Faso attack: At least 29 dead, scores freed after hotel siege," CNN, Jan. 18, 2016, http://www.cnn.com/2016/01/16/africa/burkina-faso-hotel-terrorist-attack/index.html.

116. Stephanie Linning and Julian Robinson, "Al-Qaeda 'Jihadi John' fighter with British accent claims responsibility for kidnapping Swiss nun who 'preached Christianity on Muslim lands'" *Daily Mail* (UK), Jan. 26, 2015, http://www.dailymail.co.uk/news/article-3418385/Swiss-nun-kidnapped-Mali-SECOND-time-appears-hostage-video-al-Qaeda-captors-demand-jihadis-released-secure-freedom.html

117. African Union Mission to Somalia: www.amisom-au.org.

118. Greg Mills and Dickie Davis, "Life after Al Shabbab's attack on El-Adde: How will Kenya respond?" Feb. 3, 2016, http://www.dailymaverick.co.za/article/2016-02-03-life-after-al-shabbabs-attack-on-el-adde-how-will-kenya-respond/#.VrNXn_krLIV.

119. "Islamist gunmen kill 17 in Somalia beach restaurant attack," Reuters, Jan. 22, 2016, http://www.reuters.com/article/us-somalia-attacks-idUSKCN0V00D7.

120. Jane Onyanga-Omara, "Survivor claims Boko Haram burned kids alive in attack that kills 86," *USA Today*, Feb. 1, 2016, http://www.usatoday.com/story/news/world/2016/01/31/boko-haram-attack-village/79623914/.

121. Usam Sadiq Al-Amin and Dionne Searcey, "Young Bombers Kill 58 at Nigerian Camp for Those Fleeing Boko Haram," *New York Times*, Feb. 10, 2016, http://www.nytimes.com/2016/02/11/world/africa/suicide-bomber-girls-kill-58-in-nigerian-refugee-camp.html?_r=0.

122. "Africa-Frontex Intelligence Community Joint Report," Frontex (European agency for the Management of Operational Cooperation at the

External Borders of the Member States of the European Union), January 2016, http://frontex .europa.eu/assets/Publications/Risk_Analysis/ AFIC/AFIC_report_2015.pdf.

123. The Office of the United Nations High Commissioner for Refugees, Statistics – Latest Monthly Data: http://www.unhcr.org/ pages/49c3646c4d6.html.

124. Aislinn Laing/Gulu, "A Lords Resistance Army Commander Goes on Trial but Joseph Kony Still Eludes Justice," *Time*, Jan. 21, 2016, http://time .com/4186861/lra-kony-ongwen.

BIBLIOGRAPHY

Selected Sources
Books

Cole, Peter, and Brian McQuinn, eds., *The Libyan Revolution and Its Aftermath*, Oxford University Press, 2015.
A Libya specialist at the International Crisis Group (Cole) and a doctoral student at the University of Oxford (McQuinn) chronicle the 2011 revolution that led to the toppling of Libyan dictator Moammar Gadhafi, explaining how various factions came together to make it happen.

Tadros, Samuel, *Motherland Lost: The Egyptian and Coptic Quest for Modernity*, Hoover Institution Press, 2013.
A senior fellow at the Hudson Institute, a Washington think tank, describes the major challenges faced by Egypt's several million-strong, 2,000-year-old Coptic Christian community.

Willis, Michael, *The Islamist Challenge in Algeria: A Political History*, NYU Press, 1999.
An honorary research associate at the University of Durham (U.K.) recounts the rise of the Islamist FIS political party in Algeria in the late 1980s, its success in the 1991 elections and the civil war that followed its brutal repression by Algerian authorities.

Articles

"Jihad in Africa: The danger in the desert," *The Economist*, Jan. 26, 2013, http://tinyurl.com/ p8fvp7f.
Islamist militants have carried out deadly terrorist attacks and managed to capture large swaths of territory in Algeria and Mali.

Callimachi, Rukmini, "Paying Ransoms, Europe Bankrolls Qaeda Terror," *The New York Times*, July 29, 2014, http://tinyurl.com/k8xa8az.
This investigation examines how Islamist groups increasingly resort to kidnapping Westerners to raise revenue, causing tensions among Western governments divided over the paying of ransoms.

Crowder, Nicole, "A parent, a home, a leg — former child soldiers of the LRA tell 'what I lost' during years of captivity," *The Washington Post*, May 20, 2015, http://tinyurl.com/pynycvy.
A photo documentary portrays the brutal campaign of the Lord's Resistance Army, a Christian fundamentalist group that has terrorized parts of Central Africa for 30 years.

Joscelyn, Thomas, "Terrorism in Africa: The Imminent Threat to the United States," *Long War Journal*, April 29, 2015, http://tinyurl.com/ nbbqwl2.
A senior fellow at the Foundation for Defense of Democracies in Washington explains the differences and similarities between al Qaeda and Islamic State, two jihadist organizations that are gaining a foothold in northern Africa.

Serwer, Daniel P., "Libya's Escalating Civil War: Contingency Planning Memorandum Update," Council on Foreign Relations, June 2015, http:// tinyurl.com/pl57sgo.
A professor at the Johns Hopkins School of Advanced International Studies in Washington, D.C., explains how the Libyan state has fallen apart over the past year and makes recommendations to Western governments on what they should do about it.

Reports and Studies

"Boko Haram" (interim report), United Nations High Commissioner for Human Rights, July 1, 2015, http://tinyurl.com/oe2qcd6.
This report graphically details widespread atrocities committed by the terror group in northeastern Nigeria and neighboring Cameroon, Chad and Niger.

"Jihadism in Africa — Conclusions and Recommendations," German Institute for International and Security Affairs, June 2015, http://tinyurl.com/pvc3om9.

A Berlin-based think tank analyzes the evolution of armed Islamist activity in Algeria, Libya, Nigeria, Somalia and Tunisia.

" 'Our Job Is to Shoot, Slaughter and Kill': Boko Haram's Reign of Terror in North-East Nigeria," Amnesty International, April 13, 2015, http://tinyurl.com/k9dquft.

The human rights advocacy group charts the violence perpetrated by the Nigerian terrorist group Boko Haram, providing first-hand reports from victims, including abducted children who were forced to fight and witness the mass slaughter of civilians.

"Somali Al-Shabab: It Will Be a Long War," Policy Briefing No. 99, International Crisis Group, June 26, 2014, http://tinyurl.com/ozjue4h.

This independent organization that seeks to resolve international conflicts analyzes the threat posed by Somalia-based al Shabab, which emerged in the mid-2000s as an armed Islamist group and has carried out attacks in neighboring Kenya.

Buluma, Godfrey, "Al-Shabaab: The Threat to Kenya and the Horn of Africa," United States Army War College, 2014, http://tinyurl.com/pfdekax.

An officer in the Kenyan Defense Forces analyzes the threat posed by al Shabab and makes recommendations on how to stabilize Somalia.

Wehrey, Frederic, "Splitting the Islamists: The Islamic State's Creeping Advance in Libya," Carnegie Endowment for International Peace, June 19, 2015, http://tinyurl.com/qy39udc.

A senior associate at Carnegie's Middle East program recounts the ongoing battle between various armed Islamist groups for control of Libya.

For More Information

Amnesty International, 17-25 New Inn Yard, London, EC2A 3EA, United Kingdom; +44 207-033-1500; www.amnesty.org. Nongovernmental organization that documents human-rights abuses around the world.

Brookings Institution, 1775 Massachusetts Ave., N.W., Washington, DC 20036; 202-7970-6000; www.brookings.edu. Think tank with experts on Africa and terrorism.

Carnegie Endowment for International Peace, 1779 Massachusetts Ave., N.W., Washington, DC 20036; 202-483-7600; www.carnegieendowment.org. Network of policy research centers with expertise on global security issues, a think tank with research centers around the world dedicated to advancing the cause of global peace.

Center for Strategic and International Studies, 1616 Rhode Island Ave., N.W., Washington, DC 20036; 202-887-0200; www.csis.org. Think tank specializing in defense and security matters.

German Institute for International and Security Affairs, Ludwigkirchplatz 3-4, 10719 Berlin, Germany; +49-30-88007-0; www.swp-berlin.org. Research institution focused on foreign policy and global security.

Human Rights Watch, 350 Fifth Ave., 34th Floor, New York, NY 10118; 212-290-4700; www.hrw.org. Nongovernmental organization that defends human rights around the world.

International Crisis Group, 149 Avenue Louise, Level 14, B-1050 Brussels, Belgium; +32 2 502 90 38; www.crisisgroup.org. Nongovernmental organization that works to prevent and resolve deadly conflict.

United Nations High Commissioner for Refugees, Case Postale 2500, CH-1211 Genève 2 Dépôt, Switzerland; +41 22 739 8111; www.unhcr.org. U.N. agency that leads and coordinates international action to protect refugees.

United States Commission on International Religious Freedom, 732 N. Capitol St., N.W., Suite A714, Washington, DC 20401; 202-523-3240; www.uscirf.gov. Independent commission created by the U.S. government to defend freedom of religion abroad.

4

Assessing the Threat from al Qaeda

Barbara Mantel

Sami Dayan, an al Qaeda leader in Yemen, was sentenced in April to 15 years in prison for his role in the 2012 assassination of a Yemeni general. Yemen-based Al Qaeda in the Arabian Peninsula (AQAP) is among four Sunni Muslim extremist groups that have sworn allegiance to al Qaeda leader Ayman al-Zawahiri. AQAP targets local, U.S. and other Western interests in the region and has attempted attacks against the United States.

From *CQ Researcher*,
June 27, 2014.

In late April, a CIA officer and a U.S. Special Operations commando shot and killed two armed men trying to kidnap them from a barbershop in Sana, the capital of Yemen. Officials later said the dead men were members of an al Qaeda-linked cell that had broken 19 inmates out of a Yemeni prison in February, tried to assassinate a German diplomat in April and killed a Frenchman in May.[1]

The barbershop shooting shines a light on America's clandestine operations in Yemen, where U.S. Special Operations troops train Yemeni counterterrorism forces and American commandos help target al Qaeda suspects for drone strikes.[2]

As of April 21, the United States had launched 94 drone attacks and 15 conventional air strikes in Yemen, most since 2009 under President Obama, according to the Washington-based New America Foundation, a think tank that tracks U.S. drone warfare. The drone and cruise missile strikes have killed between 669 and 887 militants and up to 87 civilians.[3]

"For the foreseeable future, the most direct threat to America at home and abroad remains terrorism," Obama told graduating cadets at the U.S. Military Academy at West Point last month.[4] And Yemen has become the center of the country's counterterrorism campaign, home to Al Qaeda in the Arabian Peninsula (AQAP), the Sunni Muslim extremist group and al Qaeda franchise that poses the most serious direct threat to the United States, according to counterterrorism officials.

"AQAP . . . has made repeated efforts to export terrorism to our homeland," Jeh Johnson, Secretary of Homeland Security, told

Al Qaeda Network Spans Africa, Middle East

Al Qaeda operates from bases in eastern Afghanistan and western Pakistan. Al Qaeda affiliates operate in Syria, the Arabian Peninsula, Somalia and parts of northwestern Africa. Groups that share the Islamist philosophy of al Qaeda but are not official affiliates include the Islamic State of Iraq and Greater Syria (ISIS)* and Boko Haram in Nigeria.

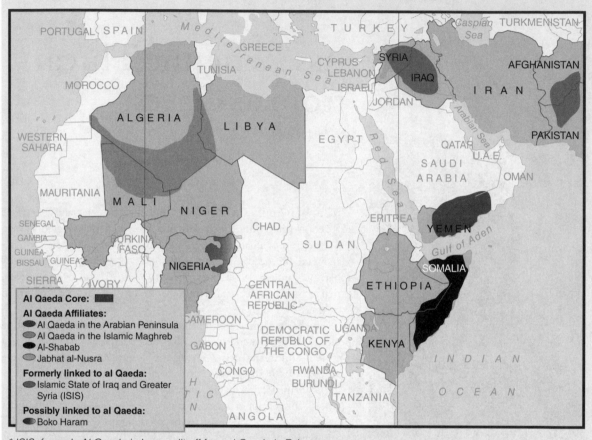

* ISIS, formerly Al Qaeda in Iraq, split off from al Qaeda in February.

Source: Colin Freeman, Barney Henderson and Mark Oliver, "Al-Qaeda map: Isis, Boko Haram and other affiliates' strongholds across Africa and Asia," The Telegraph (U.K.), June 12, 2014, http://tinyurl.com/muhhuka; "Global Terrorism Database," National Consortium for the Study of Terrorism and Responses to Terrorism, University of Maryland and the U.S. Department of Homeland Security, http://tinyurl.com/m4bfw6

Congress in May.[5] Operatives from AQAP hid bombs in printer toner cartridges being shipped aboard U.S.-bound flights in 2010, and AQAP was blamed for a suicide bomber's bungled 2009 attempt to detonate an explosive device — hidden in his underwear — aboard a Detroit-bound jet.

Al Qaeda will forever be associated in the American mind with the Sept. 11, 2001, terrorist attacks that killed 2,977 people and prompted President George W. Bush to declare war on terrorism. But today's al Qaeda is far different from the hierarchical organization that mounted the 9/11 attacks, led by Osama bin Laden operating from a safe haven in Afghanistan. Since 2004, U.S. drone strikes have killed dozens of top al Qaeda leaders hiding in neighboring Pakistan, and a U.S. Navy SEAL team killed bin Laden there in 2011.

Now experts describe a smaller, weaker, Pakistan-based al Qaeda leadership, often referred to as "al Qaeda core," operating alongside a murky far-flung network of affiliates, associates and supporters. Such groups have been attempting to control territory in northwest and eastern Africa and in Iraq, Syria and Yemen in the Middle East. They are taking advantage of the instability and civil war that emerged in some countries after the Arab Spring protest movement swept across North Africa and the Middle East in 2011, dislodging at least four dictators.[6]

These groups, which are Sunni, are also taking advantage of renewed ethnic and religious conflict stemming from the age-old struggle over which branch of Islam — Sunni or Shiite — will control the Middle East. Shiite-led Syria* and Iraq are supported by the region's major Shiite power, Iran. The rival Sunni-led governments of Saudi Arabia and the Gulf States have been supporting Sunni rebels in Syria, but not al Qaeda. Private citizens, however, have been sending money to extremists in Syria despite legal prohibitions in Saudi Arabia and Kuwait, a big source of funds.[7]

But counterterrorism experts disagree about the strength of the operational ties of the affiliates and associates to al Qaeda's core leadership, their long-term goals and whether they pose a direct threat to the West. In fact, the experts can't agree on the very nature of al Qaeda: Is it a strong terrorist network led by al Qaeda's core leadership in Pakistan, a loose network of affiliates with weakening links to core al Qaeda or more of a brand opportunistically adopted by disconnected jihadists groups?

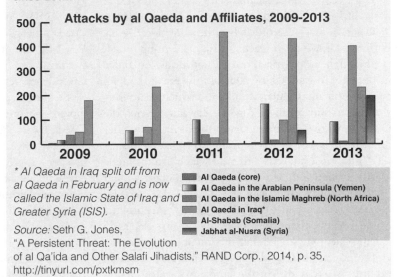

Al Qaeda Attacks Exceed 900 in 2013

Attacks by al Qaeda and its main affiliates — plus the breakaway affiliate Al Qaeda in Iraq — more than tripled from 2009 to 2013, to 929. Nearly 90 percent of the 2013 attacks were carried out by groups in Syria, Somalia and Iraq. Al Qaeda core has not launched an attack since 2012.

Attacks by al Qaeda and Affiliates, 2009-2013

* Al Qaeda in Iraq split off from al Qaeda in February and is now called the Islamic State of Iraq and Greater Syria (ISIS).

- Al Qaeda (core)
- Al Qaeda in the Arabian Peninsula (Yemen)
- Al Qaeda in the Islamic Maghreb (North Africa)
- Al Qaeda in Iraq*
- Al-Shabab (Somalia)
- Jabhat al-Nusra (Syria)

Source: Seth G. Jones, "A Persistent Threat: The Evolution of al Qa'ida and Other Salafi Jihadists," RAND Corp., 2014, p. 35, http://tinyurl.com/pxtkmsm

---

* Syria's leaders are Alawites, a Shiite sect.

"The Defense Department, the Justice Department and the State Department each have their own definition of the problem," says Christopher Swift, a fellow at the University of Virginia's Center for National Security Law.

Yet defining and understanding al Qaeda is critical to forming policy, experts say. "We can't fight an enemy that we don't know," says Katherine Zimmerman, a senior analyst for the Critical Threats Project at the American Enterprise Institute, a Washington think tank. "We need to understand the enemy to craft a strategy to defeat it."

Most analysts agree that four al Qaeda affiliates, or franchises, are part of the network. They have sworn allegiance to Ayman al-Zawahiri, bin Laden's successor, believed to be living in Pakistan, and have been recognized by him in return. They are:

- Al Qaeda in the Arabian Peninsula, whose leader, Nasir al-Wahishi, is also Zawahiri's second-in-command at al Qaeda;
- Al-Shabab, an extremist group fighting for control of Somalia;

- Al Qaeda in the Islamic Maghreb (AQIM), which aims to overthrow the Algerian government and institute an Islamic state;
- Jabhat al-Nusra, formed two years ago to overthrow President Bashar al-Assad in Syria's bloody civil war.

Until February, the Islamic State of Iraq and Greater Syria (ISIS)* — considered one of the most ruthless jihadist groups — was officially affiliated with al Qaeda. Formerly known as Al Qaeda in Iraq, the group broadened its fight into Syria and has dramatically expanded its presence in Iraq, taking control this year of the Iraqi cities of Ramadi, Falluja, Mosul and Tikrit and currently working its way south to Bagdad. Zawahiri severed ties to the group over its brutal tactics and its refusal to obey his order to leave the Syrian theater to Jabhat al-Nusra.

While most analysts agree on which groups are al Qaeda affiliates, they disagree on which other violent jihadist groups in Pakistan, the Middle East and North Africa are al Qaeda "associates." Arguments hinge on whether one believes a group shares al Qaeda's ideology — a belief in violent jihad to create an Islamic caliphate under strict Islamic law, or sharia, extending across all Muslim lands; has strong operational ties to core al Qaeda or its sworn affiliates; and potentially threatens the West.

For instance, Zimmerman and others who define al Qaeda broadly also include an alliance of militant groups called Tehrik-e Taliban Pakistan (TTP), which is fighting the military in Pakistan's tribal territories.** "TTP has worked very closely with al Qaeda leadership and shares al Qaeda's ideology," says Zimmerman. She also includes Ansar al Din, which took control of northern Mali in 2012 but was ousted by French forces in early 2013. "It seeks to install a sharia-based government in north Mali and would permit AQIM to use the region as a base of operations."

---

* ISIS is also sometimes referred to as the Islamic State of Iraq and the Levant (ISIL), or the Islamic State of Iraq and Syria.

** The TTP, also known as the Pakistan Taliban, is not directly affiliated with the Afghan Taliban, which is fighting international coalition and Afghan security forces in Afghanistan. Both groups are on U.S. foreign terrorist lists. The five detainees recently released from Guantánamo in exchange for U.S. Sgt. Bowe Bergdahl were from the Afghan Taliban, which is not formally part of al Qaeda.

Thomas Joscelyn, a senior fellow at the Foundation for Defense of Democracies, a Washington think tank, also includes Ansar al-Sharia in Tunisia, a radical Islamist group formed in 2011 and accused of a wave of political assassinations last year. "First of all, the leaders have al Qaeda dossiers, and, second, their rhetoric is openly al Qaeda," says Joscelyn. "Third, there are reports of them working with AQIM, and their social media is littered with al Qaeda propaganda." He also includes Ansar al-Sharia in Benghazi, notorious for its role in the Sept. 11, 2012, consulate attack that killed U.S. Ambassador to Libya J. Christopher Stevens and three other Americans.

But Swift says groups like Ansar al Din have only loose opportunistic ties to al Qaeda. "If you define al Qaeda by its ideology, you will find al Qaeda everywhere, which is not a terribly helpful basis for analysis," he says. "You can share the al Qaeda ideology and not have any operational link to al Qaeda and also have very different political objectives."

"Al Qaeda is largely a brand more than a coherent organization," says Robert Grenier, chairman of ERG Partners, a consultant to private security and intelligence firms, and former head of the CIA's Counterterrorism Center. "The al Qaeda brand is still very powerful and is therefore appropriated by extremist groups which share a very similar doctrine of Islam, but operationally, those organizations, most often, have . . . only very tenuous connections with al Qaeda core."

In fact, Grenier argues that even AQIM and al-Shabab, which have sworn allegiance to al Qaeda, "operate quite independently, and their specific local agendas, although maybe working in parallel, are actually quite separate."

As the world watches the ongoing civil war in Syria and the increasingly successful insurgency in Iraq, here are some of the questions being debated by counterterrorism experts and government officials:

Is al Qaeda weaker since Osama bin Laden was killed?

U.S. drone strikes and targeted assassinations have killed bin Laden, nearly three dozen of his key lieutenants and hundreds of fighters in Pakistan. "Al Qaeda's core leadership has been degraded, limiting its ability to conduct attacks and direct its followers," said a recent U.S. State Department analysis.[8]

"The drone strikes have had a severe impact on al Qaeda core in Pakistan," says former FBI Special Agent Clint Watts, a senior fellow at the Foreign Policy Research Institute, a Philadelphia-based think tank. The strikes have "really slowed down their communications and coordination."

But al Qaeda's core should not be underestimated, says Bruce Hoffman, director of Georgetown University's Center for Security Studies. It has a defined and articulated strategy and "a deeper bench of personnel than we imagined," says Hoffman. Al Qaeda is filling key spots with Pakistanis — its media arm recently has been publishing more in Urdu, Pakistan's national language, than in Arabic — and "there still are senior commanders in al Qaeda who have fought in Afghanistan against the [Soviets in the 1980s] and have gravitas and stature," he says.

Even if al Qaeda's core is replenishing its ranks and hanging on, Zawahiri is losing control of the group's affiliates, say some analysts, citing Syria as a prime example. "In recent months, a full-scale civil war has erupted within al Qaeda," said J. M. Berger, editor of *intelwire. com*, which publishes terrorism research and analysis.[9]

When Zawahiri ordered ISIS to leave Syria and allow rival affiliate Jabhat al-Nusra to spearhead al Qaeda's fight against Syrian President al-Assad, ISIS openly defied him and continued its bloody feud with Jabhat al-Nusra. ISIS then taunted Zawahiri on social media.[10] "In Syria, Zawahiri is starting to resemble a guide more than a military commander," said Berger.[11]

Daveed Gartenstein-Ross, a senior fellow at the Foundation for Defense of Democracies, disagrees with Berger. ISIS has drawn little support from other groups, he said, while Zawahiri is supported "across the al Qaeda spectrum," including by AQAP, AQIM, al-Shabab and other militant jihadist groups and "a coterie of extremist clerics."[12]

In addition, al Qaeda's leadership is still exerting some control in Syria, according to Gartenstein-Ross, with several senior al Qaeda figures "integrated into Syrian jihadists groups at the highest level." They include founding al Qaeda member Abu Firas al-Suri and al Qaeda's former head of security for counterintelligence, Abu Wafa al-Saudi.[13]

Still, Zawahiri cannot offer the deep pockets and safe haven that bin Laden could, many analysts say. In fact, most al Qaeda affiliates raise their own money, sometimes through kidnapping for ransom, such as AQIM.

In June, ISIS allegedly stole $430 million from Iraq's central bank in Mosul, which would make it the world's richest terrorist group.[14]

While core al Qaeda may be weaker, many analysts argue that the al Qaeda network, however defined, is stronger. In fact, al Qaeda affiliates — and former affiliate ISIS — control more territory today than in 2011, when bin Laden was killed and the Arab Spring began. Al Qaeda was not in Syria or Lebanon two years ago, but now Jabhat Al-Nusra and ISIS control large swaths of northeastern Syria, and ISIS is gaining considerable territory in Iraq. And both are making inroads into Lebanon.

If other groups with looser ties to core al Qaeda are included, the amount of territory under al Qaeda's control expands. Since bin Laden's death, "we've seen al Qaeda offshoots active in Mali, Mauritania, Niger and crossing the border to stage attacks in Cameroon," says Hoffman. "They have been very adept at taking advantage of lawless border areas and ungoverned or under-governed regions."

However, al Qaeda affiliates and associated groups are often their own worst enemy, says Andrew Liepman, a senior policy analyst at the Rand Corp., a think tank in Santa Monica, Calif., and a former principal deputy director of the National Counterterrorism Center. "They overstretch, they establish brutal regulations that communities don't welcome — whether it's no drinking, no smoking, no mixing of the sexes or no education of girls," he says.

For example, he cites what happened in 2012 in the northern reaches of Mali, a moderate Muslim country in West Africa. Ansar al Din and AQIM took over large swathes of territory, but when the French went in to clear them out in early 2013, the local population applauded the French — their former colonial masters — for liberating them from the harsh tactics and rules imposed by the Islamists.

And in Somalia, al-Shabab refused Western aid during the 2011 famine in southern Somalia. "The local population thought that was ridiculous, and that, combined with a pretty aggressive campaign by Kenyan and African Union troops, pushed al-Shabab into the bush between Somalia and Kenya," he says.

Guide to al Qaeda Affiliates

Four Sunni Muslim extremist groups have sworn allegiance to al Qaeda leader Ayman al-Zawahiri:

Al Qaeda in the Arabian Peninsula (AQAP): *Based in Yemen. Emerged when Yemeni and Saudi terrorists groups unified in January 2009. Targets local, U.S. and other Western interests in the Arabian Peninsula and has attempted attacks against the United States. Leader Nasir al-Wahishi is second-in-command to Zawahiri.*

Al Qaeda in the Islamic Maghreb (AQIM): *Based in Algeria. Operates in the country's coastal areas and parts of the south, as well as in Mali's northern desert regions. Founded in 1998 as a faction of Algeria's then-largest terrorist group. Algerian counterterrorism measures have reduced its ranks from more than 30,000 to fewer than 1,000. Targets local and Western interests.*

Al-Shabab: *Emerged from militant wing of Somali Council of Islamic Courts that took over most of southern Somalia in 2006. Recently weakened by Somali, Ethiopian and African Union military forces but continues lethal attacks in Somalia, Kenya and Ethiopia. Members come from disparate clans, but its senior leaders are affiliated with al Qaeda and are believed to have fought the Soviets in Afghanistan.*

Jabhat al-Nusra: *Created in January 2012 to overthrow regime of Syrian President Bashar al-Assad. Composed mostly of Syrians, but also attracts Western fighters. Controls territory in northern Syria. Islamic State of Iraq and Greater Syria (ISIS) played significant role in its founding, but the groups have engaged in a bloody feud inside Syria for the past year.*

Source: National Counterterrorism Center, www.nctc.gov.

However, al-Shabab remains lethal, as it demonstrated last September, when members stormed the Westgate Mall in Nairobi, Kenya, killing at least 67 people.

Does al Qaeda remain a threat to the West?

Al Qaeda's core leadership has not directed a successful attack against a Western target since the 2005 bombings of the London Underground transit system and a city bus, which killed 56 people, including the four suicide bombers, and injured more than 800. But it has not stopped trying. Afghan-born American resident Najibullah Zazi, who plotted to bomb the New York City subway system on the eighth anniversary of

9/11, testified that he and two co-conspirators had trained with al Qaeda in Pakistan.

"Al Qaeda has been doing its utmost to attack the United States and has not pulled any punches," according to retired U.S. Army officer Thomas Lynch, a research fellow at the National Defense University's Institute of National Strategic Studies in Washington. However, the attacks "failed repeatedly before bin Laden's death and should be expected to continue to fail now that he is dead."[15] Lynch says a seriously degraded al Qaeda core has lost its operational capability and is no longer a global threat.

What is left are Salafi-jihadist* groups operating with local agendas from Tunisia to Pakistan, many of which have existed, in one form or another, since before al Qaeda was created, says Lynch. "They will shout 'death to America' and 'death to the West,' and some will even claim to be of al Qaeda, although many do not, but their focus is on local revolution and insurgency in Muslim countries." And they lack "the capability to mount serious catastrophic terror threats in the West," he says.

But Hoffman, at Georgetown, says that "completely disregards their statements and what they have argued is their strategy." Salafi-jihadists may be focusing on local conflicts now, but that can change in the future, he says.

If any of the world's violent jihadist groups pose a threat to the West, it is AQAP, says Watts, of the Foreign Policy Research Institute. "Its capability has, however, been degraded a bit because of the drone strikes and the leaders they have lost," he says, "and

---

* Salifists are ultraconservative fundamentalist Sunni Muslims who want to return Islam to seventh-century religious traditions.

there is debate swirling about whether their master bomb maker is still alive."

Last August, the U.S. temporarily shut down 22 embassies and consulates across the Middle East and North Africa after a message was intercepted between Zawahiri and AQAP leader Nasir al-Wahishi describing a planned terror attack.[16] Although the message did not give time and location, it was "one of the most specific and credible threats I've seen perhaps since 9/11," Rep. Michael McCaul, R-Texas, chairman of the House Homeland Security Committee, said at the time.[17]

Western security officials also worry about ISIS leader Abu Bakr al-Baghdadi. He took the reins of Al Qaeda in Iraq in 2010, when it was at a low ebb, having been marginalized after the U.S. convinced Sunni Iraqis to turn against the group. However, the 2011 withdrawal of U.S. troops from Iraq breathed new life into Baghdadi's organization, which has adroitly exploited a growing Sunni rebellion against the sectarian rule of Iraq's Shiite-led government. The recent gains by ISIS in western and northern Iraq have raised alarms that it, too, could shift its focus to the West.

"Ultimately, ISIS seeks to create an Islamic state from where they would launch a global holy war," said Theodore Karasik, research director of the Institute for Near East and Gulf Military Analysis, located in Dubai, UAE and Beirut. "Perhaps that war is now beginning as Baghdadi's ISIS eclipses Zawahiri's al-Qaeda," he said.[18]

Yet ISIS has enemies, and its split with Jabhat al-Nusra favors the West, says RAND's Liepman. "Right now they are both busy trying to overthrow the Assad regime and also killing each other," he says. For instance, in just one 10-day period in May, a reported 230 militants were killed as the two groups battled one other.[19]

However, "given that both groups have at different times sworn loyalty to bin Laden and Zawahiri, what comes with that is antipathy to the West," says Liepman. "So in the longer term, who knows?" And Hoffman says competition between the two groups could lead one or the other to mount an attack on the West to boost its prestige.

Fractures have plagued other al Qaeda affiliates, as well, including al-Shabab, whose top leadership consists of committed international jihadis linked to al Qaeda and local Somali militants. Their relationship has been marked by "infighting and betrayal," and "the local radicals' cooperation has been mostly opportunistic, a method of obtaining funding, arms and training for use against domestic foes," according to Bronwyn Bruton, deputy director of the Africa Center at the Atlantic Council, a Washington think tank.[20]

"My gut instinct is absolutely, no. I can't see al-Shabab launching an attack on the U.S. It's ridiculous to me," Bruton says.

Liepman also says that, despite its fiery rhetoric, AQIM's sworn allegiance to Zawahiri is a marriage of convenience for a group that is focused on forming a regional Islamist caliphate in Algeria and neighboring states. "AQIM says they buy into the global jihad, but their actions say otherwise," says Liepman. For one thing, he points out, the group is based just across the Mediterranean from Europe but has never tried to attack there.

Hoffman says he doesn't have an explanation for why AQIM has not yet struck abroad. "But al Qaeda hadn't struck in the United States either until 9/11," he warns. (The truck bomb that exploded in a World Trade Center garage on Feb. 26, 1993, killing six people and injuring more than 1,000, was not an al Qaeda operation. Mastermind Ramzi Yousef said the attack was because of U.S. support of Israel. Yousef is the nephew of Khalid Shaikh Mohammed, who funded the attack and later joined al Qaeda and allegedly planned 9/11.)

Can the United States do more to stem al Qaeda's spread?

After ISIS surprised the West in mid-June by quickly taking over key Iraqi cities, sending Iraqi soldiers deserting in disarray, President Obama scrambled to catch up. His national security staff met around the clock, Pentagon officials briefed lawmakers, and on June 19 the president announced that he would send up to 300 military advisers to help Iraq's security forces and was prepared to launch air strikes against the Sunni militants.[21]

Meanwhile, Shiite-dominated Iran sent three battalions to Iraq to defend the government of Shiite Prime Minister Nouri Kamal al-Maliki, according to Iranian officials, while ISIS — infamous for its beheadings, brutality and repressive rules in territory it controls — threatened Karbala and Hajaf, two Iraqi cities sacred to Shiites.[22]

Analysts blamed Maliki, who they say has purged the Iraqi Army of capable leaders and centralized decision making. But many also criticize Obama's hesitation to

Taliban, Al Qaeda in Iraq Killed Most in 2013

Only three of the world's 10 most violent groups that employed terrorist tactics against noncombatants in 2013 were affiliated with al Qaeda (in gray). Among the 10, four were based in the Middle East, three in Asia, two in Africa and one in South America.

Groups That Committed Deadliest Terror Attacks, 2013

Group	Total Killed	No. of Attacks
Taliban (Afghanistan)	2,340	641
Al Qaeda in Iraq*	1,725	401
Boko Haram (Nigeria)	1,589	213
Tehrik-i-Taliban Pakistan	589	134
Al-Shabab (Somalia)	512	195
Communist Party of India — Maoist	190	203
Al Qaeda in the Arabian Peninsula	177	84
New People's Army (Philippines)	88	118
Revolutionary Armed Forces of Colombia	45	77
Bangsamoro Islamic Freedom Movement (Philippines)	23	34

Al Qaeda in Iraq split off from al Qaeda in February and is now called the Islamic State of Iraq and Greater Syria (ISIS).

Source: "Annex of Statistical Information: Country Reports on Terrorism 2013," U.S. State Department, April 2014, p. 8, http://tinyurl.com/o2s263h

arm moderate opponents of Assad in Syria when ISIS was gaining strength there, and his inability to reach an agreement with Iraq to keep a residual presence there when U.S. soldiers pulled out in 2011. Iraq had refused to grant legal immunity to U.S. troops beyond that date.[23]

"It's hugely frustrating," said Michael D. Barbero, a retired U.S. Army lieutenant general who oversaw the training of Iraqi troops from 2009 to 2011. "We knew they had chinks in their armor, and we knew they weren't going to get better once we left. And yet we didn't try hard enough to get an agreement to keep some people there."[24]

No one knows whether a U.S. presence could have prevented the recent resurgence of ISIS in Iraq, considering the Sunni population's growing antipathy for the Maliki regime's sectarian policies. But the same critique has been leveled against Obama's more recent decision to steadily pull most U.S. troops out of Afghanistan by the end of 2016, leaving only a normal military presence at the embassy. Just under 32,000 U.S. troops remain in Afghanistan, down from a 2011 peak of 100,000. In 2015, there will be 9,800. Obama announced the Afghanistan withdrawal plans in a Rose Garden speech in late May, saying the United States had struck significant blows against al Qaeda's leadership, eliminated bin Laden, and "prevented Afghanistan from being used to launch attacks against our homeland."[25]

But others worry that chaos, and large numbers of al Qaeda, will return to Afghanistan. "We're going to risk squandering the gains that we have made, just as we did in Iraq," said retired Gen. Jack Keane, Army vice chief of staff from 1999 to 2003. "We're about to repeat the same mistake again."[26]

The rugged region between the capital Kabul and the Pakistan border is of particular concern. "Even now, an al Qaeda safe haven is emerging in northeastern Afghanistan," said Rep. Mike Rogers, R-Mich., chairman of the House Permanent Select Committee on Intelligence. "And I question whether the enemy will take further advantage of the announced timeline to renew its efforts to launch new operations."[27] Rather than a firm deadline, many analysts would like to see an open-ended drawdown, contingent on the situation on the ground.

However, not everyone agrees Afghanistan should be a high priority. "While there is some al Qaeda presence remaining in Afghanistan that we should be worried about, there is far more to worry about in Syria, Iraq and Yemen," said Calif. Rep. Adam Schiff, a Democratic member of the Intelligence committee.[28]

Obama addressed those concerns in his West Point speech the day after his Rose Garden remarks, announcing establishment of a Counterterrorism Partnerships Fund (CPF) of up to $5 billion to build counterterrorism capacity and "facilitate partner countries on the front lines."[29]

However, four similar programs have been created in the past decade. "If the performance over the past three years of Iraqi forces and the likely performance of Afghan security forces is any guide, don't expect stability, transparency, effectiveness and a lack of corruption to spring forth from the barren soil of the CPF's new partners," said Gordon Adams, a professor of international relations at American University and President Bill Clinton's senior budget official for national security.[30]

Finding reliable partners will also be a challenge for the CPF, says Bruce Riedel, director of the Washington-based Brookings Institution's Intelligence Project and a former senior adviser to the last four U.S. presidents on South Asia and the Middle East.

"We don't want to support the Assad regime to fight al-Nusra. Somalia really has no effective government whatsoever, so who are you going to support there? We gave a lot of money to the Pakistani government, but is there really any evidence that we are getting much help in fighting al Qaeda? Pakistan hasn't arrested a senior al Qaeda figure since 2005," says Riedel.

Yemen is the poster child for U.S. training and intelligence support, says Riedel. "Building up the [counterterrorism] capability of the government of Yemen makes a lot of sense . . . but even in Yemen, you have a weak government."

Moreover, training foreign forces inside countries with weak governments can have unintended negative consequences, said Adams. "Just take the case of Mali, where a U.S.-trained captain, Amadou Sanogo, carried out a coup in 2012, leading to the disintegration of the Malian military, a nearly successful Islamic extremist revolt, and the need for foreign intervention."[31]

Last year, U.S. Special Operations troops began to instruct and equip "hundreds of handpicked commandos in Libya, Niger, Mauritania and Mali," according to *The New York Times*. "You have to make sure of who you're training," said Maj. Gen. Patrick J. Donahue II, commander of U.S. Army soldiers operating in Africa. "It can't be the standard, 'Has this guy been a terrorist or some sort of criminal?' but also, 'What are his allegiances? Is he true to the country, or is he still bound to his militia?'"[32]

BACKGROUND
The Beginning

"Al Qaeda and transnational jihad in general are primarily creatures of the Afghan war against the Soviets," wrote political scientist Fawaz Gerges in *The Rise and Fall of Al-Qaeda*.[33]

From 1979 to 1989, an unprecedented migration of young Muslim men, predominantly from the Middle East, descended on Pakistan and Afghanistan to wage jihad, or holy war, against the Soviet Union after its invasion of Afghanistan.[34]

They were inspired by the charismatic Sunni scholar Abdallah Azzam, a Jordanian of Palestinian descent. Azzam believed in the creation of a Muslim vanguard to fight and build a strict Islamic society ruled by sharia, or Islamic law. "Azzam's preaching and advocacy of jihad to defend Afghan Muslims persecuted by the Soviets reached audiences throughout the world via audio broadcasts, magazines and flyers," counterterrorism expert Watts, of the Foreign Policy Research Institute, wrote in a short history of al Qaeda.[35]

In 1984, Azzam set up the Services Bureau, a staging base in Peshawar, Pakistan, to recruit and transition Arab fighters, known as "Afghan Arabs," into training camps in Afghanistan. As a university student, Osama bin Laden, born in Saudi Arabia in the late 1950s to a Yemeni construction magnate, had heard Azzam lecture and agreed to finance his endeavor. Bin Laden also set up his own training camp in Afghanistan, called the Lion's Den. And he began to associate with Egyptian radicals, including Ayman al-Zawahiri, a surgeon, who came to Peshawar in 1986 to work for the Red Crescent Society, the Islamic version of the International Red Cross.

Zawahiri and Azzam had competing views of jihad, a rift that deepened in 1988 as the Soviets began withdrawing from Afghanistan, which soon plunged into civil war. Zawahiri proposed redirecting the Afghan Arabs against "apostate" Muslim regimes, starting with Egypt and Algeria. In 1981, Zawahiri had been arrested and charged with collaborating in the assassination of Egyptian President Anwar Sadat, who had signed an historic 1979 peace treaty with Israel. Not long after his release in 1984, Zawahiri took over leadership of Egyptian Islamic Jihad, a terrorist organization bent on installing religious rule.

Azzam opposed taking up arms against other Muslims and, instead, wanted to send the Arab Afghans to the Palestinian territories to reclaim his ancestral land from Israel.

Both camps bitterly vied for bin Laden's allegiance and money. But bin Laden did not share either of their priorities, wrote journalist Lawrence Wright in *The Looming Tower: Al-Qaeda and the Road to 9/11*. "At the time, he

CHRONOLOGY

1980s *Osama bin Laden establishes al Qaeda.*

1984 Sunni scholar Abdallah Azzam and bin Laden establish a staging base in Peshawar, Pakistan, for Arabs fighting Soviet troops in Afghanistan. . . . Future al Qaeda leader Ayman al-Zawahiri becomes leader of Egyptian Islamic Jihad.

1986 Bin Laden establishes training camp in Afghanistan for Arabs fighting Soviets troops. . . . He meets Zawahiri in Peshawar.

1988 Soviets begin withdrawing from Afghanistan. . . . Bin Laden founds al Qaeda, Arabic for "the base," to redirect foreign fighters to other Muslim countries.

1990s *Bin Laden and Zawahiri decide to target the West.*

1992 From Sudan, bin Laden masterminds an attack against U.S. soldiers in Yemen, but two tourists die instead.

1996 Bin Laden moves to Afghanistan as Taliban guest.

1998 Bin Laden, Zawahiri and others call for Muslims to kill Americans. . . . Al Qaeda bombs U.S. embassies in Kenya and Tanzania, killing 224; President Bill Clinton launches cruise missiles against al Qaeda training camp in Afghanistan but misses senior leaders.

2000-2005 *Al Qaeda strikes United States mainland; bin Laden goes into hiding. Smaller attacks in Spain and London follow.*

2000 Two al Qaeda suicide attackers ram an explosive-laden boat into the Navy destroyer *U.S.S. Cole* in Yemen, killing 17 U.S. sailors.

2001 Nearly 3,000 people are killed after 19 al Qaeda operatives fly hijacked jets into World Trade Center, Pentagon and a Pennsylvania field (Sept. 11); President George W. Bush declares a war on terror (Sept. 20); United States launches air strikes in Afghanistan (Oct. 7). . . . British al Qaeda follower Richard Reid tries to detonate a shoe bomb on a Paris to Miami flight (Dec. 22).

2002 Bin Laden escapes to Pakistan.

2003 Al Qaeda-linked groups blamed for bombings in Kenya, Saudi Arabia, Morocco and Turkey. . . . United States invades Iraq after Bush claims it is producing weapons of mass destruction.

2004 Alleged al Qaeda bombers attack four commuter trains in Madrid, killing 191 and injuring more than 1,800.

2005 Four al Qaeda-trained British citizens bomb London's Underground transit system and a bus, killing 56 people, including the four bombers, and injuring more than 700.

2009-Present *United States foils several al Qaeda attacks and kills bin Laden; al Qaeda affiliates focus on local conflicts.*

2009 Al Qaeda-trained Afghan-American Najibullah Zazi is arrested in New York for plot to bomb subways. . . . Nigerian Umar Farouk Abdulmutallab is arrested after trying to ignite an al Qaeda-supplied bomb hidden in his underwear aboard a U.S.-bound flight.

2011 U.S. Special Forces team kills bin Laden in Abbottabad, Pakistan. . . . Civilian protests against authoritarian rulers spread from Tunisia to the Middle East; anti-government demonstrations in Syria morph into a sectarian civil war.

2013 Al Qaeda affiliate al-Shabab storms Nairobi's Westgate Mall, killing at least 67. . . . To date, U.S. drone strikes in Pakistan have killed roughly three dozen key al Qaeda lieutenants and nearly 300 lower-level militants.

2014 Zawahiri cuts ties with the Islamic State of Iraq and Greater Syria (ISIS) for its brutal tactics and for battling another al Qaeda branch in Syria's civil war. . . . U.S. drone strikes in Yemen have killed up to 887 militants linked to Al Qaeda in the Arabian Peninsula (AQAP) and up to 87 civilians. . . . ISIS forces in Iraq take control of Mosul and Tikrit; Iraq declares a state of emergency (June). . . . Obama sends the first of 300 military advisers to Iraq and is considering air strikes against ISIS.

envisioned moving the struggle to Kashmir, the Philippines and particularly the Central Asian republics, where he could continue the jihad against the Soviet Union."[36]

In August 1988, bin Laden and a small group of associates formed a new organization called al Qaeda — Arabic for "the base" — to direct the best fighters from among the Afghan Arabs. "But it was still unclear what the organization would do or where it would go after the jihad [in Afghanistan]. Perhaps bin Laden himself didn't know," wrote Wright. "Notably, the United States was not yet on anyone's list."[37]

Global Jihad Emerges

In 1989, Azzam was killed by unknown assassins, and bin Laden returned to Saudi Arabia. In 1990 he proposed that the Saudi government allow him to use Arab veterans of the Afghan conflict — now scattered across Pakistan, Afghanistan and the Middle East — to fight Iraq, which had invaded Kuwait and threatened Saudi Arabia. The government refused, and bin Laden watched, enraged, as American troops established bases in the Saudi kingdom to protect it and expel the Iraqis from Kuwait. He soon came to see the United States as an occupying force of nonbelievers in the Arabian peninsula, home to Mecca, Islam's holiest city.

In 1992, Sudan's new Islamist-backed government invited bin Laden to move there, hoping he would invest in the country's development. Bin Laden quickly built an empire of factories and farming estates. But American troops remained in Saudi Arabia, overseeing the ceasefire with Iraq and, equally galling to bin Laden, using his ancestral home of Yemen as a stopover on their way to famine-plagued Somalia to protect U.N. aid workers from local militias.

"After all the plans al Qaeda had nurtured to spread an Islamist revolution, it was America that appeared to be waxing in influence across the region," said Wright.[38] In late December, 1992, two bombs exploded at hotels in Aden, Yemen, targeting U.S. troops. Bin Laden would claim credit for the attack, in which two Austrian tourists died, but no soldiers.

With the Yemeni attacks, "a new vision of al Qaeda was born" as a global terrorist organization, wrote Wright. "America was the only power capable of blocking the restoration of the ancient Islamic caliphate, and it would have to be confronted and defeated."[39]

In October, 1993, 18 U.S. soldiers were killed in Mogadishu, the capital of Somalia, in an incident that ended with shocking images of dead, naked American troops being dragged through the streets and their bodies burned by local insurgents. In 1996, the U.S. initiated a grand jury investigation of bin Laden's role in the "Blackhawk Down" incident, and the FBI and the CIA created a joint operation to track him down.

Meanwhile, under international pressure, Sudan expelled bin Laden, who settled in Afghanistan in 1996 as a guest of the Taliban, which had recently seized control of Kabul and implemented strict Islamic law. Zawahiri joined him in the late 1990s and officially merged Egyptian Islamic Jihad with al Qaeda.

In February 1998, bin Laden, Zawahiri and other radical jihadists declared that killing "Americans and their allies — civilians and military — is an individual duty for every Muslim who can do it in any country in which it is possible to do it." Their main complaints against the United States were: the presence of U.S. troops in the Arabian Peninsula; their fear that the United States was intent on destroying the Muslim people of Iraq through economic sanctions; and its support of Israel and corrupt dictatorships in the Middle East and North Africa.[40]

The call to arms drew a new generation of young fighters — from Europe, North Africa and the Middle East — to train with al Qaeda in Afghanistan. And it signaled a shift in Zawahiri's strategy from attacking apostate and pro-Western Muslim rulers to attacking the West.

By that time, the number of intelligence reports on al Qaeda plots was growing, but "few in the United State's government were listening," wrote terrorism analyst Seth G. Jones in *Hunting in the Shadows: The Pursuit of al Qa'ida Since 9/11*. "It took gruesome terrorist attacks to spur the government to move against bin Laden and Zawahiri."[41]

On Aug. 7, 1998, al Qaeda operatives bombed the U.S. embassies in Nairobi, Kenya, and Dar es Salaam, Tanzania, killing 224 people and injuring more than 4,500. President Bill Clinton responded by launching a cruise missile strike against a suspected al Qaeda training camp in Afghanistan, but neither bin Laden nor senior al Qaeda leaders were killed.

The embassy bombings "had a profound impact on U.S. counterterrorism efforts," wrote Jones. The CIA

Al Qaeda Seeks Weapons of Mass Destruction

While intent on attacks, the group lacks know-how, experts say.

Al Qaeda's interest in developing and using weapons of mass destruction (WMDs) dates back to the 1990s. During that decade, al Qaeda tried to purchase uranium for nuclear weapons, established a biowarfare laboratory in Afghanistan to develop weaponized anthrax and undertook a separate project to produce ricin and other chemical-warfare agents.[1]

"Those efforts were seriously disrupted by the U.S. invasion [of Afghanistan], but I don't think that al Qaeda or its affiliates and associates have completely abandoned the desire for these weapons," says Bruce Hoffman, director of Georgetown University's Center for Security Studies.

In 2003, al Qaeda put out a fatwa — an opinion handed down by an Islamic scholar — justifying the use of weapons of mass destruction. "And in 2008, Ayman al-Zawahiri" — al Qaeda's second-in-command at the time —"wrote a book and explained why WMD was still important," says Rolf Mowatt-Larssen, a senior fellow at Harvard University's Belfer Center for Science and International Affairs and a former director of intelligence and counterintelligence at the U.S. Department of Energy. Commentaries and statements from al Qaeda's core — its Pakistan-based leadership — since then suggest that "the goal is the same," he says.

But the focus of al Qaeda's core leadership and that of its affiliates diverge, says Mowatt-Larssen. Al Qaeda's core "recognizes that at the very high end there are two options: a nuclear event or a large-scale biological weapon, like anthrax," Mowatt-Larssen says. The affiliates are more interested in mid- and low-level events, such as a chemical attack on a rival's territory or an assassination using cyanide, "in order to get rid of rivals and start panic," he says.

But al Qaeda and its affiliates have not succeeded, as far as is known publicly, in effectively using weapons of mass destruction. Hoffman and Mowatt-Larssen point to several reasons for that.

First, such weapons, especially nuclear or biological ones, are difficult to develop and use. "It is really hard to get nuclear material," says Mowatt-Larssen. "There is some on the black market, but there may not be enough for terrorists to build a viable nuclear device."

Even if terrorists were about to acquire enough nuclear material, Hoffman points out, the terrorists would then "have to design a bomb and figure out how to trigger it. The technological and scientific hurdles are tremendous, and I would think that they would be insurmountable without state support."

established a special unit to plan operations against bin Laden and put a covert team in Afghanistan.[42] But bin Laden and Zawahiri eluded capture, and on Oct. 12, 2000, two al Qaeda suicide attackers rammed an explosives-laden boat into the Navy destroyer *U.S.S. Cole* in the Port of Aden, Yemen, killing 17 U.S. sailors.

The United States did not respond militarily, and al Qaeda operative Khalid Sheikh Mohammed, with bin Laden's blessing, continued to plan an attack on the U.S. homeland, which bin Laden believed would force the United States to pull out of the Middle East and lead to the establishment of conservative Islamic regimes. Mohammed, a Pakistani citizen, was captured by the CIA and Pakistan intelligence in Pakistan in 2003 and

is awaiting trial at the Guantánamo Bay military prison, accused of masterminding 9/11.

Retreat to Pakistan

Nine days after 9/11, President George W. Bush declared a "war on terror" and demanded that the Taliban turn over bin Laden and al Qaeda leaders.[43] Bin Laden "was confident that the United States would respond to the attacks in New York and Washington only with cruise missile strikes, as it had done three years earlier," wrote journalist Peter Bergen in *Manhunt: The Ten Year Search for Bin Laden from 9/11 to Abbottabad.*[44]

But the U.S. response was quick and fierce. Within a week, Congress granted Bush authority to use force

Biological weapons are difficult to fabricate and difficult to disseminate effectively, says Hoffman. "I believe the Japanese cult Aum Shinrikyo had at least on nine occasions tried to use biological weapons, and it didn't succeed," he says. "And that's why they turned to chemical weapons and sarin." The group captured worldwide attention in 1995 when it released sarin, a nerve agent, onto Tokyo subway cars, killing 12 people.

"What is the most likely WMD that al Qaeda might get its hands on? In my view: chemical," says Hoffman. "But still, you need to have a lot of it to have an effect; you've got to have a way to deliver it; it can dissipate; and you have to protect yourself."

When Tamil Tiger insurgents used chlorine gas to attack a Sri Lankan armed forces base in 1990, Hoffman explained, the wind changed direction and blew the gas back at the Tigers, who had to abort the attack.[2] And during the height of the Iraq War in 2006, Al Qaeda in Iraq used chlorine gas in its bombs, but while the explosions killed people, "the chlorine itself didn't really harm anyone," says Hoffman.

Besides finding it difficult to obtain destructive materials, al Qaeda hasn't succeeded at deploying a WMD because U.S. drone strikes have seriously degraded al Qaeda's core leadership, and security officials have been effective at preventing attacks, says Mowatt-Larssen. For example, a police raid of a London apartment in 2003 found castor oil beans — the raw material for ricin — along with production equipment and recipes for ricin, botulinum and other poisons. Two years later, a British court found a suspected al Qaeda operative arrested in connection with the raid guilty of plotting to spread ricin in public areas of the United Kingdom.[3] A year ago, Iraq said it had captured an al Qaeda cell that planned to produce mustard gas and other poisons for attacks in Iraq, Europe and the United States.[4]

In addition, while al Qaeda and its affiliates are expert in conventional weapons, they may not have personnel with expertise in chemical, biological or nuclear weapons, Hoffman says. However, the civil war in Syria could change that equation, he says. In a deal brokered by the United States and Russia in the wake of a deadly chemical attack on civilians, allegedly by the regime of Syrian President Bashar al-Assad, Assad agreed to allow Syria's chemical weapons stockpiles to be destroyed, which the United Nations announced on June 23 had been accomplished.

"What is worrisome is that veterans of the Syrian Army's chemical corps might find their way into al Qaeda's ranks in Syria and provide that expertise and knowledge," says Hoffman.

"I think it would be hardest for [al Qaeda and its affiliates] to use WMD's against the United States. I believe it is certainly becoming more of a problem in the Middle East," he says.

— *Barbara Mantel*

[1] Bruce Hoffman, "Low-Tech Terrorism," *The National Interest*, March-April 2014, p. 3, tinyurl.com/lgd4age.

[2] *Ibid.*

[3] "Killer jailed over poison plot," BBC News, April 13, 2005, http://news.bbc.co.uk/2/hi/uk_news/4433709.stm.

[4] "Iraq says captures al Qaeda chemical gas team," Reuters, June 1, 2013, http://articles.chicagotribune.com/2013-06-01/news/sns-rt-us-iraq-violence-chemicalsbre9500cg-20130601_1_mustard-gas-iraqi-kurdish-chlorine-gas.

against any "nations, organizations, or persons" involved in the 9/11 attack or that "harbored" those responsible. On Oct. 7, Bush launched air strikes in Afghanistan, and by early December, the Taliban was ousted and bin Laden and al Qaeda's core members had retreated to the Afghan mountains, where they battled U.S. and British Special Forces. Rather than pushing the United States out of Muslim lands, 9/11 had invited an invasion.[45]

In February, bin Laden and some associates slipped into Pakistan, where many hid in the relative anonymity of the bustling city of Karachi and set about rebuilding al Qaeda. But after Pakistan and the United States captured several key operatives in the next several years — including 9/11 planner Mohammed — al Qaeda's leaders retreated to northern Pakistan's lawless tribal regions, where they set up training camps, albeit on a smaller scale than in Afghanistan. Bin Laden's whereabouts were unknown.

Meanwhile, bombings of Western targets in North Africa, Europe and the Middle East demonstrated al Qaeda's reach. In some cases, governments blamed al Qaeda directly, such as for the May 12, 2003, bombings in the Saudi capital Riyadh, which killed 35 people. In other incidents, violent jihadist groups with suspected connections to al Qaeda either claimed responsibility or were blamed. Analysts still disagree about whether al Qaeda directed the March 11, 2004, bombing of commuter trains in Madrid, which killed 191 people and left at least 1,800 injured, or whether the dozens of men

Is Boko Haram Aligned with al Qaeda?

"They are boys who . . . rape women, kill children and steal from the population."

Boko Haram caught the world's attention when it kidnapped 276 schoolgirls from a remote northern Nigerian village on April 14. But the brutal Islamist insurgency has been terrorizing northeastern Nigeria and nearby border areas for years.

Since 2009, Boko Haram has killed an estimated 6,500 people, according to Bronwyn Bruton, deputy director of the Africa Center at the Atlantic Council, a Washington think tank.[1] In a particularly horrific attack in February, the group — whose name, loosely translated from the local Hausa language, means "Western education is forbidden" — attacked a secondary school in northeastern Nigeria and shot, hacked or burned to death 59 boys, many as they slept in their beds. On June 23, the group reportedly abducted at least 91 more people, including 60 girls and 31 boys.[2]

Besides students and civilians, the group has attacked police officers, soldiers, politicians, and rival religious leaders. Their attacks, and a government crackdown on the group that began in 2009, have caused an estimated 250,000 people in the region to flee their homes in the past 10 months.[3]

Last month Nigerian officials met in Paris with representatives from neighboring Chad, Cameroon, Niger and Benin to forge an agreement to share intelligence and coordinate patrol and rescue efforts in the border areas where Boko Haram operates. At a news conference after the meeting, Nigerian President Goodluck Jonathan called Boko Haram the "al Qaeda of West Africa."[4]

He is not alone in tying Boko Haram to al Qaeda. Last November, the State Department declared Boko Haram a foreign terrorist organization with "links to al-Qa'ida in the Islamic Maghreb (AQIM)."[5]

Yet some analysts say the al Qaeda label is misleading. "It is very much in President Jonathan's interest to say Boko Haram is part of the international terror movement because it then gives him a claim on international resources," says John Campbell, former U.S. ambassador to Nigeria (2004-2007) and author of *Nigeria: Dancing on the Brink*.

While the group issues statements supporting al Qaeda's goals, Boko Haram's focus is strictly local, and the organizations have no formal ties, Campbell says. "I don't doubt that you have members of Boko Haram who have talked to people who claim to be part of al-Shabab or al Qaeda in the Islamic Maghreb," he says, but Boko Haram "is a different kind of creature."

Its violence is too unfocused and brutal even for al Qaeda, says Bruton, who calls Boko Haram an African rebel group. "Al Qaeda's violence is very strategic. They use violence to send a very careful political message, whereas African rebel groups tend to be really predatory," said Bruton. Members of African rebel groups like Boko Haram "are young boys who do drugs, they are not educated . . . and they are especially known to rape women, to kill children, to steal from the local population." Al Qaeda's leaders would worry that such behavior would sully its brand, she said.[6]

Other analysts, however, agree with the State Department's assessment. "Al Qaeda affiliates' purpose is to handle local affairs," says Jacob Zenn, an analyst of African and Eurasian Affairs for The Jamestown Foundation, a Washington-based think tank. For example, "Al Qaeda in the Islamic Maghreb does mostly attacks in Algeria. Boko Haram attacks in Nigeria." Zenn calls Boko Haram a "clandestine" al Qaeda affiliate, because they haven't yet "formalized the connection to the world."

The United States, France, Britain and Israel have sent special forces and intelligence operatives to help search for the kidnapped girls, although U.S. actions are constrained by prohibitions on direct military assistance to any foreign military unit that has violated human rights. "Since 2009, the Nigerian military has been widely accused by local witnesses and human rights groups of killing thousands of people — many of them innocent civilians — in its efforts to destroy Boko Haram," said Bruton."[7]

---

arrested, mostly Moroccan, were only tenuously linked to al Qaeda.

Al Qaeda's link to the July 7, 2005, bombings of the London Underground and a city bus is much clearer:

The four British citizens, three of Pakistani descent, who detonated the bombs had trained at al Qaeda's camps in Pakistan. The explosions — the deadliest terrorist attack in British history — killed 56 people,

Boko Haram was created in 2002 in the northeastern Nigerian state of Borno by Islamist cleric Mohammed Yusuf, whom the government executed in 2009 after an armed uprising in the region. "From sermons and statements, you can say their goal is the establishment of God's kingdom on Earth through justice for the poor, achieved through the rigorous application of Islamic law, or sharia," says Campbell. The group has been unclear, however, as to whether it wants sharia law imposed nationwide or only in Nigeria's predominantly Muslim northern states, he adds.

After the government crackdown in 2009, Boko Haram splintered into several groups and became increasingly radical and brutal. The group's putative leader now is Yusuf acolyte Abubakar Shekau. Boko Haram "is a symptom of decades of failed government and elite delinquency finally ripening into social chaos," said Nigerian analyst and blogger Chris Ngwodo.[8]

While analysts disagree on Boko Haram's ties to al Qaeda, they agree that a growing Western presence in Nigeria could push the group into the arms of international jihadists. Last month, says Campbell, a northern Nigerian religious leader warned that if Western troops get involved in the fight against Boko Haram, it would "lead to an influx of foreign fighters into northern Nigeria in support of Boko Haram."

To eliminate the threat from Boko Haram, says Campbell, the Nigerian government should halt human rights abuses by its military and police, reduce government corruption and reduce the stark differences that have historically existed between the predominantly Muslim north and the mostly Christian south. For example, he points out, fewer than 20 percent of northern Nigerian women can read and write, compared to more than 80 percent in the south. "You are really asking for a country to transform itself, and that is usually hard for countries to do," says Campbell.

— *Barbara Mantel*

PIUS UTOMI EKPEI/AFP/Getty Images

A woman rallies in Lagos, Nigeria, for the release of 287 Nigerian schoolgirls captured by Boko Haram on April 14. Thought by some to be linked to al Qaeda, the brutal group reportedly abducted at least 91 more youths on June 23.

[2] Robyn Dixon, "Nigeria kidnapping: 60 girls and women, 31 boys said to be abducted," *Los Angeles Times*, June 24, 2014, http://tinyurl.com/koaafel.

[3] Ishaan Tharoor, "MAP: What Boko Haram is doing to Nigeria," *The Washington Post*, June 5, 2014, http://tinyurl.com/ku4dynn.

[4] John Irish and Elizabeth Pineau, "West Africa leaders vow to wage 'total war' on Boko Haram," Reuters, May 17, 2014, http://tinyurl.com/lzgw7nt.

[5] "Terrorist Designations of Boko Haram and Ansaru," U.S. Department of State, Nov. 13, 2013, http://tinyurl.com/m7mmky6.

[6] "Bronwyn Bruton on Boko Haram," *op. cit.*

[7] Bronwyn Bruton, "Intelbrief: Nigeria: The Limits of US Assistance," Atlantic Council, May 13, 2014, http://tinyurl.com/lerd7p7.

[8] Mohammed Aly Sergie and Toni Johnson, "Terrorist Groups: Boko Haram," Council on Foreign Relations, May 5, 2014, http://tinyurl.com/q4yvapy.

[1] "Bronwyn Bruton on Boko Haram," Atlantic Council, May 29, 2014, http://tinyurl.com/qh88yk2.

including the four suicide bombers, and injured more than 700.[46]

Unbeknown to the CIA, that same year bin Laden moved into a walled compound in Abbottabad, Pakistan,

and began relying on a few select couriers to communicate with others in the al Qaeda leadership and beyond, including al Qaeda in Iraq, which was created after the United States invaded Iraq in 2003.

AP Photo via militant website, File

ALI AL-SAADI/AFP/Getty Images

Battle for Iraq

In a photo released by the Islamic State of Iraq and Greater Syria (ISIS), militants appear to be leading away captured Iraqi soldiers dressed in plain clothes on June 14. (Top) The militants' claims that they later executed 1,700 soldiers could not be independently verified. In the sectarian conflict in Iraq, the former al Qaeda affiliate has captured several major cities and in late June appeared to be closing in on Baghdad. Also on June 14, Shiites in Baghdad (bottom) pledged to join Iraqi security forces in the fight against ISIS. The Sunni-Shiite battle over Iraq and neighboring Syria reflects a 1,000-year-old conflict between the two Muslim sects and is seen by many analysts as a proxy battle to determine whether Shiite-dominated Iran or Sunni-led Saudi Arabia will dominate the Arab world.

wrote Bergen. But by 2005, "he had grown increasingly worried about the brutal tactics of al-Qaeda in Iraq." The group blew up Shia mosques, killed fellow Sunnis, and its leader — Abu Musab al-Zarqawi — posted online the gruesome videos of hostage beheadings. Bin Laden worried that Zarqawi was harming the al Qaeda brand and publicly apologized for Zarqawi's behavior after U.S. air strikes killed him in 2006.[47]

Bin Laden was also disappointed in al Qaeda trainees' failed attempts to carry out attacks in the United States, thwarted partly by America's post-9/11 intelligence and security apparatus and partly by the trainees' own bungling. In early September 2009, Najibullah Zazi, an Afghan-American trained by al Qaeda in Pakistan, traveled from Denver to detonate bombs in the subways of New York. But he was arrested by the FBI, which had him under surveillance. On Christmas Day the same year, Nigerian Umar Farouk Abdul mutallab tried unsuccessfully to ignite a bomb hidden in his underwear as his Amsterdam-to-Detroit flight was about to land. He told investigators he had acquired the device in Yemen, home of AQAP.[48]

After those attempts, President Obama intensified the U.S. drone campaign in Pakistan, begun by President George W. Bush, and extended it to Yemen. By 2014, the controversial drone strikes — which international rights groups complained were killing innocent civilians and alienating the local population — had killed dozens of key al Qaeda lieutenants, including propagandist Anwar al-Awlaki, a U.S. citizen in Yemen, and hundreds in the middle ranks.[49]

Bin Laden was initially "ecstatic about the opportunities that the 2003 American invasion presented to establish an al Qaeda affiliate in the Arab heartland,"

Is the threat posed by former Guantánamo detainees exaggerated?

YES Bailey Cahall
Policy Analyst, International Security Program, New America Foundation

Written for CQ Researcher, June 2014

NO Daveed Gartenstein-Ross
Senior fellow, Foundation for Defense of Democracies

Written for CQ Researcher, June 2014

The May 31 release of U.S. Army Sgt. Bowe Bergdahl in exchange for five former senior Taliban officials being held at the U.S. detention facility at Guantánamo Bay, Cuba, has renewed the debate over how many former detainees end up returning to the battlefield. Days after Bergdahl's release, Sen. John McCain, R-Ariz., told Fox News that 30 percent of the released detainees "have already gone back into the fight," a figure that has been repeated by a number of other sources. But this number is a misleading conflation of the U.S. government's own estimates.

The Office of the Director of National Intelligence (ODNI) — which releases an unclassified summary report about the recidivism rates of former detainees every six months — said in January that 104 (17 percent) of the 614 detainees released from the prison have engaged in "terrorist activities," and 74 (12 percent) are suspected of doing so. Yet it is impossible to assess the validity of these numbers because the U.S. government has not publicly released the names of any of these detainees since 2009.

But even if the numbers were correctly parsed, the phrase "terrorist activities" adds to the confusion. In the public sphere, these are treated as if they were all attacks, but the ODNI combines planning and conducting attacks with financing terrorist operations and facilitating the movement of people involved in such activities.

While none of these are good, some are certainly worse than others. There is a scale to the level of threat these activities pose, but commentators act as if they are absolutes.

To be sure, some former Guantánamo detainees are quite dangerous. For example, Said Ali al-Shiri, who was transferred to Saudi Arabia in 2007, cofounded Al Qaeda in the Arabian Peninsula in 2009. And Abdullah Ghulam Rasoul emerged as a top Taliban commander after being transferred to Afghanistan and subsequently released in 2007.

Yet the men who were transferred from Guantánamo in exchange for Bergdahl are not being released freely into Afghan society. They must first spend a year in Qatar, a rich and efficient police state, and they have been banned from travel during that time.

Assuming that ban holds, by the time they are able to return to Afghanistan, there will no longer be a U.S. combat presence in the country, minimizing any potential threat they might pose to American soldiers there.

In considering whether detainees released from Guantánamo Bay pose a real threat, the debate over recidivism rates is somewhat beside the point. Enemy combatants are detained during wars because of concern that, if released, they will return to the fight. So it's worth examining the impact released detainees have had, as revealed in militant propaganda, credible media accounts and the work of scholars. It's no exaggeration to say Guantánamo detainees have had an impact on tens of thousands of lives since their release.

Former detainees have played prominent leadership roles in Islamist groups. In South Asia, they served as the Taliban's chief military commander, led Taliban forces in southern Afghanistan, served as the shadow governor in Uruzgan province and commanded thousands of fighters in Pakistan's Waziristan region. Former detainees served as the deputy commander of Al Qaeda in the Arabian Peninsula (AQAP) and as an AQAP operational commander (Othman Ahmed al-Ghamdi) and religious leader (Ibrahim al-Rubaish). A former detainee leads Ansar al-Sharia in Derna, Libya.

Detainees have been involved in numerous attacks since their release. They have orchestrated attacks against coalition forces in Afghanistan, directed a hotel bombing in Islamabad, participated in attacks in the Caucasus region and blew up a gas pipeline in Russia's Tatarstan republic. They carried out a suicide bombing in Iraq (13 dead) and oversaw a 2007 suicide attack in Pakistan (31 dead). Former detainees masterminded or participated in the kidnapping of a Saudi diplomat in 2012 and two Chinese engineers in Pakistan in 2004.

In addition, released detainees have found their way to the Syrian battlefield and served as foot soldiers or operatives in Afghanistan, Pakistan, Saudi Arabia and Yemen.

Other former detainees are involved in terrorist recruitment. This month Spanish authorities arrested Lahcen Ikasrrien for running a cell that provided fighters to the Islamic State of Iraq and Greater Syria, and others have been charged with recruitment or facilitation elsewhere.

There are serious policy questions about detention of non-state actors. Unlike state-to-state conflict, such enemies rarely wear a uniform, and conflicts may last far longer when nonstate actors are involved. But these questions must be separated from questions of fact. Many released detainees do not return to militancy. But those who do have already had a significant impact.

Arab Spring

After a nearly decade-long manhunt, on May 1, 2011, a U.S. Navy SEAL team killed bin Laden at his Abbottabad compound. "The death of bin Laden marks the most significant achievement to date in our nation's effort to defeat al Qaeda," President Obama told the nation. "His death does not mark the end of our effort. There's no doubt that al Qaeda will continue to pursue attacks against us."[50] Six weeks later, al Qaeda appointed Zawahiri as bin Laden's successor.

Bin Laden's death was soon eclipsed by the momentous events of the Arab Spring, which began five months earlier with peaceful protests in Tunisia and spread across North Africa and the Middle East. A combination of civilian protests, internal military intervention and, in the case of Libya, rebel fighting and Western military help, toppled dictators in Tunisia, Egypt, Libya and Yemen, seeming to undercut bin Laden's claim that attacking America was a necessary prelude to dislodging dictatorial regimes. Initially, at least, "al Qaeda's leaders, foot soldiers, and ideas played no role," wrote Bergen.[51]

But al Qaeda thrives where there is chaos, and the early promise of the Arab Spring has faded. While Tunisia adopted a new constitution in January and is transitioning to democracy, fighting among rival militias and a renegade general's attempted coup is pushing Libya toward civil war. Yemen's new president is battling separatist forces, and Egypt's military recently ousted a democratically elected, religiously conservative government. Anti-government demonstrations in Syria degenerated into a civil war, and the violence is spilling into Lebanon, Jordan and Iraq, where a renewed Sunni insurgency is fighting the Shiite-led government. Al Qaeda's formal affiliates, loosely tied associates and professed supporters have inserted themselves into each of these conflicts.

In January, Director of National Intelligence James Clapper told the Senate Select Committee on Intelligence that he expected worse to come: "In the three years since the outbreak of the Arab Spring, a few states have made halting progress in their transitions away from authoritarian rule. Nevertheless, political uncertainty and violence will probably increase across the region in 2014 as the toppling of leaders and weakening of regimes have unleashed ethnic and sectarian rivalries that are propagating destabilizing violence."[52]

CURRENT SITUATION
Foreign Fighters in Syria

On a Saturday afternoon in late May, a man entered the Jewish Museum in Brussels and shot and killed two Israeli tourists with a .38-caliber revolver. He then pulled an assault rifle from a black bag and killed a French museum volunteer and wounded a Belgian man.[53]

French authorities later arrested a suspect, 29-year-old Frenchman Mehdi Nemmouche, during a routine customs check as he arrived in France by bus. Officials said he had travelled to Syria last year to fight with the Islamic State of Iraq and Greater Syria (ISIS).[54]

The killings are likely the first by a European citizen returning from the Syrian conflict, according to European officials, although they could not say what role, if any, ISIS played in the attack or whether Nemmouche was motivated by his experience in Syria.[55] Nevertheless, his arrest underscores Western governments' warnings that some of the thousands of foreign fighters flowing into Syria — where many are thought to connect with ISIS or the al Qaeda affiliate Jabhat al-Nusra — could pose a terrorist threat once they return home.

"This raises concerns that radicalized individuals with extremist contacts and battlefield experience could either return to their home countries to commit violence at their own initiative, or participate in an al Qaeda-directed plot aimed at Western targets outside Syria," Matthew Olsen, director of the National Counterterrorism Center, told Congress.[56]

Since late 2011, as many as 12,000 citizens or residents from more than 80 countries have gone to Syria to fight the Assad regime, according to some analysts. "These numbers are unprecedented," says Aaron Zelin, a fellow at the Washington Institute for Near East Policy, whose own "best guesstimate" is more like 9,000. "It is unlike anything we've seen before" in Afghanistan, Iraq, Somalia or other places where foreigners have joined violent jihadist insurgencies.

About 100 foreign fighters in Syria are from the United States, and 2,000 to 3,000 are from Western Europe, the second-largest source after Arab countries, such as Tunisia, Saudi Arabia and Morocco.

Several factors explain why foreign Muslims are attracted to the Syrian war, experts say. "Obviously the biggest driver is the fact that the Assad regime is slaughtering innocent people," says Zelin, "and they view it as a religious duty to help out their brothers and sisters being killed." Syria also is relatively easy to reach.

In addition, the extremist groups, especially ISIS, are using social media extensively to lure recruits. Foreign fighters are drawn to ISIS and Jabhat al-Nusra because the groups "tend to be more inclusive, better organized and better financed than their more moderate counterparts," said Richard Barrett, senior vice president at The Soufan Group, a New York-based security consultancy. Concentrated in the north and the east, the extremists also are the first groups many foreigners meet after crossing the Turkish and Iraqi borders.[57]

Threat in the West

Not every foreigner fighting in Syria is a potential domestic terrorist. Some may choose never to return home; others will be killed. In May, a Florida man, Moner Mohammad Abusalha, possibly became the first American suicide bomber in Syria, according to the U.S. State Department. Abusalha had spent two months training with Jabhat al-Nusra.[58]

Most Western fighters who do return will never engage in domestic terrorism, if past experience is any guide, according to Thomas Hegghammer a researcher at the Norwegian Defense Research Establishment in Oslo. Hegghammer studied about 1,000 jihadists from North America, Western Europe and Australia who fought abroad between 1990 and 2010. "My data, with all its limitations, indicate that no more than one in nine foreign fighters returned to perpetrate attacks in the West," he wrote.[59] Still, extrapolating from that rate, "That is potentially 300 or more people who have gone to Syria who could be involved in attempted attacks in the West," says Zelin.

Experts say it is exceedingly difficult to determine which foreign fighters will return to become domestic terrorists. In the case of Syria, there is no uniform profile of foreign fighters, let alone those who might return home bent on violence, says Zelin. While most are young Muslim men, he says, they include converts and those born into Muslim families; immigrants and those who are European-born; and people who are poor and middle class. Education levels vary as well, says Zelin.

In addition, Western intelligence agencies have few resources in Syria to track their citizens or residents. "It's a bit of a black hole," said a U.S. counterterrorism official.[60] And back home, "most states lack the resources to identify and monitor more than a few returning fighters," said Barrett.

But even countries with generous resources are becoming overwhelmed. By the end of April, the number of people in France under surveillance was growing, "and the security forces were feeling the strain," according to Barrett.[61] With far fewer American fighters in Syria, the U.S. government might have an easier time monitoring. Last month the FBI announced it had formed a special team to identify and investigate such individuals.

Some Western nations are turning to families and friends for clues. France is setting up a network of telephone hotlines and counseling centers for family, friends and community members to report radicalized young men, and Germany is considering such a system as well.

Countries also are taking legal measures. Last month, the United States designated Jabhat al-Nusra a terrorist organization — ISIS, under its former name of Al Qaeda in Iraq, has been on the terrorist list for years — allowing anyone who fights with them to be prosecuted for knowingly providing "material support or resources" to the group.[62]

In the past year, three American citizens or permanent residents have been arrested at U.S. airports or near the Canadian border for allegedly trying to leave the country to join Jabhat al-Nusra or another al Qaeda splinter group. All have pleaded not guilty or denied the charges. Another American, Sinh Vinh Ngo Nguyen of Southern California, pleaded guilty last year to "attempting to provide weapons training to al Qaeda" after fighting alongside Jabhat al-Nusra in 2012.[63]

Britain has begun detaining returnees from Syria. Last month, Mashudur Choudhury, 31, became the first Briton convicted of preparing for a terrorist act after returning from fighting in Syria.[64] France has begun to arrest people for plotting terrorism as they try to make their way to Syria, leading some defense lawyers to claim civil liberties are being violated.

"In France all they have done is to purchase a ticket; it is impossible to foresee who will leave for the purpose of carrying out terrorism," said lawyer Pierre de Combles de Nayves.[65]

Middle East Spillover

Most foreign fighters in Syria are from predominantly Muslim countries. "I definitely think that we will see those who survive Syria and return to Saudi Arabia or Jordan or elsewhere in the region create new groups or join existing radical jihadist movements," says Riedel of the Brookings Institution, "and they will not only have the skill set acquired from having fought on battlefields, they will also have a lot of prestige as veterans of jihad."

Spillover is already occurring: The ranks of two al Qaeda-linked groups in Lebanon, Jabhat al-Nusra and the Abdullah Azzam Brigades, are filling with rebel fighters from Syria and have taken responsibility for a string of suicide attacks aimed at Hezbollah, a Lebanese Shiite Muslim political party and militant group that supports the Assad regime.

"Al Qaeda in Lebanon are like these beads," said Omar Bakri Fostok, a radical Sunni preacher based in Tripoli, pulling on a string of prayer beads. "There were individuals, but they have always lacked the thread that holds them together. They were not organized. That is now changing."[66]

In Iraq, the ISIS resurgence over the last three years is partially due to "access to a steady flow of both weapons and fighters from Syria," the National Counterterrorism Center's Olsen told Congress.[67]

In Saudi Arabia, King Abdullah decreed in February that citizens who fight in conflicts abroad will face three to 20 years in prison upon returning home. Early last month, Saudi Arabia detained 62 suspected Islamic militants with reported ties to al Qaeda groups in Syria and Yemen. They represent the largest group accused of Islamist militancy in Saudi Arabia for at least two years.[68]

Jordan has recently criminalized "joining or attempting to join armed or terrorist groups, or recruiting or attempting to recruit people" to join such groups. "Let's be frank," says Riedel. "Saudi Arabia, Jordan and Egypt are police states, and they're going to go after anyone who is coming home from this in the manner that a police state does. They're just going to round people up and put them in jail."

Some governments are taking less punitive approaches. For instance, Tunisia has established an amnesty program to integrate into society individuals who have gone to Syria but have not killed anyone. Morocco is considering a similar program. And Saudi Arabia is considering expanding its system of rehabilitation centers serving the thousands it arrested during the last wave of al Qaeda attacks in the kingdom in the mid-2000s.[69]

OUTLOOK
Improving Governance

Development is the key to countering al Qaeda and Salafi-jihadist groups, says the Atlantic Council's Bruton. For example, in Nigeria, "If the U.S. can go in and build roads, build schools, speak out against Nigerian human rights abuses and be seen as a neutral party interested in resolving legitimate grievances, that would be very helpful," she says.

"Simply by improving local governance we would start to roll back where al Qaeda is able to operate," says Zimmerman of the American Enterprise Institute. "Granted, this is broad, difficult and ill-defined, but it is what is missing." For example, when the Yemeni government clears out AQAP forces from an area, "it then needs to provide basic services — food, water, shelter," with Western help, if necessary, says Zimmerman "The Yemeni government doesn't provide much to the population, which is one reason why the population is not very loyal to the government."

Without that kind of Western strategy, "I see a very strong al Qaeda," says Zimmerman. She sees a broad sectarian war between Sunnis and Shiites across Syria and Iraq, with al Qaeda as major player; AQAP continuing along its current path; al-Shabab developing further into an East African group; and al Qaeda's resurgence in Pakistan as the United States pulls out of Afghanistan. "And, frankly, if al Qaeda moves into Afghanistan, Pakistan is not going to be pursuing it," she says.

However, Watts of the Foreign Policy Research Institute cautions that the West should not try to help develop government institutions and civil society, often called "nation building."

"I don't see how that helps us in counterterrorism," says Watts. "Mostly it creates weak democracies that become safe havens for groups like al Qaeda, which is what we're seeing in Anbar Province in Iraq."

As for ISIS' relentless advance in Iraq, he sees the group replacing al Qaeda's core leadership as the global leader of jihad, at least in the short run, especially if AQAP leader Wahishi shifts his loyalty to ISIS. But as the Iraqi Shiites, aided by the Iranians and with some Western support, repel ISIS, Watts predicts, an entirely different scenario will emerge, especially as infighting continues between ISIS and al Qaeda leadership in Pakistan.

"Al Qaeda affiliates and regional upstarts may find little incentive to hitch their group to a volatile global jihadi alliance that would only erode their local popular support without bringing in outside resources, operational capability or ideological clarity," according to Watts.[70]

Over the longer term, he says, al Qaeda affiliates and jihadi groups "would remain only very loosely connected to one another."

"Al Qaeda is being forced to change by counterterrorism pressure and by regional events," says Liepman of the Rand Corp. And the two most important events are the civil war in Syria and the upheaval in Iraq, he says. "The next couple of years will be both unstable and unpredictable for the jihadist universe, primarily because of the instability in both Syria and Iraq."

NOTES

1. Shuaib Almosawa and Eric Schmitt, "2 Yemenis Shot by Americans are Linked to Qaeda Cell," *The New York Times*, May 10, 2014, http://tinyurl.com/lvaxdf8.

2. *Ibid.*

3. "Drone Wars Yemen: Analysis," New America Foundation, April 21, 2014, http://tinyurl.com/kaxev54.

4. "Remarks by the President at the United States Military Academy Commencement Ceremony," The White House, May 28, 2014, http://tinyurl.com/o7l87wf.

5. "Testimony by Jeh Johnson, Secretary of Homeland Security," House Judiciary Committee Hearing: Oversight of the United States Department of Homeland Security, May 29, 2014, http://tinyurl.com/mwx5zen.

6. For background, see Kenneth Jost, "Unrest in the Arab World," *CQ Researcher*, Feb. 1, 2013, pp. 105-132; and Roland Flamini, "Turmoil in the Arab World," *CQ Researcher*, May 3, 2011, pp. 209-236.

7. Ben Gilbert, "Saudi Arabia walks a fine line in backing Syrian rebellion," Aljazeera America, Jan. 20, 2014, http://tinyurl.com/jwewou. For background, see Leda Hartman, "Islamic Sectarianism," *CQ Researcher*, Aug. 7, 2012, pp. 353-376.

8. "Country Reports on Terrorism 2013 — Executive Summary," U.S. Department of State, April 2014, p. 5, http://tinyurl.com/oe6wder.

9. J. M. Berger, "Debate: Is al-Qaeda a global terror threat or a local military menace?" *The Globe and Mail*, May 28, 2014, http://tinyurl.com/ohzpza2.

10. "Discord in the ranks of Al Qaeda as leader is slammed over Syria," The Associated Press, May 12, 2014, http://tinyurl.com/kvtuvdo.

11. J. M. Berger, "War on Error," *Foreign Policy*, Feb. 5, 2014, http://tinyurl.com/pbv522w.

12. Daveed Gartenstein-Ross, "Debate: Is al-Qaeda a global terror threat or a local military menace?" *The Globe and Mail*, May 28, 2014, http://tinyurl.com/ohzpza2.

13. *Ibid.*

14. Terrence McCoy, "ISIS just stole $425 million, Iraqi governor says, and became the 'world's richest terrorist group,'" *The Washington Post*, June 12, 2014, http://tinyurl.com/ljyq933.

15. Thomas Lynch, "It's Not About Al-Qaeda Anymore," *War On the Rocks*, Nov. 26, 2013, http://tinyurl.com/qhmgmwb.

16. Oren Dorell and David Jackson, "Details Emerge on al-Qaeda link to embassy closures," *USA Today*, Aug. 5, 2013, http://tinyurl.com/q4q6wrp.

17. Barbara Starr, *et al.*, "Intercepted al Qaeda message led to shuttering embassies, consulates," CNN, Aug. 4, 2013, http://tinyurl.com/lt9jo2w.

18. Terrence McCoy, "How ISIS leader Abu Bakr al-Baghdadi became the world's most powerful jihadist leader," *The Washington Post*, June 11, 2014, http://tinyurl.com/n44z5l7.

19. "Al Qaeda splinter group moves to take eastern Syrian city," Reuters, May 11, 2014, http://tinyurl.com/qdej88q.

20. Bronwyn Bruton, "The Real Reason al-Shabab Attacked a Mall in Kenya," *Defense One*, Sept. 24, 2013, http://tinyurl.com/oelke4h.

21. Mark Landler and Michael Gordon, "U.S. to Send Up to 300 Military Advisers to Iraq," *The New York Times*, June 20, 2014, http:// tinyurl.com/pybqkhe.

22. Farnaz Fassihi, *et al.*, "Iraq Scrambles to Defend Baghdad," *The Wall Street Journal*, June 13, 2014, http://tinyurl.com/k7nm5w5.

23. Kevin Sullivan and Greg Jaffe, "Collapse of Iraqi army a failure for nation's premier and for U.S. military," *The Washington Post*, June 12, 2013, http://tinyurl.com/olw2dly.

24. *Ibid.*

25. "Statement by the President on Afghanistan — Rose Garden," The White House, May 27, 2014, http://tinyurl.com/ma33ne7.

26. "How realistic is Obama's new Afghanistan timeline?" PBS Newshour, May 27, 2014, http://tinyurl.com/ppswx3y.

27. Eli Lake, "As Obama Draws Down, Al Qaeda Grows in Afghanistan," *The Daily Beast*, May 29, 2014, http://tinyurl.com/o4qmert.

28. *Ibid.*

29. "Remarks by the President," *op. cit.*

30. Gordon Adams, "Obama's Big, New Counterterrorism Plan is a Hot Mess," *Foreign Policy*, May 30, 2014, http://tinyurl.com/mnccc2v.

31. *Ibid.*

32. Eric Schmitt, "U.S. Training Elite Antiterror Troops in Four African Nations," *The New York Times*, May 26, 2014, http://tinyurl.com/opv335n.

33. Fawaz A. Gerges, *The Rise and Fall of Al-Qaeda* (2011), p. 34.

34. For background, see Thomas J. Billitteri, "Afghanistan Dilemma," *CQ Researcher*, Aug. 7, 2009, pp. 669-692.

35. Clint Watts, "The Three Versions of Al Qaeda: A Primer," Foreign Policy Research Institute, December 2013, http://tinyurl.com/p5qnz6b.

36. Lawrence Wright, *The Looming Tower: Al-Qaeda and the Road to 9/11* (2007), p. 150.

37. *Ibid.*, pp. 150, 152.

38. *Ibid.*, p. 193.

39. *Ibid.*, pp. 198-199.

40. Seth G. Jones, *Hunting in the Shadows: The Pursuit of Al Qa'ida Since 9/11* (2012), p. 46.

41. *Ibid.*, p. 47.

42. *Ibid.*, pp. 48-49.

43. President Bush Speech to a Joint Session of Congress, Sept. 20, 2001, http://tinyurl.com/3btzktw.

44. Peter L. Bergen, *Manhunt: The Ten-Year Search for Bin Laden from 9/11 to Abbottabad* (2012), p. 23.

45. For background, see Kenneth Jost, "Rebuilding Afghanistan," *CQ Researcher*, Dec. 21, 2001, pp. 1041-1064; and David Masci and Kenneth Jost, "War on Terrorism," *CQ Researcher*, Oct. 12, 2001, pp. 817-848.

46. Bergen, *op. cit.*, p. 68; Global Terrorism Database, National Consortium for the Study of Terrorism and Responses to Terrorism, http://tinyurl.com/p5b49ee.

47. Bergen, *ibid.*, pp. 138-139.

48. *Ibid.*, pp. 117-118.

49. For background, see Thomas J. Billitteri, "Drone Warfare," *CQ Researcher*, Aug. 6, 2010, pp. 653-676.

50. "President Obama's Speech on Osama Bin Laden," *Discovery News*, Feb. 11, 2013, http://tinyurl.com/o6mtsgl.

51. Bergen, *op. cit.*, p. 259.

52. James R. Clapper, "Statement for the Record: Worldwide Threat Assessment of the US Intelligence Community," Senate Select Committee on Intelligence, Jan. 29, 2014, p. 12, http://tinyurl.com/omy462h.

53. Scott Sayare, "Suspect Held in Jewish Museum Killings," *The New York Times*, June 1, 2014, http://tinyurl.com/karok85.

54. *Ibid.*

55. *Ibid.*

56. Matthew Olsen testimony, Senate Foreign Relations Committee Hearing: "Extremism and Sectarianism in Syria, Iraq and Lebanon," March 6, 2014, p. 3, http://tinyurl.com/mobzrpj.

57. Richard Barrett, "Foreign Fighters in Syria," The Soufan Group, June 2014, p. 25, http://tinyurl.com/ncv7erx.

58. Mark Mazzetti, *et al.*, "Suicide Bomber Is Identified as a Florida Man," *The New York Times*, May 31, 2014, http://tinyurl.com/kxw4vut.

ASSESSING THE THREAT FROM AL QAEDA   107

59. Thomas Hegghammer, "Should I Stay or Should I Go? Explaining Variation in Western Jihadists' Choice between Domestic and Foreign Fighting," *American Political Science Review*, February 2013, p. 10, http://tinyurl.com/oagxzwe.

60. Greg Miller, *et al.*, "American suicide bomber in Syria raises fears for U.S.," *The Washington Post*, June 2, 2014, http://tinyurl.com/p3b2r59.

61. Barrett, *op. cit.*

62. "Foreign Terrorist Organizations," U.S. Department of State, http://tinyurl.com/d9s57hn.

63. Peter Bergen, "Americans dying for al Qaeda," CNN, June 2, 2014, http://tinyurl.com/mzaep4l.

64. Kimiko De Freytas-Tamura, "Foreign Jihadis Fighting in Syria Pose Risk in West," *The New York Times*, May 30, 2014, http://tiny url.com/n7dl558.

65. Alissa J. Rubin, "Fearing Converts to Terrorism, France Intercepts Citizens Bound for Syria," *The New York Times*, June 3, 2014, http://tinyurl.com/ke6a67j.

66. Loveday Morris, "Al-Qaeda builds networks in Lebanon as security slips" *The Washington Post*, March 18, 2014, http://tinyurl.com/l7svldp.

67. Olsen, *op. cit.*

68. Rania El Gamal and Yara Bayoumy, "Saudi Arabia says uncovers al Qaeda cell plotting attacks," Reuters, May 6, 2014, http://tinyurl.com/ko52fez.

69. Aaron Y. Zelin and Jonathan Prohov, "The Foreign Policy Essay: Proactive Measures — Countering the Returnee Threat," *LawFare* (blog), May 18, 2014, http://tinyurl.com/n4qu5rv.

70. Clint Watts, "ISIS's Rise After al Qaeda's House of Cards," Foreign Policy Research Institute, March 22, 2014, http://tinyurl.com/mgo ghvk.

BIBLIOGRAPHY
Selected Sources
Books

Bergen, Peter L., *Manhunt: The Ten-Year Search for Bin Laden from 9/11 to Abbottabad*, Crown, 2012.
CNN's national security analyst traces the hunt for al Qaeda leader Osama bin Laden.

Gerges, Fawaz A., *The Rise and Fall of Al-Qaeda*, Oxford University Press, 2011.
A professor at the London School of Economics chronicles al Qaeda's emergence from local jihadist movements and its subsequent decentralization.

Jones, Seth G., *Hunting in the Shadows: The Pursuit of Al Qa'ida Since 9/11*, W.W. Norton, 2012.
A senior RAND Corp. analyst chronicles the fight against al Qaeda.

Wright, Lawrence, *The Looming Tower: Al-Qaeda and the Road to 9/11*, Vintage Books, 2007.
A journalist explains the growth of Islamic fundamentalism, al Qaeda's rise and the intelligence failures that culminated in the 9/11 terrorist attacks in the United States.

Articles

"Discord in the ranks of Al Qaeda as leader is slammed over Syria," The Associated Press, May 12, 2014, http:// tinyurl.com/kvtuvdo.
A breakaway al Qaeda affiliate strongly criticizes al Qaeda's leader Ayman al-Zawahiri for siding with rival Jabhat al-Nusra.

Almosawa, Shuaib, and Eric Schmitt, "2 Yemenis Shot by Americans are Linked to Qaeda Cell," *The New York Times*, May 10, 2014, http://tinyurl.com/lvaxdf8.
The two Yemeni men shot dead trying to kidnap two American Embassy employees in Yemen were part of an al Qaeda cell.

De Freytas-Tamura, Kimiko, "Foreign Jihadis Fighting in Syria Pose Risk in West," *The New York Times*, May 30, 2014, http://tinyurl.com/n7dl558.
Thousands of Westerners have gone to fight with radical Islamist groups in Syria, raising concerns that some may return home trained to commit violent attacks.

Gilbert, Ben, "Saudi Arabia walks a fine line in backing Syrian rebellion," Aljazeera America, Jan. 20, 2014, http://tinyurl.com/ljwewou.
Saudi Arabia forbids citizens from fighting abroad or sending money to support extremist groups in Syria, but many send funds anyway, using bank accounts in Kuwait.

Landler, Mark, and Michael R. Gordon, "Obama Orders 300 Advisors to Iraq," *The New York Times*, June 20, 2014, http://tinyurl.com/pybqkhe.

The president will deploy military advisers to help Iraqi security forces and is prepared to launch air strikes against Sunni militants.

Miller, Greg, *et al.*, "American suicide bomber in Syria raises fears for U.S.," *The Washington Post*, June 2, 2014, http://tinyurl.com/p3b2r59.
U.S. counterterrorism officials were caught unawares when a Floridian exploded a suicide bomb in Syria.

Sayare, Scott, "Suspect Held in Jewish Museum Killings," *The New York Times*, June 2, 2014, http:// tinyurl.com/ karok85.
A Frenchman accused of killing three people at a Brussels museum had fought with radical Islamist fighters in Syria.

Sullivan, Kevin, and Greg Jaffe, "Collapse of Iraqi army a failure for nation's premier and for U.S. military," *The Washington Post*, June 12, 2014, http://tinyurl.com/ olw 2dly.
The U.S.-trained Iraqi army suffered mass desertions as breakaway al Qaeda group advanced.

Reports and Studies

"Country Reports on Terrorism 2013 — Executive Summary," U.S. State Department, April 2014, http://tiny url.com/oe6wder.

The government's latest review of the state of worldwide terrorism gives a region by region breakdown of violent groups.

Barrett, Richard, "Foreign Fighters in Syria," The Soufan Group, June 2014, http://tinyurl.com/ncv7erx.
A counterterrorism expert documents the flow of foreign fighters into Syria.

Hoffman, Bruce, "Low-Tech Terrorism," *The National Interest*, March-April 2014, http://tinyurl .com/lqd4aqe.
The director of Georgetown University's Center for Security Studies analyzes the weapons terrorists choose to use.

Johnson, Jeh, Testimony before House Judiciary Committee Hearing, May 29, 2014, http://tinyurl .com/mwx5zen.
The secretary of Homeland Security outlines the terror threat inside the United States.

Olsen, Matthew, "Extremism and Sectarianism in Syria, Iraq, and Lebanon," testimony before Senate Foreign Relations Committee hearing, March 6, 2014, http://tinyurl. com/mobzrpj.
The National Counterterrorism Center director analyzes growing instability in Syria, Lebanon and Iraq.

For More Information

American Enterprise Institute, 1150 17th St., N.W., Washington, DC 20036; 202-862-5800; www.aei.org. Conservative think tank focusing on government, politics, foreign policy, economics and social welfare.

Atlantic Council, 1030 15th St., N.W., 12th Floor, Washington, DC 20005; 202-463-7226; www.atlanticcouncil.org. Centrist think tank conducting research on international affairs.

Brookings Institution, 1775 Massachusetts Ave., N.W., Washington, DC 20036; 202-797-6000; www.brookings .edu. Centrist think tank researching foreign policy, global development, economics and social policy.

Bureau of Counterterrorism, U.S. Department of State, 2201 C St., N.W., Washington, DC 20520; 202-647-4000; www.state.gov/j/ct. Helps develop and coordinate counter-terrorism strategies.

Foreign Policy Research Institute, 1528 Walnut St., Suite 610, Philadelphia, PA 19102; 215-732-3774; www.fpri.org. Conservative think tank focused on international issues.

National Consortium for the Study of Terrorism and Responses to Terrorism (START), 8400 Baltimore Ave., Suite 250, College Park, MD 20740; 301-405-6600; www.start.umd.edu. University-based research center on terrorism.

National Counterterrorism Center, Washington, DC 20511; www.nctc.gov. Government agency that analyzes terrorism intelligence and plans counterterrorism activities.

Rand Corp., 1776 Main St., Santa Monica, CA 90401; 310-393-0411; www.rand.org. Think tank focused on security, health, education, sustainability, growth and development.

5

Transnational Crime

Peter Katel

Pakistani sisters Zunera, 16, at left, and Shaista are hiding in Faisalabad after being held in a Dubai brothel for four years where they were forced to work as prostitutes. Zunera displays a scar left after she was shot in the leg while trying to escape. Sex traffickers and other criminal gangs have adapted to globalization and modern technology to set up networks for a wide range of criminal enterprises.

From *CQ Researcher*, August 29, 2014.

FAROOQ NAEEM/AFP/Getty Images

I n the last year, some 230,000 people worldwide received a startling message when they turned on their computers: "Your personal files are encrypted! . . . To obtain the private key for this computer, which will automatically decrypt files, you need to pay 300USD/300EUR/similar amount in another currency."[1]

The scam and an associated scheme paid off: Victims handed over an estimated $100 million for the cyber-extortion by Russian and Ukrainian hackers.[2]

With help from Europe and other countries, U.S. authorities pulled the plug on the "CryptoLocker" data-ransom operation. But those behind it remain free, like other Russian hackers in recent years.

Cyber-extortion is part of a much broader problem that the United Nations Office on Drugs and Crime (UNODC) calls "transnational organized crime." It includes not only cross-border hacking but also ivory and wildlife smuggling, piracy on the open seas, counterfeiting of high-end, name-brand products and trafficking in drugs, human organs, weapons and sex workers.

Statistics on the phenomenon are notoriously unreliable, partly because countries define and measure transnational criminal activity differently — or don't collect data on it at all. In its latest report, issued in 2011, the UNODC said international criminals raked in some $2.1 trillion in illicit profits in 2009.[3] But that figure is based on a 1998 International Monetary Fund (IMF) estimate of laundered crime profits. "There is currently no single method that would give clear, unambiguous and indisputable results," the U.N. agency said.

Nonetheless, official assessments suggest transnational crime is overwhelming law enforcement. Such crime "poses a significant and growing threat to national and international security, with dire

Traffickers Use Complex International Networks

Heroin trafficking routes run from Afghanistan to Europe, and cocaine travels from South America to the United States and Europe. Gun traffickers ship weapons from the United States to Mexico and from Ukraine to Africa. Traffickers in China and India supply most of Africa's counterfeit medicines, while illegal African wildlife and animal byproducts, such as ivory, travel to buyers in Southeast Asia and China.

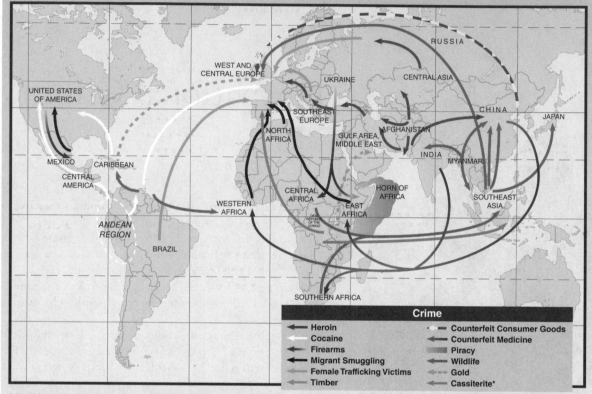

Used to make tin. Proceeds from illegal cassiterite mining operations in the Congo are used to purchase arms for rebel groups.

Source: "The Globalization of Crime," United Nations Office on Drugs and Crime, 2010, p. 2, http://tinyurl.com/lh7okrm

implications for public safety, public health, democratic institutions and economic stability across the globe," the Obama administration said in 2011.[4] "The underworld has become inextricably linked to the global economy," the UNODC said a year earlier.[5]

Some crime scholars argue, however, that transnational crime is neither new nor more of a threat than in the past. "In some ways, it was a bigger problem at earlier points in history," says Peter Andreas, a political science professor at Brown University in Providence, R.I. "In Miami in the '70s," he says, drug-money launderers

"could walk into a bank with a duffel bag of cash, no questions asked."

In addition, experts say some modern developments, such as instant Internet communication and globalization, give police and prosecutors new advantages, such as the ability to trace criminals' electronic trails, as the Justice Department did to take down CryptoLocker, which was aided by a network of computers secretly infected with malware known as "Gameover Zeus."

"We succeeded in disabling Gameover Zeus and Crypto-Locker," said Deputy U.S. Attorney General

James M. Cole, in part because of "strong working relationships with private industry experts and law enforcement counterparts in more than 10 countries."[6]

Still, transnational criminals today can inflict widespread damage more quickly than their predecessors. A month after the CryptoLocker plot was disrupted, another Russian hacking group reportedly captured an astonishing 1.2 billion user name-password combinations and more than 500 million email addresses.[7] Indeed, thousands of hackers, smugglers and other criminals benefit from today's Internet-enabled instantaneous global communications and the boom in international trade sparked by globalization.[8]

Meanwhile, Interpol, popularly imagined to be a sort of global super-police, is actually just a data exchange and training agency, and international treaties to control transnational crime have often been ineffective.

International agreements can prove less persuasive than profits. In Thailand, for instance, civilian and military officials profited from the trafficking of asylum seekers from Myanmar and Bangladesh — members of the Muslim Rohingya ethnic minority — for forced labor, according to a State Department annual report released in June on countries' efforts to comply with a U.N. anti-trafficking treaty.

"People died there every day," said Akram, a Rohingya rescued from a Thai rubber plantation last year. Thailand, also home to a thriving sex-worker trafficking industry, largely has not kept promises to improve anti-human trafficking enforcement, the report said.[9]

In other instances, countries may agree to cooperate in fighting global crime, but national sovereignty often trumps another country's request to have a foreign national arrested on his home turf. For instance, in July the Netherlands refused a U.S. request to extradite a former senior Venezuelan intelligence official indicted for alleged ties to Colombian drug traffickers.[10]

Moreover, the National Intelligence Council reported to Congress in 2011, "Terrorist organizations . . . are turning to criminal activities such as kidnapping for ransom to generate funding to continue their operations."[11] According to *The New York Times*, al Qaeda and close affiliates have received at least $125 million in payments to free kidnap victims since 2008, often paid by Western European governments and sometimes disguised as aid grants.[12]

The ransom issue took on grim new urgency with the beheading — made public by a video released on Aug. 19 — of U.S. journalist James Foley by the Islamic State, often referred to as ISIS or ISIL, the jihadist army that controls parts of Syria and Iraq. Foley's kidnappers had demanded a multimillion-dollar ransom that the United States — following longstanding policy — refused to pay. But four French and two Spanish journalists had been freed earlier after their governments paid ransoms, reported journalist David Rohde of *The Atlantic* (himself a former Taliban hostage who escaped).[13]

Criminal-terrorist links clearly arouse concern. "Boko Haram has been terrorizing the Nigerian people for years, and now they're involved in this horrific case of human trafficking," said Rep. Kay Granger, R-Texas, chair of the House State, Foreign Operations and Related Programs Subcommittee, speaking of the Islamist extremist group's April kidnapping of more than 200 schoolgirls and threat to sell them.[14] "We want to hear about how the funding this subcommittee provides is being used to confront these types of issues and what is needed for the next fiscal year."[15]

Some experts want illegal corporate activities with international consequences defined as transnational crime, such as the massive sale of investment securities composed of high-risk mortgages in the 2000s — which precipitated the 2008 financial crash. "They were sold through false representation, which is a felony, and triggered a global economic crisis," says William K. Black, a professor of law and economics at the University of Missouri-Kansas City, where he teaches on white-collar crime. "It was by far one of the largest crimes in world history."[16]

But international white-collar crime is even more complicated and difficult than prosecuting other cross-border crimes, experts say. "Trying to enforce the law is a fool's game," says Jack Blum, a lawyer and early investigator of international financial crimes based in Annapolis, Md. "It takes years, it doesn't work and prosecutors generally give up."

The internationalization of financial crime reveals "fundamentally broken processes," he continues. "In the financial world, people have just purchased a version of the latest Ferrari or Lamborghini and are tooling at 200 miles an hour, and in the background you've got a couple of cops on broken rent-a-bikes trying to catch up."

Bank of America agreed on Aug. 21 to pay $16.6 billion to settle Justice Department charges of fraud in selling mortgage-backed securities. The accusations were made in a civil case, though the department did not exclude the possibility of criminal charges against individuals. However, department officials and some outside experts say proving criminal intent by executives in cases arising from the financial crash is virtually impossible.[17] The UNODC's figures on the scope of transnational crime don't include those of financial institutions allegedly acting fraudulently.

Assertions that the financial crisis stemmed from widespread cross-border law-breaking are "ideologically motivated," says Stewart Baker, a Washington lawyer and cyber-security specialist who was assistant secretary for policy in the Homeland Security Department during the George W. Bush administration. "We certainly know that transnational corporations pose special problems for international regulation, but to add those to the category of transnational crime would probably just make the category less meaningful."

As law enforcement authorities around the globe strive to arrest and prosecute international criminals, here are some of the questions academics, police and governments are debating:

Is the danger posed by transnational crime exaggerated?

The most fundamental debate concerning transnational crime is over the magnitude of the danger it represents.

It "poses a significant challenge to the United States and democratic governments and free-market economies around the world [and] a direct and immediate threat to the national security of the United States," concluded a multi-agency assessment released by the outgoing Clinton administration in December 2000.[18] That same year the U.N. General Assembly adopted a nearly identical stance.

Five years later Moisés Naím, a prominent Washington foreign-policy specialist and then-editor in chief of *Foreign Policy*, wrote in a widely cited book: "All the evidence from the illicit trade in arms, drugs, human beings, counterfeits, money laundering . . . to say nothing of international terrorism, points us over and over to the driving force that international networks exercise in eroding the authority of states, corrupting legitimate businesses and governments and hijacking their institutions."[19]

Such alarmed tones provoked a strong counter-argument about the dangers posed by transnational crime. "What is increasing is the amount of fuss made about it and the careers built on constructing platitudes to describe it," wrote R. T. Naylor, a professor of economics at Canada's McGill University in Montreal, Quebec, a long-time scholar of illegal markets.[20]

Capitol Hill veterans such as Blum, a former staff lawyer for the Senate Antitrust Subcommittee and the Senate Foreign Relations Committee, say the grimness of some official assessments reminds him of the drug war build-up in the 1980s. "You're running a law enforcement agency, you want a budget," he says. "So you hype like crazy to make sure you have a budget."

Others share in the official alarm but acknowledge that statistics on transnational crime are unreliable for certain crimes, such as wildlife and sex trafficking. "By definition, illicit businesses don't want to be counted or sized in any kind of proper way," says Nils Gilman, associate chancellor at the University of California, Berkeley, and author of a study on black market globalization.

In one field alone — stolen art and antiquities — Interpol has estimated losses at $6 billion to $8 billion a year. "I'm extremely skeptical of all the numbers I hear," Gilman says. "The numbers are, quote-unquote, plausible, but probably because I've heard them repeated again and again."[21]

Still, cyber-crimes, he says, are genuinely new and dangerous: "The stealing of personal information is extremely disruptive and causes economic problems."

Louise I. Shelley, who directs the Terrorism, Transnational Crime and Corruption Center at George Mason University in Fairfax, Va., argues that crimes such as drug, wildlife and human trafficking clearly cause enormous damage, even if precise data is absent. "Yes, it would be better if we had data" on the many forms of illegal international activity, she says, including "data on how incredibly large the drug markets are." Citing a UNODC estimate of total transnational crime commercial volume in 2009, she said, "We don't know precisely, but we're probably talking about 7 percent of the world's trade."[22]

Yet, others say "transnational organized crime" is simply a modern term for an age-old phenomenon. "Hacking by definition is new, but it's in some ways an old crime — theft," says Brown University's Andreas.

"We come up with new words to describe these things because they exist in the cyber-world."

Similarly, smuggling is an ancient crime that has increased in volume, but not necessarily as a percentage of global trade flows, says Andreas, who wrote a 2013 book on illicit trade in U.S. history.[23] "A lot of globalization is about reducing trade barriers, which in some ways has drastically reduced incentives to smuggle," he says. "The stuff that is [still] smuggled is stuff with high taxes on it, like cigarettes."

Nevertheless, even experts who see political motives behind some official characterizations of globalized crime worry that certain schemes can have grave worldwide consequences.

Blum points to "an explosion of financial crime," citing continuing damage from a long-running scam called "prime bank instrument fraud," in which people are lured to invest in nonexistent investment instruments allegedly sanctioned by major financial institutions such as the Federal Reserve or the IMF. The U.S. Treasury Department, which has posted detailed warnings about such schemes, says they have bilked individuals and organizations around the world of billions of dollars.[24]

Instrument fraud and other financial scams existed long before the Internet, Blum acknowledges. But as early as 1998, he and colleagues were warning that criminals were setting up banks online with no fixed physical address, making enforcement all but impossible.[25]

"When people commit crimes, they do not report to some international statistics agency," Blum says. "Is it much worse? What are the trends? Without hard knowledge it is hard to say. But we can sense anecdotally that, particularly in the financial area, it's out of control."

Nikos Passas, a professor of criminal justice at Northeastern University in Boston, has a more muted view. He agrees that technology has given criminals access to instant new worldwide communication, encryption and other tools that only governments used to enjoy, and that cyber-criminality can victimize large numbers of people or institutions. But, he adds, "We do not have a paradigmatic shift. We have different vulnerabilities."

For instance, Passas says, criminals have also become more vulnerable, because globalization offers "different opportunities for control," such as recently revealed global communications monitoring by the U.S. National

Customs officials in Indonesia display methamphetamine that a German smuggler tried to bring into the country on Dec. 5, 2013. International enforcement has not put a major dent in the international illegal drug industry, according to the Congressional Research Service.

Security Agency (NSA). "The NSA has shown that. There are handles on crime; it's not like it's out of control."

Does the failure to stop drug trafficking suggest that fighting other transnational crime also will fail?

Despite decades of international anti-drug enforcement, the global illegal drug industry enjoys a steady supply of raw materials, unencumbered transportation routes and high consumer demand.

International enforcement has not put a major dent in the international illegal drug industry, the Congressional Research Service reported last year. "In 1998 . . . the United Nations committed to 'eliminating or reducing significantly' the supply of illicit drugs by 2008," the nonpartisan research agency noted last year. "In 2009, when that goal had not been accomplished, U.N. Member States agreed to recommit to achieve this goal in another decade, by 2019."[26]

Nevertheless, the prevalence of illicit drug use worldwide is "generally stable," with the total number of users "commensurate with the growth of the world population," the UNODC reported this year.[27] Although statistics on the drug trade are shaky, the agency estimates that the drug-using population ranged from as low as 162 million to as high as 324 million worldwide in 2012, or between 3.5 percent and 7 percent of the world's population.[28]

The New York-based Council on Foreign Relations said in a report last year that countries generally agree on how to define and prosecute international drug trafficking. But the "norms for law enforcement and judicial cooperation remain weak, vague or non-existent," rendering the international agreements on transnational crime essentially toothless, concluded the nonpartisan think tank.[29]

Crime specialists who favor legalizing drugs say the ineffectiveness of drug regulations proves their futility. Shrinking the drug supply through enforcement doesn't eliminate demand, they argue, and crackdowns only benefit drug traffickers. "If you succeed, what happens to the price of drugs? They go up; and profits? They go up as well — a really, really bad dynamic," says Black, of the University of Missouri-Kansas City law school. A former litigation director of the Federal Home Loan Bank Board, Black is also a former deputy director of the National Commission on Financial Institution Reform, Recovery and Enforcement, which examined the causes of the savings and loan crisis of the 1980s.

But what Black views as doomed anti-drug efforts does not necessarily mean that efforts to fight other transnational crimes will fail, he says. The United States still wields considerable global power, and financial and other crimes do not enjoy the overpowering consumer dependence on an illicit product like drugs, he says.

"We can actually create standards of conduct in areas like finance," he says. "It is hard, but . . . we know what steps to take." These include pursuing criminal prosecutions of banks that violate laws, rather than ending cases with a guilty plea and a fine, he says. In June, for instance, BNP Paribas, France's biggest bank, pleaded guilty to violating U.S. economic sanctions against Sudan and Iran and agreed to pay an $8.9 billion fine.[30]

But financial crime expert Blum says substantial differences in laws and procedures between countries pose major — and usually prohibitive — restrictions on transnational enforcement. "There is no way to compel the attendance of a witness across international borders, he says.

Technology that enabled Internet-based global banking has raced far ahead of national sovereignty laws, Blum says. "This kind of antique legal arrangement is just not working," he argues. "For all of the ways in which the Internet and the ability to wire money

instantly have improved, the law enforcement side of it is nowhere.

"There are, for example, all these mutual legal-assistance treaties," he adds. "Everybody touts them. Try to use one, and see what happens." In practice, he says, countries usually give their sovereignty priority over other countries' criminal cases, regardless of treaties.

But Gilman of UC Berkeley — citing a recent U.S.-Swiss accord designed to weaken bank secrecy in Switzerland — suggests that governments trying to deal with financial problems stemming from the financial crash of 2008-09 may be about to make transnational financial crimes a higher priority. Two years ago, "I would have said no," it's not going to happen, he says. "But the United States has cracked down on bank secrecy in Switzerland to an extent I never would have imagined."

The reason is simple, Gilman says. "Governments are desperate for revenue," he explains. "That could create a shift in tolerance. If we were able to close up the holes in the global financial system, that would severely restrict all other illicit businesses, because it would be harder to launder their money."

But even if enforcement of financial crimes is getting stricter, transnational criminals remain technologically ahead of the authorities, says Douglas Farah, an investigative reporter and consultant specializing in ties between governments and organized crime in Latin America and Africa.

For instance, he says, "The Sinaloa [drug] cartel [in Mexico] and other folks have been hiring top-grade hackers. They want to know what the police are doing, and they can pay for the best," he says. "It used to be that only a few small groups could do things like high-end encryption. But now, if you look across the transnational organized crime world, there are really sophisticated Chinese, Russian and Mexican people."

As a result, Farah says, "the law enforcement and intelligence side can't really keep up."

Should the illegal activities of banks and corporations be classified as transnational crimes?

The explosion of concern about transnational crime that followed the geopolitical and economic changes of the 1990s — such as the collapse of the Soviet Union and the rise of Asian manufacturing centers — prompted arguments about how to define international law-breaking.

Should it include only hard-core crimes such as smuggling, trafficking and cyber-hacking? Or, should transnational offenses also include illegal activities by banks and corporations?

As early as the late 1980s, criminologists had begun exploring the idea of a broader definition of crime, in a "crimes of the powerful" sub-specialty, which they dubbed "state-corporate crime."[31]

The field included crimes committed by corporations on their own initiative or on orders of a government.[32] Some scholars broadened the scope of the concept to include transnational events. Passas, of Northeastern University, cites the design, operation and quality of regulation of Japan's Fukushima nuclear plant, wrecked by a 2011 earthquake and tsunami. Citing those three factors, a Japanese parliamentary investigation called the disaster "man-made." Now shuttered, the plant continues to leak radioactive water into the ocean.[33]

"If Fukushima keeps leaking . . ., you're not going to be able to eat fish in California," Passas says, citing reports of recent major leaks. But Passas concedes that, despite persistent criticism of official handling of the disaster, what may seem like criminal behavior can only be treated as such if a country has applicable laws.

Likewise, legislative bodies would have to conclude — as he has — that some financial maneuvering is criminal. "Extraordinary risk-taking with derivatives and subprime mortgages — nobody went to jail for those things," he says. "If you know what you are doing, you [can] take advantage of the legal environment. People play with definitions; some people decide that some things are going to be left out of criminal law, even very serious misconduct that has structural and systemic implications."

Karl Lallerstedt, a co-founder of Black Market Watch, a think tank in Geneva, Switzerland, that is developing ways to track illicit cross-border trade, argues that not all unethical behavior need be defined as criminal. "You are collecting toxic debt and selling it to other people," he says, differentiating between breaking criminal laws and

Human Trafficking Varies by Region

Sexual exploitation is the most common form of human trafficking in Europe, Central Asia and the Americas, while forced labor is more prevalent in Asia, the Pacific, Africa and the Middle East.

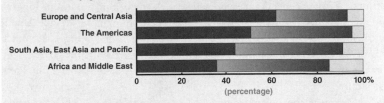

Victims of Human Trafficking and Exploitation (by Region and Percentage, 2007-2010)

* *Includes trafficking in organs and using children as child soldiers, beggars or petty criminals or as sources of body parts for rituals and/or traditional healing.*

Sexual exploitation / Forced labor / Other forms*

Source: "Global Report on Trafficking in Persons 2012," United Nations Office on Drugs and Crime, December 2012, p. 12, http://tinyurl.com/d99pyt7

not complying with government regulations and industry standards.

Lallerstedt is focusing on the smuggling of legal goods, such as untaxed cigarettes. Such economic crimes arouse little public indignation or law enforcement interest, despite their intersection with hard-core criminal activity, he says. "Illicit trade in normally legal goods is a low priority because it's not considered so sexy," he says. "Guns, drugs receive priority. But if the same groups are involved in multiple activities, and the same routes are being used, perhaps corrupting the same individuals to facilitate the movement of these products, [then] you have a synergy effect."

In an essay this year, Gilman of UC-Berkeley drew a deeper distinction between transnational businesspeople involved in legal transactions and transnational criminals intentionally breaking laws. The businesspeople — whom Gilman calls members of a "plutocratic insurgency" — seek to weaken government taxation and regulation, even as they enjoy government-provided services, he wrote.[34] Members of the "criminal insurgency" dodge law enforcement to provide goods and services that are quasi-legal in some places but illegal in others — such as illicit drugs.

"There are myriad connections between the two categories, but it's useful to keep them distinct," Gilman says. "Hedge fund managers aren't running drug or organ trafficking rings."

BACKGROUND
Slaves and Pirates

Experts today may debate what activities are transnational crimes, but they agree that certain activities clearly belong in the category — such as slavery, piracy and human trafficking. Yet, measured against the span of recorded history, such enterprises were legal and sometimes even government-sponsored or sanctioned — before they were prohibited.

Slavery was the norm in ancient Greece and Rome and subsequent early civilizations. And the massive Atlantic slave trade that enriched European colonial powers and shaped the futures of the United States and the Americas began as a state-sponsored enterprise, founded by the Portuguese crown in the early 1400s, during early explorations of coastal western Africa.[35]

By 1833, Britain — once a major slave-trading power — had banned slavery throughout its empire and begun efforts to ban it worldwide, with limited success. In 1845, for instance, the trafficking of slaves to the Spanish colony of Cuba was booming. Spain didn't abolish the trade until 1867; Portugal did so in 1869. European powers promised to prohibit slave-trading in their African colonies in the General Act of Brussels of 1890. But slavery and slave-trafficking were not definitively defined as international crimes until adoption of the Slavery Convention of 1926, amended in 1953.[36]

The transition from legal international activity to prohibited criminal act was even more complicated in the case of another crime whose roots date to antiquity — piracy.

For instance, during the 16th- and 17th-century wars for control of Atlantic and Caribbean trade and territory, Britain and France authorized "privateering" — the seizing of enemy vessels by naval entrepreneurs who would split the proceeds with their governments. Spain considered these robbers pirates, but some modern scholars say because the privateers attacked ships of their enemies, they were in a different category from pirates.[37]

As a young nation, the United States also authorized privateers against British vessels during the Revolutionary War and the War of 1812.[38]

But it was government-sanctioned piracy along the Barbary Coast of North Africa that led the new United States in 1794 to re-establish its navy, which had been disbanded after the American Revolution. The Ottoman provinces of Tripoli, Algiers and Tunis — known as the Barbary states — had been plundering European merchant ships in the Mediterranean Sea for centuries, demanding ransom for the crews or selling them into slavery.

After American independence, the pirates began seizing U.S. merchant ships and their crews, and for years the government paid ransom — or "tribute" — to retrieve them. But, Presidents Thomas Jefferson and James Madison went to war against the Barbary states — once in 1801-1805 and again in 1815 — eventually putting an end to the seizure of U.S. ships.[39]

Privateering was not outlawed internationally until a treaty signed in Paris in 1856. And, despite centuries-old prohibitions on piracy, it was not defined as a crime under international law until the Geneva Convention on the High Seas in 1958. Further international agreements were signed in 1992 and 1994.[40]

Trafficking in wildlife and animal parts, by contrast, was not recognized as a threat to certain animal species until the 20th century. In 1900, a convention signed in London represented the first international attempt to protect endangered species. That same year, President William McKinley signed the Lacey Act, designed with the same objective at the national level and later expanded to cover wildlife imported into the United States.[41]

The London treaty was ineffective, as were 1940 and 1968 conventions designed to protect wildlife in Latin America and Africa, respectively. Then, in 1973, 21 countries signed the sweeping Convention on International Trade in Endangered Species of Wild Fauna and Flora (CITES), which made trafficking in endangered or threatened wildlife a crime. Since then, 180 countries have signed on. But with a booming ivory trade threatening African elephants with extinction, the CITES treaty alone hasn't ensured that it is enforced everywhere.[42]

Similarly, international conventions on protecting intellectual property have not prevented a global boom in the trade of counterfeit products. International protection of patents, trademarks and copyrights dates to the 1883 Paris Convention for the Protection of Industrial Property. In addition, protection is now provided, at least legally, by the World Trade Organization's Agreement on Trade-Related

Aspects of Intellectual Property Rights, and — for strictly intellectual property matters, including patents, the U.N.'s World Intellectual Property Organization.[43]

Yet trade in counterfeit goods is thriving, projected next year to total up to $1.7 trillion, putting 2.5 million legitimate jobs at risk, according to the Paris-based International Chamber of Commerce.[44] Last year, the European Union seized about $1.04 billion worth of counterfeit goods, 12 percent of which was clothing. In the United States, an estimated $1.7 billion worth of counterfeit goods were seized in fiscal 2013, about 35 percent of which was clothing.[45]

China is by far the single biggest source of counterfeit products found in Europe and the United States: 66 percent of items seized in the EU originated in China, as did 68 percent of those found in the United States.[46] But, on paper at least, China is fully compliant with international copyright and trademark standards, embodied in the WTO agreement. But the U.S. trade representative said in 2012 that enforcement of trademark and patent protection remained spotty, marked by "the failure to impose deterrent penalties . . . sufficient to change behavior."[47]

Ironically, the United States was on the other side of the issue early in its history. The new country relied on British inventors, engineers and machine operators to copy technological breakthroughs in Britain's textile production, which had transformed a manual craft into a major industry. For the British, copying that technology was a crime. And even before America declared its independence, Britain had made it illegal for skilled British artisans and mechanics to emigrate to the United States and barred the export of textile machinery.[48]

But machines were smuggled into the United States anyway. Shortly after his inauguration, President George Washington declined personal involvement in establishing a Virginia factory — without discouraging the effort itself — using machines shipped illegally from Britain because it would constitute "a felony."

In the late 19th and early 20th centuries, transnational trafficking in human labor flourished in the United States and elsewhere, protected by corrupt low-level officials. Contractors working for U.S. mining and railroad companies brought in Chinese laborers, often using force or deception.[49] Although their employers didn't claim them as property, the circumstances under which they entered

the country and the conditions in which they lived and worked certainly qualified many of them as victims of what is now known as "human trafficking."

Among the victims were Chinese women brought in to work as prostitutes, followed by a stream of women from Europe known — in the language of the time — as "white slaves." Japanese and Mexican women also were smuggled in to work in big-city brothels. By one estimate, a New York gang made the current equivalent of $15 million in one year from trafficking women.

Prohibition

A 1920 U.S. law banning alcohol had the unintended consequence of creating a major smuggling industry to serve alcohol to American consumers.[50] By 1933, when Prohibition was repealed, a sizeable smuggling industry was concentrated along the Atlantic Coast and the Canadian side of the U.S. Northern border.

Even before Prohibition began, however, Congress had begun laying the groundwork for what would become, decades later, drug prohibition. In 1914 the Harrison Act regulated the distribution of cocaine and opiates — the most popular mood-altering substances apart from alcohol — by requiring that they be taxed and sold only by prescription. The Marihuana Tax Act of 1937 imposed further restrictions on drugs.[51]

The opiate and cocaine markets expanded, partly due to energetic efforts by traffickers from the United States and elsewhere, who developed international smuggling routes. France became a major source for legally produced opiates and cocaine that were diverted into the illegal transatlantic trade.[52]

The Comprehensive Drug Abuse Prevention and Control Act of 1970 classified drugs according to their potential for medical use and abuse.[53] The next year, President Richard M. Nixon told Congress that drug use had "assumed the dimensions of a national emergency" and declared "a war on drugs."[54]

But drug demand kept growing. By the early '70s, heroin production and smuggling routes were thriving from Turkey and then from Southeast Asia, where the U.S. government supported regional military forces that actually engaged in heroin trafficking.[55] Pakistan and Mexico also came to play ever-increasing roles in heroin trafficking. A growing U.S. appetite for marijuana, meanwhile, was being fed not only by supplies from Mexico,

CHRONOLOGY

1790-1912 *United States creates Navy to fight piracy and extortion in North Africa. Transnational crime appears early in U.S. history as intellectual-property theft.*

1790 President George Washington condones American copying of British industrial innovations, which British consider a crime.

1801 U.S. goes to war against Barbary pirates rather than continuing to pay ransom for kidnapped Americans.

1808 Congress outlaws international trafficking of slaves to the United States, but enforcement is lax.

1912 A New York gang makes today's equivalent of $15 million smuggling foreign women for prostitution.

1920-1933 *Alcohol prohibition spurs birth of major liquor smuggling and trafficking industry.*

1920 Congress and the states adopt the 18th Amendment, prohibiting production, importation and sale of alcoholic beverages. It is repealed 13 years later.

1926 League of Nations adopts Slavery Convention to ban slavery in all forms.

1937 Marihuana Tax Act tightens restrictions on cannabis and other drugs.

1948 U.N. bans slavery and slave trade worldwide in Universal Declaration of Human Rights.

1971-1988 *U.S. sparks war on drugs, crackdown on money laundering.*

1971 President Richard M. Nixon declares "war on drugs," saying drug use has become a "national emergency."

1975 Convention on International Trade in Endangered Species goes into effect, banning international trade in species facing extinction and limiting trade in thousands of other threatened species. It has since been signed by 180 countries.

1987 "Laundering" of proceeds from booming drug smuggling and trafficking becomes huge industry.

1988 Federal money-laundering indictment against Luxembourg's Bank of Credit and Commerce International ends in landmark $14 million fine, coinciding with Senate probe of bank's involvement in asset management for dictators and terrorists.

1991-Present *Soviet Union's collapse and rise of Asian manufacturing spur global trade boom, soon to be facilitated by international digital interconnectedness.*

1991 Soviet Union collapses.

1997 An estimated 400,000 women and children from the ex-Soviet bloc and Southeast Asia are trafficked into sex trade.

2000 White House report calls international crime a direct threat to national security. . . . U.N. adopts Trafficking in Persons Protocol, the first binding international treaty specifically criminalizing human trafficking.

2003 Seventy-seven countries sign on to Kimberly Process, a certification system designed to discourage "blood diamond" trade, which finances deadly African insurgencies and terrorist activities.

2009 Russian and Ukrainian hackers are indicted for stealing more than 160 million credit-card numbers from U.S. retailers' computer systems. . . . U.N. Security Council creates a "contact group" focused on piracy of merchant vessels off Somalia.

2013 Secretary of State Hillary Rodham Clinton says booming transnational ivory trade threatens African elephants with extinction in 10 years.

2014 Justice Department announces dismantling of CryptoLocker, computer malware that encrypted victims' data, forcing them to pay an estimated $100 million worldwide to recover it. . . . African leaders at White House summit plead for more U.S. aid against elephant and rhinoceros poachers. . . . Accused Russian hacker arrested in Maldives and flown to U.S. territory. . . . Russian-based hackers steal more than 1 billion pieces of website sign-on information.

the traditional source, but increasingly from Colombia, which also became a major source of cocaine.[56]

By the 1980s, the transnational illegal drug industry had grown to the point that its financial practices — especially its efforts to "launder" profits to disguise the source — had become as big an issue for policy-makers and journalists as trafficking itself.

In that period, the major overseas drug organizations, based in Colombia, wanted to repatriate dollars made in the United States back to their home countries and, in some cases, to invest some of it in the United States. Banks in Miami — considered the U.S. center of the drug trafficking industry — happily did business with clients bearing duffel bags stuffed with dollars.

In 1987 FBI agents arrested nine people in Miami and 32 others elsewhere for allegedly laundering $200 million, some of which had arrived at an FBI front company in boxes, suitcases and duffel bags in quantities of up to $2.5 million at a time. The front company had run the money through banks, which then wired it to accounts in Panama, Switzerland and Tokyo.[57]

In 1988, the issue of illegal international transactions took on a much bigger dimension after the Bank of Credit and Commerce International (BCCI) was indicted for laundering drug money. The Luxembourg-based bank had branches in many countries, including the United States.

In a plea bargain, two bank officials pleaded guilty to reduced charges, and BCCI was fined $14 million. More significantly, the Senate Terrorism, Narcotics and International Operations Subcommittee, led by then-Sen. John Kerry, D-Mass., now secretary of State, began investigating BCCI's handling of the assets of Panamanian strongman Gen. Manuel Noriega.[58]

The committee investigation and an indictment brought by famed New York City District Attorney Robert M. Morgenthau broke open the story of the bank's operations, which included systematic money laundering in several countries, the handling of assets of corrupt dictators, and financial operations on behalf of terrorist organizations. Morgenthau called the bank "one of the biggest criminal enterprises in world history."[59]

The case, which generated enormous press coverage, was the first to reveal what Kerry's panel called "the vulnerability of the world to international crime on a global scope that is beyond the current ability of governments to control."[60]

Globalized Crime

Such warnings intensified in the 1990s, as global mobility and international trade surged following the collapse of the Soviet Union in 1991 and the privatization of huge state-owned Russian industries, a process taken advantage of by insiders who grew rich from the deals. They soon became known as "oligarchs."

A highly developed criminal subculture, which had led a semi-clandestine existence under Soviet rule, flourished openly in the early post-Soviet years. But the professional criminals soon lost power to a new class in government and business.

"Government officials and powerful entrepreneurs . . . take their methods and sometimes their enforcers from the criminal world," wrote Stephen Handelman, a former correspondent for the *Toronto Star* and *Time* magazine, in 2001. Handelman wrote an early book on the rise of post-Soviet Russian organized crime.[61]

Western banks and institutions seemed untroubled, however, about doing business with the new breed of Russian enterprises, Handelman noted. In one of the early cases to grow out of such relationships, the Bank of New York in 2005 paid $38 million in fines and compensation to settle U.S. fraud and money laundering charges involving Russian funds.[62]

Whatever level of cooperation existed between Russian and American businesses, it did not extend, at least from the American point of view, to U.S.-Russia cooperation on the growing number of cyber-crime cases centered in Russia. In 2001, the FBI resorted to luring two Russian hackers, Vasily Gorshkov and Alexey Ivanov, to the United States by inviting them to fake job interviews. The two had stolen credit card numbers and other financial data, trying to extort money from the data owners to retrieve the information, and using stolen credit card numbers for purchases using PayPal. Ivanov was sentenced to four years, Gorshkov to three.[63]

Authorities also saw a sudden uptick in the number of people sold into the international sex industry, largely through networks operating from eastern and central Europe. A federal, multi-agency "International Crime Threat Assessment" concluded in 2000 that about 175,000 of the women and children brought into Europe and the United States in 1997 to serve in the sex trade were from former Soviet-bloc countries.[64] Even more women and children were trafficked from Southeast Asia, where an

Investigators Examine Ancient Money-Transfer Method

"Hawala" system was once suspected in 9/11 attacks.

In the aftermath of the Sept. 11, 2001, terrorist attacks on the United States, politicians, government officials and journalists struggled to understand a new enemy and how it worked. Searchers for the key to al Qaeda's organizational techniques obeyed Washington wisdom: "Follow the money."

The hunt led many to a money-transfer system that former Deputy Treasury Secretary Stuart Eizenstat called the pipeline for a "potentially significant portion of terrorist funds into or out of the U.S.," which Secretary of State Colin Powell in 2002 called "shadowy," and the *Los Angeles Times* called "a destination point for terrorists and heroin traffickers."[1]

That system had a name that sounded suitably mysterious to Western ears —"hawala." As some experts pointed out, the system was devised centuries ago, in South Asia and the Middle East, to allow merchants and travelers to transmit money without risking robbery by carrying it with them. Similar systems were known in China as Fei-Ch'ien; in India, as Hundi; and in Thailand, as Phei Kwan.[2]

But in the post-2001 atmosphere, hawalas, more than their East Asian counterparts, came to represent a key intersection between two sets of wrongdoers who needed to move money around the globe: transnational criminals and terrorists.

The fund-transfer system seemed ideal for both sets of people. As Rand Beers, then-assistant secretary of State for international narcotics and law enforcement, told a congressional subcommittee in 2002: "Terrorists and drug traffickers use similar means to conceal profits and fundraising. They use informal transfer systems such as 'hawala.'

" He added that they also used bulk cash smuggling and multiple bank accounts.[3]

The hawala system, which came to be used by people settling debts and by immigrants sending money home, is user-friendly. A person wanting to send money gives the cash to a nearby money-transfer agent, a "hawaldar" who may also be a merchant or shopkeeper. He, in turn, sends a message — today, by phone, fax or email — to a counterpart hawaldar near the intended recipient, perhaps in another country, who then pays the recipient. At some point, hawaldars who have done business with each other settle accounts, if one has paid out more to customers than the other.[4]

Because the system has no formal record-keeping requirements and is largely unregulated by governments, it seemed to pose obvious attractions for those who wanted their international transactions kept under the radar.

However, in 2004, the National Commission on Terrorist Attacks Upon the United States (the 9/11 Commission), reported that the attackers got their money in above-ground ways that were theoretically open to scrutiny by investigators. The attackers used wire transfers from Dubai, cash that some of them brought with them and ATM withdrawals in the United States from accounts in the United Arab Emirates. "Our investigation has uncovered no evidence that the 9/11 conspirators employed hawala as a means to move the money that funded the operation," the commission concluded.[5]

Osama bin Laden and his comrades did use hawalas in the 1990s when al Qaeda established itself in Afghanistan.

---

estimated 225,000 women, most under 18, were sold into the sex trade in 1997.[65]

While no one disputes that sex-worker trafficking is a big industry, statistics on human trafficking of all kinds, including workers and child soldiers, for instance, are fuzzy. In 2006, the U.S. government estimated that

600,000 to 800,000 people were trafficked across international borders. But the Government Accountability Office, the federal government's accounting arm, said there were no data to support those numbers.[66]

In any case, human trafficking had been proscribed in a U.N. General Assembly convention against transnational

But, as the commission noted, the banking system there was "antiquated and undependable."[6]

Inefficient for terrorists meant inefficient for everyone else as well, pointed out experts in the hawala system — also known to academics as informal funds transfer (IFT). "Overregulation and coercive measures will not be effective," Mohammed El-Qorchi, a senior economist for the International Monetary Fund, argued in 2002, "because they might push IFT further underground. . . . They will not, in isolation, succeed in reducing the attractiveness of the hawala system. As a matter of fact, as long as there are reasons for people to prefer such systems, they will continue to exist and even expand."[7]

Nikos Passas, a professor of criminal justice at Northeastern University in Boston, who has been researching the hawala system and its counterparts since the 1990s, acknowledged that it can be used by criminals and, in principle, by violent extremists. But he said in a 2005 report to the Dutch Ministry of Justice that he had "encountered no instance of terrorist finance in the U.S. or Europe" through these informal systems. "In South Asia and Africa, there are such instances," he added, "but this is mostly because of the general use of [hawala-type systems] for all kinds of transfers and payments."[8]

Passas argued that the post-2001 focus on hawalas as potential channels for financing terrorism and crime could bring about a cure worse than the disease: a shift to more modern methods of transferring money that include gift cards, manipulation of invoices to hide transfers, use of brokerage accounts and credit and debit cards. "The problem is that even less is known" about these systems' vulnerabilities, he wrote. "Instead of increasing transparency of fund transfers and reducing crime, the authorities' efforts may produce the opposite result."[9]

Still, officials remain wary of hawalas' below-the-radar quality, even though the intense political and law enforcement focus on them has faded since the immediate post-9/11 period.

"I don't think that the notion of hawalas or of informal financial services is in and of itself problematic," Daniel Glaser, assistant Treasury secretary for terrorist financing and financial crimes, said at a panel discussion last year at the Center for Strategic and International Studies in Washington. "The problematic aspect of it is the non-transparent aspect of it, which then makes it subject to abuse by people who we wouldn't want to have access to this financial system."[10]

— *Peter Katel*

[1] "President George W. Bush [and others] Delivers Remarks at the Treasury Department's Financial Crimes Enforcement Network," *FDCH Political Transcripts*, Nov. 7, 2001; Josh Meyer, "Cutting Money Flow to Terrorists Proves Difficult," *Los Angeles Times*, Sept. 28, 2003, http://tinyurl.com/lh8jqey.

[2] Nikos Passas, "Demystifying Hawala," *Journal of Scandinavian Studies in Criminology and Crime Prevention*, 2006, http://tinyurl.com/lp82tj2; Mohammed El-Qorchi, "Hawala," Finance & Development, International Monetary Fund, December 2002, http://tinyurl.com/mkrhx7d.

[3] Rand Beers, "Narco-Terror: The Worldwide Connection Between Drugs and Terror," testimony to Senate Judiciary Committee, Subcommittee on Technology, Terrorism and Government Information, Federal News Service, March 13, 2002, http://tinyurl.com/k5qgu9x.

[4] *Ibid.*

[5] "The 9/11 Commission Report," National Commission on Terrorist Attacks Upon the United States, 2004, pp. 224, 237, 499, http://tinyurl.com/49xkf.

[6] *Ibid.*, p. 171.

[7] El-Qorchi, *op. cit.*

[8] Nikos Passas, "Informal Value Transfer Systems and Criminal Activities," Ministerie van Veiligheid en justitie [Ministry of Security and Justice, the Netherlands], p. 36, http://tinyurl.com/kuqxzjp.

[9] *Ibid.*, p. 38; Nikos Passas, "Informal Value Transfer Systems, Terrorism and Money Laundering," Report to the National Institute of Justice, November 2003, p. 17, http://tinyurl.com/k96bvzb.

[10] "The Center for Strategic and International Studies Holds the Global Security Forum 2013, Panel on What Role Financial Power Should Play in National Security," *CQ Transcriptions*, Nov. 5, 2013.

organized crime in 2000. The treaty defined transnational organized crime as "money-laundering, corruption, illicit trafficking in endangered species of wild flora and fauna, [and] offences against cultural heritage," as well as human trafficking. It called on governments to recognize the links between international criminal activities and terrorism.[67]

Terrorism and Crime

After the Sept. 11, 2001, terrorist attacks in the United States, governments and international organizations quickly switched their anti-transnational crime efforts to focus on criminals' connections to terrorism.

Criminals Want Corrupt States — But Good Roads, Too

Transnational crime requires reliable global connections and banking systems.

What more could an internationally minded criminal want than a country whose government is essentially nonexistent, where a crime boss is free to conduct his business without fear of policemen's prying eyes?

A lot more, it turns out. Experts say crooks need the same basic government services — such as dependable electricity, decent roads and reliable Internet connections — as law-abiding citizens.

"The ideal locale for a transnational criminal organization is one which boasts many of the advantages of a strong, functioning state, such as modern infrastructure and communications, a banking system and enough rule of law to make life generally predictable," writes Patrick Radden Keefe, a journalist and author specializing in international crime.[1]

Fear of transnational organized crime surged during the post-Cold War period when the specter of "failed states" loomed as an international menace. In the 1990s, the breakdown of all government in Somalia, where a small-scale U.S. military intervention came to grief, seemed to represent the danger.

Failed states became a bigger concern after the Sept. 11, 2001, terrorist attacks in the United States, perpetrated by extremists hiding out in Taliban-controlled Afghanistan. As then-President George W. Bush's 2002 national security strategy document declared: "America is now threatened less by conquering states than we are by failing ones."[2]

Although armed extremism led the list of fears, crime was not far behind. By 2006, the Bush administration was warning that "weak and impoverished states and ungoverned areas" were "susceptible to exploitation by terrorists, tyrants and international criminals."[3]

Since then, though, crime experts have been drawing distinctions between collapsed or nascent states and weak ones, and weak ones with good connections to the rest of the world and those lacking such links.

For instance, barely governed states are good spots for smugglers of drugs, guns and people, Stewart M. Patrick, now director of the International Institutions and Global Governance Program at the Council on Foreign Relations think tank, wrote in 2006. "Criminal groups have become adept at exploiting weak-state capacity in conflict zones, such as Colombia or the DRC [Democratic Republic of Congo], where political authority is contested or formal institutions have collapsed."[4]

But selling products, or laundering profits, requires communications and transportation networks and functioning banks, Patrick added. Thus, "South Africa and Nigeria have become magnets for transnational and domestic organized crime," he wrote, because they have working infrastructures. "Togo has not."

Nigeria, as it happens, is ranked as shakier, overall, than Togo in this year's global ranking of "fragile states" by *Foreign Policy* magazine and the Fund for Peace, a think tank and advocacy organization favoring alternatives to armed conflict. But Nigeria comes out somewhat better than Togo in terms of the quality of its public services.[5]

How comfortable transnational criminals feel in a country also depends on the extent to which they can forge

Even though al Qaeda — the group behind the 9/11 attacks — had political and religious objectives, investigations showed that its logistical machinery had a structure that copied or even overlapped with transnational criminal networks. "Transnational organized crime and international terrorism increasingly share both organizational and operational characteristics and at times even partner with one another," Thomas M. Sanderson, deputy director of the Center for Strategic and International Studies' Transnational Threat Initiative, wrote in 2004.[68]

In West Africa, *Washington Post* correspondent Farah had reported in November 2001 that al Qaeda was

corrupt ties to law enforcement officials and politicians. This has long been an issue in some Latin American countries, including the gang violence-plagued Central American nations — El Salvador, Honduras and Guatemala — the countries from which thousands of women and children have been seeking refuge by crossing the U.S. border in recent weeks. The region's gangs — with help from some corrupt police — are deeply involved in transnational drug trafficking.[6]

Trafficking relies on a thriving culture of political corruption. A former Guatemalan president, Alfonso Portillo, was sentenced in May to more than five years in a U.S. federal prison after pleading guilty to money laundering conspiracy (using U.S. banks). El Salvador's attorney general announced in June that he was investigating Defense Minister David Munguia Payes for allegedly selling military weapons to gangs, an investigation the military had tried to block. And Honduras has earned a reputation from the State Department's human rights investigators and others as a center of widespread government corruption.[7]

The three countries are grouped with a predominantly African contingent as the world's most fragile states, according to the *Foreign Policy*-Fund for Peace rankings. But they also have adequate communications and transportation networks. In fact, Honduran Foreign Minister Mireya Aguero Corrales told NPR in July, the city in her country with the highest homicide rate is also its business capital. "If you go to San Pedro Sula . . . you see a prosperous city," she said. "It's where the business centers are. Many international brand names have their maquilas [assembly plants] there."[8]

For some analysts, the attention paid to the link between fragile states and transnational crime distracts from what they see as the bigger problem of transnational criminal behavior in major institutions in wealthy countries. Swiss bankers recently told *The New York Times* about traveling to the United States to recruit clients interested in shielding their assets from the Internal Revenue Service by using Switzerland's fabled bank secrecy. Clients would use code names to call

from pay phones, the bankers said. And the bankers' laptops were set up to allow easy and instant erasing of data.[9]

Author Keefe, in fact, argued that Switzerland and other tax havens had found a legal way around the issue of criminality. "In these jurisdictions, the rule of law manages to accommodate criminality," he wrote. "The corruption is written into the law itself."

— Peter Katel

[1] Patrick Radden Keefe, "The Geography of Badness: Mapping the Hubs of the Illicit Global Economy," in Michael Miklaucic and Jacqueline Brewer, eds., *Convergence: Illicit Networks and National Security in the Age of Globalization* (2013), p. 102, http://tinyurl.com/qfodcxg.

[2] Quoted in Michael J. Mazarr, "The Rise and Fall of the Failed-State Paradigm," *Foreign Affairs*, January/February, 2014, http://tinyurl.com/myoo4ds; Michael Bowden, *Black Hawk Down: A Story of Modern War* (1999).

[3] "The National Security Strategy of the United States of America," The White House, March 2006, p. 33, http://tinyurl.com/ms7unhb.

[4] Stewart M. Patrick, "Weak States and Global Threats: Fact or Fiction?" *The Washington Quarterly*, Spring 2006, p. 39, http://tinyurl.com/ljejp62.

[5] "Fragile States," *Foreign Policy*, 2014, http://tinyurl.com/m3wdvpk.

[6] Jo Tuckman, " 'Flee or die': violence drives Central America's child migrants to US border," *The Guardian*, July 9, 2014, http://tinyurl.com/k3sgahk; Steven S. Dudley, "Drug Trafficking Organizations in Central America: Transportistas, Mexican Cartels and Maras," Woodrow Wilson International Center for Scholars, University of San Diego, May 2010, http://tinyurl.com/7auevqs.

[7] "US court sentences former president of Guatemala to prison for taking bribes," The Associated Press (*The Guardian*), May 22, 2014, http://tinyurl.com/k7v9mvq; Seth Robbins, "El Salvador's Military: Arms Dealer to the Maras?" *InSight Crime*, June 16, 2014, http://tinyurl.com/q37g56b; Elisabeth Malkin, "Lawmakers Ask State Dept. to Review Support for Honduras," *The New York Times*, May 29, 2014, http://tinyurl.com/pwdg8rh.

[8] "Honduras Foreign Minister: U.S. Should Address Root Causes of Migration," NPR, July 25, 2014, http://tinyurl.com/ltmqdm5.

[9] Doreen Carvajal, "Swiss Banks' Tradition of Secrecy Clashes With Quests Abroad For Disclosure," *The New York Times*, July 8, 2014, http://tinyurl.com/nzr83u5.

earning millions by buying diamonds from Sierra Leonean guerrillas at below-market prices and selling them in Europe.[69] Former CIA and military officials gave similar accounts to NBC News in 2005, but a State Department deputy assistant secretary said in 2006, "We have not been able to verify those reports."[70]

However, international outrage over the trade in "blood diamonds" — diamonds trafficked to finance brutal civil wars in Liberia and Sierra Leone — led to creation in 2003 of the Kimberly Process, a system endorsed by 77 countries designed to certify diamonds as unconnected with trafficking by warring insurgents.

Meanwhile, rapid expansion of Internet connectivity and e-commerce in the early 2000s led to the parallel growth of Internet-enabled global crime. By 2005, investigators said criminal networks based in former Soviet-bloc countries, Russia above all, were deeply involved in trading bulk quantities of personal-identity information from stolen credit cards and online accounts. Experts pointed to a combination of poverty and, given a still-strong educational system, superior technological skills.[71]

As data piracy expanded, so did the ancient crime of piracy on the high seas. The first half of 2009 alone saw a total of 240 pirate attacks, most involving the hijacking of shipping vessels by Somalis operating in the Red Sea and Gulf of Aden.[72]

But international cooperation — based on common agreement that the pirates had to be stopped — made a difference. By May 2013, Somali piracy had effectively ended, without a single successful hijacking during the previous 12 months. Armed guards on ships, naval deployments by NATO, the EU, China, Russia and other countries and prosecutions of more than 1,000 pirates helped to end Somali piracy.[73]

Meanwhile, world attention had turned to high finance after the burst housing bubble precipitated a global financial crisis in 2008, when the value of investment securities backed by subprime mortgages plunged.[74] The crash prompted debate over where to draw the line between high-risk financial maneuvers involving billions of dollars and crime and vividly illustrated how interconnected the world economy had become.

CURRENT SITUATION

Arresting Russians?

The alleged leader of a hacker ring accused of reaping at least $2 million by stealing and reselling credit card information siphoned from U.S. business computer systems is awaiting trial in Seattle.[75]

Roman V. Seleznev, 30, a Russian, was grabbed in July in the Maldives, a popular Indian Ocean tourist destination, apparently by U.S. law enforcement agents. He was flown to the U.S. Pacific island territory of Guam, where a judge ordered him transferred to Seattle. He had been indicted there in 2011 for alleged bank fraud, computer hacking, identity theft and related charges. He

was indicted separately in Nevada in 2012 on similar charges, and faces up to 30 years in prison.[76]

Declaring that Seleznev had been "kidnapped," the Russian foreign ministry said, "We consider this the latest unfriendly move from Washington."[77]

The arrest came only five weeks after Justice Department officials fingered another Russian as head of the CryptoLocker ransom scheme. Then, news broke of the massive theft of more than 1 billion pieces of website sign-on data — a scheme also allegedly centered in Russia.[78]

But as the circumstances of Seleznev's capture had made clear, U.S. authorities cannot count on Russia arresting alleged cyber-crooks accused of crimes in the United States.

Meanwhile, as Russian aggression in Ukraine worsened relations between the two countries, Russia in August announced that former U.S. National Security Agency analyst Edward Snowden could stay another three years in Russia. Snowden has been in Russia since 2013, when he released classified documents that revealed massive, worldwide electronic surveillance by the NSA. The Justice Department has charged him with theft and violations of the Espionage Act.[79]

But even before Snowden's Russia stay was extended, the United States had been unable to get Russian help in major hacking cases. "The FBI has tried to get cooperation, the State Department has asked for help and nothing happens," said Richard Clarke, who was special adviser for cybersecurity in the George W. Bush administration, "so law enforcement options are pretty negligible."[80]

U.S.-Russia discussions reportedly have centered on Russian and Ukrainian hackers that the Americans believe stole more than 160 million credit card numbers from Neiman Marcus and other retailers in the past seven years. A 2009 indictment in New Jersey against five of them was unsealed last year.[81] Two of the five were arrested at U.S. request while vacationing in the Netherlands in 2012.[82]

Russian police did arrest two people in June — a teenage boy and a 23-year-old man — for allegedly mounting a small-scale "ransomware" scheme targeting Apple devices.[83]

Russia is not the only country greeting U.S.-requested arrests coolly. In July, the United States had a former Venezuelan military intelligence official arrested in Aruba, a former Dutch colony in the Caribbean, 15 miles from the Venezuelan coast. U.S. indictments accused Hugo Carvajal of business ties to Colombian drug traffickers who shipped drugs to the United States via Venezuela.[84]

Is the transnational organized crime threat exaggerated?

YES

Peter Andreas
*Professor of Political Science and
International Studies, Brown University*

Written for *CQ Researcher,* August 2014

Illicit cross-border activities, ranging from drug trafficking to money laundering, are often lumped under the frustratingly vague term "transnational organized crime." In standard accounts, globetrotting criminals are increasingly sophisticated, organized and powerful. Governments, in contrast, are increasingly overwhelmed, outsmarted and outmaneuvered.

At first, this portrayal seems accurate. Transnational organized crime routinely defies borders, mocks laws and corrupts and sometimes violently challenges authorities. But by neglecting the past, we grossly distort our view of the present. Contrary to conventional wisdom, states have struggled with this challenge for centuries.

For the most part, transnational crime is a fuzzy new term for an old practice: smuggling. Although the speed, content, methods and organization of smuggling have varied greatly across time and place, the basic activity has not fundamentally changed. Even though the global reach of some smuggling groups has accelerated with the integration of the global economy, the image of an octopus-like network of crime syndicates that runs the underworld is fiction. Even the most sophisticated smuggling schemes tend to be defined more by fragmentation and loose, informal networks than by concentration and hierarchical organization. And no so-called drug cartel actually fits the definition of a cartel.

We are often told that the volume of organized transnational criminal activity has surged in recent decades. Of course, we have no idea how true those statistical claims are — they tend to be assertions and guesstimates rather than reliable and verifiable empirical evidence. Still, cross-border organized crime would simply have to keep pace with the illicit economy to grow at an impressive rate. But that does not necessarily mean it has increased as an overall percentage of global economic transactions. Indeed, the liberalization of trade in recent decades has sharply reduced incentives to engage in smuggling practices designed to evade taxes and tariffs, historically the backbone of illicit commerce.

The historical amnesia that too often afflicts the debate is nowhere more evident than in the depiction of our borders as increasingly overrun and overwhelmed — with the U.S.-Mexico line cited as a particularly glaring illustration. Yet, there was never a golden age of border security. Popular political calls to "regain control" of the border falsely imply that it was ever actually under control. And by historical standards, this border is in fact far more controlled than ever before.

NO

Louise I. Shelley
*Director, Terrorism, Transnational Crime and
Corruption Center, George Mason University*

Excerpted from Shelley's book, *Dirty Entanglements: Corruption, Crime and Terrorism* (Cambridge University Press, 2014)

The threat of transnational organized crime is all too real. That entangled threat of crime, corruption and terrorism now commands high-level attention because of (1) its endemic nature in many diverse regions of the world, especially in conflict regions; (2) the financial success and extensive influence of nonstate actors on governments, often by means of corruption; (3) the increasing economic role of criminals and terrorists both as employers and participants in the local and global economy; (4) the deleterious impact of crime and terrorism on communities and the political order; and (5) the incapacity of state and multinational organizations to successfully challenge transnational criminals and terrorists at the national, regional and global levels.

Contemporary illicit trade, a key component of the crime-terror relationship, is different from smuggling in previous millennia. Smuggling has existed since the dawn of history, when states began to raise revenues by imposing taxes on the movement of goods. Yet today's illicit trade carried out by criminals, terrorists and corrupt officials affects millions, if not billions, of lives by doing irreversible damage to the planet and to existing communities, whether by eliminating species or forests or spreading contagious diseases or components of weapons of mass destruction.

The future will see new kinds of dirty entanglements and groups, such as the recently established relationships between the criminal gangs of Central America and the drug cartels. State-level conflicts do not necessarily deter business relations among nonstate actors. The desire to make money in the illicit economy transcends long-term hostilities, and in the future we will continue to see such strange, strategic partnerships and new and possibly now unimaginable entanglements. In the future, identities may be more blurred.

Dirty entanglements are unfortunately on a growth trajectory. The forces contributing to their rise — including increased populations without a future, growing income inequality, increased migration and displacement, poor governance, absence of the rule of law, continuing civil unrest and conflict and climate change — show no signs of abating.

In our highly interconnected world, diverse communities must work together to counter the scourge of corruption, crime and terrorism. Unfortunately, until now, without a whole-of-society perspective, we have made little progress globally against the dirty entanglements.

The Venezuelan government said Carvajal had been "kidnapped." The Dutch government, which handles matters for Aruba, decided to release Carvajal, who had a diplomatic passport.[85]

Threatened Wildlife

Transnational crime is becoming a major issue in relations between African and Asian countries and the rest of the world, as the demand for smuggled animal parts from endangered and threatened species skyrockets. Much of the increased demand, especially for elephant ivory, is being spurred by an expanding middle class in China, where carved ivory is highly prized.[86]

During a White House summit for leaders from 50 African countries in August, U.S. officials held high-level talks on how to combat the booming illegal regional trade in wildlife. "The elephants are killed in Tanzania," Tanzanian President Jakaya Kikwete said at a panel discussion with several counterparts and U.S. Interior Secretary Sally Jewell. "But the consignment [of ivory] came from Kampala, Uganda, and moved through Mombasa [Kenya's main port]. So there is definitely need for working together."[87]

The flourishing demand for ivory has devastated Africa's elephant and rhinoceros populations. Rhino horns are erroneously believed to have medicinal powers and are popular for making dagger handles in Yemen. At least 1,000 rhinos were killed last year, as were 20,000 African elephants (and 35,000 the year before), according to former Deputy Interior Secretary David J. Hayes.[88] Ivory trafficking alone is threatening African forest elephants with extinction within 10 years, then-Secretary of State Hillary Clinton said last year.[89]

The recent Washington discussions didn't yield any definitive results. However, the U.S. government has been helping African governments beef up their wildlife protection programs via training, equipment and uniforms. Still, African leaders at the summit asked for more: helicopters in Namibia, night-vision goggles in Tanzania, infrared scanners in Togo and military support in Gabon.[90]

"Well-armed, well-equipped and well-organized networks of criminals, and corrupt officials exploit porous borders and weak institutions," Obama said in February as he introduced a White House strategy to enhance enforcement of anti-wildlife trafficking laws, including diplomatic initiatives to promote international cooperation.[91]

The Justice Department also is targeting ivory and rhino horn dealers. In the past two months:

- Federal agents arrested a Canadian dealer on charges of smuggling more than $500,000 worth of both products from the United States;
- A Miami-based dealer pleaded guilty to brokering the sale of rhino horn;
- A Texas dealer pleaded guilty to conspiring to traffic horn and ivory; and
- Two men in separate cases were sentenced to 30 and 70 months, respectively, for involvement in major ivory and horn trafficking enterprises.[92]

The 70-month sentence — the longest ever in a U.S. wildlife smuggling case — was imposed on a Chinese businessman convicted of heading a smuggling enterprise that shipped $4.5 million worth of African rhino horn and ivory from the United States to China. Zhifei Li admitted he smuggled 30 rhino horns that were used to make drinking cups. Folk tradition in China and other Asian countries holds that drinking from horn cups brings good health.[93]

"If you are able to stop the market for ivory and rhino horns, definitely you will be able to save these species," Tanzanian President Kikwete said at the White House summit.[94]

OUTLOOK
Grim Future

Crime expert Blum says international financial crimes seem likely to continue to be a growth industry. "Countries are not going to cooperate" against financial crooks, he says, citing the tendencies to prize national sovereignty over other countries' criminal cases. "They're going to sign all kinds of agreements and ignore them."

And national differences on what crimes should be priorities seem likely to persist. For instance, the United Nations and several other countries define organ trafficking as illegal, but the international organ-brokering trade is prospering due to lax enforcement in many countries.[95]

Still, shifting political winds offer occasional chances to crack down on some transnational crimes, says Passas of Northeastern University. "It becomes a lot easier when old friends fall out," he says, citing the cases of former U.S. allies Panamanian strongman Noriega, Iraqi dictator Saddam Hussein, Libyan dictator Moammar Gadhafi and Egyptian dictator Hosni Mubarak. "They had all been involved for ages in corrupt financial misconduct," Passas says. "We protected them, and then they were behind bars or killed."

International politics can also complicate efforts to pressure other countries into cracking down on transnational crime. The State Department's harsh evaluation this year of Thailand's anti-human trafficking efforts led to that country's inclusion on a list of 23 countries deemed not complying with minimum standards or making significant efforts to improve. Inclusion on the list means the U.S. president can order foreign aid withheld.

But last year, Obama waived sanctions against China, Russia and Uzbekistan while imposing full sanctions on Cuba, Iran and North Korea — which already have hostile relations with the United States and receive no aid. Partial sanctions were applied to Congo, Equatorial Guinea, Eritrea, Sudan, Syria and Zimbabwe, whose relations with the U.S. are tense.

As for Thailand and other countries in its category, "You certainly wouldn't want to halt any assistance that's going specifically to increasing the capacity of our partners in those governments to fight human trafficking or to help its victims," Luis CdeBaca, the ambassador-at-large of the State Department's office that monitors and combats human trafficking, said at a June briefing.[96]

Moreover, says reporter Farah, in a post-Cold War world with two major superpowers no longer dominating international relations, crime-linked governments can more easily develop alliances without worrying about crackdowns from major powers.

Policymakers and law enforcement should focus on criminal-government ties, "especially in an age of resource constraint," Farah says, urging a focus on crime that poses major threats rather than the relatively less dangerous variety. "You have to be somewhat realistic about what is always going to be out there — handbag counterfeiting, even fairly high-end narcotrafficking."

Andreas of Brown University predicts that enforcement of laws against cyber-crime, which can victimize millions of people and businesses at a time, will become increasingly important. "The debate used to focus primarily on the drug issue," he says. "Drugs are still quite prominent but don't monopolize the debate like they used to."

When it comes to cyber-crime, former Homeland Security official Baker argues that time is not on the criminals' side. "It is harder and harder to hide your ID consistently in cyberspace," he says. "It will be increasingly possible to ID these people."

And all high-level hackers don't enjoy ironclad protection against arrest, Baker says. They may be out of danger as long as they're in Russia or elsewhere in the old Soviet bloc, but, "The old Soviet Union is not that much fun. They will travel, and they will get busted. My hope is that we will eventually begin to weed out at least the less disciplined cyber-criminals."

In addition, cyber-tools may become a bigger part of law-enforcement's arsenal. Lallerstedt of Black Market Watch says an international agreement may soon require cigarette firms to use technology enabling them to "track and trace" every pack in order to deter smuggling, which costs governments an estimated $30 billion a year in lost cigarette tax revenue.[97]

"I'm not saying it's a magic bullet," he says. "But the further ahead you look, the more monitoring and track-and-tracing options are available."

Nevertheless, other transnational crime-watchers see much less reason for hope when looking at the big picture. Transnational criminals likely will continue reaping the benefits of inconsistent enforcement, efficient trade routes and ready markets for their goods, says Shelley of George Mason University.

"The future is grim," she says. "At the rate we're going: Goodbye rhino, goodbye elephant; welcome, trafficked people."

NOTES

1. Eric Geier, "How to rescue your PC from ransomware," *PCWorld*, Jan. 13, 2014, http:// tinyurl.com/oj9myjc.

2. Matt Apuzzo, "Secret Global Strike Kills 2 Malicious Web Viruses," *The New York Times*, June 3, 2014, http://tinyurl.com/lhk254d.

3. "Estimating Illicit Financial Flows Resulting from Drug Trafficking and Other Transnational Organized Crimes," U.N. Office on Drugs and Crime, October 2011, p. 7, http://tinyurl. com/p64lrda.

4. "Transnational Organized Crime: A Growing Threat to International and National Security," in "Strategy to Combat Transnational Organized Crime," The White House, July 25, 2011, http://tinyurl.com/3t5jwtg.

5. "The Globalization of Crime: A Transnational Organized Crime Threat Assessment," U.N. Office on Drugs and Crime, 2010, p. ii, http://tinyurl.com/p64lrda.

6. "Memorandum of Law," U.S. v. Evgeniy Mikhaliovoch Bogachev, (copy on Justice Department website, undated), http://tinyurl.com/pm9zufj; "U.S. Leads Multi-National Action Against 'Gameover Zeus and 'CryptoLocker' Ransomware . . .," U.S. Justice Department, June 2, 2014, http://tinyurl.com/nbdxqoh.

7. Nicole Perlroth and David Gelles, "Russian Hackers Amass Over a Billion Passwords," The New York Times, Aug. 5, 2014, http://tinyurl.com/qd8ucqn.

8. For background, see the following CQ Researchers: John Felton, "Small Arms Trade," June 19, 2012, pp. 281-304; Robert Kiener, Human Trafficking and Slavery," Oct. 16, 2012, pp. 473-496; Sarah Glazer, "Organ Trafficking," July 19, 2011, pp. 341-366; and Peter Katel, "Mexico's Drug War," Dec. 12, 2008, pp. 1009-1032.

9. Quoted in Andrew R.C. Marshall, "Thai police target human traffickers but rescued Rohingya may face more abuse," Reuters, Feb. 13, 2014, www.reuters.com/article/2014/02/13/us-thailand-rohingya-id USBREA1C0FB20140213. "Trafficking in Persons Report 2014," U.S. Department of State, 2014, pp. 372-376, http://tiny url.com/kw2yz8y.

10. Tim Dees, "What Do Interpol Agents Really Do," Slate, July 1, 2013, http://tinyurl.com/k7mskqf; Jim Wyss, "Top Venezuela official accused in drug case averts U.S. extradition, heads back home," The Miami Herald, July 27, 2014, http://tinyurl.com/oeqnuxl.

11. Quoted in John Rollins and Liana Sun Wyler, "Terrorism and Transnational Crime: Foreign Policy Issues for Congress," Congressional Research Service, June 11, 2013, pp. 2-3, http://tinyurl.com/ptk4y5m.

12. Rukmini Callimachi, "Paying Ransoms, Europe Bankrolls Qaeda Terror," The New York Times, July 29,

2014, http://tinyurl.com/nupg66w. For background see Barbara Mantel, "Assessing the Threat from Al Qaeda," CQ Researcher, June 27, 2014, pp. 553-576.

13. Rukmini Callimachi, "Before Killing James Foley, ISIS Demanded Ransom from U.S.," The New York Times, Aug. 20, 2014, http://tinyurl.com/nf8q5tx; David Rohde. For background, see Frank Greve, "Combat Journalism," CQ Researcher, April 12, 2013, pp. 329-352.; David Rohde, "How the U.S. and Europe Failed James Foley," The Atlantic, August 2014, http://tinyurl.com/n9ojb4g.

14. Aminu Abubakar and Josh Levs, " 'I will sell them,' Boko Haram leader says of kidnapped Nigerian girls," CNN, May 6, 2014, http://tinyurl.com/lcgxyvh.

15. "Rep. Kay Granger Holds a Hearing on United States Assistance to Combat Transnational Crime Budget for F.Y. 2015," House Subcommittee on State, Foreign Operations and Related Programs, CQ Transcriptions, May 7, 2014.

16. For background, see Kenneth Jost, "Financial Misconduct," CQ Researcher, Jan. 20, 2012, pp. 53-76.

17. John Cassidy, "The Justice Department's 'War' on Wall Street: Still No Criminal Charges," The New Yorker, Aug. 8, 2013, http://tinyurl.com/qym7ned; Christina Rexrode and Andrew Grossman, "Record Bank of America Settlement Latest in Government Crusade," The Wall Street Journal, Aug. 21, 2014, http://tinyurl.com/ktlhgpa.

18. "International Crime Threat Assessment, Introduction," The White House, December 2000, http://tinyurl.com/oema9cf.

19. Moisés Naím, Illicit: How Smugglers, Traffickers, and Copycats are Hijacking the Global Economy (2005), Kindle edition, no page number available.

20. R. T. Naylor, Counterfeit Crime: Criminal Profits, Terror Dollars, and Nonsense (2014), p. 31.

21. "ICE Homeland Security Investigations: Efforts to Combat Illicit Trafficking in Stolen Art, Antiquities and Cultural Property," U.S. Department of State, press conference, Sept. 6, 2013, http://tinyurl.com/ngywyan.

22. "Transnational organized crime: the globalized illegal economy," U.N. Office on Drugs and Crime, undated, http://tinyurl.com/ko36hqa.

23. Peter Andreas, *Smuggler Nation: How Illicit Trade Made America* (2013).

24. "Prime Bank Instrument Fraud," U.S. Treasury Department, undated, http://tinyurl.com/33pjqs.

25. Jack A. Blum, *et al.*, "Financial Havens, Banking Secrecy and Money Laundering," U.N. Office on Drugs and Crime, 1998, http://tiny url.com/mrwzdec.

26. Liana Sun Wyler, "International Drug Control Policy: Background and U.S. Responses," Congressional Research Service, Aug. 13, 2013, p. 9, http://tinyurl .com/q7dx88c.

27. *Ibid.*

28. "World Drug Report 2014," U.N. Office on Drugs and Crime, Executive Summary, p. 1, http://tinyurl. com/lsm7hgr.

29. "The Global Regime for Transnational Crime," Council on Foreign Relations, updated June 25, 2013, http://tinyurl.com/nxqt9bz.

30. Ben Protess and Jessica Silver-Greenberg, "BNP Paribas Admits Guilt and Agrees to pay $8.9 Billion Fine to U.S.," *The New York Times*, June 30, 2014, http://tinyurl.com/pp4tsn4.

31. Kris Lasslett, "A Critical Introduction to State-Corporate Crime," International State Crime Initiative, Oct. 21, 2010, http://tinyurl.com/ pyf9cyb.

32. *Ibid.*

33. Quoted in Tsuyoshi Inajima, Jacob Adelman and Yuji Okada, "Fukushima Disaster Was Man-Made, Investigation Finds," Bloomberg, July 5, 2012, http://tinyurl.com/c4ju2ut; "Water leaks continue to plague No. 5 reactor at Fukushima plant," Asahi Shimbun, July 20, 2014, http://tinyurl.com/ l5bp7en.

34. Nils Gilman, "The Twin Insurgency," *The American Interest*, June 15, 2014, http://tinyurl.com/qh2d3yc.

35. Hugh Thomas, *The Slave Trade: The Story of the Atlantic Slave Trade: 1440-1870* (1997), pp. 25-31; 48-67.

36. *Ibid.*, pp. 649-783, 787-790; Peter P. Hinks, *et al.*, eds., *Encyclopedia of Antislavery and Abolition* (2007), Vol. 2, pp. 502-503; "Slavery Convention," Office of the High Commissioner for Human Rights, United Nations, http://tinyurl.com/lln3u26.

37. "Counterpiracy under International Law," Geneva Academy of International Humanitarian Law and Human Rights, August 2012, p. 11, http://tinyurl .com/mfqu7as.

38. Andreas, *op. cit.*, pp. 50-56, 83-88.

39. For background, see Alan Greenblatt, "Attacking Piracy," *CQ Researcher*, Aug. 1, 2009, pp. 205-232. Also see Michael A. Palmer, "The Navy: The Continental Period, 1775-1890," Naval History and Heritage Command, http://tinyurl.com/lk5nouf.

40. "Counterpiracy under International Law," *op. cit.*, p. 11.

41. For background, see Robert Kiener, "Wildlife Smuggling," *CQ Researcher*, Oct. 1, 2010, pp. 235-262.

42. *Ibid.*; "What is CITES?" Convention on International Trade in Endangered Species of Wild Fauna and Flora," undated, http://tinyurl.com/aggl3od.

43. "WIPO — A Brief History," World Intellectual Property Organization, undated, http://tinyurl.com/ kclcpc4.

44. "Estimating the global economic and social impacts of counterfeiting and piracy," International Chamber of Commerce, http://tinyurl.com/mqg8nte.

45. "Intellectual Property Seizures Statistics, Fiscal Year 2013," U.S. Customs and Border Protection, undated, http://tinyurl.com/n6wth8n; "Report on EU customs enforcement of intellectual property rights: Results at the EU border, 2013," European Commission, 2014, http://tinyurl.com/n997qvy.

46. *Ibid.*

47. "2012 Special 301 Report," Office of the United States Trade Representative, April 2012, p. 27, http://tinyurl.com/cxywwn2.

48. Andreas, *op. cit.*, pp. 63-73.

49. Quoted in *ibid.*, p. 101.

50. See Daniel Okrent, *Last Call* (2010).

51. Steven B. Duke and Albert C. Gross, *America's Longest War: Rethinking Our Tragic Crusade Against Drugs* (1993), pp. 85-86.

52. Andreas, *op. cit.*, pp. 262-265.

53. *Ibid.*

54. Quoted in Andreas, *op. cit.*, p. 274.

55. Cornelius Friesendorf, *US Foreign Policy and the War on Drugs: Displacing the Cocaine and Heroin Industry* (2007), p. 70.

56. Andreas, *op. cit.*, pp. 275-308.

57. *Ibid.*; Leslie Maitland Werner, "Scores Arrested in Money-Laundering," *The New York Times*, June 13, 1987, http://tinyurl.com/kjmuko3.

58. Michael Wines, "Washington at Work; A Crusader Driven by Outrage," *The New York Times*, Aug. 22, 1991, http://tinyurl.com/mbq5sxe.

59. Quoted in David Sirota and Jonathan Baskin, "Follow the Money," *Washington Monthly*, September 2004, http://tinyurl.com/48edh.

60. "The BCCI Affair," Senate Foreign Relations Committee, December 1992, http://tinyurl.com/l66kb55.

61. Stephen Handelman, *Thieves in Power: The New Challenge of Corruption* (2001), http://tinyurl.com/mg4dnhb; James O. Finckenauer and Yri A. Voronin, "The Threat of Russian Organized Crime," U.S. Department of Justice, June 2001, http://tinyurl.com/qjcq49a.

62. *Ibid.*, Handelman; Timothy L. O'Brien, "Bank Settles U.S. Inquiry Into Money Laundering," *The New York Times*, Nov. 9, 2005, http://tinyurl.com/l8qnzzo.

63. "Russian Man Sentenced for Hacking into Computers in the United States," U.S. Attorney, District of Connecticut, July 25, 2003, http://tinyurl.com/p4utjal.

64. "Trafficking in Women and Children," in "International Crime Threat Assessment," *op. cit.*

65. *Ibid.*

66. "Human Trafficking: Better Data, Strategy, and Reporting Needed to Enhance U.S. Antitrafficking Efforts Abroad," U.S. Government Accountability Office, July 18, 2006, http://tinyurl.com/8aavx4b.

67. "General Assembly resolution 55/25, United Nations Convention Against Transnational Organized Crime," Nov. 15, 2000, p. 2, http://tinyurl.com/24d4ftw.

68. Thomas M. Sanderson, "Transnational Terror and Organized Crime: Blurring the Lines," *SAIS Review*, Winter-Spring, 2004, http://tinyurl.com/qh4vor9.

69. Douglas Farah, "Al Qaeda Cash Tied to Diamond Trade," *The Washington Post*, Nov. 2, 2001, p. A1 (not online in complete form).

70. "Press Briefing on Conflict Diamonds," U.S. State Department, Dec. 5, 2006, http://tinyurl.com/o8tty5a; Chris Hansen, "Liberia's former president, a friend to terror?" Dateline NBC, July 17, 2005, http://tinyurl.com/nanml6y.

71. For background, see Peter Katel, "ID Theft," *CQ Researcher*, June 10, 2005, pp. 517-540; "Russian organised crime: The EU perspective," Library Briefing, Library of the European Parliament, March 4, 2011, http://tinyurl.com/c5momso; Alissa de Carbonell, "Ex-Soviet hackers play outsized role in cyber crime world," Reuters, Aug. 22, 2013, http://tinyurl.com/ne5hav6.

72. For background, see Alan Greenblatt, "Attacking Piracy," *CQ Researcher*, Aug. 1, 2009, pp. 205-232.

73. "No Somali pirate hijacking in nearly a year, says UN," The Associated Press (*The Guardian*), May 3, 2013, http://tinyurl.com/ppeh6xj.

74. For background, see Marcia Clemmitt, "Mortgage Crisis," *CQ Researcher*, Nov. 2, 2007, pp. 913-936.

75. "Judge won't free Russian accused of hacking in US," The Associated Press (*The Washington Post*), Aug. 1, http://tinyurl.com/pbwlodc.

76. Nicole Perlroth, "After Arrest of Accused Hacker, Russia Accuses U.S. of Kidnapping," *The New York Times* (Bits Blog), July 8, 2014, http://tinyurl.com/psufbch; "Russian National Arraigned on Indictment For Distributing Credit Card Data Belonging to Thousands of Card Holders," U.S. Attorney's Office, Western District of Washington, Aug. 8, 2014, http://tinyurl.com/onkvo97.

77. *Ibid.*

78. Perlroth and Gelles, *op. cit.*

79. Peter Finn and Sari Horwitz, "U.S. charges Snowden with espionage," *The Washington Post*, June 21, 2013, http://tinyurl.com/ke39l9k; Alec Luhn and Mark Tran, "Edward Snowden given permission to stay in Russia for three more years," *The Guardian*, Aug. 7, 2014, http://tinyurl.com/l5udg5g. For background the following *CQ Researchers* by Chuck McCutcheon: "Whistleblowers," Jan. 31, 2014,

pp. 97-120, and "Government Surveillance," Aug. 30, 2013, pp. 717-740.

80. Quoted in Michael Riley, "Neiman Marcus Breach Linked to Russians Who Eluded U.S.," Bloomberg, April 6, 2014, http://tinyurl.com/kpmljn8.

81. *Ibid.*; *United States of America v. Vladimir Drinkman, et al.*, July 25, 2013, http://tinyurl.com/l3ujjrj.

82. Maud Van Gaal and David Voreacos, "Hacker Goes to Top Dutch Court in U.S. Extradition Fight," Bloomberg, May 9, 2014, http://tinyurl.com/q6xqhxv; Ted Sherman, "Russian hacker pleads not guilty, denied bail in massive data breach case," [Newark, N.J.] *Star-Ledger*, Aug. 12, 2013, http://tinyurl.com/lfepfxg.

83. Lucian Constantin, "Hackers behind iPhone ransom attacks arrested in Russia," *PCWorld*, June 10, 2014, http://tinyurl.com/qxn9lde.

84. William Neuman, "Venezuelan officers Linked to Colombian Cocaine Traffickers," *The New York Times*, July 28, 2014, http://tinyurl.com/n3o4e9t.

85. Quoted in Ray Sanchez, "Aruba releases Venezuelan ex-general wanted in U.S.," CNN, July 28, 2014, http://tinyurl.com/mq7hjfx.

86. Kiener, "Wildlife Smuggling," *op. cit.*

87. Quoted in "African leaders in Washington: How Do We Win the War on Poaching?" *The Dodo*, Aug. 7, 2014, http://tinyurl.com/kzjpwxo; Juliet Eilperin, "Obama praises U.S.-Africa summit as an 'extraordinary event,' " *The Washington Post*, Aug. 6, 2014, http://tinyurl.com/m6tdd4j.

88. David J. Hayes, "Illegal Wildlife Trafficking and the U.S.-Africa Summit," *National Geographic* (blog), Aug. 6, 2014, http://tinyurl.com/okx532k.

89. Suzanne Goldenberg, "US to destroy ivory stocks in effort to stop illegal elephant poaching," *The Guardian*, Sept. 9, 2013, http://tinyurl.com/qg5ab6e.

90. Hayes, "Illegal Wildlife Trafficking," *op. cit.*; "African Leaders in Washington," *op. cit.*

91. "National Strategy for Combating Wildlife Trafficking," The White House, February, 2014, http://tinyurl.com/mm2fw3a.

92. "Law Enforcement Stories and News Releases," U.S. Fish and Service, (varied dates), http://tinyurl.com/k4fr2dp.

93. "Ringleaders of International Rhino Smuggling Conspiracy Sentenced in New Jersey To 70 Months in Prison," U.S. Attorney's Office, District of New Jersey, May 27, 2014, http://tinyurl.com/lepnc56.

94. Quoted in "U.S.-Africa summit on wildlife poaching addresses Asian demand," Agence France-Presse (*South China Morning Post*), Aug. 7, 2014, http://tinyurl.com/kgxdn2x.

95. "Trafficking for Organ Trade," United Nations, undated, http://tinyurl.com/o7bn5hd; Kevin Sack, "Transplant Brokers in Israel Lure Desperate Kidney Patients to Costa Rica," *The New York Times*, Aug. 17, 2014, http://tinyurl.com/mldhslg.

96. "Briefing on the Trafficking in Persons Report 2014," *op. cit.*

97. Martine Geller, "Big Tobacco squares up as EU rules aim to track every cigarette," Reuters, June 18, 2014, http://tinyurl.com/m443vrf.

BIBLIOGRAPHY

Selected Sources

Books

Andreas, Peter, *Smuggler Nation: How Illegal Trade Made America*, Oxford University Press, 2013.
A Brown University political scientist concludes that transnational crime is far from a new phenomenon in the United States.

Miklaucic, Michael, and Jacqueline Brewer, eds., *Convergence: Illicit Networks and National Security in the Age of Globalization*, National Defense University Press, 2013, www.ndufoundation.org/file/pdf-test/Convergence.pdf.
National security-oriented researchers analyze ties between international criminals and religious extremists.

Naím, Moisés, *Illicit: How Smugglers, Traffickers and Counterfeiters are Hijacking the Global Economy*, Anchor Books, 2005.
The then-editor of Foreign Policy magazine argues that transnational criminals are ahead of governments and legitimate businesses in technology and trade expertise.

Naylor, R.T., *Counterfeit Crime: Criminal Profits, Terror Dollars, and Nonsense*, McGill-Queen's University Press, 2014.

A professor of economics at Montreal's McGill University who has long specialized in black markets, smuggling and money laundering questions the ideas and information underlying anti-transnational crime enforcement.

Shelley, Louise I., *Dirty Entanglements: Corruption, Crime, and Terrorism*, Cambridge University Press, 2014.
A crime scholar examines links between transnational crime and terrorist networks.

Articles

Blue, Violet, "CryptoLocker's crimewave: A trial of millions in laundered Bitcoin," *ZDNet*, Dec. 22, 2013, http://tinyurl.com/njymdlh.
A reporter for a computer security publication provides a detailed account of how hackers last year held computer users' data hostage.

Callimachi, Rukmini, "Paying Ransoms, Europe Bankrolls Qaeda," *The New York Times*, July 29, 2014, http://tinyurl.com/k8xa8az.
An investigative reporter says European governments pay hefty sums for kidnapped citizens, thus financing terrorists.

Carvajal, Doreen, "Swiss Banks' Tradition of Secrecy Clashes With Quests Abroad for Disclosure," *The New York Times*, July 8, 2014, http://tinyurl.com/nzr83u5.
Swiss bankers used techniques familiar to spies and crooks in recruiting clients interested in shielding their assets, a Europe-based correspondent reports.

Cawley, Margaret, "Phone Tap Shows US — El Salvador MS13 Connections," *InSight Crime*, Oct. 29, 2013, http://tinyurl.com/n4wlepd.
One of the major street gangs terrorizing Central America closely coordinates its activities, including extortion, with its U.S. branch, according to a website specializing in Latin American crime analysis.

Gilman, Nils, "The Twin Insurgency," *The American Interest*, June 15, 2014, http://tinyurl.com/qh2d3yc.

An associate chancellor at the University of California, Berkeley, argues that both criminals and the wealthy pressure governments in order to avoid taxes and regulation.

Perlroth, Nicole, and David Gelles, "Russian Hackers Amass Over a Billion Internet Passwords," *The New York Times*, Aug. 5, 2014, http://tinyurl.com/qas8ovb.
Technology reporters disclosed a security firm's conclusion that Russian cyber-crooks had penetrated more than 400,000 websites to steal user names and passwords.

Reports and Studies

"Comprehensive Study on Cybercrime," United Nations Office on Drugs and Crime, February 2013, http://tinyurl.com/nrxbrtl.
The world's primary anti-transnational crime monitoring agency concludes (in a report formally still in draft form) that the borderless nature of global interconnectedness is hampering anti-cybercrime enforcement.

"Elephants in the Dust: The African Elephant Crisis," United Nations Environmental Programme, *et al.*, 2013, http://tinyurl.com/qzmpntr.
Four U.N. and nongovernmental organizations report on the devastating effects of ivory trafficking on Africa's rapidly dwindling elephant population.

"Estimating Illicit Financial Flows Resulting From Drug Trafficking and Other Transnational Organized Crimes," United Nations Office on Drugs and Crime, October 2011, http://tinyurl.com/p64lrda.
The agency estimates total revenue from transnational crime, while acknowledging such statistics are problematic.

Miraglia, Paula, Rolando Ochoa and Ivan Briscoe, "Transnational organised crime and fragile states," Organization for Economic Cooperation and Development, October 2012, http://tinyurl.com/qef2zuy.
A Paris-based international economic monitoring organization says transnational crime poses grave dangers to unstable countries but argues that repressive countermeasures are unproductive.

For More Information

Black Market Watch, Geneva, Switzerland; www.black marketwatch.org. Think tank that is developing methods for gauging the magnitude of illicit trade.

Brookings Institution, 1775 Massachusetts Ave., N.W., Washington, DC 20036; 202-797-6000; www.brookings .edu/research/topics/crime. Think tank that studies, among other things, cyber-piracy and anti-money laundering strategies.

Insight Crime, Center for Latin American and Latino Studies, American University, 4400 Massachusetts Ave., N.W., Washington DC 20016; 202-885-6178; www .insightcrime.org. U.S. office of a Medellín, Colombia-based site that reports and analyzes Latin American crime news and trends.

Institute for Security & Development Policy, Västra finnbodavägen 2, 131 30 Nacka, Sweden; 46 (0) 8-41056960; www.isdp.eu/issues/organized-crime.html.

Stockholm-based nongovernmental research center that studies transnational crime.

Terrorism, Transnational Crime and Corruption Center, George Mason University, 3351 Fairfax Dr., MS3B1, Arlington, VA 22201; 703-993-9757; http://policy-tracc .gmu.edu. Think tank that publishes research on international crime.

Transnational Threats Project, Center for Strategic and International Studies, 1616 Rhode Island Ave., N.W., Washington, DC 20036; 202-887-0200; http://csis.org/ program/transnational-threats-project. National-security think tank that studies transnational crime, especially its connections to armed extremism.

United Nations Office On Drugs and Crime (UNODC), Vienna International Centre, Wagramer Strasse 5, A 1400 Vienna, Austria; 43-1-26060; www.unodoc.org. Publishes major studies on the scope and revenue of transnational crime.

6

Resurgent Russia

Brian Beary

Demonstrators in Ukraine's capital, Kiev, protest on Dec. 7, 2013, after President Viktor Yanukovych backed out of a trade deal with the European Union, reportedly under pressure from Russian President Vladimir Putin. Moscow wants Ukraine to join the Eurasian Economic Union, a Russian-dominated free-trade coalition. Clashes in Ukraine between police and protesters have turned increasingly violent, and fears are mounting that the country may be on the brink of civil war. On Jan. 28, the prime minister and cabinet resigned, and restrictions on political protest imposed weeks earlier were rescinded.

From *CQ Researcher*,
February 7, 2014;
updated January 2015, February 2016.

O n a visit to Moldova in September 2013, Russian Deputy Prime Minister Dmitry Rogozin did not mince words. "Energy supplies are important in the runup to winter," he told his hosts. "I hope you won't freeze."

Rogozin's words were a veiled threat, say experts on the region, implying that if the former Soviet republic signs the major pacts that it had just negotiated with the European Union (EU), Russia might cut off its gas supply.[1]

Moldova, a small, poor country in southeastern Europe, depends heavily on Russian natural gas. Nevertheless, Moldova is refusing to cave to Russian pressure — for now. But its far bigger neighbor to the north, Ukraine, also an ex-Soviet republic, is heeding Moscow's warnings. In November 2013, Ukrainian President Viktor Yanukovych decided not to continue pursuing closer ties with the EU, just days before he was due to sign an accord with the EU at a much-heralded summit in Vilnius, Lithuania, capital of yet another ex-Soviet republic. In Ukraine, ongoing mass protests against Yanukovych's move have led to the prime minister's resignation.

Still reeling from Yanukovych's abandonment, Swedish Foreign Minister Carl Bildt, whose country is one of the 28 EU members, predicted that Ukraine's decision would lead it "not west or east, but down," adding, "it's a fairly brutal game being played" by Russia.[2]

The tug-of-war between Russia and the EU over Moldova and Ukraine has been going on since 2008, when the EU began enticing Russia's neighbors into its economic sphere via its Eastern Partnership initiative. The new program promised Eastern European countries access to Western Europe's huge market if they first made their governments more efficient, democratic and less corrupt.

VIKTOR DRACHEV/AFP/Getty Images

Although the EU did not offer them full membership, it didn't exclude the possibility.

Russia was always suspicious of the Eastern Partnership but began to ramp up its opposition in late 2013, apparently after realizing that newly concluded EU trade pacts with Russia's former neighbors could pull the post-Soviet nations irrevocably into the EU's orbit. "Moscow has rediscovered the real nature of the EU: the prospect that one day Ukraine [along with the other ex-Soviet Union countries] . . . could begin to work its way up the rankings of corruption or doing business and, with time, even outdistance Russia," according to Olaf Osica, director of the Centre for Eastern Studies in Warsaw, Poland.[3]

The Russians are especially wary of the EU initiative because in 2004 and 2007, 10 former Central and East European communist nations joined the EU, and many of them now have strained relations with Moscow. In fact, several of those nations are the most ardent supporters of the Eastern Partnership. And nations such as Poland and Lithuania have painful memories of Russian domination during the Cold War era. Having fought so hard for independence from Russia, they look at Russia's economic revival in the 2000s and early 2010s and its growing geopolitical activism with unease. Such strained relations are the clearest illustration of Moscow's simmering tensions with the West that are being triggered by the increasingly assertive stance that Russia has taken in its neighborhood and beyond.

Russia strongly denies that it pressures its neighbors. Alexey Drobinin, senior counselor at the Russian Embassy in Washington, says, for instance, that a 2013 Russian ban on imports of Moldovan wine and spirits is justified on "very hard evidence" that it's needed to protect Russian consumers from unsafe food products. "There was no political calculation involved," he says.[4]

But Moldova's government sees things differently. "This is a crucial time for my country," said Moldovan Foreign Minister Natalia Gherman. While her governing party wants to join the EU, the Communist Party — the main opposition — sides with Russia, she said. The communists prefer that Moldova reject the EU and instead join the new Russian-sponsored Eurasian Economic Union (EEU), a free-trade and economic coalition similar to the EU, but which would be dominated by Russia. Gherman dismissed the EEU as "economic and political nonsense." The EU's market of 500 million people is far bigger and better than anything Russia could offer with its nascent free-trade zone, she said.[5]

Moldova continues to have a pro-EU government but one that faces persistent opposition to this stance from the signficant pro-Russian segment of the population.[6]

Gunnar Wiegand, a senior EU diplomat, said it was "regrettable" that Russia has wrongly concluded that the new EU trade pacts would harm Russian interests. "It has become almost an obsession" for Russia, said Wiegand, who negotiated many of the accords.[7]

While Russia is no longer a superpower, it remains a significant international economic force, with its strength heavily concentrated in the energy sector. It is the world's top exporter of natural gas, No. 2 in oil and No. 3 in coal.[8] In fact, the EU gets about 30 percent of its oil, gas and coal imports from Russia. But Russia relies even more on the EU; European Union countries buy about 80 percent of Russia's gas exports, 70 percent of its oil exports and 50 percent of its coal exports.[9]

"We are more dependent on the EU than the EU is dependent on us," said Mikhail Kalugin, head of the economic section at the Russian Embassy in Washington.[10]

Beyond Europe, Russia has elevated itself from the marginal player it became after the Soviet Union collapsed in 1991 to a power that is now increasingly shaping events in geopolitical hotspots, notably the Middle East. For instance, Russia brokered a deal in 2013 to avert a U.S.- and French-led military strike on Syria after Syrian leader Bashar al-Assad allegedly launched a gas attack on his own people in the Syrian civil war, killing some 1,400.[11] In September 2015, it launched airstrikes in Syria, claiming it was joining the Western-led coalition to defeat the Islamic State (ISIS) terrorist group which has gained a foothold there.[12]

U.S.-Russian relations today are at their lowest ebb since the Cold War. In addition to supporting the EU in the struggle for Eastern Europe, the United States has condemned Russia's worsening human rights record under President Vladimir Putin, including a 2013 law banning "homosexual propaganda." Putin also has irked Washington by giving temporary political asylum to Edward Snowden, a former National Security Agency (NSA) contractor who in the summer of 2013 revealed that the NSA was conducting mass surveillance

Russia's Neighbors Lean Toward Europe or China

Several former members of the Soviet bloc say Moscow is pressuring them to join the Eurasian Economic Union (EEU), a free-trade coalition patterned after the European Union (EU) but dominated by Russia. Protests broke out in Ukraine in November 2015 after its government reneged on a commitment to sign trade pacts with the EU, reportedly after Russia pressured Ukraine to join the EEU instead. Russia denies pressuring its neighbors, but experts say the EEU is designed to keep Russia's former satellite states out of EU's economic grasp.

Economic Coalition Membership of Russia and Its Neighbors

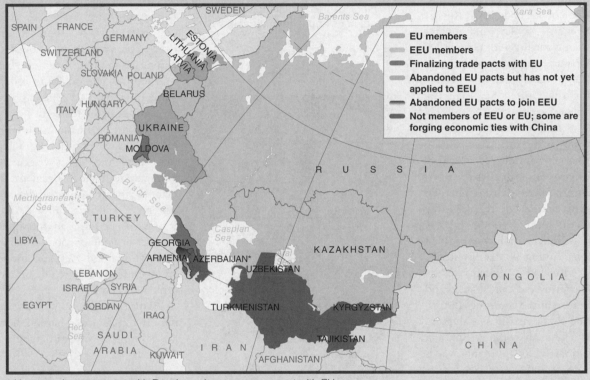

Legend:
- EU members
- EEU members
- Finalizing trade pacts with EU
- Abandoned EU pacts but has not yet applied to EEU
- Abandoned EU pacts to join EEU
- Not members of EEU or EU; some are forging economic ties with China

* Has security agreement with Russia and energy agreement with EU

programs on U.S. and foreign citizens' phone and e-mail records as well as on the communications of foreign heads of state.[13]

The eruption of militant Islamist violence in the Middle East following the 2011 Arab Spring uprisings — including in Syria — has spurred Russia to become more assertive in the region, given that its own southern border is a hotbed of Islamist-inspired terrorism, both inside Russia (in Chechnya and Dagestan) and in nearby countries such as Uzbekistan. And with the United States

having completed the drawdown of its combat troops from Afghanistan in December 2014, Russia has boosted its military presence among its southern neighbors that flank Afghanistan, fearing that Afghanistan will again become a haven for global jihadists.[14]

The world's eyes were on Russia in February 2014 when it hosted the Winter Olympic Games in the Black Sea resort town of Sochi. There were fears of terrorist attacks following suicide bombings, carried out by suspected Islamist terrorists, of a train station and trolley bus in the Russian city of Volgograd in December 2015 that killed 34 people and wounded many more.[15] President Putin ramped up security, determined to avoid any more embarrassing incidents or attacks and the Games proceeded without incident.[16]

Russia's spotty human-rights record has come under scrutiny. In a not-so-subtle jab at Russia's new anti-gay law that equates homosexuality with pedophilia, Obama put two openly gay athletes in the delegation representing the United States in the opening ceremony at Sochi.[17]

Russia's relations with China, which had grown frosty during Russia's communist era, have improved since they both embraced capitalism. The two giant nations are trading more manufactured goods and raw materials and have resolved longstanding border disputes.

Fiona Hill, director of the Center on the United States and Europe at the Brookings Institution think tank in Washington, says China has eclipsed Russia in industrial output and wants Russian raw materials for its manufacturing sector. China is busy increasing trade and investments in Central Asian markets that were once part of the Soviet Union, especially Turkmenistan and Uzbekistan. Kazakhstan, Kyrgyzstan and Tajikistan, however, retain close ties to Russia as well.[18]

Meanwhile, China's economic influence in Russia's vast Siberia region is growing as Russian residents emigrate westward and

Russia Trails U.S., China on Growth

Russia's total output of goods and services — its gross domestic product (GDP) — and its GDP growth rate in 2015 trailed those of the United States and China. However, Russia's GDP per capita was almost twice that of China's. Much of Russia's wealth comes from exports of its abundant natural gas.

Economic Data for Russia, U.S. and China, 2015

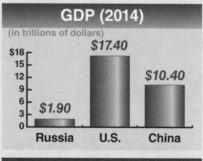

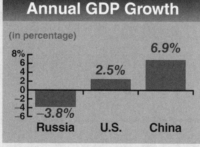

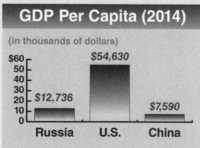

Source: World Bank, Global Economic Prospects, January 2016.

China boosts its investment in the region, often bringing in Chinese migrant workers in the process. China has provided $25 billion to extend Russia's Eastern Siberia Pacific Ocean pipeline to Asia in return for guaranteed supplies of Siberian crude oil.[20]

To the south, Russia and energy-hungry India have been strengthening economic ties. The two countries have collaborated on Russian projects to export liquefied natural gas to India. Russia also has sold military equipment to India, while India has sold generic pharmaceuticals to the Russians.[21]

In addition, Russia has forged closer links with Brazil, with joint projects planned on cybersecurity and space technology. Brazil also is planning to buy Russian air defense systems.[22] And in Southeast Asia, Russia is emerging as an important supplier of military goods, notably to Myanmar and Vietnam, and is an investor in offshore oil and gas exploration projects.[23]

As Russia increasingly asserts itself in its region and beyond, here are some key questions being debated:

Is Russia trying to recreate the Soviet bloc?

The Russian government strongly denies that it aims to revive the defunct Soviet Union. Drobinin at the Russian Embassy says unequivocally: "No. It is not possible to recreate what existed 25 years ago, and there is no intention to do so."

Lee Feinstein, U.S. ambassador to Poland from 2009-12 and now a fellow at the German Marshall Fund of the United States, says,

"Circumstances today are completely different than in Soviet times. Putin is no democrat, and he is consolidating his power, but Russia is not a Stalinist totalitarian state. There is greater scope for individuals" — for instance, to travel and do business.

Drobinin says that since Putin was re-elected president in 2012 (he was president from 2000-08 and prime minister from 1999-2000 and 2008-12), he has actively promoted the Eurasian Economic Union. "We see our closest neighbors as our closest partners," Drobinin says. "We treat them as equals and do not interfere in their domestic affairs."

Andrey Slepnev, trade minister at the Eurasian Economic Commission (the EEU's rule-making body), has also sought to dispel what he called an "urban legend" that "we are trying to reconstitute the Soviet Union." The EEU is an economic rather than a political initiative, Slepnev said during a 2013 visit to Washington.[24]

A Russian journalist who asks not to be named because his media outlet bars him from giving on-the-record interviews, says, "Russia does not wish to be a military superpower again. But it would like to play a bigger role in the world than it did in the 1990s," particularly in its immediate neighborhood. "Russia is behaving no differently than the U.S. does in Latin America" when Washington concludes trade agreements with countries that include provisions not directly linked to trade, he argues.

But Archil Gegeshidze, the Georgian ambassador to the United States, believes Russia goes way beyond what countries typically seek through trade agreements. He says Russia is trying to create various groupings of former Soviet republics, with Russia as the center of gravity. Whether it is the Commonwealth of Independent States (CIS), a group of nine former Soviet bloc countries set up in the dying days of the Soviet Union to retain some form of ties between those nations, or the newer EEU initiative, "the idea is the same," and "it is always a political project."

Georgia, which was the last country to join the CIS, did so under pressure, Gegeshidze says, and formally left the CIS in 2009 shortly after a Georgia-Russia war fought over control of Georgia's secessionist regions, Abkhazia and South Ossetia. The two countries have not had diplomatic relations since then, although talks are ongoing to restore ties.[25]

Asked if Russia is resurrecting its past political union with its neighbors, Brookings' Hill, a British national who has lived in Russia and speaks Russian, says, "It depends what you mean by the Soviet bloc. If you mean a rigid political and security bloc, the answer is no. But Russia does want to retain its influence in the Soviet region." For instance, she says, Russia is insisting that its neighbors not join any other economic or political bloc such as the EU Eastern Partnership. Russia argues that being part of both trading blocs simultaneously is incompatible because of how trade agreements work, such as having a common customs code.

Armen Sahakyan, founder and president of the Eurasian Research Analysis Institute, a new Armenia-based think tank, cites Russia's neighbor Belarus as evidence that Russia is not trying to create a new political union. Belarus for years has been pushing the idea of a reconfigured Soviet Union, but Putin has shown little interest in the concept, he says. "Russia wants something more similar to the EU," he says.

But Jacek Saryusz-Wolski, a Polish member of the European Parliament, believes Russia is trying to create a "closed economic union" similar to the Comecon, the Soviet trading bloc that existed during the Cold War between the Soviet Union and Central and Eastern European nations. The new EEU will be "very protectionist" with high tariffs and nontariff barriers against the rest of the world, he predicts. "But in the next stage Russia will go for a political union just like the USSR," he says.

If Russia really does intend to recreate the Soviet Union, the growing economic might of China could derail its plans. "When the Russians look eastward they are fighting a losing battle if they are fighting at all," said the late Alexandros Petersen, an adviser at the Woodrow Wilson International Center for Scholars in Washington. Petersen edited a Web forum on China's presence in Central Asia until he was killed in the Jan. 17, 2014, Taliban bombing of a Lebanese restaurant in Kabul, Afghanistan.[27] China has concluded multiple trade and investment deals with Kazakhstan, Kyrgyzstan, Turkmenistan and Uzbekistan, including roads, railways, pipelines, power plants and refineries. Such deals are "completely changing the game in the region," Petersen said.[28]

By contrast, Russian investment in Central Asia is "almost nothing," Petersen said. Leaders in Central Asia tend to prefer deals with China, he said, because China

Russia Faces Backlash Over Immigration Policies

Millions of migrants from former Soviet republics fill low-skilled jobs.

Thousands of Russians took to the streets of Moscow in October 2013 in violent anti-immigrant protests sparked by the fatal stabbing of a Russian man by an allegedly illegal immigrant from Azerbaijan. Immigrants' stores were looted, more than a thousand rioters and 200 illegal immigrants were detained and Moscow Mayor Sergei Sobyanin called for "radical decisions" by the Russian government to address immigration policy.

Russia may no longer have a political union with its neighbors as in the Soviet era, but that has not stopped several million workers from the former Soviet republics from flocking to Russia in search of higher-paying jobs.[1]

Many ordinary Russians resent the immigrants. An opinion poll from summer 2013 found that 53 percent wanted tighter immigration laws.[2] And anti-immigrant sentiment is on the rise. For example, 70 percent oppose migrant workers taking catering jobs, up from 54 percent in 2006.[3]

But with a relatively low birth rate, high death rate and an unemployment rate of about 5 percent, Russia has a labor shortage. To fill jobs, it relies on labor from poorer nations in the former Soviet Union. Because of their historical ties with Russia, these workers can enter the country and find work, many without an official work permit.

Chinese employers investing in Russia have brought in thousands of Chinese workers, who, unlike Central Asian migrants, require visas to enter the country.[4]

Many Central Asian women have taken fast-food jobs that Russian students previously held. And central Asian men from countries such as Tajikistan and Kyrgyzstan fill thousands of construction jobs. Armen Sahakyan, executive director of the Washington branch of the Eurasian Research Analysis Institute, an Armenia-based think tank, says many workers employed to build facilities for the Winter Olympic Games in Sochi were non-Russians.

Russia also has experienced an influx of ethnic Russians from other regions, especially Central Asia. They are mainly descendants of people who emigrated there in the 1700s and 1800s, when the Russian Empire was expanding southward. When the republics where they live emerged as independent nations in the early 1990s, the new countries made their native languages, not Russian, the official tongue. This has made it harder for Russian-speaking residents to prosper — notably in government, where the native tongue is often required.[5]

Since a separatist conflict erupted in eastern Ukraine in April 2014, led by pro-Russian Ukrainians opposed to the new government's pro-Western orientation, there has been a large influx of refugees from this region into Russia, with more than 97,000 Ukrainians granted temporary protection in Russia in the first half of 2015.[19]

Some migrants come from countries that have strained relations with Russia. A prime example is Georgia, which fought a war with Russia in 2008 over Georgia's two separatist

is more respectful of their sovereignty than Russia. The five Central Asian republics — Kazakhstan, Kyrgyzstan, Tajikistan, Turkmenistan and Uzbekkistan (the so-called 'Stans) — were fully integrated into the Soviet Union until its dissolution in 1991.

Is Russia helping to bring peace to the Middle East?

Russia unquestionably is taking a more active role in the major Middle Eastern conflict zones — Afghanistan, Egypt, Iran and Syria. But experts disagree on whether Moscow is trying to bring peace to the region.

The Russian Embassy's Drobinin insists that it is. Russia has been "very cooperative" with the United States on Syria and Iran, he says. "We have played an important role in creating the conditions to settle the issues in both cases." Russia is motivated by "our opposition to the rise of violent extremism," he adds, and while "we do not take sides" in the five-year Syrian civil war, Moscow believes the Assad regime "is a legitimate government."

regions, Abkhazia and South Ossetia, which Russia supports. Of a total population of 5 million Georgians, an estimated[1] million work in Russia, says Archil Gegeshidze, the country's U.S. ambassador. Most went to Russia in the 1990s when the Georgian economy was failing. Many began trading agricultural products. "Georgians in Russia tend not to assimilate as easily as some other groups," Gegeshidze says. "They like to keep their ties to Georgia."

Fiona Hill, director of the Center on the United States and Europe at the Brookings Institution in Washington, sees similarities between Russia and the United States in that migrant workers in both countries tend to come from poorer regions and take manual jobs. For example, landscaping is a niche for migrants in Russia as it is for Latino migrants in the United States.

But Hill is quick to highlight one major difference. "Russia is more strategic than the U.S. in the way it uses immigration in its foreign policy," she says. For example, she says, Russia uses migrant workers' remittances — money they send back home — to advance its geopolitical goals. As petty revenge against Georgia and Moldova for aligning themselves with the European Union (EU) and NATO, Russia has threatened to block Georgians and Moldovans from using the banking system to wire money home, Hill says. Russia distrusts NATO and wants the former Soviet republics to reject the EU and instead join Russia's nascent free-trade zone, the Eurasian Economic Union.

Remittances from migrant workers comprise about 12 percent of Armenia's gross domestic product (GDP), Sahakyan says. Tajikistan, a small, poor former Soviet republic, has some 900,000 migrant workers in Russia. Their $3.6 billion in remittances in 2012 accounted for half of Tajikistan's GDP that year.[6]

Some Russians want immigration policies to give preference to ethnic Russians and warn that allowing so many migrants from overwhelmingly Muslim Central Asia into the country could foment Islamist terrorism.[7] Russian President Vladimir Putin said in summer 2013 that immigrants from the former Soviet Union were able to assimilate. "On the whole," he said, "our policy in the migration sphere should be more flexible, certainly ensuring the rights of our indigenous citizens, but it should be more flexible so to attract labor resources at least."[8]

— Brian Beary

[1] "Illegal migrants may be banned from entering Russia for 10 years," Xinhua General News Service, April 4, 2013, http://en.ria.ru/russia/20130404/180446 936.html.

[2] "More than half of Russians support toughening of immigration laws in relation to citizens of CIS — research" Central Asian News Services, Aug. 15, 2013, http://bnews.kz/en/news/post/153656/.

[3] "Russians develop hard feelings towards immigrants — poll," Central Asia General Newswire, Aug. 1, 2013.

[4] Evgeny Kuzmin, "Migrant Workers Finding Opportunity in Russian Far East," Inter Press Service News Agency, Aug. 6, 2013, www.ipsnews.net/2013/08/ migrant-workers-finding-opportunity-in-russian-far-east/.

[5] See sidebar on ethnic Russians of Central Asia in Brian Beary, "Emerging Central Asia," *CQ Global Researcher*, Jan. 17, 2012, pp. 29-56.

[6] "Ratification of Russian military base deal provides Tajikistan with important security guarantees," *Jane's Intelligence Weekly*, Oct. 2, 2013, www.janes. com/article/27898/ratification-of-russian-military-base-deal-provides-tajikistan-with-important-security-guarantees.

[7] "Russian analysts: immigrants, guest workers fertile ground for radical Islamism," Interfax News Agency, May 14, 2013, http://interfaxreli.customers.ru/?act=news&div=10454.

[8] "Putin says Russia needs more flexible approach to immigration," BBC Worldwide Monitoring, June 11, 2013.

Russia's pivotal role in brokering the September 2013 deal that persuaded Assad to give up his chemical weapons shows that "we have achieved something," he argues. And Russia, along with the United States, is the key mediator in the "Geneva II" peace conference that began in Switzerland that aims to end the brutal civil war in Syria, which has killed hundreds of thousands of people and created millions of refugees.

But Saryusz-Wolski, of the European Parliament, says the chemical weapons deal that Russia cobbled together

is "a trap" that gives "a free hand to Assad to continue in power." He rejects the idea that Russia wants peace in the Middle East. Moscow's true goal is to "keep things boiling" so oil and gas prices remain high, which suits Russia, being that it is such a big energy supplier, he argues. Since the fall of 2014, a sharp and continuous decline in global oil prices has hit Russia hard, sending its economy into a deep recession.[29]

Armenian scholar Sahakyan suggests a different motivation behind Russia's support for Assad. "Russia is

Europe, China Are Key Russian Trading Partners

Despite trying to steer its neighbors away from the European Union trading alliance and into its Eurasian Economic Union, Russia remains heavily dependent on trade with Europe. Germany is Russia's second-largest supplier of imports (behind China), which totaled $314 billion in 2012. Machinery and transportation equipment, chemicals and agricultural commodities top its list of imports. The Netherlands, Germany and Italy are among the top four biggest buyers of Russian commodities, with natural gas and other fuel, metals and chemicals comprising the biggest shares of Russia's $525 billion in exports in 2012.

Russia's Top Trade Partners in 2014[26]

Share of Exports (total exports = $433 billion)		Share of Imports (total imports = $254 billion)	
Netherlands	13.7%	China	17.8%
China	7.5	Germany	11.5
Germany	7.5	United States	6.5
Italy	7.2	Italy	4.4
Turkey	4.9	Japan	3.8
Japan	4.0	France	3.8
South Korea	3.7	South Korea	3.2
Poland	3.2	United Kingdom	2.7
United Kingdom	2.3	Poland	2.5
Finland	2.3	Turkey	2.3
United States	2.1	Netherlands	1.8

Source: Federal State Statistics Service of the Russian Federation

professed right to retain nuclear weapons to deter any potential attack from Iran. But later in the year, he seemed to reverse course, calling on Israel to dismantle its nuclear arsenal. The Israeli news magazine *Jerusalem Report* suggested that Putin's U-turn was him pandering to "Russia's allies in the Shi'ite axis [to] convince them to remain loyal."[30]

Many experts say Russia's opposition to Islamist militancy in the Middle East is sincere and stems from the instability generated in Russia by terrorist attacks by militants from the Caucasus region. Separatist wars in Chechnya in the 1990s caused the death, injury or displacement of 150,000 people, including 8,000 Russians.[31] Russia has been very willing to help neighboring governments in Central Asia to suppress radical Islam — for instance by clamping down on groups such as the Islamic Movement of Uzbekistan.

"Yes, Russia wants peace and stability in the Middle East. It does not want the blowback from the Sunni Muslim uprisings that stemmed from the Arab Spring," says Brookings' Hill. Moscow would like "strong, secular, authoritarian leaders" who serve as a "nice lid to put on" social tensions and conflicts in the region.

"They see democracy as messy and being at the root of all the problems there [in the Middle East] today," she adds. That explains why Russia welcomed the overthrow of Egypt's democratically elected Muslim Brotherhood government in a coup in July 2013 and concluded arms deals with the Egyptian military junta that deposed Mohamed Morsi, the Islamist leader.

According to Feinstein of the German Marshall Fund, Russia's role across the region has been "mixed." Sometimes, he says, Russia has been "a very clear impediment to addressing regional concerns." In Syria, Moscow has gone "from being very obstructionist to being pragmatic."

still a naval power and would like a base in the Mediterranean," he says. Syria's western coastline is on the Mediterranean, and Russia has maintained a naval facility in the port city of Tartus since the early 1970s. While Russia's role in the Middle East had been decreasing until recently, he adds, Russia now wants to stem its waning influence in the region.

Georgian Ambassador Gegeshidze agrees with Sahakyan that Russia's primary interest in the Middle East is neither peace nor stability but "access to the warmer seas," namely the Mediterranean Sea and Indian Ocean, which he notes has been Russia's desire since tsarist times (1547-1917).

Putin has sent mixed signals in his dealings with arch enemies Iran and Israel. Despite historically having been more aligned with Iran, Putin for most of 2013 tried to improve relations with Israel, promising to support its

Despite the chemical weapons deal, for which Russia was widely praised by the West, during most of 2011-13, Russia was strongly criticized for blocking U.N. Security Council sanctions against Assad.[32] Meanwhile, Russia has been "cooperative" in Afghanistan, Feinstein says, by providing a corridor for NATO to move troops and supplies into the war-torn country. And in Iran, Moscow "has been pragmatic so far," he says, by supporting an international deal finalized in July 2015 that will end trade sanctions on Iran imposed over its nuclear program in return for Iran reining in the program.[33]

Russia's overall strategy, Feinstein says, is that "it wants allies to the extent that it can have them" to maintain influence globally.

Should the United States take a tougher stance with Russia?

Views are sharply divided on how the United States should respond to a Russia that is increasingly flexing its muscles on the global stage, in particular in Eastern Europe and the Middle East.

According to Sharyl Cross, a Russian foreign policy scholar and director of the Kozmetsky Center at St. Edward's University in Austin, Texas, "we should scale down our expectations" of the relationship. It is wrong to "look at everything as a new chapter in the Cold War," she said, because it remains unclear what direction Russia is actually taking.[34]

She advocated a pragmatic approach in which the two powers collaborate closely in the big regional hotspots such as the Middle East. Cooperation on defense policy is even possible, she maintained. For instance, the West "should take more seriously" former President Dmitry Medvedev's proposal for NATO and Russia to jointly conclude a pan-European Security Treaty, she said. First floated in 2008, the proposal gained little traction in the United States.

U.S. Secretary of State John Kerry has also called for pragmatism. "Russia and the U.S. are in full agreement on a number of points" in the Syrian peace talks, he said, specifically that "there isn't a military solution." Kerry and Russian Foreign Minister Sergey Lavrov agreed that al Qaeda-linked rebel groups in Syria had no place at the "Geneva II" peace talks, which have been taking place for several years without any breakthrough.[35]

Armenian scholar Sahakyan says it does not make a lot of sense for the United States to get tougher with Russia. Imposing economic sanctions "would make little difference because there is so little U.S.-Russian trade," he says. On the other hand, he says, Russia can help the United States fight Islamist extremists in the Middle East.

In Europe, however, Russia has opposed NATO plans — in the works since 2009 — to install missile interceptors and radar equipment across Europe in such places as Poland and Romania, which were once part of the pro-Soviet bloc. Sahakyan says NATO should realize that "there will be a backlash" if it ignores Russia's opposition to the NATO plan. Russia responded already, placing missiles in Kaliningrad, a small Russian region wedged between NATO member states Lithuania and Poland.[36] "I don't think taking a tougher line with Russia will achieve much," Sahakyan says.

But Saryusz-Wolski, the Polish member of the European Parliament, strongly disapproves of America's current pragmatic approach toward Russia, accusing Obama of moving "too much into the realm of *realpolitik* in dealing with Russia and away from a values-based policy." Referring to Obama's so-called strategic pivot to Asia, he says, it would be better if the United States "stopped withdrawing from Europe." However, he concedes that the prevailing view in Washington "that Europe should count on itself more . . . is in a way right, but it makes Europe feel less comfortable."[37]

Recent Russian military maneuvers in Europe worry Urmas Reinsalu, Estonia's minister of defense, who noted that Russia has doubled its strategic weapons in Europe during the past four years. He urged the United States to hold onto the nuclear weapons it still keeps in Belgium, Italy, the Netherlands and Turkey as a deterrent to Russia.[38]

Georgian Ambassador Gegeshidze also is in the get-tough-with-Russia camp. "In Georgia, we have been watching Russia for centuries, and our experience prompts us to think that Russia only listens to tougher language," he says. "Russia can never be a genuine strategic partner of the U.S. because, for that, you need to share values," whereas Russia is growing increasingly authoritarian.

However, "the U.S. does not have a lot of carrots and sticks to use" with Russia because its relations are primarily security-based, rather than trade-based, says Brookings' Hill. "The only way for the U.S. to get tough with Russia is to get closer to the EU, because the EU does a huge amount of trade with Russia." Since the summer of 2013, the U.S. has been negotiating a free-trade agreement with the EU, which is its biggest trade partner.[39]

Hill says the EU and United States can and should together take a tougher stance against Russia for bullying its neighbors into joining the EEU. And the United States does have at least one sanction at its disposal, she says, namely visa bans. There has been a massive increase in the number of special "government official" passports issued by the Russian government in recent years, she says. Moscow is very keen for Russians to attain visa-free travel wherever possible, so the West does have some leverage in that regard, she says.

The United States could also object to what Hill calls Russia's misuse of World Trade Organization (WTO) food safety rules to punish its neighbors by banning their products from Russian markets. For instance, shortly after Moscow banned Moldovan wine and spirits, and just days before the November 2013 EU summit in Vilnius, Russia threatened to ban Polish fruit and vegetables, again on food safety grounds. Poland is one of the leading EU members supporting the free-trade deals the EU has negotiated with Georgia, Moldova, and Ukraine.[40]

Hill categorically rejects as "a complete sham" Russian officials' claims that these bans are justified on public-health grounds. Food safety standards are quite poor in Russia, she argues, citing the numerous severe bouts of food poisoning she suffered during the years she lived there.

BACKGROUND
Russia's Rise

The first Russian state, based in Kiev, the capital of modern Ukraine, emerged in the ninth century.[41] Originally a Viking settlement, Kiev was situated on a trade route from Scandinavia to Byzantium, now Istanbul.[42]

In 988 Prince Vladimir, the ruler of Kiev, adopted the Byzantine form of Christianity, planting the seed for Orthodox Christianity to become the dominant religion among Russians. Kiev developed into a major center of Christian learning in the 1000s and early 1100s. Meanwhile, two other Russian city states, Novgorod and Moscow, began to develop as economic centers.

During the Mongol invasions of Russian territories in the early 1200s, the army of Batu Khan, the grandson of Genghis Khan, plundered Kiev. The Mongols quickly established dominion over the Russians and were referred to as The Golden Horde.

During the 1300s Moscow eclipsed Kiev as the dominant Russian principality, and in 1478 Moscow's ruler, Prince Ivan III, conquered Novgorod. Moscow grew increasingly powerful in the 1500s. Defended by semi-autonomous soldiers called Cossacks, Moscow introduced an efficient tax collection system and instituted serfdom, a system of feudal dependency that forbade peasants from moving away from their lord's estate. In return for protection, some land to sustain themselves and some autonomy over their daily affairs, peasants were obliged to perform hard labor and pay taxes and were at times subject to military service.

Ivan IV, who reigned from 1533 to 1584 and was known as Ivan the Terrible, became the undisputed leader of Russia through his strong, harsh leadership and adopted the title of tsar (from the Roman word caesar).[43] Paranoid about plots against him, he was unusually cruel in suppressing perceived dissent, according to one historian, sending soldiers out on "black horses, each carrying a dog's head and a broom . . . to sniff out treachery and sweep it away. Supposed traitors were tortured or murdered."[44]

A series of weak leaders succeeded Ivan, with the next similarly strong tsar emerging in the late 1600s. Peter I, who became known as Peter the Great (1682-1725), captured the Baltic provinces from Sweden in 1709 at the Battle of Poltava. Peter established the most extensive diplomatic relations with European governments Russia had ever had until that point. He imported the best military technologies from Europe, established a new capital city, St. Petersburg, on the Baltic, and created Russia's first permanent army.

Catherine II (1762-1796) — known as Catherine the Great — conspired with Austria and Prussia to dismember Poland in the late 1700s, leading Russia to annex parts of modern-day Belarus, Lithuania, Poland and Ukraine. She also instituted a new legal code that greatly improved the effectiveness of the Russian government and introduced a new system for consulting her subjects over proposed laws, in which an expanded array of social groups was involved in the process.

CHRONOLOGY

988-1917 *Russia emerges as the world's largest country, ruled by powerful tsars.*

988 Prince Vladimir, ruler of the Russian city state of Kiev, converts to Byzantine (Orthodox) Christianity. His conversion leads to Orthodox Christianity becoming Russia's dominant religion.

1547 The ruler of Moscow, Ivan IV, known as Ivan the Terrible, is crowned tsar, marking the culmination of Moscow's emergence as the dominant Russian power.

1703 Tsar Peter the Great establishes a new capital, St. Petersburg, on the Baltic Sea.

1917 The last tsar, Nicholas II, is deposed and later murdered as the communist Bolshevik party seizes power.

1918-1991 *Russian-dominated Soviet Union industrializes and becomes one of the world's two superpowers, along with the United States.*

1922 Union of Soviet Socialist Republics (USSR) is formed as a multi-ethnic, atheistic, communist state in which Russia is the largest and most powerful republic.

1928 Soviet leader Josef Stalin launches the first of several five-year plans, which transform the USSR from a mainly agricultural to a predominantly industrial country.

1945 USSR emerges as a victor in World War II, resulting in an expansion of its territory and influence in Eastern Europe. The expansion marks the onset of the Cold War, a rivalry for global dominance between the United States and USSR.

1955 Eight communist countries of Central and Eastern Europe, including the USSR, sign the Warsaw Pact military alliance, bolstering Soviet sway over the region.

1985 New Soviet leader Mikhail Gorbachev initiates a policy of greater openness called glasnost that encourages the Warsaw Pact nations to realign themselves westward geo-politically.

1991 USSR is dissolved after the 1989 fall of the Berlin Wall and two years of protests in former Soviet republics. Fifteen sovereign republics emerge from the former Soviet Union.

1992-2014 *After an initial period of economic and political turmoil, Russia stabilizes economically and becomes more assertive on the global stage.*

1992 Russian lawmakers privatize state-owned-enterprises, resulting in the country's rapid transformation from communism to capitalism.

1999 Vladimir Putin, a senior adviser to President Boris Yeltin, is appointed prime minister of Russia, marking the beginning of his ascent to power.

2004 European Union (EU) and NATO expand to Russia's western border, and former communist bloc nations join the pro-Western economic and military alliance.

2008 Russian opposition to Georgia's bid to join NATO triggers a war that ends with Russia tightening control over Georgia's secessionist republics, Abkhazia and South Ossetia.

2010 Russia signs a new nuclear weapons reduction treaty, START, with the United States.

2012 Russia joins the World Trade Organization. . . . Putin easily wins re-election as president amid accusations from international observers that the result was pre-determined.

2013 Russia's relations with the EU deteriorate over EU plans to conclude free trade and association pacts with several former Soviet republics, including Ukraine. . . . Armenia announces it will join a Russian-sponsored customs union instead of signing a trade pact with the EU (September). . . . To avoid a U.S.-French crackdown on Syria, Russia brokers a deal whereby Syria will give up its chemical weapons arsenal. . . . Ukraine ditches its planned EU deal amid Western accusations of Russian intimidation (November).

(Continued)

(Continued)

2014 Russia hosts the Winter Olympics in Black Sea resort town of Sochi, casting a spotlight on the country's human rights record (February). . . . Russia exploits power vacuum in neighboring Ukraine by annexing Crimea (March). . . . Pro-Russian separatists in eastern Ukraine declare independent republics of Donetsk and Lugansk (April). . . . Passenger plane shot down in eastern Ukraine killing all 298 aboard and leading the EU and U.S. to impose economic sanctions on Russia (July). . . . Russia concludes agreements with China and Mongolia aimed at forging closer economic ties (August). . . . Russia signs peace agreement with EU and Ukraine in Minsk to end separatist conflict in eastern Ukraine (September). . . . Falling oil prices and sanctions cause Russian ruble's value to tumble (December)

2015 Russian-led Eurasian Economic Union (EEU) enters into force with goal of reducing trade barriers between founding members Armenia, Belarus, Kazakhstan and Russia (January 1). . . . Kyrgyzstan joins EEU (May 1). . . .

Russia involves itself in Syrian civil war by launching airstrikes against Sunni Muslim militants (September 30). . . . Islamic State terrorist group blows up Russian passenger plane in midair in Egypt, killing all 224 aboard (October 31). . . . Russian-Turkish relations fracture over Turkey's downing of a Russian military plane (November 24) on Turkey-Syria border. . . . EU extends trade sanctions on Russia until July 2016 (December 21).

2016 Russia imposes trade sanctions on Ukraine as EU-Ukraine free trade pact takes effect (January 1). . . . Russia's economy forecast to shrink 0.7 percent year-to-year, following 3.8 percent contraction in 2015 with global oil prices and value of Russian currency continuing to tumble (January). . . . Russia announces reduction in troop totals deployed to the Central Asian republic of Tajikistan (January 30).

Russia Plays Leading Role in Separatist Conflicts

In 1807 a pact with French Emperor Napoleon I gave Russia control of Finland. By this time Russia had grown into the world's largest country, stretching from the Baltic to the Black Sea and all the way to the Pacific Ocean. In the 1800s Russia extended its territory and influence in Eastern Europe, the Caucasus and the Balkans through various wars against the Ottoman Empire, which was slowly disintegrating. Around the same time, it gained control of the mainly ethnically Turkic peoples of Central Asia, wrenching the local mini-kingdoms called khanates from the British and Persians, a tussle referred to by historians as "The Great Game."[45] In the 1860s Russia expelled between 1 and 2 million Circassian people from their native western Caucasus.[46]

The completion of the Trans-Siberian Railway in 1903 boosted Russia's expanding industrial sector, which was producing a growing urban working class, from which developed socialist-oriented political parties, including the Bolsheviks and Mensheviks. A humiliating defeat for Russia in a war with newly emergent Japan in 1904-05 stymied Russia's ambition of gaining influence over Korea, Chinese Manchuria and the Far East.

That loss also helped to trigger a revolution that forced Tsar Nicholas II (1894-1917) to set up a parliament, called the Duma. During World War I (1914-1918) Russia fought on the side of France and the United Kingdom against the German-Austro-Hungarian-Turkish alliance. The Russians suffered massive casualties, leading to two revolutions in 1917 in which Nicholas was deposed and later murdered and Bolshevik leader Vladimir Lenin came to power. He established a "dictatorship of the proletariat," as advocated by the founders of Marxist political ideologies, including Karl Marx himself, laying the foundation for the multi-ethnic Soviet Union. Many non-Russian peoples who lived in the defunct Russian Empire tried to establish independent republics, but Lenin suppressed such moves. In 1922, they became part of the new, Russian-dominated Union of the Soviet Socialist Republics (USSR).

The Soviet Era

Lenin, who died in 1924, was succeeded by Josef Stalin, a high-ranking Georgian-born official who in 1922 had become general secretary of the Communist Party. Stalin boosted industrial production through a series of five-year plans, which began in 1928, and forced the collectivization of farms.

When middle-class farmers from Ukraine and Kazakhstan resisted, Stalin brutally repressed them, with millions murdered or deported to labor camps in Siberia. Stalin also devised an elaborate system of keeping files on Communist Party members, which he used to devastating effect in the late 1930s, when he conducted wide-scale purges, eliminating anyone he viewed as a potential threat.

During World War II (1939-45), the Soviets joined France, the United Kingdom and United States in defeating the German-Japanese alliance. Some 27 million Soviet soldiers and civilians were killed — or 14 percent of the population.[47] The war enabled Stalin to regain territories ceded to Germany in World War I, notably the three Baltic nations of Estonia, Latvia and Lithuania, and parts of modern-day Belarus. In addition, Stalin pushed Central and Eastern European nations, including East Germany, into the Comecon economic union, as well as a military alliance, the 1955 Warsaw Pact. In 1946 Britain's former wartime prime minister, Winston Churchill, famously described the alliance as creating an "Iron Curtain" between Western Europe and the region.

The period between 1945 and the fall of the Berlin Wall in 1989 became known as the Cold War, in reference to the intense geopolitical rivalry that existed between the Soviet Union and the United States, the world's two superpowers. Among the tensest episodes were the 1948-49 Berlin Airlift, in which the U.S. military flew supplies into West Berlin to foil a Soviet blockade; the 1962 Cuban Missile Crisis in which the United States threatened war if the Soviets did not remove missiles they had placed in Cuba; and the Soviet invasion of Afghanistan in 1979, which sparked a U.S. boycott of the 1980 Moscow Olympic Games.[48]

When Stalin died in 1953, he was succeeded by Nikita Khrushchev, who denounced Stalin's extreme political repression but retained his socialist policies. Khrushchev made some economic adjustments, though, such as giving Russian families their own apartments and expanding state welfare benefits. Abroad, Khrushchev kept a firm grip on the Soviet satellite states, notably sending troops to quell an anti-communist uprising in Hungary in 1956.

After the Soviet politburo peacefully ousted Khrushchev in 1964, the new leader, Leonid Brezhnev, deployed troops to Czechoslovakia in 1968 to suppress the so-called Prague Spring, a movement to introduce democracy and liberalize personal freedom. High oil prices in the 1970s enabled Russia to maintain its status as a military superpower, but its economy stagnated and its public finances deteriorated accordingly.

A new chapter began when Mikhail Gorbachev became the Soviet leader in 1985. He dramatically improved relations with the West, signing major disarmament treaties with President Ronald Reagan. Gorbachev adopted a so-called *glasnost* policy to allow greater freedom of speech, a policy that reverberated throughout the Warsaw Pact nations. East European countries began to throw off Soviet domination, beginning with Poland, which held partly free and fair elections in June 1989.

The toppling of the Berlin Wall in November 1989 marked the end of the Cold War as Bulgaria, Czechoslovakia, East Germany, Hungary and Romania quickly joined Poland in abandoning communism and becoming free-market democracies. Lithuania's declaration of independence from the Soviet Union in March 1990 marked the beginning of the end of the USSR, which was officially dissolved on New Year's Eve in 1991, and all 15 Soviet republics emerged as independent countries.

Chaos and Resurgence

After the Soviet Union collapsed, Russia plunged into trauma and chaos. Economically, it embraced a model of unfettered capitalism that enriched a relative few but slashed the living standards of many ordinary Russians. Price controls were relaxed and state-owned enterprises privatized.

Russia also had to deal with an internal war in the early 1990s, when Chechnya, a southern republic in the mountainous Caucasus region, tried to secede. Russian troops eventually suppressed the uprising, but violence in the region persists.

Boris Yeltsin, Russia's president from 1991-1999, struggled to keep order at home while trying to build good relations with the rest of the world. In the mid-1990s Russia, Ukraine and the United States agreed to

Russia Plays Leading Role in Separatist Conflicts

Moscow sees itself as a protector, but others view it differently.

When the word "separatist" is mentioned in relation to Russia, it usually conjures up the conflict with Chechnya, the predominantly Muslim republic in Russia's mountainous Caucasus region that tried unsuccessfully to secede in the 1990s.

But Russia is a pivotal player in five other separatist conflicts — in Abkhazia and South Ossetia in Georgia, Nagorno-Karabakh in Azerbaijan, Transnistria in Moldova and the Donetsk and Lugansk regions in eastern Ukraine — which remain unresolved.[1] In each case, Russia provides some support to the separatists — military, diplomatic, economic or a combination — a thorn in the side of the countries from which the regions have seceded.

Russia was devastated to lose Azerbaijan, Georgia, Moldova and 11 other republics when the Soviet Union was dissolved. Russia and Georgia fought a brief war in 2008, and in retaliation Russia recognized Abkhazia and South Ossetia as independent countries in their secessionist dispute with Georgia. Russia also maintains about 1,000 troops in Transnistria, even though Russia does not share a border with Transnistria as it does with Abkhazia and South Ossetia.[2]

Georgia's U.S. ambassador, Archil Gegeshidze, says "two competing narratives" explain Russia's role in the conflicts. In the pro-Russian view, people in the breakaway republics align themselves with Russia because of their common histories, and Russia supports them as a "moral obligation," Gegeshidze says. Russia's opponents, he adds, say it "always

uses these conflicts as a lever over the former Soviet republics to prevent them from jumping out of the Russian orbit."

While media reports often refer to Abkhazia and South Ossetia in one breath, Gegeshidze says they are different. Most South Ossetians speak Georgian and are culturally close to Georgians, but South Ossetia is too weak economically to be a self-sustaining country, he says. By contrast, the Abkhazians "have more choices" about whether or not to go it alone, he says, because their land is more fertile, they have access to the sea and Russian is the dominant language. Still, Gegeshidze says, ethnic Abkhaz control the government but are outnumbered by ethnic Armenians and Georgians in Abkhazia. So the Abkhaz are glad to have Russia's protection.

Svante Cornell, director of the Central Asia-Caucasus Institute at Johns Hopkins University in Washington, has argued that Russia uses these conflicts to keep the countries within its sphere of influence.[3] For instance, Cornell pointed out that Russia has already warned that if Moldova continues to forge closer ties with the European Union against Russia's wishes, Russia would support separatists in Moldova's Transnistria region.

Russia can do the same with Nagorno-Karabakh, which is officially part of Azerbaijan but populated by ethnic Armenians who would welcome Russia's protection, Cornell said. Regional experts believe concern about the future of Nagorno-Karabakh was a major factor in Armenia's sudden decision in September 2013 to abandon

begin eliminating their nuclear arsenals, resulting in Ukraine becoming a nuclear-weapons-free country.

Yeltsin appointed Putin as his prime minister in 1999, and Putin took over the presidency from Yeltsin in 2000. Higher oil prices in subsequent years gave Putin sufficient revenues to cement his grip on power. In addition, he placed control of the giant energy company Gazprom back in government hands, further strengthening his political power.[49] In foreign policy, Putin was far

less friendly than Yeltsin toward the West. He opposed the U.S.-led Iraq War in 2003, the NATO-sponsored secession of Kosovo from Serbia in 2008 and the U.S. plan to install a missile defense system in Eastern Europe in the mid-2000s.

Putin also resented NATO's expansion to his doorstep in 2004, when Estonia, Latvia and Lithuania joined the Western military alliance. In addition, he viewed with unease the European Union's expansion in

a trade agreement negotiated with the EU and instead join the Russian-backed Eurasian Economic Union (EEU).

Armen Sahakyan, founder and executive director of the Washington office of the Eurasian Research Analysis Institute, an Armenia-based think tank, says Russia's goal in these conflicts is "to preserve the status quo" because doing so allows it to retain influence. As for Georgia, Sahakyan suggests Moscow might give Abkhazia and South Ossetia back to Georgia if it agreed to join the EEU. And it could do the same with Transnistria, he says.

The key other player is the 28-member European Union. In June 2014, Georgia and Moldova defied Russia's warnings by signing comprehensive free-trade and association agreements with the EU. But it is unclear how these accords will be applied in the frozen conflicts.

Gunnar Wiegand, a senior EU diplomat, said the visa-free regime the EU is offering Moldova would apply to Moldovans living in Transnistria. And Transnistrians also would benefit from lower import tariffs under the EU trade pact, since most of Moldova's heavy industry is in Transnistria.

As for the broader question of who will govern these regions in the long term, the stalemate has become so entrenched that the answer remains unclear. With the EU adopting its trade incentives "carrot" approach, in contrast to Moscow's "stick" approach, Russia's attraction for the region's residents remains its "hard power," while the EU's attraction remains its "soft power," Cornell says.

— *Brian Beary*

---

[1] For a full account of these conflicts, see Brian Beary, *Separatist Movements* (2011).

[2] David M. Herszenhorn, "Russia Putting a Strong Arm On Neighbors," *The New York Times*, Oct. 22, 2013, www.nytimes.com/2013/10/23/world/europe/russia-putting-a-strong-arm-on-neighbors.html?_r=0.

Separatist Conflicts Fester in Russia's Southwest

Russia provides some support for separatist movements in three former Soviet republics on its southwestern border near Sochi, site of this month's Winter Olympic Games. The four so-called "frozen" separatist conflicts are in Georgia, where Abkhazia and South Ossetia want to secede; Azerbaijan, where separatists are active in Nagorno-Karabakh; and Moldova, where the breakaway region of Transnistria is located.

Source: Brian Beary, various open sources online.

[3] Cornell spoke at an event titled, "Pushback to Putin's Eurasian Dream? The Looming Facedown between China, the EU and Russia," at the School of Advanced International Studies, Johns Hopkins University, Washington D.C., Dec. 4, 2013.

2004 and 2007, when it accepted as members eight former communist nations from Central and Eastern Europe.[50] The new EU member states were staunchly pro-American and eagerly contributed troops to the U.S.-led Iraq War.

Constitutionally limited to two consecutive terms, Putin handpicked his prime minister, Dmitry Medvedev, to succeed him. Medvedev was elected in March 2008 with 70 percent of the vote.[51] With a softer style, Medvedev helped to warm Russia's relations with the West. A major achievement was conclusion of a new nuclear arms reduction treaty (START) in 2010.[52]

Medvedev was aided by Obama's election as president in November 2008, especially after the Obama administration vowed to "hit the reset button" and work to improve U.S.-Russian relations. The two cooperated in combating militant Islam in Afghanistan, with Russia

KAREN MINASYAN/AFP/Getty Images

An Armenian soldier in the self-proclaimed republic of Nagorno-Karabakh guards the border with Azerbaijan near the town of Martakert. Nagorno-Karabakh is officially part of Azerbaijan but populated by ethnic Armenian separatists, who would welcome Russia's protection. Concern about the future of Nagorno-Karabakh is seen as a major factor in Armenia's sudden decision in September 2013 to abandon a trade agreement negotiated with the European Union and instead join the Russian-backed Eurasian Economic Union.

granting the NATO mission there access to transport corridors that allowed NATO military personnel and equipment to travel from bases in the Baltic through Russia.

During the Arab Spring uprisings in 2011, Russia chose not to veto a U.N. Security Council move to deploy a NATO military mission in Libya. That mission led to the removal from power of Libyan leader Moammar Gadhafi in the summer of 2011. Meanwhile, the United States backed Russia's bid to join the WTO, giving it enhanced access to world markets for trade and investment purposes.[53]

Tensions ran high, however, when Georgia and Ukraine made bids to join NATO, which the United States supported but Russia firmly opposed. The situation was a contributing factor in the Russia-Georgia war that erupted in summer 2008, which ended with Russia tightening its control over Georgia's two secessionist regions, Abkhazia and South Ossetia.

U.S.-Russian relations soured in 2012, as the two countries could not reconcile their competing plans to develop new missile-defense systems in Europe.

As the United States began withdrawing its troops from Afghanistan in 2011, Russia began boosting its military presence in Central Asia. For instance, in September 2012 Moscow persuaded Tajikistan to allow Russian military bases there to remain open until 2042 by extending its existing lease.[54] Putin, who had been prime minister under Medvedev, was easily re-elected president for six more years in May 2012. His return to the presidency quickly led to a chilling of relations with the West, due both to Putin's more confrontational style as well as Western criticism of his human-rights record, for instance on freedom of the press.

Russian-U.S. relations became further strained in summer 2013 after NSA contractor Snowden was granted political asylum in Russia after disclosing details of the NSA's mass surveillance programs of U.S. and foreign citizens.

"It's not our fault that he found himself in Russia," says the Russian Embassy's Drobinin. He insists that Moscow was legally required to examine Snowden's claim for asylum and could not send him back to the United States, since the two countries do not have an extradition treaty.

Meanwhile, the atmosphere in Eastern Europe began heating up as the EU and Russia competed for influence in the region. Moldova has aligned itself more closely with the EU since 2009, when a strongly pro-Western government was elected, replacing the ruling communists. This caused tension in Moldova's relations with Moscow, especially after Russia in September 2013 banned Moldovan wine and spirits, officially due to public-health concerns.

In the fall of 2013, Ukraine became an even bigger battleground between Russia and the EU, when the EU urged Kiev to sign an association and trade agreement. However, the EU also demanded the release from prison of Ukrainian opposition leader Yulia Tymoshenko for medical treatment in Germany — something the Ukrainian government refused to do.

Meanwhile, on Sept. 3, 2013, Armenian President Serzh Sargsyan announced Armenia would join the Russian-backed EEU instead of signing trade and association pacts it had concluded with the EU.[55] The decision came as a shock: Even Armenian diplomats in Washington were blindsided by the sudden shift that occurred after conversations between Sargsyan and Putin.

CURRENT SITUATION

Tensions in Ukraine

Ukraine was plunged into turmoil when President Yanukovych refused to sign the trade and association agreements with the EU. Popular protests focused around Independence Square in Kiev snowballed after the Vilnius summit, in a movement dubbed Euro-Maidan in Ukrainian, or "Euro-Square." Clashes between the police and protesters turned increasingly violent — and even militant — with widespread arrests and several deaths and beatings reported.

On Jan. 28, 2014, the prime minister and cabinet resigned, and restrictions on political protest imposed weeks earlier were rescinded.[56] Obama, in his State of the Union speech on Jan. 28, 2014, said, "In Ukraine, we stand for the principle that all people have the right to express themselves freely and peacefully, and have a say in their country's future."[57]

By contrast, media coverage in Russia of the protests characterized the demonstrators as violent rioters. Voice of Russia, the government-owned broadcaster, alleged that the protests were being spearheaded by "well-organized radical groups — mainly, football ultras, professional raiders and militants who have undergone special training."[58]

The backlash in Ukraine soured Russia's relations with the rest of Europe. An EU-Russia summit did go ahead as planned in Brussels on Jan. 28, 2014 and was attended by President Putin, EU Commission President Jose Manuel Barroso and EU Council President Herman Van Rompuy. However, given the dire state of their relations, the meeting was confined to a working lunch between the leaders. In the post-summit press conference, President Van Rompuy said the European integration offers to Ukraine, Georgia or Moldova were "fully compatible" with Russia's interests. Putin said, "We would most likely abolish [our] preferential measures for Ukraine if it signs the [EU] association agreement."[59]

The Russian Embassy's Drobinin insisted: "it was Ukraine's decision taken in their national interests" not to sign the EU deal and that it was "misleading" to claim that Russia exerted pressure on Kiev.

Drobinin conceded that the EU-Ukraine deal would, however, hurt Russia's economy by causing EU goods to flood duty-free into the Russian market through Ukraine, after being stamped with a "Made in Ukraine" label.

But Judy Dempsey, a scholar at the Carnegie Endowment for International Peace, said "Putin is desperate to hold on to [Ukraine], knowing full well that if Ukraine goes over to the EU, Russia's own bulwarks against the EU's creeping democratic influence will crumble."[60]

The U.S. administration intensified diplomatic efforts to persuade the East European countries to align themselves with the EU. Secretary of State Kerry, for instance, visited Moldova in December 2013, and U.S. Assistant Secretary of State for European and Eurasian Affairs Victoria Nuland made numerous trips to the region.

"The United States stands with you in search of . . . the European future that you have chosen and you deserve," Nuland said, addressing the media in Kiev on Dec. 11, 2013 after meeting with Yanukovych. "It is still possible to save Ukraine's European future," and "the world is watching."[61]

The Vilnius summit debacle, where Yanukovych decided at the last minute he would not sign the trade deal with the EU, made EU leaders bolder and blunter about their feelings. EU leaders Van Rompuy and Barroso said jointly that they "strongly disapprove of Russia's position and actions" regarding Ukraine.

The U.S. Senate responded similarly, passing a resolution on Jan. 7, 2014 referring to "Russian economic coercion" in Ukraine and urging U.S. and EU leaders "to continue working together to [move] Ukraine toward a future in the Euro-Atlantic community."[62]

Welcoming the resolution, Deputy Assistant Secretary of State Thomas Melia said, "I believe the embers that sparked the protests in late November are still burning and will not be easily extinguished."[63] Nuland, his State Department colleague, added, "There is, also, a good deal of disinformation in Russia about the effect that the EU's Eastern Partnership could have on its economy and arrangements with neighbors."[64]

Meanwhile, Georgia and Moldova, which at the Vilnius summit initialed their EU trade deals — a preliminary step before signing the accords — grew more determined than ever to conclude them despite or perhaps because of the harsh warnings from Moscow. Armenian scholar Sahakyan says Georgia and Moldova may have less to fear from Russian economic retaliation than Ukraine because they are less economically dependent on Russia.

Nevertheless, he says, heavy-handedness from Russia is "not smart" because it hurts Russia's relations with the West. Armenia's government, he points out, could still turn back to the EU if Russia does not provide it with the security guarantees it wants.

Hot Spots and Winter Games

As NATO wound down its presence in Afghanistan, Russia moved in to fill the security vacuum. Its new extended lease on a military base in Tajikistan means that 7,000 Russian troops will stay on to help the Tajiks deal with any potential militant Islamist threats. The Tajik government worries about militants crossing the porous borders it shares with Afghanistan and Pakistan.[65]

Russia also is donating $1.1 billion in military weapons to Kyrgyzstan and paying $4.5 million a year to lease the country's Kant airbase for use by the Russian military. The United States, in contrast, is closing its Kyrgyz base at the Manas Transit Center.

"The underlying political message is that Russia is a more durable security partner than the U.S.," according to *Jane's Intelligence Review,* the security magazine.[66]

In Syria and Iran, Russia managed to maintain a working relationship with the EU and United States, as evidenced by the Nov. 23, 2013, preliminary deal on Iran's nuclear program that the EU brokered. Carnegie Endowment for International Peace scholars Andrew Weiss and Dmitri Trenin said the United States and Russia are in an era of "purely transactional relations against the background of deep mutual mistrust" and that "this may be the 'new normal' in U.S.-Russian relations."[67]

However, tensions between NATO and Russia continued to mount on the issue of missile defense. Talks to develop a joint system, which began in 2010, became hopelessly deadlocked. Russia wants NATO's missile defense system to be operationally linked to Russia's, while NATO prefers to limit such cooperation to information-sharing between the NATO and Russian command-and-control centers. NATO also is resisting Russia's demand for a legal guarantee that the NATO missile defense system would not be used against Russia.[68]

Russia's new short-range ballistic missiles deployed in Kaliningrad could theoretically be used to destroy NATO's planned radar facility and missile interceptor in neighboring Poland. The missiles have a range of about 250 miles.[69] Artis Pabriks, defense minister of Lithuania, a NATO member state that borders Kaliningrad, said, "We have followed these events for quite some time, and this is not a surprise for us," but added that "it creates unnecessary political tension and suspicions and reduces mutual trust because we don't see reason why Russians would need such weapons here. . . . I think it's just to show who is the boss in the region."[70]

In February 2014, the world spotlight turned to the southern Russian resort city of Sochi for the Winter Olympics. Russia spent $51 billion on the games, more than eight times the amount spent for the previous Winter Olympics in Vancouver, Canada.[71]

In efforts to burnish his image in the run-up to the Olympics Putin in December 2013 released longtime jailed businessman Mikhail Khodorkovsky and two anti-Putin activists from the pop band Pussy Riot.[72]

Security was exceptionally tight at the Games as there were fears that Islamist terrorists would strike but the Games ultimately took place without any security incident. By the end of 2014, Sochi was experiencing a new boost in tourism as the sudden fall in the Russian ruble's value on currency markets caused Russians to forego foreign travel and vacation at home instead.[73] The boost for the tourism industry was also an effort by Russians to prop up their economy after it slid into recession over the course of 2014 due to falling oil prices and the impact of sanctions that the EU and U.S. imposed in retaliation for Russia's actions in Ukraine.

Continuing Tensions

Russia is likely to continue trying to enhance its voice in major international forums. With its WTO membership sealed, Russia now has its sights set on joining the Organization for Economic Co-operation and Development, a Paris-based coalition of 34 developed nations that works to promote democracy and free markets. In order to be allowed to join, Russia will need to prove to the members, which are almost all advanced economies, that it has a genuinely free market and open economy, one where businesses have confidence they can come and invest in a corruption-free, legally certain

Should the United States take a tougher stance with Russia?

YES

ARIEL COHEN
Senior Research Fellow In Russian And Eurasian Studies, Heritage Foundation

Written for *CQ Researcher*, February 2014

With the U.S. Olympic team now in Sochi and Washington engaged in intensive talks with Moscow on the Syrian cease-fire and Iran's nuclear program, this is a good time to examine the U.S.-Russia relationship.

The Obama administration's ballyhooed Russian "reset" was an abysmal failure. There is no shared threat assessment and no mutual understanding between the United States and Russia on how to deal with the changing geopolitical environment. Instead, Russia's anti-U.S. foreign policy tilt prevents diplomatic cooperation. Because Russia still views America as a "principal adversary" — a Cold War legacy — it wants to constrain America's diplomatic and military maneuverability.

Flush with oil cash, Putin has chosen to build up Russia's military power, launching a $700 billion rearmament program, including massive nuclear missile modernization. Meanwhile, he has nearly eliminated U.S. missile defenses in Europe. He also has successfully confronted the Bush and Obama administrations over Iran, effectively saved Syrian President Bashar al-Assad and supported a "deal" over the future of Iran's atomic program that brings Tehran to the threshold of nuclear statehood.

Moscow wants to see U.S. power diminished in Eurasia, the Middle East and Europe. Putin's vision includes domination over the former Soviet bloc as an independent pole in a "multi-polar world." Russia's pressures on Ukraine and Georgia continue unrelentingly, aimed at bringing Kiev and Tbilisi into Moscow's fold, most likely through the Eurasian Economic Union, a post-Soviet satellite state system not unlike the Warsaw Pact.

President Obama should ask the National Security Council to conduct a bottom-up review of Russia policy. He also should strengthen ties with former Soviet bloc countries concerned about their independence, such as Azerbaijan, Georgia, Kazakhstan, Turkmenistan, Ukraine and Uzbekistan, and provide economic advice and political-military cooperation if requested. That would be particularly timely, since the United States plans to withdraw troops from Afghanistan later this year.

Russia's intransigent foreign policy will require the administration to provide global leadership and consistent, robust pushback when U.S. interests are at stake. Disagreements over security concerns and geopolitics hinder U.S.-Russian cooperation in counterterrorism, nonproliferation, global security and business. Moscow's anti-U.S. approach means tough times for U.S.-Russian relations. But when engaging Moscow, the United States must guard its national security interests, not engage in a self-deluding, feel-good policy exercise.

NO

ARMEN SAHAKYAN
Executive Director Washington, D.C. Branch, Eurasian Research Analysis Institute

Written for *CQ Researcher*, February 2014

When discussing the question of taking a tougher stance with Russia one must bear in mind two important questions. First, what is the trigger to adopt such a policy? And second, will the policy lead to any favorable outcomes for the United States?

Recently, a widely cited reason has been Russia's ambition to form the Eurasian Economic Union (EEU) by Jan. 1, 2015. It is expected to be an economic union of five former Soviet states that will break down internal trade barriers, adopt a common tariff on foreign goods and other such free-trade measures. The United States has long been a proponent of free trade and globalization, yet it is alarmed with the idea of the EEU. The U.S. motive thus becomes questionable and the adoption of a harsher policy toward the EEU would likely hurt the U.S. international image as the torchbearer on free trade. It would be wiser to further develop friendly relations with the EEU states and ensure their continued integration into the world economy.

As for the second question — whether getting tough on Russia will produce a favorable outcome — I see it as counterproductive for the United States, which needs a strong Russia in the region and should be on favorable terms with it, considering the looming pullout of U.S. and coalition forces from Afghanistan.

Russia also has key roles to play regarding the ongoing instability in Syria and the fight against terrorism. As a permanent Security Council member, Russia also is instrumental in matters affecting the entire world. Should U.S.-Russia relations deteriorate, it would be much harder to reach a consensus on a wide range of issues, further destabilizing the balance of power.

Even if we were to disregard all of those considerations, it is doubtful that a tougher policy would be effective, since the United States does not have many "buttons" that it can push to pressure Russia. Russia and the United States do not have the deepest economic ties. The same underdeveloped relations exist on many other fronts, and it is questionable whether economic or other types of pressure would yield any favorable outcomes.

A cost-benefit analysis would show that the United States will be better off by further deepening its ties with Russia, cooperating in anti-terrorism and other areas and facilitating the EEU's integration with other trading blocs, such as NAFTA, the EU and others.

Russian police officers were a major presence at the 2014 Winter Olympic Games in Sochi, Russia. Sochi lies in the Caucasus region, a hotbed of Muslim radicalism. Islamist-inspired terrorists said they planned to attack the games, although no attack took place. Russian President Vladimir Putin has firmly opposed such groups in the past.

environment. Given the well-documented governance problems in the country, convincing them will be no small task.[74]

Russia also is expected to consolidate its historical hold over the Arctic region.[75] Norway's defense minister, Ine Eriksen Soreide, said in January 2014 that Russia's increased military activity in the Arctic was "cause for concern" and that NATO and Russia "do not see eye to eye" over joint naval exercises in the Arctic. "Small things can spark tensions," Soreide cautioned, pointing out that Norway shared a 122-mile land border and 466-mile sea border with Russia.[76]

As for Russia's ultimate goal regarding the Eurasian Economic Union, "We want to create a common [trading] space from Lisbon to Vladivostok," says Kalugin, of the Russian Embassy in Washington. Thus, the EU is part of Russia's plan as well, with the EU's 28 member states remaining Russia's top trading partners, Kalugin stresses.

Some demographers predict that Russia eventually will lose control of Siberia as Russians continue migrating out of the area and are replaced by Chinese migrant workers. But the Russian Embassy's Drobinin disputes such predictions. "Siberia is not some kind of promised land," he says. "It is really hard to live there," given its harsh climate and remoteness.

Four former Soviet-bloc countries that are now members of the EU — Estonia, Latvia, Lithuania and Poland — will be leading the resistance to Russia's attempts to extend its influence into its Soviet-era sphere. "We were under occupation for 50 years," said Vydas Gedvilas, the speaker of the Lithuanian Parliament. "Now we are doing everything in our power to get these countries closer to the EU."[77]

Similarly, Estonian Defense Minister Reinsalu urged NATO to keep its door open to new members and for the United States to retain a military presence in Europe.[78] The State Department's Nuland has urged the EU to leave the welcome mat out for Ukraine,.[79]

Russia's recent arm-twisting "will ultimately lead to disaster" in its foreign relations, predicted Stephen Blank, a senior fellow for Russia at the American Foreign Policy Council, a Washington think tank. Refusing "to recognize the sovereignty and independence" of Armenia, Georgia, Kyrgyzstan and Ukraine makes the region "fundamentally unstable" and "under constant threat of war," Blank argued.[80]

Frederick Starr, chairman of the Central Asia-Caucasus Institute at Johns Hopkins University in Washington DC, called Putin's policy "an absurd replay of Alexander III's" eastward expansion of the Russian Empire in the late 1800s, which culminated in the Russian revolution of 1905.[81]

"Everything is possible — both a drift of the former Soviet [countries] toward Russia, combined with the inward collapse of its states and societies," according to Olaf Osica, director of the Warsaw-based Centre for Eastern Studies, "as well as increasing opposition by the [Eastern Partnership] countries against the Kremlin's conduct."[82]

EPILOGUE

In the two years since this report was published, Russia has continued to pursue a muscular foreign policy. This has included annexing Crimea, a region in neighbouring Ukraine, in 2014, an action that triggered a freeze in Russia's relations with the European Union and United States. Then in 2015, Russia turned its gaze southward to the Middle East, choosing to become involved in Syria's civil war by launching airstrikes against Sunni Muslim militants there. Meanwhile, global oil prices nosedived from $100 to $30 a barrel, sending the Russian economy into deep recession due to its heavy dependence on oil exports for revenue. The oil price plummet, coupled with trade wars waged on multiple fronts stemming from its overseas interventions, put Russian public finances under severe strain by early 2016.

On February 22, 2014, a political vacuum was created in Ukraine by the sudden flight from Kiev of Ukraine's pro-Russian President, Viktor Yanukovych, in response to weeks of mounting pro-Western protests, which had begun to turn violent.[83] Russian President Vladimir Putin exploited the vacuum by engineering the annexation of Ukraine's predominantly ethnic Russian region, Crimea, on March 19.[84] In addition, two pro-Russian regions in eastern Ukraine, Donetsk and Lugansk, declared their secession in early May, causing a conflict to erupt in which separatist rebels whom Russia supported were pitted against the Ukrainian military, which tried unsuccessfully to take back control of the two breakaway regions.[85] Presidential elections in Ukraine on May 25, 2014, were won convincingly by a pro-Western candidate, Petro Poroschenko, which cemented Ukraine's drift away from Russia.[86]

The EU and U.S. condemned Russia's actions in Ukraine and as the year progressed, they rolled out successively more stringent sanctions in response. After a Malaysia Airlines passenger plane was shot down on July 17 – most likely by accident by pro-Russian separatists — killing all 298 aboard, most of whom were Dutch nationals, the 28 member countries of the EU restricted trade with Russia in the energy, defense and banking sectors. In retaliation, Russia banned imports of EU agricultural products.[87]

A regional polarization ensued in which some former Soviet bloc countries, notably Georgia, Moldova and Ukraine, oriented themselves westwards by concluding and implementing free trade agreements with the EU.[88] By contrast, the post-Soviet bloc nations Armenia, Belarus, and Kazakhstan joined Russia in an alternative free trade bloc called the Eurasian Economic Union, which came into being on January 1, 2015. Kyrgyzstan became the Union's fifth member on May 8, 2015.[89] The EU and U.S. viewed this nascent free trade bloc with suspicion because of Russia's economic dominance of it and thus refrained from entering into talks about potential trade opportunities.

In addition to flexing its muscles on its immediate border, a new foreign policy chapter was opened on September 30, 2015 when Russia launched airstrikes in Syria, a country where hundreds of thousands have been killed and millions have fled in an increasingly complex conflict that has raged since 2011.[90] Russia claimed to be helping the Western-led coalition which, since summer 2014, has conducted airstrikes against the Islamic State (ISIS) militant group after ISIS suddenly captured swaths of territory in Iraq and Syria. The U.S. alleged that the true purpose of the Russian airstrikes was less about depleting ISIS and more about hitting the Sunni Muslim Arab rebels who are fighting against the troops of Syrian President Bashar al-Assad. Russia is a long-standing ally of Assad.

Blowback for the Syria intervention came quickly, with ISIS on October 31 exploding a bomb on a Russian passenger plane as it flew tourists back home from their holiday in Egypt in an attack that killed all 224 aboard.[91] On November 24, Turkey, which disapproved and distrusted Russia's military intervention in its neighbour Syria, shot down a Russian military plane, claiming it had momentarily entered Turkish airspace. The plane downing episode led to a rupture in Russian-Turkish relations with Russia imposing trade sanctions against Turkey in retaliation. Thus, Russian tour operators were restricted from arranging tours to Turkey, Turkish businessmen restricted from visiting Russia for business fairs, and plans shelved to build a pipeline to transport Russian gas across the Black Sea to energy-hungry Turkey.[92]

One bright spot on another otherwise bleak foreign policy horizon was Russia's participation, along with China, France, Germany, the United Kingdom and the U.S., in EU-brokered talks on Iran's nuclear program, which culminated in a final agreement being clinched on July 14, 2015.[93] The agreement, which aims to prevent Iran acquiring nuclear weapons, gave the green light to a gradual lifting of trade sanctions against Iran in return for Iran scaling back its civil nuclear program.

While the EU and U.S. trade sanctions have hurt Russia's economy, the dramatic drop in global oil prices has dealt it an even more serious blow. In early 2014, oil had been selling for $100 a barrel but by February 2016 the price had nosedived to $30.[94] Consequently, Russia's economy grew by 0.6 percent in 2014, contracted by 3.8 percent in 2015, and is forecast to contract a further 0.7 percent in 2016.[95] The Russian ruble has lost half its value on currency markets, down from 35 rubles to the dollar in February 2014 to nearly 80 rubles to the dollar in February 2016. With the EU, Russia's main trading partner, deciding on December 21, 2015, to extend trade sanctions against it until July 2016, and oil prices predicted to stay low in the near term, there seems to be little respite on the economic horizon.[96]

"It's a long, slow crisis with no chance of recovery" said Natalia Zubarevich, Professor of Geography at Moscow State University, of the economic outlook. While spending on the Russian military has skyrocketed and amounts to a third of the federal budget, Zubarevich predicted that the government would soon be forced to cut back military spending due to the rising public deficit. The Russian people are bracing themselves for years of hardship, she said, although she doubted that they would turn against Putin in anger over their plight as he is perceived as being "above the crisis."[97]

The worsening state of the public finances was likely a factor in the Russian government's January 2016 announcement that it was scrapping plans to boost its troop presence in the Central Asian Republic of Tajikistan, which lies in a region where Islamic terrorism is a chronic threat. Rather than raising troop levels to 9,000 as signaled in 2015, Russia has decided to downsize the deployment to 3,000-5,000.[98] Meanwhile, while Russia is struggling to follow through on planned economic investments in Central Asia, including a hydropower plant in Kyrgyzstan, due to its financial constraints, China's investment in that region continues to grow.[99]

The separatist conflict in eastern Ukraine continues to flare up sporadically, despite ceasefire agreements having been signed in September 2014 and February 2015 in Minsk, the capital of neighboring Belarus. Many residents in the affected regions have fled to Russia, with 97,000 refugees arriving in the first half of 2015 alone.[100] Meanwhile, in Moldova, a small country nestled between Romania and Ukraine which also was once a part of the Soviet Union, there are signs of a Ukraine-style east-west divide occurring. While a new, pro-Western government was sworn into office in January 2016, a large chunk of the Moldovan population is pro-Russian and a long sliver of Moldovan territory, Transnistria, functions as a pro-Russian separatist enclave.[101]

The next key date on Russia's political calendar is September 18, 2016, when parliamentary elections are scheduled to happen. President Putin's term of office will run until 2018.

NOTES

1. "Rogozin Warns Moldova on Relations," Reuters, Sept. 5, 2013, Reuters, www.themoscowtimes.com/business/article/rogozin-warns-moldova-on-relations/485526.html.

2. Foreign minister Bildt was speaking at a conference entitled, "The European Union's Eastern Partnership: What to Expect at Vilnius," hosted by the Brookings Institution in Washington, D.C., on Nov. 21, 2013, www.brookings.edu/events/2013/11/21-european-union-eastern-partner-ship-vilnius.

3. See Olaf Osica, "The Eastern Partnership: Life Begins after Vilnius," Center for European Analysis, Dec. 13, 2013, http://cepa.org/content/eastern-partnership-life-begins-after-vilnius.

4. T.J., "Why has Russia banned Moldovan wine?" *The Economist*, Nov. 25, 2013, www.economist.com/blogs/economist-explains/2013/11/economist-explains-18.

5. Minister Gherman was speaking at a discussion on the EU Eastern Partnership, organized by the European Institute in Washington, D.C., on Sept. 18, 2013.

6. Howard Amos, "'Moldova, The New Ukraine: Pro-Russian Street Protests in Moldova Set to Escalate," *International Business Times*, Jan. 28, 2016, http://www.ibtimes.com/moldova-new-ukraine-pro-russian-street-protests-moldova-set-escalate-2284250.

7. Wiegand was speaking at an event entitled, "The EU's Eastern Partnership in Light of Present Challenges," hosted by Johns Hopkins University in Washington, D.C., Jan. 16, 2014.

8. Presentation by Mikhail Kalugin, head of economic section, Embassy of Russia to the United States, at discussion entitled, "Securing Northern Europe's Energy Independence: A Finnish Perspective," organized by the European Institute, Washington, D.C., Dec. 19, 2013.

9. *Ibid.*

10. *Ibid.*

11. See Human Rights Watch, "Attacks on Ghouta," Sept. 10, 2013, www.hrw.org/node/118725/.

12. Ed Payne, Barbara Starr and Susannah Cullinane, "Russia launches first airstrikes in Syria," CNN,

Sept. 30, 2015, http://www.cnn.com/2015/09/30/politics/russia-syria-airstrikes-isis/index.html.

13. For background, see Chuck McCutcheon, "Government Surveillance," *CQ Researcher,* Aug. 30, 2013, pp. 717-740.

14. "Ratification of Russian military base deal provides Tajikistan with important security guarantees," *Jane's Intelligence Weekly,* Oct. 2, 2013, www.janes.com/article/27898/ratification-of-russian-military-base-deal-provides-tajikistan-with-important-security-guarantees.

15. "Russia: 2 suspects arrested in bombing," The Associated Press, Jan. 30, 2014, www.lasvegassun.com/news/2014/jan/30/russia-2-suspects-arrested-suicide-bombing/.

16. "Winter Olympics: Russia launches Sochi security clampdown," BBC News, www.bbc.co.uk/news/world-europe-25633632.

17. Kelly Whiteside, "Obama sends message by naming Sochi Olympic delegation," *USA Today,* Dec. 20, 2013, www.usatoday.com/story/sports/olympics/sochi/2013/12/17/white-house-sochi-olympics-delegation-to-include-gay-athlete/4051581/.

18. Brian Beary, "Emerging Central Asia," *CQ Global Researcher,* Jan. 17, 2012, pp. 29-56.

19. UNHCR, "Mid-Year Trends 2015," http://www.unhcr.org/56701b969.html.

20. Helen Robertson, "Russia's energy trade with China to quadruple by 2025," *Petroleum Economist,* October 2013, www.petroleum-economist.com/Article/3258056/Russias-energy-trade-with-China-to-quadruple-by-2025.html.

21. MK & Danfes, "Putin's India Visit Furthers Indo-Russian Ties," *The Day After,* Jan. 1, 2013; also see "Indian Generic Drugmakers Pile Into Russian Market," *Business Monitor International,* March 14, 2013, www.pharmaceuticalsinsight.com/file/158892/indian-generic-drugmakers-pile-into-russian-market.html.

22. Matthew Smith, "Brazil, Russia agree to space and cyber collaboration," *Jane's Defence Industry,* Nov. 1, 2013, www.janes.com/article/28518/brazil-russia-agree-to-space-and-cyber-collaboration.

23. Jon Grevatt, "Russia increases defence industrial presence in Myanmar, Vietnam," *Jane's Defence Weekly,* March 5, 2013, www.janes.com/article/11244/russia-increases-defence-in dustrial-presence-in-myanmar-vietnam.

24. Andrey Slepnev, minister for trade, Eurasian Economic Commission, speaking at Center for Strategic and International Studies in Washington, D.C., at a discussion entitled "The Future of the Eurasian Economic Union," Oct. 31, 2013.

25. "Next Round Of Georgian-Russian Talks Moved To March," Feb. 8, 2016, Radio Free Europe/Radio Liberty, http://www.rferl.org/content/georgia-russia-talks-prague-postponed/27538292.html.

26. Source: Russian Federation, Federal State Statistics Service: http://www.gks.ru/bgd/regl/b15_12/IssWWW.exe/stg/d02/27-06.htm

27. On Jan. 17, 2014, Alexandros Petersen was shot dead while dining at a popular Lebanese restaurant in downtown Kabul, Afghanistan. Petersen was the victim of an anti-Western terrorist attack carried out by Taliban militants that killed 21 people.

28. Petersen was speaking at an event entitled "Pushback to Putin's Eurasian Dream? The Looming Facedown between China, the EU and Russia," School for Advanced International Studies, Johns Hopkins University, Dec. 4, 2013.

29. "Global Economic Prospects: Spillovers amid Weak Growth," World Bank, January 2016, http://www.worldbank.org/content/dam/Worldbank/GEP/GEP2016a/Global-Economic-Prospects-January-2016-Spillovers-amid-weak-growth.pdf.

30. Zvi Magen, "Putin flexes his muscles," *The Jerusalem Report,* Oct. 7, 2013, www.jpost.com/Jerusalem-Report/The-Region/Putin-flexes-his-muscles-326954.

31. David Des Roches, "Russia in the Middle East: Help or Hinderance?" *The Diplomatic Insight,* Dec. 31, 2012.

32. Rick Gladstone, "Friction at the U.N. as Russia and China Veto Another Resolution on Syria Sanctions," *The New York Times,* July 19, 2012, www.nytimes.com/2012/07/20/world/middleeast/russia-and-china-veto-un-sanctions-against-syria.html?_r=0.

33. Jethro Mullen and Nic Robertson, "Landmark deal reached on Iran nuclear program," CNN, July 14, 2015, http://www.cnn.com/2015/07/14/politics/iran-nuclear-deal/index.html.

34. Professor Cross spoke at the "Round Table on the NATO-Russian Relationship," Woodrow Wilson International Center for Scholars, Jan. 10, 2014.

35. "Press Availability with U.S. Secretary of State John Kerry, Russian Foreign Minister Sergey Lavrov and UN Special Representative Lakhdar Brahimi," Paris, France, Jan. 13, 2014, www.state.gov/secretary/remarks/2014/01/219604.htm.

36. "Kaliningrad: European fears over Russian missiles," BBC News, Dec. 13, 2013, www.bbc.co.uk/news/world-europe-25407284.

37. For background, see Roland Flamini, "U.S.-Europe Relations," *CQ Researcher*, March 23, 2012, pp. 277-300.

38. Reinsalu made his comments at a discussion entitled "Ten Years in NATO; Twelve Years in Afghanistan: An Estonian Perspective on the Future of NATO," Center for Strategic and International Studies, Jan. 6, 2014, http://csis.org/event/ten-years-nato-twelve-years-afghanistan.

39. See Brian Beary, "U.S. Trade Policy," *CQ Researcher*, Sept. 13, 2013, pp. 765-788.

40. "Russia may ban import of Polish fruits and vegetables," Voice of Russia, Nov. 16. 2013, http://voiceofrussia.com/news/2013_11_16/Russia-may-ban-import-of-Polish-fruits-and-vegetables-5949/.

41. For background on Russian history, see Kenneth Jost, "Russia and the Former Soviet Republics," *CQ Researcher*, June 17, 2005, pp. 541-564.

42. For a concise overview of Russian history, see Geoffrey Hosking, *Russian History: A Very Short Introduction* (2012).

43. See Jason McClure, "Russia in Turmoil," *CQ Researcher*, Feb. 21, 2012, pp. 81-104.

44. Hoskings, *op. cit.*, p. 22.

45. Jost, *op. cit.*

46. Walter Richmond, *The Circassian Genocide* (2013).

47. McClure, *op. cit.*

48. For background, see Roland Flamini, "Dealing With the 'New' Russia," *CQ Researcher*, June 6, 2008, pp. 481-504.

49. McClure, *op. cit.*

50. For background, see Brian Beary, "The New Europe," *CQ Global Researcher*, Aug. 1, 2007, pp. 181-210.

51. Flamini, "Dealing With the 'New' Russia," *op. cit.*

52. *Ibid.*

53. For details of Russia's WTO membership obligations, see "Office of the United States Trade Representative's Report on Russia's Implementation of the WTO Agreement," December 2013, www.ustr.gov/sites/default/files/Russia-WTO-Implementation-Report%20FINAL-12-20-13.pdf.

54. See Beary, "Emerging Central Asia," *op. cit.*

55. David M. Herszenhorn, "Russia Putting A Strong Arm On Neighbors," *The New York Times*, Oct. 23, 2013, www.nytimes.com/2013/10/23/world/europe/russia-putting-a-strong-arm-on-neighbors.html?_r=0.

56. "Ukraine's protests: Praying for peace," *The Economist*, Jan. 30, 2014, www.economist.com/news/europe/21595512-government-resigns-opposition-protesters-remain-defiantly-streets-praying.

57. "Obama's 2014 State of the Union address: transcript," ABC News, Jan. 28, 2014, www.cbsnews.com/news/obamas-2014-state-of-the-union-address-full-text/.

58. "Who is who in pro-EU protests events in Ukraine?" Voice of Russia, Jan. 30, 2014, http://voiceofrussia.com/2014_01_30/Who-is-who-in-pro-EU-protests-events-in-Ukraine-4142/.

59. Joanna Sopinska, "Expert consultations on Eastern Partnership agreements," *Europolitics*, Jan. 29, 2014.

60. Judy Dempsey, "Is This Ukraine's Turning Point?" *Carnegie Europe*, Dec. 9, 2013, http://carnegieeurope.eu/strategiceurope/?fa=53847.

61. "Remarks to the Media Following Meeting With President Yanukovych," U.S. Department of State, Dec. 11, 2013, www.state.gov/p/eur/rls/rm/2013/dec/218604.htm.

62. "S.RES.319 — Expressing support for the Ukrainian people in light of President Yanukovych's decision not to sign an Association Agreement with the European Union," U.S. Senate Resolution approved by unanimous consent on Jan. 7, 2014, http://thomas. loc.gov/cgi-bin/query/D?c113:3:./ temp/~c113vhuJWD::

63. Thomas O. Melia, deputy assistant secretary, Bureau of Democracy, Human Rights and Labor, statement to the Senate Foreign Relations Committee hearing on the situation in Ukraine, Jan. 15, 2014.

64. *Ibid.*

65. "Ratification of Russian military base deal provides Tajikistan with important security guarantees," *Jane's Intelligence Weekly,* Oct. 2, 2013, www.janes.com/ article/27898/ratification-of-russian-military-base-deal-provides-tajikistan-with-important-security-guarantees.

66. "Neighbourhood watch: Russia's response to insecurity in Central Asia," *Jane's Intelligence Review,* Dec. 1, 2013.

67. Dmitri Trenin and Andrew S. Weiss, "Dealing With the New Normal in U.S.-Russian Relations," Carnegie Endowment for International Peace, Dec. 20, 2013, http://carnegie.ru/2013/12/20/dealing-with-new-normal-in-u.s.-russian-relations/gwto.

68. Brooks Tigner, "NATO-Russian missile defence talks deadlocked," *Jane's Defence Weekly,* Nov. 27, 2013, www.janes.com/article/30935/nato-russian-missile-defence-talks-deadlocked.

69. "Russian missile deployment to Kaliningrad does not heighten war risk but will cause decline in diplomatic relations," *Jane's Intelligence Weekly,* Dec. 18, 2013.

70. Steve Gutterman, "Russia has stationed Iskander missiles in western region: reports," Reuters, Dec. 16, 2013, www.reuters.com/article/2013/12/16/ us-russia-missiles-idUSBRE9BF0W020131216.

71. "Sochi: Olympic Flame in the Caucasus," teleconference, Woodrow Wilson Center for International Scholars, Washington, D.C., Jan. 13, 2014.

72. Masha Gessen, "Don't be fooled by Putin," CNN, Dec. 21, 2013, www.cnn.com/2013/12/21/opinion/ gessen-putin-khodorkovsky/.

73. Karoun Demirjian, "Russian economic crisis helps save Putin's post-Olympic dream at Sochi," *Washington Post,* Jan. 18, 2015, www.washingtonpost.com/world/ europe/russian-economic-crisis-helps-save-putins-post-olympic-dream-at-sochi/2015/01/17/d8c7bbd8-92b1-11e4-a66f-0ca5037a597d_story.html.

74. Chris Weafer, "Russia's Path to Progress Goes Through OECD," *The Moscow Times,* Dec. 11, 2013, www.themoscowtimes.com/opinion/article/ russias-path-to-progress-goes-through-oecd/491391 .html#ixzz2s0B47xi9.

75. See Brian Beary, "Race for the Arctic," *CQ Global Researcher,* August 2008, pp. 213-242.

76. Soreide made her comments at a discussion entitled "Writing NATO's Next Chapter: The View from Norway," Center for Strategic and International Studies, Jan. 9, 2014, http://csis.org/event/writing-natos-next-chapter.

77. Gedvilas made his remarks at a discussion on the EU's Eastern Partnership, European Institute, Sept. 18, 2013.

78. Reinsalu, *op. cit.*

79. Statement to the Senate Foreign Relations Committee hearing on the situation in Ukraine, Jan. 15, 2014.

80. Blank was speaking at a conference entitled, "Pushback to Putin's Eurasian Dream? The Looming Facedown between China, the EU and Russia," School of Advanced International Studies, Johns Hopkins University, Dec. 4, 2013.

81. Starr was speaking at a conference entitled: "Pushback to Putin's Eurasian Dream? . . ." *ibid.*

82. Osica, *op. cit.*

83. Andrew Higgins and Andrew E. Kramer "Archrival Is Freed as Ukraine Leader Flees," *New York Times,* Feb. 22, 2014, http://www.nytimes.com/2014/02/23/ world/europe/ukraine.html?_r=0.

84. "Russia's annexation of Crimea is 'armed robbery,' says Ukrainian PM Yatsenyuk," *Euronews,* March 21, 2014, http://www.euronews.com/2014/03/21/ russia-s-annexation-of-crimea-is-armed-robbery-says-ukrainian-pm-yatsenyuk.

85. Mark MacKinnon, "In Ukraine, Donetsk People's Republic lurches to life," The Globe and Mail, May 12, 2014, http://www.theglobeandmail.com/news/world/in-ukraine-donetsk-peoples-republic-lurches-to-life/article18621492/.

86. "Petro Poroshenko wins Ukraine's presidential election, exit polls show," Associated Press, May 25, 2014, http://www.cbc.ca/news/world/petro-poroshenko-wins-ukraine-s-presidential-election-exit-polls-show-1.2653513.

87. "Russia bans fruit, veg. meat, fish, dairy imports from EU and US," RTE News, Aug. 8, 2014, http://www.rte.ie/news/2014/0807/635600-russia-sanctions/.

88. "Joint Declaration of the Eastern Partnership Summit (Riga, 21-22 May 2015)," European Union External Action Service, http://eeas.europa.eu/eastern/docs/riga-declaration-220515-final_en.pdf.

89. Malika Orazgaliyevau "Kyrgyzstan Joins Eurasian Economic Union," The Astana Times, May 14, 2015, http://astanatimes.com/2015/05/kyrgyzstan-joins-eurasian-economic-union/.

90. Ed Payne, Barbara Starr and Susannah Cullinane, "Russia launches first airstrikes in Syria," CNN, Sept. 30, 2015, http://www.cnn.com/2015/09/30/politics/russia-syria-airstrikes-isis/index.html.

91. "Exclusive: EgyptAir mechanic suspected in Russian plane crash" Reuters, Jan. 29, 2016, http://www.reuters.com/article/us-egypt-crash-suspects-idUSKCN0V712V.

92. Shaun Walker, "Russia imposes sanctions on Turkey over downed plane," The Guardian, Nov. 26, 2015, http://www.theguardian.com/world/2015/nov/26/hollandes-anti-isis-talks-with-putin-complicated-by-downing-of-russian-jet.

93. Jethro Mullen and Nic Robertson, "Landmark deal reached on Iran nuclear program," CNN, July 14, 2015, http://www.cnn.com/2015/07/14/politics/iran-nuclear-deal/index.html.

94. Global oil prices indicator: www.oil-price.net

95. "Global Economic Prospects: Spillovers amid Weak Growth," World Bank, January 2016, http://www.worldbank.org/content/dam/Worldbank/GEP/GEP2016a/Global-Economic-Prospects-January-2016-Spillovers-amid-weak-growth.pdf.

96. Bryan McManus, "EU extends sanctions against defiant Russia" Reuters, Agence France Presse, Dec. 21, 2015, http://news.yahoo.com/russia-slams-eu-extending-sanctions-instead-cooperating-terrorism-161125588.html.

97. Comments made at event entitled, "Natalia Zubarevich: Russian Financial Crisis Comes to the Regions," at the Woodrow Wilson International Center for Scholars, Feb. 4, 2016, https://www.wilsoncenter.org/event/natalia-zubarevich-russian-financial-crisis-comes-to-the-regions.

98. Farangis Najibullah, "Cash Crunch, Stretched Military Spur Russian Troop Cuts Near Afghan Frontier," Radio Free Europe / Radio Liberty, Feb. 5, 2016, http://www.rferl.org/content/russia-troops-cuts-tajikistan-afghanistan-border/27534647.html.

99. Stephen Blank, "Russia Losing Ground Across Central Asia," Eurasia Daily Monitor Vol. 13, No. 26, Feb. 8, 2016, http://www.jamestown.org/programs/edm/single/?tx_ttnews%5Btt_news%5D=45077&cHash=d9ae176a76135a00889cc62adc3be119#.VrvCr_IrLIU.

100. UNHCR, "Mid-Year Trends 2015," http://www.unhcr.org/56701b969.html.

101. Howard Amos, "Moldova, The New Ukraine: Pro-Russian Street Protests in Moldova Set to Escalate," International Business Times, Jan. 28, 2016, http://www.ibtimes.com/moldova-new-ukraine-pro-russian-street-protests-moldova-set-escalate-2284250.

BIBLIOGRAPHY

Selected Sources

Books

Bullough, Oliver, *The Last Man in Russia*, Basic Books, 2013.
In a mix of travelogue, sociological study and biography, a British journalist and author who lived for several years in Russia describes contemporary Russian society.

Hill, Fiona, and Clifford G. Gaddy, *Mr. Putin: Operative in the Kremlin*, Brookings, 2013.
A senior fellow at the Brookings Institution, a major Washington think tank, assesses Vladimir Putin's leadership of Russia.

Hosking, Geoffrey, *Russian History: A Very Short Introduction,* **Oxford University Press, 2012.**
An emeritus professor of Russian history at University College London provides a succinct history of Russia, from its medieval origins to contemporary events.

Judah, Ben, *Fragile Empire: How Russia Fell in and out of Love With Vladimir Putin,* **2013.**
An associate fellow at the European Council on Foreign Relations sketches a revealing portrait of the Russian leader.

Mankoff, Jeffrey, *Russian Foreign Policy: The Return of Great Power Politics,* **Rowman & Littlefield Publishers, 2011.**
A fellow at the Center for Strategic and International Studies examines how Russian foreign policy has developed since the end of the Cold War.

Stent, Angela E., *The Limits of Partnership: US-Russian Relations in the Twenty-First Century,* **Princeton University Press, 2014.**
The director of the Center for Eurasian, Russian and East European Studies at Georgetown University describes U.S.-Russian relations since the collapse of the Soviet Union.

Articles

Dempsey, Judy, "Is This Ukraine's Turning Point?" Carnegie Europe, Dec. 9, 2013, http://carnegieeurope.eu/strategiceurope/?fa=53847.
A journalist and scholar assesses where Ukraine may be headed geopolitically.

Des Roches, David, "Russia in the Middle East: Help or Hinderance," *The Diplomatic Insight,* **Dec. 31, 2012, pp. 19-20, http://thediplomaticinsight.com/wp-content/uploads/2013/01/december-2012-magazine.pdf.**
An associate professor at the National Defense University examines Russia's role in current Middle Eastern politics.

Jones, Stephen, "Reaching the Summit: Implications of Vilnius for Georgia," The Central Asia-Caucasus Analyst, Dec. 11, 2013, http://cacianalyst.org/publications/analyticalarticles/item/12879-reaching-the-summit-implications-ofvilnius-for-georgia.html.
A professor of Russian studies at Mount Holyoke College examines the consequences of Georgia's initialling major trade and association pacts with the EU in November 2013.

Leigh, Michael, "Ukraine's Pivot to Europe?" German Marshall Fund of the United States, Nov. 13, 2013, www.realclearworld.com/articles/2013/11/13/ukraines_pivot_to_europe.html.
A senior adviser to the German Marshall Fund of the United States, a nonpartisan organization that promotes trans-Atlantic cooperation, explains Ukraine's dilemma in deciding whether to align itself with Russia or Europe.

Lindberg, Todd, "A Bear in the Desert: Why did the Obama administration allow a Russian resurgence in the Middle East?" *The Weekly Standard,* **July 1, 2013, www.weeklystandard.com/articles/bear-desert_736859.html.**
A research fellow at the conservative Hoover Institution criticizes President Obama for allowing Russia to reassert itself in the Middle East.

Osica, Olaf, "The Eastern Partnership: Life Begins after Vilnius," Center for European Analysis, Dec. 13, 2013, http://cepa.org/content/eastern-partnership-life-begins-after-vilnius.
A director of the Centre for Eastern Studies in Warsaw urges the EU to try to keep Georgia and Moldova on their current pro-EU path.

Trenin, Dmitri, and Andrew S. Weiss, "Dealing With the New Normal in U.S.-Russian Relations," Carnegie Endowment for International Peace, Dec. 20, 2013, http://carnegie.ru/2013/12/20/dealing-with-new-normal-in-u.s.russian-relations/gwto.
Two scholars outline how Russia's U.S. relations deteriorated in 2013.

Reports and Studies

"Report on Russia's Implementation of the WTO Agreement," Office of the U.S. Trade Representative, December 2013, www. ustr.gov/sites/default/files/Russia-WTO-ImplementationReport%20FINAL-12-20-13.pdf.
The U.S. agency that negotiates trade agreements reports on how Russia is complying with its obligations at the World Trade Organization, which Russia joined in 2012.

"U.S.-Russia Bilateral Presidential Commission — 2013 Joint Report," United States Department of State, December 2013, www.state.gov/documents/organization/219326.pdf.
The report describes the main areas where the United States and Russia cooperate bilaterally.

For More Information

The Atlantic Council, 1030 15th St., N.W., 12th Floor, Washington, DC 20005; 202-778-4952; www.atlantic council.org. Think tank that promotes the trans-Atlantic relationship, conducts research on defense, economic and foreign policies.

Brookings Institution, 1775 Massachusetts Ave., N.W., Washington, DC 20036; 202-797-6000; www.brookings.edu. Centrist think tank with a unit that studies relations between the United States and Europe.

Carnegie Moscow Center, 16/2 Tverskaya, Moscow 125009, Russia; +7 495-9358904; www.carnegie.ru. Division of the Washington-based Carnegie Endowment for International Peace that does research and promotes debate on post-Soviet Russia and Eurasia.

Embassy of the Russian Federation to the United States of America, 2650 Wisconsin Ave., N.W., Washington, DC 20007; 202-298-5700; www.russianembassy.org. Official representative of the Russian government in the United States.

Eurasian Economic Commission, Ul. Letnikovskaya 2, Moscow 115114, Russia; +7 495 669 2400 ext. 4117. Regulatory body of the Eurasian Economic Union; aims to develop a free-trade area in Russia and the former Soviet republics.

German Marshall Fund of the United States, 1744 R St., N.W., Washington, DC 20009; 202-683-2650; www.gmfus .org. Foundation with several Russia-specialist scholars that promotes trans-Atlantic relations.

Heritage Foundation, 214 Massachusetts Ave., N.E., Washington, DC 20002; 202546-4400; www.heritage.org. Conservative think tank that focuses in part on U.S.-Russia relations.

School of Advanced International Studies, Johns Hopkins University, Nitze Building, 1740 Massachusetts Ave., N.W., Washington, DC 20036; 202-663-5600; www.sais-jhu.edu. Foreign policy-oriented institution with expertise in the Central Asian-Caucasus region.

Woodrow Wilson Center for International Scholars, Ronald Reagan Building and International Trade Center, One Woodrow Wilson Plaza, 1300 Pennsylvania Ave., N.W., Washington, DC 20004; 202-691-4000; www.wilsoncenter .org. Think tank with longstanding interest in Russia and Eastern Europe.

7

Robotic Warfare

Daniel McGlynn

The Campaign to Stop Killer Robots calls for a ban on further development of lethal autonomous weapons at a demonstration in London on April 23, 2013. The group, along with some other nongovernmental organizations, deems such weapons immoral and unsafe. Supporters of autonomous weaponized robots — which do not yet exist — say their use will save soldiers' lives and reduce civilian deaths.

From *CQ Researcher*, January 23, 2015.

Last spring the Russian military announced it is developing a new kind of guard to secure five ballistic missile bases: robots.

The latest reports say the machines, which tote cameras, sensors and laser-guided rangefinders along with heavy machine guns and small arms, will be operational by 2020.[1] They will be able to travel at more than 30 miles an hour, cover large distances or go dormant for days at a time. And they are being designed to operate fully autonomously — meaning they can kill intruders without human intervention.[2]

Russian military leaders, like their counterparts in other countries, see technology as a way to make war and national security safer and cheaper. In 2013, Russian Deputy Prime Minister Dmitry Rogozin, announcing plans for new military robot labs, said, "We have to conduct battles without any contact, so that our boys do not die, and for that it is necessary to use war robots."[3]

In South Korea a robotic sentry patrols the demilitarized zone along the North Korean border. The robot can carry weapons and operate autonomously, but for now it only patrols semi-autonomously, with a human operator in control.[4]

The United States, already a pioneer in the development of military drone aircraft, leads the world in robotic weapons research and development. But at least 40 other countries — including China, Israel and Great Britain — also are developing unmanned weapons. Even countries not often characterized as militarily aggressive, such as the Netherlands, are developing robotic weapons, signaling that an autonomous weapons arms race may be under way.[5]

Autonomous Weapons Budget to Shrink

Federal funding for all unmanned weapons systems is expected to peak at $5.3 billion in 2015 and fall to $4.7 billion in 2017 before climbing slightly in 2018. Autonomous aircraft, such as drones, receive most of the unmanned systems budget, while ground systems receive the least — $13 million in 2014 — an amount expected to grow fivefold by 2018.

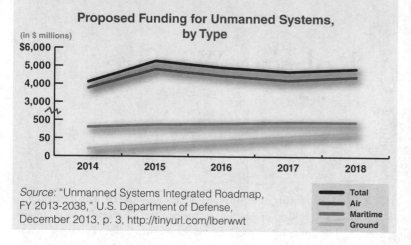

Proposed Funding for Unmanned Systems, by Type

(in $ millions)

Source: "Unmanned Systems Integrated Roadmap, FY 2013-2038," U.S. Department of Defense, December 2013, p. 3, http://tinyurl.com/lberwwt

The push toward warfighting robots is occurring against a backdrop of other military innovations that mirror commercial, technological advances in areas such as sensing, computing and materials science. For example, the U.S. Marine Corps is experimenting with Kevlar underwear, the Navy is building a fleet of autonomous boats using algorithms developed for NASA's Mars Rover and Army scientists are developing 3D-printed food that can be customized to match the nutritional needs of individual soldiers.[6]

In 2013, the U.S. robot maker Boston Dynamics, now owned by Google, unveiled Atlas, a humanoid robot that is 6 feet tall and weighs 330 pounds. The Defense Advanced Research Projects Agency (DARPA) developed the robot for search and rescue operations and other emergency situations.[7]

Futuristic technology is also under development for weapons systems. The Navy just tested a large ship-mounted laser that can blow targets out of the air or water. "This is the first time in recorded history that a directed-energy weapons system has ever deployed," said Rear Admiral Matthew Klunder, chief of naval research.[8]

Meanwhile, the Air Force is trying to update its aging stealth-bomber fleet with new long-range strike aircraft that could eventually be flown without a human pilot onboard.[9] And the Army is retooling its ground robots and developing, among other things, a surveillance robot small enough to fit in a backpack and durable enough to be thrown over a wall or into building harboring enemy soldiers or other threats.

These emerging technologies are changing military tactics. Rapid responses, precision strikes and real-time data and intelligence gathering are encouraging the development of weapon systems that can identify and eliminate threats with some degree of autonomy. Such unmanned weapons, like armed robots preprogrammed to complete a mission, are better insulated from cybersecurity threats such as communications jamming, because after launch they would not need further instructions.

But the technology under development is raising legal and ethical questions. While proponents say increased battlefield technology might limit collateral damage and allow for precision strike, critics contend lethal technology could be abused, or it might perform in unintended ways. They fear that conflicts might begin merely because weapon systems have become so automated.

A key issue surrounding the development of weaponized military robots, or lethal autonomous weapon systems (LAWS), is defining what autonomous means.

"There is no internationally agreed definition of autonomous weapon systems," according to an International Committee of the Red Cross summary of the most recent international talks about how military robots can best be regulated. For the purposes of the meeting, the report said, autonomous weapon systems were defined as "weapons that can independently select and attack targets, i.e., with autonomy in the 'critical functions' of acquiring, tracking, selecting and attacking targets."[10]

Robotic weapons are divided into three classes, depending on what level of human interaction they involve:

- In-the-loop — semi-autonomous systems, such as homing munitions fired by a human operator, that search by themselves for a preprogrammed target, such as a tank or a ship;
- On-the-loop — automated systems supervised by a human operator, such as existing missile defense systems; and
- Out-of-the loop — systems that, once activated, can analyze their surroundings and take action without human intervention.

Fully autonomous weapons that do not need human control to complete tasks or missions do not exist yet, but they are the topic of international debate. Some nongovernmental organizations, such as the Campaign to Stop Killer Robots and the International Committee for Robot Arms Control, are calling for outright bans on further development of lethal autonomous weapons systems.

"The biggest question is whether it is morally acceptable to delegate killing to a machine," says Heather Roff, a University of Denver political scientist who specializes in international ethics. "Is it desirable to create an algorithm to target human beings, or planes or ships that are carrying human beings — is that morally palatable?"

In a 2013 report, Christof Heyns, special rapporteur on extrajudicial, summary or arbitrary executions for the United Nations, called for a moratorium on development of such weapons.[11] "They raise far-reaching concerns about the protection of life during war and peace," said the report. "This includes the question of the extent to which they can be programmed to comply with the requirements of international humanitarian law and the standards protecting life under international human rights law. Beyond this, their deployment may be unacceptable because no adequate system of legal accountability can

Would You Believe Invisible Camouflage?

The U.S. military and defense contractors are developing non-weapon technologies, including body armor and invisible camouflage, to better equip soldiers.

Type	Innovation	Description
Body Armor	Tactical Assault Light Operator Suit (TALOS)	Flexible Kevlar suit soaked in polyethylene thickening fluid; suit becomes rigid when struck by bullets; includes hydraulic frames on arms and legs for increased strength and speed, plus wearable electronic computer display.
Virtual Reality Training	Multi-platform training system	Program combines multiple virtual training simulation platforms into a streamlined synthetic environment; soldiers-in-training would have customized avatars matching their skills and perform activities mimicking real-world operations.
Food	3D printing	Soldiers to be equipped with sensors monitoring their nutrient levels, and nutrient-dense sheets in powdered or liquid forms could be "printed" on command using 3D printing technology.
Camouflage	Invisibility	Material developed by a Canadian company bends light waves around a user wearing it, reportedly rendering the person invisible.

Sources: Tom Bowman, "Special Ops Envisions 'Iron Man'-Like Suit To Protect Troops," NPR, Aug. 5, 2013, http://tinyurl.com/lfoulyo; Tonya Johnson, "Liquid Body Armor," Army News Service, undated, http://tinyurl.com/yaj7heu; Meghan Neal, "The Army Goes Cyberpunk, Embraces Virtual Battlefields and Killer Robots," VICE, Jan. 22, 2014, http://tinyurl.com/nc5btqs; Aarti Shahani, "Army Eyes 3-D Printed Food For Soldiers," NPR, Nov. 4, 2014, http://tinyurl.com/lzqh95q; Sebastian Anthony, "Canadian camouflage company claims to have created perfect invisibility cloak, US military soon to be invisible," ExtremeTech, Dec. 14, 2012, http://tinyurl.com/c7j8rvr

be devised, and because robots should not have the power of life and death over human beings."[12]

After two long wars in Iraq and Afghanistan — during which remote-controlled military robots were used regularly for the first time — the U.S. military is deciding how best to incorporate unmanned warfighting systems into its tactics. But the Department of Defense has directed its forces to carefully review all weapons systems capable of autonomous action before they are used, and requires, for now, that a human remain in the loop in some capacity.

Meanwhile, new weapons systems that are inching closer to complete autonomy continue to be developed. Defense contractor Lockheed Martin recently tested a long-range missile capable of autonomously changing course to avoid detection and then select its target based on preprogramed criteria.

No international standards spell out what kinds of operations robotic weapons are allowed to perform. But, military experts and analysts say the move toward autonomous weapons and other military machinery will make war and tactical training safer for soldiers and civilians.

"We've seen an explosion of unmanned vehicles used in the military environment for the past decade, because people see the value in them for saving lives and saving money," says Paul Scharre, a fellow at the Center for a New American Security, a nonpartisan national security and defense policy think tank in Washington, and director of the 20YY Warfare Initiative, which studies how technology will influence future warfare.

"Automation . . . can reduce training costs," Scharre says. "They spend a lot of time in the military training pilots on how to take off and land, particularly in the Navy on aircraft carriers, but that problem is now solved with the X-47B," he says, referring to the Navy's new unmanned plane that can safely take off and land on an aircraft carrier.[13]

Besides saving lives and money, robotic military machines might also be better and "smarter" than people, especially when operating in chaotic wartime conditions, says Ronald Arkin, a professor of robotics and a robo-ethicist at the Georgia Institute of Technology. "I believe they can fit into a new class of precision-guided munitions that can reduce casualties and be used more efficiently than current weapons."

As military and arms control experts, ethicists, roboticists and human rights advocates debate the use of robotic weapons, these are some of the questions they are asking:

Are lethal autonomous weapons ethical?

Building, distributing and deploying robots that do not require direct human control to kill raise many ethical questions. Chief among them is whether a machine should be programmed to take human life.

"Depriving people of human life is very serious and shouldn't be carried out by a machine," says Peter Asaro, professor of media studies at The New School in New York City and a cofounder of the International Committee for Robot Arms Control, a group of legal, ethics and technology experts concerned about the development and proliferation of lethal autonomous weapons. "Inappropriate lethal force is seen as an injustice."

Proponents of robotic warfare, like Arkin of the Georgia Institute of Technology, disagree. War is brutal, they say, but smarter weapons systems may be able to limit civilian casualties and collateral damage. "It is not my belief that an unmanned system will be able to be perfectly ethical in the battlefield, but I am convinced that they can perform more ethically than human soldiers," Arkin told *The New York Times*. [14]

"We are not talking about weapons of mass destruction," Arkin told *CQ Researcher*. "They will be specialized platforms to do specific jobs like clearing mine fields or clearing buildings or counter-sniper operations, but they will not operate in a Terminator-like fashion. It's not about winning wars. It's about protecting noncombatants in the battlespace. Under certain circumstances these machines can be used to protect lives."

Asaro counters: "It may be the case that some machines in the future might be better at the task of limiting noncombatant casualties. Even if that is the case, these systems will not be able to take the moral responsibility of taking a life."

Beyond whether it is ethically acceptable for autonomous machines to kill, experts also are debating whether robots equipped with advanced artificial intelligence — the ability to sense, learn and adapt — can make moral decisions. Morality is not a data point that can be coded into a computer program, they say.

"First of all, we might think that morality is just not the kind of thing that can be codified in strict rules,"

Ryan Jenkins, a war and technology ethicist at California Polytechnic State University, wrote recently. "For many people, morality is something that has to be felt or intuited. . . . If that's right, it seems like computers could never navigate the moral universe as well as (some) humans do. There could be no computer sages or saints of the likes of the Buddha or Martin Luther King Jr."[15]

Scharre, of the Center for a New American Security, cautions against lumping all applications of autonomous robots into one category, especially since sophisticated, fully autonomous artificial intelligence is still years — maybe decades — away.

"Part of the problem is the gravitational pull from science fiction. It never ends well for the people in science fiction movies," Scharre says. "When robots get weapons, the people and machines don't live harmoniously. How do we have a paradigm where autonomy is good and helpful, like with the use of precision weapons, . . . without getting to a level of bad autonomy that we don't want? It requires a nuanced view; it's not so much about limiting autonomy as it is about limiting the type of autonomy. One equivalent is a driver-assisted car. It will be safer, but we wouldn't let the car choose its own destination."

Ethicists also are grappling with questions of responsibility and accountability. Currently, troop commanders may be liable for any war crimes committed by soldiers under their command. But the accountability systems for machines that deviate from the rules of war are less clear.

However, Kenneth Anderson and Matthew Waxman, legal experts at the Hoover Institution, a conservative security think tank at Stanford University, think that principles of accountability for lethal autonomous weapon systems can be developed as the technology matures. "It would be unfortunate to sacrifice real-world gains [such as] reduced battlefield harm . . . in order to satisfy [a] principle that there always be a human to hold accountable," they wrote in a 2013 paper. "It would be better to adapt mechanisms of collective responsibility borne by a 'side' in war."[16]

Could autonomous weapons systems make war more likely?

Advances in military technology are making warfare faster, cheaper and more precise. But some analysts worry that the same factors that make robotic weapons attractive to military leaders might also shape the politics surrounding decisions to go to war.

"More than 40 countries, including potential adversaries such as China, are working on robotics technology," wrote Reuters world affairs columnist Bernrd Debusmann, "which leaves one to wonder how the ability to send large numbers of robots, and fewer soldiers, to war will affect political decisions on force versus diplomacy. You need to be an optimist to think that political leaders will opt for negotiation over war once combat casualties come home not in flag-decked coffins but in packing crates destined for the robot repair shop."[17]

In many cases political leaders must persuade the public that going to war is a good idea and worth risking soldiers' lives. But in his report to the U.N., Heyns, the special rapporteur on executions, wrote that the lowered risks to a nation deciding to go war might make military actions short of war — such as engaging terrorists — seem normal and no longer requiring public debate.

"Due to the low or lowered human costs of armed conflict to States with LARS [lethal autonomous robots] in their arsenals, the national public may over time become increasingly disengaged and leave the decision to use force as a largely financial or diplomatic question for the state, leading to the 'normalization' of armed conflict," he wrote. "LARs may thus lower the threshold . . . for going to war or otherwise using lethal force, resulting in armed conflict no longer being a measure of last resort."[18]

Heyns added that "presenting the use of unmanned systems as a less costly alternative to deploying 'boots on the ground' may . . . in many cases be a false dichotomy. If there is not sufficient support for a ground invasion, the true alternative to using unmanned systems may be not to use force at all."[19]

But other experts point out that such arguments were made in the past, when other forms of military technology — including gunpowder and aerial bombs — were introduced. Going to war, they say, is not solely about having strategic or tactical advantages or an arsenal of the latest technology but part of a complex process involving legal and ethical, as well as strategic, considerations.

"Technologies that reduce risks to human soldiers (or civilians) may also facilitate desirable — even morally imperative — military action," the Hoover Institution's Anderson and Waxman wrote in their paper arguing for

An unarmed Predator drone operated by U.S. Customs and Border Protection is readied for a surveillance flight from Fort Huachuca, Ariz., on March 7, 2013. The U.S. Air Force flew Predators for the first time in Kosovo in 1999. The unarmed drones proved useful in gathering intelligence. Later drones equipped with precision bombs were used widely in the Afghanistan and Iraq wars.

incremental regulation of autonomous weapons systems rather than an immediate ban. "More broadly, trying to reduce warfare and the resort to force by seeking to control the availability of certain weapon systems — particularly those that might make war less risky or less damaging in its conduct — is the tail wagging the dog: How much war occurs and at what intensity and level of destructiveness depends on a slew of much more significant factors, ranging across law, politics, diplomacy, the effectiveness of international institutions, the nature of threats and many other things."[20]

Some experts argue that allowing robotic weapons to proliferate would lead to hair-trigger reactions when international disputes arise. Indeed, uncertainty persists about what would happen if opposing autonomous weapons began engaging one another. The decision to go to war then might be made not by political or military leaders but by algorithms preprogrammed to react.

Asaro of the International Committee for Robot Arms Control compares the dangers inherent in such algorithms to those of automated stock market trading. In 2010, he notes, an automated algorithm triggered a so-called flash crash of the U.S. stock market, causing billions of dollars of losses before humans could respond.

"One of the leading strategic military advantages for using lethal autonomous robots is that they can match the increased tempo of modern warfare, and they can respond to threats more rapidly," Asaro says. But, he adds, "In a mathematical and physical sense, these systems are unpredictable. We don't really know what they are going to do when they engage with other complex systems."

Moreover, Asaro says, "There are practical worries about killer robots — really bad things might come of it. There might be regional and global strategic arms races, between Pakistan and India or China and the U.S., and the kind of instability that that can cause. You could initiate conflict automatically without human intervention."

Should lethal autonomous weapons be banned?

Some experts and advocates from nongovernmental organizations — such as the International Committee for Robot Arms Control, Human Rights Watch and the Campaign to Stop Killer Robots want a permanent ban on all lethal autonomous weapon systems capable of identifying, targeting and engaging targets without direct human control. Existing international humanitarian and human rights laws governing war do not provide an adequate legal structure for lethal autonomous weapons, they say.

They note that certain other weapons systems — such as chemical and biological weapons, landmines and blinding lasers — have been effectively banned by the Geneva Conventions, a series of international agreements created in, and continuously updated since, 1864. The conventions define the rules of war and outline a system of accountability.

Banning lethal autonomous weapons systems, disarmament advocates say, would be better than creating new laws because it would provide a clear message that the ethical risks and the potential of humans losing control of how and why wars are fought are not worth the gains of quicker and more precise military action. And it would stop future development of such automated weapons systems, rather than delaying rule-making until after the weapons are in use.

"A blanket ban [on lethal autonomous weapons] has a wide-range effect, has greater obligations and creates a stronger stigma against using them," says Bonnie Docherty, a senior researcher at Human Rights Watch, an international nongovernmental organization that advocates for human rights, and an instructor at Harvard Law School's International Human Rights Clinic. "If you only regulate them, there is an increased likelihood that militaries will use them in ways they are not supposed to."

The Convention on Certain Conventional Weapons (CCW) was adopted in 1980 to regulate the use of several types of destructive weapons, such as incendiary weapons and napalm. Since then it has been ratified by 115 countries, including the United States. The law is guided by two overarching principles: distinction and proportionality.

Distinction requires that weapons be designed so that they can be used in ways that allow them to distinguish between enemy combatants and noncombatants and avoid unnecessary civilian casualties. Landmines, for example, are considered indiscriminate because there is no way of knowing who will activate them — an enemy soldier or a child who accidentally wanders into a minefield. Proportionality means the number of causalities and the damage inflicted on noncombatants must be weighed against potential strategic or tactical military gains. Under the convention, military actions that cause high civilian casualties with little strategic gain can be prosecuted as war crimes.

International humanitarian law — a body of treaties, directives and legally binding agreements enacted since World War II and enforced by the U.N. and other international nongovernmental organizations — applies during wartime and is used to prosecute war crimes. Human rights law, which was also developed through a series of international agreements and treaties after World War II, applies equally during war and peace and broadly covers the right to life, equality and other fundamental human rights.[21]

Autonomous robotic weapons threaten human rights because they may not have adequate intelligence and

Weapons Technologies of the Future

The U.S. military and defense contractors are developing advanced technologies, lethal and non-lethal, for use in armed conflicts.

Weapon	Military Branch	Description
Laser technology	Navy	Laser Weapon System (LaWS) uses heat from lasers to incinerate moving and stationary targets; mounted on ships.
Electromagnetic waves	Navy	Microwave generators, vehicle-mounted dishes and cruise missiles use pulses of electromagnetic waves to disable vehicles, weapons and electrical grids.
Heat-powered "Active Denial System"	Marines	Non-lethal weapon that transmits heat to locations up to 1,000 meters (six-tenths of a mile) away; arrives in sudden, uncomfortable waves; to be used for mob dispersal, checkpoint and perimeter security and infrastructure protection.
Hypersonic cruise missiles	Air Force, Navy	Can travel up to 300 miles in five minutes by compressing air into a combustion chamber; would be used for executing surprise strikes.

Sources: Kris Osborn, "Navy Declares Laser Weapons Ready to Protect Ships in Persian Gulf," *Military.com*, Dec. 10, 2014, http://tinyurl.com/pdstwgn; Sharon Weinberger, "Electronic warfare: The ethereal future of battle," BBC, April 4, 2013, http://tinyurl.com/lvlkeah; Paul McLeary, "US Army Studying Replacing Thousands of Grunts with Robots," *DefenseNews*, Jan. 20, 2014, http://tinyurl.com/qjoc3b7; "US military unveils non-lethal heat ray weapon," *The Sydney Morning Herald*, March 12, 2012, http://tinyurl.com/mrqzf8z; Alexander Soule, "Raytheon quietly developing new cruise missile technolgy," *Boston Business Journal*, Sept. 24, 2013, http://tinyurl.com/mnqznca

judgment to deal with complicated life-and-death situations, said a report by Human Rights Watch. Further, the report said, the lack of a clear accountability structure might make them illegal.

"International human rights law applies in both peace and war, and it regulates the use of force in situations other than military operations and combat," the report said. And it "tends to have more stringent standards for

Courtesy iRobot Inc. (both)

Soldiers' Little Helper
The Boston-based iRobot company designs military robots such as the 110 FirstLook, launched in 2011 for use in special operations. The small robot can be thrown over walls and into buildings before troops enter to provide surveillance (top). Once inside a building, the robot can use its camera to search for explosives and other hazards to troops (bottom).

regulating the use of lethal force, typically limiting it to where needed to defend human life and safety. Therefore, the challenges of developing a fully autonomous weapon that would comply with international law and still be

useful are even greater when viewed through a human rights lens."[22]

However, other experts warn that an outright ban on weapons with autonomous capabilities will hamper technological innovation and could eliminate potentially life-saving uses of robotic military machines. The Hoover Institution's Anderson and Waxman argue that because fully autonomous weapons capable of taking lethal action without human input don't exist yet in a fully functioning form, current rules of war can be adapted to newer forms of technology as they develop.

"Sensible regulation of these systems as they emerge is both possible and desirable," wrote Anderson and Waxman. "But regulation has to emerge along with the technologies themselves, and against the backdrop of a world that will likely come to adopt, over coming decades, technologies of autonomy for self-driving vehicles, or advanced nursing or elder-care robots, or any number of other technologies that evolve from being increasingly automated to performing some functions with genuine machine autonomy. With many of these technologies, however, the machine will take actions with potentially lethal consequences — and it will happen largely because people conclude over successive decades that machines can sometimes do certain tasks better than humans can."[23]

Part of the legal debate surrounding lethal autonomous weapons focuses on Article 36 of Additional Protocol I, written in 1977 to clarify the Geneva Conventions of 1949. The article requires that any new weapon system be tested and reviewed to ensure that it does not violate the rules of distinction or proportionality: In other words, it cannot indiscriminately target people and must operate at a scale that is appropriate for the conflict.

International law experts question whether Article 36 could effectively ensure that lethal autonomous weapon systems will meet the criteria of distinction and proportionality outlined in international humanitarian law. Evaluating a weapon may sound simple, they say, but distinguishing between a weapon's design and how it is used is complicated.

BACKGROUND
Technological Advances

The emergence of "digital warriors" is the "most important weapons development since the atomic bomb," writes

> **The new precision weapons were not infallible. On July 3, 1988, after some skirmishes with Iranian naval vessels in the Persian Gulf, the U.S. guided missile cruiser *Vincennes* mistakenly shot down Iran Air Flight 655, killing all 290 people on board, including 66 children.**

Peter Singer, an expert on warfare at the New America Foundation think tank and author of *Wired for War*, about the role of technology in the future of warfare.[24] He was referring to robotic weapons in general, not necessarily autonomous ones.

Technological innovation has always been a part of warfare, and it has usually been controversial.

During the Crusades of the Middle Ages, the crossbow was a new battlefield weapon. In 1139, Pope Innocent II prohibited Christians from using the crossbow because it disrupted traditional combat tactics and caused increased casualties. But soldiers adopted the weapon anyway, because it was so effective.

Later that century, when gunpowder was first used in Europe, the Catholic Church again issued a ban, calling weapons that used gunpowder demonic. Like the crossbow, however, the papal ban was ignored.[25]

For centuries military leaders have employed scientists, engineers and academics to devise better tactical tools to win strategic advantages. For example, Singer writes, in 1820 the French and British militaries used a giant mechanical calculating machine called the Arithmometer — a forerunner of the computer — to map out the trajectory of cannonballs.[26]

Unmanned combat machines were first used in World War I. A remote-controlled armored tractor, created by Caterpillar just before the end of the war, was modified to carry explosives and became known as a land torpedo. And an unmanned plane called the Kettering Bug, which could fly by itself, could crash into an enemy target 50 miles away and explode.[27]

By World War II, wireless remote-controlled technology was further developed, and unmanned systems became more sophisticated. The Germans built 8,000 small, unmanned, tank-like vehicles, called Goliaths, which were loaded with explosives and launched at enemy troops and bunkers.[28]

One of the U.S. military's first experimental drone programs was Operation Aphrodite, in which a human crew would pilot an explosive-laden bomber during take off and then bail out. After that the bomber would be remotely guided into important targets that were beyond normal bomber range.

The drone's first target was a powerful German super cannon threatening London. On Aug. 12, 1944, the United States launched a loaded bomber from England, but the unstable explosives blew up before the crew could eject, killing them. The pilot was Joseph Kennedy Jr., the son of former U.S. ambassador to Great Britain and businessman Joseph P. Kennedy Sr. and brother of former President John F. Kennedy.[29]

The political fallout from the high-profile failure of the early drone program caused the U.S. military to stop experimenting with unmanned systems. Later, advances in computing and guided munitions, or smart bombs, would clear the way for future unmanned military systems and robotic weapons.

After World War II (1939-45) and during the Cold War the United States became a leader in development of precision strike weapons. By the beginning of the Vietnam War (1955-1975), the United States military started using precision weapons for aerial bombings.

According to a report prepared for Congress about precision weapons, "Between 1968 and 1973, for example, the Air Force and Navy expended more than 28,000 laser guided bombs in Southeast Asia, mainly against bridges and transportation checkpoints."[30] The guided missiles and bombs were used in addition to massive airborne bombing assaults, in which unguided bombs were dropped on large areas in hopes of hitting targets. The advances in guidance systems brought more precision to battle and created less collateral damage.

The new precision weapons were not infallible, however. On July 3, 1988, after some skirmishes with Iranian naval vessels in the Persian Gulf, the U.S. guided missile cruiser *Vincennes* mistakenly shot down Iran Air Flight 655, killing all 290 people on board, including 66 children.[31] The Navy vessel was using a new Aegis radar system that identified aircraft according to preprogramed guidelines. Although the plane was not on an attack heading and was

CHRONOLOGY

1914-1950s *World wars bring advances in weapons technology and firepower.*

1914-18 World War I begins the age of modern warfare and the early use of remote-controlled weapons.

1920s The word "robot" is first used by Czech writer Karel Capek in "Rossum's Universal Robots," a play about the dangers technological innovation poses to humanity; robot derives from the Czech word for forced labor.

1939-45 World War II inspires advances in military science and technology, including more experiments with unmanned systems, and introduces new weapons, such as the atomic bomb. The scale of destruction caused by the war inspires the codification of international humanitarian and human rights law.

1950 British mathematician Alan Turing posits the concept of artificial intelligence, asking, "Can machines think?"

1958 The Pentagon's Advanced Research Projects Agency (later renamed the Defense Advanced Research Projects Agency, or DARPA) is founded during the height of the Cold War to develop technologies to compete with Soviet science and engineering capabilities.

1968 U.S. military begins using guided bombs in Southeast Asia during the Vietnam War.

1980s-1990s *Advanced missiles and drones appear on the battlefield.*

1980 Members of the U.N. meet to discuss the Geneva Convention on Certain Conventional Weapons, adding to a larger body of international humanitarian law; it limits the deployment of landmines, booby traps, incendiary devices and other weapons that can indiscriminately harm civilians.

1988 U.S. Navy tests a Harpoon anti-ship missile with early self-guidance capabilities; the unarmed missile mistakenly hits an Indian freighter, killing a crew member. In a separate incident a Navy crew using a computer-controlled missile system misidentifies and shoots down Iran Air Flight 655, killing 290 civilians.

1990-1991 During the Persian Gulf War, the United States deploys unmanned aircraft on a limited basis; Iraqi troops surrender to Navy Pioneer drones.

1998 The Convention on Certain Conventional Weapons bans blinding laser weapons.

2000s-Present *With the U.S. fighting wars in Iraq and Afghanistan, the role of unmanned weapons grows.*

2001 Congress sets a goal for the military: By 2010, one-third of its long-range attack aircraft are to be unmanned and one-third of its ground combat vehicles by 2015. The goal has not been met yet. . . . Army begins unmanned ground-vehicle program. . . . PackBot robots search the World Trade Center after Sept. 11 terrorist attacks. . . . War in Afghanistan begins.

2003 Iraq War starts; use of unmanned ground systems follows.

2007 U.S. deploys SWORDS, the first weaponized ground robot, in Iraq; it is recalled a year later, reportedly for acting erratically.

2009 International Committee for Robot Arms Control forms to draw attention to robotic warfare's ethical and legal issues.

2010s The international community begins discussing how best to develop preemptive regulations for lethal autonomous weapon systems. . . . The conflicts in Afghanistan and Iraq wind down for U.S. forces, and the military begins reorganizing.

2012 Defense Department requires autonomous and semi-autonomous weapons to be controlled by "appropriate levels of human judgment."

2013 U.N. holds first meeting on lethal autonomous weapons.

2014 U.N. members meet again to discuss regulating robotic weapons.

April 2015 Signatories to Convention on Certain Conventional Weapons plan to meet to discuss potential robotic warfare regulations.

broadcasting signals marking it as a civilian flight, the radar system misidentified the plane as an Iranian F-14.

"Even though the hard data was telling the crew that the plane wasn't a fighter jet, they trusted what the computer was telling them more," writes Singer. "Aegis was on semiautomatic mode, but not one of the 18 sailors and officers on the command crew was willing to challenge the computer's wisdom. They authorized it to fire."[32] The *Vincennes* was the only military vessel in the area that did not need prior permission from fleet commanders to fire, because military leaders trusted the computer system to properly identify targets.[33]

By the 1990-1991 Persian Gulf War the United States had further developed its precision weapon arsenal, begun using cruise missiles and increased the use of laser guided bombs. On the first night of the war, the U.S. military was able to destroy the Iraqi air force while it was still on the ground and blow up strategic bridges to control the flow of enemy combatants.

"The results were striking," according to the report prepared for Congress. In previous conflicts, it might take hundreds of bombing runs with unguided weapons to destroy dozens of targets. Using precision weapons, the U.S. military destroyed 41 strategic Iraqi bridges in four weeks.[34]

Indeed, unmanned technology had developed to a point where military leaders felt comfortable using it on the battlefield. The army converted M-60 tanks into unmanned rigs to clear Iraqi minefields. The Air Force used a drone to fly surveillance operations, and the Navy deployed Pioneer drones to spot targets for massive battleship cannons shelling Iraq.

Iraqi troops soon learned that if they heard the buzzing of a Pioneer drone overhead, shelling was close behind. "In one case, a group of Iraqi soldiers saw a Pioneer flying overhead and, rather than wait to be blown up by a 2,000-pound cannon shell, waved white bed sheets and undershirts at the drone," writes Singer. "It was the first time in history that human soldiers surrendered to an unmanned system."[35]

By 1999, precision weapons had improved still more and were used in the U.S. military's operations as part of a NATO alliance in Kosovo, where they were trying to stop a war between Serbians and ethnic Albanians in the former Yugoslavia.[36] By then, the introduction of a Global Positioning System (GPS) for guiding bombs was a major advancement for weapons systems. Computer-generated coordinates controlled guidance, rather than the laser-guided systems used in the past, enabling nighttime and foul-weather operations. With a $20,000 kit that included a GPS device, tailfins and sensors, the military could convert unguided bombs into precision weapons. During NATO's 78-day air campaign in Kosovo, hundreds of bombs were dropped with an accuracy rate of more than 90 percent.[37]

In Kosovo, the Air Force flew unmanned Predator drones for the first time. They weren't equipped with weapons but proved a very useful tool for gathering intelligence.[38]

But the advanced military hardware was only as precise as the human intelligence it received. On May 7, 1999, a U.S. B-2 bomber dropped two 2,000-pound bombs on the Chinese Embassy in Belgrade, killing three Chinese citizens, injuring 20 and straining international relations.[39] The bombs hit the target they were programmed to hit, but the building had been mistakenly identified as a military supply depot.

Nevertheless, the reliance on precision guided munitions continued to grow during the conflicts in Iraq and Afghanistan in the early 2000s. Precision weapons were paired with remotely piloted drones, allowing for targeted operations. According to the report for Congress, "The use of precision strike has influenced warfare to such an extent that military forces now have the capability of accurately targeting specific individuals. There is also the inherent ability to limit collateral damage by picking the right-sized weapon for the respective target."

The U.S. military's dominance in the development and use of precision weapons is eroding, however. Russia, China and other nations with advanced military capabilities also have precision weapons. In 2006, for the first time, a non-state actor — Hezbollah, an Islamist militant group based in Lebanon — used guided antitank and antiship cruise missiles against Israeli forces.[40]

Military Robots

When the United States went to war in Afghanistan in 2001 and Iraq in 2003, American ground forces arrived without the support of robotic weapons. A decade later, U.S. forces had deployed more than 6,000 ground robots to aid with surveillance and bomb detection and destruction.[41]

One of the first ground robots used in Iraq was manufactured by iRobot, a Boston-based company

Army War Games Take on Techie Twist

Advocates say video games give recruits "mental flexibility."

The U.S. military — incubator of the Internet, GPS, computers and many other global technologies — is less known for its educational innovations.

But literacy training and, later, occupational training have long been cornerstones of U.S. military indoctrination. When the Continental Army was shivering at Valley Forge during the American Revolution, Gen. George Washington tried to teach his troops to read and write by having them read the Bible.

"During times of war, when large numbers of lower-skilled inductees have nearly overwhelmed the military's capacities, the armed forces have been a seedbed for new teaching methods and tools," Corey Mead, an assistant professor of English at Baruch College in New York, wrote in his 2013 book, *War Play*, a look at educational technology in the military. "In particular, military research and funding have been the primary drivers of educational technology since World War II, including the computers-in-the-schools movement that began in the early 1980s and laid the groundwork for the [use] of high technology in classrooms today."[1]

Video games and, more recently, virtual training grounds are the latest incarnations of the U.S. military's drive to educate its troops. By 2015, the Department of Defense was projected to spend an estimated $24.1 billion on developing the technology to make virtual reality and gaming useful training tools.[2]

The Army has its own online training video game called "America's Army" that multiple soldiers can play simultaneously. To connect with potential recruits, the Army allows non-military players to participate as well. Digital war games like "America's Army" serve as contemporary versions of earlier pro-military propaganda, such as posters and movies depicting military life as adventurous and heroic.[3] According to MIT research, "The free-to-play game has become a more effective recruiting tool for the Army than all other Army advertisements combined."[4]

Describing a virtual reality training ground called "FlatWorld," in which large digital images are projected onto screens inside a warehouse, Mead writes: "Onto the screen (that is, the "flat") was projected the computer-animated version of a deserted city street lined with squat gray residential buildings, a white mosque with two minarets, telephone wire and palm trees. A Middle Eastern carpet covered the floor of the room, with pieces of concrete and wrecked furniture heaped in one corner. Broken ceiling panels hung overhead."

He continues, "Just then a computer-animated helicopter roared in overhead and began strafing the street, as insurgents and U.S. soldiers appeared along the road, each group firing at the other. One insurgent popped up in the open doorway where the American officer had been. He pointed his machine gun in my direction and started firing, and the wall to my left began sending out virtual clouds of plaster dust, which cleared to reveal pockmarks where the bullets had lodged."[5]

In addition to preparing for combat scenarios, the military's video games and virtual reality training are used for cultural training and to help veterans cope with post-traumatic

founded by three MIT roboticists. One of the company's first commercial successes was the Roomba, a robot that vacuums floors. In 1998, iRobot won a grant from DARPA to develop a small ground robot for the U.S. military. In 2001, iRobot sent a PackBot to help search the World Trade Center for victims after the Sept. 11 terrorist attacks.

The following year the PackBot was used in Iraq to help troops dismantle improvised explosive devices (IEDs).

The Boston company also designed other military robots, such as the 110 FirstLook, launched in 2011 to be used in special-operations scenarios. The small robot can be thrown over walls and into buildings before troops enter to provide surveillance.[42]

The robots were especially helpful in Afghanistan and Iraq, where enemy troops conducted so-called asymmetrical warfare — using unconventional weapons such as IEDs and fighting in urban areas surrounded by

stress. Champions of these games as training tools say that learning to process and translate rapidly changing visual data is crucial for soldiers today. Recent wars have not been fought on traditional battlefields where two massive armies face off against one another, but instead they have been fought against backgrounds where combatants may not be easy to identify, or with civilian populations nearby.

"Against this chaos and clutter, somebody who can pick a key piece of information out of a scene and decide in a split second what to do about it is a strategically important person for the army," Mead wrote.[6]

Young enlisted soldiers who grew up playing video games are proving to be well suited to some of the military's new roles, including operating robotic systems from afar. The ability to manage many streams of data while multitasking is another asset. "This experience," wrote Peter Singer, an expert on the future of warfare and security at the New America Foundation, a think tank in Washington, and author of *Wired for War*, "gives kids not just more smarts, but a certain mental flexibility that translates especially well in the complex fights of today's wars. As two retired Marine officers describe what they saw in Iraq, 'Battles are won by young enlisted men, not by generals poring over maps as in World War II.' "[7]

But Singer said that video game and virtual reality training do have drawbacks. "As the Air Force colonel who led a Predator squadron explains, the younger troops flying drones may be more talented, but there is a cost: 'The video game generation is worse at distorting the reality of it [war] from the virtual nature. They don't have that sense of what is really going on,' " according to the colonel as quoted by Singer.

The colonel, Singer said, "believes that the virtual nature of the games makes the consequences seem unreal."[8]

— *Daniel McGlynn*

A virtual battlefield is displayed on a giant screen as American soldiers test a digital war game at Fort Leavenworth, Kan., on Oct. 25, 2012.

Shane Keyser/Kansas City Star/MCT via Getty Images

[1] Corey Mead, *War Play: Video Games and the Future of Armed Conflict* (2013), p. 36.

[2] *Ibid.*, p. 7.

[3] Alex Rayner, "Are video games just propaganda and training tools for the military?" *The Guardian*, March 18, 2012, http://tinyurl.com/phjaeuj.

[4] Jeremy Hsu, "For the U.S. military, video games get serious," *LiveScience*, Aug. 19, 2010, http://tinyurl.com/mg3kaxv.

[5] Mead, *op. cit.*, p. 2.

[6] *Ibid.*, p. 55.

[7] Peter Singer, *Wired for War* (2009), p. 366.

[8] *Ibid.*, p. 367.

noncombatants. As a result, U.S. military officials began buying robots such as the Talon, a remotely operated, tracked vehicle capable of carrying loads (such as a heavy machine gun) over a variety of terrain.

In 2007 the United States deployed its first armed military robots in Iraq. Called Special Weapons Observation Remote Direct-Action System (SWORDS), the robots used Talon platforms equipped with an M249 machine gun. The three SWORDS robots never fired at enemy troops and were pulled from Iraq a year later, leading to widespread but unconfirmed media stories that the armed robot was unpredictable.[43]

By early 2014, as the wars in Iraq and Afghanistan were winding down, the Robotic Systems Joint Program Office, which directed robotics programs for the Marines and Army, was reorganized and transferred to the Army's combat support and combat service support divisions, according to Michael Clow, a spokesman for

Do Today's Rules of War Fit Tomorrow's Conflicts?

Geneva Conventions define allowable weapons and tactics.

Today's rules of war are composed of a series of treaties and agreements collectively known as international humanitarian law. Specific rules about tactics, weapons and treatment of combatants and noncombatants — including defining those roles — are laid out in a series of agreements called the Geneva Conventions.

The first international agreement establishing some basic ground rules was adopted in 1864 in what is considered the first Geneva Convention. It closely followed the work of Henri Dunant, a Swiss businessman and activist who founded the International Committee of the Red Cross following the Crimean War in Europe and was discussed as the American Civil War was underway.[1]

Called the Geneva Convention for the Amelioration of the Condition of the Wounded in Armies in the Field, the agreement focused on caring for the sick and wounded during wartime. It protected caregivers and allowed the Red Cross and ambulances to enter war zones as neutral parties.

Meetings in The Hague between 1899 and 1907 established protocols for protecting prisoners of war and defined such locations as hospitals and schools as off-limits for hostile targeting.[2] Other conventions were written after World War I (1914-18), in which millions died from newly deployed weapons such as machine guns, tanks and mustard gas. In 1925, for example, the Geneva Gas Protocol banned poisonous gas and biological weapons from the battlefield.

In 1949, four years after the end of World War II (1939-45), four additional Geneva Conventions were written. They covered the treatment of wounded and sick soldiers found on land, shipwrecked or stranded. Additional rules covered the treatment of prisoners of war and of civilians during armed conflict.[3]

In 1977, the Hague conventions were updated and amended again. Called the Additional Protocols I and II, the new provisions further defined allowable weapons systems and tactics during conflicts. Article 36 of Protocol 1 required a review process for all new weapon systems. It also outlined the principles of distinction, proportionality and precaution, requiring military leaders to ensure that:

- Weapon systems and tactical maneuvers distinguish civilians from combatants;
- Calculated civilian losses are not disproportional to a strategic military gain;
- Targets are verified and civilian populations are warned before military action.

In 1980, the Convention on Certain Conventional Weapons banned the use of specific weapon systems that violated the rules laid out three years earlier.[4] For example,

the Army's robotics program. The Army is currently retiring 60 percent of its aging ground robots while it plans and develops more standardized unmanned ground systems.

Banned Weapons

As disarmament and arms control advocates call for a preemptive ban on lethal autonomous weapons systems, they point to existing treaties banning chemical weapons, landmines and blinding laser weapons.

"I think chemical weapons are a good analogy," says Asaro, of the International Committee for Robotic Arms Control. "In the 19th and early 20th century, people thought that chemical weapons would be a cleaner, more efficient form of war."

But the use of chemical weapons — during World War I and more recently against civilians by Syrian President Bashar al-Assad in the Syrian civil war — is now considered barbaric by the international community.[44] The Chemical Weapons Convention (CWC), which went into effect in

it banned weapons that produced fragments invisible to X-ray, restricted the use of landmines and booby traps (a separate 1999 treaty calls for a complete ban on antipersonnel mines) and barred incendiary weapons such as napalm. In 1995, an additional protocol banned blinding laser weapons, and in 2003 a fifth protocol established responsibilities for unexploded ordinance used during war.[5]

All nations have signed the 1949 Geneva Conventions, but not all have agreed to every subsequent international war rules treaty.[6] Still, the rules tend to set standards of acceptable behavior and are known as customary laws. The United States refused to sign the 1997 ban on landmines but has stopped exporting or deploying them. Military officials say landmines can be important weapons and don't want to be prohibited from ever using them again.[7]

Those calling for a complete prohibition on robotic weapons cite the bans on landmines, incendiary weapons and blinding lasers as precedent. But some legal experts argue that new protocols wouldn't be needed to accomplish such a ban.

"Additional Protocol I has the real framework, and any new weapons that are developed have to fit in that framework," says Laurie Blank, a law professor and director of the International Humanitarian Law Clinic at Emory University School of Law in Atlanta. "It establishes what a lawful weapons is, and the lawful use of weapons systems. Those rules apply if you use a knife, or if you use the most high-tech weapons."

— *Daniel McGlynn*

British soldiers in France in June 1944 inspect three German remote-controlled "Goliath" mini-tanks loaded with explosives.

[2] David Greenberg, "Fighting fair: The laws of war and how they grew," *Slate*, Jan. 27, 2002, http://tinyurl.com/lsh2gc6.

[3] Trombly, *op. cit.*

[4] The convention's full name is "Convention on Prohibitions or Restrictions on the Use of Certain Conventional Weapons Which May Be Deemed to Be Excessively Injurious or to Have Indiscriminate Effects."

[5] For background, see "The Convention on Certain Conventional Weapons" at http://tinyurl.com/42wfo3.

[6] "2013 Annual Report, States Party to the Geneva Convention and their additional protocols," International Committee of the Red Cross, http://tinyurl.com/mlseg8p.

[7] For background, see Robert Kiener, "Dangerous War Debris," *CQ Researcher*, March 1, 2010, pp. 51-78.

[1] Maria Trombly, "A brief history of the laws of war," Society of Professional Journalists, 2003, http://tinyurl.com/mcalch8.

1997, prohibits the use of chemical weapons as well as their production, possession and transfer. "With the support of 188 states around the world [including the United States], the CWC is one of the most widely adhered-to international treaties, and it has come to symbolize the idea that it is possible to 'civilize' the conduct of war — seemingly against all odds," wrote Richard Price, a professor of political science at the University of British Columbia.[45]

The Convention on the Prohibition of the Use, Stockpiling, Production and Transfer of Anti-Personnel Mines and on Their Destruction, also known as the mine ban treaty, went into effect in 1999 for the 162 countries that have signed it.[46] It prohibits the production, transfer and use of antipersonnel landmines because they violate international humanitarian law prohibitions against weapons that are indiscriminate — that target soldiers and civilians alike. Nations committed to the treaty have pledged not to produce or use landmines, to clear their respective territory of mines, and to establish economic opportunities for civilian victims of landmines.

The U.S. Army used iRobot PackBots during the wars in Iraq and Afghanistan to help troops dismantle improvised explosive devices (IEDs). The small ground robot was developed by the Boston-based iRobot company with a grant from the Pentagon's Defense Advanced Research Projects Agency. In 2001, a PackBot was used to help search the World Trade Center for victims after the Sept. 11 terrorist attacks.

The United States and 35 other countries have not agreed to the ban. U.S. officials say landmines are strategically critical for maintaining the Demilitarized Zone between North and South Korea and that they reserve the right to use them in military operations there.[47]

However, the chemical weapons and landmine treaties came too late to stop the years of indiscriminate deaths and injuries caused by landmines. Banning lethal autonomous weapon systems is entirely different, disarmament experts say, because they haven't been deployed yet.

That makes it challenging for those advocating a ban, says Docherty, the Harvard Law School lecturer and senior researcher for Human Rights Watch. "There are no causalities to tell stories or document," she says. On the other hand, "It should be easier for nations to give these weapons up, because they are not yet using them."

The U.N.'s Protocol on Blinding Laser Weapons is a good precedent for a preemptive ban, Docherty says. Written in the mid-1990s and in effect since 1998, it was in response to weapons research conducted by the U.S.

Air Force and others, which sought to devise a way to destroy human vision from a distance.

The rationale behind the weapons, according to the *Bulletin of the Atomic Scientists*, was that blinding an enemy was useful because the injured fighter would require assistance, which would occupy other combatants.[48] Before the laser weapons were used in combat, however, they were banned. Other laser weapon research continues, though, such as the massive laser cannon recently tested by the U.S. Navy.[49]

In 2009, an international group of academics concerned about the proliferation of robotic weapon systems and the potential development of lethal autonomous weapon systems, founded the International Committee for Robot Arms Control. In 2012, Human Rights Watch began publishing reports about the unregulated development of autonomous weapon systems.

In 2012 the U.S. Department of Defense ordered that a human operator must be "in-the-loop" and maintain control of any robotic weapons. But while the directive provides current guidance, it is not a permanent policy.

In 2013, the Campaign to Stop Killer Robots — a coalition of nongovernmental organizations and disarmament groups, including Human Rights Watch — was launched.

CURRENT SITUATION
International Debate

Policymakers, military leaders and ethicists continue to debate how to regulate autonomous weapon systems in a way that encourages positive outcomes — such as limiting noncombatant casualties — and minimizes the risks of unleashing uncontrolled killer robots.

"As we plan for the future, we've determined that advanced autonomy-enabled technologies will play an even greater role in keeping our soldiers safe."

— *Paul D. Rogers,
Director, U.S. Army Tank Automotive
Research Development and
Engineering Center*

Can lethal autonomous weapons be operated ethically?

YES — Ronald Arkin
Professor of Robotics, Georgia Institute of Technology

Excerpted from statement at a meeting of robotics and legal experts convened by the International Committee of the Red Cross in Geneva, Switzerland, March 26-28, 2014

Multiple potential benefits of intelligent war machines have already been declared by the military, including: a reduction in friendly casualties; force multiplication; expanding the battlespace; extending the soldier's reach; the ability to respond faster given the pressure of an ever increasing battlefield tempo; and greater precision due to . . . constant video surveillance that enables more time for decision-making and more eyes on target. This argues for the inevitability of development and deployment of lethal autonomous systems from a military efficiency and economic standpoint, unless limited by [international humanitarian law].

Past and present trends in human behavior in the battlefield regarding adhering to legal and ethical requirements are questionable at best. Unfortunately, humanity has a rather dismal record in ethical behavior in the battlefield. Potential explanations for the persistence of war crimes include: high friendly losses leading to a tendency to seek revenge; high turnover in the chain of command leading to weakened leadership; dehumanization of the enemy through the use of derogatory names and epithets; poorly trained or inexperienced troops; no clearly defined enemy; unclear orders . . . ; youth and immaturity of troops; external pressure, e.g. for a need to produce a high body count of the enemy; and pleasure from the power of killing or an overwhelming sense of frustration. There is clearly room for improvement, and autonomous systems may help address some of these problems.

Robotics technology, suitably deployed, may assist with the plight of the innocent noncombatant caught on the battlefield. If used without suitable precautions, however, it could potentially exacerbate the already existing violations by human soldiers. While I have the utmost respect for our young men and women soldiers, modern warfare puts them in situations in which no human being was ever designed to function. In such conditions, expecting strict adherence to the laws of war seems unreasonable and unattainable by a significant number of soldiers. Battlefield atrocities have been present since the beginnings of warfare, and despite the growth of [international humanitarian law] over the last 150 years or so, these tendencies persist and are well documented, even more so in the days of CNN and the Internet. The dangers of abuse of unmanned robotic systems in war, such as the Predator and Reaper drones, are well documented; they occur even when a human operator is directly in charge.

NO — Peter Asaro
Professor of Media Studies, The New School; Cofounder, International Committee for Robot Arms Control

Excerpted from statement at a meeting of robotics and legal experts convened by the International Committee of the Red Cross in Geneva, Switzerland, March 26-28, 2014

It is necessary to avoid legalism here — the view that morality and legality are equivalent. If we are to extend the existing body of [international humanitarian law], the best place to start is with moral reflection. As a global community, we may hold different moral values and theories, but historically we have been able to come to broad-based agreement on certain moral issues. The U.N. Declaration of Human Rights (1948) is a significant example. It is valuable to consider autonomous weapon systems from a variety of moral theories and perspectives. I believe that taking such an approach leads us to a convergence of various views and perspectives on the conclusion that the best option for regulating autonomous weapon systems is a prohibition on their use.

So what are the moral questions that arise beyond existing law with regard to permitting autonomous weapon systems to kill human beings? Insofar as we define autonomous weapon systems as systems capable of selecting targets and directing violent force against [them] without meaningful human control, then autonomous weapon systems are significantly different than other weapons. . . . There are weapons in use in which particular objects and people are not consciously targeted by the operator of the weapon, including artillery. However, there is still a human who makes a targeting decision.

In giving over the responsibility to make targeting decisions to machines, we fundamentally change the nature of the moral considerations involved in the use of violent force. While it is claimed that a human will write the computer program the autonomous weapon system will follow, there is no way for a programmer to anticipate every situation and circumstance of the use of force, or the moral values and military necessity for the use of force in those future instances. At best, such a program might approximate the choices made by humans. To be clear, a programmed system would not be conducting the moral reasoning of human beings, at least for the foreseeable future. Moral reasoning requires an ability to view a situation from multiple and conflicting perspectives, weigh incomparable values against each other, including the significance and value of human life, and to choose a course of action that one can take responsibility for. While moral reasoning is a challenge for humans, and they often fall short, it is impossible for algorithms.

While there are still no clear-cut solutions to robotic warfare policy questions, most nations, including the United States, agree rules are needed governing the use of lethal autonomous weapons.

Cuba, Ecuador, Egypt, Pakistan and the Vatican have expressed support for a preemptive ban on fully autonomous weapons, according to an annual report by the Campaign to Stop Killer Robots. But they have yet to execute that commitment into law or policy. And several countries have indicated "they see a need to draw the line at some point," the report said.[50]

Meanwhile, the United States and United Kingdom have policies permitting the development of autonomous weapons systems as long as human operators continue to maintain some control. Much of the current discussion focuses on defining what, exactly, is meant by autonomous weapons systems and what degree of human control should be required.

"One of the things that clouds discussion of autonomy is a lack of precision. It would be nice if everyone discussing this could have an agreed-upon lexicon," says Scharre, of the Center for a New American Security. "When you say fully autonomous, one person is picturing a Roomba [the robotic vacuum cleaner] and another person is picturing a Terminator." There are important differences between automated, automatic and autonomous, he points out.

In November, at a U.N. meeting in Geneva, member states of the Convention on Certain Conventional Weapon called for " 'meaningful human control' of lethal weapons to be enshrined in international law," but the precise definition of that principle has yet to be clarified.[51]

Mary Wareham, advocacy director of the Arms Division of Human Rights Watch, says, "This topic of meaningful human control is an organizing point: What is the nature of human control over existing systems, and what makes them acceptable? This will be part of the talks this year."

Meanwhile, advocacy groups and NGOs are working to educate and inform the general public about the role of robots in the future of warfare, and their campaign for a ban is gaining momentum. "The Campaign to Stop Killer Robots has gathered supporters more quickly than any other disarmament movement," a reporter noted in *Foreign Affairs*. "It took the campaign just six months to get on the U.N. agenda; other campaigns took at least five years."[52]

The Robotic Age

Several militaries already use defensive weapons systems that automatically respond to threats. The United States operates the Patriot Missile Defense System, for instance, and Israel has its Iron Dome, a mobile defense system. Both are designed to automatically launch rockets to intercept inbound missiles or aircraft.

"They are used because the time of engagement is too fast for people to be in the loop," Scharre says. "Some of the systems have been used for decades, but used relatively narrowly, [such as] to defend places where there are people."

Proponents of unmanned military weapons cite the successful and controlled use of automated defensive weapons as a model of how future robotic weapons systems might work and argue that banning autonomous weapons systems can be harmful. "Robotics has an ever-disappearing horizon of definitions," says Georgia Institute of Technology's Arkin.

The success and sophistication of automated weapons defense systems stands in contrast to the state of technology for other kinds of military robots. Automated missile systems work because they are programmed to perform one task over and over in a confined operational window. Other military robots, such as those that detect bombs, monitor troop movements and conduct underwater surveillance, are not as successful, mainly because many warfighting tasks require heightened situational awareness.

The Red Cross report lists the technological limitations of military robots:

- They are unreliable because they are not adaptable and break down easily;
- They still rely heavily on human input to correct mistakes; and
- There are no standard methodologies to test and validate autonomous systems.

But perhaps the greatest barrier to development of autonomous weapon systems, the report said, "is the limited ability of autonomous robotic systems to perceive the environment in which they operate."[53]

However, the rapid pace of technological innovation, particularly in robotics and artificial intelligence, suggests that military robots might transition quickly from handling repetitive tasks to sensing, learning and making decisions.

"Even though today's unmanned systems are 'dumb' in comparison to a human counterpart, strides are being made quickly to incorporate more automation at a faster pace than we've seen before," said Paul Bello, director of the cognitive science program at the Office of Naval Research.[54]

Military robot technology is developing quickly in part because of the high demand for nonmilitary commercial robotic systems for manufacturing and industrial processes. Amazon, the Internet retailer, uses Kiva shipping robots to move cargo around its vast warehouses. Last year Google purchased eight robotics companies, including Boston Dynamics, which builds the human-looking Atlas robot for the Defense Advanced Research Projects Agency (DARPA).

"Unlike during the Cold War, when advanced technologies . . . stemmed largely from government-directed national security research and development strategies, the movement toward the Robotic Age is not being led by the American military-industrial complex," wrote Robert Work and Shawn Brimley, security experts at the Center for a New American Security, in a report about current trends that will shape the future of warfare.

"Companies focused on producing consumer goods and business-to-business services are driving many other key enabling technologies, such as advanced computing and 'big data,' autonomy, artificial intelligence, miniaturization, additive manufacturing [3D printing and related technologies] and small but high-density power systems." Such technologies evolving in the commercial computing and robotics sectors "could be exploited to build increasingly sophisticated and capable unmanned and autonomous military systems."[55]

Meanwhile, the Army alone invested $730 million in robots during the last decade in Iraq and Afghanistan, and the military is in the midst of reorganizing its robotics programs.[56] The Army operates roughly 3,000 ground robots — the Talon IV, PackBot 510 and the Dragon Runner are the most popular — for basic reconnaissance and bomb and hazardous material detection and destruction. The Army is developing standardized requirements for future robotic platforms in order to reduce training and maintenance costs, says Clow, the Army spokesman.

As part of the standardization, the Army is also developing a common robotic individual (CRI), "a lightweight, back-packable robot" that can support reconnaissance,

urban scouting, explosive detection and other missions, Clow says.

Eighty-seven of the 119 nations that have signed the Convention on Certain Conventional Weapons have met several times to begin discussions on potential robotic warfare regulations.[57] They plan to meet again this April to continue the talks.

OUTLOOK
Future of the Force

Whether it is driving the family car, performing surgery or fighting in wars, robots are likely to play an increased role in many future activities, particularly if the tasks are boring, repetitive or dangerous.

Many military experts are enthusiastic about the role robots may play in reducing troop casualties. "As we plan for the future, we've determined that advanced autonomy-enabled technologies will play an even greater role in keeping our soldiers safe," said Paul D. Rogers, director of the U.S. Army Tank Automotive Research Development and Engineering Center at the Detroit Arsenal, in Warren, Mich.[58]

Meanwhile, U.S. military leaders view unmanned robotic weapons systems as critical in maintaining military strength as military budgets shrink. In January, Army Gen. Robert Cone, who leads the Training and Doctrine Command, said, "I've got clear guidance to think about what if you could robotically perform some of the tasks in terms of maneuverability, in terms of the future of the force." With the Army considering reducing the size of a brigade — its most basic, self-sufficient, fighting unit — from 4,000 to 3,000 troops, robotic and unmanned systems could play a key role in that transition, the general said.[59]

What is less clear is whether military robots in the future will be allowed to carry weapons, and if so, what kinds of weapons. And despite increased public engagement about the ethical and legal challenges inherent in autonomous weapons systems, the outcome of the battle for a ban on robotic weapons also is unclear.

"Whether or not this kind of regulation is realistic in the near future is another question — despite the best efforts of groups like International Committee for Robot Arms Control there appears to be little political will to regulate autonomous weapons," Chantal Grut, an international law consultant, wrote in the *Journal of Conflict and Security Law.* "Contrary to rudimentary systems like landmines, autonomy is also a cutting-edge technology — it is only within the near grasp of some states.[60]

"So long as some states maintain a significant military advantage by having access to such technology," she continued, "and as long as such technology is primarily being used against non-state actors, then the international community seems unlikely to find the kind of political will needed to explicitly address these questions in a convention framework."[61]

Some experts question whether the sophisticated hardware used in military applications could be applied to nonmilitary purposes, such as policing or border security. In the United States, research funded by the Department of Homeland Security has reached "heights not seen since the *Sputnik* era," says *Wired for War* author Singer, quoting *Popular Science* magazine.

"Autonomous weapon systems are entering the battlefields of the future, but they are doing so one small automated step at a time" military law experts Anderson and Waxman wrote. "The steady march of automation . . . is frankly inevitable, in part because it is not merely a feature of weapons technology but of technology generally — anything from self-driving cars to high-frequency trading programs dealing in the financial markets in nanosecond intervals too swift for human intervention."

"Automation in weapons technology is also inevitable," they continued, "as a response to the increasing tempo of military operations and political pressures to protect not just one's own personnel but also civilian persons and property."[62]

NOTES

1. "Battle robots to guard Russian missile silos by 2020," *Moscow Times*, Aug. 18, 2014, http://tinyurl.com/kalvug6.

2. David Hambling, "Armed Russian robocops to defend missile bases," *New Scientist*, April 23, 2014, http://tinyurl.com/kyeqksp.

3. *Ibid.*

4. Denise Garcia, "The case against killer robots: Why the United States should ban them," *Foreign Affairs*, May 10, 2014, http://tinyurl.com/n2k3xlt.

5. *Ibid.*; see also: "Robots go to war: March of the Robots" *The Economist*, June 2, 2012, http://tinyurl.com/85hmj87.

6. Jeff Schogol, "Marines in Afghanistan get ballistic underwear," *Stars and Stripes*, June 23, 2011, http://tinyurl.com/6eoklmm. See also Jeremy Hsu, "U.S. Navy tests robot boat swarm to overwhelm enemies," *IEEE Spectrum*, Oct. 5, 2014, http://tinyurl.com/koeubf8; Aarti Shahani, "Army eyes 3D printed food for soldiers," NPR, Nov. 4, 2014, http://tinyurl.com/lzqh95q; see also Peter Katel, "3D Printing," *CQ Researcher*, Dec. 7, 2012, pp. 1037-1060.

7. Will Knight, "Meet Atlas, the robot designed to save the day," *MIT Technology Review*, July 12, 2013, http://tinyurl.com/k5rh88r. Bernd Debusmann, "Killer robots and a revolution in warfare," Reuters, April 22, 2009, http://tinyurl.com/cs2kcp.

8. Mark Thompson, "Zap wars: U.S. Navy successfully tests laser weapon in the Persian Gulf," *Time*, Dec. 10, 2014, http://tinyurl.com/pyfsw3u.

9. Bill Sweetman, "Is the Pentagon's $55 billion stealth bomber too big a secret?" *The Daily Beast*, Sept. 22, 2014, http://tinyurl.com/ll2zhqh. Also see Robert Burns, "Hagel on farewell tour to promote next-gen bomber," The Associated Press, Jan. 14, 2015, http://tinyurl.com/k9bzmsq.

10. "Autonomous weapon system: technical, military, legal and humanitarian aspects," International Committee of the Red Cross, Nov. 1, 2014, http://tinyurl.com/n4fmfe9.

11. John Markoff, "Fearing bombs that can pick whom to kill," *The New York Times*, Nov. 11, 2014, http://tinyurl.com/kyr6ez4.

12. Christof Heyns, "Report of the Special Rapporteur on extrajudicial, summary or arbitrary executions," United Nations General Assembly, April 9, 2013, http://tinyurl.com/bu9c5o4.

13. Craig Whitlock, "Navy lands drone aboard aircraft carrier for first time," *The Washington Post*, July, 10, 2013, http://tinyurl.com/la6yz5j.

14. Cornelia Dean, "A soldier, taking orders from its ethical judgment center," *The New York Times*, Nov. 24, 2008, http://tinyurl.com/ou494fg.

15. Ryan Jenkins, "The Ethics of Killer Robots," E-International Relations, July 23, 2014, http://tinyurl.com/plm6b98.

16. Kenneth Anderson and Matthew Waxman, "Law and ethics for autonomous weapon systems," Hoover Institution, 2013, http://tinyurl.com/n7d2usv.

17. Debusmann, *op. cit.*

18. Heyns, *op. cit.*

19. *Ibid.*

20. Anderson and Waxman, *op. cit.*

21. For background, see U.N. Office of the High Commissioner for Human Rights, http://tinyurl.com/dllogu.

22. "Shaking the foundations: The human rights implications of killer robots," Human Rights Watch and International Human Rights Clinic, Harvard Law School, 2014, http://tinyurl.com/l63dtuw.

23. Anderson and Waxman, *op. cit.*

24. Peter Singer, *Wired for War* (2009), p. 10.

25. Cathal J. Nolan, *The Age of Wars of Religion, 1000-1650* (2006), p. 703.

26. Singer, *op. cit.*, p. 45.

27. *Ibid.*, p. 47. For background, see Thomas J. Billitteri, "Drone Warfare," *CQ Researcher*, Aug. 6, 2010, pp. 653-676.

28. *Ibid.*, p. 47.

29. *Ibid.*, p. 49.

30. Randy Huiss, "Proliferation of Precision Strike: Issues for Congress," Congressional Research Service, May 14, 2012, http://tinyurl.com/mdzhv9o.

31. Max Fisher, "The forgotten story of Iran Air flight 655," *The Washington Post*, Oct. 16, 2013, http://tinyurl.com/nnjfb9x.

32. Singer, *op. cit.*, p. 125.

33. *Ibid.*

34. Huiss, *op. cit.*

35. Singer, *op. cit.*, p. 57.

36. For background, see "NATO's role in Kosovo," www.nato.int/kosovo/history.htm.

37. Huiss, *op. cit.*

38. *Ibid.*

39. Martin Kettle, "CIA takes rap for embassy attack," *The Guardian*, April 9, 2000, http://tinyurl.com/m9jmj38.

40. Huiss, *op. cit.*

41. Erik Sofge, "America's Robot Army: Are unmanned fighters ready for combat?" *Popular Mechanics*, Dec. 18, 2009, http://tinyurl.com/y7xkrpv.

42. For background on iRobot company history, see http://tinyurl.com/kt5cqzo.

43. Erik Sofge, "The inside story of the SWORDS armed robot 'pullout' in Iraq: Update," *Popular Mechanics*, Oct. 1, 2009, http://tinyurl.com/ks6zctl.

44. Anthony Deutsch, "Exclusive: Syria reveals more chemical weapons to watchdog — sources," Reuters, Sept. 17, 2014, http://tinyurl.com/qx9fhnx.

45. Richard Price, "How chemical weapons became taboo," *Foreign Affairs*, Jan. 22, 2013, http://tinyurl.com/pehablm.

46. For background, see Robert Kiener, "Dangerous War Debris," *CQ Researcher*, March 1, 2010, pp. 51-78.

47. Joaquim Moreira Salles, "The United States pledges to give up landmines, just not everywhere," ThinkProgress, Sept. 23, 2014, http://tinyurl.com/ly4rv6c.

48. Dan Drollette Jr., "Blinding them with science: Is the development of a banned laser weapon continuing?" *Bulletin of the Atomic Scientists*, Sept. 14, 2014, http://tinyurl.com/mjqzf8q.

49. *Ibid.*

50. "2014: A year of progress," Campaign to Stop Killer Robots, http://tinyurl.com/nxdnw56.

51. Ed Pilkington, "Killer robots need to be strictly monitored, nations warn at UN meeting," *The Guardian*, Nov. 13, 2004, http://tinyurl.com/lk4ce7c.

52. Garcia, *op. cit.*

53. "Autonomous weapon systems: technical, military, legal and humanitarian aspects," *op. cit.*, p. 13.

54. Patrick Tucker, "The military wants to teach robots right from wrong," *The Atlantic*, May 14, 2014, http://tinyurl.com/m7u8hgu.

55. Robert O. Work and Shawn Brimley, "20YY: Preparing for war in the robotic age," Center for a New American Security, January 2014, http://tinyurl.com/ot6l3vq.

56. Joe Gould, "U.S. Army works toward single ground robot," *DefenseNews*, Nov. 15, 2014, http://tinyurl.com/ljkg9op.

57. For a complete list of the treaty's members, see http://tinyurl.com/mqg5dos.

58. David McNally, "Army researchers envision future robots," U.S. Army Public Affairs, Nov. 3, 2014, http://tinyurl.com/klvwfc3.

59. Paul McLeary, "U.S. Army studying replacing thousands of grunts with robots," *DefenseNews*, Jan. 20, 2014, http://tinyurl.com/k8ro5a8.

60. Chantal Grut, "The challenge of autonomous lethal robotics to international humanitarian law," *Journal of Conflict and Security Law*, Winter 2013, http://tinyurl.com/mqshu29.

61. *Ibid.*

62. Anderson and Waxman, *op. cit.*

BIBLIOGRAPHY

Selected Sources

Books

Mead, Corey, *War Play: Video Games and the Future of Armed Conflict*, Houghton Mifflin Harcourt, 2013.
An English professor explains how history and technology meet in the U.S. military's video game and virtual reality training programs.

Singer, Peter, *Wired for War*, Penguin Books, 2009.
An international security expert and scholar examines how technology, largely robotics, is changing the way wars are fought and the people who fight them.

Articles

Garcia, Denise, "The Case Against Killer Robots: Why the United States Should Ban Them," *Foreign Affairs*, May 10, 2014, http://tinyurl.com/n2k3xlt.
A political scientist argues that the United States should take the lead against lethal autonomous weapon systems.

Greenberg, David, "Fighting Fair: The laws of war and how they grew," *Slate*, Jan. 17, 2002, http://tinyurl.com/lsh2gc6.
A professor of history and journalism traces the development of international humanitarian law over the past 150 years.

Grut, Chantal, "The Challenge of Autonomous Lethal Robotics to International Humanitarian Law," *Journal of Conflict and Security Law*, February 2013, http://tinyurl.com/p3c7yly.
A legal expert outlines some of the legal and ethical challenges inherent in the development and deployment of robotic weapons.

Markoff, John, "Fearing Bombs That Can Pick Whom to Kill," *The New York Times*, Nov. 11, 2014, http://tinyurl.com/o6u9v9d.
A technology journalist explains the latest developments in robotic weapons.

Sofge, Erik, "America's Robot Army: Are Unmanned Fighters Ready for Combat?" *Popular Mechanics*, Dec. 18, 2009, http://tinyurl.com/y7xkrpv.
A journalist provides a technical overview of the U.S. military's ground robots.

Tucker, Patrick, "The Military Wants to Teach Robots Right From Wrong," *The Atlantic*, May 14, 2014, http://tinyurl.com/m7u8hgu.
A journalist explains the complexities of developing artificial intelligence capable of moral judgment.

Reports and Studies

"Autonomous Weapon Systems: Technical, Military, Legal and Humanitarian Aspects," International Committee of the Red Cross, November 2014, http://tinyurl.com/nez5gpy.
The report offers a lengthy summary of some of the issues covered during an international meeting of experts on robotic warfare in Geneva in late March 2014. It includes notes on the topics discussed and speeches given.

"Losing Humanity: The Case Against Killer Robots," Human Rights Watch and the International Human Rights Clinic, Nov. 12, 2012, http://tinyurl.com/bnrw592.
This is the first of two reports published by Human Rights Watch, an international nongovernmental organization, in partnership with Harvard Law School's International Human Rights Clinic. The report outlines some general issues related to the potential conflict between human rights law and lethal autonomous weapons systems.

"Shaking the Foundations: The Human Rights Implications of Killer Robots," Human Rights Watch

and the International Human Rights Clinic, May 12, 2014, http://tinyurl.com/nvf2us5.
This second of two reports explains some of the human rights concerns and potential threats to international law by autonomous weapons development.

"Unmanned Systems Integrated Roadmap FY 2013-2038," Department of Defense, 2013, http://tinyurl.com/lberwwt.
The Department of Defense lays out the technical details and strategic justifications for developing unmanned systems across all branches of the military.

Anderson, Kenneth, and Matthew Waxman, "Law and Ethics for Autonomous Weapons Systems: Why a Ban Won't Work and How the Laws of War Can,"

Hoover Institution, 2013, http://tinyurl.com/n7d2usv.
Two law experts from the conservative Hoover Institution, a public policy think tank based at Stanford University, outline how the existing laws of war are equipped to regulate military robots, and how creating a ban now would stifle innovation.

Work, Robert O., and Shawn Brimley, "20YY: Preparing for War in the Robotic Age," Center for a New American Security, January 2014, http://tinyurl.com/ot6l3vq.
Two researchers at a nonpartisan think tank that focuses on defense and national security policy urge the United States to quickly adopt the next generation of war-fighting technology, including robotic weapons.

For More Information

Campaign to Stop Killer Robots, www.stopkillerrobots.org. Coalition of disarmament and human rights advocacy groups that seeks to ban lethal autonomous weapons systems.

Center for New American Security, 1152 15th St., N.W., Suite 950, Washington, DC 20005; 202-457-9400; www.cnas.org. Security policy think tank and creator of the 20YY Initiative, a research project that focuses on the future of warfare and the role of robotic weapons.

Hoover Institution, 434 Galvez Mall, Stanford University, Stanford, CA 94305-6010; 650-723-1754; www.hoover.org. Conservative public policy think tank that advocates for individual freedoms and a strong national defense.

Human Rights Watch, 350 Fifth Ave., 34th floor, New York, NY 10118-3299; 212-290-4700; www.hrw.org. International nongovernmental organization that researches and reports human rights abuses and provides education and advocacy work worldwide.

International Committee for the Red Cross, 19, avenue de la Paix, 1202 Geneva, Switzerland; 41-22-734-60-01;

www.icrc.org. International NGO that provides humanitarian assistance to victims of war and violence.

International Committee for Robot Arms Control, http://icrac.net. Committee of experts from a variety of backgrounds who are concerned about the development and proliferation of autonomous weapons.

New America Foundation, 1899 L St., N.W., Suite 400, Washington, DC 20036; 202-986-2700; newamerica.net. Nonpartisan public policy institute and think tank that focuses on technology and security issues.

Office of Naval Research, 875 N. Randolph St., Arlington, VA 22217; 703-696-5031; www.onr.navy.mil/. Science and technology research department for the Navy and Marine Corps that is investigating new robotic weapon systems.

U.S. Army Program Executive Office, Combat Support and Combat Service Support, 6501 E. 11 Mile Rd., Warren, MI 48397-5000; www.peocscss.army.mil/. Army office that is responsible for ground robotics program.

8

European Unrest

Brian Beary

Police use water cannons on May 4, 2014, to douse protesters in Brussels, Belgium, who were making the controversial gesture known as the quenelle, which many consider an inverted Nazi salute and a sign of anti-Semitism. As the 28-nation European Union struggles to emerge from recession, it has been hit by waves of Middle Eastern and African refugees and increasing political and social unrest, including rising anti-Semitism. In Greece, the neo-Nazi Golden Dawn party has become a significant political force.

From *CQ Researcher*,
January 9, 2015.

NICOLAS MAETERLINCK/AFP/Getty Images

Nigel Farage, leader of Britain's far-right U.K. Independence Party (UKIP), was fuming. Stuck in traffic for hours in early December, he missed a £25 a-head meet-and-greet with grassroots supporters.

Bristling, he told a television interviewer: "It took me six hours and 15 minutes to get here — it should have taken three-and-a-half to four. This is nothing to do with professionalism. What it does have to do with is a population that is going through the roof because of open-door immigration."[1]

The British media, predictably, went to town on the comment. *The Daily Mirror* published a list of "next things Nigel Farage will blame on immigrants," which included "burned the toast, rainy weather [and] lost his homework."[2]

Back in July, Hungary's prime minister, Viktor Orban, gave a speech in Baile Tusnad, a Romanian town in an area inhabited by several million ethnic Hungarians, that shocked many observers. "We are searching for, and we are doing our best to find, parting ways with Western European dogmas, making ourselves independent from them." Orban said. "A democracy is not necessarily liberal. . . . We have to abandon liberal methods and principles of organizing a society."[3] Moreover, added the leader of a country that belongs to both NATO and the European Union (EU), "Today, the stars of international analyses are Singapore, China, India, Turkey and Russia."[4]

Struggling to emerge from recession and gripped by a wave of Middle Eastern and African refugees, the EU's 28 member countries are experiencing increasing social and political unrest. Jews have been attacked in some countries, often by radicalized, jobless

Muslim immigrant youths, and the neo-Nazi Golden Dawn party — which has its own black-shirted militia — has become a significant political force in Greece.[5] And, far-right nativist, anti-immigrant, anti-EU parties scored some stunning wins in last May's European Parliament election.*

German Chancellor Angela Merkel used her New Year's Eve address to the nation to urge Germans not to follow the Dresden protest leaders, who she said "have prejudice, coldness, even hatred in their hearts."[6]

Meanwhile, as indicated by Orban's comments, some former Soviet-bloc countries — even ones now belonging to the EU — are questioning whether centrally controlled economic systems work better than Western-style free markets, leading some observers and U.S. government officials to voice concern about the future of multicultural tolerance, democracy and economic liberalism in Europe.

Brent Hartley, deputy assistant secretary of State for European and Eurasian affairs, told a U.S. congressional hearing on the status of Hungarian democracy that his office had complained to the Hungarian government about its new undemocratic laws. "Unfortunately, our message went unheeded," said Hartley.[7]

In the May EU parliamentary election, the far-right National Front party came in first in France, while Britain's UKIP, founded in 1993 to push for withdrawal from the EU, also won big. In Germany and Greece, neo-Nazis were elected, while in Hungary, the virulently anti-Roma Jobbik party gained seats.**

"We like to think of Europe as the cradle of democracy. But it is also the cradle of the world's most totalitarian regimes," Dimitris Christopoulos, a professor of social and political science at Panteion University, in Athens, Greece, said at a recent conference. Europe's political elites have mismanaged the economy, and the sudden rise in immigration is fueling a rise in extremist dissent, he said.

---

* The European Parliament — directly elected by EU citizens every five years — is empowered to pass laws in a wide array of policy areas, from protecting the environment and workers' rights to setting EU farm subsidy levels.

** The Roma, often called gypsies, are an ethnic group with its own language and distinct culture that migrated from India to Europe 1,000 years ago.

However, the election did not represent a clean sweep by the far right. Votes for the Netherlands' anti-immigrant Party for Freedom fell 4 percent from the previous European election in 2009, and far-right parties in Romania and Bulgaria lost ground.

"It is a complex situation," Christopoulos explained, in which countries such as Austria and the Nordic states are performing reasonably well economically but still seeing a rise of the far right, while others badly bruised in the 2008-09 recession — such as Ireland, Portugal and Spain — have no neo-Nazi party.[8]

In 2014, the EU economies grew by barely more than 1 percent overall, compared to 2.2 percent in the United States, 5.6 percent in India and 7.4 percent in China.[9] Unemployment remains stubbornly high, around 10 percent EU-wide and 25 percent in Greece and Spain.[10] In France, policymakers seem unable to revive the sputtering economy, and Marine Le Pen — who took over the National Front leadership from her father, Jean-Marie, in 2011 — has benefited from the situation.

Meanwhile, some 216,300 non-Europeans requested asylum in the EU in the first six months of 2014 — up 23 percent over the same period in 2013.[11] Many arrive on smuggler's ships such as the two craft that made international headlines in late December and early January after the crews abandoned them in rough seas off the Italian coast. More than 1,500 illegal migrants, mostly Syrian Kurds, were on the ships, which were boarded by Italian rescue teams and steered to safety.[12]

Along with anti-immigrant sentiment, anti-Semitism is rising in parts of Europe. Violent protests erupted last summer in France and Germany after Israel launched a military incursion into Gaza. Western Europe is seeing more "physical attacks by radical Muslims" on Jews and Jewish sites and properties, according to Andrew Srulevitch, director of European Affairs for the Anti-Defamation League (ADL), a New York-based organization that combats anti-Semitism. In Central and Eastern Europe, "our concerns are more about political parties who are anti-Semitic," he said.[13]

Anti-Muslim sentiment is growing as well, especially in Germany, where 200,000 refugees, many from Muslim-majority countries such as Afghanistan and Iraq, arrived in 2014, more than in any other EU country. In

EU Nearly Doubled Since 2004

Membership in the European Union (EU) grew from 15 nations to 28 in the last 10 years. In addition to Croatia, which joined in 2013, the EU added Bulgaria and Romania in 2007 and 10 others — including the Czech Republic, Hungary and Poland — in 2004. Some experts believe concerns over the EU's expanding geographic breadth and lawmaking powers have fueled the growing political and popular unrest in Europe.

Source: "Member states of the EU," European Union, undated, http://tinyurl.com/3jsomd9. Map by Lewis Agrell.

the eastern German city of Dresden, thousands of people attended rallies in December organized by a new movement called Patriotic Europeans Against the Islamization of the West — known as PEGIDA. Several recent violent Islamist attacks, such as the fatal Jan. 7 shooting of 12 people at the Paris offices of the French satirical newspaper *Charlie Hebdo*, are exacerbating anti-Muslim sentiment, experts say.[14]

Some political analysts say that nativism also is on the rise, due to anxiety about the rising inflow of immigrants and the EU's rapid expansion in both lawmaking powers and geographic reach — from just six countries in 1957 to 28 in 2013. "When the EU was conceived, people didn't think about it growing into a single market of more than 500 million people, each citizen having the freedom to live and work in any country," says Michael Geary, a global fellow in contemporary European politics at the Woodrow Wilson International Center for Scholars in Washington.

The rise of nativist parties is heightening fears of countries reverting to authoritarianism, considered unthinkable a decade ago. Hungarian leader Orban's repudiation of liberal democracy is raising alarm bells, including in the United States, a strong advocate of EU enlargement as a means to cement democracy and alliances. A U.S. congressional hearing on the Hungarian situation featured testimony by a member of Orban's Fidesz party, József Szajer. Sweeping constitutional changes enacted since Orban was elected in 2010 — such as requiring religions to get parliamentary approval to be officially recognized — were legal, he said, because the party has a two-thirds majority in parliament and can amend the constitution as it wishes.[15] But many are worried about the ease and frequency with which the parliament is changing the Hungarian constitution to strengthen the party's control.

Yet the EU is "not doing anything about it," contended Cas Mudde, associate professor of political science in the School of Public and International Affairs at the University of Georgia and author of a book on far-right European parties. Speaking at a conference in Washington in November, Mudde warned that other

Far Right and Far Left Gained Ground in 2014

Although centrists occupy the largest share of seats in the European Parliament, far-right and so-called non-attached groups won a combined 16 percent of the seats in parliamentary elections last May, while the European United Left/Nordic Green Left groups won 7 percent.

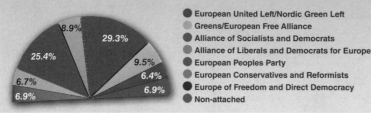

European Parliament Seats Controlled by Each Group, 2014

- ● European United Left/Nordic Green Left
- ● Greens/European Free Alliance
- ● Alliance of Socialists and Democrats
- ● Alliance of Liberals and Democrats for Europe
- ● European Peoples Party
- ● European Conservatives and Reformists
- ● Europe of Freedom and Direct Democracy
- ● Non-attached

What the Parties Represent

There are seven official political groups within the European Parliament, in addition to non-attached groups that comprise their own category. Groups vary by political ideology as follows:

Political Extremists

Far Right — Europe of Freedom and Direct Democracy, a eurosceptic, nationalistic group dominated by the anti-European Union UK Independence Party (UKIP) and Italy's anti-austerity Five Star Party.

Far Left — European United Left/Nordic Green Left; includes established communist parties and newer leftist movements that seek to reconstruct a new European Union with more socialist economic policies.

Non-Attached — Have not joined or formed any specific political group, though most are from far-right parties that do not have enough affiliated members of parliament to form their own political group; includes France's National Front, an anti-immigration, nationalist group, and Greece's neo-Nazi Golden Dawn party.

Centrist Groups

Alliance of Liberals and Democrats for Europe — Includes members from nearly all EU countries; embraces pro-EU, pro-business policies.

Alliance of Socialists and Democrats — Main center-left group; includes French and Italian socialists and the UK Labour Party.

European Conservatives and Reformists — Eurosceptic group led by the UK Conservatives that includes far-right parties from Denmark, Finland and Germany.

European Peoples Party — Center-right Christian Democrat parties with large delegations in Germany and Poland; supports economic and political integration of European countries.

Greens/European Free Alliance — Environmentalists and regional separatists, including the Scottish and Catalan pro-independence parties.

Source: "Size of Political Groups in the EP," European Parliamentary Research Service, Oct. 21, 2014, http://tinyurl.com/lnv3lzh

countries, such as Romania, may follow Orban's lead, justifying their actions by saying, "Well, Hungary did it."[16]

Russia's forcible seizure of Crimea from Ukraine last year has exacerbated European anxieties and created new economic pain as retaliatory trade sanctions imposed by the two sides kick in.

Meanwhile, the radical left also is forging ahead in much of Europe. In Greece, a new party, Syriza, has become the country's largest, eclipsing the "old" socialist and communist left. It campaigns against Greece's post-recession economic bailout deal with the European Union, which required severe cutbacks in public spending and job layoffs.

In Germany, Die Linke (The Left), founded in 2007 on a platform to replace capitalism with democratic socialism, is trying to overtake the Social Democrats. In Spain, Podemos (We Can), established in 2014 to oppose EU austerity policies, won 8 percent of the vote in the May European Parliament elections. In Ireland, the two centrist parties that have governed since independence nearly a century ago could lose power, as the far-left, nationalist Sinn Fein has soared to 25 percent in the polls.

As Europe grapples with these political and social trends, here are some of the questions being raised:

Is political extremism growing in Europe?

The success of the far right and far left in many countries in last May's European Parliament elections triggered headlines around the world about rising extremism.

But the reality is more complicated than that, says the University of Georgia's Mudde, who contends that Europe's old political elites are fueling a false narrative about an extremist surge.[17] While many media outlets reported last year's elections as a political "earthquake," extremist parties' gains were not so dramatic and were limited to certain places, like Hungary, he argues.

"The election was really a victory for Marine Le Pen," whose National Front members comprise 42.5 percent of all the far-right votes in all EU countries, he said. And while the far right gained seats in Austria, Denmark, France, Germany, Greece and Sweden, he continued, it lost in Belgium, Bulgaria, Italy, the Netherlands, Romania, Slovakia and the U.K.[18] In addition, although Germany's neo-Nazi National Democratic Party (NDP) won a seat for the first time, that was only because a few weeks before the vote, the German constitutional court removed the 3 percent threshold needed for parties to win a seat. The NDP's voting share was only 1 percent.

Dieter Dettke, a German national who specializes in European integration and transatlantic relations as an adjunct professor at Georgetown University's School of Foreign Service, cites the rise of the Jobbik opposition party in Hungary as evidence of a rise in extremism. Established in 2003 and led by 36-year-old former history teacher Gabor Vona, Jobbik won 21 percent of the vote in Hungary's 2014 national parliamentary elections. But Jobbik does not hold a monopoly on nativist, anti-capitalist views. Hungary's ruling Fidesz party also is increasingly embracing these ideologies, he points out.

Péter Krekó, director of the Political Capital Institute, a Budapest-based think tank, likened Hungarian Prime Minister Orban to Turkey's president, Recep Tayyip Erdogan, who, when first elected prime minister in 2002, was moderate and pro-Western but gradually embraced nativist conservatism. "The political attractiveness of the Western model is eroding, and populist politicians who have made many efforts to gain the support of the West one or two decades ago are now abandoning the Western path," Krekó said.[19]

While extremism has been a stock feature in Western Europe since the 1980s, it is a newer phenomenon in Central and Eastern Europe, having emerged in the post-communist era.

"How governments managed their transition from a state-controlled economy to a market-driven, democratic country" is key in determining whether political extremism will take root, Georgetown's Dettke says. In countries that managed this transition successfully — such as the Czech Republic, Estonia and Poland — anti-free market, nativist movements are marginal, he says. But in countries that failed to properly manage the transition — such as Bulgaria, Hungary and Romania — the far right is stronger because it exploits widespread disillusionment with reforms that have not improved peoples' daily lives. The extremist parties tend to blame non-natives and ethnic minorities such as the Roma for these failures — along with the EU, since many of the reforms stem from EU membership.

Given the high level of extremism in Eastern Europe, manifested in a resurgence of nationalism and anti-foreigner sentiment, some question whether the National Front and UKIP should be considered extremists.

"Le Pen and Farage are populists, not extremists," says the Wilson Center's Geary. "They take the popular concerns being voiced, such as the expanding role of the EU, and shape them into a populist image."

Geoffrey Harris, a British national who is deputy head of the Washington-based European Parliament Liaison Office with the U.S. Congress in Washington, says that while these parties "have become so popular it is becoming hard to dismiss them as extremists." Harris has researched the phenomenon for more than three decades while working for the European Parliament and co-wrote a book on Europe's far right.

Wolfgang Münchau, associate editor of the *Financial Times*, has argued that new hard-left parties, such as Die Linke in Germany and Podemos in Spain, are not, in fact, extremists. They are simply demanding an end to the pro-austerity policies that EU governments have embraced since a sovereign debt crisis began in late 2009. Rather than extremist views, he contended, their calls for higher levels of public sector investment and debt restructuring reflect a "global consensus" on what economic policies the EU should adopt.[20]

With the EU's single currency area, the eurozone, experiencing negligible or zero economic growth over a sustained period, governments should be restructuring their debts, Münchau wrote.[21]

A demonstrator in Budapest, Hungary, equates the far-right Jobbik party with the ruling Fidesz party of Prime Minister Viktor Orban, which increasingly is embracing similarly extreme policies. Demonstrators marched a few days before the April 6, 2014, general parliamentary election, in which Jobbik won 21 percent of the vote. The phrase at the bottom of the placard reads "No vote for hatred."

Do immigrants pose an economic threat to Europe?

Two distinct types of immigration are occurring in the EU: Workers from poorer EU countries, mostly in Eastern Europe, are heading west, lured by higher-paying jobs; and refugees fleeing conflict and economic hardship in the Middle East and North Africa are also heading to Western Europe. Each is the source of heated debate among both politicians and the public.

Hungary's Orban has blamed immigration for the poor state of Europe's economy. "Western Europe [is] so preoccupied with solving the situation of immigrants that it forgot about the working class," he said. Repeating a frequent claim by those opposed to a liberal immigration policy, Orban said: "Many [immigrants] became free-loaders on the back of welfare systems."[22] The EU's 507 million citizens have a limited legal right to claim welfare benefits in whatever EU country they choose to live in.

The National Front's Le Pen told *Euronews* recently that immigration has been "devastating" for France. France simply does not have the capacity to absorb more immigrants, she said. Asked what to do with the current influx of refugees, her answer was firm: "They can go home. I'm here to save the skin of the French people. . . . We can't make room. We can't, because there's no more room."[23]

Immigrants' share of France's population has increased gradually, from 3.7 percent in 1921 to 8.7 percent by 2011. Meanwhile, France's unemployment rate is 10 percent, the EU average.[24]

A lawyer who at one time represented immigrants, Le Pen insisted she did not wish to demonize immigrants who were already in France but criticized pro-immigration policymakers. "We've always said we've nothing against immigrants but rather those who made them come here," she said. The political elites gave immigrants the false impression "that there was work in Europe," she charged, leading "them to believe that it was Eldorado."

By contrast, London's conservative mayor, Boris Johnson, said immigrants boost the economy but must be integrated into British society. "The country benefits massively from immigration, but people need to be British," said Johnson, who himself has a cosmopolitan background, having been born in New York, with British, German and Turkish ancestry. "They need to speak English, . . . to be loyal to this culture, to this country, to our institutions, to our society, to the Queen, to the rule of law — all the things that make us British," including "a sense of humor."[25]

Georgetown's Dettke says whether immigrants are an economic threat depends on the policies their host countries adopt toward them. For example, he notes, Germany has often been criticized in the past for making it difficult for immigrants who have lived there for many years to gain citizenship, although in 1999 the government made it somewhat easier. Germany is sometimes compared negatively to France, where immigrants can obtain a French passport more easily.

However, Dettke contends that Germany has integrated immigrants into its economy better than some EU countries. "The millions of Turks who immigrated to Germany are not an underclass," he says. By contrast, France housed most of its North African immigrants in high-rise apartment blocks on the outskirts of cities, Dettke says, leading to the emergence of impoverished suburban ghettos that make it difficult for immigrants to assimilate into wider French society or access well-paying jobs.[26]

But Germany's roughly 3 million residents of Turkish background also have had difficulties integrating. When Turks were first invited to immigrate as "guest workers" in the 1960s due to a labor shortage, the German government did not realize for decades that they were there to stay. As a result, comprehensive integration policies were developed only recently.

While the nativist right blames the slow recovery of Europe's economy on immigration and alleges immigrants strain social welfare systems, the Wilson Center's Geary says there is little evidence to support this claim. "In fact," he says, "immigrants are less likely to claim benefits than the rest of the population," at least in the United Kingdom, according to his research.

According to University College London's Centre for Research and Analysis of Migration, immigrants in the U.K. put less strain on social welfare systems than native-born Britons: 34.2 percent of immigrants claim benefits, compared to 37.2 percent of natives.[27] Immigrants who arrived in the U.K. since 2000 have made a positive net fiscal contribution to the British economy, in contrast to natives, whose net fiscal contribution has been negative, the center found.[28] Immigrants from Central and Eastern European countries particularly made a net positive contribution, the research showed, because of their industriousness and high rate of employment.

Geary also points out that the British government has successfully marketed London's multicultural nature as a tool to attract tourists, making immigration more of a revenue generator than an economic drain. And in neighboring Ireland, he notes, many Polish immigrants returned home when the Polish economy picked up, just as Ireland slipped into recession.

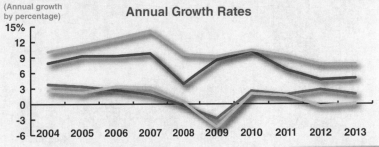

EU Struggles to Recover From Recession

The 28-member European Union (EU) has recovered more slowly from the 2008-09 global recession than China, India and the United States, contributing to rising political and social unrest, some experts say. From 2010 to 2013, the U.S. economy grew at an annual rate of about 2 percent while the EU economy shrank in 2012 and grew by just 0.1 percent in 2013.

Annual Growth Rates

(Annual growth by percentage)

China
India
United States
European Union

Source: "World Databank, GDP growth (annual %)," World Bank, accessed Dec. 16, 2014, http://tinyurl.com/lewnjgb

In general, he says, immigrants in Europe "are adding pressure on the system, but they are not a threat to it," he says. "The situation is manageable."

Has EU centralization and geographic expansion fueled political extremism?

In addition to doubling its membership over the past 20 years, the EU has greatly expanded its powers — with its sphere of responsibility now covering economic, environmental, foreign, monetary and social policies.

In addition, the EU's financial bailouts of deeply indebted countries such as Greece and Portugal that were initiated in 2010-12 have created a backlash, said Timo Lochocki, a transatlantic fellow of the German Marshall Fund of the United States.[29] The Alternative For Germany party, which won 7.1 percent in last year's European Parliament elections, was created in 2013 specifically in opposition to the bailouts.

The bailouts have been an extremely touchy subject for Germans, who are providing €190 billion ($227 billion), or 38 percent, of the €500 billion ($597 billion) European Stability Mechanism, a rescue fund created in 2012. A survey in September measuring German "angst" levels

EU Asylum Applications Rising

Germany received more than 130,000 applications for political asylum through the first 10 months of 2014, more than double its total for all of 2012 and about 20 percent more than in 2013. Sweden (62,000 applications in 2014) and Italy (42,000) have also received more asylum applications each year since 2012.

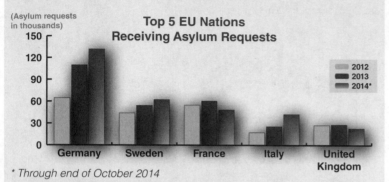

(Asylum requests in thousands)

Top 5 EU Nations Receiving Asylum Requests

2012
2013
2014*

Germany   Sweden   France   Italy   United Kingdom

* Through end of October 2014

Source: "Asylum applications lodged in selected countries in Europe, North America, Oceania and Asia, 2014," U.N. High Commissioner for Refugees, updated Dec. 2, 2014, http://tinyurl.com/ocg9wbu; "Asylum Trends, First half 2014," U.N. High Commissioner for Refugees, Oct. 9, 2014, p. 18, http://tinyurl.com/navcxn3

found that six in 10 were concerned about the impact of the bailouts on German taxpayers, compared to fewer than four in 10 who were worried about the ongoing conflict between Russia and Ukraine.

"People have their own view, which differs from those of the politicians and people in charge of economic and monetary policy, who say debt is under control and the bailout policy is working," said Manfred Schmidt, a politics professor at the University of Heidelberg.[30]

In Finland, the populist Finns party, which also opposes the EU bailouts, has become one of the nation's largest, with a strong chance, say pundits, of gaining enough votes to form part of a coalition government after upcoming national parliament elections in April. But unlike the National Front and Greece's neo-Nazi Golden Dawn party, says Finns party leader Timo Soini, the Finns party is not anti-immigrant.[31] Comprising the bedrock of his supporters, he says, are "mostly working-class men, aged 35 to 54 years — taxi drivers."

In the U.K., ex-parliamentarian Ford said, "It's not primarily a hatred of the EU, but rather that of the self-absorbed political class encapsulated in UKIP's [slogan]: 'No more immigration, no more EU, no more cosmopolitan condescension from London liberal elites.'"[32]

Thus, the message is subtly different from the overt racism encapsulated in the older British National Party (BNP), whose support is declining. "UKIP is not the BNP; its voters share the same social profile, yet because it is seen first and foremost as a 'hard' eurosceptic [anti-EU] party, it has a reputational shield that allows it to introduce into public discourse the racism and xenophobia that was rejected when its mouthpiece was . . . the BNP," said Ford.[33]

Similarly, in Germany, the long-established neo-Nazi NDP has lost ground to the more anti-EU-oriented Alternative For Germany. And France's Marine Le Pen has distanced herself from the more crude, overtly racist and anti-Semitic rhetoric favored by her father Jean-Marie, the longtime National Front leader whom she succeeded in 2011.

Some cite a disappointing 42.5 percent voter turnout in last year's European Parliament elections — the lowest since direct elections began in 1979 — as evidence of Europeans' disillusionment with the EU. But EU supporters point out that turnout was even lower — just 36.6 percent — in the U.S. congressional elections in November, yet Congress' overall legitimacy is not called into question.[34]

The European Commission, which regularly conducts polls on the EU's popularity, claims there is support for more, not fewer, decisions to be taken at the Europe-wide level. In a 2014 poll of the general population, 72 percent of respondents said they want the EU to make decisions on environmental policy and 59 percent on immigration policy. Asked if they wanted an EU army, respondents were almost evenly split, with 46 percent in favor and 47 percent against. The EU's critics, however, regularly cast doubt on the reliability of commission polls, claiming the questions are written to elicit the most EU-friendly response possible.[35]

In a recent speech to the European Parliament, Pope Francis rebuked what he regarded as the elitism of the EU leadership. As the European Union has expanded, he said, "there has been growing mistrust on the part of citizens towards institutions considered to be aloof, engaged in laying down rules perceived as insensitive to individual peoples, if not downright harmful."[36]

The University of Georgia's Mudde drew a distinction between parties that are EU-sceptic and those that are anti-democratic, such as Golden Dawn. The latter are doing best in countries such as Greece, where the democratically elected government is not providing basic services such as health care and social welfare.

The Wilson Center's Geary blames EU skepticism on the recession rather than expansion of the EU's territory and powers. "The collapse of the EU economy is the key reason behind the rise of extremism," he says. "It has been easy for the populists to hook in youth with their messages because young people are less trusting of the ruling elites."

Geary notes that countries that joined the EU in the early 2000s, such as Poland, did not go into recession after joining. "The problem is more to do with bad fiscal management in the old EU member states," he says.

BACKGROUND
Rise of Fascism

The roots of extremist, anti-democratic forces in contemporary Europe can be traced to the emergence of communism and fascism in the early 1900s. Although generally viewed as ideological enemies, with fascism heavily motivated by a hatred of communism, both ideologies supported the establishment of a totalitarian state propped up by parallel, party-based institutions.

The communists were the first to achieve this goal, with the successful 1917 Bolshevik Revolution in Russia, which led to the founding of the Soviet Union. While several communist uprisings occurred in continental Europe at the time, such as in Munich and Hungary, they were short-lived and failed to take root elsewhere.[37] However, the communists' seizure of power in Russia sent shockwaves throughout Europe and proved a boon for nascent fascist parties.

After World War I, the redrawing of Europe's political map at the Paris Peace Conference in 1919, with clear "winners" and "losers," also fueled fascism, says Georgetown's Dettke. In Germany and Hungary, fascists exploited seething resentment over the loss of large chunks of territory that those nations had historically governed, coupled — in Germany's case — with an obligation to compensate other countries for the damages caused during the war.

In 1922, fascists first took power in Italy after Benito Mussolini was appointed prime minister. Fascism also took root in France. The Cross of Fire (Croix-de-Feu) and Doriot movements, which differentiated themselves from communist parties by having strong nationalist leanings, were the most prominent manifestations of French fascism.

Europe was a hotbed of anti-Semitism at the time. Jews were typically blamed for territorial losses and accused of perpetrating communist revolutions (in fact, several communist leaders were Jewish). But anti-Semitism has had a much longer history. It had religious roots — with Christians blaming Jews for Jesus' crucifixion — and economic ones. Jews, often barred from joining guilds and owning land, became moneylenders, making them easy targets for demonization. And falsehoods about Jews were disseminated, such as that they carried out ritual murders during Passover.

The spread of such rumors was often a prelude for anti-Jewish riots and murders. In 1905, an anti-Semitic hoax, *The Protocols of the Elders of Zion*, was published in Russia, claiming that Jewish leaders were plotting world conquest. The book influenced the thinking of Adolf Hitler, an Austrian who became the leader of the National Socialist German Workers' Party (the Nazi Party) in Germany in 1921.[38]

Hitler came to power in Germany in 1933 after the Nazis emerged as the largest party in national elections. The German economy was in a shambles, suffering from both the worldwide depression that followed the 1929 Wall Street crash and the crippling war reparations it was forced to pay the victors of World War I. The Nazis, with virulently anti-Semitic, xenophobic rhetoric, successfully tapped into popular anger over the situation. Hitler quickly imposed a dictatorship, after parliament passed the Enabling Act giving him power to unilaterally enact laws.[39]

Hitler and Mussolini signed a military pact just before World War II broke out in September 1939. Through a combination of political coercion and military conquest, by 1942 they had extended some form of fascist rule through most of continental Europe. The nadir for Europe was the Holocaust, the carefully planned murder of 6 million Jews by the Germans that involved collaboration with many other European nations, including the Netherlands, France and Poland.

Cold War Divisions

As Europe rebuilt itself after World War II, far-right movements gained only marginal support. In Central and Eastern Europe, they were suppressed by communist governments, which were allied mostly with the Soviet Union.

During this period, many fascist leaders were either imprisoned or went into exile. Throughout much of Western Europe, multiparty democracies took hold. While far-right parties were able to compete in elections, they gained little popular support. Fascist governments remained in power in Spain and Portugal until the 1970s: A revolution toppled the fascist regime in Portugal in 1974, and Spain transitioned peacefully to democracy after longtime dictator Gen. Francisco Franco died in 1975.

Racism began to re-emerge in the 1960s and '70s as immigrants arrived in large numbers from former European colonies in Africa and Asia that were transitioning to independence, such as the Congo, Indonesia and Libya. These migrants included Europeans who immigrated out of fear of being persecuted in the newly independent countries. This was notably the case in Algeria, which was a French administrative unit rather than a colony.

However, most of the immigrants were ethnic African, Asian and Afro-Caribbean peoples lured by the prospect of higher living standards in Europe. In West Germany, millions arrived from Turkey, invited by the government as "guest workers" under a 1961 agreement with Turkey aimed at filling a labor shortage.[40] These immigration waves fomented social tensions as host countries struggled to integrate and assimilate them.[41] Some neo-Nazi groups surfaced, often identifiable by their members' shaved heads, earning them the nickname "skinheads."

The government responded by banning symbols such as the Nazi swastika that undermine the constitutional, democratic system. German courts regularly had to interpret the ban and decide what specific symbols and parties are legal or prohibited.

By the 1980s, a new generation of far-right parties and leaders had sprung up, including in Austria, Belgium, Denmark, France, Italy, the Netherlands and the U.K. According to the European Parliament's Harris, who researched the groups at the time, "There was still a real bridge between these new parties and the original Nazi and fascist groups. The continuity between them was quite fascinating."

He attributes their rise to "disillusioned left-wing voters," noting that "the extreme right gets an opportunity when the left is unconvincing." In other words, working-class voters who typically would align themselves with left-wing parties switch allegiances to far-right parties when leftist parties fail to deliver well-paying jobs and strong social protections. In France, for instance, Harris noted how urban ghettos developed under the leadership of a socialist president, François Mitterrand, which National Front leader Jean-Marie Le Pen skillfully exploited. Le Pen, a gifted public speaker, won 15 percent in the 1988 presidential elections.[42]

While the EU traces its origins to the establishment of a European Coal and Steel Community in 1951, its powers and policy responsibilities were relatively limited. For instance, there was still no single currency. The Brussels-based EU institutions thus were not a major focus of the far right's energies, Harris says.[43]

Europe Reunited

Beginning in 1989, the single-party, authoritarian, communist regimes in Central and Eastern Europe were replaced or toppled. When the Soviet Union collapsed at the end of 1991, the end of the Cold War ushered in an era of multiparty elections and free-market economics.

For the first time since World War II, expressions of extreme nationalism and xenophobia were allowed in Central and Eastern Europe. By the mid-2000s, ultra-nationalists had established political parties — such as Ataka in Bulgaria, Jobbik in Hungary and Greater Romania Party in Romania — that were regularly winning seats in parliament.

In Western Europe, far-right ideologues profited from simmering social tensions that arose from a new wave of mostly Muslim immigrants from the Middle East and North Africa, many of whom were asylum-seekers.

CHRONOLOGY

1900-1945 *Totalitarianism rises in Europe.*

1905 *The Protocols of the Elders of Zion*, an anti-Semitic hoax purporting to show Jewish leaders plotting world domination, is published in Russia, fueling anti-Semitism.

October 1917 Communists overthrow Russia's tsars, in Bolshevik Revolution; they establish the Soviet Union, replacing the fledgling democracy with a totalitarian dictatorship.

1919 Paris Peace Conference following World War I inadvertently sows the seeds for the rise of fascism and World War II by harshly punishing losing countries.

1922 Italy's Benito Mussolini becomes Europe's first fascist leader; he soon dismantles constitutional democracy.

1933 Nazi leader Adolf Hitler is elected German chancellor; he quickly installs a fascist dictatorship.

1945 The world learns about the Holocaust, Nazi Germany's systematic murder of 6 million Jews. After the war, Germany is split in two, and the Soviet Union begins its domination over Eastern Europe.

1948-2007 *Eastern and Western Europe split, with the east dominated by Soviet Union, then reunify.*

1949 The Council for Mutual Economic Assistance (Comecon), a Soviet-led economic pact between communist-led countries in Central and Eastern Europe, is founded. . . . The North Atlantic Treaty Organization (NATO), a military alliance between Canada, the United States and Western Europe's free-market democracies, is established as a counterweight.

1960 Independence movement in European colonies in Africa, Asia and the Caribbean gains momentum, triggering large-scale immigration from the former colonies to Europe and the rise of anti-immigrant, racist sentiment.

1988 Jean-Marie Le Pen, the anti-Semitic, racist leader of France's far-right National Front Party, wins 14 percent of the vote in presidential election.

1989 Communist governments in Central and Eastern Europe are replaced or ousted, ushering in multiparty elections and painful transitions to free-market economies. . . . Berlin Wall falls.

1999 Jörg Haider's Freedom Party finishes second in Austria's legislative elections, marking the first time since World War II that a far-right party enters national government in Europe.

2002 Jean-Marie Le Pen reaches the final round in France's presidential election but loses to Jacques Chirac, who wins 82 percent of the vote.

2008-2017 *Far right surges during European recession.*

2008 Global financial crisis hits Europe.

2010 Hungary elects a strongly nationalistic government, which begins to amend the constitution in ways critics say erodes democracy.

2012 Neo-Nazi Golden Dawn party wins 7 percent of the votes in Greece's national parliamentary elections.

2013 British Prime Minister David Cameron announces that if re-elected he will hold a referendum allowing voters to decide whether the U.K. should leave the European Union (EU).

2014 Russia annexes Crimea from Ukraine without the latter's consent. (March). . . . Far-right parties come in first in European Parliament elections in France and the U.K. (May). . . . Refugees fleeing war-torn Iraq and Syria pour into Europe (August). . . . In an independence referendum, Scots opt to remain part of the U.K. (September). . . . EU Court of Justice says countries may limit immigrants' welfare benefits. . . . A far-right bid in the European Parliament to oust the newly elected European Commission (the EU's executive arm) is easily defeated (November).

2017 U.K. voters are due to decide on continued EU membership. . . . Presidential elections are scheduled in France, with the National Front given a strong chance to reach the final round.

Anti-Semitism Re-emerges in Europe

The Israeli-Palestinian conflict has added fuel to the problem.

"Hamas, Hamas: Jews to the gas," demonstrators on Kurfürstendamm, a main avenue in Berlin, chanted last summer, protesting Israel's military incursion into Gaza in July. In Rome protesters urged the boycott of Jewish businesses; in London a supermarket manager briefly pulled Kosher products from shelves, and in Brussels a synagogue was firebombed.

"Seventy years after the Holocaust, many Jews in Europe no longer feel safe," Deborah Lipstadt, a professor of modern Jewish history and Holocaust studies at Emory University, wrote in a *New York Times* op-ed.[1]

In France, home to Europe's largest Jewish community — half a million — numerous, well-publicized violent incidents have occurred in recent years. And in the United Kingdom, which has Europe's second-largest Jewish population of 300,000, the number of anti-Semitic incidents fell in recent years but surged again in July after the Gaza incursion.[2]

Surveys by the European Union's Agency for Fundamental Rights have found that 29 percent of European Jews had considered emigrating to Israel because they did not feel safe, with 76 percent saying anti-Semitism had worsened over the past five years in their home countries.[3] In Germany, the nation's 120,000 Jews "are nervous," Andrew Srulevitch, director of European Affairs at the Anti-Defamation League (ADL), a U.S.-based Jewish advocacy group, told a recent conference at Georgetown University on the rise in anti-Semitism.[4]

Modern European anti-Semitism has two roots: In parts of Eastern Europe, the old, racially motivated hatred of Jews has re-emerged. In Western Europe, opposition to Israeli government policies toward the Palestinians has periodically re-ignited anti-Jewish sentiment, especially after Arab-Israeli flareups such as the one in July.

Sarah Fainberg, a professor of government at Tel Aviv University and a French national, called the anti-Israel argument "the Israelization of anti-Semitism." Advocates for Jews say those who argue they are not anti-Semitic just because they disagree with Israel's policies are walking a thin line. In the "new anti-Semitism," hatred of Israel is used to disguise hatred of Jews, said Hannah Rosenthal, the former U.S. special envoy for combating anti-Semitism.[5]

Stephen Pollard, editor of the *Jewish Chronicle*, agrees. "These people [in France] were not attacked because they were showing their support for the Israeli government," he said. "They were attacked because they were Jews, going about their daily business."[6]

Stacy Bernard Davis, a U.S. State Department official who works on preventing religious persecution, told the Georgetown conference: "Even if you have peace in the Middle East, it won't wipe out anti-Semitism that has been here for millennia."[7]

But Akiva Eldar, a veteran Israeli journalist, is critical of those who suggest that anyone who condemns Israel's occupation of the Palestinian territories in Gaza and West Bank is anti-Semitic. "The cry of 'Help, anti-Semitism' distracts from the cry of 'Help, occupation,' " he wrote in *Al Monitor*, an online magazine on Middle Eastern affairs. The actual data shows that Jewish emigration from Europe is more of a trickle than an exodus, and comparing anti-Semitism in today's Europe to the fascist-dominated 1930s is a "wild exaggeration," he said.[8]

Anti-Semitic attitudes are most widespread in Eastern and Southern Europe, according to an ADL worldwide survey, with Greece (17th), Poland (26th), Bulgaria (27th) and Hungary (30th) the EU countries with the most anti-Semitism.[9] In addition, the EU's Agency for Fundamental Rights found that anti-Semitic offenses and complaints have increased over the decade ending in 2013.[10]

In Italy, the neo-fascist National Alliance led by Gianfranco Fini, from the northern Italian city of Bologna — a communist stronghold — steadily grew. Fini advocated stricter controls on immigration and more stringent law-and-order policies.

In Austria, the populist Freedom Party led by a charismatic, young politician, Jörg Haider, dubbed by some a "yuppie fascist," reached its zenith in the 1999 elections when it tied for second place with the center-right Peoples Party. The two formed a coalition government, but the

Fainberg said some Jews leaving France have been frightened by several attacks on synagogues and Jewish businesses, especially last summer, usually perpetrated by second- or third-generation Muslim immigrants. In one high-profile instance, pro-Palestinian rioters attacked a synagogue and Jewish-owned shops in the northern Paris suburb of Sarcelles, known as "Little Jerusalem."[11] Between January and August last year, 4,556 French Jews became Israeli citizens, she noted.[12]

Some French anti-Semitism is directed at ultra-orthodox Jews, whose numbers, ironically, are growing just as some secular French Jews are leaving France, Fainberg said. "These people live in ghettos," she said. "They do not inhabit the public space. It is not a positive thing." Jean-Yves Camus, director of the Observatory of Political Radicalization at the Foundation Jean-Jaurès, a socialist think tank in Paris, downplayed the emigration of French Jews. Only about 3,000 of the nation's 500,000 Jews left in 2014, he noted, adding that anti-Semitic violence was no longer being driven by the old far-right but by Muslim fundamentalists.[13]

Muslim attacks on French Jews peaked in the early- to mid-2000s, often spurred by extremist imams exploiting discontent among jobless Muslims living in public housing in Parisian suburbs. The French government responded by passing religious anti-discrimination laws and expelling half a dozen radical imams.[14]

Dieter Dettke, a German national and an adjunct professor at Georgetown University who specializes in European integration, has researched the rise of xenophobia in Hungary, home to 80,000 Jews. Although anti-Semitism has been growing there, it has not risen in neighboring Germany, Dettke says. "After World War II, Hungarian fascism was less discredited than German fascism," he says.

Europe's Jews have been persecuted for more than 1,000 years, punctuated by the mass expulsion of Jews from Portugal and Spain in the 1490s, Russian pogroms in the late 1800s and the murder of 6 million Jews during the Nazi Holocaust of World War II.[15]

"Anti-Semitism is the oldest hate in the world," Walter Reich, former director of the U.S. Holocaust Memorial Museum, in Washington, said in October. "After the Holocaust, anti-Semitism did not disappear. It went on a kind of a vacation. It went silent."[16]

— *Brian Beary*

[1] Deborah Lipstadt, "Why Jews Are Worried," *The New York Times*, Aug. 20, 2014, http://tinyurl.com/krfqrlu.

[2] See "Anti-Semitic Incidents Report 2013," Community Security Trust, 2014, http://tinyurl.com/krjbz6y.

[3] Adam LeBor, "Exodus: Why Europe's Jews Are Fleeing Once Again," *Newsweek*, July 29, 2014, http://tinyurl.com/oz7xk9s.

[4] Srulevitch was speaking at a seminar on anti-Semitism at Georgetown University on Sept. 9, 2014.

[5] LeBor, *op. cit.*

[6] *Ibid.*

[7] Davis was speaking at a seminar on anti-Semitism at Georgetown University on Sept. 9, 2014.

[8] Akiva Eldar, "Anti-Israelism, not anti-Semitism, voiced in Europe," *Al Monitor*, Aug. 27, 2014, http://tinyurl.com/ozxa35a.

[9] "Global Survey of Anti-Semitic Attitudes — Executive Summary," Anti-Defamation League, 2014, http://tinyurl.com/kunqm54.

[10] "Antisemitism: Summary overview of the data available in the European Union," European Union Agency for Fundamental Rights, October 2014, http://tinyurl.com/kdk84do.

[11] Kim Willsher, "French officials decry rioters who target synagogue, Jewish shops," *LA Times*, July 21, 2014, http://tinyurl.com/o8flwlh.

[12] Fainberg was speaking at a seminar on anti-Semitism at Georgetown University on Sept. 9, 2014.

[13] Jean-Yves Camus was speaking at the "2014 Human Rights Agenda" conference, organized by the New York-based NGO Human Rights First, on a panel entitled, "The Future of Europe in a Time of Political Extremism."

[14] "The Lost Territories of the Republic," American Jewish Committee, April 2006, http://tinyurl.com/m5ztn3o.

[15] "Antisemitism: Summary overview of the data available in the European Union," *op. cit.*

[16] Reich was speaking at a seminar on the rise of anti-Semitism, organized by the Woodrow Wilson International Center for Scholars, in Washington, D.C., on Oct. 22, 2014.

Freedom Party — plagued by infighting and schisms — began hemorrhaging support in the 2000s.

In Belgium's mostly Dutch-speaking region of Flanders, the far-right, secessionist Flemish Bloc party grew steadily. It was led by Filip de Winter, a controversial figure who defended Flemish nationalists who had collaborated with the Nazis during World War II. The party peaked in the mid-2000s, winning about 25 percent of the Flemish vote. The party was deliberately excluded from government due to an anti-extremist pact called the *cordon sanitaire*

Is Hungary Sliding Toward Authoritarianism?

Viktor Orban's government has made radical changes.

When the ex-communist countries of Central and Eastern Europe were joining the European Union (EU) in the 2000s, Europe's political elites assumed EU membership would ensure their progress toward becoming free-market democracies. But today's situation in Hungary has put that assumption in doubt.

In a speech last July, Hungarian Prime Minister Viktor Orban lavished praise on China and Russia for their "star" systems of government, which he contrasted with the "corruption, sex and violence" of the United States and its "liberal values."[1]

Since his election as prime minister in 2010 after his party won 53 percent of the votes in parliamentary elections, Orban has eradicated many checks and balances in Hungary's political system, taken over ownership of private pension funds in order to cut the public deficit, imposed high taxes on sectors with strong foreign investment and increased state involvement in the economy.

The July speech "reinforced his reputation as a leader who is happy to scandalize critics at home and in the EU, while striving to radically overhaul Hungary and strengthen it through relations with partners to the east," wrote Irish journalist Daniel McLaughlin.[2]

Orban is "a perfect populist who exploits the chameleon nature of populism like no other," wrote Péter Krekó, director of the Political Capital Institute, a Budapest-based think tank. The prime minister started out as a radical liberal favoring free-market economics, switched to a more statist-populist position advocating greater government involvement in the economy in 2002 and has shifted toward authoritarianism since 2010, Krekó said.[3]

After leaving communism behind in 1989, Hungary saw its economy contract by 18 percent over the next three years and by 6.4 percent between 2008 and 2009. Orban aims to replace Hungary's debt-laden welfare state with a "workfare of state," in which fewer people rely on state handouts.[4]

Swept into power with a two-thirds majority in parliament, Orban's ruling Fidesz party rode a wave of mass public dissatisfaction with the previous government, which was mired in economic failure and political corruption. The Fidesz-controlled parliament moved swiftly to consolidate its control of the country, passing a law requiring "balanced reporting" by media outlets — with "balanced" defined by a specially appointed commission — and establishing fines for transgressors.

The parliament also gave itself authority to decide what religions to officially recognize.[5] The law has forced more newly established religions in Hungary to reapply for recognition, putting their future in the hands of parliamentarians, while older, established religions have retained their official status.

Civil liberties advocates and conservative evangelical churches have united in opposing the new law. They claim it discriminates among churches and flouts human rights conventions by sanctioning only religions deemed to pose no threat to "national security."

On another front, the parliament passed a law that dismissed hundreds of judges and prosecutors by lowering the mandatory retirement age from 70 to 62. The European Court of Justice later struck down the law for violating EU anti-age-discrimination legislation.[6]

Parliament also restricted the Constitutional Court's power to review draft constitutional amendments or religious freedom claims. Moreover, it banned speech that violates the dignity of the "Hungarian Nation," which Human Rights First, a New York-based advocacy group, says has been used to target Hungary's Roma minority. The Roma (also known as gypsies), an ethnic minority dispersed widely across Europe, suffer from longstanding discrimination and marginalization from the majority populations where they live, including Hungary.[7]

While Orban's Fidesz party won re-election in 2014 with 44.5 percent of the vote, its share of total votes declined by 8 percent from 2010.

Some Hungarians are anxious about their government's increasingly interventionist policies. For example, a protest in November against a new plan to eliminate private pension funds attracted several thousand. Protest organizer Zoltán Vajda said: "The money I have in the private pension fund is mine, not somebody else's, but mine, or if I die it is for my children or my wife. If the government feels that the private pension system is not working well, they can start a discussion about it."[8]

Former President Bill Clinton also is sounding an alarm over Hungary. "The Hungarian prime minister said he likes authoritarian capitalism," Clinton said in September. "That's just a way to say, 'I don't want to give up power.' In general, these types want to stay eternally in power and make money."[9]

Orban has effectively tapped into still-simmering public resentment over the post-World War I Treaty of Trianon, when Hungary was forced to cede two-thirds of territory it historically had ruled, occupied by 3 million Hungarians, to parts of what are now Romania, Serbia and Slovakia. Soon after being elected, Orban extended citizenship to ethnic Hungarians living in these "annexed territories," offending the governments of those countries.

Dieter Dettke, an adjunct professor of political science at Georgetown University who has published a study on Hungarian politics, said many extreme nationalists in Hungary are embracing a nativist ideology called Turanism. It contends that the roots of the Hungarian nation lie in the East and that Hungary should thus leave the EU and align with Asian countries. Turanist-inspired rock groups, such as Hungarica and Karpathia, express a yearning to create a "Greater Hungary," Dettke said.

Tamas Bodoky, editor-in-chief of *Atlatszo.hu*, an investigative journalism non-governmental organization (NGO), criticized Orban's handling of internal dissent. "Nobody gets shot, but the government labels the NGOs as serving 'foreign interests,'" he told a conference in December. "It's the Russian recipe against NGOs," he said, referring to how the Russian government has forced NGOs receiving funding from abroad to register as "foreign agents."[10]

Bodoky also excoriated the EU as having done nothing except "expensive public relations work" to stop the authoritarian creep in Hungary. Asked what the United States should do, Bodoky said: "If Europe is reluctant, then the U.S. should speak out."

— *Brian Beary*

ATTILA KISBENEDEK/AFP/Getty Images

Prime Minister Viktor Orban of Hungary gave a controversial speech last July in which he praised China and Russia and criticized the "corruption, sex and violence" of the United States.

[2] Daniel McLaughlin, "Orban alarms critics with plan for an 'illiberal' Hungary," *Irish Times*, July 31, 2014, http://tinyurl.com/mhzjhmj.

[3] Péter Krekó, "More Hungarys in eastern Europe?" Open Democracy, Aug. 27, 2014, http://tinyurl.com/pflt7od.

[4] Csaba Tóth, "Full text of Viktor Orbán's speech at Băile Tuşnad (Tusnádfürdő) of 26 July 2014," *The Budapest Beacon*, July 29, 2014, http://tinyurl.com/op8t8ue.

[5] Dieter Dettke, "Hungary's Jobbik Party, the Challenge of European Ethno-Nationalism and the Future of the European Project," Centre for International Relations/Wilson Center, 2014, http://tinyurl.com/oe98bbp.

[6] Gabriele Steinhauser, "EU Court Rules Against Hungary Retirement Law," *The Wall Street Journal*, Nov. 6, 2012, http://tinyurl.com/pt8h6kt.

[7] "We're not Nazis, but . . . ," Human Rights First, August 2014, http://tinyurl.com/oz2ql92.

[8] "Hungarians protest as the government moves against private pension schemes," *Euronews*, Nov. 26, 2014, http://tinyurl.com/k8ockf3.

[9] Joëlle Stolz, "Bruxelles, face au déficit démocratique hongrois," *Le Monde*, Sept. 29, 2014, http://tinyurl.com/ojmsbyt.

[10] Bodoky was speaking in Washington at the "2014 Human Rights Agenda" conference on Dec. 9, 2014, organized by New York-based Human Rights First, on a panel entitled, "The Future of Europe in a Time of Political Extremism." See video recording of the discussion uploaded to YouTube at http://tinyurl.com/o9y7pjh.

[1] "Viktor Orbán's Speech, Tusnádfürdő, 26 July 2014, German English Subtitles," YouTube, July 26, 2014, http://tinyurl.com/laqf46k.

(sanitary cordon) forged by the other parties. Since 2010, it has been eclipsed by another secessionist — but not racist — Flemish party, the New Flemish Alliance.

Anti-Semitism flared sporadically, often along with anti-Zionism (opposition to the existence of a Jewish state in Israel/Palestine). A unique coalition formed on this issue between Muslim immigrant youths — often stirred up by radical Muslim imams in France — who sympathized with the fate of stateless Palestinian Arabs, and leftist European intellectuals, who accused the Israeli government of committing grave human rights abuses against the Palestinians. In France, home to many discontented, jobless North African immigrants, high-profile incidents of anti-Semitic violence occurred, such as the 2006 youth gang torture and murder of a young Jewish man, Ilan Halimi, in Paris.[44]

Meanwhile, the EU's powers were expanded in a series of intergovernmental treaties, making it increasingly a target of criticism from the far right. In 2007, the EU established the Agency for Fundamental Rights, based in Vienna, to collect reliable and comparable data on racism and anti-Semitism.

Economic Turmoil

The global financial crisis of 2008-09 plunged Europe into deep recession from which it has yet to fully recover. Extremist movements have popped up, usually in countries worst hit by the crisis, such as financially struggling Greece, where the far-right, racist Golden Dawn party emerged as a political force in 2012, winning 7 percent of the vote in national parliamentary elections, compared to just 0.29 percent in 2009.

Golden Dawn grew out of a magazine of the same name, launched in 1980 by Nikolaos Michaloliakos, a hardline nationalist who supported the Greek military junta that ruled from 1967-74 and who was convicted in 1978 on weapons possession charges. The party uses Nazi rhetoric, adopted a swastika-like symbol and has its own black-shirted militia, some of whom have been implicated in the murder and torture of immigrants, according to Human Rights First, a New York-based anti-extremist group.[45] Golden Dawn has tapped into anti-immigrant sentiment that began in the 1990s, when large numbers of Albanians moved to Greece.

After Greece agreed to an EU bailout and austerity program in 2010 to avoid defaulting on soaring sovereign

debts, Golden Dawn became a significant party at the national level.[46] However, the hard-left, anti-austerity party, Syriza, became the main opposition in 2012, winning more than twice as many votes as Golden Dawn.

While extremist manifestations were mostly peaceful, an attack in affluent Norway in 2011 shocked the world. Right-wing extremist and loner Anders Breivik, disgruntled over his government's liberal immigration policies, murdered 77 teenagers at the summer camp of the center-left Labor Party's youth wing.[47]

In the U.K., which has seen more than a million new migrant workers arrive from Eastern Europe, the populist right has channeled its energies into anti-immigrant and anti-EU rhetoric. Conservative Prime Minister David Cameron was accused by many of pandering to the far right when he announced, in January 2013, plans to hold a referendum in 2017 to give the British people the option of leaving the EU entirely (they joined in 1973).

Cameron has said that he personally would like Britain to remain in the EU and that if his party is re-elected in 2015 he will renegotiate the terms of Britain's EU membership to claw back some powers from Brussels to London. But rather than stopping the hemorrhaging of support from his party, the referendum announcement seemed to boost the ranks of UKIP, which came in first in the European elections last May, winning 27 percent of the vote.

Germany was spared the worst of the recession, in part due to a successful reform of its labor markets in the early 2000s, making it less financially onerous for employers to hire new workers, and also cutting benefits for the long-term unemployed. These reforms helped bolster Germany's position as a leading global exporter of manufactured goods. But it has not been immune to threats of political disruption.

The long-established pro-business, pro-EU Free Democrats, the historically favored coalition partner of Chancellor Angela Merkel's center-right Christian Democrats, risks being supplanted by the far-right, anti-EU Alternative For Germany. Georgetown University's Dettke believes that the Free Democrats, which lost all its seats in the 2013 German election, are being punished by Germans for supporting EU-mandated austerity, which has included slashing welfare benefits.

In Italy, the populist, anti-austerity Five Star Movement party, led by former comedian Beppe Grillo, also is riding an anti-austerity wave, winning 25 percent of the vote in the 2013 national elections.

In Eastern Europe, the Baltic countries and Poland seem to have benefited the most from EU membership, while Bulgaria, Hungary and Romania have been struggling. Hungary's far-right Jobbik party has gained support but still trails Orban's ruling Fidesz party. With these two parties competing for the same electoral base, they are more rivals than allies.

In the runup to the May 2014 European Parliament elections, Orban engaged in a skillful tactical maneuver — alleging that Jobbik was receiving secret funding from Russia — aimed at stemming the party's rise.[48] The ploy seems to have worked: While Jobbik still won 15 percent of the vote, it was 6 percent less than its support in the national elections a month earlier.

CURRENT SITUATION

Recent Immigration

After years of a weak EU economy and steady inflows of refugees and economic migrants from troubled regions, immigration fatigue and anxiety are setting in among Europeans.

The flow of refugees — often via smugglers' ships — from Iraq and Syria has risen especially since last summer, when the Islamic State terrorist group, also known as ISIL and ISIS, captured large swaths of territory in the region.[49] On Nov. 28, more than 700 migrants fleeing Syria on a smuggler's vessel were forced to dock on the Greek island of Crete after their ship broke down.[50] North African immigrants have been crossing the Mediterranean in large numbers too, often landing in places such as Sicily and Malta, which are ill-equipped to handle such large influxes.

According to the U.N. High Commissioner for Refugees, four countries — France, Germany, Italy and Sweden — received more asylum applications in 2014 than the rest of the 28 EU member states. Germany has taken in tens of thousands of Syrian refugees since the civil war there erupted in 2011. In one Swedish town — Sodertalje — 30,000 of its 90,000 residents now come from the Middle East. With a rapidly developing housing shortage, Sodertalje Mayor Boel Godner said, "The question that has come up lately is: Can the

welfare system bear us all?"[51] Central and Eastern European countries are seeing smaller influxes.[52]

European governments are conflicted over whether to grant the newcomers refugee status, move them to a nearby country better able to accommodate them or deport them as illegal immigrants. In Denmark, there is talk of limiting the stay of asylum-seekers to one year instead of granting them permission to stay for an unlimited period.[53] The five countries that collectively received 75 percent of the refugees in the first half of 2014 — France, Germany, Poland, Spain and the U.K. — have asked the EU Commission to propose new rules for redistributing refugees more evenly.[54]

Responsibility for controlling the EU's external border is another source of discord. Countries such as Italy, which spends millions of euros to try to stop illegal immigration, would like the issue treated more as an EU-wide problem, given that once the migrants arrive in one EU country they are fairly free to travel elsewhere in Europe.

Meanwhile, the Luxembourg-based EU Court of Justice delivered an important ruling on Nov. 11 on the right of immigrants from one EU country to claim welfare benefits when they move to another EU country. The court ruled in favor of the German government, which had denied a Romanian woman's request for unemployment benefits on the grounds that she had not tried to find a job.[55] According to Geary of the Wilson Center, some governments — notably the U.K. — likely will use the ruling to further limit social benefits for immigrants.

New Leadership

Despite some major gains in last May's European Parliament elections, the far right is now struggling to consolidate its wins.

To wield real power in the European Parliament, political parties must form a coalition of at least 25 members from no fewer than seven countries. This alliance-forging process has exposed how riven the far right is with mutual antipathy, distrust and rivalries.

Two competing factions — one led by France's Le Pen and the Netherlands' Party For Freedom leader Geert Wilders, who opposes what he calls the Islamization of the West, and the other by UKIP's Farage — each tried to woo far-right parliament members into their camp.

AT ISSUE

Is far-right political extremism growing in Europe?

YES
Péter Krekó
Director, Political Capital Institute, Budapest, Hungary; Co-chair, EU Radicalisation Awareness Network's PREVENT Working Group; Senior lecturer, EötvösLoránd University of Sciences, Budapest

Written for *CQ Researcher*, January 2015

The far right is on the rise in Europe, with more domestic and foreign support and more impact on the mainstream. In the 2014 European Parliament elections last May, support grew for the far right's ethno-nationalistic agenda and for populist right-wing parties' anti-European Union (EU) agenda. Right-wing and anti-EU parties now have more than 13 percent of the European Parliament seats. They range from Germany's openly neo-Nazi NDP to Italy's eurosceptic-populist Five Star movement.

The anti-EU Europe of Freedom and Direct Democracy group of populist leader Nigel Farage has 6.4 percent; the non-affiliated far-right members of groups such as the French Front National, Greek Golden Dawn or Hungarian Jobbik have 6.9 percent.

Far-right or populist eurosceptic parties came in first in European Parliament elections in France and the U.K. and second in Hungary. Extremist politics in Europe pose a number of dangers. For example, several far-right supporters (along with many on the far left) want to undermine U.S.-EU relations by opposing NATO membership and the Transatlantic Trade and Investment Partnership.

Another danger lies in the far right's capacity to provoke and sharpen ethnic conflicts. In Eastern Europe they target mainly the Roma minority; in Western Europe, Muslim immigrants and immigrants from the poorer Eastern European countries.

The far right increasingly has an impact on the mainstream. In Hungary, the governing Fidesz party implemented several measures pushed by Jobbik, a radical nationalist party, including dual citizenship for ethnic Hungarians and extra taxes on banks and multinational companies. Meanwhile, the burqa ban in France, restrictions on immigration in Denmark and efforts toward forced integration in the Netherlands demonstrate the impact of far-right rhetoric on governments. In Denmark, the far right was practically in government for a decade; in Sweden it just brought down the government.

And many far-right parties openly support President Vladimir Putin's Russia with votes, statements and information. These parties can help Russia in destabilizing the EU and pushing the Kremlin narrative in international politics.

The strengthening of the far right does not justify apocalyptic visions: We are not in the 1930s again, and there is no "fascist plague" in Europe. But as the far right in Europe shifts from neo-fascism to more moderate neo-populism, it can increase both its appeal and impact.

NO
Cas Mudde
Associate Professor, School of Public and International Affairs, University of Georgia; Author: Populism in Europe and the Americas and Political Extremism

Written for *CQ Researcher*, January 2015

The idea that economic crises lead to more support for far-right parties goes back to Adolf Hitler's rise to power during the Great Depression. However, the link is largely false. Just as Hitler was one of few fascists to profit from the global economic collapse, the French National Front (FN) is among the minority of far-right parties today to grow significantly as a consequence of the recent global recession.

A comparison of national electoral results of far-right parties before and after the recession shows only marginal growth, mostly the result of a couple of highly successful parties. Roughly as many far-right parties lost as won electoral support. And the few that won big in recent years were almost all well established; some simply recovered from a pre-crisis dip in support, such as the Austrian Freedom Party (FPÖ) and the FN. Perhaps most telling is that only one of the five "bailout countries" in the European Union has a moderately successful far-right party: Greece.

The situation in the European Parliament is similar. The European elections of May 2014 were not an "earthquake." Depending on the broadness of the definition of "far right" — mainly whether the UK Independence Party (UKIP) is included — far-right parties won between 6.8 and 10.3 percent of the vote, an increase of roughly 1-2 percent. If UKIP is excluded, the far right holds 51 seats, up 17 from 2009.

Overall, far-right parties gained representation in just 10 of the 28 EU member states. In six they gained extra seats, in seven they lost seats. In three East European countries they lost representation altogether. In short, the far right is not growing significantly in Europe, but only in a few European countries.

The reason is both simple and somewhat paradoxical: During an economic crisis, most people prioritize socioeconomic issues like unemployment. For far-right parties, such issues are secondary to sociocultural issues like immigration. Hence, people who sympathize with far-right parties on sociocultural issues like multiculturalism will look for an alternative on socioeconomic issues. In countries less hard hit by the economic crisis, like Austria and Sweden, socioeconomic issues will dominate the public debate less, leaving more space for far-right parties to convince their potential electorate that the real issues are sociocultural (e.g. European integration) rather than socioeconomic (e.g. austerity).

Ultimately, only Farage could get the requisite number to form a political group, leaving Le Pen and Wilders stranded as "non-attached," meaning their parties get no funding from Parliament and must scramble for speaking time in floor debates.

Neither Le Pen nor Farage was willing to accept the more extremist positions of Hungary's Jobbik and Greece's Golden Dawn, further splintering the far right's representation. The Nordic countries have a solid and growing populist right representation. The Swedish Democrats joined Farage's group, while the Danish People's Party and the Finns Party joined the European Conservatives and Reformists, a softer eurosceptic group led by the U.K.'s Conservatives.

When a new EU Commission, led by former Luxembourg Prime Minister Jean-Claude Juncker, took office on Nov. 1, far-right members introduced a no-confidence motion against the commission, using a tax evasion-related scandal called Luxleaks as their justification. It was easily defeated on Nov. 27, with 101 voting for and 461 against.

Welcoming the loss, a German member of Parliament, Manfred Weber, vowed that the Parliament would "not allow" Farage and Le Pen to "continue playing their little political games."

Despite the large margin of victory, Harris of the EU Parliament's liaison office in Washington offers a warning. He says that the mainstream parties that saved Juncker should avoid lapsing into a typical "cozy consensus" that "gives the non-mainstream parties an easy way" to argue that a self-perpetuating ruling elite in Brussels fails to address the needs of ordinary citizens.

Russian Influence

In the wake of Russia's 2014 annexation of Crimea and support for pro-Russian separatist rebels in Eastern Ukraine, relations between the EU and the United States are warmer, but both are now estranged from Russia.

The EU and the United States imposed financial and economic sanctions on Russia, which quickly retaliated by banning imports of EU and U.S. food.[56]

German Chancellor Merkel warned that Russia's actions in Crimea and eastern Ukraine "called the whole of the European peaceful order into question," and said she feared the creation of a Cold War-style zone of influence in Europe. In a speech to the Lowry Institute for International Policy Studies in Sydney, Australia, she said, "This isn't just about Ukraine. This is about Moldova [and] Georgia, and if this continues then one will have to ask about Serbia, and one will have to ask about the countries of the Western Balkans."[57]

Since the trouble in Ukraine, some Central and Eastern European countries, such as Estonia, Latvia and Lithuania, have ensconced themselves more firmly in the pro-NATO camp. But others are questioning where their true allegiance lies. Slovakian Prime Minister Robert Fico likened the possible deployment of NATO troops to Eastern Europe in response to Russian incursions into Ukraine to the 1968 Soviet invasion of Czechoslovakia.

"Slovakia has its historical experience with participation of foreign troops. Let us remember the 1968 invasion. Therefore this topic is extraordinarily sensitive to us," he said.[58] Even in more pro-NATO Poland, the new prime minister, Ewa Kopacz, has asked her foreign minister to urgently revise policy toward Russia to avoid setting "unrealistic goals" in Ukraine.[59]

"A big chunk of the NATO alliance has quietly begun to lean toward Moscow," wrote Jackson Diehl, deputy editorial page editor of *The Washington Post.*

In a recent interview with Euronews television, France's Le Pen made no secret of her admiration for the current Russian regime. "I share at least a part of Vladimir Putin's economic vision," she said. "We welcomed the arrival of a government that did not serve the 'apparatchiks' and which developed a patriotic economy," and showed a "cool head" in standing up to the EU and United States in the Ukraine crisis.[60]

Krekó, of the Political Capital Institute, said "Russia has a lot of allies in the European Parliament, but they are not really homogenous." Eight of the 14 far-right parties in the Parliament were openly pro-Russian, including parties in Austria, Belgium, France, Greece, Hungary and Italy, he claimed. "They are looking for an alternative to EU-U.S. hegemony," one that fits with their "anti-Western, nationalist, traditionalist" ideologies.[61]

Jean-Yves Camus, director of the Observatory of Political Radicalization at the Foundation Jean Jaurès, a French socialist think tank in Paris, said he was "pretty sure" Russia had lent €9 billion ($11 billion) to France's National Front, while the Austrian Freedom Party was getting support from "top-ranking officials in Russia, if not from President Putin himself."[62] However, the recent slide of the Russian economy, with the ruble rapidly losing value and a recession forecast for 2015, will likely test this new allegiance between Europe's far right and Putin.

OUTLOOK

Economic 'Nuclear Winter'?

As Europe continues to receive tens of thousands of new asylum seekers, social tensions will likely remain — and possibly increase — in the coming years, as host countries attempt to integrate them all.

Since many of the refugees are Muslim, the influx could increase Islamophobia or exacerbate anti-Semitism, if discontented Muslim immigrant youths remain at the vanguard of anti-Jewish sentiment in Europe. Whether native-born Europeans turn against immigrants will depend on whether the economy picks up steam and creates more jobs, according to some experts.

With commentators speaking of a "lost decade" for Europe economically, experts see little cause for optimism in the current climate. There is growing apprehension and suspicion of EU institutions, once viewed as beacons of peace and prosperity. Eurosceptic populist parties continue to insist that Brussels is trying by stealth to transform itself into a super-state.

However, EU Commission President Juncker, who will be in office until at least 2019, adamantly denies that goal. "The European people don't want a United States of Europe, and that is something I don't want either," Juncker told a dinner audience in Washington. "I could imagine a Europe of concentric circles, with a strong core of fully integrated member states and with other member states on the outer circles."[63]

Juncker is developing a $358 billion infrastructure investment plan aimed at hauling Europe out of the economic doldrums. The International Monetary Fund is urging the EU to pursue such a plan, cautioning against continuing with more "self-defeating" deficit and debt-reduction austerity policies.[64]

The Financial Times' Münchau warned that the "establishment parties of the center-left and the center-right are allowing Europe to drift into the economic equivalent of a nuclear winter." On the other hand, he predicted, the hard-left parties will do well in upcoming elections because they are the only ones advocating debt restructuring. But rather than allow such voices into

government, he said, there may be more "grand coalitions" of center-left and center-right parties, such as Chancellor Merkel's post-2013 government. For instance, a strong showing by Spain's Podemos party in 2015 could push the country's center-right popular and center-left socialist parties into a similar arrangement.[65]

Meanwhile, human rights groups and Europe's closest ally, the United States, are concerned that new EU member countries could backslide on democracy. Georgetown's Dettke has noted how "leverage over full EU member states is much weaker than it is over candidates for membership."[66]

Dettke says "the EU made a big mistake by canceling all of its pro-democracy civil society funding programs for candidate countries once they joined, in a misguided belief that the transition to democracy was complete and irreversible once countries had acceded to the EU. This has given far-right radicals such as Hungary's Jobbik an open field to operate in." He recommends the EU develop new programs to engage civil society and youth groups on EU-related issues in countries where extremism has gained a foothold. "That is the kind of initiative that I would like to see post-enlargement, instead of just more regulations from Brussels," he says.

The Political Capital Institute's Kreko argued in August that the leaders of Romania (Victor Ponta) and Slovakia (Robert Fico) were most likely to follow Orban's example in Hungary. "The EU needs leaders who have the courage to confront national politicians that seem to have abandoned its key values," Kreko said.[67]

Some, like Dettke, see the 2014 secession referenda in Spain and Scotland — although unsuccessful — as a sign of things to come if a rise in regionally based secessionist movements goes hand-in-hand with a rise in EU-sceptic nationalism. Both the Catalan and Scottish separatists have said that they would like to remain inside the EU if they do manage to forge independent countries. The EU "serves well as a common roof, even if nationalist or separatist movements are filled with grievances against their own governments," said Dettke.

Meanwhile, Le Pen makes no secret of her ambition to become the first democratically elected leader of a far-right party in Europe since World War II. "I'm preparing the great democratic upset that's going to happen in the next presidential election for sure," she said.[68]

NOTES

1. "Nigel Farage in UKIP event no-show due to 'immigration'," BBC News, Dec. 7, 2014, http://tinyurl.com/kkeex2x.

2. Frankie Goodway, "Factchecking Nigel Farage's traffic jam — how many immigrants WERE on the M4?" *Daily Mirror* (UK), Dec. 8, 2014, http://tinyurl.com/ke2t5o8.

3. Viktor Orban, prime minister of Hungary, July 26, 2014 speech: http://tinyurl.com/laqf46k.

4. *Ibid.*

5. "We're not Nazis, but . . . ," Human Rights First, August 2014, http://tinyurl.com/oz2ql92.

6. Andrew Marszal, and agencies, "Angela Merkel attacks 'prejudice' and 'hatred' of German Islamisation marches," *The Telegraph*, Dec. 31, 2014, http://tinyurl.com/nfu7u7m.

7. Hartley was testifying at a hearing of the U.S. Congress Commission on Security and Cooperation in Europe on March 19, 2014, http://tinyurl.com/n9kkbsn.

8. Christopoulos was speaking on a panel entitled "The Future of Europe in a Time of Political Extremism" at a conference organized by Human Rights First.

9. Brian Beary, "IMF puts probability of eurozone recession at nearly 40%," *Europolitics*, Oct. 7, 2014.

10. "World Economic Outlook — October 2014 edition," online database, International Monetary Fund, http://tinyurl.com/37ha3q.

11. "Asylum trends, first half 2014: Levels and Trends in Industrialized Countries," U.N. High Commissioner for Refugees, http://tinyurl.com/mh7wp3s.

12. See Frances D'Emilio, "For the second time this week, smugglers abandon migrant-packed ship in treacherous seas off Italian coast," The Associated Press, *National Post*, Jan. 2, 2015, http://tinyurl.com/mv3fys2; and Ben Rossington, "Smugglers left 1,000 immigrants aboard cargo ship on deadly collision course with the coast," Dec. 31, 2014, http://tinyurl.com/lulw9qr.

13. Srulevitch was speaking at a conference on anti-Semitism at Georgetown University on Sept. 16, 2014.

14. "Anti-Islam 'Pegida' march in German city of Dresden," BBC News, Dec. 16, 2014, http://tinyurl.com/lsj7j62. Maïa De La Baume and Dan Bilefsky, "Gunmen in Paris Kill 12 at Offices of Satirical Newspaper Charlie Hebdo," *The New York Times*, Jan. 7, 2015, http://tinyurl.com/l86y5vu.

15. Joszef Szajer was testifying at a hearing before the U.S. Congress' Committee for the Organization of Security and Co-operation in Europe, on March 19, 2013.

16. Mudde was giving a presentation entitled, "The Far Right, the 2014 European Elections, and the Euroscepticism Debate" at The George Washington University on Nov. 14, 2014.

17. *Ibid.*

18. Mudde classified the British National Party as a far-right party but not UKIP.

19. Péter Krekó, "More Hungarys in eastern Europe?" Open Democracy, Aug. 27, 2014, http://tinyurl.com/pflt7od.

20. Wolfgang Münchau, "Radical left is right about Europe's debt," *Financial Times*, Nov. 24, 2014, http://tinyurl.com/ka58t6o.

21. Münchau, *op. cit.*

22. Orban, *op. cit.*

23. "Le Pen: I admire 'cool head' Putin's resistance to West's new Cold War," *Euronews*, Dec. 1, 2014, http://tinyurl.com/mvvq44g.

24. Data comes from National Institute of Statistics and Economic Studies (France), www.insee.fr.

25. Ben Riley-Smith, "Boris Johnson: Nigel Farage's decision to blame M4 traffic on immigration is like 'effluent' and 'sewage,' " *Daily Telegraph*, Dec. 8, 2014, http://tinyurl.com/m3bfrk4.

26. For background, see Sarah Glazer, "Europe's Immigration Turmoil," *CQ Researcher*, Dec. 1, 2010, pp. 289-320.

27. Frankie Goodway, "How many immigrants do claim benefits?" *Mirror* (U.K.), http://tinyurl.com/nq49x8x.

28. "Positive economic impact of UK immigration from the European Union: new evidence," UCL Centre for Research and Analysis of Migration (CReAM),

Nov. 5, 2014, http://tinyurl.com/kexs7u3; Press release summarizing key findings of academic article by Christian Dustmann and Tommaso Frattini, "The Fiscal Effects Of Immigration To The UK," *The Economic Journal*, Nov. 5, 2014, http://tinyurl.com/mj43qb5.

29. Timo Lochocki, "The Unstoppable Far Right?" German Marshall Fund of the United States, September 2014, http://tinyurl.com/owtwrf7.

30. Stephen Brown, "Euro bailouts cause Germans more angst than Ukraine — poll," Reuters, Sept. 4, 2014, http://tinyurl.com/prmy22n.

31. Soini was speaking at a press luncheon organized by the Finnish embassy in Washington, D.C., in January 2014.

32. Glyn Ford, "Left faces political car crash," *Tribune*, Nov. 14, 2014, http://tinyurl.com/lel84u4.

33. *Ibid.*

34. Fivethirtyeight, Blog post, November 2014, www.fivethirtyeight.com.

35. "Future of Europe — Special Eurobarometer 413," European Commission, March 2014, http://tinyurl.com/kqzyolo.

36. Pope Francis was speaking to the European Parliament and Council of Europe, Strasbourg, Nov. 25, 2014, http://tinyurl.com/jvzzd7s.

37. For background on early 20th century European fascist movements, see Ernst Nolte, *Three Faces of Fascism* (1966).

38. For background, see Sarah Glazer, "Anti-Semitism in Europe," *CQ Researcher*, June 1, 2008, pp. 149-181.

39. For background, see Mary Cooper, "Europe's New Right," *CQ Researcher*, Feb. 12, 1993.

40. Matthias Bartsch, Andrea Brandt and Daniel Steinvorth, "Turkish Immigration to Germany: A Sorry History of Self-Deception and Wasted Opportunities," *Spiegel Online International*, Sept. 7, 2010, http://tinyurl.com/ordqpzy.

41. Cooper, *op. cit.*

42. *Ibid.*

43. For background, see Roland Flamini, "U.S.-Europe Relations," *CQ Researcher*, March 23, 2012, pp. 277-300.

44. Glazer, "Anti-Semitism in Europe," *op. cit.*

45. We're not Nazis, but . . . ," *op. cit.*

46. *Ibid.*

47. Jon Stone, "Far-right terrorist Breivik tries to set up fascist network from his prison cell," *The Independent* (UK), Dec. 24, 2014, http://tinyurl.com/pzc7f8h.

48. Mitchell A. Orenstein and Péter Krekó, "A Russian Spy in Brussels." *Foreign Affairs*, May 29, 2014, http://tinyurl.com/p58pexp.

49. For background, see Barbara Mantel, "Assessing the Threat from al Qaeda," *CQ Researcher*, June 27, 2014, pp. 553-576.

50. "700 ISIS refugees rescued after ship breaks down," TVNV, Nov. 28, 2014, http://tinyurl.com/o25z4b6.

51. Joanna Kakissis, "Sweden's Tolerance Is Tested By Tide Of Syrian Immigrants," National Public Radio, Dec. 5, 2014, http://tinyurl.com/npqdywe.

52. "Asylum trends, first half 2014: Levels and Trends in Industrialized Countries," *op. cit.*

53. "Denmark to rein in refugees fleeing from ISIS," Bloomberg, Oct. 8, 2014, http://tinyurl.com/mmt9xkw.

54. Nathalie Vandystadt, "Migration: European project will collapse without solidarity. Interview with MEP Kashetu Kyenge (S&D, Italy)," *Europolitics*, Nov. 6, 2014.

55. Alison Smale, "Court Lets E.U. Nations Curb Immigrant Welfare," *The New York Times*, Nov. 11, 2014, http://tinyurl.com/p6qrfap.

56. Sam Ro and Michael B. Kelley, "It's official: Russia Bans Food Imports From The US And The EU," *Business Insider*, Aug. 7, 2014, http://tinyurl.com/mpx434c.

57. Roland Oliphant, "Angela Merkel warns Russia could seek to destabilise 'whole of the European peaceful order,' " *The Telegraph*, Nov. 7, 2014, http://tinyurl.com/pmdj5qo.

58. Jan Lopatka "Slovak PM follows Czechs in ruling out foreign NATO troops," Reuters, June 4, 2014, http://tinyurl.com/mgyqja8.

59. Jackson Diehl, "Eastern Europeans are bowing to Putin's power," *The Washington Post*, Oct. 12, 2014, http://tinyurl.com/q58lwuw.

60. Le Pen, *op. cit.*

61. Krekó was speaking at a conference at the Woodrow Wilson International Center for Scholars in Washington, D.C., on July 11, 2014.

62. Camus was speaking on a panel entitled, "The Future of Europe in a Time of Political Extremism" at the "2014 Human Rights Agenda" conference, organized by Human Rights First.

63. Juncker was speaking at the Cosmos Club in Washington, D.C., on April 19, 2013, organized by the European Institute.

64. Beary, *op. cit.*

65. Munchau, *op. cit.*

66. Dieter Dettke, "Hungary's Jobbik Party, the Challenge of European Ethno-Nationalism and the Future of the European Project," Center For International Relations, Wilson Center, 2014.

67. Krekó, *op. cit.*

68. Le Pen, *op. cit.*

BIBLIOGRAPHY
Selected Sources
Books

Ignazi, Piero, *Extreme Right Parties in Europe*, Oxford University Press, 2003.
A professor of political science at the University of Bologna outlines the ideology of far-right groups, differentiating terms like "populist" and "radical" and charting their evolution from the pre-World War II times.

Mudde, Cas, *Populist Radical Right Parties in Europe*, Cambridge University Press, 2007.
A Dutch political scientist provides an overview of far-right parties in Europe, including how their ideologies can differ, depending on which country they are based in and how they have evolved over time.

Nolte, Ernst, *The Three Faces of Fascism*, Henry Holt & Co., 1966.
In this seminal work, a German philosopher and political scientist explains how fascism emerged in Europe in the early 1900s — especially in France, Germany and Italy — and how it compares to communism.

Wistrich, Robert S., *A Lethal Obsession: Anti-Semitism from Antiquity to the Global Jihad*, Random House, 2010.
A professor of modern European history at the Hebrew University of Jerusalem charts the long history of hatred of Jews, which stretches back more than 2,000 years.

Articles

Mounk, Yascha, "Europe's Jewish Problem: The Misunderstood Rise of European Anti-Semitism," *Foreign Affairs*, Sept. 17, 2014, http://tinyurl.com/q423j5b.
A doctoral candidate in government at Harvard University debunks some misunderstandings about what lies behind a recent resurgence of anti-Semitism in Europe.

Dettke, Dieter, "Hungary's Jobbik Party, the Challenge of European Ethno-Nationalism and the Future of the European Project," Centre for International Relations/Wilson Center, 2014, http://tinyurl.com/oe98bbp.
An adjunct professor of German politics and European integration at Georgetown University's Center for Security Studies examines Hungary's far-right Jobbik party.

Halikiopoulou, Daphne, and Sofia Vasilopoulou, "Support for the Far Right in the European Parliament Elections: A Comparative Perspective," *The Political Quarterly*, Vol. 85, Issue 3, 2014, pp. 285–288.
The success of far-right parties in the May 2014 European Parliament elections is analyzed, showing how the far-right won in countries such as Denmark and Hungary but failed to gain traction in others, such as Ireland and Spain.

Krekó, Péter, "More Hungarys in eastern Europe?" Open Democracy, Aug. 27, 2014, http://tinyurl.com/pflt7od.
The director of a Budapest-based think tank warns that authoritarianism could return to Europe if it remains passive in the face of worrying developments in Hungary, including radical changes made by prime minister Viktor Orban.

Lochocki, Timo, "The Unstoppable Far Right?" German Marshall Fund of the United States, September 2014, http://tinyurl.com/owtwrf7.
A transatlantic fellow of the German Marshall Fund argues that moderate European parties fuel extremism by embracing populist policies.

Packer, George, "The Quiet German," *The New Yorker*, Dec. 1, 2014, http://tinyurl.com/kxszpsf.
A journalist charts the rise of Europe's most powerful leader: German Chancellor Angela Merkel.

Visser, Mark, Marcel Lubbers, Gerbert Kraaykamp and Eva Jaspers, "Support for radical left ideologies in Europe," *European Journal of Political Research*, Vol. 53, Issue 3, 3013, pp. 541–558.
Four scholars analyze support for far-left parties in 32 European countries, drawing on survey data from 2002-10.

Reports and Studies

"Asylum trends, first half 2014: Levels and Trends in Industrialized Countries," United Nations High Commissioner for Refugees, Sept. 3, 2014, http://tinyurl.com/mh7wp3s.
The regularly updated statistical database of the UNHCR shows how Europe has experienced a spike in new asylum claims over the past year, notably from the Middle East.

"Future of Europe — Special Eurobarometer 413," European Commission, March 2014, http://tinyurl .com/kqzyolo.
The European Union's executive arm reports on a survey it conducted of European citizens' opinions of what powers the EU should have.

"Global Survey of Anti-Semitic Attitudes," Anti-Defamation League, 2014, http://tinyurl.com/pzes476.
A New York-based organization that combats anti-Semitism reports on a worldwide survey it conducted of public attitudes toward Jews.

"We're not Nazis, but . . . ," Human Rights First, August 2014, http://tinyurl.com/oz2ql92.
A U.S.-based advocacy group explains why the United States should care about the success of far-right political parties in Greece and Hungary.

For More Information

Delegation of the European Union to the United States, 2175 K St., N.W., Washington, DC 20037; 202-862-9500; www.eurunion.org/eu. The EU's representative office in the United States; seeks to foster good relations with the U.S. government and public.

The European Institute, 1001 Connecticut Ave., N.W., Suite 220, Washington, DC 20036; 202-895-1670; www .europeaninstitute.org. Public-policy organization that seeks to foster the trans-Atlantic relationship.

European Parliament Liaison Office with U.S. Congress, 2175 K St., N.W., Suite 600, Washington, DC 20037; 202-862-4734; www.europarl.europa.eu/us/view/en/home .html. European parliament's official representation in the United States; aims to foster closer relations with Congress.

The European Policy Centre, Residence Palace, 155 rue de la Loi, B-1040, Brussels; +32-2-231-0340; www.epc.eu.
Independent think tank that promotes European integration through analysis and debate.

European Union Agency for Fundamental Rights, Schwarzenbergplatz 11, A-1040, Vienna, Austria; +43-1-580-300; www.fra.europa.eu. Collects and analyzes data and advises EU institutions on promoting and protecting fundamental rights.

German Marshall Fund of the United States, 1744 R St., N.W., Washington, DC 20009; 202-683-2650; www.gmfus .org. Established by the German government in 1972 to promote trans-Atlantic relations.

Human Rights First, 75 Broad St., 31st Floor, New York, NY 10004; 212-845-5200; www.humanrightsfirst.org. Human rights advocacy group whose activities include monitoring the emergence of extremist groups.

Margaret Thatcher Center for Freedom, The Heritage Foundation, 214 Massachusetts Ave., N.E., Washington, DC 20002; 202-546-4400; www.thatchercenter.org. Trans-Atlantic-relations division of the conservative Heritage Foundation think tank; provides a critical view of the European Union.

United States Holocaust Memorial Museum, 100 Raoul Wallenberg Place, S.W., Washington, DC 20024; 202-488-0400; www.ushmm.org. Recounts the story of the mass murder of Jews during World War II and assists those seeking to learn about the Holocaust.

Woodrow Wilson Center for International Scholars, Ronald Reagan Building and International Trade Center, One Woodrow Wilson Plaza, 1300 Pennsylvania Ave., N.W., Washington, DC 20004; 202-691-4000; www.wilsoncenter.org. Think tank with a longstanding interest in Russia and Eastern Europe.

9

Restoring Ties with Cuba

Peter Katel

A vintage American car used as a taxi passes a crumbling building outside Havana. President Obama's plan to ease trade restrictions with Cuba comes at a critical time for the island's tottering economy. Wages are low and Venezuela has scaled back crucial shipments of low-cost oil.

From *CQ Researcher*,
June 12, 2015.

The meeting looked too ordinary to have taken a half-century to arrange: two men in business suits sitting a few feet apart in a room at the Panama City, Panama, convention center. But the crowd of reporters and the live TV coverage testified to the importance of the meeting between President Obama and Cuban President Raúl Castro. The once-unlikely encounter — held in April during the regionwide Summit of the Americas — served to prove that an attempt Obama announced last December to normalize U.S.-Cuban relations was still underway.

"I truly believe that as more exchanges take place, more commerce and interactions resume between the United States and Cuba, that the deep connections between the Cuban people and the American people will reflect itself in a more positive and constructive relationship between our governments," Obama said. Even so, he acknowledged that "deep and significant differences" remain.[1]

Castro endorsed the new approach but sounded an even more cautious note. "When I say that I agree with everything the president has just said, I include that we have agreed to disagree," the Cuban leader said. "No one should entertain illusions. . . . Our countries have a long and complicated history."[2]

That history took a sharp turn into mutual antagonism more than a half-century ago, when in 1959 rebels led by Raúl's older brother, Fidel, who would soon proclaim himself a Marxist-Leninist, ousted a U.S.-backed dictator and turned Cuba — a mere 90 miles from Florida — into a communist state allied with the Soviet Union. In 1962, after Cuba expropriated U.S.-owned business, the United States broke off diplomatic relations and imposed a trade

213

Wary Neighbors

Cuba lies just 90 miles from Key West, Fla., but the island nation and the United States have been far apart since 1961, when Cuba's new communist government expropriated U.S.-owned businesses. That prompted the United States to break off diplomatic relations and impose trade and travel restrictions. New moves by President Obama may help bridge the economic and political distance between the two countries.

Cuba at a Glance

Population: 11.27 million (2013)

Area: 42,803 sq. miles

GDP: $68.23 billion (2011)

Per Capita Income: $5,890 (2011)

Life Expectancy: 79 years (2013)

Adult Literacy Rate: 99.8% (2012)

Legislature: National Assembly of Peoples Power, 612 members

Key Trading Partners:

• *Exports* — *Venezuela (43%), Canada (8.8%), Netherlands (8.7%), China (6.5%)*

• *Imports* — *Venezuela (33%), China (10.4%), Spain (8.3%), Brazil (4.2%), Mexico (3.5%)*

Sources: Mark P. Sullivan, "Cuba: Issues for the 114th Congress," Congressional Research Service, May 20, 2015, p. 4, http://tinyurl.com/pva8497; data from "World Development Indicators, Cuba," The World Bank, http://tinyurl.com/33zt 2ohand and "The World Factbook, Cuba," U.S. Central Intelligence Agency, http://tinyurl.com/yum8e3

Obama's attempt to thaw relations with Cuba has the support of many U.S. foreign policy experts and Latin American countries, along with business interests eager for trade opportunities. But Obama's goals for his Cuba policy go far beyond opening up trade. He also wants to spark a push for democracy and free enterprise in Cuba. That has led even some supporters of Obama's Cuba policy to warn against hopes for vast improvements in U.S.-Cuba relations in the near future.

"People are saying that this is magic, that 55 years of hostility will be gone," says Carmelo Mesa-Lago, emeritus professor of economics and Latin American studies at the University of Pittsburgh and a leading expert on the Cuban economy. "No, no, no. I am happy, but at the same time I am very skeptical."

To help warm relations with Cuba, Obama has removed the country from a U.S. list of terrorism-supporting nations. He also has loosened red tape for travelers to Cuba, but only for approved purposes that do not include tourism — although U.S. tourists are going anyway.

In addition, Obama has eased, but not fully lifted, the long-standing embargo on trade. Among the changes: Building materials for private home construction and digital communications equipment can be exported. And travelers will be able to use U.S. credit and debit cards in Cuba. Meanwhile, talks are underway between Washington and Havana to re-establish full diplomatic relations between the two countries.

embargo on the island nation, along with travel and other restrictions in place ever since.[3]

The easing in tensions comes at a critical time for Cuba. The country will soon face a future without a

Castro in charge for the first time since the revolution: President Castro is 84 years old; and Fidel — whom Raúl replaced as president in 2008 but who still exerts influence — is 88. Meanwhile, Cuba, with 11 million people, has a tottering economy. Private businesses — and the jobs that go with them — remain scarce despite a modest reform effort by Raúl Castro. Meanwhile, Cuba's main foreign lifeline, petroleum giant Venezuela, which has provided oil to Cuba on favorable terms for years, is in desperate economic straits, leading it to cut shipments to the island.

Given Cuba's weaknesses, Obama's critics argue that he gave away too much for too little in the way of Cuban social and political reform. "I always felt that the embargo was a pressure point," Rep. Albio Sires, D-N.J., a Cuban-American, said at one of several congressional hearings this year on the new policy, "and that we would take the embargo off when we get some concessions — especially concessions that led to a free economy . . . where people could have free elections."[4]

Obama's defenders say easing the embargo is appropriate. "Whatever bad I have to say about the Cuban system, which is a lot, the Cuban system is no threat to the United States," says Ted Henken, a Latin American studies professor at Baruch College in New York, "whereas we have a lot we are doing to them."

Although both sides talk about a new relationship, Obama and Castro have vowed to maintain fundamental principles. In Cuba's case, that means maintaining state control of society, including most business and all industry. Yet the new U.S. travel and trade rules are explicitly designed to facilitate travel by Americans training Cuban private businesses, and to spur Internet growth in Cuba.[5]

But the extent to which Cuba, where only 5 percent of the population has Internet access, will accept U.S. efforts to promote private business and Internet use remains unclear.

Some experts say the most aggressive action the United States could take is what it did — open more trade and communication channels, thereby reversing the old-school view that unrelenting isolation of Cuba will force it to change. "The hard-line is engagement," says Marifeli Pérez-Stable, a sociology professor at Florida International University and a longtime scholar of Cuba policy.

Indeed, many critics contend that U.S. trade and travel sanctions have essentially helped the Cuban government

suppress dissent and remain in power. "It's so ironic," says Vicki Huddleston of Santa Fe, N.M., a retired diplomat who headed the U.S. Interests Section in Havana from 1999 to 2002. "Under the embargo, we didn't allow communications equipment to be exported — TV, iPads, cellphones." Yet, she adds, "it is much easier to control a country when you control communications."

But Jaime Suchlicki, a University of Miami history professor and the director of the university's Cuba Transition Project, notes that countries that have tried to engage Cuba with trade and travel also have failed to spark ideological change in the island nation. "Europeans have been trying this for 50 years — investing in Cuba, sending tourists," he says. "Is Cuba more democratic?"

American officials say they have no illusions that increasing travel and commerce will by itself make Cuba a more open society. "No country ever became a democracy simply because of trade or tourists," Thomas Malinowski, an assistant secretary of State for human rights, told a Senate Foreign Relations subcommittee in February.[6]

Still, the moves by Obama and Raúl Castro mark a clear attempt to break from a historical pattern of hostility and conflict. If talks to re-establish full diplomatic relations succeed, quasi-embassies established by the United States and Cuba in each other's capitals could become full-fledged embassies. But even that step is not simple. Cuba's president recently reiterated longtime aversion to U.S. diplomats in Cuba providing training to journalists who want to work outside the government-owned-and-operated media.[7]

James Cason, mayor of Coral Gables, Fla., who headed the U.S. Interests Section in Havana from 2002 to 2005, says Cuba doesn't want a fully functional U.S. embassy, with diplomats talking to a wide range of Cubans, including dissidents — "all those kinds of things that we consider normal, that diplomats do around the world."

In this country, despite some objections to Obama's moves, widespread opposition hasn't surfaced — even in Miami-Dade County, the unofficial Cuban-American capital and traditionally a bulwark of anti-Castro sentiment. In a poll conducted last year, before Obama's announcement, 52 percent of the county's Cuban-Americans opposed the embargo, and 68 percent supported full diplomatic relations with Cuba.

Nationally, support for Obama's actions runs even stronger, including among Republicans. Sixty-eight percent of respondents to a poll late last year supported ending the trade embargo; among Republicans, support was at 57 percent, though 47 percent of Republicans opposed establishing full diplomatic relations.[8]

The shift in attitude may reflect a loss of hope that the hard-line policy against Cuba was working. Even Cason, a fierce critic of Obama's Cuba policy, concedes, "The embargo has not been effective in bringing political change." He adds, "But neither has any other policy."

As scholars, human-rights activists, business officials and politicians consider the administration's rapprochement with Cuba, here are some of the questions being debated:

Is the United States getting too little in return for Obama's Cuba initiative?

So far, most of the moves in the U.S.-Cuba normalization effort have come from the American side. Since last December, when Obama announced the policy shift, the administration has released from prison three members of a Cuban spy ring and allowed them to return to Cuba (though he did not release a high-level U.S. spy for Cuba in the U.S. Defense Intelligence Agency); removed Cuba from the "state sponsors of terrorism" list; and loosened restrictions on trade and travel with Cuba, including expanding the list of goods that can be exported to Cuba and allowing U.S. travelers to use American credit and debit cards on the island.[9]

In return for the U.S. prisoner releases, the Cuban government freed 53 prisoners that American negotiators said had been held for political reasons; it also freed USAID contractor Alan P. Gross and a Cuban intelligence officer, Rolando Sarraff Trujillo, who reportedly

Cuban-Americans Favor Renewed Ties

Nearly 70 percent of Cuban-Americans living in Miami supported re-establishing diplomatic ties with Cuba, six months before President Obama announced plans to normalize U.S.-Cuban relations.

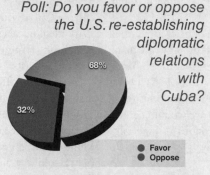

Poll: Do you favor or oppose the U.S. re-establishing diplomatic relations with Cuba?

68%

32%

● Favor
● Oppose

Source: "2014 FIU Cuba Poll," Cuban Research Institute, Florida International University, 2014, p. 11, http://tinyurl.com/n2mhcce

had spied on his country for the CIA.[10]

Obama was able to initiate the moves that resulted in the exchanges because the embargo — often seen as a law that only Congress can change or repeal — includes administrative measures that a president can loosen or tighten. "It is necessary to dispose of any misapprehension that the president has no authority to normalize relations with Cuba," Washington lawyer Robert Muse wrote last year in a piece that, in effect, laid out the road map Obama is following.[11]

Critics charge that Obama's moves are hugely disproportional in Cuba's favor. "I always think it's a mistake in foreign policy to give it away for nothing," Rep. Gerry Connolly, D-Va., said at a House Foreign Affairs Committee hearing in February.[12]

But Roberta S. Jacobson, assistant secretary of State for Western Hemisphere affairs, replied that a "transactional" approach with Cuba on human rights would be counterproductive. "The problem with that is they won't trade for anything," she said. "And we will end up still not helping the Cuban people." She added, "We're not letting up on human rights."[13]

Some who favor Obama's policy decisions agree that Cuba has not taken actions of equivalent scope — but that it has no reason to do so. "You shouldn't expect to get something for not behaving badly anymore," says Muse, who specializes in laws affecting Cuba. "We were violating international norms" by sanctioning a country that did not pose a threat to the United States.

Critics of the Obama policy argue in part that the administration should not have eased sanctions until Cuba turned over fugitives from U.S. justice who have long resided on the island.

John S. Kavulich II, president of the U.S.-Cuba Trade and Economic Council, a New York-based

Seizures of Migrants on the Rise

The U.S. Coast Guard has interdicted — halted and sent home — nearly 1,500 Cuban migrants in the first four months of 2015. Interdictions peaked in 2007 before declining for three years during the 2007-2009 recession, largely because of diminished economic prospects in the United States and aggressive prosecution of human smugglers, according to officials. Interdictions began rising again in 2011 as the U.S. economy improved.

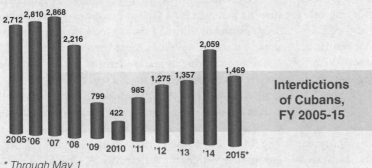

Interdictions of Cubans, FY 2005-15

* Through May 1

Source: Mark P. Sullivan, "Cuba: Issues for the 114th Congress," Congressional Research Service, May 20, 2015, p. 44, http://tinyurl.com/pva8497; data from "Total Interdictions — Fiscal Year 1982 to Present," U.S. Coast Guard, updated May 1, 2015, http://tinyurl.com/oe7wqj4

nonpartisan organization serving companies interested in doing business in Cuba, acknowledges that restoration of full diplomatic relations would be "a big win for Cuba." Cuba could then tell foreign governments and businesses, "'We told you the Americans wanted to come back,'" Kavulich says. "It makes it easier for Cuba to market itself."

Obama, who rejects the regime-change language of his predecessor, President George W. Bush, describes his policy shift as a way to promote greater political and economic freedom for Cubans. But critics say Obama's policy stands no chance of success on that score. "I think we were snookered," says ex-diplomat Cason. "I don't think the Cubans want normalization. They want diplomatic relations. What they really want is to get loans from the U.S. government. That's why they want to be off the terrorist list."

Regardless of whether Cuba would be able to obtain loans, Cason argues that Cuban officials have no intention of loosening their communist system. "These 85-year-old guys," he says, referring to the Castro brothers, "have said

to us, 'We'll take your money, but we're not going to change politically or economically.'"

Pérez-Stable of Florida International University, agrees the Cuban government won't jeopardize its hold on power. But, she adds, past U.S. hopes for rapid and fundamental change were misplaced. "Given that the old policy didn't bring Cuba to respect human rights, didn't provoke the Cuban people en masse to go out on streizeets to call for change," Pérez-Stable says, "this policy is betting that it's not going to happen overnight."

The Castro government's apparent determination not to reciprocate could make it hard for the United States to further improve relations with Cuba, says the University of Pittsburgh's Mesa-Lago. Noting a speech by Raúl Castro at the Panama summit, where he defiantly reasserted Cuba's revolutionary ideology and condemned U.S. interventions in the Americas, Mesa-Lago says, "All these things that Raúl and the Cuban government are doing don't help on the key issue, which is lifting the embargo, because he is giving ammunition to those who are against that action."[14]

Mesa-Lago adds, "This is a time when Cuba has to do something; if it doesn't, it will be reinforcing the view that Obama is not getting anything in return."

Will improved U.S.-Cuba relations reduce Cuban migration to the United States?

A steady outflow of Cubans to the United States marked the past half-century of hostile relations between the two nations. Cubans started fleeing the island when the revolution began. Their numbers reached about 78,000 in 1962, and by 1979, the total number who had made it to the United States was in the "hundreds of thousands," according to the nonpartisan Congressional Research Service.[15]

However, mass departures from Cuba in 1980 and 1994 led to U.S.-Cuban agreements designed to hold down the number of unauthorized migrants.[16] A 1994 U.S. commitment to issue at least 20,000 visas a year — thereby providing a legal alternative to fleeing Cuba without authorization — helped slow migration but didn't stop it.

This year, nearly 9,500 Cubans entered the United States, both by sea and across the U.S.-Mexico border during the first quarter. During the same period last year, approximately 4,200 entered.[17]

The United States exerts a magnetic pull in the form of the Cuban Adjustment Act of 1966, which gave Cuban refugees a status enjoyed by immigrants from no other country. They are allowed to remain in the United States for one year, at which point they are eligible for permanent residency, or "green card" status, which allows them to apply for citizenship later. The law's underlying assumption is that Cubans fleeing the island are political refugees.[18]

Because the recent increase followed Obama's December announcement of his new Cuba policy, many experts speculate that Cubans fear the Cuban Adjustment Act will soon disappear or be made more restrictive. "I think they're going to tighten it," the University of Miami's Suchlicki says, "so that it applies to political dissenters, not just to anyone who says, 'I want to stay.'"

The U.S.-Cuba thaw has introduced a new element into the migration equation: the possibility that Cubans' rising expectations will erode into disappointment.

"People in Cuba for the past four months have been reintroduced to the word 'hope,'" says Henken of Baruch College. "That is dangerous for any government, because you've got to deliver on that hope."

Cuban government actions in the past several years have dampened hopes for growth of the island's private sector. "They have increased taxes if you have more than five employees, for example," says Henken. "A number of entrepreneurs have called it quits; those people are certainly potential migrants."

Piero Gleijeses, a professor of U.S. foreign policy at the Johns Hopkins School of Advanced International Studies, dismisses such assessments, however. "I don't think Cubans expect dramatic change overnight," he says, arguing that improvements in Cuban living conditions depend on whether Washington continues to loosen commercial restrictions.

But former diplomat Cason says another migration surge could easily arise if normalization talks run into problems. "The Cubans always threaten a rafter crisis when things get out of hand," he says, a reference to the thousands of Cuban refugees who have crossed into Florida on rickety, homemade rafts and other craft. And public discontent with the failure of normalization to provide more than a limited benefit to ordinary Cubans could encourage the Cuban government to promote a mass exodus, he speculates. "There is not much," he says, "that the average Cuban can make from tourism."

The University of Pittsburgh's Mesa-Lago, noting what he sees as U.S. sensitivity to mass migration, hypothesizes that the potential for a Cuban exodus may have encouraged Obama to shift U.S. policy in hopes of promoting improved conditions there. Mesa-Lago acknowledges that conditions favoring migration remain: Since the revolution, it has become easier for Cubans to leave the island legally. Along with the 1994 visa deal, Cuba in 2013 relaxed its rules on off-island travel, making it possible for Cubans intending to emigrate to leave legally.

Still, some Cubans take to the sea. The Cuban government blames the Adjustment Act, calling it the *ley asesina* — murderous law.[19] But Pérez-Stable of Florida International University scoffs at Cuba's expressions of concern for its citizens who take to the high seas on unsafe craft. "The Cuban government doesn't do anything," she says. "Every time I go to Southcom [the U.S. Southern Command military base, headquartered in Miami], I say publicly say, 'Thank you for saving so many Cuban lives.'"

Is Obama's policy shift designed to thwart Russian or Chinese influence on Cuba?

The collapse of the Soviet Union in 1991 hit Cuba hard, given its decades of dependence on Soviet loans and subsidies. But after the post-Soviet period, Cuba found a new source of support in Venezuela, headed since 1999 by fervent ideological allies. Now Venezuela is facing its own economic crisis, intensified by the recent plunge in world oil prices.

Venezuelan oil shipments to Cuba — on highly favorable terms — dropped from a reported 100,000 to 70,000 barrels a day as the oil giant shifted its petroleum to the world market for a better price.[20]

In addition to relying on cheap Venezuelan oil, Cuba has been receiving an estimated $5.4 billion a year from Venezuela for the services of 40,000 Cuban professionals, most of them doctors and other health care workers, according to the centrist Brookings Institution think

Win McNamee/Getty Images

Alan Gross, a USAID contractor, was arrested in Cuba in late 2009 for bringing digital communications equipment to Cuban citizens without Cuban government permission. He was sentenced to 15 years in prison and released in December 2014 in a prisoner swap.

tank in Washington. "Replacing dependence on the Soviet Union with dependence on Venezuela simply creates a new vulnerability," analysts Ted Piccone and Harold Trinkunas of Brookings' Latin America Initiative wrote last year.[21]

In this perilous economic climate, Cuba has been turning back to Russia for help — renewing concerns among U.S. conservatives about a new alliance between the two countries.

In July 2014, on a visit to Cuba, Russian President Vladimir Putin announced that Russia had canceled 90 percent of a $32 billion debt to Russia that dated to Soviet times. On the same trip, three Russian corporations signed trade deals with Cuba, including a $1.6 billion agreement to build four power plants on the island.[22]

In addition, Russia reopened an electronic listening post at a Cuban base called Lourdes that the Soviet Union used during the Cold War to spy on U.S. communications.[23]

The re-energized relationship between Cuba and Russia comes amid tensions between Moscow and the West over the conflict in Ukraine between pro-Russian separatists and the U.S.- and NATO-backed Ukrainian government. The conflict has stirred fears in Europe and the United States of a Russian invasion of Ukraine, leading them to pressure Putin to stay out of the Western-backed country, and has deeply chilled relations between Washington and Moscow.[24]

Carl Meacham, Americas program director at the Center for Strategic and International Studies, a Washington think tank on security matters, told *The Miami Herald* that Putin's visit to Cuba was a message that "if the United States and NATO pushes in on Ukraine, Russia can push in on Cuba."[25]

Some experts see the erosion of Venezuelan support of Cuba — whose low-cost oil program has extended to 13 other countries as well — as the single biggest factor that pushed Cuba into negotiations with the United States. "Countries want to be less reliant on Venezuela at a time Venezuela has less resources to provide for them," Avinash Persaud, London-based chairman of Intelligence Capital, a wealth-management firm, and Elara Capital, an investment bank, told Bloomberg News. "In the case of Cuba, they don't want this to be another Soviet Union where their dependency suddenly disappears."[26]

China's economic stake in Cuba is larger than Russia's, even though Russian ties with Cuba are deeper on a political, personal and cultural level because of the historic alliance between Cuba and the Soviets. China is Cuba's biggest creditor, and its $1.4 billion worth of trade with the island makes it Cuba's second-largest trading partner, after Venezuela.[27]

China finances the manufacturing of Chinese-brand consumer electronics and appliances on the island, and it has invested $6 billion in Cuban oil and gas refining projects. Still, Chinese economic involvement is far below its potential — largely, Chinese officials have said, because Cuban quality-control standards are unacceptably low. Adrian H. Hearn, a sociologist at the China Studies Center at the University of Sydney in Australia, wrote that Chinese leaders told Fidel Castro as far back as 1995 that economic pragmatism ranked higher in their eyes than ideological compatibility.[28]

"The United States already knows that China is not going to put any real investment in Cuba until the leaders of Cuba get the Cuban economy in order," says Pérez-Stable. And as for Russia's recent overtures? "Putin has his hands full" in places other than Cuba, she says.

The bottom line, Pérez-Stable says, is that the attempt by Obama and Raúl Castro to normalize U.S.-Cuba relations has little to do with third countries. "Mainly this is about the United States and Cuba," she says, adding that the Cuban revolution stalled the possibility that Cuba and the United States could build a more equitable relationship, one that overcame the bitterness of past U.S. military occupation of the island and later political and economic influence there.

"The United States has learned to deal with Central America, with the English- and Spanish- and French-speaking Caribbean," she says. "Cuba missed that boat."

Cason says that even if the United States is concerned about Russian involvement in Cuba, Obama's new policy won't do anything to counter it. "Look at what Cuba has done: invited Russia back into Lourdes to listen to all our phone calls again," he says.

As for China, it serves largely as a negative example of the consequences of economic liberalization, Cason says: The Castro regime wants "to keep the economic conditions of Cubans as low as possible and as equal as possible. Otherwise economic change will lead to political pressure, which they've seen in China."

BACKGROUND
Revolution and Reprisal

Cuban revolutionaries led by Fidel Castro toppled the U.S.-supported dictatorship of Fulgencio Batista in 1959. Overseer of a corrupt, inefficient government in a deeply unequal society, Batista was opposed by wide swaths of Cuban society.

Castro and his allies also channeled nationalist resentment of the dominating role that the United States had played in Cuba since Spain's ouster as colonial ruler in 1898. From 1903 to '34, the U.S.-Cuba relationship was defined by a treaty known as the "Platt Amendment." It gave the United States the right to intervene in Cuba to restore order — which it did on several occasions.[29]

Republican President Dwight D. Eisenhower and Vice President Richard M. Nixon had always suspected Castro of being an anti-American radical, but Castro's calls for deep economic and social changes convinced them that the charismatic Castro indeed was a grave danger to U.S. interests. In November, 1959 Eisenhower signed off on a policy of destabilizing the Castro government, which set the CIA to developing a plan for armed insurgency in Cuba — a plan Eisenhower approved in March 1960. Meanwhile, the CIA made plans to assassinate Castro.[30]

In October 1960, as Castro was nationalizing U.S. oil refineries on the island and seizing other properties owned by American citizens and corporations, Eisenhower banned all trade with Cuba except for food and medicine.[31]

Invasion plans continued under Democratic President John F. Kennedy, who took office in 1961. Despite misgivings, Kennedy gave the go-ahead for the so-called exiles' brigade of 1,500 men to go ashore at *Playa Girón*, known on U.S. maps as the Bay of Pigs.[32] The operation was a fiasco. Cuban forces crushed the invasion, and at the end of the fighting the Cuban government held 1,214 invaders as prisoners.[33]

Private individuals coordinating with the Kennedy administration negotiated for the prisoners' release. In 1962, most were freed in exchange for $53 million worth of food, medicine and other goods, plus $2.9 million in cash.[34]

In between the invasion and prisoner release, the United States and the Soviet Union came to the brink of nuclear war in October 1962 after the discovery of Soviet nuclear missiles in Cuba. The two superpowers peacefully resolved the "missile crisis," with the Soviets withdrawing the weapons and the United States pledging not to invade Cuba. Castro, who had not been consulted by his Soviet allies about the missile withdrawal, was furious at the weapons' removal.[35]

Meanwhile, the Kennedy administration continued Operation Mongoose, a CIA program of sabotaging Cuban factories, farms and ships in hopes of sparking a counter-revolution. The administration also continued an Eisenhower-era program of trying to kill Castro, on at least two occasions subcontracting the job to Mafia bosses with Cuban contacts. In 1963, the administration set in motion its last assassination effort aimed at Castro. The assassination of President Kennedy weeks later, on Nov. 22, 1963, ended the plot.[36]

Secret Talks

In the mid-1970s, Henry Kissinger, secretary of State under Republican President Gerald R. Ford, opened exploratory talks with the Castro government designed to lead to resumption of diplomatic relations.[37]

Ford's predecessor, Nixon, who became president in 1969 but resigned in disgrace in 1974, had refused to deal with Cuba on anything but unavoidable issues. These included the hijackings of airliners to Cuba by U.S. radicals being pursued on criminal charges, as well by common criminals. Above all, the United States wanted American hijackers returned to the United States. Cuba

Cubans who fled from Cuba by boat celebrate after arriving in Key West, Fla., on May 5, 1980. Some 125,000 Cubans came to the United States via the so-called Mariel boatlift.

wanted U.S. prosecutions of Cubans who hijacked planes or boats to the United States. Negotiations led to a formal agreement in 1973 under which hijackers would be tried in the country that they reached, or extradited to their home countries.[38]

As Ford and Kissinger pursued normalization, each country had a list of conditions for forging a new relationship. On the U.S. side, these included compensation for property seized from U.S. citizens after the revolution; release of Americans held in Cuban prisons; and reduced Cuban support for Latin American revolutionary movements.[39] Cuba wanted an end to the trade embargo; cancellation of U.S. spy plane overflights; and removal of restrictions on trade with Cuba by U.S. companies' foreign subsidiaries.[40]

The international climate seemed to favor normalization, partly because a growing number of Latin American countries opposed U.S. demands that they impose sanctions on Cuba.[41]

In response, Ford loosened the embargo by ending a ban on foreign aid to countries whose ships or airplanes were used in trade with Cuba.[42] But Ford's wish for full restoration of U.S.-Cuba ties failed. Americans blamed Cuban military action in Africa, in which Cuban troops backed the revolutionary government of Angola against an invasion by apartheid-era South Africa. Angolan forces siding with the invasion were trained and advised by the United States.[43] In 1976, Cuban diplomats said Cuba would not sacrifice its foreign policy to achieve better relations with the United States.[44]

That same year, the in-flight bombing of a Cuban airliner killed the country's entire Olympic fencing team and all other passengers and crew. The bombing was carried out by the head of a Cuban exile organization, the Coordination of United Revolutionary Organizations, which the FBI categorized as "terrorist," and an ex-CIA operative, Luis Posada Carriles. A furious Castro blamed the CIA for the attack and ruled out "collaboration of any kind" between the two countries for the time being.[45]

Refugee Crisis

Despite those developments, Ford's successor, Democratic President Jimmy Carter, was even more intent on improving relations with Cuba.[46]

Signaling his willingness to negotiate a new relationship, Carter effectively ended the ban on U.S. citizens' travel to Cuba, and his administration took the first step toward each country opening an "interests section" in the other's capital city.[47]

On the Cuban side, the government in 1978 allowed Cuban exiles to come back to visit. More than 100,000 Cuban-Americans took advantage of the new policy in 1979 — a development with unexpected consequences. At a time of deepening hardship in Cuba, with sugar and tobacco crops failing, the exiles seemed prosperous and content.[48]

Hence a growing number of economically desperate Cubans stole or hijacked boats to reach the United States. Once there, the 1966 Cuban Adjustment Act made them automatically eligible for lawful permanent residence.[49]

Meanwhile, some Cubans tried a different tactic — breaking into the grounds of Latin American embassies in Havana to claim asylum. After an April 1, 1980, incident at the Peruvian Embassy, Castro angrily ordered barriers and guard posts outside the embassy torn down — a message that if Peru maintained its policy of granting asylum, it would be overwhelmed by asylum-seekers. Indeed, over the next three days, 10,000 people flocked to the embassy grounds. Castro called the embassy refugees *escoria* — scum, or social misfits.[50]

But Castro soon turned his crisis into a major headache for the United States. He announced that Cubans who wanted to leave should gather at the port of Mariel, west of Havana — and that Cuban-Americans should head there with boats to pick them up. Hundreds of Cuban-Americans and others sailed for Mariel, ignoring

State Department warnings that they were breaking immigration law.[51]

Under Carter's orders, the U.S. Coast Guard finally cracked down, seizing vessels heading for Cuba. But, by then, more than 1,000 craft were already at Mariel. All told, 125,266 Cubans reached the United States in what became known as the Mariel boatlift.[52]

The 'Special Period'

The administration of Republican President Ronald Reagan (1981-89), who voiced strong anti-communist views during his two terms in office, coincided with developments that had major effects on U.S.-Cuba policy. During Reagan's early years in office, wars in Central America involving Cuban-backed guerrillas in El Salvador and a Cuban-supported revolutionary government in Nicaragua, preoccupied the new administration.

In 1981, the Cuban government sent word that it had cut its arms shipments to the Salvadoran guerrillas and to the new Nicaraguan government and that Cuba publicly supported diplomatic efforts to end the Central American conflicts. But the Reagan administration, convinced that Cuba's stance reflected weakness and fears of U.S. military action, hardened its resistance to the Castro regime and stopped pursuing normalization talks. In 1982, the Reagan administration restored the ban on most U.S. travel to Cuba.[53]

A new anti-Castro lobbying organization, the Miami-based Cuban American National Foundation (CANF), successfully lobbied Congress to set up a U.S. government radio station aimed at Cuba. Radio Martí (named after Cuban independence hero José Martí) began broadcasting in May 1985. Castro, who considered Radio Martí a propaganda effort aimed at destabilizing Cuba, responded by suspending the migration agreement and stopping Cuban-Americans' visits to Cuba. The migration agreement was restored in 1987.[54]

By the early '90s, the collapse of the Soviet Union left Fidel Castro's Cuba more vulnerable than ever. Shortly before the Soviet Union officially dissolved on Dec. 25, 1991, its last leader, Mikhail Gorbachev, announced an end to all military aid to Cuba by Jan. 1, 1992. Castro called the decision a "betrayal."[55]

With Cuba suddenly dependent on trade outside the vanished Soviet bloc, CANF raced to push for passage of the Cuban Democracy Act. The legislation aimed to reimpose the ban on trade with Cuba by foreign subsidiaries of U.S. corporations, among other measures. Republican President George H. W. Bush signed the bill in 1992.[56]

Democratic President Bill Clinton, who inherited the post-Cold War world, said he wanted to normalize relations with Cuba. However, when running for office, he had supported the Cuban Democracy Act, given the political importance of Florida, where anti-normalization Cuban-Americans constituted a major voting bloc.[57]

Meanwhile, Cuba was wracked by economic crisis — which the Castro government designated the "Special Period in Time of Peace," — marked by the disappearance of Soviet subsidies for energy and other essentials.[58]

Growing privation led thousands of Cubans to flee the island on anything that floated. In August 1994, after a series of boat hijackings, Castro — blaming the United States for welcoming fleeing Cubans — said Cubans were free to leave. In one day alone, the Coast Guard picked up more than 3,200 Cubans at sea, many of them on home-made rafts. The total number of *balseros* — rafters — that year reached nearly 40,000.[59]

The Clinton administration began taking rescued Cubans to the U.S. Navy base at Guantánamo, Cuba, where they could apply for immigration to the United States or other countries.*

As the refugee flow continued, the United States and Cuba agreed to discourage sea migration. Eventually, the United States decided that Cubans who reached U.S. soil would be accepted into the country, but that those rescued at sea would be sent back.[60]

A new crisis damaged U.S.-Cuban relations even more seriously. In 1996, aircraft from Brothers to the Rescue, a Miami-based outfit that sent small planes over the Straits of Florida to spot fleeing Cubans and alert the Coast Guard, began dropping anti-Castro leaflets over Cuba itself. Cuba warned repeatedly that it would shoot down planes violating Cuban airspace. Cuban MiG fighters carried out the threat in February of that year, downing two of three Brothers planes, killing all four aboard.[61]

Clinton then signed a bill he had opposed — the Cuban Liberty and Democratic Solidarity Act, known as "Helms-Burton" after its Republican sponsors, Sen. Jesse

---

* Guantanamo, located on Cuban soil. was permanently leased to the United States under the Platt Amendment for a Navy installation; Cuba has long demanded the return of Guantanamo.

C H R O N O L O G Y

1959-1976 *U.S.-Cuba relations deteriorate after Cuban revolution.*

1959 Revolutionaries led by Fidel Castro overthrow Fulgencio Batista.

1960 President Dwight D. Eisenhower orders CIA to train a Cuban exile force to land in Cuba and imposes trade embargo with Cuba, except for food and medicine.

1961 CIA-trained Cuban exiles invade island, are routed at Bay of Pigs.

1962 Cuban missile crisis brings U.S., Soviet Union to brink of nuclear war.

1963 CIA shelves plan to assassinate Castro after President John F. Kennedy is killed.

1973 United States and Cuba agree to put airplane hijackers on trial or extradite them. . . . Secretary of State Henry Kissinger OKs secret talks with Cuba.

1975 President Gerald R. Ford lifts ban on aid to countries whose planes and ships are used in Cuba trade. . . . U.S. halts further moves to improve relations because of Cuban military activity in southern Africa.

1976 Cuban exiles, one CIA-trained, blow up a Cuban airliner; Castro blames CIA.

1977-1996 *President Jimmy Carter seeks to normalize relations with Cuba, but President Ronald Reagan takes tougher approach.*

1977 Carter ends travel ban to Cuba for U.S. citizens.

1978 Cuba allows Cuban exiles to return for visits.

1980 Mariel "boatlift" ferries more than 125,000 Cubans to U.S.

1981 Cuba reduces arms shipments to Central American guerrillas. . . . Anti-Castro Cuban-American National Foundation becomes influential on U.S. policy.

1985 U.S. anti-Castro radio station, Radio Martí, begins broadcasting to Cuba. . . . Cuba suspends migration agreement and halts Cuban-Americans' visits to Cuba.

1987 Cuba renews migration agreement.

1992 President George H. W. Bush signs bill reimposing Cuba trade ban on foreign subsidiaries of U.S. corporations. . . . Soviet Union ends all military aid to Cuba.

1993-2002 *Cuban migration to U.S. accelerates.*

1993 After Soviet collapse, number of Cubans fleeing reaches nearly 40,000.

1994 Castro declares Cubans free to leave, and thousands take to sea. . . . U.S. "wet foot-dry foot" policy sends Cubans back who don't reach land.

1996 Cuban fighters shoot down two small planes from a Cuban rescue group. . . . President Bill Clinton signs Helms-Burton measure, stiffening economic embargo.

2003-Present *President Obama seeks fresh start with Cuba.*

2003 George W. Bush administration openly encourages Cuban dissidents. . . . Cuba arrests 75 regime dissidents.

2008 Castro retires; his brother Raúl is tapped as his successor.

2009 Obama calls for "new beginning" with Cuba, eases travel restrictions. . . . Cuba arrests USAID contractor Alan Gross for distributing communications gear to Cubans.

2011 Gross is sentenced to 15 years in prison for subversion.

2013 Cuba eases restrictions on foreign travel for Cubans.

2014 Obama announces plan to restore diplomatic relations with Cuba and loosen embargo. . . . Cuba, U.S. swap Gross for remaining "Cuban Five" prisoners; Cuba frees 53 political prisoners.

2015 Raúl Castro and Obama meet in Panama. . . . Cuba removed from list of terrorism-sponsoring countries. . . . Talks held to open embassies in Havana, Washington.

Claims Against Cuba Complicate Relations

Havana owes billions, but experts say creative solutions are possible.

Decades of political hostility, economic embargo, covert war and espionage represent only a few of the obstacles facing the United States and Cuba as they attempt to patch up their relationship.

Billions of dollars also stand between the two countries.

The money represents claims against the Cuban government. Filings by American citizens and companies that reported losing money and property to the revolutionary Cuban government after it took power in 1959 make up one category of demands. The Foreign Claims Settlement Commission, attached to the U.S. Justice Department, certified 5,913 of these claims, totaling $1.9 billion. With interest tacked on, the figure is $7 billion.[1]

Claims vary enormously in their nature and amount. The single biggest is a $267.5 million demand by Cuban Electric Co., a onetime U.S.-owned utility. Claims of companies that no longer exist pass to the firms' buyers.

Claims by individuals include Isaac Kabbany's, who is owed $1,053.80, plus interest, because he had opened a savings account at a Havana branch of the National City Bank of New York during a 1957 trip to Cuba.[2]

Such individual claims could be settled relatively easily, experts say, and they represent only a relatively small part of the total. But the billions of dollars in corporate claims are a lot of money for a poor island nation with big financial troubles.

Cuba owes the so-called Paris Club of wealthy, mostly European nations an estimated $16 billion. Until last year, Cuba owed even more — $32 billion — to Russia, a liability dating from the decades when the Soviet Union subsidized the Cuban economy. Russian President Vladimir Putin solved the problem by canceling most of the debt.[3]

Settlement possibilities exist for corporate claims, however. One approach: Companies could get tax breaks in return for investing in Cuba. "Cuba could say, 'We'll give you

an income tax holiday, an import duty holiday,' " says John S. Kavulich II, president of the U.S.-Cuba Trade and Economic Council, a New York-based nonpartisan organization that provides information to businesses interested in doing business with Cuba. "The claims are not a huge obstacle if the Cuban government wants to get creative."

But the U.S. government now represents the claimants, and it would have to allow individual firms to negotiate with Cuba. "If it's wise, the United States will encourage and facilitate that type of thing," says Robert L. Muse, a Washington lawyer specializing in U.S. laws on Cuba relations.

A further complication would arise if a bill introduced in the U.S. Senate by opponents of the Obama administration's Cuba policy in May becomes law. Co-sponsored by Marco Rubio, R-Fla., and David Vitter, R-La., the legislation would require the Cuban government to settle all certified claims before the United States could ease any sanctions on Cuba.[4]

For all the potential stumbling blocks in settling these U.S.-certified claims, they may be the simplest of the money issues affecting U.S.-Cuba relations.

Two other kinds of claims raise major political and legal issues. The first involves judgments issued by U.S. courts in lawsuits by relatives of Americans killed by the Cuban government. In 2001, federal judges awarded a total of $96.7 million to the families of three of the four Cuban-Americans killed when Cuban air force fighters shot down their small planes over international waters in 1996. And in 2007, two women collected a total of $90.9 million by order of a federal court. One was the daughter of an American CIA contractor pilot shot down during the 1961 Bay of Pigs invasion; the other was the daughter of an American businessman who smuggled arms into Cuba and was executed by firing squad.[5]

Helms of North Carolina and Rep. Dan Burton of Indiana. The measure imposed new sanctions on foreign countries and corporations that did business in Cuba. It also allowed U.S. citizens to sue foreign companies that bought or sold properties expropriated from Cubans or Americans after

the revolution. Clinton signed the bill in the presence of relatives of the four dead pilots.[62]

But, in his second term, Clinton eased restrictions on travel between the two countries and raised the amounts that Cuban-Americans could legally send in cash

The lawsuits were filed under a 1996 law allowing Americans victimized by state-sponsored terrorism to sue countries on the U.S. list of state terrorism sponsors. In 2002, Congress allowed judgments in these cases to be paid from Cuban government funds in U.S. bank accounts frozen since the early 1960s.[6]

Months after a federal judge in New York rejected an attempt to keep the funds frozen, Cuba's foreign ministry in 2007 called such payouts "a new robbery of our frozen funds" in which "the United States government acted in total complicity with the plaintiffs."[7] Regardless of judicial and congressional decisions, "the Cuban government does not recognize the jurisdiction of North American courts to judge the Republic of Cuba," the ministry said.[8]

An even more controversial category of claim is made up of lawsuits filed by people who were Cuban citizens when their property allegedly was seized by the revolutionary government.

No registry of these lawsuits exists. But the judgments levied by state courts, most in Miami-Dade County, Fla., which has a large Cuban-American population, could reach as high as $30 billion, Muse estimates.

Winners of these judgments say they reflect the U.S. legal system at its finest. "I am very happy with this finding," Gustavo Villoldo told *The Miami Herald*. "It's justice." The Bay of Pigs and CIA veteran won in 2011 what is reportedly the single biggest judgment against the Cuban government — $2.8 billion — to compensate for the seizure of his family's properties and his father's 1959 suicide — a result, he claimed, of the expropriations and official harassment.

Villoldo and the others who have made claims of this type have not collected the money. Whether they ever will be able to is unclear. "It is going to be very difficult for them to collect," Antonio C. Martinez II, a New York lawyer specializing in the issue, told *The Tampa Tribune*. One reason, he said, is that Cuba will have its governmental immunity against collecting on foreign judgments restored.[9]

Muse calls these lawsuits "bogus," however, because they center on actions that occurred on foreign soil, involving people who weren't American citizens when the Cuban government actions in question occurred. But, he says, unless the U.S. government takes action to invalidate the judgments, they could endanger improved U.S.-Cuba relations.

"[If] we want scheduled U.S. airlines to fly to Cuba, the Cubans will naturally want reciprocity," he says. "The minute a Cuban airliner touches down [in the United States], it's going to be gang-swarmed by lawyers with writs to collect on judgments."

— *Peter Katel*

[1] "Program Overview," Foreign Claims Settlement Commission, Feb. 3, 2015, http://tinyurl.com/ousthhd; Mark P. Sullivan, "Cuba: Issues for the 114th Congress," Congressional Research Service, p. 48, http://tinyurl.com/ph2kwzc.

[2] "Section II Completion of the Cuban Claims Program Under Title V of the International Claims Settlement Act of 1949," Foreign Claims Settlement Commission of the United States, 1972, pp. 351, 414; "In the Matter of the Claim of Isaac M. Kabbany," Foreign Claims Settlement Commission of the United States, July 14, 1967, http://tinyurl.com/p2esn7r.

[3] Andrey Ostroukh and José de Córdoba, "Russia Writes Off Cuba Debt," *The Wall Street Journal*, July 12, 2014, http://tinyurl.com/q4bkqlz; Daniel Trotta, "Paris Club chief in Cuba to expedite negotiations," Reuters, March 6, 2015, http://tinyurl.com/o7tuhtm.

[4] "2 US Senators Would Require Cuba to Address Claims," Voice of America, May 20, 2015, http://tinyurl.com/oa4aau6.

[5] "Cuba slams payment for American Bay of Pigs dead," Reuters, *The Washington Post*, Jan. 10, 2007, http://tinyurl.com/o5vchmf.

[6] Jennifer K. Elsea, "Suits Against Terrorist States by Victims of Terrorism," Congressional Research Service, Aug. 8, 2008, p. 1, http://tinyurl.com/ojns3sy.

[7] "Cuba jamás renunciará a su derecho," Juventud Rebelde, Jan. 10, 2007, http://tinyurl.com/o7hwlxp; Madeline BarM-s Diaz, "Federal judge orders Cuba payout," *Sun-Sentinel*, Nov. 18, 2006, http://tinyurl.com/pkh8cjp.

[8] *Ibid.*

[9] Paul Guzzo, "Lawsuits block Cuba's path to normalization," *The Tampa Tribune*, Jan. 24, 2015, http://tinyurl.com/pl5flng.

(remittances) to relatives and friends in Cuba. The final years of the Clinton years were also marked by a furious fight over the fate of Elián González, a 5-year-old rafter rescued from the sea, where his mother died. Many Miami Cubans demanded that he be allowed to stay with Miami relatives. But the Cuban and U.S. governments finally agreed to reunite him with his father in Cuba.[63]

The administration of Republican President George W. Bush, though focused on wars in the Middle East, included Cuba in what it called its "democracy promotion"

Baseball, the Goodwill Ambassador

U.S., communist rival share a love of the popular sport.

U.S.-Cuban animosities never loosened one of the strongest ties between the neighboring countries: a love of baseball.

Now, as the two governments attempt to forge a new relationship, the U.S. baseball world is jumping with excitement over the possibility that more Cuban players might be able to join U.S. teams.

The island is "a great source of talent," Major League Baseball Commissioner Rob Manfred told *The Wall Street Journal* in March. "We've seen the level of interest that quality Cuban players have generated among major-league clubs. And secondly, Cuba is a country where baseball is part of the culture."[1]

Fidel Castro, for one, never let his political views of the United States stand in the way of his love of baseball, which he played on an amateur level.[2]

And many Cuban players who wanted to play in the majors didn't let the Cuban government stand in their way.

Cuba abolished professional baseball soon after the 1959 revolution and barred its players from joining other leagues. Like all Cubans, players required special permits to travel off the island, so players wanting to compete in the big leagues had no choice but to find their own ways out of Cuba. Those who did were barred from playing in Cuba again or competing on the national team.[3]

At least 22 Cubans are now playing in the majors, a trend that began — in modern times — in 1991, when Rene Arocha, a pitcher on the Cuban national team, stayed in the United States during a team trip. He eventually joined the St. Louis Cardinals. Today's players include Yasiel Puig and Alex Guerrero of the Los Angeles Dodgers; Rusney Castillo, who was promoted to the Boston Red Sox this year from the Triple-A Pawtucket Red Sox; and star pitcher Aroldis Chapman of the Cincinnati Reds.[4]

These players and nearly all others competing on U.S. teams left Cuba illegally. Like Arocha, they usually did so while traveling abroad with Cuban teams. One Cuban-American agent involved in the clandestine business of arranging defections spent 13 years in prison in Cuba after he was arrested in 1996 for trying to help Orlando "El Duque" Hernández depart. Hernández later escaped Cuba by speedboat and became a star pitcher for the New York Yankees and other teams.[5]

"With every impediment you can imagine," says Milton Jamail, an Austin, Texas-based expert on Latin American baseball, "somehow supply and demand have been met at this level. Imagine if the market were an open market."

Traditionally, the Cuban government treated defecting players as traitors, and they were never mentioned in the state-owned national press. More recently, however, one of Cuba's hottest prospects, 19-year-old switch-hitting infielder Yoan Moncada, left the island legally last year by quitting his team, then obtaining an exit visa and passport from the government. The Boston Red Sox organization signed him to a $31.5 million contract, a record for a foreign amateur player, and slated him to start out on a Sox minor-league team.[6]

If U.S.-Cuba relations improve to the point that Cuban players can legally leave, Jamail says, U.S. teams might be able to set up training academies for young prospects. Academies already exist in the Dominican Republic and Venezuela, two other nations with strong baseball traditions. "Cubans now don't have access to the technology we have," Jamail says. "They may not see the potential in a player that one of our organizations would see."

Jamail, a retired professor of political science at the University of Texas, Austin, and a consultant to the Tampa Bay Rays, suggests that in the more immediate future, "a player could stay in Cuba until he was 23 and play for the national team, and then be free to play for Major League Baseball."

But Roberto González Echevarría, a professor of Hispanic and comparative literature at Yale and a historian of Cuban baseball, argues that unless and until Cuba abandons its Soviet-style political and economic system, no

U.S.-Cuba baseball arrangements will be fair to players. Under an exception that Cuba opened last year to the pro sports ban, Cuban players now compete on Japanese professional teams, he notes.[7] But "the agent for them is the state," he says. "It's not a free contract arrangement, and, of course, the regime keeps a substantial amount of the money" paid on the player's contract.

González Echeverría also has doubts about an academy system. "This creates a sense among young men that this is the way to go, not to study."

That warning is often heard among major-league critics who say academies exploit disadvantaged youths dreaming of striking it rich in baseball. But even some critics say academies can be run correctly, without mistreating the poor youths who go through them. "The higher-end facilities," historian Rob Ruck of the University of Pittsburgh wrote of the scene in the Dominican Republic, "offer comfortable quarters and competent instruction."[8]

Cubans have been playing baseball on the island since the 19th century. Contrary to legend, the sport didn't arrive with U.S. Marines who occupied the island from 1899 to 1902, but with a young Cuban who had studied in the United States and co-founded the Habana Base Ball Club, Cuba's first team, in 1868.[9]

The sport took off. One baseball reference site lists 190 Cuban-born players for U.S. teams since the sport became formally organized, including members of pre-World War I clubs. But before 1947, only light-skinned Cubans were allowed on the then-racially segregated U.S. big-league teams.[10]

The chasm between the link with the United States expressed on baseball fields, and the political challenge to the United States embodied in the Cuban revolution, led González Echeverría to argue in his Cuban baseball history that the baseball attachment is the deeper one between the two countries. "Cuban national, cultural, and political identities can only be carved out of their involvement with the United States," he wrote. "All the paeans to the Soviet Union in the recent past, to the sister countries of the Communist bloc, to the Third World, and to Latin America . . . never truly reflected the people's feelings."[11]

— Peter Katel

Yasiel Puig of the Los Angeles Dodgers is among at least 22 Cuban baseball players now in the major leagues. Almost all left Cuba illegally, usually while traveling abroad with Cuban teams.

Denis Poroy/Getty Images

[1] Quoted in Brian Costa, "MLB Likely to Play Exhibition Game in Cuba," *The Wall Street Journal*, March 19, 2015, http://tinyurl.com/mw9eqc3.

[2] "Rare Video: Fidel Castro Plays Baseball (1959)," Open Culture, posted June 11, 2014, http://tinyurl.com/n9t6mod.

[3] Daniel Trotta and Junko Fujita, "Cuba opens pipeline of baseball talent to Japan, U.S. left out," Reuters, July 3, 2014, http://tinyurl.com/oae6p4b.

[4] Julie Marie Bunck, "The Politics of Sports in Revolutionary Cuba," in Irving Louis Horowitz and Jaime Suchlicki, eds., *Cuban Communism*, Ninth Edition (1998), pp. 475-495; James C. McKinley Jr., "What Price Glory? A Special Report; Cuban Players Defect, but Often With a Cost," *The New York Times*, April 25, 1999, http://tinyurl.com/pj9a27m.

[5] Christopher Rhoads, "Baseball Scout's Ordeal: 13 Years in Cuban Prison," *The Wall Street Journal*, April 24, 2010, http://tinyurl.com/osu9n48.

[6] McKinley, *op. cit.*; Jesse Sanchez, "Infield prospect Moncada leaves Cuba," MLB.com, June 30, 2014, http://tinyurl.com/nfn2bkw; Gordon Edes, "Red Sox introduce Yoan Moncada," ESPN, March 14, 2015, http://tinyurl.com/pnle3kk; Jesse Sanchez, "Source: Red Sox land Cuban prospect Moncada for $31.5M," MLB.com, Feb. 23, 2015, http://tinyurl.com/nevacx4.

[7] Trotta and Fujita, *op. cit.*

[8] Rob Ruck, "Baseball's Recruitment Abuses," *Americas Quarterly*, Summer 2011, http://tinyurl.com/pkaqxhs.

[9] Milton H. Jamail, *Full Count: Inside Cuban Baseball* (2000), pp. 16-17.

[10] *Ibid.*, p. 11; "190 players born in Cuba," BaseballReference.com, undated, http://tinyurl.com/mj3hryp.

[11] Roberto González Echevarría, *The Pride of Havana: A History of Cuban Baseball* (1999), Kindle edition.

Sven Creutzmann/Mambo photo/Getty Images

Raúl Castro, right celebrates after Cuba's National Assembly elected him president in 2008 to succeed his brother, Fidel, at left. A major question hangs over Cuba's future: How will the island change after the two founding-generation revolutionaries are gone?

campaign. U.S. diplomats in Havana gave shortwave radios to dissidents. But the Cuban government in 2003 arrested 75 oppositionists and sentenced them to prison terms of up to 28 years for working with the United States against their country.[64]

In 2006, an announcement that Fidel Castro was seriously ill and had handed power to his brother, Raúl, prompted a wave of speculation that Cuba's legendary leader was dying or dead. Fidel remained alive, but he retired for good in 2008, and the National Assembly, Cuba's parliament, elected Raúl to succeed his brother as president.[65]

When Democrat Obama began his first term in 2009 he called for a "new beginning with Cuba." The administration allowed U.S.-based musicians and other artists to travel to Cuba and granted U.S. visas to Cuban artists.

However, the new tone didn't halt U.S. efforts that the Cuban government considered subversive. In late 2009, Alan Gross, a USAID contractor, was arrested for bringing digital communications equipment to Cuban citizens without Cuban government authorization. He was eventually sentenced to 15 years in prison and released only last December in the recent prisoner exchange. Gross now actively supports Obama's new Cuba policy.[66]

In one sign that Raúl Castro was trying to make some changes, Cuba in 2013 canceled its decades-old policy of requiring Cubans to have exit permits to travel off the island.[67]

CURRENT SITUATION
Embassies and Terrorism

American and Cuban negotiators continue dickering over the conditions for re-establishing full diplomatic relations, one of the key aims Obama announced when he introduced his new Cuba policy in December.

After two days of talks at the State Department in late May, the most recent of four sessions on conditions under which each country would open an embassy in the other, the sides failed to reach agreement.[68]

Neither country disclosed sticking points, but the top U.S. negotiator, Jacobson, the assistant secretary of State for Western Hemisphere affairs, told the Senate Foreign Relations Committee that the United States wants to "ensure a future U.S. embassy will be able to function more like other diplomatic missions in Cuba and elsewhere in the world."[69]

At a previous hearing, Jacobson spoke more explicitly, saying that U.S. diplomats would "hopefully [have] the ability to travel throughout the country and see more people, and support more people." Presently, she said, "we can't really move outside of Havana."[70]

State Department officials have acknowledged that a U.S. embassy in Havana might operate under conditions similar to those imposed by two other communist countries, China and Vietnam, which restrict U.S. diplomats' travel outside the capitals.[71]

While the talks have not yielded a final deal, the fact that negotiations have continued results from an action that the Obama administration formally took in May — removing Cuba from the small list of countries categorized by the United States as sponsors of terrorism.[72] Obama announced the decision to strike Cuba from the list days after meeting with Castro, acting on a recommendation from the State Department.

"Circumstances have changed since 1982, when Cuba was originally designated as a state sponsor of terrorism because of its efforts to promote armed revolution by forces in Latin America," the department said.[73]

Will the new Cuba policy strengthen human rights in Cuba?

YES   Tom P. Malinowski
Assistant Secretary of State, Bureau of Democracy, Human Rights, and Labor

From testimony before the Senate Foreign Relations Committee, Feb. 3, 2015

The promotion of universal human rights and the empowerment of all Cubans must be the bedrock of our policy toward Cuba. President Obama has made clear that it will be.

The most immediate result of this policy shift — the release from prison of 53 activists who are now back with their families and able to continue their brave work — is unambiguously a good thing. The released men and women included all Cubans designated by Amnesty International as "prisoners of conscience," and many known to my bureau to have been prosecuted for peaceful expression, association and assembly in Cuba.

The release of these political prisoners does not of itself change anything in Cuba. Cuba remains a one-party state that tries to stifle virtually all political, cultural and economic activity that it does not control.

And let's be clear: None of this — Cuba's repression, its poverty, its isolation — is the fault of the United States or of the embargo. The responsibility lies with the Cuban government.

At the same time, after 50 years of experience with the embargo, we have to face the hard truth that it has not weakened the repressive apparatus of the Castro government. It has not strengthened Cuba's civil society. It has not given us the leverage we need to press for change, or the Cuban people the hope they crave. The Castro government has been happy in its isolation. The Cuban people have not.

At the same time, over many years of working on this issue, I have seen how the Castro government has turned our policy against us, and how this has helped an authoritarian form of government survive so close to our shores. . . .

For decades, in capitals around the world, the Cuban government has succeeded in making our embargo and its isolation from the United States a bigger issue than its own repression. We have to acknowledge that, over the years, shifting the blame to America has worked for the Castro government. It is not going to work any more.

If our new policy succeeds in empowering the Cuban people to shape their political destiny, then the Cuban government may respond by cracking down harder in the short run, but the Cuban people will have the best opportunity in more than half a century to freely determine their own future in the long run.

NO   Sen. Robert Menendez, D-N.J.

From remarks before the Senate Foreign Relations Committee, Feb. 3, 2015

Eighteen months of secret negotiations produced a bad deal for the Cuban people. In my view, we've compromised bedrock principles for virtually no concessions.

I don't want to relive years of engagement with China that has brought us forced abortions, prison camp labor, one-child policy, ethnic cleansing in Tibet, exile of the Dalai Lama and, most recently, repression in Hong Kong's democracy. From those engagements, maybe we can say that we're doing business with China, but we can't really hold up democracy and human rights as a great success story of that engagement. If that's what we hope for the Cuban people, then it's a sad day.

At the end of the day, 53 political prisoners were released while so many more remain in jail. I'm also concerned that the 53 prisoners were not released unconditionally and continue to face legal hurdles and that several of them have been rearrested. And the Cuban people still have zero guarantees for any basic freedoms.

I'm concerned that the president announced that the International Committee of the Red Cross and the United Nations would be granted access in Cuba, yet we know from the State Department briefings that they will be allowed to travel to Havana, but only to discuss prison conditions with regime officials and won't be given access to Cuban jails or Cuban prisoners, which does nothing to improve human rights conditions in Cuba.

I'm concerned that there was not one substantial step toward transparent, democratic elections, improved human rights, freedom of assembly or the ability to form independent political parties and independent trade unions. Ironically, just two weeks after the announcement, the regime arrested more than 50 people who tried to speak about the hopes for the future of their country.

The harsh reality [is that] heroic individuals inside of Cuba struggle to create a greater space for civil society, human rights and democracy. And we sort of sweep that away: People will say, "I know there are violations," and then we go to, "Let's do business, let's travel."

Dissidents on the island still don't have access to the Internet and other forms of communication because, even if you think the law allows the investment of U.S. dollars to provide the link to the island, there is no guarantee that the government of Cuba will permit such linkages to ultimately take place.

In its most recent report on global terrorism, published last year, the department said there was "no indication that the Cuban government provided weapons or paramilitary training to terrorist groups."[74]

Congressional foes initially said they would try to block Obama's action on the terrorism list. But Rep. Ileana Ros-Lehtinen, R-Fla., acknowledged in late April — following an analysis by the nonpartisan Congressional Research Service — that the laws authorizing the list and its related sanctions did not provide a way for Congress to prevent Obama's action.[75]

Apart from symbolic value, ending Cuba's official classification as a terrorism-supporting state carries real value for Cuba, says Kavulich of the U.S.-Cuba Business Council. "Their cost of borrowing immediately decreases," he says. "One of the factors that banks, companies, governments use to determine liability is risk. The Cubans now can say, 'No longer do we have the U.S. government trying to harm us' " by counting Cuba as a sponsor of terrorism.

Seeking Fugitives

Cuba's hospitality to American fugitives who have long resided there, including a prison escapee convicted of killing a New Jersey state trooper, remains a U.S. grievance against Cuba.

Opponents of the administration's policy shift on Cuba tried to persuade the State Department that Cuba should remain on the terrorism list because it harbors fugitives. "It is essential to recognize that the Castro regime has a long track record of providing sanctuary to terrorists and harboring U.S. fugitives who have murdered American citizens," Sen. Robert Menendez, D-N.J., wrote to Secretary of State John Kerry in February. "Before Cuba is removed from the list . . . American fugitives must be brought back to face justice in the U.S."[76]

But the State Department reported in 2009 that Cuba had not "provided safe haven to any new U.S. fugitives wanted for terrorism since 2006." The precise number of U.S. fugitives in Cuba is unknown.[77]

Menendez' letter — later echoed by New Jersey Republican Gov. Chris Christie — cited a State Department figure of 70 as of 2007. But the *Sun-Sentinel* of Fort Lauderdale, Fla., reported an additional 50 fugitives from fraud, theft and drug trafficking charges, as well as 500 Cuban-born fugitives who could be anywhere, including their homeland.[78]

The main focus is on a handful of politically charged cases. The highest-profile fugitive is Joanne Chesimard, a member of the so-called Black Liberation Army (BLA), who was convicted of killing New Jersey state trooper Werner Foerster during a 1973 traffic stop. The BLA was tied to bank robberies, bombings and killings of police officers in the 1970s.[79]

U.S. diplomats say they have repeatedly demanded Chesimard's extradition. But Cuba steadfastly refuses. "I can say it is off the table," Gustavo Machín, deputy director for American affairs at the Cuban foreign ministry, told Yahoo News. Machín said Cuba had granted Chesimard political asylum.[80]

Conversely, Cuba has long demanded the extradition of Luis Posada Carriles, a former CIA asset who escaped from jail in Venezuela, where he was charged with having planned and carried out the 1976 Cuban airliner bombing that killed the country's Olympic fencing team. Posada Carriles was acquitted in El Paso, Texas, in 2011 of lying to immigration authorities and has been living in Miami. In 1998, he told *The New York Times* that he had planned bombing attacks in Havana in 1997 in which an Italian tourist was killed.[81]

The list of fugitives also includes a Puerto Rican independence activist convicted of bomb-making and an African-American separatist charged in the killing of a New Mexico state police officer.[82]

The latter, Charlie Hill, hinted in a recent interview with CNN in Havana that he might return voluntarily or not resist extradition.[83]

Boom and Realities

Whatever the future of U.S.-Cuba relations, an immediate result of the new U.S. policy is an American tourism boom in Cuba.

A University of Havana economist found a 36 percent increase in the number of Americans arriving in Cuba this year, through May 9, compared with the same period last year. According to the economist's research, 51,458 Americans with no relatives on the island have arrived this year, nearly 14,000 more than the 37,459 during the first five months of 2014.[84]

Roughly one-third of the visitors arrived via third countries, including Mexico and the Bahamas, to evade what remains of a U.S. prohibition on tourism.[85]

But Washington lawyer Muse told The Associated Press that the Obama administration is not actively enforcing the prohibition. "They favor engagement," he said. "That's why they take this liberalized approach to travel."[86]

Alongside the tourists, Cuba is seeing a parade of U.S. politicians and businesspeople eager for the opportunities that loosened restrictions on trade might provide. Over the past several months, known visitors include Democratic Gov. Andrew Cuomo of New York, heading a trade delegation, and a delegation of about two dozen Texas farmers and food exporters.[87]

But Americans aren't the only business visitors. "Everyone else around the world is anticipating the dropping or loosening of the embargo, so they are quickly moving to get ahead of us," says James Williams, president of a newly formed anti-embargo advocacy group, Engage Cuba. "We're going to be boxed out."

However, some Cuba experts acknowledge that while opportunities exist, they are not as extensive as some Americans may believe. "The business payoff is not very big; it is very, very small," says Henken of Baruch College, a specialist in the emerging Cuban private sector. "It is very important for everyone involved or interested to take a chill pill — the market is relatively minuscule, the embargo is still in place, the Cuban government is one of the worst in the world to do business with."

Further, it is far from clear how accepting Cuba will be of the new trade parameters that the Obama administration set. Expanded export categories include building materials for private-home construction, farm equipment for small-scale farmers and unspecified "goods for use by private-sector Cuban entrepreneurs."[88]

But moves that President Castro began in 2008 to encourage Cuba's tiny private sector have been slow to produce results, specialists say. "It is possible that a conflict exists within Cuban leadership," wrote the University of Pittsburgh's Mesa-Lago. "The most advanced members push for the reforms but the hard-liners — fearful of delegation and loss of economic power and a 'snowball' effect — attach controls, regulations and taxes which they justify by arguing that they avoid wealth concentration."[89]

Tourism, already an established industry, might be one exception. Brian Chesky, CEO of Airbnb, a company that brokers vacation stays in private homes, told Bloomberg that the firm saw the number of Cubans signed up to host visitors increase from 1,000 to 2,000 in about six weeks. "I don't think we've ever had a market grow as fast as Cuba," he said.[90]

OUTLOOK
Pressure for Change

A major question hangs over Cuba policy: How will the island change when Fidel and Raúl Castro die?

President Castro, formerly the longtime defense minister and armed forces chief, has said that his present term, which ends in 2018, will be his last. His expected successor is First Vice President Miguel Díaz-Canel. Unlike the Castros, the 55-year-old, who was trained as an engineer, does not have an extensive military background beyond his standard armed forces service. But as a government official in provinces with tourism projects, he worked with the military, which has been branching out into business and industrial development.[91]

The military has a holding company, GAESA, which is reported to control 20 percent to 40 percent of the Cuban economy and is headed by President Castro's son-in-law. Its firms include telecommunications, import-export and retail operations. An army colonel, formerly with GAESA, now runs CIMEX, Cuba's biggest company, which is both the receiving agent for foreign remittances and a real estate firm that rents properties to foreigners.[92]

Whether Díaz-Canel in fact inherits the presidency, Suchlicki of the University of Miami argues that President Castro has set the course for the future — and, Suchlicki says, that course is military domination of the economy and the country as a whole.

As head of the armed forces, Raúl Castro spearheaded military involvement in the economy, he notes. "What he wants to do is finish his couple of years, then pass it on to Canel and his [Raúl's] son. . . . Then, more Americans come, more tourists. 'You want to invest? Here is general so-and-so; he's going to be partner in the shoe industry.' "

But pressure for change from Cuba's citizenry may be unstoppable, others argue. Henken of Baruch College says the new Obama policy likely will add to that pressure. Noting that new U.S. trade moves include encouraging export of digital communications technology and software, he says, "The Cuban government cannot keep denying access to the Internet and getting away with it. The United States can play a role there in promoting a business opportunity."

Meanwhile, all signs point to the United States maintaining its support for human rights activists. Cuba has long complained that the United States is hypocritical on that subject, and some experts agree. "The moral argument is a huge joke," says Gleijeses of the Johns Hopkins School of Advanced International Studies. "We have just re-established military aid to the government of Egypt, and the president of Egypt is a mass murderer. Does Cuba repress political dissent? Sure, but what is the relevance to the United States? If we are concerned about that, we should start with Egypt."

Within Cuba, however, the country's long alliance with the repressive Soviet Union is now an accepted — if sensitive — topic of discussion. Distribution has been allowed of a book by Cuban novelist Leonardo Padura that raises the issue by examining Cuba's ties to the Soviet ideology espoused by the late Soviet dictator Joseph Stalin. The book "exposes the hideous legacy of Stalinism, which for decades amounted to a state religion in Cuba," wrote journalist Jon Lee Anderson, a former Havana resident.[93]

But several countries have retained their communist systems, at least politically, while opening their markets. China and Vietnam provide useful road maps for maintaining a one-party, politically controlled state alongside a capitalist economy, some Cuba-watchers argue.

Some even say that Chinese investment in Cuba has pushed the island nation in a more capitalist direction. "Chinese support for Cuba's [economic] liberalization agenda is prompting the Western Hemisphere's only communist nation toward alignment with international norms," Hearn of the China Studies Center wrote in 2012.[94]

But Michael Shifter, president of Inter-American Dialogue, a Washington think tank, rejects the notion of an Asian model for Cuba. "Cuba is its own case," he says. "Whatever happens there is not going to be the China path or Vietnam path. It is an island that is close to the United States; there is a history of nationalism. It is distinctive."

Still, he adds, "I don't think anyone knows what the political future of Cuba will be."

NOTES

1. "Remarks by President Obama and President Raúl Castro of Cuba Before Meeting," The White House, April 11, 2015, http://tinyurl.com/noplp26.

2. *Ibid.*

3. Hugh Thomas, *Cuba: The Pursuit of Freedom* (1971), p. 1373; Daniel P. Erikson, *The Cuba Wars: Fidel Castro, the United States and the Next Revolution* (2008), pp. 139-140.

4. "Cuba: Assessing the Administration's Sudden Shift," House Foreign Affairs Committee, CQ Transcriptions, Feb. 4, 2015; Pietro Pitts, "U.S.-Cuba Deal Shows Venezuelan Oil Giveaways Running Out," Bloomberg, Dec. 19, 2014, http://tinyurl.com/otpedg5; Carmelo Mesa-Lago, "Institutional Changes of Cuba's Economic-Social Reforms," Brookings Institution, University of Havana, August 2014, http://tinyurl.com/oub36qq.

5. Emily Parker, "Cuba's uneasy Internet connection," Reuters, April 8, 2014, http://tinyurl.com/pqhpbrr.

6. Senate Committee on Foreign Relations, Subcommittee on Western Hemisphere, Transnational Crime, Civilian Security, Democracy, Human Rights and Global Women's Issues, CQ Transcriptions, Feb. 3, 2015.

7. Patrick Oppmann, "Cuban official: 'This could be last round' of talks leading to embassies reopening," CNN, May 18, 2015, http://tinyurl.com/q8n76ow.

8. "2014 FIU Cuba Poll: How Cuban Americans in Miami View U.S. Policies Toward Cuba," Florida International University, 2014, http://tinyurl.com/oalzpry; Scott Clement, "Poll: Support increases for lifting Cuba embargo, travel restrictions," *The Washington Post*, Dec. 23, 2014, http://tinyurl.com/p33zyhr.

9. "Fact Sheet: Charting a New Course on Cuba," The White House, Dec. 17, 2014, http://tinyurl.com/ojuge6h; Randal C. Archibold and Julie Hirschfeld Davis, "Cuba to Be Removed From U.S. List of Nations That Sponsor Terrorism," *The New York Times*, April 14, 2015, http://tinyurl.com/mqllnys; Frances Robles and Julie Hirschfeld Davis, "U.S. Frees Last of the 'Cuban Five,' Part of a 1990s Spy Ring," *The New York Times*, Dec. 17, 2014, http://tinyurl.com/naxu5qx; Mark Mazzetti, Michael S. Schmidt and Frances Robles, "Crucial Spy in Cuba Paid a Heavy Cold War Price," *The New York Times*, Dec. 18, 2014, http://tinyurl.com/mj7ktdo; Brian Latell, "New revelations about Cuban spy Ana Montes," *The Miami Herald*, Aug. 2, 2014, http://tinyurl.com/omguug4.

10. Matt Spetalnick, David Adams, Lesley Wroughton, "Cuba has freed all 53 prisoners as agreed in U.S. deal: U.S. officials," Reuters, Jan. 12, 2015, http://tinyurl.com/oax3jvf; Mazzetti, Schmidt, Robles, *ibid.*

11. Robert Muse, "U.S. Presidential Action on Cuba: The New Normalization?" *Americas Quarterly*, 2014, http://tinyurl.com/ord7gpe. "Cuban Embargo: Selected Issues Relating to Travel, Exports, and Telecommunications," U.S. General Accounting Office, December 1998, http://tinyurl.com/on85tdo.

12. "Cuba: Assessing the Administration's Sudden Shift," House Foreign Affairs Committee, CQ Transcriptions, Feb. 4, 2015.

13. *Ibid.*

14. "Raúl Castro en la Cumbre de las Américas . . . ," CubaDebate, April 11, 2015, http://tinyurl.com/qxjbjb8.

15. Ruth Ellen Wasem, "Cuban Migration to the United States: Policy and Trends," Congressional Research Service, p. 1, http://tinyurl.com/ykb2w4h.

16. *Ibid.*, pp. 1-5.

17. U.S. Customs and Border protection figures supplied by agency.

18. Wasem, *op. cit.*, p. 2.

19. "Acerca de la Ley de Ajuste Cubano," Cuba vs. Bloqueo, undated, http://tinyurl.com/ogu28c2.

20. Pitts, *op. cit.*; Ted Piccone and Harold Trinkunas, "The Cuba-Venezuela Alliance: The Beginning of the End?" Brookings Institution, June 2014, http://tinyurl.com/nugy2j3.

21. Piccone and Trinkunas, *ibid.*

22. Olga Tanas and Anna Andrianova, "Russia Writes Off 90% of Cuba Debt as Putin Meets Castros," Bloomberg, July 11, 2014, http://tinyurl.com/p55te4c.

23. "Russia 'to reopen Lourdes spy base in Cuba," BBC, July 16, 2014, http://tinyurl.com/nl47jrp.

24. David M. Herszenhorn, "Ukraine Repels Separatists in Fierce Fighting, Poroshenko Says," *The New York Times*, June 5, 2015, http://tinyurl.com/pezbqxw.

25. Quoted in Juan O. Tamayo, "Russia-Cuba love affair on again," *The Miami Herald*, July 19, 2014, http://tinyurl.com/opyl42h.

26. Quoted in Pitts, *op. cit.*; "Single point of failure," *The Economist*, Oct. 4, 2014, http://tinyurl.com/nzqa3a4.

27. Marc Frank, "Cuba hopes for more investment as Chinese president arrives," Reuters, July 21, 2014, http://tinyurl.com/optf7hh.

28. Adrian H. Hearn, "China, Global Governance and the Future of Cuba," *Journal of Current Chinese Affairs*, 2012, http://tinyurl.com/o4ytxr9.

29. "Platt Amendment (1903)," Ourdocuments.gov, http://tinyurl.com/nckozro; Thomas, *op. cit.*, pp. 444-462, 789-802; Julia E. Sweig, *Cuba: What Everyone Needs to Know* (2012), pp. 8-35.

30. Jim Rasenberger, *The Brilliant Disaster: JFK, Castro, and America's Doomed Invasion of Cuba's Bay of Pigs* (2011), pp. 45-51; Tim Weiner, *Legacy of Ashes: The History of the CIA* (2008), pp. 180-182; William M. LeoGrande and Peter Kornbluh, *Back Channel to Cuba: The Hidden History of Negotiations Between Washington and Havana* (2014), pp. 27-33.

31. Patrick J. Haney and Walt Vanderbush, *The Cuban Embargo: The Domestic Politics of an American Foreign Policy* (2005), Kindle edition.

32. Thomas, *op. cit.*, pp. 1301-2, 1360-71; Weiner, *op. cit.*, pp. 186-87, 199-200.

33. Thomas, *op. cit.*, pp. 1303-4; Tim Weiner, "C.I.A. Bares Its Bungling in Report on Bay of Pigs Invasion," *The New York Times*, Feb. 22, 1998, http://tinyurl.com/cuxd8tf; LeoGrande and Kornbluh, *op. cit.*, p. 47.

34. LeoGrande and Kornbluh, *ibid.*, pp. 47-53, 58-61.

35. Thomas, *op. cit.*, pp. 1412-1414.

36. Weiner, *op. cit.*, pp. 186-187, 199-200, 240-241.

37. LeoGrande and Kornbluh, *op. cit.*, pp. 119-154.

38. *Ibid.*, pp. 123-125; "U.S.-Cuba Hijacking Agreement, 1969-February 1973, #142, Memorandum," U.S. State Department, http://tinyurl.com/pwv7vjd.

39. LeoGrande and Kornbluh, *op. cit.*, pp. 130-131.

40. *Ibid.*, pp. 130-131.

41. Haney and Vanderbush, *op. cit.*; "The Situation of Cuba in the OAS and the Protection of Human Rights," Organization of American States, Secretariat for Legal Affairs, April 25, 2003, pp. 1-2, http://tinyurl.com/kam5e52.

42. Haney and Vanderbush, *ibid.*

43. LeoGrande and Kornbluh, *op. cit.*, p. 145.

44. *Ibid.*, p. 147.

45. *Ibid.*, p. 153.

46. *Ibid.*, p. 158.

47. *Ibid.*, pp. 162-163; Mark P. Sullivan, "Cuba: U.S. Restrictions on Travel and Remittances," Congressional Research Service, April 10, 2015, p. 1, http://tinyurl.com/nnb25yt.

48. *Ibid.*, LeoGrande and Kornbluh, pp. 214-215.

49. *Ibid.*, p. 215.

50. *Ibid.*, pp. 216-217; quoted in Mirta Ojito, *Finding Mañana: A Memoir of a Cuban Exodus* (2005), p. 117.

51. *Ibid.*, LeoGrande and Kornbluh, p. 217.

52. Ojito, *op. cit.*, p. 258.

53. LeoGrande and Kornbluh, *op. cit.*, pp. 225-230. Sullivan, *op. cit.*, p. 1.

54. LeoGrande and Kornbluh, *op. cit.*, pp. 244-245, pp. 247-248; "Radio Marti Authorization," *CQ Almanac*, 1982, http://tinyurl.com/q7yz5ne.

55. Quoted in ibid, LeoGrande and Kornbluh, *op. cit.*, p. 265; Serge Schmemann, "End of the Soviet Union; the Soviet State, Born of a Dream, Dies," *The New York Times*, Dec. 26, 1991, http://tinyurl.com/o58zdyp.

56. *Ibid.*, LeoGrande and Kornbluh, *op. cit.*, p. 270.

57. Haney and Vanderbush, *op. cit.* Kindle edition, no page numbers.

58. Daniel P. Erikson, *The Cuba Wars: Fidel Castro, the United States, and the Next Revolution* (2008), p. 234.

59. LeoGrande and Kornbluh, *op. cit.*, pp. 281-282; Wasem, *op. cit.*, p. 1.

60. *Ibid.*, pp. 279-299.

61. *Ibid.*, pp. 304-313.

62. *Ibid.*, pp. 305, 314-315.

63. *Ibid.*, pp. 343-344. Ed Vulliamy, "Elián González and the Cuban crisis: fallout from a big row over a little boy," *The Guardian*, Feb. 20, 2010, http://tinyurl.com/ogq6qp3.

64. *Ibid.*, pp. 359-361.

65. *Ibid.*, pp. 365-368.

66. "Cuba Releases American Alan Gross After 5 Years in Prison," The Associated Press, *The Huffington Post*, Dec. 17, 2014, http://tinyurl.com/kkwrm94; "What Was Alan Gross Doing in Cuba?," FactCheck.org, Dec. 23, 2014, http://tinyurl.com/kjm7nxb; Felicia Schwartz, "After Jail in Cuba, Alan Gross to Work for U.S.-Cuba Opening," *The Wall Street Journal*, May 3, 2015, http://tinyurl.com/q43297b.

67. Tracy Wilkinson, "Cubans no longer need special exit permit to travel off island," *Los Angeles Times*, Jan. 15, 2013, http://tinyurl.com/orqchkx.

68. Michael R. Gordon and Randal C. Archibold, "U.S. and Cuban Negotiators Can't Quite Seal a Deal," *The New York Times*, May 22, 2015, http://tinyurl.com/pyjvqyn.

69. Roberta S. Jacobson, testimony before the Senate Foreign Relations Committee, May 20, 2015, CQ Congressional Testimony.

70. House Foreign Affairs Committee, *op. cit.*

71. Patricia Zengerle and Lesley Wroughton, "U.S. embassy in Cuba likely to operate in restrictive environment," Reuters, May 20, 2015, http://tinyurl.com/n4tmm46.

72. Mimi Whitefield, "Cuba removed from U.S. terrorism list," *The Miami Herald*, May 28, 2015, http://tinyurl.com/qaugzbf.

73. "Recommendation to Rescind Cuba's Designation as a State Sponsor of Terrorism," U.S. State Department, April 14, 2015, http://tinyurl.com/n7shb3l;. Archibold and Davis, *op. cit.*

74. "Country Reports on Terrorism 2013," U.S. State Department, April 2014, p. 19, http://tinyurl.com/nlxbv8x.

75. Mimi Whitefield, "Republicans won't challenge Cuba's removal from terrorism list," *The Miami Herald*, April 23, 2015, http://tinyurl.com/qg7asrc; Dianne E. Rennack, "State Sponsors of Acts of International Terrorism — Legislative Parameters: In Brief," Congressional Research Service, April 15, 2015, pp. 5-6, http://tinyurl.com/oo2l7sk.

76. Letter, Sen. Robert Menendez to Secretary of State John Kerry, Feb. 26, 2015, http://tinyurl.com/pawjkg4.

77. "State Sponsors of Terrorism," in "Country Reports on Terrorism 2008," U.S. State Department, April 30, 2009, http://tinyurl.com/qxbx75d.

78. Megan O'Matz and Sally Kestin, "U.S. has no idea how many fugitives Cuba's harboring," *Sun-Sentinel*, Jan. 31, 2015, http://tinyurl.com/pw8l2w6; Ted Hesson, "Chris Christie wants Cuba to hand over Tupac's godmother," *Fusion*, April 21, 2015, http://tinyurl.com/qeqfe6p.

79. Michael Isikoff, "Castro government: We will never return fugitive cop killer to U.S.," Yahoo News, March 2, 2015, http://tinyurl.com/p6em8lm; Hesson, *ibid.*

80. Quoted in Isikoff, *ibid.*

81. "US court acquits Cuba militant Luis Posada Carriles," BBC, April 8, 2011, http://tinyurl.com/oa5a5sc; "Posada Carriles Stars in Anti-Castro Rally in Miami," *Havana Times*, Dec. 21, 2014, http://tinyurl.com/nbhvuqk.

82. Michael Coleman, "NM fugitive in Cuba sought in killing of officer wants to return," *Albuquerque Journal*, April 10, 2015, http://tinyurl.com/ppq3zhc; Meghan Keneally, "These American Fugitives May Be Hiding Out in Cuba," ABC News, Dec. 19, 2014, http://tinyurl.com/kcc7s2l.

83. Patrick Oppmann, "Admitted hijacker dreams of home after 43 years hiding out in Cuba," CNN, April 9, 2015, www.cnn.com/2015/04/09/americas/us-cuba-fugitive-charlie-hill/Oppmann.

84. "US travel to Cuba surges 36% following thaw in diplomatic relations," The Associated Press, *The Guardian*, May 26, 2015, http://tinyurl.com/m4zr37d.

85. "Fact Sheet: Charting a New Course on Cuba," The White House, Dec. 17, 2014, http://tinyurl.com/l4wkqvw.

86. Quoted in "US travel . . . ," *op. cit.*

87. Alfredo Corchado, "Texans hoping to turn U.S.-Cuba thaw into cold cash," *The Dallas Morning News*, April 24, 2015, http://tinyurl.com/o4hdfd8; Susanne Craig, "Seeking Business, Cuomo Heads to Cuba With a New York Trade Delegation," *The New York Times*, April 19, 2015, http://tinyurl.com/omrg777.

88. "Fact Sheet . . . ," *op. cit.*

89. Mesa-Lago, *op. cit.*, p. 23.

90. "Cuba is Airbnb's Fastest Growing Market: CEO," *BloombergBusiness*, May 11, 2015, http://tinyurl.com/nnout7m.

91. Damien Cave, "Raúl Castro Says His New 5-Year Term as Cuba's President Will Be His Last," *The New York Times*, Feb. 24, 2013, http://tinyurl.com/k7t8l85; Damien Cave and Victoria Burnett, "As Castro Era Drifts to Close, a New Face Steps In at No. 2," *The New York Times*, Feb. 27, 2013, http://tinyurl.com/o66m3cl.

92. William M. LeoGrande, "The Party and the Army: Civil-Military Relations in Cuba," *World Politics Review*, June 26, 2014, http://tinyurl.com/nkhcu7h; "Trying to make the sums add up," *The Economist*, Nov. 11, 2010, http://tinyurl.com/o4kgjfs; Damien Cave, "Cuba's Reward for the Dutiful: Gated Housing," *The New York Times*, Feb. 11, 2014, http://tinyurl.com/p6m2asy; Alejandro Castro Espín: "Cuba Will Never Return to Capitalism," *Havana Times*, Feb. 24, 2015, http://tinyurl.com/ps3c5to.

93. Jon Lee Anderson, "Private Eyes: A crime novelist navigates Cuba's shifting reality," *The New Yorker*, Oct. 21, 2013, http://tinyurl.com/n43jlwk.

94. Hearn, *op. cit.*

BIBLIOGRAPHY
Selected Sources
Books

Hufbauer, Gary Clyde, and Barbara Kotschwar, *Economic Normalization With Cuba: A Roadmap for US Policymakers*, **Peterson Institute for International Economics, 2014.**
Two international economists explain how the United States could help Cuba develop a successful capitalist economy.

LeoGrande, William M., and Peter Kornbluh, *Back Channel to Cuba: The Hidden History of Negotiations Between Washington and Havana*, **University of North Carolina Press, 2014.**
From interviews and previously undisclosed documents, an American University political scientist (LeoGrande) and

a National Security Archive specialist (Kornbluh) chronicle postrevolutionary U.S.-Cuba diplomatic history.

Pérez-Stable, Marifeli, ed., *Looking Forward: Comparative Perspectives on Cuba's Transition,* **University of Notre Dame Press, 2007.**
In studies still relevant today, scholars explore the possible roads Cuba could take after revolutionary leader Fidel Castro dies.

Sweig, Julia E., *Cuba: What Everyone Needs to Know,* **Oxford University Press, 2012.**
A Latin America specialist at the Council on Foreign Relations provides a guide to Cuban history and the country's relations with the United States.

Articles

"A long game in Havana," *The Economist,* **March 7, 2015, http://tinyurl.com/pxymazz.**
The British newsmagazine argues that Cuba will not rush into a new relationship with the United States for fear of political disruption.

Adams, David, and Zachary Fagenson, "Cuban immigration surges after thaw in US-Cuban relations," Reuters, May 13, 2015, http://tinyurl.com/pxwkzbk.
U.S. Customs and Border Patrol numbers show a rise in Cuban immigration since President Obama's policy shift.

Archibold, Randal C., "American Released by Cuba Plays Role as U.S. Relations With Havana Thaw," *The New York Times,* **May 2, 2015, http://tinyurl.com/kqmgl23.**
Alan Gross, released by Cuba in a prisoner exchange with the United States, is becoming an advocate for normalization.

Cave, Damien, "Cuba's Reward for the Dutiful: Gated Housing," *The New York Times,* **Feb. 11, 2014, http://tinyurl.com/p6m2asy.**
A Latin America correspondent explores the Cuban military's increasing involvement in business and industry.

DeYoung, Karen, "As normalization talks begin, Cubans begin anticipating changes to come," *The Washington Post,* **Jan. 24, 2015, http://tinyurl.com/o85e8s7.**
Ordinary Cubans respond positively to warming ties with the United States while members of the governing elite are divided, a veteran correspondent reports.

Garcia, Anne-Marie, "Diplomats, business people flood Cuba amid warmer US ties," The Associated Press, May 10, 2015, http://tinyurl.com/qh7ugq4.
Foreign diplomats and businesspeople, seeing benefits to a new Cuba-U.S. relationship, trek to Havana.

Garrett, Laurie, "How Cuba Could Stop the Next Ebola Outbreak," *Foreign Policy,* **May 6, 2015, http://tinyurl.com/kyhhm2v.**
A journalist proposes that the United States help finance Cuba's medical training program for world health care workers, in an effort to prevent another Ebola epidemic.

Padgett, Tim, "Obama's Top Negotiator In CubaSays Human Rights, Private Sector Will Be U.S. Drumbeat," WLRN, Jan. 28, 2015, http://tinyurl.com/o7hlj6x.
A State Department official vows to continue advocating for human rights in Cuba.

Shifter, Michael, "What's Next for Cuba?" *Politico Magazine,* **Dec. 21, 2014, http://tinyurl.com/pyjmhmk.**
The president of a Washington think tank on Latin America cautions that restoring U.S.-Cuba relations will be long and complicated.

Whitefield, Mimi, "Ferry service to Cuba may return to the Florida Straits," *The Miami Herald,* **May 5, 2015, http://tinyurl.com/nn3yjg9.**
Washington approves five companies' proposals to provide ferry service to Cuba.

Reports and Studies

Mesa-Lago, Carmelo, "Institutional Changes of Cuba's Economic-Social Reforms," The Brookings Institution, University of Havana, August 2014, http://tinyurl.com/oub36qq.
An expert on the Cuban economy concludes that post-2008 economic reforms have not delivered tangible improvements for most Cubans.

Sullivan, Mark P., "Cuba: Issues for the 114th Congress," Congressional Research Service, April 17, 2015, http://tinyurl.com/pva8497.
A nonpartisan analysis says that while economic change on the island is possible, the Cuban government will keep tight political control.

For More Information

The Brookings Institution, 1775 Massachusetts Ave., N.W., Washington, DC 20036; 202-797-6000; www.brookings.edu/research/topics/cuba. Centrist think tank that sponsors research on Cuba and holds panel discussions, available on Web recordings.

Center for a Free Cuba, 1725 DeSales St., N.W., Suite 600, Washington, DC 20036; 202-463-8430; www.cuba-center.org/. Advocacy group for Cuban dissidents that opposes Obama policy shift on Cuban relations.

Cuban American National Foundation, 2147 S.W. 8th St., Miami, FL 33135; 305-592-7768; http://canf.org/. Formerly hard-line organization that supports a complete lifting of restrictions on family remittances to Cuba.

Cuban Research Institute, Florida International University, Modesto A. Maidique Campus, Deuxième Maison (DM) 445, 11200 S.W. 8th St., Miami, FL 33199; 305-348-1991; https://cri.fiu.edu/. University think tank that sponsors research on Cuban history, politics and society.

Granma International, www.granma.cu/idiomas/ingles/. English-language Web version of Cuba's state-owned daily, which presents the Cuban government's views on U.S. policy.

Inter-American Dialogue, 1211 Connecticut Ave., N.W., Suite 510, Washington, DC 20036; 202-822-9002; www.thedialogue.org/cuba. Washington think tank that focuses on connecting Cuban businesses to international financial institutions.

Washington Office on Latin America, 1666 Connecticut Ave., N.W., Suite 400, Washington, DC 20009; 202-797-2171; www.wola.org/program/cuba. Human-rights-oriented research and advocacy organization that supports the U.S. policy shift.

10

U.S. Global Engagement

Peter Katel

A girl is carried to safety in Aleppo, Syria, after being wounded by a reported barrel bomb dropped by government forces on April 27, 2014. At least 150,000 people — one-third of them civilians — have been killed in the three years of fighting between government forces and the rebels seeking to unseat President Bashar al-Assad. President Obama backed off military action against Assad after he agreed to destroy his chemical weapons.

ZEIN AL-RIFAI/AFP/Getty Images

From *CQ Researcher*,
May 16, 2014.

In May, yet another foreign official came to Washington to act out a time-honored ritual: pleading for help in overthrowing a hated dictatorship.

This time the supplicant was Munzer Akbik, chief of staff in the Opposition Coalition seeking to depose Syrian President Bashar al-Assad. Although the rebels have received some U.S. weapons, they want more.[1]

"There is a wide range of sophisticated weaponry that can make a difference on the ground, [such as] missiles, the anti-aircraft, anti-tank missiles and maybe some kind of guided weaponry and heavy artillery," Akbik said.[2]

In the 1980s, Afghans fighting a Soviet invasion, Nicaraguans opposing a left-wing government and Bosnians facing assault by Serbian forces all came to Washington with similar requests.[3] Four decades earlier, as Nazi Germany bombed London, British Prime Minister Winston Churchill was unable to visit Washington personally, but he still pleaded successfully for help getting U.S. weapons, despite Americans' resistance to entering World War II prior to Japan's 1941 attack on Pearl Harbor.[4]

Akbik came to Washington at a time of multiple foreign crises: Pro-Russian separatists are fighting Ukrainians over territory; a rapidly militarizing China is asserting claims to lands held by neighbors; and the U.S. and several other nations are attempting to limit Iran's nuclear development.

As the world's economic and military superpower, the United States engages overseas in those regions and others in many

Unrest Spreads in Ukraine

Ukrainian troops and pro-Russian protesters have clashed in eastern and southwest Ukraine. Russia annexed the Crimean Peninsula in southern Ukraine in March.

about military action," says James F. Jeffrey, a former U.S. ambassador to Iraq in the Obama administration, who also served in the National Security Council in the George W. Bush administration. "But I don't think anybody recently has done a good job of explaining to the American public why it is that the Russia action in Crimea matters," says Jeffrey, now a distinguished visiting fellow at the Washington Institute for Near East Policy. "There is a serious public education case to be done here."

In fact, the administration is also wary of the public mood as it confronts pressure to intervene, treaty responsibilities to allies, humanitarian obligations and its own caution about military action. "America must not succumb to the temptation to turn inward," Defense Secretary Chuck Hagel said in a speech in Chicago in early May, likening public opinion now to antiwar sentiment before World War II. "We are a great nation because we engage in the world."[6]

ways — diplomatically, economically, militarily — and does so for many reasons, including opposing its foes, supporting its allies, protecting its economic self-interest and providing humanitarian assistance. But Americans are increasingly unhappy at the prospect of more U.S. involvement in foreign crises.

A *Wall Street Journal*/NBC poll in April found that nearly half (47 percent) of respondents want the United States to be less active internationally — a much higher share than in previous years. The Pew Research Center, in a survey released late last year, found "the most lopsided balance in favor of the U.S. 'minding its own business'" since the question was first asked in 1964 — 52 percent of respondents.[5]

Some foreign-policy experts welcome the public skepticism. It matches their own rejection of the doctrine of American "exceptionalism" as justification for intervention. "What nation doesn't think it is exceptional?," asks Melvin Goodman, a former CIA and State Department analyst of Soviet affairs who now directs the National Security Project at the liberal Center for International Policy in Washington. "We've carried too much of the international burden."

Other, more hawkish, experts argue that the public, though understandably wary after more than a decade of war in Iraq and Afghanistan, should be persuaded to support some actions overseas. "Americans are gun-shy

Still, the Obama administration has generally emphasized diplomacy. The United States and some allies eased sanctions on Iran last year to encourage negotiations with its longtime foe. The negotiations — which included Russia and China — are continuing. They aim to ensure that Iran develops nuclear capabilities for peaceful purposes only. But President Obama's Iran diplomacy faces constant, deep-seated skepticism by a key U.S. ally, Israel. That attitude was reflected in March when overwhelming bipartisan majorities in the House (394 members) and Senate (83) signed letters demanding crippling sanctions against Iran if the negotiations fail.[7] (Secretary of State John F. Kerry's most recent attempt to broker peace between Israel and the Palestinians collapsed in late April.[8])

The administration also avails itself of harder-edged forms of overseas engagement. Asian allies' worries over China's military expansion — its military budget is due to grow by 12.2 percent this year — have sparked U.S. plans to send additional forces to the region.[9] To deal with the crisis in Ukraine, the administration has imposed selective sanctions against some Russian oligarchs and companies.

Engagement can also include small-scale intervention. In early May, Obama sent U.S. law enforcement and military experts to Nigeria to help find almost 300 Nigerian schoolgirls kidnapped by a brutal Islamist militia, Boko Haram.[10]

Neither that action nor the others has aroused U.S. public opposition. What Americans do clearly oppose is major military action. The problem is "intervention fatigue," say two staff members at the Council on Foreign Relations, a New York-based think tank stemming from the Iraq and Afghan wars.[11]

Obama cited that factor in pushing back against critics who call his foreign policy too timid. "Most of the foreign policy commentators that have questioned our policies would go headlong into a bunch of military adventures that the American people had no interest in participating in and would not advance our core security interests," he told reporters during an April tour of Asia.[12]

Obama himself saw his attempt at limited military action in the Middle East turn out badly. American airstrikes in 2011 were critical to toppling Moammar Gadhafi, a move that Obama justified at the time as a moral imperative, saying he refused "to wait for images of slaughter and mass graves." But jockeying for power after the U.S.-aided overthrow of the Libyan dictator left al Qaeda-influenced militias in a strong position — strong enough to attack the U.S. Consulate in Benghazi and kill Ambassador J. Christopher Stevens and three security guards.[13]

Last year, after having warned the Syrian regime not to cross a "red line" by using chemical weapons, Obama considered and then rejected a Syria airstrike, following what U.S. and United Nations officials in August 2013 called convincing evidence of a chemical attack that the United States said killed more than 1,400 people, including children. All told, at least 150,000 people have been killed in the Syrian War.[14]

Most Want U.S. to "Mind Its Own Business"

Fifty-two percent of Americans agree that the U.S. should "mind its own business internationally." The proportion of Americans favoring less involvement in other countries' foreign affairs has grown by 22 percentage points since 2002.

Percentage of Americans Who Agree U.S. Should "Mind its own business internationally and let other countries get along the best they can on their own."

Source: "America's Place in the World 2013," Pew Research Center, Dec. 3, 2013, p. 107, http://tinyurl.com/lz3mh2y (The September 2001 survey was conducted before the 9/11 attacks.)

In the wake of that chastening experience, Obama not only turned away from military action against the Syrian government but then teamed up with Russia to try to solve at least the chemical-weapons element of the Syrian crisis. Although Russia is Syria's major ally and single biggest arms supplier, it agreed with the United States in September that Syria should surrender all its chemical weapons for destruction.[15]

Some critics say that Obama's retreat from military action in Syria amounted to giving Russian President Vladimir V. Putin a green light in Ukraine. David Adesnik, a visiting scholar at the conservative American Enterprise Institute, a Washington think tank, argues a modified version of that critique, noting that Russia had behaved aggressively under Obama's predecessor George W. Bush, and that Obama had tried for a "reset" to prompt warmer relations with Russia.[16] "That was a big mistake," he says, but "Syria didn't have a salutary effect" on Putin's calculations of U.S. steadfastness.

The Ukraine crisis has America's Eastern European allies growing increasingly nervous about Russia's territorial intentions.

In a show of strength aimed at Russia, 600 U.S. paratroopers have begun training with Eastern European forces, and a dozen F-16 fighter jets have been deployed to Poland. The military exercises involve fellow members of the North Atlantic Treaty Organization (NATO), a military alliance the United

States helped form at the start of the Cold War to deter Soviet aggression in Europe.[17]

Ukraine, a former Soviet republic that has been an independent nation since 1991, borders Russia. Since last year, Ukraine has been torn between Ukrainians who want to deepen ties to Europe and those who want to solidify ties with Russia. This spring, Russia annexed the Crimean Peninsula. The country's east has become a battleground for pro-Russian separatists, at least some of them Soviet or Russian military veterans, and the Western-oriented government.[18]

Those who fear a revival of Soviet territorial ambition have been wary ever since Putin first became Russia's president in 2000. A former Soviet intelligence officer, he has never retracted what many interpret as a sign of nostalgia for the days of Soviet power — his often-quoted view, in a 2005 speech, that "the collapse of the Soviet Union was a major geopolitical disaster of the century."[19]

Historical echoes are sounding in the United States as well. The top Republican interventionist, Sen. John McCain, R-Ariz., calls for supplying weapons to Ukraine. And he has denounced the administration policy on Syria, demanding military action, but short of "boots on the ground." McCain argued, "Our policies should be determined by the realities of the moment, not by today's isolationism dictated by the past."[20]

As foreign-policy experts watch the latest developments in Ukraine, Syria, Asia and elsewhere, these are some of the issues they are debating:

Should the U.S. military intervene in Ukraine?

With its Cold War echoes, the U.S.-Russia confrontation over Ukraine may offer the clearest test of Americans' attitudes toward U.S. intervention in international crises, and whether economic and diplomatic approaches are sufficient, or military engagement is called for. In confronting Russia, the United States is opposing the former command center of the old Soviet empire, and at the same time trying to reassure Eastern European allies that once were ruled by Soviet puppet governments.

Since the 1990s and early 2000s, those countries, including Ukraine's biggest neighbor to the west, Poland, have been members of NATO, which was born in the Cold War, and pledged to the mutual defense of any

member that comes under attack.[21] American forces are participating in NATO exercises in Poland and other ex-Soviet neighbors. The Obama administration so far has drawn the line at supplying arms to Ukraine or taking direct military action.[22]

But the administration, in addition to leveling sanctions at some Russians, has agreed to provide $1 billion in loan guarantees to Ukraine.[23] Those are in addition to a $17 billion loan from the International Monetary Fund, of which the United States is a major member, and $15 billion in other financing from the United States and other sources.[24]

The aid bolsters pro-Western Ukrainians in their demands for closer ties to Europe — demands that led them to oust elected President Viktor Yanukovych early this year. He had rejected a previously agreed upon trade agreement with the European Union that would have oriented Ukraine's economy toward Europe rather than Russia.[25] Protesters also called for better government and denounced corruption by Yanukovych and his cronies.[26]

After Yanukovych vacated the presidency, Putin supported efforts in Crimea (part of Russia until 1954) to secede from Ukraine. He then promoted annexation of Crimea.[27]

Then the Crimea scenario appeared to start replaying in eastern Ukraine, where ties to Russia are believed strong. Talks in Geneva between U.S. Secretary of State Kerry, Russian Foreign Minister Sergey Lavrov and representatives of Ukraine and the European Union yielded an agreement to de-escalate, but pro-Western and pro-Russian groups struggling in the streets of Ukraine ignored the deal.[28]

In early May, Obama made clear that he rejects any military intervention in Ukraine. "We want to see a diplomatic resolution to the situation in Ukraine," he said at a White House press conference with German Chancellor Angela Merkel. "But we've also been clear that if the Russian leadership does not change course, it will face increasing costs as well as growing isolation — diplomatic and economic."[29]

Andrew J. Bacevich, a professor of international relations and security studies at Boston University who is a West Point graduate and retired Army colonel, says the administration's measured approach properly reflects the importance of the current Ukraine clash to U.S. national-security priorities. "The classic definition of a vital interest is: Is it a place or an issue you are willing to die for?," he says. "I think the American people would probably have some doubts there."

Adesnik at the American Enterprise Institute argues that survey data about U.S. public opinion on global engagement show more nuance than skeptics acknowledge. "There's a lot of contradictory evidence," he says, acknowledging the support for the go-it-alone approach but pointing out that Americans also want their country to remain a superpower. He cites Pew survey numbers that show 56 percent of respondents believe the United States should remain the sole military superpower while 72 percent support a shared global leadership role for the United States.[30]

Adesnik also acknowledges that the public opposes military action that would place troops at risk. "But the best way to stay out of war is to indicate you're not afraid of war," he adds. "American behavior — always reaching out to your enemies — did contribute to Putin's behavior. It led him to think that Obama is always going to resort to that."

But Stephen F. Cohen, a historian of the Soviet Union and emeritus professor at Princeton and New York University, argues that debates among foreign-policy specialists over Obama's approach to the Ukraine crisis fail to take into account details of the Russia-Ukraine conflict, including the ouster of elected president Yanukovych. "The government in Kiev hasn't got a shred of legitimacy," he says. "It came to power by overthrowing a constitutionally elected president, though he may have been a very bad guy."

Between the toppling of a pro-Russian president and the expansion of NATO in Russia's neighborhood beginning in the 1990s, Cohen argues, Putin has a case for worrying about encirclement. Between that Russian case and U.S. fears of Russian aggression toward NATO allies, Cohen says, "That is where you sit down and negotiate."

If the U.S. reduces its global involvement, will China and Russia step in?

Behind demands or pleas for a more aggressive, military-oriented response to the crises in Ukraine and Syria — and whatever future conflicts may emerge — is concern that the United States may lose the superpower status it has held since World War II and the preeminent global

position it has occupied since the fall of the Soviet Union in 1991. Russia's actions in Ukraine, its key roles in the Syria chemical-weapons deal and Iran nuclear negotiations, as well as China's economic might and its recent territorial aggressiveness, are amplifying concerns about U.S. global strength.

Putin is likely to continue to resist a geopolitical order in which U.S.-dominated NATO extends to Russia's borders. In 2007, he said in what observers interpreted as a jab at the United States: "There are those who would like to build a unipolar world, who would themselves like to rule all of humanity."[31]

Significantly, given Moscow's insistence on dangers to ethnic Russians in Ukraine, in his 2005 speech calling the Soviet collapse disastrous, Putin said that when the empire fell, "Tens of millions of our co-citizens and compatriots found themselves outside Russian territory."[32]

By April of this year, Russian Foreign Minister Lavrov picked up the theme, warning that Russian citizens would treat any attack on Russian-speakers in Eastern Ukraine as an attack on Russia.[33]

At that time, Obama was beginning a tour of Asia that grew out of his policy of shoring up U.S. allies over what is seen as a long-term military and political challenge by China. "There's a widely held view in the region that the U.S.-China relationship is tipping toward being much more confrontational," Bonnie S. Glaser, a senior adviser for Asia at the Center for Strategic and International Studies, told Bloomberg News.[34]

The confluence of the Russia and Asia events underlined the concerns of some experts that a diminishing U.S. presence in global affairs would be replaced by China or Russia or the two together.

But even some of those most alarmed at what they see as U.S. disengagement draw clear distinctions between Russia and China and their potential for expanding their presence. "Russia is not really interested in or really integrated into the outside world," says former U.S. Ambassador to Iraq Jeffrey of the Washington Institute for Near East Policy. "China is different — very integrated into the outside world." But Russia, otherwise economically disconnected, is a vital supplier of petroleum to Europe.

China may be connected, but it is not indispensable, because its economy centers on manufacturing, which can be done elsewhere, argues Bruce Jones, director of the International Order and Strategy Project at the centrist Brookings Institution think tank. "The threat to American leadership is greatly exaggerated," he says. "In the next 10 or 15 years, the Chinese economy will be as large as the United States' but not as influential."

As for Russia, Jones says, it arouses no global allegiance, especially among its fellow members of the so-called BRICS countries (Brazil, Russia, India, China, South Africa). "The notion that Russia is leading some anti-American coalition in the BRICS is facile," he says. "China is not about to be led; India is not about to be led."

But other global-engagement partisans argue that possible new threats from old Cold War foes have more to do with U.S. withdrawal than with Russian or Chinese muscle-flexing. "There is more danger that there will be no leader," says Adesnik of the American Enterprise Institute. "Imagine what the sanctions effort on Iran would be without the United States to take the lead. Other countries only get convinced to sign up when the United States says, 'We are going to lead.'"

Adesnik does agree with the skeptics who question the leadership capabilities of America's two big rivals. "No one wants to be led by China and Russia," he says. "They are not at the forefront of solving problems."

But Goodman at the Center for International Policy argues that the Obama administration's "pivot" to Asia amounts to a direct challenge to China in the form of Cold War-style containment. "That is what China fears. We have more subtle reminders available than to announce a pivot."

Still, Goodman says, little chance exists of a Russia-China alliance against the United States. "There is too much mutual suspicion along that 6,000-kilometer border."[35]

Is the post-Cold War vision of the U.S. as the "indispensable nation" still valid?

As secretary of State in the Clinton administration, Madeleine Albright in 1998 coined what has become a favored description among global engagement partisans of America's place in the world: the "indispensable nation."

At the time, the administration was preparing for possible military action against Iraqi dictator Saddam Hussein, to enforce a United Nations resolution that he relinquish weapons of mass destruction. Asked by host Matt Lauer on the NBC "Today" show what she would tell the parents of U.S. military personnel "being asked to clean up a mess for the rest of the world," Albright said:

"But if we have to use force, it is because we are America; we are the indispensable nation. We stand tall and we see further than other countries into the future, and we see the danger here to all of us. I know that the American men and women in uniform are always prepared to sacrifice for freedom, democracy and the American way of life."[36]

When she spoke, the Soviet Union's collapse had ended the Cold War, NATO had begun expanding to countries of the former Soviet empire, the administration had intervened in Bosnia and was about to press for NATO airstrikes on Serbia. The United States had also grappled with issues of post-Cold War engagement in other parts of the world. In 1990-91, President George H. W. Bush had assembled a multinational alliance to reverse an Iraqi invasion of Kuwait, a key world oil supplier. But in 1994, the United States took no action to stop the genocide in Rwanda, a moral failure for which President Bill Clinton eventually took responsibility.

In 2003, just months after the start of the Iraq War, President George W. Bush lauded the United States as the exemplar of democratic government: "It is no accident that the rise of so many democracies took place in a time when the world's most influential nation was itself a democracy."[37]

But in 2011, when Obama was announcing the downshifting of the U.S. campaign in Afghanistan, he captured what seemed to be the public mood after years of war: "America, it is time to focus on nation-building here at home."[38]

The otherwise hawkish former U.S. Ambassador to Iraq Jeffrey summarizes that mood, shared by Obama, Americans in general, and himself: "Never, ever try to change the internal situation in a country by putting thousands of ground troops in."

However, he contends, the reality is that the United States is indeed indispensable. Americans should understand that the nation's seemingly inexhaustible supply of cheap imported goods grows out of U.S. power. "We're the world's reserve currency; people pour money into this country," he says. "These things all flow from the U.S. position in the world."

Ted Galen Carpenter, a senior fellow for defense and foreign policy studies at the conservative-libertarian Cato Institute, responds that U.S. economic power is being eroded by the very military strength that "indispensability" advocates champion. "We're in severe danger of draining the strength of the economy to preserve all of these commitments in the world," he says.

In any event, Carpenter argues, the entire indispensability concept amounts to "national narcissism." The reality, he says, is that the idea of one indispensable nation no longer fits global reality. "The world is becoming more multipolar economically and militarily," he says, "and this notion of the indispensable nation is becoming obsolete."

But Jones at Brookings argues that the growing power of other nations doesn't change the fact that "we have far greater power and influence than any actor out there." Those who reject this view "underestimate American power and overestimate the challenge posed by rising powers," he says.

Still, historian Cohen says, the indispensability doctrine is so deeply ingrained in the diplomatic corps, and in the schools that train Foreign Service officers, that it may be ineradicable. "That is the orthodoxy," he says, "An alternative point of view hasn't existed, so far in my adult lifetime, partly because of the Cold War, when you could argue that America was indispensable."

The American Enterprise Institute's Adesnik says that despite assumptions that Americans are now deeply anti-interventionist, "Public opinion rides the roller coaster of events."

Citizens now may not be in favor of intervention, he says, but, "Americans will respond much more vigorously when the perception of a threat is clear, and they have leaders who hold that America must take a leading role."

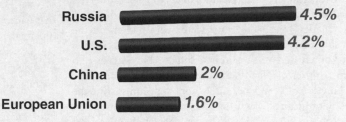

Russia, U.S. Are Biggest Military Spenders

Russia spent 4.5 percent of its gross domestic product (GDP) on its military in 2012, while U.S. expenditures were slightly lower. In total, however, the $645.7 billion U.S. military budget that year was 11 times Russia's and six times China's.

Military Expenditures as Percentage of GDP, 2012

Russia	*4.5%*
U.S.	*4.2%*
China	*2%*
European Union	*1.6%*

Source: "Military expenditure (% of GDP)," World Bank, http://tinyurl.com/mckxvjq

BACKGROUND
Isolationism Defeated

The United States grew slowly into its global superpower role. President Thomas Jefferson, in his 1801 inaugural speech, famously called for "honest friendship with all nations, entangling alliances with none." Nonetheless, the young nation expanded across the continent, and later into the Caribbean and Pacific, claiming Puerto Rico and the Philippines as possessions in 1898.[39]

But World War I, which began in 1914, called for judgments far more complicated than those involved in claiming new territory. On one side, Britain and France had deep ties to the United States. But sympathy for Germany ran strong among German-Americans and Irish-Americans (the latter because Germany was fighting archenemy Britain). American public opinion turned against Germany with publication of the "Zimmermann telegram," in which a German diplomat proposed returning formerly Mexican U.S. territory to Mexico in return for Mexico backing Germany.[40] The U.S. entered the war in 1917.

Twenty years after World War I ended in 1918, Americans were again debating whether to intervene in Europe. The period leading up to the forced U.S. entry into World War II in 1941 was marked by a fierce fight between President Franklin D. Roosevelt and anti-interventionists from right and left. Roosevelt himself took pains to avoid publicly declaring himself in favor of intervention until the war in Europe was well under way.[41]

U.S. debate intensified after Germany began the war by invading Poland in 1939, prompting Britain and France — allies of Poland — to declare war on Germany.

About two months later, a *Fortune* magazine poll of Americans found only 20 percent of respondents favored aid to European democracies.

An especially vocal group, the America First Committee, called for U.S. neutrality. America First's star spokesman was Charles Lindbergh, the aviator who had made the first solo trans-Atlantic flight. He was one of the country's best-known and most admired figures. He was also an open admirer of Nazi Germany and its anti-Semitism.

America First was resolutely anti-communist. But the U.S. Communist Party also opposed intervention, in obedience to orders from Moscow. Soviet Premier Josef Stalin and German Chancellor and Nazi Party leader Adolf Hitler had signed a non-aggression pact in 1939, under which Germany and the Soviet Union divided Poland and the Soviet Union took over the Baltic states.[42] Hitler was able to go to war with Poland, France and Great Britain without having to worry — for the time being — about fighting the Soviet Union, too.

Between April and June 1940, Germany invaded and occupied France, Belgium, the Netherlands, Norway and Denmark. Seeing German aggression as likely to erode isolationist sentiment, Roosevelt unveiled his interventionist intentions. It was a "delusion," he said in a 1940 speech, to believe that the United States could be "a lone island in a world dominated by the philosophy of force."[43]

The war took a turn when Germany betrayed its nonaggression pact and invaded the Soviet Union in June 1941. In the United States, Communist opposition to intervention ended immediately, and party members became the fiercest of hawks. The Japanese bombing of Pearl Harbor on Dec. 7, 1941, ended debate among the other anti-interventionists. Isolationism became a discredited, fringe ideology.

Cold War

The post-World War II era was marked by a bipartisan consensus among U.S. and allied leaders that U.S. action on behalf of friendly governments or against unfriendly ones was a good thing.[44]

Friendly governments were those that sided with the United States against the Soviet Union. A third category of "nonaligned" countries, including India, maintained ties with both sides.[45] Because the big Cold War players

all had nuclear weapons that could destroy one another, they did not battle directly — a restraining mechanism called "mutual assured destruction."[46]

A U.S. doctrine called "containment" also shaped Cold War policy. It called for "counterforce" against the Soviet Union in the form of diplomacy and covert action, instead of war. The doctrine was formulated, though not under that name, in 1946 by George F. Kennan, then the No. 2 diplomat in the U.S. Embassy in Moscow. "If situations are properly handled," Kennan wrote, "there need be no prestige-engaging showdowns."[47]

Instead, the opposing sides faced off in proxy wars and coups in smaller countries. Soviet dictator Stalin had started off after World War II by installing puppet regimes throughout Central and Eastern Europe, as well as the eastern half of Germany. These moves followed tacit recognition of Soviet preeminence in that region in the closing months of the war by the three major wartime allies, the United States, Great Britain and the Soviet Union. Roosevelt, Stalin and British Prime Minister Winston Churchill sealed that pact during a historic meeting at the Crimean resort of Yalta.[48]

By 1949, relations between the Soviet Union and the West had deteriorated to the point that the United States and 11 major allies formed NATO to resist Soviet expansion. The Soviet bloc in turn formalized its military and political ties through the 1955 Warsaw Pact.[49]

From the U.S. side, much of the early Cold War involved secret operations by the then-new Central Intelligence Agency (CIA), formed in 1947. These operations included:

- The 1953 overthrow of Iran's elected prime minister, Mohammed Mossadeq, on the ground that he could pave the way for a Soviet takeover of the oil-rich country.[50]

- The 1954 toppling of the elected government of President Jacobo Arbenz of Guatemala, whom the United States considered a communist sympathizer.

- Involvement in the overthrow and execution of the elected prime minister of Congo, Patrice Lumumba, whom the United States considered a communist dupe.

- A failed 1961 attempt to overthrow Cuba's Soviet-allied prime minister, Fidel Castro, which ended in defeat at the island's Bay of Pigs.

In the same year as the Cuba disaster, the Soviet-allied government of East Germany — then a separate country — erected a concrete wall separating the eastern and western sectors of Berlin. The Berlin Wall became a symbol of East-West hostility.[51]

The most dangerous moment in the Cold War came in 1962, after the United States learned that Soviet nuclear missiles had been shipped to Cuba. Negotiations between President John F. Kennedy and Soviet leader Nikita S. Khrushchev averted catastrophic nuclear conflict.[52]

Meanwhile, U.S. military advisers had been working with the government of South Vietnam since 1955 in an effort to strengthen South Vietnam, then a separate nation, against North Vietnam, a communist ally of the Soviet Union and China. U.S. involvement was based on what President Dwight D. Eisenhower in 1954 called the " 'falling domino' principle" — that North Vietnamese victory would lead to communist victories elsewhere in Southeast Asia.[53]

In 1964, a confrontation between U.S. warships and North Vietnamese vessels in the Tonkin Gulf led President Lyndon B. Johnson to order U.S. combat forces into Vietnam. By the time U.S. military operations ceased in 1973, 2.7 million U.S. military personnel had served in Vietnam.[54]

The war polarized the United States for the rest of the 1960s and the early '70s, and its effects arguably still influence America's global stance. There were huge anti-war demonstrations, a wave of resistance to the military draft and a political debate that tore apart the Democratic Party in 1968. Among those marked by the conflict were Sen. McCain, a Navy pilot held prisoner by North Vietnam for more than five years, and Secretary of State Kerry, a Navy veteran who became a leader of Vietnam Veterans Against the War.[55]

In 1973, following years of U.S. negotiations with the North Vietnamese, the United States withdrew military forces. Two years later, North Vietnam defeated the U.S.-allied government. The war had cost the lives of more than 58,000 American military personnel and between 1.5 million and 3.8 million Vietnamese troops and civilians.[56]

Beginning in 1979, a series of upheavals in the Middle East and Latin America opened a new era of U.S. engagement. The Iranian revolution of 1979 toppled Mohammad Reza Shah Pahlavi, a longtime U.S. ally. An Islamist government hostile to the West in general and the United States in particular took power.

West Berliners watch East German border guards demolishing a section of the Berlin Wall on Nov. 11, 1989, to open a link between East and West Berlin. Erected in 1961 by communist East Germany, the wall became a symbol of Cold War hostility between the East and West. The dramatic tear-down of the wall by Berliners from both East and West Berlin presaged the implosion of the Soviet Union two years later.

That same year, the Soviet Union invaded neighboring Afghanistan to prop up a friendly government, and Nicaraguan revolutionaries aided by Cuba overthrew President Anastasio Somoza, recently abandoned as a U.S. ally. The revolutionary government in turn eventually was opposed by right-wing guerrillas, known as contras. In neighboring El Salvador, a war between the government and a left-wing guerrilla army soon intensified.[57]

With the Cold War still very much in progress, the Reagan administration (1981-89) responded to these events both openly and covertly with military and intelligence operations. In Afghanistan, the administration expanded a Carter administration CIA program to aid guerrilla forces opposing the Soviet invaders. (The Soviets withdrew in defeat in 1989.) Meanwhile, the CIA aided the contras, and U.S. military advisers assisted the Salvadoran army.

Intense political debate over Nicaragua led to a congressional ban on assistance to the contras. But U.S. Marine Lt. Col. Oliver North, a National Security Council staffer, helped devise a plan in which the United States sold weapons to Iran in return for the release of U.S. hostages held by pro-Iranian forces in Lebanon. Then, profit from the arms deal was funneled to the contras.[58]

The scheme, known as Iran-Contra, blew up into the Reagan administration's worst scandal. North was indicted for lying to Congress and trying to destroy evidence. He was convicted on three counts in 1989 and sentenced to two years probation.[59]

Soviet Collapse

The Soviet empire began imploding in the late 1980s. The dramatic tear-down of the Berlin Wall by Berliners from both east and west in 1989 symbolized the process. Germany was reunited the following year.[60] The Soviet Union formally dissolved in 1991.

The end of the Cold War, which had defined U.S. foreign policy for decades, led to a search for a new guiding principle. President George H. W. Bush in 1990 and 1991 laid out a vision of a "new world order" in which "the rule of the law, not the law of the jungle, governs the conduct of nations."[61]

Despite hopes, the end of the Cold War did not bring global peace.[62]

Shortly before the Soviet collapse, Iraqi dictator Saddam Hussein in 1990 invaded the tiny oil kingdom of Kuwait. In response — and to protect world oil power Saudi Arabia — Bush assembled a 670,000-strong military alliance of 39 countries dominated by the United States, which contributed 425,000 personnel.[63]

The Persian Gulf War lasted less than three months. Because the war was brief, and because the United States was not acting alone and was fighting a tyrant, no major antiwar movement developed. The war ended with the rout of Iraqi troops from Kuwait, but Bush did not try to topple Hussein. The United States encouraged Shiite and Kurdish Iraqis who rose up against Hussein at war's end, but they got no U.S. aid, and many were slaughtered or fled Iraq.[64]

A subsequent crisis in Europe provoked intense debate about the extent of U.S. involvement overseas. After the collapse of the Soviet Union, Yugoslavia (which had been made up of modern-day Croatia, Montenegro, Serbia, Slovenia, Bosnia and Herzegovina, and Macedonia) disintegrated. The region fell into war and what was called "ethnic cleansing" — the removal, accompanied by massacres, of ethnic or religious minorities from areas claimed by a majority population.

The conflict centered on Bosnia. In 1992 Muslim Bosnians and Croats voted for independence, but Serbia wanted to keep Bosnia. Bosnian Serbs besieged Sarajevo, a historic city defended by Muslims. Serb artillery attacks, sniper killings

and a food blockade drew world attention and prompted some U.S. public figures to denounce U.S. inaction.

The U.N. sent a protective force, which set up so-called safe havens for Muslims, including one in the Bosnian village of Srebrenica. But in 1995, Serb forces overran the village, after U.N. troops were overwhelmed. More than 7,000 Muslim men were massacred. No slaughter on such a scale had taken place in Europe since World War II.

U.S. experience engaging — or not — in other nations influenced the American reaction. Srebrenica followed the horrific 1994 genocide in Rwanda, which the United States and other nations didn't try to stop; members of the Hutu ethnic majority slaughtered hundreds of thousands of members of the Tutsi ethnic group.[65] Clinton later acknowledged his administration's non-reaction to Rwanda as a failure.[66]

Among the reasons analysts have pointed to for the Clinton administration's failure to intervene in Rwanda was a 1993 military catastrophe during a raid by U.S. special-operations forces during a humanitarian mission to Somalia.[67] The mission, chronicled in the book and film "Black Hawk Down," ended in 18 American deaths. Video of a dead American being dragged through the streets of Mogadishu seemed to illustrate the dangers of humanitarian operations in violent environments.[68] But Samantha Power, then a journalist and now the U.S. ambassador to the U.N., rejected this reasoning in a detailed, scathing account of the U.S. failure to act in Rwanda.[69]

Finally jolted into action by the Srebrenica massacre, the Clinton administration helped launch a NATO bombing campaign against Serb forces. After Clinton pressured Serbia to sign a peace deal, in late 1995 he ordered 20,000 U.S. troops to Bosnia to join a NATO peacekeeping force. To do so, he overcame strong congressional resistance, especially but not exclusively among Republicans. Opponents questioned the U.S. national interest in bringing peace to the Balkans.[70]

In 1999, another phase of the Balkan crisis erupted over Kosovo, a Serbian province with an ethnic Albanian majority population. NATO, dominated by its senior member, the United States, began an air campaign of more than five months against Serbian forces, including bombing the Serbian capital, Belgrade.

The United States also took military action in 1998 with cruise missile attacks in Afghanistan and Sudan. The targets were said to be linked to terrorist leader Osama

CHRONOLOGY

1939-1962 *World War II is followed by decades-long Cold War.*

1939 World War II begins in Europe; only 20 percent of Americans favor aiding European democracies.

1941 United States enters World War II after Japan bombs Pearl Harbor; war lasts until 1945.

1949 United States joins 11 other countries to form North Atlantic Treaty Organization (NATO).

1961 CIA-sponsored invasion of Cuba at Bay of Pigs aimed at toppling regime of Fidel Castro turns into debacle.... Soviet satellite East Germany erects Berlin Wall.

1962 Conflict over Soviet nuclear missiles in Cuba leads United States and Soviet Union to brink of nuclear war.

1964-1985 *U.S. divided over military involvement in Vietnam; upheaval shakes Middle East, Latin America.*

1964 President Lyndon Johnson orders U.S. combat forces into South Vietnam.

1973 Peace talks with North Vietnam lead to U.S. military withdrawal.... Chilean military, encouraged by CIA, overthrows left-leaning president.

1979 Iranian revolution topples U.S.-backed Shah and installs religious regime hostile to United States.... Soviet Union invades Afghanistan.... Leftist Nicaraguan rebels overthrow government.

1985 Reagan administration aides begin scheme known as Iran-Contra to sell arms to Iran in return for freeing of U.S. hostages held in Lebanon, with profit to be used for U.S. aid to Nicaraguan rebels fighting left-wing government.

1989-1999 *Soviet Union falls, ending Cold War and touching off new round of global conflicts.*

1989 East Germany scraps travel restrictions on its citizens, leading to fall of Berlin Wall.

1991 Soviet Union dissolves.

1992 Yugoslavia falls apart along ethnic and religious lines, sparking armed conflict over Serbian attempt to hold onto breakaway Bosnia.

1995 NATO intervenes in Bosnia; peace talks held in Dayton, Ohio, end conflict.

1997 Three former Soviet Bloc members including Poland join NATO, a move Russia sees as hostile.

1999 Prompted by United States, NATO launches air campaign against Serbia over its actions in breakaway Kosovo province.

2001-Present *Terrorists attack United States; turmoil wracks Middle East, Eastern Europe.*

2001 Sept. 11 terrorist attacks prompt calls for aggressive U.S. response.

2003 George W. Bush administration launches war to overthrow Iraqi dictator Saddam Hussein.

2011 Syrian revolt begins . . . Libyan uprising begins.... President Obama orders airstrikes against Libyan government, aiding rebel victory.

2012 U.S. Ambassador J. Christopher Stevens and three embassy staffers killed by armed militants in Benghazi, Libya.... Obama declares that Syrian government use of chemical weapons would mark a "red line."

2013 Syria uses chemical weapons against civilians; Obama backs off military action.... Administration makes deal with Russia to remove chemical arms from Syria.... Ukrainian citizens protest President's Viktor Yanukovych's rejection of European Union trade deal.

2014 Ukrainian uprising topples president.... Russia supports Crimea secession from Ukraine, then annexes Crimea.... U.S. contributes troops to NATO exercises to reassure Russia's Eastern European neighbors.... Obama administration begins supplying some Syrian rebels with weapons.... Pro-Russian separatists effectively take over much of eastern Ukraine.

U.S. Weighs Interests of Allies

Saudis speak out about Syria; Europeans worry about Ukraine.

Managing international friends and allies may be harder than being commander in chief of the world's biggest military machine.

Take Saudi Arabia, a major American ally. Twenty-four years ago, the United States assembled an enormous multinational military force, in large part to protect Saudi Arabia — successfully — from attack by Iraqi dictator Saddam Hussein, who had invaded neighboring Kuwait.

But last year, the Saudi monarchy was so furious at the United States and other world powers for not intervening in Syria that the kingdom refused a seat on the United Nations Security Council. "Allowing the ruling regime in Syria to kill and burn its people by the chemical weapons, while the world stands idly . . . is also irrefutable evidence and proof of the inability of the Security Council to carry out its duties and responsibilities," the Saudi government said in announcing its move.[1]

The Saudis are both a world oil power and a center of the majority Sunni branch of Islam. Fellow Sunnis are the bulk of the rebel militias fighting the Syrian government, which is controlled by members of the minority Alawite Muslim sect, a splinter group of the Shiite branch of Islam.

If the Saudis were trying to make sure that President Obama got the message to step up aid to the Syrian rebels, they succeeded. In March, Obama traveled to Riyadh, the Saudi capital, where he personally told Saudi King Abdullah that the United States remained determined to back non-jihadist forces among the Syrian rebels.[2]

Weeks later, Harakat Hazm ("Movement of Steadfastness"), a Syrian rebel formation of 5,000 fighters that the United States considers moderate, received the first shipment of U.S. BGM-71 antitank missiles.[3]

While the Syrian civil war forces the administration to weigh the dangers of supplying advanced weaponry that could fall into the hands of anti-Western extremists against the need to maintain ties with Saudi Arabia, Obama faces equally tough choices involving America's European allies in the Ukraine crisis.

For one thing, the European Union (EU) is divided over how aggressively to hit back at Russia over its actions in Ukraine. Consequently, EU sanctions have been more limited than American measures. In Germany, Europe's economic powerhouse, the business establishment is openly opposing tougher EU sanctions.

Germany has more companies doing business with Russia — about 6,200 firms — than the rest of the EU combined, and it depends on Russia for about one-third of its gas and oil.[4] All in all, the 28 EU countries did 267.5 billion euros ($371.8 billion) worth of trade with Russia in 2012, the latest figures available. European countries import 84 percent of Russia's oil exports and about 76 percent of Russia's natural gas. They export 123 billion euros ($192.7 billion) worth of goods to Russia.[5]

"There's no question that Germany's economic interests would be best served by avoiding sanctions," Klaus-Jürgen Gern, an economist at a German think tank, the Kiel Institute for the World Economy, told *The Wall Street Journal*.[6]

German Chancellor Angela Merkel, appearing in Washington with Obama in early May, has so far maintained unity with Obama while delaying stronger economic measures against Russia. At a joint press conference, she said that if Russia disrupts a Ukrainian election scheduled for May 25, "We will not have a choice but to move forward with additional, more severe sanctions."[7]

She added that among EU countries "some are more vulnerable than others to potential Russia retaliation."[8]

Poland, a fellow EU member, also gets about 30 percent of its gas from Russia, but it takes a tougher line toward the Russians. "Russia needs our money more than we need its gas," Foreign Minister Radoslaw Sikorski told *The Washington Post*.[9]

Poland, whose history as a Soviet satellite is still fresh in the minds of Sikorski and other leaders, played a major part in demanding and receiving U.S. military reassurance in

bin Laden, who had just orchestrated deadly bombings of U.S. embassies in Tanzania and Kenya. His network, al Qaeda, had not yet become universally known.[71]

Major Wars

The Sept. 11 attacks on the United States by al Qaeda operatives opened a period in which the United States

the form of NATO military exercises on Polish soil that began in April. Poland had sent troops to back the United States in Afghanistan and Iraq, Sikorski reminded *Foreign Policy* magazine. "Now we feel it's payback time."[10]

In Asia, Obama is carrying out another balancing act — protecting the interests of friendly and allied countries while not alarming the region's giant, China. "We're not interested in containing China," Obama said in April. He was on a trip promoting the administration's "pivot to Asia" — reassurances to Asian countries worried about signs of Chinese expansionism, such as claims to non-Chinese territory as well as to sovereignty in air and coastal zones.[11]

To reassure China's neighbors, Obama signed a pact with the Philippines allowing greater access to its military bases by U.S. troops, ships and aircraft. Previously, the administration began deploying 2,500 Marines to Australia. And the first of four new U.S. coastal warships assigned to patrol Pacific waters near China has begun its mission.[12]

Although the deployments send a clear message of support for Asian allies dealing with territorial disputes, Obama added that the message isn't meant provocatively. "My hope is, is that at some point we're going to be able to work cooperatively with China as well," he said in Manila, "because our goal here is simply to make sure that everybody is operating in a peaceful, responsible fashion."[13]

— Peter Katel

President Obama and German Chancellor Angela Merkel hold a news conference at the White House on May 2, 2014. Merkel said if Russia disrupts a Ukrainian election scheduled for May 25, Germany would impose "more servere sanctions."

[1] Quoted in Robert F. Worth, "Saudi Arabia Rejects U.N. Security Council Seat in Protest Move," *The New York Times*, Oct. 18, 2013, http://tinyurl.com/m2rkubz.

[2] Michael D. Shear and Michael R. Gordon, "Obama Offers Assurance to Saudis on Syria Stance," *The New York Times*, March 28, 2014, http://tinyurl.com/ll3augt.

[3] Liz Sly, "Syrian rebels who received first U.S. missiles of war see shipment as 'an important first step,' " *The Washington Post*, April 27, 2014, http://tinyurl.com/ljavuxj.

[4] Matthew Karnitschnig, "German Businesses Urge Halt on Sanctions Against Russia," *The Wall Street Journal*, May 1, 2014, http://tinyurl.com/khedgms.

[5] "Russia's trade ties with Europe," BBC, March 4, 2014, http://tinyurl.com/mlw8ddl; "Russia, trade," European Commission, updated Nov. 19, 2013, http://tinyurl.com/oufrlx7.

[6] Quoted in Karnitschnig, *op. cit.*

[7] "Full Transcript: Obama, Merkel Press Conference," *The Wall Street Journal*, May 2, 2014, http://tinyurl.com/l6nzk82.

[8] *Ibid.*

[9] Lally Weymouth, "Talking with Poland's foreign minister about the Ukraine crisis and Russia's next moves," *The Washington Post*, April 18, 2014, http://tinyurl.com/kqmk9kd.

[10] Quoted in Michael Weiss, "Can Radek Sikorski Save Europe?" *Foreign Policy*, April 30, 2014, http://tinyurl.com/mk3nk28.

[11] Quoted in Mark Landler, "On a Trip That Avoids Beijing, Obama Keeps His Eye on China," *The New York Times*, April 26, 2014, http://tinyurl.com/mzcv753; Ian Johnson, "The China Challenge," *New York Review of Books*, May 8, 2014, http://tinyurl.com/q7cymxu.

[12] Matt Siegel, "As Part of Pact, U.S. Marines Arrive in Australia, in China's Strategic Backyard," *The New York Times*, April 4, 2012, http://tinyurl.com/879fnxs; Kirk Spitzer, "New Warship Gives U.S. Pivot Some Punch," *Time*, March 21, 2013, http://tinyurl.com/nz72fq7. For background, see Reed Karaim, "China Today," *CQ Researcher*, April 4, 2014, pp. 289-312.

[13] "Remarks by President Obama and President Benigno Aquino III," transcript, The White House, April 28, 2014, http://tinyurl.com/qg75rpo.

moved beyond small-scale, limited military operations to full-fledged global war against Muslim jihadists.

But unlike the short Persian Gulf War, the wars in Afghanistan (2001 to the present) and Iraq (2003-2011)

Probable GOP Candidates Debate Intervention

"The most interesting debate is in the Republican Party."

Foreign policy arguments among potential candidates in the 2016 Republican presidential primary largely amount to feints and jabs, with no full-scale fights. But the debate among Republicans concerning interventionism overshadows any foreign policy argument among Democrats, at least so far.

Republicans all express varying degrees of opposition to the Democratic Obama administration's foreign policy. Arizona Sen. John McCain, the most outspoken critic, has charged the administration with running "a feckless foreign policy where nobody believes in America's strength anymore." And Sen. Lindsey Graham of South Carolina called Obama a "weak and indecisive president that invites aggression."[1]

Nevertheless, McCain already lost a presidential election in 2008, and Graham is not on any list of expected Republican presidential contenders. Among potential candidates, Kentucky Sen. Rand Paul stands in the middle of the Republican foreign policy argument. The political heir to his libertarian father, former Rep. Ron Paul, R-Texas, the younger Paul does not embrace McCain-Graham style hawkishness. But he also has been trying to distance himself somewhat from his father's hard-line stand against involvement in almost any foreign conflict.

Notably, in an opinion piece in *The Washington Post* in April, Paul sought to explain a 2012 vote of his concerning Iran. Paul had cast the lone vote against a Senate resolution opposing "any United States policy that would rely on efforts to contain a nuclear weapons-capable Iran." That is, the resolution opposed any U.S. acceptance of Iran possessing or being able to make nuclear weapons.[2]

In his op-ed, he wrote, "I am not for containment in Iran." He added that his 2012 vote had been misunderstood. "It is . . . dumb, dangerous and foolhardy to announce in advance how we would react to any nation that obtains nuclear weapons. Real foreign policy is made in the middle, with nuance; in the gray area of diplomacy, engagement and reluctantly, if necessary, military action."[3]

The Republican often mentioned as Paul's opposite on foreign affairs, Sen. Marco Rubio of Florida, criticizes the Obama administration for, in effect, overdoing nuance and diplomacy. "One lesson we should take from the current crisis in Ukraine is that when authoritarian regimes sense weakness and opportunity they will exploit it," Rubio wrote in *Foreign Policy* magazine.[4]

Between Rubio and Paul, some conservative foreign policy strategists leave no doubt whom they favor. "On one hand you have Rubio, who embraces the model of American leadership that has sustained global peace," Danielle Pletka, vice president of foreign and defense studies at the conservative American Enterprise Institute, told *National Journal.* "And then you have Rand Paul who wants to spend less money to do less with the world. I see this as a genuine competition of ideas."[5]

Pletka is a member of the Committee on the Present Danger, an advocacy group from the Republican neoconservative wing that was founded in the Cold War and now is devoted to promoting antiterrorism policy.[6]

Paul has derided the neoconservatives, who provided much of the ideological and bureaucratic thrust for the post-Sept. 11 campaigns in Afghanistan and Iraq.[7] In Paul's words: "To this crowd, anyone who doesn't clamor first for the military option is somehow an isolationist. The irony is that the crowd that claims they want to engage often opposes diplomatic engagement."[8]

Veteran public opinion analyst Andrew Kohut, founding director of the Pew Research Center, has argued that the public is not demanding foreign policy aggressiveness. "The GOP's difficulty with exploiting public discontent with Obama's handling of foreign policy," he wrote, "is that the president's unwillingness to be more assertive in Syria or Ukraine reflects the public's mood — including Republicans."[9]

James F. Jeffrey, a former ambassador in the Obama administration who also served in President George W. Bush's National Security Council, argued that Republicans still need

ran long and cost thousands of lives. More than 4,400 American and civilian defense employees died in Iraq, and more than 2,317 in Afghanistan and nearby countries.[72]

The United States originally went to war in Afghanistan to topple the Muslim fundamentalist Taliban government, which was hosting al Qaeda — a move

"a policy of activism that doesn't immediately default to the neocons," who held sway during the Bush administration. He added, "Between George W. Bush and Rand Paul, more and more Republicans are saying Rand Paul."

Writing in early 2013, before Rand Paul had made much of an impression, Daniel W. Drezner, a professor of international politics at Tufts University's Fletcher School of Law and Diplomacy, argued even more strongly that the neoconservatives had done major damage to the GOP. "Since the knee-jerk Republican response has been to call for military action anywhere and everywhere trouble breaks out," he wrote, "the American people have tuned out the GOP's alarmist rhetoric."[10]

On the Democratic side, the top potential nominee so far is also the leader in foreign policy experience among presidential hopefuls in both parties. Former Secretary of State Hillary Rodham Clinton has been characterized by some left-liberals as a hawk, having supported stepping up the U.S. campaign in Afghanistan, using airstrikes in Syria and intervening in Libya.

Foreign policy expert Stephen F. Cohen, a historian of the Soviet Union and an emeritus professor at New York and Princeton universities, points to a lack of diplomacy in a recent statement by Clinton likening Russian President Vladimir V. Putin's insistence on protecting the rights of ethnic Russians in other countries to Adolf Hitler's pre-World War II strategy of using the defense of ethnic Germans as a pretext for war.[11]

"She says he's like Hitler," Cohen says, asking how Clinton would able to meet with Putin after a comment so insulting.

Still, Cohen says, "The most interesting debate is in the Republican Party, with Rand Paul trying to move into the mainstream with his less interventionist perspective."

— *Peter Katel*

Sen. Rand Paul, R-Ky., left, has distanced himself from hardline stands against foreign involvement. Sen. Marco Rubio, R-Fla., at right, claims the Obama administration is overdoing nuance and diplomacy.

[4] Marco Rubio, "I Come Bearing . . . Reassurance," *Foreign Policy*, April 24, 2014, http://tinyurl.com/lfuvny9.

[5] Beth Reinhard and Ben Terris, "The GOP's Identity Crisis: Marco Rubio Versus Rand Paul," *National Journal*, March 15, 2013, http://tinyurl.com/pyapllr.

[6] "Committee on the Present Danger," http://tinyurl.com/m68l9r5.

[7] James Mann, *Rise of the Vulcans: The History of Bush's War Cabinet* (2004).

[8] David Adesnik, "Rand Paul bravely attacks a battalion of straw-men," American Enterprise Institute, Jan. 17, 2014, http://tinyurl.com/ozpabbv.

[9] Andrew Kohut, "Is Attacking Obama's Foreign Policy a Winning Strategy?," *Politico*, April 29, 2014, http://tinyurl.com/oldw6ke.

[10] Daniel W. Drezner, "Rebooting Republican Foreign Policy," *Foreign Affairs*, January-February 2013, www.cfr.org/world/rebooting-republican-foreign-policy/p29717.

[11] Philip Rucker, "Hillary Clinton's Putin-Hitler comments draw rebukes as she wades into Ukraine conflict," *The Washington Post*, March 5, 2014, www.washingtonpost.com/politics/hillary-clintons-putin-hitler-comments-draw-rebukes-as-she-wades-into-ukraine-conflict/2014/03/05/31a748d8-a486-11e3-84d4-e59b1709222c_story.html.

[1] Michael Hirsh, "The GOP's Foreign Policy Problem," *National Journal*, March 6, 2014, http://tinyurl.com/kvj4qeg.

[2] Ben Brumfield and Ted Barrett, "U.S. Senate votes to fund the federal government, strengthens resolve on Iran," CNN, Sept. 22, 2012, http://tinyurl.com/loklnps.

[3] Rand Paul, "Where I stand on containing Iran," *The Washington Post*, April 15, 2014, http://tinyurl.com/nh8f8yq.

that enjoyed widespread post-9/11 public support. The war in Iraq was launched to overthrow Hussein and seize what were said to be his nuclear and chemical weapons. After these weapons were determined not to exist, the war became a campaign to establish a democratic government — a development that President

George W. Bush said would encourage democracy throughout the Middle East.[73]

As casualties mounted, so did opposition, though not to anti-Vietnam War levels. One reason may have been that young men did not face the military draft, which had been abolished in 1973.[74] Nonetheless, ending the Iraq war was one of the major planks in Obama's successful 2008 presidential campaign.

After the U.S. withdrawal from Iraq, conflict between the country's Shiite-majority government, established with U.S. help, and members of the Sunni minority, including jihadists, intensified. The Shiites and the Sunnis are the two major branches of Islam, and relations between them remain contentious in the Middle East.[75]

The Afghan War, which began first, did not yield a definitive victory over the Taliban, which became a guerrilla army after it was removed from the government. Jihadist attacks elsewhere continued, and al Qaeda remains a feared terrorist network.[76] Indeed, Muslim extremists now have a new field of battle in Syria.

During the ensuing pro-democracy surge in the Middle East known as the "Arab Spring," Libyans rose up in 2011 against the 42-year dictatorship of Moammar Gadhafi.[77] Obama, urged on by Libyan and American supporters of the revolt, and acting under authority of a U.N. resolution, ordered a U.S. air campaign that established a no-fly zone over Libya — grounding its air force — and attacked some government forces. "Operation Odyssey Dawn" assured the revolution's success eight months after it began.[78]

Although the Libya operation seemed at first to show the positive results of small-scale intervention, it was followed by a jihadist attack on the U.S. consulate in Benghazi in 2012 that killed Ambassador J. Christopher Stevens and three other Americans.[79]

CURRENT SITUATION

Sanctioning Putin

Eastern Ukrainian cities remain a battleground between pro-Russia and pro-Ukrainian government forces. But with events moving at a dizzying pace, Ukrainians and foreign observers alike are trying to decode statements by Russian President Putin that seem to indicate a willingness to tamp down the potential for all-out war.

In early May, Putin announced that he would pull back an invasion-ready force of 40,000 Russian troops, plus warplanes, that had been stationed on the Russian side of the border. NATO and officials of the provisional Ukrainian government in Kiev were not taking the statement at face value.[80]

Nevertheless, Putin did strike a tone different from his previous belligerence. "I simply believe that if we want to find a long-term solution to the crisis in Ukraine, open, honest and equal dialogue is the only possible option," he said at a Kremlin press conference.[81]

One immediate question was the practical effect of a May 11 referendum in two eastern Ukrainian provinces, which pro-Russians announced as showing overwhelming support for autonomy from the Ukrainian government in Kiev. Another was whether the Kiev government would be able to hold a nationwide presidential election on May 25.[82]

While debate continues on whether the United States and its allies should intervene militarily, the Obama administration and the European Union are expanding the list of individuals and companies targeted by economic sanctions.[83] "The goal is to change [Putin's] calculus with respect to how the current actions that he's engaging in in Ukraine could have an adverse impact on the Russian economy over the long haul," Obama said in late April.[84] The United States has frozen assets, banned commerce and imposed other sanctions against numerous Russian politicians, companies and business figures.

Whatever the long-range effect of sanctions, so far they seem of no consequence on the ground in eastern Ukraine. Pro-Russia separatists have taken over a series of towns and cities, and the country's acting president acknowledged in late April that the provisional government's security services have been "helpless" against these groups, which U.S. officials say are controlled by Russian special forces.[85]

Sanctions by the European Union have been kept minimal, to avoid hurting some of its members' considerable business ties with Russia, including imports of Russian oil and natural gas.[86] The EU in March and April imposed visa bans and asset freezes on 48 Russian politicians and military commanders.

EU sanctions haven't included business figures or companies. "Some EU countries may have been reluctant

Is the Obama administration responding effectively to the Ukraine crisis?

YES
John Kerry
Secretary of State

Excerpted from Senate Foreign Relations Committee hearing, April 8, 2014

What we see from Russia is an illegal and illegitimate effort to destabilize a sovereign state and create a contrived crisis with paid operatives across an international boundary.

Our preference, and the preference of our friends and allies, is de-escalation and a diplomatic solution. But Russia should not for a single solitary second mistake the expression of that preference as an unwillingness to do what is necessary to stop any violation of the international order.

At NATO last week, and in all of my conversations of the past weeks, it is clear that the United States and our closest partners are united in this effort, despite the costs, and willing to put in effect tough new sanctions on those orchestrating this action and on key sectors of the Russian economy in energy, banking, mining. They are all on the table. And President Obama has already signed an executive order to implement these actions if Russia does not end its pressure and aggression on Ukraine.

It must be the reality that the United States and our allies will not hesitate to use 21st century tools to hold Russia accountable for 19th century behavior. It doesn't have to be this way. But it will be this way if Russia continues down this provocative path.

We have made it clear that Russia needs to take concrete steps to disavow separatist actions in eastern Ukraine, pull back its forces outside the country, which they say they have begun to do with the movement of one battalion, and demonstrate that they are prepared to come to these discussions, to do what is necessary to de-escalate.

So, Russia has a choice: to work with the international community to help build an independent Ukraine that could be a bridge between East and West, not the object of a tug of war, that could meet the hopes and aspirations of all Ukrainians. Or, they could face greater isolation and pay the costs for their failure, to see that the world is not a zero-sum game.

His [Putin's] oligarchs are not able to travel to various places. They're losing money. The ruble has gone down 7 percent. There's an impact in Europe. I think [Putin has] had a massive change in public opinion in Ukraine. People who once felt better about Russia don't today. He has united many Ukrainians, even those who are Russian-speaking, against Russia.

NO
Sen. John McCain, R-Ariz.
Member, Senate Foreign Relations Committee

Excerpted from Senate Foreign Relations Committee hearing, April 8, 2014

My hero, Teddy Roosevelt, used to say talk softly, but carry a big stick. What [the Obama administration is] doing is talking strongly and carrying a very small stick, in fact, a twig.

What has been done so far as a result of the Russian dismemberment of Ukraine in violation of a treaty that they signed in return for the nuclear inventory of Ukraine, which was then the third largest nuclear power? Some individual sanctions, some diplomatic sanctions, a suspension — not removal from the G-8. And, now, more threats to come.

I predicted that Putin would go into Crimea because he couldn't bear to give up Sevastopol, because he is what he is.

And I am now very concerned, because of our lack of response, whether he will foment discontent in the manner which he is now, which will then demand autonomy for parts of eastern Ukraine.

And when a foreign minister of Russia lies to your face, once, twice, three, four times, I would be reluctant to take his word for anything.

So, here we are with Ukraine being destabilized, a part of it dismembered, and we won't give them defensive weapons.

We don't want to provoke? We don't want to provoke Vladimir Putin by giving these people the ability to defend themselves after their country has been dismembered and there is provocations going on? That, I say to you, is the logic of appeasement.

I want to know, and I think the American people should know, and maybe most importantly, the people of Ukraine should know why won't we give them some defensive weapons when they're facing another invasion, not the first, but another invasion of their country. It is just beyond logic.

When we don't give people assistance to defend themselves, then it — just as the Syrian decision — it reverberates throughout the entire world. I would like to know why it is not at least under serious consideration to give them some defensive weapons.

[The administration's] view of what the Ukrainians need is vastly different from what the Ukrainians think they need, which is a sovereign right to try to defend themselves, which is something that we have done historically, helping people who are struggling against overwhelming odds.

to do so given the important economic ties many EU countries have with such persons and institutions," the nonpartisan Congressional Research Service reported in March.[87]

Speaking more bluntly, an unnamed senior European official told *The Wall Street Journal*: "There's still a lot of nervousness in Europe about heading in that direction. They don't want to burn bridges with the Kremlin."[88]

From the Russian side, Putin and his officials shrugged off the punitive actions. "Sanctions are not effective in the contemporary world and are not bringing the desired outcome," Putin said in April.[89]

U.S. political debate on sanctions has been sparse so far. In April, some Republicans on the Senate Foreign Relations Committee expressed skepticism to Kerry about the measures' effectiveness. "They mocked our last set of sanctions," said Sen. Ron Johnson, R-Wis.[90]

Kerry disputed that, adding, "I think it's clear that we have huge capacity to have an impact. . . . [Russians] are not incapable of analyzing America's capacity here with respect to banking and finance and movement of people."[91]

Meanwhile, McCain was the only committee member to advocate arming the Ukrainians.

Obama appears committed to managing the crisis so that it doesn't lead to full-scale confrontation. *The New York Times* reported that the president has told visitors privately that Ukraine is not a big issue for most Americans.[92]

A late-April survey by Pew and *USA Today* found that 53 percent of respondents supported stepping up economic and diplomatic sanctions against Russia. But 62 percent opposed sending arms to the Ukrainian government.[93]

Syria: Ballots and Bombs

With war ravaging his country, Syrian President Assad is preparing for a June 3 election — or something resembling an election — that he is universally expected to win overwhelmingly.

When he stood for election to his second term in 2007, Assad was the sole candidate. Official results showed him winning 97.29 percent of the vote. He first became president after his father, Hafez Assad, died in 2000. Between father and son, the Assads have ruled Syria since 1979.[94]

This time, Assad will be one of seven contenders, but none of the others is believed to stand a chance. Election law requires candidates to have lived in Syria continuously for 10 years, effectively barring exiled oppositionists.[95]

As the election nears, the Obama administration has stepped up its controlled efforts to aid some of the rebels fighting the Assad government. Obama has in recent months defined Syria policy in humanitarian terms as "helping the Syrian people" facing the "repressive regime" of Assad.[96]

Nevertheless, Obama has not backed off his refusal to send in U.S. troops or take other direct military action. "America is not the world's policeman," he said in September. "Terrible things happen across the globe, and it is beyond our means to right every wrong."[97]

Together with Saudi Arabia, the administration has shipped a small number of advanced anti-tank missiles to rebel militias deemed "moderate," *The Wall Street Journal* reported in April. In the context of the Syrian war, moderate means not commanded by Islamist extremists.[98]

The new arms reportedly represent a test to determine whether the recipients can be trusted with anti-aircraft weapons, which they have long demanded. American officials have been reluctant, because of the potential danger to civilian aircraft. But events such as the bombing of a school by Syrian government aircraft in the city of Aleppo — killing at least 17 students and two teachers — have ratcheted up the pressure on the administration.[99]

Speaking early last year, before the chemical weapons deal with Russia, Obama cited the practical and even moral "limitations" on U.S. action. "What offers the best prospect of a stable post-Assad regime?" he asked. "And how do I weigh tens of thousands who've been killed in Syria versus the tens of thousands who are currently being killed in the Congo?"[100]

Decades of civil war in Congo have cost millions of lives. Last year, the U.N. formed its first offensive military force, allied with the Congolese government military, to fight rebels.[101]

The Syrian civil war began more than three years ago, after Assad ordered his military to crush anti-government demonstrations. By now, the armed opposition reportedly consists of as many as 1,000 groups of varied sizes, made up of an estimated 100,000 fighters, representing a wide variety of religious and political views.[102]

Complications involved in determining which opposition groups the United States should support begin with the presence of a strong religious aspect to the Syrian war. Assad and his top supporters belong to the Alawite religious minority, an Islamic sect with an ancestral tie to Shiism. Sunnis, the majority sect of Islam, make up the backbone of the anti-Assad forces.[103]

Some rebels are supported by Sunni militants and al Qaeda-linked extremists who represent an extremist Sunni fringe. The government in turn is relying in part on the highly organized and combat-ready Hezbollah ("Party of God") militia from Lebanon. The Iranian-supported Shiite force has fought two wars with Israel, previously its main enemy.[104]

In addition, Assad government forces receive weapons and fighters directly from Iran, the target of longstanding U.S. and international efforts to curb its nuclear-development program. These are shipped by aircraft that pass through Iraqi airspace. To complicate the situation further, Iraq's Shiite-majority government, which has extensive ties to Iran, was installed with the help of the U.S. government during the war to topple Sunni dictator Saddam Hussein. Speaking to *The New Yorker* magazine, Iraqi Prime Minister Nouri al-Maliki defined the Syrian war as a conflict between Assad and al Qaeda, with the former preferable to the latter. "There is no more moderate opposition in Syria," he said.[105]

The administration, though cautious about which groups to aid, does not agree. Nevertheless, a persistent criticism of the administration's Syria policy is that there was a missed chance to help rebels early in the war. "We had an opportunity before the fundamentalists," says former CIA and State Department analyst Goodman. "We had a humanitarian obligation from the outset."

However, he acknowledges, there was no public support. Referring to Obama's cancellation of airstrikes in favor of negotiating the chemical-weapons deal, Goodman said the president "marched right up to the brink and looked behind him and there was no one behind him."

OUTLOOK
Cautious Posture

The future of Ukraine and of relations with Russia, the outcome of the Syrian civil war, and the possibility of a definitive Iranian nuclear agreement remain highly uncertain, but some analysts argue that Americans' aversion to major military operations abroad is likely to continue.

"The American public, because of Iraq and Afghanistan, has been shocked into an isolationist mentality," says former ambassador Jeffrey.

But others say the American public is not categorically opposed to U.S. involvement in global affairs. "As frustrated as the public is with foreign policy, it isn't ready to abandon internationalism or to embrace unilateralism," said a Council on Foreign Relations analysis that accompanies the 2013 Pew survey.[106]

The analysis cited 72 percent support for shared world leadership, and 56 percent approval of the United States maintaining military supremacy. Nevertheless, Pew found support for going alone (38 percent) higher than at any time in nearly 50 years, except for 2009, when 44 percent supported that view.[107]

A major unknown is how the public would respond to a major attack against the United States or against U.S. interests abroad. The overwhelming support for a military response after the Sept. 11 attacks points to one possibility.

Sudden, catastrophic events aside, how public officials analyze the present can affect the course they set for U.S. policy. Carpenter of the Cato Institute, for one, argues that politicians ignore the strength of anti-interventionist public opinion at their peril. "If you continue to defy public opinion in the long term, that is likely to have political consequences," he says, adding, "In this case I think the public is correct."

Some argue that public caution about interventionism is well-founded. "This is the hundredth anniversary of World War I," says Bacevich of Boston University, pointing to a conflict that participants thought would be over in a matter of months. "The lesson of that is that once control is lost, it is difficult to restore order."

NOTES

1. Michael R. Gordon and Eric Schmitt, "Rebels to Ask for Antiaircraft Missiles," *The New York Times*, May 7, 2014, http://tinyurl.com/nhpm3zm.

2. *Ibid.*

3. Bernard Gwertzman, "Afghans Put Case Before All Forums," *The New York Times*, June 19, 1986, http://tinyurl.com/o45wea9; Norman Kempster, "Bosnian Leaders brings Arms Plea to U.S.," *Los Angeles Times*, Jan. 31, 1995, p. A4.

4. "Lend-Lease and Military Aid to the Allies in the Early Years of World War II," U.S. Department of State, Office of the Historian, undated, http://tinyurl.com/ln4d573.

5. "Public Sees U.S. Power Declining as Support for Global Engagement Slips: America's Place in the World 2013," Pew Research Center, Dec. 3, 2013, pp. 5, 20, 39, http://tinyurl.com/lz3mh2y; Janet Hook, "Americans Want to Pull Back From World Stage, Poll Finds," *The Wall Street Journal*, April 30, 2014, http://tinyurl.com/nst3umr.

6. "Secretary of Defense Chuck Hagel, Chicago Council on Global Affairs," U.S. Department of Defense, May 6, 2014, http://tinyurl.com/pcyb6bw.

7. Rebecca Shabad, "Congress fires warning shot at Iran," *The Hill*, March 18, 2014, http://tinyurl.com/myr8rlo; Robert J. Einhorn, "Preventing a Nuclear-Armed Iran: Requirements for Comprehensive Nuclear Agreement," Brookings Institution, March 2014, pp. 1-2, http://tinyurl.com/m689brf; Dan Roberts, "Obama admits Israel has good reason for skepticism over Iran nuclear deal," *The Guardian*, Nov. 24, 2013, http://tinyurl.com/nk7uxpb.

8. William Booth and Ruth Eglash, "Kerry's nine-month quest for Middle East peace ends in failure," *The Washington Post*, April 29, 2014, http://tinyurl.com/k2vpju3.

9. David J. Lynch, "China Challenges Obama's Asia Pivot With Rapid Military Buildup," Bloomberg, April 22, 2014, http://tinyurl.com/lkumsre.

10. Pamela Constable, "White House to send specialists to help recover abducted Nigerian schoolgirls," *The Washington Post*, May 6, 2014, http://tinyurl.com/nxwsbpb.

11. "Public Sees U.S. Power Declining," *op. cit.*, pp. 52-54.

12. "Remarks by President Obama and President Benigno Aquino III of the Philippines in Joint Press Conference," The White House, April 28, 2014, http://tinyurl.com/qg75rpo.

13. Mimi Hall, "Obama cites 'responsibility' of U.S. in Libya intervention," *USA Today*, March 28, 2011, http://tinyurl.com/ocafhb9; David D. Kirkpatrick, "A Deadly Mix in Benghazi," *The New York Times*, Dec. 28, 2013, http://tinyurl.com/lqeqtyv.

14. Joby Warrick, "More than 1,400 killed in Syrian chemical weapons attack, U.S. says," *The Washington Post*, Aug. 30, 2013, http://tinyurl.com/ksj2lc2. "Syria chemical attack: What we know," BBC, Sept. 24, 2013, www.bbc.com/news/world-middle-east-23927399. Reuters, April 1, 2014, www.reuters.com/article/2014/04/01/us-syria-crisis-toll-idUSBREA300YX2014041.

15. Michael R. Gordon, "U.S. and Russia Reach to Destroy Syria's Chemical Arsenal," *The New York Times*, Sept. 14, 2013, http://tinyurl.com/nytjlha; "Russia in the Syrian Conflict," *Russian Analytical Digest*, June 10, 2013, pp. 8-9, http://tinyurl.com/oxgp83m.

16. Mark Silva, "Obama's Russian Reset Lost in Putin's Translations," Bloomberg, April 3, 2014, http://tinyurl.com/pk4a5s6.

17. Sgt. A. M. LaVey, "173rd paratroopers arrive in Poland, Baltics for unscheduled exercises," *Army.mil*, April 30, 2014, http://tinyurl.com/lbx9oej; Griff Witte, "After Russian moves in Ukraine Eastern Europe shudders, NATO to increase presence," *The Washington Post*, April 18, 2014, http://tinyurl.com/msbuwlz; for background, see Roland Flamini, "Future of NATO," *CQ Researcher*, Jan. 1, 2009, pp. 1-26.

18. C. J. Chivers and Noah Sneider, "Behind the Masks in Ukraine, Many Faces of Rebellion," *The New York Times*, May 3, 2014, http://tinyurl.com/kreeybb; for background, see Brian Beary, "Resurgent Russia," *CQ Researcher*, Feb. 7, 2014, pp. 121-144.

19. "Annual Address to the Federal Assembly of the Russian Federation," President of Russia, April 25, 2005, http://tinyurl.com/ns5c6k4.

20. "Remarks by Sen. John McCain on Mass Atrocities in Syria as World Commemorates Anniversary of Rwandan Genocide," Official Website of U.S. Sen. John McCain, April 10, 2014, http://tinyurl.com/oxcpv5y; Sangwon Yoon,. Sangwon Yoon, "Losing

Syrian Rebels Press in Washington for Better Arms," Bloomberg, May 6, 2014, http://tinyurl.com/ lu9dk6v. Sean Sullivan, "McCain: Obama would face impeachment if he puts 'boots on the ground' in Syria," *The Washington Post*, Sept. 6, 2013, www.washingtonpost.com/blogs/ post-politics/wp/2013/09/06/mccain-obama-would-face-impeachment-if-he-puts-boots-on-the-ground-in-syria.

21. "Collective defence," North Atlantic Treaty Organization, undated, http://tinyurl.com/ co3p5vp.

22. Adam Entous, "U.S. Balks at Ukraine Military-Aid Request," *The Wall Street Journal*, March 13, 2014, http://tinyurl.com/mqcj9cu.

23. "Treasury Secretary Lew Announces Signing of $1 Billion Loan Guarantee Agreement for Ukraine," U.S. Department of State, April 14, 2014, http:// tinyurl.com/o9pjq6f.

24. Michael R. Gordon, "Kerry Takes Offer of Aid to Ukraine and Pushes Back Against Russian Claims," *The New York Times*, March 4, 2014, http:// tinyurl.com/n34e4jv; Ian Talley, "IMF Approves $17 Billion Emergency Aid for Ukraine's Economy," *The Wall Street Journal*, April 30, 2014, http://tinyurl.com/mrgnpb6.

25. Ian Traynor and Oksana Grytsenko, "Ukraine suspends talks on EU trade pact as Putin wins tug of war," *The Guardian*, Nov. 21, 2013, http:// tinyurl.com/mmxpjgs; "Why is Ukraine in turmoil?," BBC News, Feb. 22, 2014, http:// tinyurl.com/pxrf62y.

26. Kathy Lally, "Mansion was only a fixer-upper, Yanukovych says," *The Washington Post*, Feb. 28, 2014, http://tinyurl.com/l4twebj.

27. Henry Chu and Sergei L. Loiko, "Tensions escalate as Russia presses claim for Ukraine's Crimea," *Los Angeles Times*, March 7, 2014, http://tinyurl.com/ nhbuooy.

28. Julian Borger and Alec Luhn, "Ukraine crisis: Geneva talks produce agreement on defusing conflict," *The Guardian*, April 17, 2014, http:// tinyurl.com/p774zod; Thomas Grove and Aleksander Vasovic, "New Russia sanctions threats

as Ukraine stalemate goes on," Reuters, April 18, 2014, http://tinyurl.com/lv8s2sc.

29. "Remarks by President Obama and German Chancellor Merkel in Joint Press Conference," The White House, May 2, 2014, http://tinyurl.com/ kd7ggec.

30. "Public Sees U.S. Power Declining . . .," *op. cit.*, pp. 19, 22.

31. Chris Baldwin, "Putin says Russia threatened by 'unipolar world,' " Reuters, Nov. 5, 2007, http:// tinyurl.com/lpw7d3t.

32. "Annual Address to the Federal Assembly of the Russian Federation," *op. cit.*

33. Jay Solomon and Andrey Ostroukh, "Russia's Foreign Minister Sergei Lavrov Warns Ukraine," *The Wall Street Journal*, April 24, 2014, http:// tinyurl.com/m8k3vb3.

34. David J. Lynch, "China Challenges Obama's Asia Pivot With Rapid Military Buildup," Bloomberg, April 22, 2014, http://tinyurl.com/kc9gh4k.

35. For background, see Reed Karaim, "China Today," *CQ Researcher*, April 4, 2014, pp. 289-312.

36. "Transcript: Albright Interview on NBC-TV," USIS Washington File, Feb. 19, 1998, http:// tinyurl.com/oeyqz2d.

37. "Remarks by President George W. Bush at the 20th Anniversary of the National Endowment for Democracy," National Endowment for Democracy, Nov. 6, 2003, http://tinyurl.com/4r62tdv.

38. Scott Wilson, "Obama announces plan to bring home 33,000 'surge' troops from Afghanistan," *The Washington Post*, June 22, 2011, http://tiny url.com/6xpdnka.

39. David A. Lake, *Entangling Relations: American Foreign Policy in its Century* (1999), p. 3; Thomas Jefferson, "Inaugural Address," The American Presidency Project, March 4, 1801, http://tiny url.com/p38qgqq.

40. Justus D. Doenecke, *Nothing Less Than War: New History of America's Entry into World War I* (2011), pp. 1-18; 195-196; 149; 276; "Zimmermann Telegram," Our Documents, National Archives, http://tinyurl.com/ofnks2z.

41. Except where otherwise noted, this subsection is drawn from Susan Dunn, *1940: FDR, Willkie, Lindbergh, Hitler — the Election amid the Storm* (2013).

42. "German-Soviet Pact," United States Holocaust Memorial Museum, updated June 10, 2013, http://tinyurl.com/8gs6efm.

43. Franklin Delano Roosevelt, "'Stab in the Back' Speech," Miller Center, University of Virginia, June 10, 1940, http://tinyurl.com/q3z48v8.

44. Except where otherwise noted, this subsection is drawn from Tim Weiner, *A Legacy of Ashes: The History of the CIA* (2008).

45. "The India-Pakistan War of 1965," U.S. Department of State, Office of the Historian, undated, http://tinyurl.com/kbboxbl; "Bandung Conference (Asian-African Conference), 1955," U.S. Department of State, Office of the Historian, undated, http://tinyurl.com/mapu3jl.

46. Robert Jervis, "The Dustbin of History: Mutual Assured Destruction," *Foreign Policy*, Nov. 1, 2002, http://tinyurl.com/pv9cp2q.

47. Tim Weiner and Barbara Crossette, "George F. Kennan Dies at 101; Leading Strategist of Cold War," *The New York Times*, March 18, 2005, http://tinyurl.com/q8eg9g9; "Kennan and Containment, 1947," U.S. Department of State, Office of the Historian, undated, http://tinyurl.com/o6qqj3q; George Kennan, "Telegram . . . to the Secretary of State," Feb. 22, 1946, http://tinyurl.com/mw4k3nq.

48. "The Yalta Conference, 1945," U.S. Department of State, Office of the Historian, undated, http://tinyurl.com/mwuxwgu.

49. The NATO founding countries were: Belgium, Canada, Denmark, France, Iceland, Italy, Luxembourg, the Netherlands, Norway, Portugal, the United Kingdom, United States; "Member countries," North Atlantic Treaty Organization, undated, http://tinyurl.com/muurlsu; "A Short History of NATO," North Atlantic Treaty Organization, undated, http://tinyurl.com/knxknrh; "1955: Communist states sign Warsaw Pact," BBC, http://tinyurl.com/ywdx7o; "The Warsaw Security Pact," May 14, 1955, Avalon Project, Yale Law School, http://tinyurl.com/men7dor.

50. Weiner, *op. cit.*, pp. 92-105.

51. Frederick Taylor, "The Berlin Wall: A Secret History," *History Today*, February 2007, http://tinyurl.com/muqkgfy.

52. "The Cuban Missile Crisis: The 40th Anniversary," National Security Archive, The George Washington University, undated, http://tinyurl.com/p2wml5p.

53. "The Quotable Quotes of President Dwight D. Eisenhower," Eisenhower National Historic Site, undated, http://tinyurl.com/laxv8hb; "The Domino Theory," GlobalSecurity.org, undated, http://tinyurl.com/9v283vh.

54. Marc Selverstone and David Coleman, "Gulf of Tonkin, 1964: Perspectives from the Lyndon Johnson and National Military Command Center Tape," Miller Center, University of Virginia, undated, http://tinyurl.com/kgek74h; Andrew Gelman, "How Many Vietnam Veterans Are Still Alive?," *The New York Times*, March 25, 2013, http://tinyurl.com/qckaec4.

55. Michael Kranish, "With antiwar role, high visibility," *The Boston Globe*, June 17, 2003, http://tinyurl.com/flfx; "John Kerry Then: Hear Kerry's Historic 1971 Testimony Against the Vietnam War," Democracy Now!, Feb. 20, 2004, http://tinyurl.com/yl2gd4l; Todd Gitlin, *The Sixties: Years of Hope, Days of Rage* (1987).

56. John Tirman, "Why do we ignore the civilians killed in American wars?," *The Washington Post*, Jan. 6, 2012, http://tinyurl.com/7cwuq8h, www.archives.gov/research/military/vietnam-war/casualty-statistics.html.

57. Kate Doyle and Emily Willard, "'Learn from History,' 31st Anniversary of the Assassination of Archbishop Romero," National Security Archive, March 23, 2011, http://tinyurl.com/ky8npps.

58. "The Iran-Contra Affair," American Experience, WGBH, undated, http://tinyurl.com/3djty9z.

59. "Final Report on the Independent Counsel for Iran/Contra Matters," U.S. Court of Appeals, Chapt. 2, Aug. 4, 1993, http://tinyurl.com/5eee9.

60. Klaus Dahmann, "Fall of the Berlin Wall and Reunification (1989-1990)," *Deutsche Welle*, April 22, 2013, http://tinyurl.com/qe6axmk.

61. "George H. W. Bush — Foreign Affairs," Miller Center, University of Virginia, undated, http://tinyurl.com/l6evb78.

62. Archie Brown, "Reform, Coup and Collapse: The End of the Soviet State,: BBC, updated Feb. 17, 2011, http://tinyurl.com/6zxyv88.

63. "Gulf War Fast Facts," CNN, Sept. 15, 2013, http://tinyurl.com/mxjdmww.

64. Chronology, Gulf War, (drawn from Rick Atkinson, *Crusade: The Untold Story of the Persian Gulf War* (1993), Frontline, PBS, undated, http://tinyurl.com/d8w3jxf; Thomas E. Ricks, Fiasco: *The American Military Adventure in Iraq* (2006), pp. 5-6; "No-fly zones: The legal position," BBC, Feb. 19, 2001, http://tinyurl.com/btbrxlt.

65. "Rwanda: How the genocide happened," BBC, Dec. 18, 2008, http://tinyurl.com/yksb33z.

66. Samantha Power, "Bystanders to Genocide," *The Atlantic*, Sept. 1, 2001, http://tinyurl.com/lduvwob.

67. Walter Clarke and Jeffrey Herbst, "Somalia and the Future of Humanitarian Intervention," *Foreign Affairs*, March/April 1996, http://tinyurl.com/kaet69a.

68. Mark Bowden, *Black Hawk Down* (1999).

69. Power, *op. cit.*

70. "Balkan Accord: The Address; Clinton Lays Out his Case for U.S. Troops in Balkans," *The New York Times*, Nov. 28, 1995, http://tinyurl.com/ks55323; Katherine Q. Seelye, "Balkan Accord: In Congress," *The New York Times*, Dec. 14, 1995, http://tinyurl.com/mtje8zk.

71. James Bennet, "U.S. Cruise Missiles Strike Sudan and Afghan Tarets Tied to Terrorist Network," *The New York Times*, Aug. 21, 1998, http://tinyurl.com/k22kecs.

72. "Operation Iraqi Freedom . . . Operation Enduring Freedom, U.S. Casualty Status," updated May 9, 2014, http://tinyurl.com/29va4fp; Matt Spetalnick, "Obama, Karzai accelerate end of U.S. combat role in Afghanistan," Reuters, Jan. 12, 2013, http://tinyurl.com/b3ks34e; Michael Holmes, "Inside Iraq: Two years after U.S. withdrawal, are things worse than ever?," CNN, Jan. 15, 2014, http://tinyurl.com/o5btyxs.

73. "Remarks by President George W. Bush at the 20th Anniversary of the National Endowment for Democracy," National Endowment for Democracy, Nov. 6, 2003, http://tinyurl.com/4r62tdv.

74. Sanford Gottlieb, "The Anti-Iraq War Movement is a Far Cry From Vietnam," Pacific News Service, Sept. 21, 2005, http://tinyurl.com/ljbq957; David Crary, "Iraq and Vietnam: Contrasting Protests," The Associated Press, March, 21, 2007, http://tinyurl.com/oxnfkd3; Andrew Glass, "U.S. military draft ends, Jan. 27, 1973," *Politico*, Jan. 27, 2012, http://tinyurl.com/o74rs26.

75. For background, see Leda Hartman, "Islamic Sectarianism," *CQ Researcher*, Aug. 7, 2012, pp. 353-376.

76. For background, see Peter Katel, "The Iraq War: 10 Years Later," *CQ Researcher*, March 1, 2013, pp. 205-232.

77. Ian Black, "Barack Obama, the Arab Spring and a series of unforeseen events," *The Guardian*, Oct. 21, 2012, http://tinyurl.com/my8zqqt.

78. Adam Nossiter and Kareem Fahim, "Revolution Won, Top Libyan Official Vows a New and More Pious State," *The New York Times*, Oct. 23, 2011, http://tinyurl.com/c7c9vwm; Jeremiah Gertler, "Operation Odyssey Dawn (Libya): Background and Issues for Congress," Congressional Research Service, March 30, 2011, http://tinyurl.com/6draa8z.

79. Kirkpatrick, *op. cit.*

80. C. J. Chivers and David M. Herszenhorn, "Separatists in Ukraine Vow to Proceed With Autonomy Vote," *The New York Times*, May 8, 2014, http://tinyurl.com/kem4bm5.

81. Neil MacFarquhar, "Putin Announces Pullback From Ukraine Border," *The New York Times*, May 7, 2014, http://tinyurl.com/l2x8nyb.

82. Chivers and Herszenhorn, *op. cit.* Andrew E. Kramer and Alan Cowell, "Ukraine Authorities Dismiss Referendums as 'Farce,' " *The New York Times*, May

12, 2014, www.nytimes.com/2014/05/13/world/europe/ukraine.html?hp&_r=0.

83. MacFarquhar, *op. cit.*

84. "Remarks by President Obama and President Benigno Aquino III . . .," *op. cit.*

85. Alison Smale and Andrew Roth, "Ukrainian Says That Militias Won the East," *The New York Times*, April 30, 2014, http://tinyurl.com/kuwjsdk.

86. Jay Solomon, William Mauldin and Colleen McCain Nelson, "U.S., Europe Impose New Sanctions on Russia," *The Wall Street Journal*, April 29, 2014, http://tinyurl.com/ln2l78g.

87. Steven Woehrel, "Ukraine: Current Issues and U.S. Policy," Congressional Research Service, May 8, 2014, p. 7, http://tinyurl.com/pbcw576; Ilya Arkhipov and Anton Doroshev, "U.S. Sanctions Will Unite Russian Elite, Putin Aide Says," *Bloomberg Businessweek*, April 28, 2014, http://tinyurl.com/mvjj5x2.

88. Jay Solomon, *et al.*, *op. cit.*

89. Arkhipov and Doroshev, *op. cit.*

90. "Hearing of the Senate Foreign Relations Committee," www.foreign.senate.gov/imo/media/doc/04%2008%202014,%20International%20Affairs%20Budget1.pdf.

91. *Ibid.*

92. Peter Baker, "In Cold War Echo, Obama Strategy Writes Off Putin," *The New York Times*, April 19, 2014, http://tinyurl.com/lqka2jx.

93. "Bipartisan Support for Increased U.S. Sanctions against Russia," Pew Research Center, April 28, 2014, http://tinyurl.com/kzr7ndm.

94. "Syrians Vote For Assad in Uncontested Referendum," The Associated Press, May 28, 2007, http://tinyurl.com/npcwke4; "Hafez al-Assad, obituary," *The Guardian*, June 14, 2000, http://tinyurl.com/m8qqdhz.

95. Dominic Evans, "Assad seeks re-election as Syria war rages," Reuters, April 28, 2014, http://tinyurl.com/pcbj95h.

96. "Remarks by President Obama and President Benigno Aquino III . . .," *op. cit.*; "Full Transcript: President Obama's Sept. 10 speech on Syria," *The*

Washington Post, Sept. 10, 2013, http://tinyurl.com/ns5njac.

97. *Ibid.* (Obama speech)

98. Ellen Knickmeyer, Maria Abi-Habib, Adam Entous, "Advanced U.S. Weapons Flow to Syrian Rebels," *The Wall Street Journal*, April 18, 2014, http://tinyurl.com/m5lz3wt.

99. Anne Barnard and Hwaida Saad, "Children's Art at Syria School, and Then a Bomb," *The New York Times*, April 30, 2014, http://tinyurl.com/k9l37u8; Ben Hubbard, "Syrian Election Announced; Rebels Report New Weapons," *The New York Times*, April 21, 2014, http://tinyurl.com/kffs2ms.

100. Franklin Foer and Chris Hughes, "Barack Obama Is Not Pleased," *The New Republic*, Jan. 27, 2013, http://tinyurl.com/bkc5eev.

101. Jonathan Saruk, "Africa's deadliest war enters new phase,: *USA Today*, Aug. 21, 2013, http://tinyurl.com/kdgzcbe; "Measuring Mortality in the Democratic Republic of Congo," International Rescue Committee, 2007, http://tinyurl.com/mju56np.

102. Liam Stack, "In Slap at Syria, Turkey Shelters Anti-Assad Fighters," *The New York Times*, Oct. 27, 2011, http://tinyurl.com/3b35yhn; "Syria crisis: Guide to armed and political opposition," BBC, Dec. 13, 2013, http://tinyurl.com/ms45abz.

103. Martin Chulov and Mona Mahmood, "Syrian Sunnis fear Assad regime wants to 'ethnically cleanse' Alawite heartland," The Guardian, July 22, 2013, http://tinyurl.com/kytqyd8; "The sectarian divisions in Syria's violent uprising," CBC News, July 19, 2012, http://tinyurl.com/k2svd4w; for background, see Leda Hartman, "Islamic Sectarianism," *CQ Researcher*, Aug. 7, 2012, pp. 353-376.

104. Mona Alami, "Hezbollah takes lead in pounding Syrian rebels," *USA Today*, Feb. 27, 2014, http://tinyurl.com/pwyex8s; Alison Smale, "Flow of Westerners to Syria Prompts Security Concerns," *The New York Times*, Jan. 15, 2014, http://tinyurl.com/pzno7bx.

105. Dexter Filkins, "What We Left Behind," *The New Yorker*, April 28, 2014, http://tinyurl.com/mo2lo23.

106. "Public Sees U.S. Power Declining . . .," *op. cit.*, pp. 6, 52-54.

107. *Ibid.*, pp. 18, 21.

BIBLIOGRAPHY

Books

Bacevich, Andrew J., *The Limits of Power: The End of American Exceptionalism*, Holt Paperbacks, 2009.
A Boston University political scientist and former Army colonel warns that the deep-seated American belief in global superiority is disastrous.

Gaddis, John Lewis, *The Cold War: A New History*, Penguin Books, 2006.
A Yale University historian considered the leading scholar of the Cold War distills his past work into a narrative account of the entire period.

Jones, Bruce, *Still Ours to Lead: America, Rising Powers, and the Tension Between Rivalry and Restraint*, Brookings Institution Press, 2014.
The decline in U.S. influence following the 2008 financial crisis shouldn't be confused with total eclipse, argues a foreign-policy specialist at the centrist think tank, who writes that the United States is in "a category of one."

Lesch, David W., *Syria: The Fall of the House of Assad*, Yale University Press, 2013.
The United States is far more limited in what it can do to bring peace to Syria than many foreign-policy experts believe, argues a Trinity University historian who met repeatedly with Assad earlier in his rule.

Weiner, Tim, *Legacy of Ashes: The History of the CIA*, Anchor, 2008.
A *New York Times* national security correspondent recounts the Cold War's numerous cloak-and-dagger battles.

Articles

Bendavid, Naftali, "Syria Making Good Progress in Chemical Weapons Removal," *The Wall Street Journal*, April 25, 2014, http://tinyurl.com/kuc6lw9.
Even amid war and rising tensions with Russia — a key architect of the Syria chemical weapons deal — removal of the weapons is proceeding well.

Cohen, Stephen F., "Cold War Again: Who's Responsible?" *The Nation*, April 1, 2014, http://tinyurl.com/ouyhq9n.
A leading critic of U.S. policy toward Russia argues that current tensions grow out of post-Cold War NATO expansion, not any territorial ambitions by Russian President Vladimir Putin.

Costigliola, Frank, "What Would Kennan Say to Obama?" *The New York Times*, Feb. 27, 2014, http://tinyurl.com/kmc8wco.
The late George F. Kennan, once the leading U.S. Cold War strategist, would warn President Obama against maintaining the role of world policeman and advise him that aggressive measures against a foe can lead to war, writes a University of Connecticut professor who edited Kennan's diaries.

Fisher, Max, "American isolationism just hit a 50-year high. Why that matters," *The Washington Post*, Dec. 4, 2013, http://tinyurl.com/ldb26uf.
A foreign-policy blogger argues that results of a survey showing public disengagement from international affairs represent a powerful trend among Americans.

Kaplan, Fred, "Eastern Promises," *Slate*, April 23, 2014, http://tinyurl.com/n435xp6.
President Obama's attempt to refocus U.S. foreign policy on Asia is a good idea, a journalist specializing in national security writes, but presidential plans don't dictate the course of events, in this case the Ukraine crisis.

Landler, Mark, "On a Trip That Avoids Beijing, Obama Keeps His Eye on China," *The New York Times*, April 26, 2014, http://tinyurl.com/nv8zht4.
Obama's trip to Asia was also marked by the balancing of neighbors' fears of China with the U.S. need to maintain a working relationship with the Asian giant.

Sorokin, Vladimir, "Let the Past Collapse on Time!" *New York Review of Books*, May 8, 2014, http://tinyurl.com/ondzqbf.
A novelist who was a dissident in Soviet times and who remains in Moscow writes that the end of communism in Russia did not vanquish Soviet-style rule.

Reports

"Oral Update of the independent international commission of inquiry on the Syrian Arab Republic," U.N. Human Rights Council, March 18, 2014,

www.ohchr.org/Documents/HRBodies/HRCouncil/
CoISyria/OralUpdate18March2014.pdf.
The UN commission recounts the most blatant and
shocking human-rights violations committed during a
horrific civil war now in its fourth year.

**"Public Sees U.S. Power Declining as Support for
Global Engagement Slips," Pew Research Center,
Dec. 3, 2013, http://tinyurl.com/pqfsrre.**
The most comprehensive survey to date on U.S. public
opinion concerning global engagement, which tracks

shifts in American attitudes toward the world over
decades, is sparking interest in the foreign-policy and
political communities.

**Woehrel, Steven, "Ukraine: Current Issues and
U.S. Policy," Congressional Research Service,
May 8, 2014, www.fas.org/sgp/crs/row/RL33460
.pdf.**
A Europe specialist in Congress' nonpartisan research
arm reports on the most recent developments in Ukraine,
and Congressional response to date.

For More Information

American Enterprise Institute, 1150 17th St., N.W., Washington, DC 20036; 202-862-5800; www.aei.org/policy/foreign-and-defense-policy/. Conservative Washington think tank that includes interventionist-oriented scholars and analysts.

Brookings Institution, 1775 Massachusetts Ave., N.W., Washington, DC 20036; 202-797-6105; www.brookings.edu. A centrist research and advocacy center with a foreign affairs wing that studies international economic and human rights issues.

Carnegie Endowment for International Peace, 1779 Massachusetts Ave., N.W., Washington, DC 20036; 202-483-7600; www.carnegieendowment.org. Longtime centrist institution that maintains satellite offices in Beirut, Moscow, Brussels and elsewhere.

Cato Institute, 1000 Massachusetts Ave., N.W., Washington, DC 20001; 202-842-0200; www.cato.org. Libertarian think tank that opposes military solutions to problems.

Center for International Policy, 2000 M St., N.W., Suite 720, Washington, DC 20036; 202-232-3317; www.ciponline.org. Liberal think tank that advocates demilitarization and action against human-rights abuse.

Council on Foreign Relations, 58 E. 68th St., New York, NY 10065; 212-434-9400; cfr.org. A foreign-policy think tank including former senior diplomats.

11

Manipulating the Human Genome

Jill U. Adams

Reprinted from Cell, Volume 156, Chapter 4, Yuyu Niu et. al., "Generation of Gene-Modified Cynomolgus Monkey via Cas9/RNA-Mediated Gene Targeting in One-Cell Embryos," 836-843, 2014, with permission from Elsevier.

A new genetic engineering technology called CRISPR enables researchers to manipulate the genomes of living cells by replacing one gene with another. The technique is so advanced that it has led many scientists to fear it will soon be used to alter human embryos. Those fears were heightened last year when Chinese researchers altered the genomes of monkey embryos and brought two of them, shown above, to successful live births.

From *CQ Researcher*, June 19, 2015.

The international scientific community was stunned when a group of Chinese researchers revealed in April that they had used a new genetic technology to try to fix a defective gene that causes thalassemia, a serious blood disorder — by tinkering with the genomes of human embryos.[1]

The embryos were nonviable, meaning they could never produce live births. But the attempt to genetically alter a human embryo's genome — the genetic make-up of an organism, carried in the DNA — stepped over an ethical boundary that many scientists and ethicists say should never be crossed.

"It is highly irresponsible for a few scientists to take it upon themselves to yank this treacherous genie out of its bottle," said Marcy Darnovsky, who directs the Center for Genetics and Society, a nonprofit public interest organization in Berkeley, Calif., that studies how genetic technologies affect social justice and human rights. "This is a watershed moment in determining whether human genetic technologies will be used in the public interest and for the common good, or in ways that are dangerous and socially pernicious."[2]

The Chinese scientists had used a new gene-editing technology called CRISPR, which allows them to edit the genomes of living cells by cutting out one gene and replacing it with another, much like the "find/replace" function in word processing software. Before gene editing was developed, scientists only could add or silence certain genes — not replace them.[3]

Because CRISPR is more precise, faster and easier to use than older technologies, many scientists feared it was just a matter of

Many Nations Restrict Gene Editing

Twenty-nine nations (among 39 nations surveyed) ban research on human germline gene modification, either through legislation (25) or non-binding guidelines (4). The process involves inserting artificially modified genes into human DNA. Policies in 10 other countries are regarded as ambiguous (9) or restrictive (1). In the United States, the Food and Drug Administration closely regulates clinical trials using the technology, and the National Institutes of Health refuses to fund germline research on human embryos.

Policies for Germline Gene Modification for Reproduction, by Country*
(Non-colored countries were not surveyed)

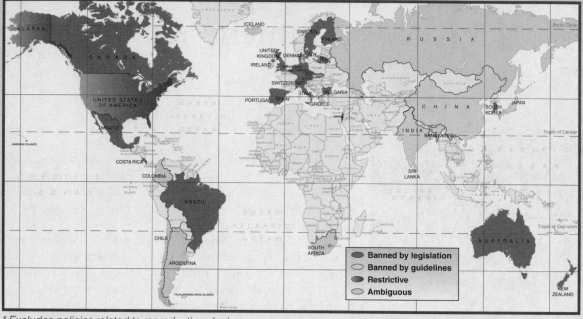

* Excludes policies related to reproductive cloning

Source: Motoko Araki and Tetsuya Ishii, "International regulatory landscape and integration of corrective genome editing into in vitro fertilization," *Repoductive Biology and Endorcrinology,* Nov. 24, 2014, http://tinyurl.com/pumn8a8

time before someone used the technology to alter viable human embryos — something that 29 countries have banned. Those fears were heightened the previous year, when a different team of Chinese researchers reported they had altered the genomes of monkey embryos and brought two of them to successful live births. Using the technology in fertilized eggs means the infant monkeys will carry the edited genome in every cell. If they survive to adulthood and reproduce, they will pass on the altered genomes to all their descendants.[4]

Critics worry that the two studies — and rumors that genome engineering is being conducted on viable human embryos in labs outside of China — point toward a frightening new world in which scientists manipulate the laws of nature to create "designer humans," forever changing future generations. Others are concerned that modifying the human germline — the eggs, sperm, and embryos which carry unique human genetic codes — could revive the notorious eugenics movement of the early 20th century, which aimed to create a perfect "master race."

Yet, scientists and ethicists are not of a single mind on genomic research. Many want a moratorium or permanent worldwide ban on human germline engineering. Others say such moves, however laudable, would be unenforceable. And some argue that the techniques — if used responsibly — could help humankind by eliminating certain genetic diseases and disorders.

Since CRISPR's emergence three years ago, it has been used by biomedical researchers to create so-called animal models of human diseases using typical laboratory species such as mice, rats and monkeys. It also is being used by clinicians to develop new gene therapies, which attempt to correct genetically based diseases in adults.

But if CRISPR and similar technologies are used to alter human genomes, the new human beings created would have artificially inserted genes in every cell and tissue in their bodies — including their eggs or sperm. Thus, the edited genome would be passed on to all the descendants of these engineered humans, and little is known about the potential long-term effects.

Many scientists want at least a temporary ban on using the technology in the human genome. "A temporary ban is a good idea," says Guoping Feng, a professor of neuroscience at the Massachusetts Institute of Technology. "There is no reason to do this in humans right now. We are not ready." Still, he adds, "I can't say that future development won't be a different case. If changing a defective gene in a human embryo is beneficial, if it prevents genetic disease, there's no reason not to use it."

But Darnovsky equates human germline engineering with reproductive cloning of humans — "two things that should be prohibited." Reproductive cloning made headlines in 1996, when Scottish researchers cloned a sheep, named Dolly. Genetic material from an adult sheep was inserted into an unfertilized egg, emptied of

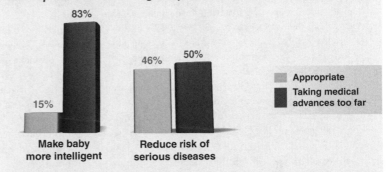

Most Oppose Gene Alteration for Intelligence

An overwhelming majority of adults say that modifying genetic characteristics to make a baby more intelligent is "taking medical advances too far." But fewer are negative about genetic treatment to reduce the risk of serious diseases in a baby: Half oppose genetic changes for this purpose and a nearly equal share (46 percent) say it would be appropriate.

Percentage of U.S. Adults Who Say Changing a Baby's Genetic Makeup for the Following Purposes Is . . .

83%

50%

46%

15%

Make baby more intelligent

Reduce risk of serious diseases

Appropriate

Taking medical advances too far

Source: "Public and Scientists' Views on Science and Society," Pew Research Center, Jan. 29, 2015, p. 57, http://tinyurl.com/m7ktyng

its own DNA and implanted into a surrogate mother sheep. The result was a lamb that carried the same genome — making it an identical twin — of the adult donor sheep. A raucous scientific and ethical debate followed, with critics voicing concerns that someone would try to clone a human.[5] In response, the Council of Europe, which sets human rights and legal standards for 28 European countries, and the United Nations banned human cloning; the U.S. government has imposed limits on human embryo research but no explicit ban.[6]

Darnovsky says genomic editing of human embryos should not be allowed for several reasons: The technology is new, and the risks of a mistake are magnified by the fact that the genetic changes would be passed along to offspring. There is also a question of consent — who gets to decide the biological features of a future human being? And human germline engineering would mark a whole new level of human alteration of nature.

"What happens if traits viewed as socially undesirable are merely problems to be solved in a system that makes

New Gene Therapies Show Promise

Successes slowly emerge after years of mixed results.

A new type of gene therapy holds promise for helping patients with diseases that result from inherited gene variants.

In gene therapy, scientists attempt to place a healthy gene into a cell to override or replace a disease-causing gene. Typically, that is done by inserting the desired gene into a virus, which then can worm its way into a cell's DNA.

Such so-called viral vectors have only been able to introduce new genes, not get rid of problem ones. New techniques, however, use carriers designed to recognize a specific address on the recipient DNA, cut out the section with the problem gene and replace it with the new and improved gene. The carriers are either proteins (the zinc finger nuclease and the TALEN methods) or RNA strands (called the CRISPR method).[1] *

Researchers are still refining the new techniques for treating inherited diseases such as sickle cell anemia and cystic fibrosis. However, the zinc finger nuclease strategy has reached the human clinical trial stage and is being used to target a gene involved in the progression of HIV infection.

In 2014, researchers at the University of Pennsylvania treated blood from 12 HIV-infected patients with zinc finger nucleases designed to disrupt the gene that enables the disease to progress. The treated blood was then transfused back into the patients, who subsequently generally showed increased T-cell counts, indicating an improvement in their immune systems.[2]

The new techniques have revived hope for gene therapy solutions to genetic disease. In the past, unexpected and sometimes tragic complications have arisen from gene therapies using viral vectors.

In a successful early trial in 1990, two girls from Ohio were treated with gene therapy to help them boost their immune systems. They suffered from a form of Severe Combined Immune Deficiency (SCID) — sometimes referred to as the "bubble-boy" disease. The condition is caused by an enzyme deficiency that left the girls unable to fight infections such as colds and flu. Researchers took white blood cells from the girls, added working genes for the missing enzyme and then infused the corrected white blood cells back into the patients.[3]

Nine years later, however, another youth — Jesse Gelsinger, 18 — underwent gene therapy to fix an enzyme problem called ornithine transcarbamylase deficiency, which led to a buildup of toxins in his body. Unlike the Ohio girls, he got worse after the treatment and died four days later from a reaction to the virus used to deliver the new gene.[4]

---

* Zinc finger nucleases (developed by Sangamo Biosciences in Richmond, Calif.) are protein complexes engineered so that one end of the molecule finds a specific address on cellular DNA and the other end makes a cut. Attaching a gene to the protein gives the cell something with which to repair the cut; thus, a new gene is put in the proper place. TALEN uses a different, easier-to-make kind of protein carrier for inserting genes. CRISPR uses RNA carriers to ferry new genes; they are easy, fast and cheap to create in the lab.

'fitting the mold' a biological possibility?" said Darnovsky's Center of Genetics and Society.[7]

CRISPR's co-inventor, Jennifer Doudna, a professor of molecular and cell biology at the University of California-Berkeley, acknowledged the concerns. "The idea that you would affect evolution is a very profound thing," she said.[8] Still, she and others contend that CRISPR can be used in valuable ways that don't involve human embryos, such as creating laboratory animals with known genetics for research or developing therapies for use in non-reproductive tissue.

Some scientists see a potential benefit of using the technology in human embryos. Certain genetic diseases, which can be passed down in families, are caused by a mutation in a single gene. Correcting the defect by cutting out the mutated gene and inserting a functional one in its place at the embryonic stage could remove the threat of a child developing that disease. It also could

Partly because of Gelsinger's youth and the fact that he had been managing his condition reasonably well with diet and medicine, the case raised ethical issues about how well subjects in clinical trials understand the risks they take. Often, clinical trials do more to advance scientific knowledge than to cure individual patients' maladies. After Gelsinger's death, many gene therapy trials were halted while the Food and Drug Administration and National Institutes of Health investigated safety and informed consent.

Since then, gene therapy has experienced more successes and more failures. The treatment has reversed blindness in patients with leber congenital amaurosis who lack a protein necessary for normal vision.[5] But in 2007, a woman with rheumatoid arthritis died after receiving her second infusion of an experimental gene therapy. Jolee Mohr's death in Springfield, Ill., was attributed to the treatment and, like Gelsinger, she was not at great risk of death or disability from her disease.[6]

Criticism of gene therapy again ran high. "The record of gene transfer has been worse than disappointing," wrote Marcy Darnovsky, executive director of the Center for Genetics and Society, which advocates for responsible uses of genetic technology, and Stuart Newman, professor of cell biology at New York Medical College. "In truth, gene therapy has harmed more people than it has helped."[7]

Since then, gene therapy has progressed slowly, gradually accumulating successes, using both old and new methods. "Whenever there's a new technology, it goes from a peak of inflated expectations, to a trough of disillusionment, to a slope of enlightenment, and a plateau of productivity," said Bruce Levine, an immunologist at the University of Pennsylvania. "Gene therapy is now in the enlightenment stage."[8]

— *Jill U. Adams*

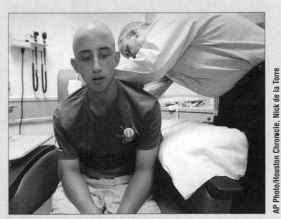

Bone cancer sufferer James Ragan is examined before getting an injection of stem cells at Methodist Hospital's Center for Cell and Gene Therapy in Houston.

AP Photo/Houston Chronicle, Nick de la Torre

[1] Susan Young, "Genome Surgery," *MIT Technology Review*, Feb. 11, 2015, http://tinyurl.com/m28mrcf.

[2] Sara Reardon, "Gene-editing method tackles HIV in first clinical test," *Nature News & Comment*, March 5, 2014, http://tinyurl.com/o2q8nds; Pablo Tebas *et al.*, "Gene Editing of CCR5 in Autologous CD4 T Cells of Person Infected with HIV," *The New England Journal of Medicine*, March 2014, http://tinyurl.com/l94otkh.

[3] Ricki Lewis, *The Forever Fix: Gene Therapy and the Boy Who Saved It* (2012), pp. 71-93.

[4] *Ibid.*, pp. 52-58.

[5] *Ibid.*, pp. 263-265.

[6] Sheldon Krimsky and Jeremy Gruber, eds., *Biotechnology in Our Lives* (2013), pp. 109-113.

[7] *Ibid.*, p. 110.

[8] Laura Cassiday, "Medical research: Gene-therapy reboot," *Nature Jobs*, May 2014, http://tinyurl.com/pbzzo8m.

prevent the mutant gene — for instance, for Huntington's disease or cystic fibrosis — from being passed on to grandchildren and great grandchildren.

As the genetic underpinnings of more complex diseases become better understood, they could possibly be prevented, said Craig Mello, a Nobel laureate and professor of genetics at the University of Massachusetts, Worcester. "In the distant future, I could imagine that altered germlines would protect humans against cancer, diabetes and other age-related problems," he said.[9]

Yet, many scientists argue that modern society already can prevent hereditary diseases by using in vitro fertilization (IVF) combined with embryonic screening and selection, known as preimplantation genetic diagnosis (PGD). For instance, if both parents carry the gene for cystic fibrosis, their child has a 1 in 4 chance of developing the disease. Those parents could use PGD to

In vitro fertilization (IVF) enabled Australian parent Lyn Martin to give birth to her son Reilly after her husband, Scott, died of cancer. Before his death, he contributed sperm that was frozen for later use to fertilize an egg from his wife. In the United States, an estimated 60,000 so-called test-tube babies are born each year using IVF.

screen the embryos in advance for the disease, discarding those with the diseased genes.[10]

"We already have PGD," says Edward Lanphier, president and CEO of Sangamo BioSciences, a biotechnology company in Richmond, Calif., that develops gene therapies. "We cannot think of any therapeutic or humanitarian justification for modifying the human germline."

Scientists generally agree that the risks from using CRISPR in human embryos are unknown and potentially great and that no benefits have been demonstrated. The big question is: Who gets to decide when and how to move forward with the technology in humans?

Geneticists have been anxious to reach consensus about regulating the technology's use in humans. In addition to safety and ethical issues, many researchers worry about damage to science's reputation if the technology is used recklessly. "We need a really strong international consortium to set up guidelines," Feng says. Currently, there are too many unsolved problems, he adds. So those charging ahead with human embryo research are being irresponsible in ways that could harm future efforts to harness the technology, he says. "The Chinese study is already damaging the field."

Feng hopes to use CRISPR to create animal models of autism, a complex neurodevelopmental disorder. Feng is focusing his research on autism's genetic component. "We want to engineer human mutations into animal models" that can provide better insights into why autism occurs and how it can be treated, he says.

Lanphier's company is developing another type of gene-editing technology that, in theory, could be used to edit human germline cells, but the process is not as cheap and easy as CRISPR, so scientists had not been worried about it being used in human embryos. Sangamo BioSciences is conducting phase 2 gene therapy studies using zinc finger nuclease technology on adult cells to block HIV from getting into the cells.

As geneticists, scientists, ethicists and policymakers consider developments in germline engineering, here are some of the questions being debated:

Should human germline engineering be banned on safety grounds?

Prominent U.S. scientists want the worldwide scientific community to agree to a ban or at least a moratorium on genetic manipulation in human germline cells. Their biggest reason: No one knows the full consequences of such alterations.

The potential health risks for the newly created life are unknown. And because the gene is altered in every tissue of the body, it could change functions in multiple organs at different stages of development. The safety implications for an individual's offspring also are uncertain.

"We worry about people making changes without the knowledge of what those changes mean in terms of the overall genome," said David Baltimore, Nobel laureate and professor emeritus at the California Institute of Technology. "I personally think we are just not smart enough — and won't be for a very long time — to feel comfortable about the consequences of changing heredity, even in a single individual."[11]

The Center for Genetics and Society cites "profound health risks to future children" as a primary reason for the United States to join other countries in prohibiting research on modifying human germline cells, whether sperm, eggs or early-stage embryos.

The center continues: "Altering the genomes of our offspring — not just the first generation but all later ones as well — means irreversibly changing every cell in their bodies, forever. The risks of such biologically extreme experimentation would be huge, from the early stages of embryonic development through the life span. Even with the latest gene-editing tools, "off-target effects" [unintended gene deletions] are an unsolved problem, and even if genes can be added or deleted in the right place, we can't predict what those added or deleted genes might do in the cell or the organism."[12]

In fact, off-target effects have been documented, as have so-called mosaic effects, which create differing genomes among the cells of a multicell embryo.

The Chinese researchers who developed twin genetically engineered monkeys reported several imperfect genetic results. The baby monkeys are being closely monitored, but it's not known what impact the unintended genetic defects will have on them. Off-target effects might mean disease or malfunctioning organs. The consequences of mosaic genomes in the primates also are unknown; the researchers chose not to bring the mosaic embryos to term.[13]

The Chinese experiment with the human genomes also reported off-target and mosaic effects, which potentially could cause any number of developmental or birth defects — including premature death — had the embryos been implanted. Not all of the embryos even survived the gene-editing procedure.[14]

"The results just underline the level of immaturity of this research," said George Daley, a stem-cell researcher and professor of biological chemistry at Harvard Medical School. "There is no way this should be used" outside of the laboratory.[15]

Other scientists say the consequences of editing the genome in human embryos can be learned through

Glossary of Key Terms

Chromosome — The physical structure that contains DNA, packaged with proteins; humans have 23 pairs of chromosomes.

Cloning — A process by which a genetically identical twin of a gene or organism is created.

CRISPR — A new genetic engineering technology that allows scientists to edit the genomes of living cells by cutting out one gene and replacing it with another.

DNA, or deoxyribonucleic acid — The molecule that carries the genetic code of organisms.

Gene editing — A process by which a gene is inserted, deleted or replaced with another gene.

Genome — The genetic code of an organism, carried in the DNA.

Germline — The reproductive cells of an organism, found in the sperm, egg and fertilized egg or embryo.

IVF (in vitro fertilization) — The joining of egg and sperm in a laboratory rather than in a human womb.

Mosaic effects — The creation of differing genomes among the cells of a multicell embryo, caused during gene editing.

Off-target effects — Unintended gene deletions caused during gene editing.

PGD, or preimplantation genetic diagnosis — A method of preventing hereditary diseases by using in vitro fertilization (IVF) combined with embryonic screening and selection.

Recombinant DNA — A DNA chain that contains material from two or more sources, created in a laboratory.

careful and methodical research. They also say some risk may be acceptable, especially compared to the risk of known genetic diseases. Human germline engineering might be a good alternative to current treatment of certain genetic diseases, they say.

"The mindful thing to do would be not to put unnecessary hampers on basic research," said Ethan Bier, a professor of biological sciences at the University of California, San Diego. "But to move to clinical use — that is a political decision and needs consensus."[16]

George Church, a professor of genetics at Harvard Medical School, agreed a moratorium should be placed on human germline engineering, but only until "safety issues are cleared up and there is a general consensus that it is okay."[17] The Chinese study was not unethical, he said, because the human embryos were not viable.[18] He also pointed out that the Chinese researchers did not

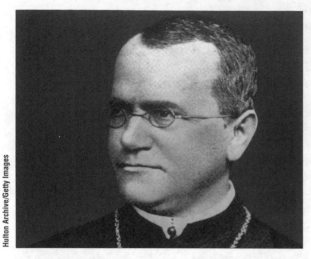

Gregor Mendel, an Austrian monk, conducted his now-famous experiments with pea plants in the 1850s. Mendel's work, though not widely read during his lifetime, was rediscovered at the turn of the 20th century, energizing a rising eugenics movement in the United States.

use the latest CRISPR techniques — new and improved methods that have much lower rates of off-target effects.

Church also noted that many people originally objected to in vitro fertilization (IVF) — the joining of egg and sperm in a laboratory rather than a human womb — until it was shown to be safe.[19]

Alta Charo, a professor of law and bioethics at the University of Wisconsin, Madison, acknowledges that the risks are more far-reaching with germline engineering than with so-called gene therapy techniques in which scientists alter a living patient's nonreproductive genes to treat a genetic disease. Because the genes are nonreproductive, those treatments will not affect the patient's offspring.

"If a mistake only affects an individual, it might be tragic, but only for the individual," Charo says. "If a mistake can affect multiple generations, then the uncertainty is heightened, and there's potential for magnification of the harm. The risk-benefit analysis will look quite different."

However, Charo says, multigenerational effects are not unique to human germline engineering. Exposures to certain environmental pollutants can have epigenetic effects — that is, a chemical in the environment can affect one's genome, thereby altering one's health as well as the health of one's offspring.

Hank Greely, director of the Center for Law and the Biosciences at Stanford University, in Palo Alto, Calif., argues that the medical justification for germline engineering is thin at best. Couples facing genetic diseases in their children can use in vitro fertilization and embryo selection — preimplantation genetic diagnosis, or PGD — to "choose a different embryo that doesn't have the disease," he said.[20]

However, the cost of those techniques — often not covered by health insurance — can be prohibitive for many patients, running about $20,000 for one attempt.[21]

Should human germline engineering be banned on ethical grounds?

Some scientists see a bright ethical line between using CRISPR and other gene-editing technologies in gene therapy — inserting therapeutic treatments in the cells and tissues of adult patients suffering from genetic diseases — and altering the human genetic code by inserting new genes into reproductive cells.

"We need to truly ban this from a moral standpoint," said Eric Lander, a professor of biology at the Massachusetts Institute of Technology. At the very least, Lander said, the moral issue should be fully discussed. "We should forbid this for at least a while — not by law, but by agreement."[22]

"Most people believe that there's no reason to go there," says Sangamo CEO Lanphier. "The only basis would be for enhancement" — in other words, eugenics.

"It's one thing to tinker with corn or mice," Lanphier says. "Humans, however, are a unique species. And as a society, as a culture, it's plain that eugenics is considered as ethically and morally inappropriate."

Darnovsky, from the Center for Genetics and Society, agrees. "People do have a gut instinct. Opinion polls show that most people don't want parents to control the traits that they pass on."

However, Matthew Porteus, a cancer biologist at Stanford, sees controlling children's traits for medical reasons as beneficial if research leads to improved methods and better outcomes. "There is no benefit in my mind of having a child born with a devastating genetic disease," he said.[23]

Other scientists agree that if research advances to the point where scientists can quantify the risks of editing the genome in human embryos, then appropriate risk-benefit

CHRONOLOGY

1850s-1940s *Researchers explore the concept of inherited characteristics.*

1859 English naturalist Charles Darwin's *The Origin of Species* includes the idea of passing on heritable traits.

1866 Austrian monk Gregor Mendel publishes paper on principles of inheritance after experiments on pea plants.

1883 English scientist Francis Galton coins the term eugenics and advocates applying knowledge of inherited traits to improve the human race.

Early 1900s Groups in the United States advocate eugenics, including laws to sterilize criminals and imbeciles.

1933-1945 German Chancellor Adolf Hitler adopts the idea of eugenics to create an Aryan "master race," leads the Nazis to kill some 11 million people, including 6 million Jews.

1950s-1990s *Understanding of genetics and the human genome advances.*

1953 American James Watson and Englishman Francis Crick describe the molecular structure of DNA — a double helix — for which they win the Nobel Prize nine years later.

1972 Scientists recombine DNA from two different species and insert it into a host cell.

1975 Scientists meet in Asilomar, Calif., to discuss concerns with manipulating DNA in living organisms.

1976 National Institutes of Health (NIH) establishes Recombinant DNA Advisory Committee to assess research that mingles DNA from different organisms.

1978 Louise Brown, the world's first test-tube baby, is born in England, the result of in vitro fertilization.

1983 First disease gene — for Huntington's disease — is mapped.

1990 First successful gene therapy clinical trials improve the immune function of children with Severe Combined Immune Deficiency. . . . Scientists develop preimplantation genetic diagnosis (PGD), which allows them to screen embryos fertilized *in vitro* for known genetic diseases before implanting them in the mother's womb.

1996 The birth of Dolly the sheep in Scotland marks the first reported successful cloning of a mammal from an adult cell.

1999 Gene therapy suffers a huge setback with the death of 18-year-old Jesse Gelsinger of Tucson, Ariz., during a clinical trial to test the safety of gene therapy to correct an enzyme defect.

2000-Present *New genetic technology makes it possible to alter the genome of a human embryo, raising safety and ethics questions.*

2000 PGD is used to conceive a "savior sibling," able to donate suitable stem cells to help his sister.

2003 The human genome is completely sequenced by competing groups led by Francis S. Collins, then director of The National Human Genome Research Institute, and Craig Venter, a former NIH scientist who founded Celera Genomics.

2012 American Jennifer Doudna and Frenchwoman Emmanuelle Charpentier develop CRISPR, a gene-editing technique that is faster and cheaper than earlier ones.

2014 Researchers in China successfully edit monkey embryos and bring infant monkeys to term.

2015 Scientists, bioethicists and legal experts meet in Napa, Calif., to discuss responsible uses of the CRISPR technology. In a statement in *Science*, they advocate caution and open discussion. . . . American scientists publish a call in *Nature* for a moratorium on editing human embryos for either research or clinical applications. . . . Chinese researchers use human germline engineering to alter the genome in non-viable human embryos. . . . NIH says it will not approve federal funds for research using human embryos. . . . The National Academy of Sciences is planning to hold an international conference this fall to review current scientific knowledge on germline manipulation, with a goal of devising policy recommendations.

analyses could be done. MIT's Feng points out that the current practice of using in vitro fertilization and embryo selection — PGD — establishes a precedent for editing the genes in human embryos after science achieves an acceptable level of safety and efficacy.

"If there's no way to select a healthy embryo, and we can go in and correct a genetic mutation to prevent severe disease or disability, why wouldn't we?" he asks. "The whole goal is clear: to prevent disease." As for making "superhumans," Feng says, "To make stronger, smarter people? No, I don't support that."

Darnovsky acknowledges that some genetic diseases cannot be prevented with PGD. "But those examples are few and far between," she says. And, she adds, there are other avenues, such as using healthy sperm or egg from a donor so the baby is genetically related to one parent but not to the one with the genetic disease. "Being able to create a healthy baby who is a full relative [of both parents] is a benefit, but it's not a medical necessity," she says.

Beyond the risks, there are two other moral and ethical objections to human germline engineering, says bioethicist Charo. First, she says, there are emotional or instinctive concerns "that we're interfering or altering some essential something to our native selves." Although these are real concerns, their logic is not as easy to analyze as safety issues, she adds, because they have to do with religious or spiritual beliefs.

Charo points out that this is not new: People have similar gut reactions to genetically engineered food, even though little to no evidence exists that it is unhealthy or unsafe. Other objections have to do with controlling human nature. "It's the sense that humans shouldn't have so much control, that things should be left to nature or fate or a deity," Charo says. She says this feeling, even if strong, is also difficult to employ as an argument against moving forward.

The Roman Catholic Church draws a clear boundary between using gene therapy for an individual patient and modifying the human germline. "Whatever genetic modifications are effected on the germ cells of a person will be transmitted to any potential offspring," the Vatican's Congregation for the Doctrine of the Faith, which promulgates Catholic doctrine, stated in 2008. "Because the risks connected to any genetic manipulation are considerable and as yet not fully controllable, in the present state of research, it is not morally permissible to

act in a way that may cause possible harm to the resulting progeny."[24]

Other religious traditions share this objection to experimentation on human embryos because they believe that life begins with fertilization. "I don't think it is right to try to determine an embryo's intrinsic worth by debating when human life begins," said Yuval Levin, a scholar with the Ethics and Public Policy Center, which relies on Judeo-Christian moral traditions to take ethical stands on societal issues. "The protection of human life comes first."[25]

Moreover, he continued, "To the extent that the debate is about whether it is acceptable to destroy a living human being for the purpose of science — even for the purpose of helping other human beings — I think that, in that sense, the embryo is our equal."[26]

Can human germline engineering be regulated worldwide?

With the advent of simpler, more precise gene-editing techniques, the capacity to change the human genome for generations becomes more widely accessible. While 40 countries explicitly ban altering the DNA in human reproductive cells or in embryos, many others — including the United States — do not.

The U.S. Food and Drug Administration (FDA), which monitors clinical trials for new medicines and technologies, and the National Institutes of Health (NIH), which oversees most federally funded biomedical research, restrict research and development of the practice.

Specifically, the FDA must approve any clinical trial of human embryo editing and only after a reasonable expectation of safety has been demonstrated. The NIH severely limits research in human embryos, partly in response to groups that see experimentation with human embryos as unethical because they consider human life as beginning at fertilization. The NIH's recombinant DNA advisory committee, which assesses all research that mingles DNA from different organisms, also reviews any work involving human gene transfers.[27]

Bioethics expert Charo says the current FDA and the NIH policies are sufficient to keep research and development of human germline engineering at bay for now, giving the scientific community and the nation time to debate the issues.[28]

In response to the Chinese human embryo study, NIH Director Francis Collins said the agency will not approve any research study that edits human germline cells at this time.[29]

Others contend that the United States should have a more explicit ban on editing the human genome. Darnovsky of the Center for Genetics and Society, notes that in addition to the individual countries that ban the practice, several international human rights treaties do so as well. "The U.S. is the outlier — it's the only scientifically advanced country that does not prohibit this," he says.

However, it is unclear that an explicit U.S. ban would have any influence on countries that do not have similar policies. And the human embryo experiment in China demonstrates that current policies and international agreements are not sufficient to stop a research lab eager to try the next new thing.

Rumors of the Chinese experiment prompted several prominent U.S. scientists to lead a discussion of what, when and how research on gene editing in human embryos should be done. An editorial in the international journal *Nature* called for an immediate ban on research and development in human genome-editing, says lead author Lanphier, the Sangamo CEO, who has 30 years' experience in the pharmaceutical and biotechnology industry and chairs the Alliance for Regenerative Medicine, a Washington, D.C.-based organization of biotechnology companies involved in gene therapy and stem cell work as well as patient advocacy groups and research institutions. "We called for a moratorium on research until we could have a broad-based, inclusive discussion among scientists and ethicists about whether there's any therapeutic or humanitarian justification to alter the human germline," he says. "We cannot think of any."

Such a moratorium would cover research in human embryos but not in animals, Lanphier says. In the editorial he urges the international scientific community to come together and decide how to proceed.[30]

A second editorial, authored by 18 scientists and bioethicists and published a week later in the international journal *Science*, called for caution but stopped short of recommending a ban on human germline manipulation in research-only scenarios. The authors recommended clear avenues of open communication and transparent research in order to evaluate the efficacy and specificity of CRISPR genome engineering technology, emphasizing that "such research is essential to inform deliberations about what clinical applications, if any, might in the future be deemed permissible."[31]

Some countries, such as China, with extensive biomedical research programs also lack regulations to monitor research practices, including human embryo research, said CRISPR inventor Doudna.[32] She helped convene a conference in January in Napa, Calif., from which the *Science* editorial was developed.

George Annas, a medical ethicist and legal expert at Boston University, said talk of imposing moratoriums or proceeding cautiously can go only so far. As the Chinese experiments demonstrate, he said, "a moratorium comes too late and is unenforceable."[33]

Although most scientists agree bans or moratoriums are unenforceable and would be of questionable influence in countries with lax regulation, a precedent does exist. In 1975, when the powers of genetic engineering first became apparent, more than 100 people gathered in Asilomar, Calif., to discuss the technology's implications and advocated for proceeding with extreme caution.

"We asked at that time that nobody do certain experiments, and in fact nobody did, to my knowledge," said Nobel laureate Baltimore, who attended both the Asilomar conference and this year's Napa conference. The Napa conference participants hoped to assert a similar "moral authority," he said.[34]

BACKGROUND
Early Genetics

Genetics dates back to the 1850s when Austrian monk Gregor Mendel conducted his now-famous pea plant experiments. Before then, people encouraged particular traits in livestock, plants and domestic animals by selecting and breeding individuals with desirable qualities. But it was unknown how those traits were transferred.

Indeed, the English naturalist Charles Darwin based his theory of evolution on the idea that traits are passed on from one generation to the next. He published his scientific treatise on the subject, *The Origin of Species*, in 1859, before Mendel's work was complete. A key feature of his theory was that variation of certain traits within a species — for

Twin Mice May Provide Clues to Cures

Epigenetics is the study of factors beyond DNA that change traits.

Identical twin agouti mice can look very different from each other. That makes them ideal subjects for scientists studying epigenetics, a field that holds promise for understanding human development and treating disease.

Epigenetics is the science of genetic control via factors outside of a person's DNA sequence. Epigenetic factors can determine which genes in a cell get turned on or off. They may explain why some people have an autoimmune disease or why identical twins are not perfectly identical. Such factors are very much a part of normal physiology; they also contribute to disease processes.[1]

As scientists have learned more about epigenetics, they have begun testing medical treatments using that knowledge to treat certain cancers, according to Randy Jirtle, one of the Duke University geneticists involved in the agouti mice study.[2] "The umbrella of epigenetics basically covers and affects every biological field that we have. Every one of them," Jirtle said during a 2014 interview. "We are right now in the process . . . of line-by-line decoding the programs of life. There isn't anything bigger than this. . . . It's that fundamentally important."[3]

The easiest way to see the effects of epigenetics is by differences in identical twins. The cells of identical twins carry exactly the same genome — down to the last DNA "letter." But twins usually have certain physical features that

allow others to tell them apart. They can also develop different diseases — even diseases with a strong genetic component, such as schizophrenia. If one twin has schizophrenia, his or her counterpart has only a 50 percent chance of also developing the disease.[4]

The twin phenomenon has been studied in great detail in agouti mice, a type of rodent that shows striking differences in identical twins. One mouse can be small with brown fur, and its twin can be obese with yellow fur. Because they have identical genomes, scientists have surmised that certain genes get turned on and others do not.

For example, in normal-weight agouti mice, researchers have discovered that a particular gene has been turned off. In 2007, Duke University scientists found that a chemical compound called a methyl group bonded to the DNA at that gene's site and kept the gene from being read. In obese mice, there was no methyl group bonded to that gene, so the gene was active, triggering obesity and yellow coloring.[5]

Environmental influences can alter the amount of DNA methylation, as it's called, and thus affect physical development. Exposing pregnant agouti mice to certain chemicals can alter the degree of DNA methylation in their offspring. For example, when the Duke scientists exposed pregnant mice to bisphenol A (BPA), a chemical that makes plastic hard and clear, the baby mice had less DNA methylation and thus were more likely to be obese than

instance, the size and shape of a finch's beak — provided survival advantages for some finches over others. The inheritance part of his theory said that such advantageous traits would be passed on to the next generation.[35]

However, Darwin had no knowledge of genes. Mendel was the first to methodically study how various traits were inherited, using pea plants as his model organism. He cross-pollinated pea plants with varying characteristics, such as those that bore yellow or green peas and those that produced smooth or wrinkled seeds. Mendel wanted to learn whether a cross-bred baby pea plant would show a blend of its parents' traits — such as yellow-green peas or slightly wrinkled seeds. Instead, he found that the cross-bred plants tended to closely resemble one of the two parental strains.

A primary principle of Mendelian genetics is that some traits are dominant. When Mendel went on to breed his first-generation plants with smooth seeds, he found that some second generation plants produced wrinkled seeds. So, even though smooth seeds are a dominant version of the trait, wrinkled seeds can still show up. It was puzzling that two smooth seed-producing plants could produce a wrinkled seed-producing offspring.

Mendel made careful genealogical charts and noted the frequency of this particular oddity — one in four of the second-generation plants. He hypothesized that pea plants carried some element of the trait from each parent and that one was dominant within each pair of trait elements. But in mixed breeding some offspring inherited

were unexposed mice.[6] A 2010 experiment, in which Australian researchers allowed pregnant agouti mice to drink alcohol, found more DNA methylation at the gene for fur color and other sites.[7]

Agouti mice are a convenient animal model to test the effects of environmental exposure to DNA methylation because the results are easily observed. But it remains unclear what DNA methylation and other epigenetic factors do in developing humans. Many human fetuses get exposed to BPA or alcohol, for instance. But the effects can't be directly studied because to do so in a controlled setting would require exposing one group of women to a harmful substance that might harm their children.

However, a natural experiment in how outside influences affect pregnancies occurred during World War II in Nazi-controlled Netherlands, where food shortages were widespread. Women who went hungry during the last trimester of their pregnancies tended to have babies with low birth weights. Women who suffered from hunger earlier in their pregnancies but were better fed later had normal weight babies. Moreover, the small babies remained underweight, on average, throughout their lives, and the normal-weight babies were more likely to become overweight as adults.

Thus, something about the timing of privation set up susceptibility toward obesity later in life. In addition, the grandchildren of the starved women showed lingering effects, suggesting that some aspect carried on into the next generation.[8]

— *Jill U. Adams*

Genetically identical twin agouti mice can look very different from each other, which makes them ideal subjects for scientists doing epigenetics engineering research.

[1] Nessa Carey, *The Epigenetics Revolution* (2012), pp. 1-10.

[2] "Epigenetics: Expert &A," NOVA ScienceNOW, Nov. 1, 2007, http://tinyurl.com/nelywcn.

[3] "What's Next Health — A Conversation with Randy Jirtle," Robert Wood Johnson Foundation, YouTube, Dec. 1, 2014, http://tinyurl.com/ok6dc9a.

[4] Carey, *op. cit.*, pp. 77-78.

[5] Jill U. Adams, "Obesity, epigenetics, and gene regulation," *Nature Education*, 2008, http://tinyurl.com/797jxqm.

[6] *Ibid.*

[7] Carey, *op. cit.*, p. 95.

[8] *Ibid.*, pp. 2-4.

two of the non-dominant element, resulting in a trait showing up that didn't outwardly exist in either parent.[36]

This theory turned out to be correct. Those trait-carrying elements are now called alleles, which are variant forms of a gene.

Rise of Eugenics

It didn't take long until breeding to encourage desirable traits or discourage undesirable ones was considered in the context of bettering the human race. This notion enchanted many educated people in the late 1800s and early 1900s. Though the proposition took many forms, efforts to improve human characteristics at a population-wide level fell under a single term — eugenics.

Englishman Francis Galton, a distant relation of Darwin who was heavily influenced by Darwin's ideas, coined the word, which means well-born or of good stock. Galton wrote about applying breeding strategies long used in animals to humans. "Consequently, as it is easy . . . to obtain by careful selection a permanent breed of dogs or horses gifted with peculiar powers of running . . .," he wrote, "so it would be quite practicable to produce a highly gifted race of men by judicious marriages during several consecutive generations."[37]

Mendel's work was not widely read during his own lifetime but was rediscovered at the turn of the century, long after his death in 1884. His meticulous scientific depiction of heredity further galvanized the eugenics movement.[38]

Aftermath of Eugenics

German women hold babies in a Nazi eugenics center, in January 1939 (top). Inspired by the American eugenics movement in the early 20th century, Germany's Nazi party, led by Adolf Hitler, took eugenics and the idea of racial purity to a horrifying degree, killing an estimated 11 million people before and during World War II. Hitler sought to create an Aryan "master race" based on Nordic features, such as blue eyes and blond hair. Laura Gerald, chairwoman of North Carolina's Eugenics Compensation Task Force (bottom), announces on Jan. 10, 2012, that the panel voted to pay $50,000 to each surviving person who had been sterilized under the state's now-reviled eugenics program. Soon afterward, state lawmakers passed a law to compensate the victims. More than 7,000 people in North Carolina — mainly African-Americans or poor or disabled people — were sterilized between 1929 and 1976. Eugenics took root in many regions of the United States, partly in response to changes in the American population wrought by waves of immigrants.

The promise of eugenics took root in many regions of the United States as proponents worked to pass laws allowing sterilization or castration of criminals and those classified as imbeciles. By 1909, Indiana, Washington, Connecticut and California had ratified measures to prevent so-called undesirables from procreating.[39] After World War I (1914-1918), the eugenics movement spread, in part in response to changes in the American population after waves of immigrants had arrived in the country.

The purported appeal of keeping certain races pure, particularly Nordic lines, spilled over into immigration policy, leading to strict limits on people coming from Southern Europe and Asia.[40] Eugenics organizations sprouted seemingly everywhere. They included the Race Betterment Foundation in Michigan and the Eugenics Research Association in New York. These groups worked to pass sterilization laws and create registries of pedigreed people.[41] The American Eugenics Society, founded in 1923, soon had 29 local chapters.[42]

In the 1930s and '40s, Germany's Nazi party took eugenics and race-purifying ideas to the ultimate degree, killing an estimated 11 million people, including 6 million Jews. German Chancellor Adolf Hitler, the party's leader, was inspired by the American eugenics movement and came to power with a quest to create an Aryan "master race" based on Nordic features such as blond hair and blue eyes.[43] After revelations about the death camps and other horrors of Hitler's Holocaust, however, eugenics was widely condemned. Several instances of "ethnic cleansing" have occurred since then, including in Rwanda in 1994 and the former Yugoslavia in the 1990s.

Now, the word eugenics is wholly pejorative, since it calls to mind one of the worst periods of human history. The term comes up as a fierce reminder of the potential dangers of new genetic technologies, especially those with the potential to create so-called "designer babies."

In Vitro Fertilization

Louise Brown was born in England on July 25, 1978 — the world's first so-called test-tube baby. An egg extracted from her mother had been successfully fertilized in a laboratory and re-inserted into her mother's womb. Since then an estimated 5 million babies have been born using in vitro fertilization (IVF) — a boon for couples facing infertility.[44]

When that first historic IVF was achieved, critics condemned it as unnatural and immoral. Now the technology is widely practiced and accepted, although it is criticized as available only to the wealthy. A single IVF cycle — often not covered by insurance — costs about $12,000 for a one in three chance of success. That means most women face the cost of multiple cycles.[45]

So far, the cost and difficulty of IVF are high-enough hurdles that the practice is not widespread. Though the number of recipients is rising — approximately 60,000 IVF babies are born in the United States each year — IVF leads to fewer than 2 percent of U.S. births.[46]

IVF produces fertilized embryos that never get implanted. They can be frozen for future use, donated to infertile couples, destroyed or donated for medical research.[47] The NIH allows experiments on human embryos only under certain circumstances. In the 1990s, an advisory group — the Human Embryo Research Panel — took up the question of whether IVF embryos should be covered under existing protections for human subjects in research. They decided protection was warrented if the embryo was to be implanted in a woman's uterus.[48]

In the 1990s, IVF was used to help couples who were carriers of severe genetic diseases, such as Duchenne muscular dystrophy or cystic fibrosis.

Babies inherit one set of chromosomes from the mother and one from the father. The chances that a baby gets a disease-causing combination can be either 1 in 2 or 1 in 4, depending on the disease. Using PGD — or embryo-selection — technology, a single cell is taken from an eight-cell embryo and tested for the presence of a known disease-causing genetic mutation. Only embryos free of mutations are implanted in the mother's womb.[49]

Clinical use of PGD now is used to detect more than 170 conditions.[50] Soon after its introduction, however, PGD became an easy way not only to weed out certain traits, but to select desirable ones. For instance, selecting embryos on the basis of gender is now a choice (at additional cost) for couples undergoing IVF in the United States but is banned for nonmedical reasons in the U.K.[51]

In 2000, the parents of Adam Nash, born in Colorado in 2000, used PGD to design a perfect sibling to help their sick daughter. Using PGD, the parents selected embryos for implantation that met two conditions: They did not have the gene that causes Fanconi anemia and they would be a suitable match for an older sibling with the disease who needed a stem cell transplant. The afflicted girl's bone marrow was diseased; her brother's blood containing healthy stem cells could revive it. The procedure worked, but was controversial as it was considered designing a baby.[52]

Cloning Controversy

Debate triggered by the 1996 revelation that a sheep in Scotland named Dolly was the first successfully cloned mammal has died down to a quiet simmer.

Scientists created Dolly by taking the genetic material from an adult sheep cell and placing it in an unfertilized sheep egg from which the genetic material had been removed. The manipulated egg was then implanted into a surrogate mother sheep and brought to term.

Scientists, ethicists and policymakers across the globe debated Dolly's cloning, partly because of safety and ethical concerns over the procedure itself and partly because of fear that somebody would use a similar procedure to clone a human — a prospect widely viewed then as unsafe and unethical.

Cloning's safety concerns focused on the poor outcomes with mammals, potential harms that are considered unethical to inflict on humans. With mammals, cloning fails more often than it succeeds. Many cloned animals have been born with abnormalities and died within weeks or months.[53] Dolly died at age 6; the average sheep lives 12 years.[54]

Current research efforts are focused on improving the percentage of successes.[55] Today, ranchers and farmers produce cloned livestock with desirable genetics; the animals are used mostly for breeding stock.[56] In 2008 the FDA declared that meat and milk from cloned animals were safe.[57]

Beyond safety concerns, religious conservatives warned that the Dolly experiment could eventually lead to the creation of human embryos never intended for life. Scientists conducting so-called therapeutic cloning create embryos that are a source of embryonic stem cells that could be used to regenerate tissues or organs in human patients. A newer cloning technique developed in 2007 skirts ethical issues over using embryonic cells by directly creating embryonic-like stem cells from skin cells.[58]

In response to recent human embryo studies by Chinese researchers, Francis S. Collins, director of the National Institutes of Health, said the agency will not, at this time, approve any research study that edits human germline cells. The NIH severely limits research in human embryos, partly in response to groups that see experimentation with human embryos as unethical.

As for human cloning, the National Bioethics Advisory Commission in the United States declared it morally unacceptable a year after Dolly's birth. The commission based its position primarily on potential harm to the resulting child. In 2001, the National Academy of Sciences published a report recommending a ban on human cloning, based primarily on safety concerns.[59] Congress held hearings on human cloning but never passed legislation.

Claims of successful human cloning, including by the Raelian religious sect in 2002, have been discredited. The Raelians believe humans were created by extraterrestrials.[60] In 2006, a Korean scientist who claimed he had cloned a human embryo was determined to have fabricated the results of his experiment.[61]

In 2005, the United Nations adopted a resolution banning human cloning in ways that are "incompatible with human dignity."[62] The ban lacked legal force, however, and was ambiguous on therapeutic cloning.[63]

Recombinant DNA

The scientists who met at the 1975 Asilomar conference to discuss the health and environmental risks of manipulating DNA in living organisms focused on DNA combined from different individuals or species — what's known as recombinant DNA. The scientists generally agreed that the new technology — also called genetic engineering — was promising, but more important, they considered whether restrictions were needed on how research and development might progress.

Prior to the conference, Nobel Prize winner Paul Berg, an American biochemist and now professor emeritus at Stanford University, had used a virus to introduce new genes into cells, but the virus was known to cause cancerous tumors in laboratory animals. People were concerned that the virus might escape researchers' control and infect people with a cancer-causing agent. Berg subsequently called for a voluntary moratorium on potentially hazardous recombinant DNA experiments. The tumor-causing virus was later replaced by different viruses and bacteria.

In light of growing concerns, Berg convened the conference, with the backing of the National Academy of Sciences and the National Institutes of Health, and invited a broad array of scientists to talk about whether a moratorium or other regulations were needed to proceed safely and with the public trust.

The NIH also convened a Recombinant DNA Advisory Committee (RAC), which still oversees new genetic technologies.[64]

Twenty years later, Berg reviewed the significant progress made in the field of recombinant DNA since the conference. "The use of the recombinant DNA technology now dominates research in biology," he wrote. "It has altered both the way questions are formulated and the way solutions are sought. The isolation of genes from any organism on our planet, alive or dead, is now routine. Furthermore, the construction of new variants of genes, chromosomes and viruses is standard practice in research laboratories, as is the introduction of genes into microbes, plants and experimental animals."[65]

Indeed, recombinant DNA technology has led to a booming biotechnology industry and to countless advances in biology. It still creates controversy, however, as has occurred with the widespread introduction of genetically engineered foods such as corn, soybeans and wheat.[66]

Insulin for diabetics is another important product resulting from genetically engineered DNA. It was first produced at Genentech, one of the first biotechnology companies, in the late 1970s. The human insulin gene was spliced into a common bacterial strain, which led to more efficient methods of producing insulin. Previously, insulin had been extracted from the pancreatic glands of livestock.[67]

Should human germline engineering be banned?

YES
Marcy Darnovsky
Executive Director, and Jessica Cussins Project Associate, Center for Genetics and Society

Written for *CQ Researcher*, June 2015

Producing genetically modified human beings — engineering the traits of future children — would represent an extreme biological and social experiment, with the altered genes and traits passed on forevermore. Crossing this threshold is medically unnecessary and dangerously unacceptable for seven safety and social reasons:

1. Profound health risks to future children. Genetically modifying the human germline — reproductive cells (sperm, eggs or embryos) — means irreversibly changing every cell in the resulting offspring and all subsequent generations. The risks of such biologically extreme experimentation would be huge, from the early stages of embryonic development through the life span.

2. Thin medical justification. In nearly every case, people at risk of passing on genetic diseases can have healthy and genetically related children without manipulating genes, using the embryo-screening technique known as preimplantation genetic diagnosis or PGD.

3. Treating human beings like engineered products. Who has the right to decide the biological future of another human being? It's one thing for parents to offer their kids opportunities like music lessons or extra coaching; it's quite another to force them into a pre-determined biological mold.

4. Violating the common heritage of humanity. Our shared humanity is the starting point for every struggle for equality. UNESCO's Universal Declaration on the Human Genome and Human Rights, unanimously passed by 77 national delegations, declares that the "human genome underlies the fundamental unity of all members of the human family, as well as the recognition of their inherent dignity and diversity."

5. Undermining the policy agreements among democratic nations. More than 40 countries and the Council of Europe prohibit genetic alterations that extend to future generations. The United States should join this international consensus.

6. Eroding public trust in responsible science. Scientists working on gene therapy and regenerative medicine are rightly worried that germline engineering will provoke a backlash against important scientific efforts to treat disease. We can and should encourage beneficial applications of genetic technologies, and condemn pernicious ones.

7. Reinforcing inequality, discrimination and conflict. The social and commercial dynamics in which human germline modification would develop could exacerbate existing health disparities and take structural inequality to a whole new (molecular) level.

NO
George Church
Professor of Genetics, Harvard Medical School

Written for *CQ Researcher*, June 2015

All new medical technologies are effectively banned from clinical use until proven safe and effective relative to alternatives. Tests in human cells, then animals and then small phase 1 clinical trials must show promise before the Food and Drug Administration OKs larger trials and ultimately general use. Should we ask for a ban on top of that ban — to discourage the usual path to approval? For germline editing, alternatives include preimplantation genetic diagnosis (PGD) or gene therapy after birth using somatic, or nonreproductive, cells.

Those alternatives might turn out to be less safe/effective than germline editing, such as when both parents have only the undesired DNA variants. Also, off-target effects in any of the billions of cells included in post-natal gene therapy could trigger cancer. Sperm precursor cell clusters (each grown from a single engineered cell) screened for zero off-target effects should be a billion times lower-risk than independently modifying billions of cells in somatic gene therapy. Engineered sperm also would avoid the wasted embryos of PGD that many couples find unacceptable.

Society permits many practices that dramatically influence future generations: PGD, vaccines, education, finances and cultural norms. Some of these are reversible in principle, but not in practice. For example, it would be hard to prevent future generations from inheriting automobile technologies, despite the fact that they cause 1.2 million deaths per year worldwide. The issue is not just about "future generations," but about benefits versus risks. To ensure safety, experiments need to be done in an approved order and with great transparency. This sort of testing is not in the far-off future.

As for concerns about changing the genetics of future generations, that is already happening through PGD, so why should germline engineering be treated differently? And it would help those parents who would not benefit from PGD or who have moral objections to creating unimplanted embryos that result from PGD. Wouldn't it impact public trust in science if those who cannot use PGD were prevented from using a safe alternative?

Germline therapy inevitably is no different from other therapies. And it could eventually reduce health care costs and thus health disparities. Moreover, it does not violate human dignity and diversity, as some argue, any more than PGD does. Indeed, the preponderance of countries — nearly 80 percent — have not prejudged the effectiveness of germline therapy by banning it.

Jennifer Doudna, co-creator of the new gene-editing technology CRISPR, acknowledges ethical concerns about manipulating the human genome. But she and other scientists contend that CRISPR can be used in valuable ways that don't involve human embryos, such as developing therapies for use in non-reproductive tissue.

More recently, bacteria have been engineered to do the complex enzymatic work of converting biomass into biofuels, producing more economically viable alternatives to fossil fuels.[68] Bacteria are used in genetic engineering because they have small genomes that are easy to manipulate. They also can be grown in industrial-size petri dishes where they serve as mini factories for making medicines or biofuels.

The first genetically engineered or transgenic mouse was created in the mid-1970s, proving that it could be done and opening the door to breeding mice with specific genetic signatures.[69] Now there are hundreds of strains of mice available from companies that breed the rodents for scientific research.[70]

Once scientists figured out how to splice genes into mammalian tissue and get the genes to function as desired, they began focusing on gene therapy. The first attempts at gene therapy in humans occurred in the 1990s but were limited to manipulating the genome in adult somatic — nonreproductive — cells, such as blood cells, and not in human germline cells.[71]

Now the latest genetic engineering techniques, including CRISPR and zinc finger nucleases, allow editing of individual genes, so researchers can delete a gene and replace it with any gene of choice. Since CRISPR was first described in 2012 it has been used by scientists to alter the embryos of fruit flies, silkworms, zebrafish, frogs, mice, rats and rabbits, all being used for research.[72]

CURRENT SITUATION
Regulatory Holes

When Nobel Prize winner Berg, CRISPR co-inventor Doudna and a large group of other scientists, bioethicists and legal experts met at the January conference in Napa, they discussed responsible uses of CRISPR technology and noted that neither the FDA nor the NIH regulate research in private laboratories. Those labs could manipulate human embryos using CRISPR, as the Chinese did.

From the discussions — and in response to rumors that human germline engineering was being conducted in laboratories outside of China — some conference participants called for a moratorium on editing the human embryo genome for clinical applications in opinion pieces in U.K.-based *Nature* and U.S.-based *Science*. But they differed on whether research on human embryos — without bringing a child into the world — should be permitted.

But Doudna said even if scientists from developed countries agree on how best to regulate human germline engineering, it is unclear whether that would have any impact on other countries. "Can we police their activities? Absolutely not," said Doudna. "Can we get buy-in from leading scientists around the world by people they respect in the U.S.? I think that's possible. Is it probable? I don't know."[73]

NIH's Recombinant DNA Advisory Committee, which oversees gene transfer experiments and reviews proposals for federal research funding, monitors gene editing experiments in human non-reproductive cells. The panel made clear in 2002 that it would not consider proposals involving modifying the human germline. While private companies need not get approval from the committee, they are encouraged to do so.[74]

FDA policies guide human experiments involving genetically modified cells, but the agency does not have regulations explicitly covering human germline alterations.[75] Indeed, current FDA policy is restricted to gene therapy — using adult non-reproductive cells — with no mention of the use of reproductive cells.[76]

Advocates of banning human germline engineering say this regulatory patchwork is troublesome. NIH's policies don't cover privately funded research, and FDA policy does not mention gene transfer protocols in human embryos.[77]

Proponents of a more explicit U.S. policy on human germline engineering highlight the fact that a variety of international groups have taken clear and firm stands. For instance, the United Nations adopted a statement with a testament to the dignity of the human genome, including this line: "In a symbolic sense, it is the heritage of humanity."[78]

The Council of Europe stated: "An intervention seeking to modify the human genome may only be undertaken for preventive, diagnostic or therapeutic purposes and only if its aim is not to introduce any modification in the genome of any descendants."[79]

Human Research

The lead researcher for the Chinese team that used a new genetic technology to edit the human embryo genome defends his work as providing meaningful scientific data.

"We wanted to show our data to the world so people know what really happened with this model, rather than just talking about what would happen without data," said Junjiu Huang of Sun Yat-sen University in Guangzhou.[80] He said he used nonviable embryos to skirt the ethical issues around human germline engineering.

In fact, their findings were mostly negative, he said. The attempted editing was successful in only 14 percent of embryos. "If you want to do it in normal embryos, you need to be close to 100 percent," Huang says. "That's why we stopped. We still think it's too immature."[81]

The researchers also reported mosaic and off-target effects, meaning edited genes varied among cells of growing embryos and some genes were unintentionally edited.

"I believe this is the first report of CRISPR . . . applied to human pre-implantation embryos and, as such, the study is a landmark, as well as a cautionary tale," said Harvard stem-cell researcher Daley. "Their study should be a stern warning to any practitioner who thinks the technology is ready for testing to eradicate disease genes."[82]

Medical ethicist Annas of Boston University says neither the negative results nor the scientists' rationales justify their work. "The fact that the researchers think that they followed ethical guidelines simply speaks to their inability to take the ethics of human embryo research seriously," said Annas.[83]

Meanwhile, rumors persist of other human embryo experiments underway. "I do worry about stuff like designer babies because it feels like there's this shift towards this use of the technology becoming more of a reality," said

Paul Knoepler, a stem-cell researcher at the University of California, Davis. "But then [this] paper" — the Chinese study in human embryos — "makes me think that would probably be sort of disastrous."[84]

OUTLOOK
Life's Blueprints

No one can be sure how the debate over human germline engineering will unfold over the next decade. In the past, some new genetic technologies have become widely adopted and others, such as human cloning, have been halted over safety concerns.

Human germline engineering could follow the path of genetic engineering, which has moved forward by leaps and bounds, or fail to progress because of safety issues.

At a conference in Atlanta in May, called Biotech and the Ethical Imagination or BEINGS, featured panelists ranged from the science fiction author Margaret Atwood to Harvard psychology professor Steven Pinker. Like the Napa and Asilomar conferences, BEINGS was primarily about holding open discussions and coming to some kind of consensus statement on what checks and balances should be applied to research that gets involved with the blueprints of life on Earth.

"They're pinning down the questions that need to be asked — it's a conversation that has to happen," Atwood said. "In the end, we're trying to decide what kind of house we all want to live in."[85]

Other conversations are taking place in religious circles. Some Catholics object to any manipulation of embryos, arguing that they have intrinsic value equivalent to that of fetuses, children and adults. A recent article in the *National Catholic Register* states, "In truth, embryonic stem-cell research, human cloning and, now, the tinkering with the DNA of future generations would not be possible without the manufacturing of human life in the laboratory. Let us not forget that the 86 embryos used in [Chinese scientist] Huang's research were created by IVF. Many argue that these 86 lives were abnormal, so it was permissible to destroy them in research. The Church resoundingly rejects that argument — because every human life is valuable."[86]

Some scientists call for a more formal examination of the safety and ethical issues involved in modifying the human germline. The National Academy of Sciences, known for its objective policy studies and reports, has announced plans to hold an international summit on the topic this fall where a panel of experts will review current scientific knowledge on germline manipulation, with a goal of devising policy recommendations.[87]

"I think that in 10 years there will be dramatic improvement in the technology and development of similar but better technologies in the sense of efficiency and safety," says autism researcher Feng. "We probably will see quite a few clinical trials based on these new technologies in stem cells or somatic cells to correct genetic mutations that cause severe disorders."

Bioethicist Charo says, "I can honestly say that I am not sure, except to be certain that the technology will have advanced in precision and accuracy, and that the range of potential applications will expand accordingly."

NOTES

1. David Cyranoski and Sara Reardon, "Chinese scientists genetically modify human embryos," *Nature News & Comment*, April 22, 2015, http://tinyurl.com/kjv6hxh.

2. "Public interest group condemns human germline modification efforts, supports research moratorium, calls for US prohibition," Center for Genetics and Society, March 19, 2015. http://tinyurl.com/nfn7ehr.

3. Andrew Pollack, "A powerful new way to edit DNA," *The New York Times*, March 3, 2014, http://tinyurl.com/nqvj9xz.

4. Christina Larson and Amanda Schaffer, "Genome editing," *MIT Technology Review*, April 23 2015, http://tinyurl.com/porh76w.

5. Robin McKie, "Scientists clone adult sheep," *The Guardian*, Feb. 23, 1997, http://tinyurl.com/nwch6qa.

6. "Worldwide reproductive cloning bans," Women's Bioethics Project, May 2009, http://tinyurl.com/o6mtrvj.

7. "Genetically Modified Humans? Seven Reasons to Say 'No,' " Center for Genetics and Society, May 7, 2015, http://tinyurl.com/nffjsrv.

8. Quoted in Andrew Pollack, "Jennifer Doudna, a Pioneer Who Helped Simplify Genome Editing," *The New York Times*, May 11, 2015, http://tinyurl.com/n28klgk. Douda's co-inventor was Emmanuelle Charpentier, a professor at the Helmholtz Centre for Infection Research and the Hannover Medical School in Germany and the Laboratory for Molecular Infection Medicine at Umeå University, Sweden.

9. Quoted in David Cyranoski, "Ethics of embryo editing divides scientists," *Nature News & Comment*, March 18, 2015, http://tinyurl.com/oohkfrn.

10. "Cystic Fibrosis," Genetic Science Learning Center, undated, http://tinyurl.com/ojagc5u.

11. Pollack, "A powerful new way to edit DNA," *op. cit.*

12. "Genetically Modified Humans? Seven Reasons to Say 'No,' " *op. cit.*

13. Larson and Schaffer, *op. cit.*

14. Cyranoski and Reardon, *op. cit.*

15. Quoted in Dan Vergano and Azeen Ghorayshi, "Chinese study of human embryos raises fears of designer babies," *BuzzFeed News*, April 22, 2015, http://tinyurl.com/pdm6byx.

16. Quoted in C. Simone Fishburn, "Strategy: Lines in the sand," *BioCentury*, March 26, 2015, http://tinyurl.com/nwel5o7.

17. Cyranoski, "Ethics of embryo editing divides scientists," *op. cit.*

18. Quoted in Tina Hesman Saey, "Editing Human Germline Cells Sparks Ethics Debate," *Science News*, May 6, 2105, http://tinyurl.com/pwen9e9.

19. Cyranoski, "Ethics of embryo editing divides scientists," *op. cit.*

20. Quoted in Larson and Schaffer, "Genome editing," *op. cit.*

21. Jennifer Gerson Uffalussy, "The Cost of IVF: 4 things I learned while battling infertility," *Forbes*, Feb. 6, 2014, http://tinyurl.com/pffqax3.

22. Quoted in Fishburn, *op. cit.*

23. Quoted in Hesman Saey, "Editing Human Germline Cells Sparks Ethics Debate," *Science News*, *op. cit.*

24. "Instruction Dignitas Personae on Certain Bioethical Questions," Congregation for the Doctrine of the Faith, Sept. 8, 2008, http://tinyurl.com/4fkxm2.

25. "The Case Against Embryonic Stem Cell Research: An interview with Yuval Levin," Pew Research Center, July 17, 2008, http://tinyurl.com/obcvytz.

26. *Ibid.*

27. The webmaster of Gene Therapy Net, D.A. Bleijs, PhD, has a scientific background in molecular biology and immunology.

28. Francis S. Collins, "Statement on NIH funding of research using gene-editing technologies in human embryos," National Institutes of Health, April 29, 2015, http://tinyurl.com/mf7jz3q.

29. Edward Lanphier *et al.*, "Don't edit the human germ line," *Nature News & Comment*, March 26, 2015, http://tinyurl.com/pwplupo.

30. David Baltimore *et al.*, "A prudent path forward for genomic engineering and germline gene modification," *Science*, April 3, 2015, http://tiny url.com/onql89f.

31. Fishburn, *op. cit.*

32. Quoted in Vergano and Ghorayshi, *op. cit.*

33. Quoted in Nicholas Wade, "Scientists Seek Ban on Method of Editing the Human Genome," *The New York Times*, March 19, 2015, http://tinyurl.com/od9dsuy.

34. Steven Potter, *Designer Genes* (2010), p. 5.

35. Ilona Miko, "Gregor Mendel and the principles of inheritance," *Nature Education*, 2008, http://tinyurl.com/22rc6oa.

36. Steven Potter, *Designer Genes* (2010), p. 136.

37. Edwin Black, *War Against the Weak* (2003), p. 27.

38. *Ibid.*, pp. 63-68.

39. "Eugenics movement reaches its height," PBS, http://tinyurl.com/3zca5.

40. Edwin Black, *War Against the Weak* (2003), pp. 87-90.

41. PBS, *op. cit.*

42. Black, *op. cit.*, pp. 270-276.

43. Kate Brian, "The amazing story of IVF: 35 years and five million babies later," *The Guardian*, July 12, 2013, http://tinyurl.com/qcxur63.

44. Gerson Uffalussy, *op. cit.*

45. Michaeleen Doucleff, "IVF Baby Boom: Births from Fertility Procedures Hit New High," NPR, Feb. 18, 2014, http://tinyurl.com/q5d67bq.

46. Laura Beil, "What happens to extra embryos after IVF?" CNN, Sept. 1, 2009, http://tinyurl.com/qcq7d55.

47. Rebecca Dresser, "Genetic Modification of Preimplantation Embryos: Toward Adequate Human Research Policies," *The Milbank Quarterly*, March 2004, Vol. 82, No. 1, http://tinyurl.com/pzor2eg.

48. Potter, *op. cit.*, p. 9.

49. Leslie Pray, "Embryo Screening and the Ethics of Human Engineering," *Nature Education*, 2008, http://tinyurl.com/lrlyyvz.

50. Peter Braude *et al.*, "Preimplantation Genetic Diagnosis," *Nature Reviews Genetics*, December 2002, http://tinyurl.com/oy7ywvu.

51. Potter, *op. cit.*

52. D. Elsner, "Just another reproductive technology? The ethics of human reproductive cloning as an experimental medical procedure," *Journal of Medical Ethics*, 2006, http://tinyurl.com/ogjj8ua.

53. For background, see Brian Hansen, "Cloning Debate," *CQ Researcher*, Oct. 22, 2004, pp. 877-900.

54. "First cloned sheep Dolly dies at 6," CNN.com, Feb. 14, 2003, http://tinyurl.com/pythgpb.

55. Juliano Rodrigues Sangali *et al.*, "Development to Term of Cloned Cattle Derived from Donor Cells Treated with Valproic Acid," PLoS ONE, June 24, 2014, http://tinyurl.com/q3ur8am.

56. Juliette Michel, "US Company in Iowa churns out 100 cloned cows a year," *The Tico Times*, June 29, 2014, http://tinyurl.com/q6sl8lg.

57. "Cloning," National Human Genome Research Institue, June 2015, http://tinyurl.com/po2vypz.

58. Andrew Pollack, "Cloning is Used to Create Embryonic Stem Cells," *The New York Times*, May 15, 2013, http://tinyurl.com/p7g65q9.

59. "Cloning/Embryonic Stem Cells," National Human Genome Research Institute, April 2006, http://tinyurl.com/apry7.

60. Anne Berryman, "Who are the Raelians?" *Time*, Jan. 4, 2003, http://tinyurl.com/po5jwj2.

61. "Timeline of a controversy," *Nature News and Comment*, Dec. 19, 2005, http://tinyurl.com/oswju6d.

62. Timothy Caulfield, "Human cloning a decade after Dolly," *Canadian Medical Association Journal*, Feb. 27, 2007, http://tinyurl.com/nurprxq.

63. Colum Lynch, "U.N. Backs Human Cloning Ban," *The Washington Post*, March 9, 2009, http://tinyurl.com/4su4zw.

64. Nelson Wivel, "Historical Perspectives Pertaining to the NIH Recombinant DNA Advisory Committee," *Human Gene Therapy*, January 2014, http://tinyurl.com/pdyww3k.

65. Paul Berg and Maxine Singer, "The recombinant DNA controversy: Twenty years later," The Proceedings of the National Academy of Sciences, September 1995, http://tinyurl.com/pdyww3k.

66. For background, see Jason McLure, "Genetically Modified Food," *CQ Researcher*, Aug. 31, 2012, pp. 717-740.

67. "First Successful Laboratory Production of Human Insulin Announced," press release, Genentech, Sept. 6, 1978, http://tinyurl.com/pwpo3b6. Also see Erika Gebel, "Making insulin," *Diabetes Forecast*, July 2013, http://tinyurl.com/nmb4pho.

68. Kevin Bullis, "Genetically Modified Bacteria Produce 50 Percent More Fuel," *MIT Technology Review*, Oct. 3, 2013, http://tinyurl.com/nncktmn.

69. For background, see David Masci, "Designer Humans," *CQ Researcher*, May 18, 2001, pp. 425-440.

70. "Catalog of Transgenic Mice," The Jackson Laboratory, accessed June 8, 2015, http://tinyurl.com/owbnatt.

71. Masci, *op. cit.*

72. Jeffrey D. Sander and J. Keith Joung, "Crispr-Cas systems for editing, regulating and targeting genomes," *Nature Biotechnology*, March 2014, http://tinyurl.com/omj4pbl.

73. Quoted in Fishburn, *op. cit.* Susan Young Rojahn, "Monkeys Modified with Genome Editing," *MIT Technology Review*, Jan. 30, 2014, http://tinyurl.com/nf589s6.

74. Dresser, *op. cit.*

75. *Ibid.*

76. "Guidance for Industry: Guidance for Human Somatic Cell Therapy and Gene Therapy," U.S. Food and Drug Administration, March 1998, http://tinyurl.com/cooum73.

77. "Genetically Modified Humans? Seven Reasons to Say 'No,'" *op. cit.*

78. "Universal Declaration on the Human Genome and Human Rights," UNESCO, Nov. 11, 1997, http://tinyurl.com/y8mhezy.

79. "Convention for the Protection of Human Rights and Dignity of the Human Being with regard to the Application of Biology and Medicine: Convention on Human Rights and Biomedicine," Council on Europe, Dec. 1, 2009, http://tinyurl.com/ns4shn3.

80. Quoted in Cyranoski and Reardon, *op. cit.*

81. *Ibid.*

82. *Ibid.*

83. *Ibid.*

84. *Ibid.*

85. Quoted in Azeen Ghorayshi, "Does Biotech Need Limits?" *BuzzFeed News*, May 19, 2015, http://tinyurl.com/klcf7ob.

86. Rebecca Taylor, "It's Time to Become Pro-life 3.0," *National Catholic Register*, May 12, 2015, http://tinyurl.com/pahbqzj.

87. "National Academy of Sciences and National Academy of Medicine announce initiative on human gene editing," National Academy of Sciences, May 18, 2015, http://tinyurl.com/q4z66u4.

BIBLIOGRAPHY
Selected Sources
Books

Black, Edwin, *War Against the Weak: Eugenics and America's Campaign to Create a Master Race*, Four Walls Eight Windows, 2003.
An investigative journalist gives an in-depth account of the eugenics movement in the United States in the first part of the 20th century.

Carey, Nessa, *The Epigenetics Revolution: How Modern Biology Is Rewriting Our Understanding of Genetics, Disease, and Inheritance,* **Columbia University Press, 2012.**
A specialist in genetics and molecular biology uses her scientific background to write about epigenetics, which explains some curiosities of life and provides new ways to understand disease.

Krimsky, Sheldon, and Jeremy Gruber, eds., *Biotechnology in Our Lives: What Modern Genetics Can Tell You About Assisted Reproduction, Human Behavior, Personalized Medicine, and Much More,* **Skyhorse Publishing, 2013.**
Two leaders of the Council for Responsible Genetics, a social scientist and a lawyer, offer a collection of essays on current issues in biotechnology from their organization's publication *GeneWatch.*

Lewis, Ricki, *The Forever Fix: Gene Therapy and the Boy Who Saved It,* **St. Martin's Press, 2012.**
A science writer provides compelling narratives about the failures and successes of early gene therapy trials.

Potter, Steven, *Designer Genes: A New Era in the Evolution of Man,* **Random House, 2010.**
A developmental biologist writes on the science and ethics of humans manipulating their own genomes.

Articles

Baltimore, David, *et al.,* **"A prudent path forward for genomic engineering and germline gene modification,"** *Science,* **April 3, 2015, http://tinyurl.com/onql89f.**
A group of scientists and ethicists write a position statement on restricting human germline engineering.

Cyranoski, David, "Ethics of embryo editing divides scientists," *Nature News & Comment,* **March 18, 2015, http://tinyurl.com/n998l7h.**
Cyranoski delineates the range of views that U.S. scientists hold about restrictions on gene editing in human embryos.

Cyranoski, David, and Sara Reardon, "Chinese scientists genetically modify human embryos," *Nature News & Comment,* **April 22, 2015, http://tinyurl.com/kjv6hxh.**

The authors report on Chinese researchers who claim to have altered the genomes of human embryos — a scientific first.

Fishburn, C. Simone, "Strategy: Lines in the sand," *BioCentury,* **March 26, 2015, http://tinyurl.com/nwel5o7.**
A trade magazine reviews various calls by scientists to build consensus on restricting human germline modification.

Ghorayshi, Azeen, "Does Biotech Need Limits?" *BuzzFeed News,* **May 19, 2015, http://tinyurl.com/klcf7ob.**
Scientists, bioethicists and forward thinkers (including novelist Margaret Atwood) gathered for wide-ranging conversations about the goals and limits of 21st-century biotechnology.

Lanphier, Edward, *et al.,* **"Don't edit the human germ line,"** *Nature News & Comment,* **March 26, 2015, http://tinyurl.com/pwplupo.**
A group of scientists and bioethicists call for a moratorium on human germline engineering for both research and clinical purposes.

Regalado, Antonio, "Engineering the perfect baby," *MIT Technology Review,* **March 5, 2015, http://tinyurl.com/ktv7e5c.**
A science reporter describes in depth how new gene-editing techniques might be used in human embryos — and talks with scientists who are interested in such research.

Taylor, Rebecca, "It's time to become pro-life 3.0," *National Catholic Register,* **May 12, 2015, http://tinyurl.com/owuhv9f.**
Catholic publication outlines possible religious objections to genetic engineering, based on the sanctity of human life.

Young, Susan, "Genome Surgery," *MIT Technology Review,* **Feb. 11, 2015, http://tinyurl.com/m28mrcf.**
Young reports on new tools that have opened up options for gene editing.

Reports and Studies

Berg, Paul, and Maxine Singer, "The recombinant DNA controversy: Twenty years later," *The Proceedings*

of the National Academy of Sciences, September 1995, http://tinyurl.com/oyjg2fh.
Two scientists discuss the landmark Asilomar Conference, an early gathering of scientists and others to discuss recombinant DNA and its impact on advances in genetic technology within a societal context.

Liang, Puping, *et al.*, "CRISPR/Cas9-mediated gene editing in human tripronuclear zygotes," *Protein and Cell*, May 2015, pp. 363-372, http://tinyurl.com/pdsf562.
Researchers in China say that they have used the CRISPR gene-editing technique to alter the genome of human embryos.

For More Information

Alliance for Regenerative Medicine, 525 Second St., NE, Washington, DC 20002; 202-568-6240; http://alliancerm.org. Global advocacy group for regenerative and advanced therapies; fosters research, development and commercialization of treatments.

Center for Genetics and Society, 1936 University Ave., Suite 350, Berkeley, CA 94704; 510-665-7760; www.geneticsandsociety.org. Information and public affairs organization that encourages responsible uses and effective societal governance of human genetic and reproductive technologies.

Ethics and Public Policy Center, 1730 M St., N.W., Suite 910, Washington, DC 20036; 202-682-1200; http://eppc.org/. A think tank that applies Judeo-Christian moral tradition to public policy issues in the United States.

Innovative Genomics Initiative, 188 Li Ka Shing Center, Berkeley, CA 94720; 510-664-7110; innovativegenomics.org. Collective of laboratories working together toward common research goals in genome engineering and genetic editing.

National Academy of Sciences, 2101 Constitution Ave., N.W., Washington, DC 20418; 202-334-2000; www.nasonline.org/. Private organization of America's leading researchers; publishes policy reports with science-based advice.

National Institutes of Health, Office of Science Policy, 6705 Rockledge Dr., Suite 750, Bethesda, MD 20817; 301-496-9838; http://osp.od.nih.gov. Advises the NIH director on matters of significance to the agency, the research community and the public.

Sangamo BioSciences Inc., Point Richmond Tech Center II, 501 Canal Blvd., Richmond, CA 94804; 510-970-6000; www.sangamo.com. Biopharmaceutical company focused on the research, development and commercialization of engineered zinc finger DNA-binding proteins targeting genetic and infectious diseases.

Stanford Center for Biomedical Ethics, 1215 Welch Rd., Modular A, Stanford, CA 94305; 650-723-5760; http://bioethics.stanford.edu/. Research and education center that serves as a scholarly resource for emerging ethical issues in medicine.

12

Free Speech at Risk

Alan Greenblatt

Egyptian political satirist Bassem Youssef arrives at the public prosecutor's office in Cairo on March 31, 2013. Police questioned Youssef for allegedly insulting then-President Mohammed Morsi and Islam. The government filed charges against hundreds of Egyptian journalists but dropped them earlier this month. Free-speech advocates worry that journalists, bloggers and democracy supporters worldwide are being intimidated into silence.

KHALED DESOUKI/AFP/Getty Images

From *CQ Researcher*,
April 26, 2013; updated February 2016.

It wasn't an April Fool's joke. On April 1, 2013, "Daily Show" host Jon Stewart defended Egyptian political satirist Bassem Youssef, who had undergone police questioning for allegedly insulting then-President Mohammed Morsi and Islam.

"That's illegal? Seriously? That's illegal in Egypt?" Stewart said on his Comedy Central show. "Because if insulting the president and Islam were a jailable offense here, Fox News go bye-bye."

Stewart was kidding, but Youssef's case drew attention from free-speech advocates who worried Egypt's nascent democracy was according no more respect toward freedom of expression than the regime it had replaced.

The U.S. Embassy in Cairo, which had linked to Stewart's broadcast on its Twitter feed, temporarily shut down the feed after Egyptian authorities objected to it. Egypt's nascent government also filed charges against hundreds of journalists, although Morsi subsequently asked that they all be dropped.

Freedom of the press became even more restricted, however, two years later when Morsi's successor, Abdel Fattah al-Sisi, enacted a new counterterrorism law making it a crime to publish or promote news about terrorism that contradicts the government's statements.[1]

Concerns are widespread that commentators, journalists, bloggers — and, yes, even comedians — are being intimidated into silence and increasingly imprisoned or killed. And not just in Egypt.

Free speech, once seen as close to an absolute right in some countries, is conflicting with other values, such as security, the

Democracies Enjoy the Most Press Freedom

Democracies such as Finland, Norway and the Netherlands have the most press freedom, while authoritarian regimes such as Turkmenistan, North Korea and Eritrea have the least, according to Reporters Without Borders' 2012 index of global press freedom. European and Islamic governments have enacted or considered new press restrictions after a recent phone-hacking scandal in Britain and Western media outlets' irreverent images of the Prophet Muhammad triggered deadly protests by Muslims. Myanmar (formerly Burma), which recently enacted democratic reforms, has reached its greatest level of press freedom ever, the report said.

Press Freedom Worldwide, 2013

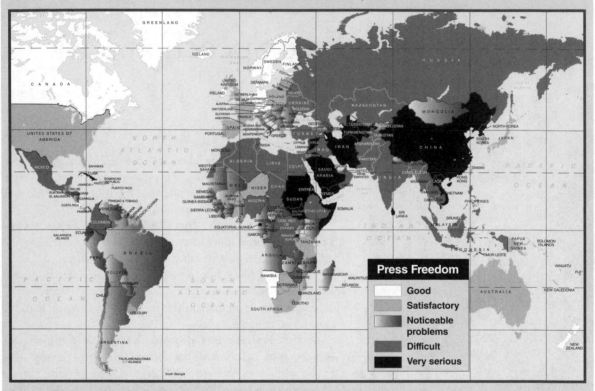

Source: "Freedom of the Press Worldwide in 2013," Reporters Without Borders, http://index.rsf.org/#!/

protection of children and the desire not to offend religious sensibilities, not just in the Middle East but in much of the world, including Western Europe.

In many cases, freedom of speech is losing. "Free speech is dying in the Western world," asserts Jonathan Turley, a George Washington University law professor. "The decline of free speech has come not from any single blow but rather from thousands of paper cuts of well-intentioned exceptions designed to maintain social harmony."[2]

In an era when words and images can be transmitted around the world instantaneously by anyone with a cell phone, even some American academics argue that an absolutist view of First Amendment protections couldn't be expected to prevail. Several made that case after protests broke out in several Muslim countries in September 2012 over an American-made video uploaded to YouTube defamed the Prophet Muhammad.

Even the administration of President Obama, who defended the nation's free-speech traditions before the United Nations that month in the wake of video backlash, supported a 2011 U.N. resolution to create an international standard to restrict some anti-religious speech. And, under Obama, the Justice Department has prosecuted a record number of government employees who have leaked sensitive documents, discouraging potential whistleblowers from exposing government waste, fraud or abuse.[3]

"Wherever you look, you see legislation or other measures seeking to reassert state control over speech and the means of speech," says John Kampfner, author of the 2010 book *Freedom for Sale*.

In the United Kingdom and Australia, government ministers in 2013 proposed that media outlets be governed by new regulatory bodies with statutory authority. Facing opposition, the UK set up a process to oversee "self-regulation" by the press and Australian officials backed off. [4]

A 2010 media law in Hungary created a regulatory council with wide-ranging powers to grant licenses to media outlets and assess content in a way that Human Rights Watch says compromises press freedom.[5]

"Not only is legislation such as this bad in and of itself, but it is crucial in sending a green light to authoritarians who use these kind of measures by Western states to say, whenever they are criticized by the West, 'Hey, you guys do the same,'" says Kampfner, former CEO of Index on Censorship, a London-based nonprofit group that fights censorship.

Some observers have hoped the growth of social media and other technologies that spread information faster and more widely than previously thought possible could act as an automatic bulwark protecting freedom of expression. "The best example of the impact of technology on free speech is to look at the Arab Spring," says Dan Wallach, a computer scientist at Rice University, referring to the series of upheavals starting in 2011 that led to the fall of autocratic leaders in Tunisia, Egypt, Yemen and Libya.[6]

But as studies by Wallach and many others show, countries such as China and Iran have been building firewalls to block sensitive information and track dissidents.[7] "The pattern seems to be that governments that fear mass movements on the street have realized that they might want to be able to shut off all Internet communications in the country and have started building the infrastructure that enables them to do that," said Andrew McLaughlin, a former White House adviser on technology.[8]

In January 2013, a French court ordered Twitter to help identify people who had tweeted racist or anti-Semitic remarks, or face fines of 1,000 euros (about $1,300) per day. The San Francisco-based company refused to comply, citing First Amendment protections for free speech.[9]

But even though Twitter appealed the French court order, the microblogging site just two months previously had blocked the account of a neo-Nazi group called Besseres Hannover, or Better Hanover, which had been charged with inciting racial hatred. Twitter said it was the first time it had used technology to monitor and withhold content based on a given country's concerns and laws.

And in late 2015, Twitter published guidelines regarding the removal and moderation of hostile or offensive language. The company thereby further inflamed the debate over freedom of speech, particularly earlier this year when it stripped the verification status of a controversial journalist for violating those rules.[10]

Meanwhile, government arrests of journalists and mob attacks against them continue to rise. Journalists are being arrested more often than in previous years in countries such as Russia and Turkey, and increasingly murdered in countries like Syria and Turkey. In 2012, mobs attacked journalists in Mali and Canada — among other countries — for what the protesters perceived as their blasphemous coverage of Islam. Blasphemy prosecutions have become more common, especially in predominantly Islamic countries such as Pakistan, where blasphemy laws apply only to comments about Islam or Muhammad, not to derogatory comments about Christianity, Judaism or other world religions.[11]

"There have been attempts to pass so-called religious-sensibility laws, which are, in fact, a way of curbing press freedom and expression," says Robert Mahoney, director of the Committee to Protect Journalists, a New York-based nonprofit group that promotes press freedom.

In one widely covered case, three members of the Russian punk rock band Pussy Riot were found guilty of hooliganism motivated by religious hatred in 2012. They had been arrested after a performance in Moscow's main cathedral, in which they profanely called for the Virgin Mary to protect Russia against Vladimir Putin, who was returned to the presidency soon after the performance.

Number of Journalists Killed on the Rise

Seventy journalists were killed in 2012, nearly half of them murdered, a 43 percent increase from 2011. A total of 232 journalists were imprisoned in 2012, the highest number since the Committee to Protect Journalists began keeping track in 1990. Experts say a select group of countries has fueled the increase by cracking down on criticism of government policies.

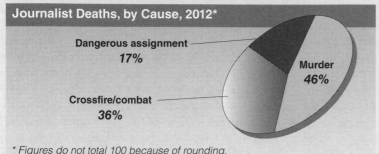

Journalist Deaths, by Cause, 2012*

Dangerous assignment
17%

Murder
46%

Crossfire/combat
36%

* Figures do not total 100 because of rounding.

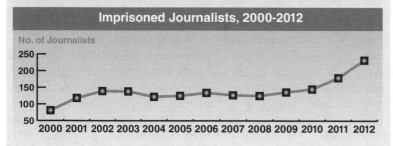

Imprisoned Journalists, 2000-2012

No. of Journalists

2000 2001 2002 2003 2004 2005 2006 2007 2008 2009 2010 2011 2012

Source: "Attacks on the Press," Committee to Protect Journalists, 2013, www.cpj.org/attacks/

As people monitor the health of free expression around the globe, here are some of the questions they're debating:

Has technology made speech freer?

As Arab protesters took to the streets — and the Internet — in 2011 in countries such as Tunisia and Egypt, everyone from commentators for serious foreign-policy journals to "The Daily Show" asked whether the world was witnessing a "Twitter revolution."

Social-media sites such as Twitter and Facebook were used by activists both as organizing tools and as a means of communication with the outside world.

Tunisians got an alternative picture from Facebook, which remained uncensored through the protests, and they communicated events to the rest of the world by posting videos to YouTube and Dailymotion," Ethan Zuckerman, a researcher at Harvard University's Berkman Center for Internet and Society, wrote in 2011. "It's likely that news of demonstrations in other parts of the country disseminated online helped others conclude that it was time to take to the streets."[13]

The three were sentenced to two years in a prison colony, but one member was released on probation before being sent to prison.[12]

In more open societies, laws meant to protect against hate speech, Holocaust denial and offenses against religious sensibilities also can end up limiting what people can talk and write about.

Free-speech laws traditionally have been about the protection of unpopular and provocative expression. Popular and uncontroversial opinions usually need no protection. But in the past several years, free-speech protections have been fading away.

"The new restrictions are forcing people to meet the demands of the lowest common denominator of accepted speech," Turley contends.

Unquestionably, new-media tools have made it easier for activists to spread their messages farther and faster than was conceivable during the days of the mimeograph machine, or even the fax. "What's happening with new technology is that it's making publication of these stories easier, and they're reaching a bigger audience," says Mahoney, the Committee to Protect Journalists deputy director.

"Twenty years ago, you'd struggle to get published in a local newspaper," Mahoney says. "Now, as a journalist, you've got far more platforms open to you, and you can get it out."

And not just journalists. From Libya and Iran to Syria and Myanmar, activists and average citizens are able to disseminate text, images and video all over the world, ensuring that their voices can be heard even at moments when regimes are violently cracking down on them.

Social media and other technological tools have become so omnipresent that former Rep. Tom Perriello, D-Va., worries that people become addicted to the online dialogue rather than reaching out to broader populations. "My pet peeve is that people think that social media can replace traditional organizing," says Perriello, President of the Center for American Progress Action Fund, part of a liberal think tank in Washington.

And even free-speech advocates readily admit that, in a broader sense, technology can be a two-edged sword. "Suddenly, you have the ability to reach people all over the world and communicate in ways that you never could before, and that's wonderful," says Eva Galperin, global policy analyst with the Electronic Frontier Foundation (EFF), a San Francisco-based group that promotes an unrestricted Internet. "But it also allows government surveillance on a scale that was never before possible."

Journalists find that their e-mail accounts have been hacked by "state-sponsored attackers" in countries such as China and Myanmar.[14] Mobile phones become surveillance devices.

"Modern information technologies such as the Internet and mobile phones . . . magnify the uniqueness of individuals, further enhancing the traditional challenges to privacy," according to a study published in 2013 by researchers from MIT and other universities that exposed the ease of tracking individual cellphone users. "Mobility data contains the approximate whereabouts of individuals and can be used to reconstruct individuals' movements across space and time."[15]

Authoritarian regimes also use technology to access dissidents' computers, installing malware that tracks their movements online, according to Galperin. "It records all of their keystrokes and can use the microphones and cameras on the computers, circumventing all attempts to use encryption," she says.

It's not just dictatorships. Galperin notes that EFF's longstanding lawsuit against the National Security Agency for using warrantless wiretaps in the United States is "now old enough to go to school." And many of the surveillance tools used by authoritarian regimes are made by U.S. companies, she points out.

ATTILA KISBENEDEK/AFP/Getty Images

A free-speech activist in Budapest, Hungary, protests against a new media law on March 15, 2011. The law set up a regulatory council with wide control over media outlets and content, a power that Human Rights Watch says compromises press freedom. Pictured on the poster is the revered poet of Hungary's 1848-1849 revolution, Sandor Petofi.

In the United Kingdom, initially in response to a phone-hacking scandal that led to government investigations and a national debate about press abuses, Home Secretary Theresa May repeatedly has pushed legislation to require Internet service providers and mobile phone services to collect and retain data on user activity. A recent version of her measure essentially would change how state, police, as well as spies can capture private messages or other data to monitor potential threats to national security.[16]

Iran, which saw its own "Twitter revolution" during a spasm of post-election protests in 2009, has attempted to keep a "Halal Internet," free of unclean influences and information from the outside world.

In March 2013, Iran's Ministry of Information and Communications Technology blocked software used by millions of Iranians to bypass the state's elaborate Internet filtering system. "A collection of illegal virtual private networks, or VPNs, was successfully closed off by the ministry, making visits to websites deemed immoral or politically dangerous — like Facebook and Whitehouse. gov — nearly impossible," *The New York Times* reported.[17]

China, which already had tough Internet restrictions, also began blocking VPNs, sparking increasing frustration among multinational companies as well as artists, entrepreneurs and professors. And it instituted new regulations requiring foreign companies to store data within the country and allow the government access.[18]

Governments and Internet users are engaged in an unending game of cat and mouse, Kampfner says, with each trying to advance technology in ways that gives its side the upper hand.

"There's something called Tor, an open-source project that aims to break through all those barriers, whether in China or Iran or anywhere else," says Wallach, the computer scientist at Rice University. "Tor keeps getting more and more clever about hiding what they're doing, and regimes like Iran get more and more clever about blocking them regardless."

But as many commentators have noted, free speech online depends not only on government policies and court rulings, but on private companies such as Twitter, Facebook and Google. These companies repeatedly have been called on to block posts by terrorists and unpopular or banned political parties, and recently they have been responding.

Facebook in January 2016 launched an "Initiative for Civil Courage Online" stating the company would seek to remove hate speech from its site, with a specific focus on Germany where many users had expressed disdain for foreigners and migrants amid the influx of more than a million Syrian refugees. Twitter and Google also pledged support in the effort.[19]

Google has responded to many other requests as well. It reported that it had received requests from governments to take down more than 12,000 items on YouTube alone during the second part of 2014. It said it complied with about half of the requests.[20]

"At the end of the day, the private networks are not in any way accountable if they choose to censor or prevent individuals from accessing services," says Katherine Maher, director of strategy and communications for Access, a New York-based digital-rights group.

"The Internet is not something different," Maher says. "It is just an extension of the area in which we live."

Should religious sensibilities be allowed to limit free expression?

When an assassin's bullet narrowly missed the head of Lars Hedegaard, suspicion immediately fell on Muslims, since Hedegaard, a former newspaper editor in Denmark, has been an anti-Islam polemicist.

But a number of Danish Muslims condemned the February 2013 attack and rose to defend Hedegaard. "We Muslims have to find a new way of reacting," said Qaiser Najeeb, a Dane whose father had emigrated from Afghanistan. "We don't defend Hedegaard's views but do defend his right to speak. He can say what he wants."[21]

For free-speech advocates, it was a refreshing reaction — particularly in a country where Muslim sensitivities have run high since the 2006 publication of cartoons caricaturing the Prophet Muhammad in a Danish newspaper.

"For those, like me, who look upon free speech as a fundamental good, no degree of cultural or religious discomfort can be reason for censorship," writes British journalist and author Kenan Malik.

"There is no free speech without the ability to offend religious and cultural sensibilities."[22]

In recent years, a growing number of people around the globe have been prosecuted on charges of blasphemy or offending cultural sensibilities through hate speech. According to the International Humanist and Ethical Union (IHEU), only three people were arrested for committing blasphemy via social media between 2007 and 2011, but more than a dozen such arrests occurred in 10 countries in 2013.[23]

Turkish pianist Fazil Say, for instance, was given a suspended sentence of 10 months in jail in April 2013 for posting tweets considered blasphemous, while Gamal Abdou Massoud, a 17-year-old Egyptian, was sentenced to three years for posting blasphemous cartoons on Facebook.

"When 21st-century technology collides with medieval blasphemy laws, it seems to be atheists who are getting hurt, as more of them go to prison for sharing their personal beliefs via social media," says Matt Cherry, editor of the IHEU report.

In Pakistan, those accused of blasphemy often fall victim to violence — before they even get their day in court. Dozens have been killed after being charged with blasphemy over the past 20 years. In November 2012, a mob burned Farooqi Girls' High School in Lahore after a teacher assigned homework that supposedly contained derogatory references to Muhammad.

"Repeating the blasphemy under Pakistan law is seen as blasphemy in itself," says Padraig Reidy, news editor for the Index on Censorship. "You have these bizarre cases where evidence is barely given but people are sentenced to death."

Even criticizing Pakistan's blasphemy law can be dangerous. Sherry Rehman, the Pakistani ambassador to the United States, received death threats after calling for changes in the law, while two like-minded politicians were assassinated.[24]

In Pakistan, free speech is pretty much limited to those hanging around cafes and literary festivals, says Huma Yusuf, a columnist for the Pakistani newspaper Dawn. "The threat of blasphemy — a crime that carries the death penalty — has stifled public discourse," she writes.[25]

YouTube was blocked throughout Pakistan beginning in September 2012, after an anti-Muslim video was uploaded to the site. Thousands of other websites also were blocked, allegedly for containing pornographic or blasphemous content. "In truth, most had published material criticizing the state," according to Yusuf. In January 2016, Google launched a local version of the site in Pakistan which allows the government to block and remove material it deems offensive.[26] In countries such as Pakistan and Egypt, the line between blasphemy laws designed to protect against religious offense and those meant to punish minorities and stifle dissent is highly porous. "There have been attempts to protect religious sensibility which are in fact a way of curbing press freedom and expression," says Mahoney, of the Committee to Protect Journalists.

In the West, worries about offending religious and cultural sensibilities have sometimes trumped free-speech concerns. "Denigration of religious beliefs is never acceptable," Australian Prime Minister Julia Gillard stated before the United Nations in 2012. "Our tolerance must never extend to tolerating religious hatred."[27]

Gillard emphasized her disdain for speech that incites hatred and violence, which has become a common concern among Western politicians. "Western governments seem to be sending the message that free-speech rights will not protect you" when it comes to hate speech, writes Turley, the George Washington University law professor.[28]

Hate speech is intended to incite discrimination or violence against members of a particular national, racial or ethnic group, writes Aryeh Neier, a former top official with the American Civil Liberties Union, Human Rights Watch and the Open Society Institute.

But, Neier notes, "It is important to differentiate blasphemy from hate speech. The proclivity of some elsewhere to react violently to what they consider blasphemous cannot be the criterion for imposing limits on free expression in the U.S., the United Kingdom, Denmark or the Netherlands (or anywhere else)."[29]

In 2012 and 2013, the human rights group American Freedom Defense Initiative (AFDI) ran anti-Muslim ads on public transportation systems around the United States. Posters that appeared on San Francisco buses, for example, included a picture of Osama bin Laden and a made-up quote from "Hamas MTV" that said, "Killing Jews is worship that brings us closer to Allah."

After New York's Metropolitan Transit Authority tried to block the ads in 2012, Federal District Judge Paul A. Engelmayer ruled that the agency had violated AFDI's First Amendment rights.

"Not only did [he] rule that the ads should be 'afforded the highest level of protection under the First Amendment,' he went on to offer some eye-opening examples," writes *San Francisco Chronicle* columnist C. W. Nevius. "Engelmayer said an ad could accuse a private citizen of being a child abuser. Or, he suggested, it could say, 'Fat people are slobs' or 'Blondes are bimbos' and still be protected."[30]

Subsequent federal court rulings on similar anti-Muslim ads by the group were mixed. In 2015, a federal circuit appeals court upheld a county decision in Washington state to bar the group from posting ads on buses that had photos of wanted terrorists and claimed the FBI offered $25 million reward for the capture of each of them.[31] But a federal district court judge ruled in April 2015 that a similar ad by the group that was barred by New York's Metropolitan Transportation Authority was protected by the First Amendment.[32]

Blasphemy Laws Proliferate

Videos and cartoons mocking the Muslim Prophet Muhammad have prompted many countries to enact strict anti-blasphemy laws. Christians and Muslims have used the laws to prosecute people seen as insulting religion. Blasphemy laws in Muslim countries usually refer only to defaming Islam, and punishments can include the death penalty. Many cases involve comments or videos posted on social media such as Twitter and YouTube.

Examples of Recent Blasphemy Cases

Country	Law
Austria	Prohibits disparaging a religious object, society or doctrine.
On Dec. 11, 2010, Helmut Griese, 63, was convicted for offending his Muslim neighbor by yodeling while mowing his lawn; the neighbor claimed Griese was imitating the Muslim call to prayer. On Jan. 22, 2009, politician Susanne Winter was fined $24,000 for saying Muhammad was a pedophile because he had a 9-year-old wife.	
India	Allows up to three years in prison for insulting religion or religious beliefs.
On April 21, 2012, the Catholic Church filed a complaint against Sanal Edamaruku, the founder of the reason-based organization Rationalist International, after he exposed a "miracle" by showing water from a statue of Jesus was coming from a leaky drain. On Nov. 19, 2012, college student Shaheen Dhada and a friend were arrested for complaining on Facebook that Mumbai had been shut down for the funeral of the leader of the Hindu nationalist party.	
Iran	Bars criticism of Islam or deviation from the ruling Islamic standards.
Web designer Saeed Malekpour, 35, a Canadian, served four years on death row in Iran for "insulting Islam." He was arrested while visiting his dying father in Iran in 2008 because a photo-sharing program he created while in Canada was used by others to download pornography. The death sentence was suspended in 2012 after Malekpour "repented."	
Netherlands	Penalizes "scornful blasphemy" that insults religious feelings.
On March 19, 2008, Dutch cartoonist Gregorius Nekschot was arrested for insulting Muslims in his drawings. On Jan. 21, 2009, politician Geert Wilders was put on trial because his film "Fitna" compared Islam and Nazism. He was acquitted.	
Pakistan	Bans blasphemy, including defiling the Quran and making remarks against the Prophet Muhammad.
In 2011 the governor of Punjab and the minister for minority affairs were assassinated because they opposed the country's blasphemy laws. On June 22, 2011, 29-year-old Larkana resident Abdul Sattar was sentenced to death and fined $1,000 for sending text messages and blaspheming the Quran, Muhammad and other Islamic figures during a phone conversation.	
United Kingdom	Prohibits "hate speech" against religious groups.
On March 4, 2010, philosophy tutor Harry Taylor was sentenced to six months in prison, 100 hours of community service and fined €250 ($337 at the time) for leaving anti-Christian and anti-Islam cartoons in an airport prayer room.	

Source: International Humanist and Ethical Union, December 2012

A federal appeals court in 2015 upheld Massachusetts Bay Transportation Authority ban on such ads, stating they were demeaning to Muslims. (Following the MBTA's decision, it instituted a new rule in December 2015 that bars any ads referring to political issues or stating opinions on "economic, political, moral, religious or social issues."[33])

Lawyers for AFDI looked to the U.S. Supreme Court to take up the Massachusetts case, but in January the high court declined.[34]

Should the United States promote free speech abroad?

Because of the First Amendment and the history of its interpretation, the United States has what comes closest to absolute protection of free speech of any country on Earth. And many believe free expression is not only essential to democracy but a value Americans should help export to other countries.

At a 2011 Internet freedom conference in The Hague, then-Secretary of State Hillary Rodham Clinton said, "The United States will be making the case for an open Internet in our work worldwide."

"The right to express one's views, practice one's faith, peacefully assemble with others to pursue political or social change — these are all rights to which all human beings are entitled, whether they choose to exercise them in a city square or an Internet chat room," Clinton said. "And just as we have worked together since the last century to secure these rights in the material world, we must work together in this century to secure them in cyberspace."[35]

But the right to free expression that is taken for granted in the United States is not shared around the world. Some people — including some Americans — worry that the United States risks offending governments and citizens in other nations by preserving free-speech rights — including the right to racist and blasphemous speech — above nearly every other consideration.

Such voices have been prominent when Americans have exercised their free-speech rights in ways that offend others. Threats to burn the *Quran* — as well as actual *Quran* burnings— by Florida pastor Terry Jones led to deadly riots in the Muslim world in 2010 and 2011. Last fall, video portions from an anti-Muslim film called "Innocence of Muslims" triggered riots in several predominantly Muslim nations.

Speaking to the United Nations two weeks later, President Obama explained that the U.S. government could not ban such a video because of free-speech rights enshrined in the U.S. Constitution.

"Americans have fought and died around the globe to protect the right of all people to express their views, even views that we profoundly disagree with," Obama said. "We do not do so because we support hateful speech, but because our founders understood that without such protections, the capacity of each individual to express their own views and practice their own faith may be threatened."[36]

While reality, some commentators said it was foolish to expect other nations to understand the American right to unbridled speech. "While the First Amendment right to free expression is important, it is also important to remember that other countries and cultures do not have to understand or respect our right," Anthea Butler, a University of Pennsylvania religious studies professor, wrote in *USA Today*.[37]

Americans must remember that "our First Amendment values are not universal," cautioned Eric Posner, a University of Chicago law professor.

"Americans need to learn that the rest of the world — and not just Muslims — see no sense in the First Amendment," Posner wrote in *Slate*. "Even other Western nations take a more circumspect position on freedom of expression than we do, realizing that often free speech must yield to other values and the need for order. Our own history suggests that they might have a point."[38]

Access' Maher, who has consulted on technology issues with the World Bank and UNICEF, notes that even other Western nations tend to hold free-speech rights less dear, viewing them within a context not of personal liberty but a framework where they risk infringing on the rights of others. "This often leads to robust debates about incitement, hate speech, blasphemy and their role in the political discourse, often in a manner

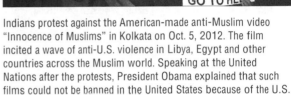

Indians protest against the American-made anti-Muslim video "Innocence of Muslims" in Kolkata on Oct. 5, 2012. The film incited a wave of anti-U.S. violence in Libya, Egypt and other countries across the Muslim world. Speaking at the United Nations after the protests, President Obama explained that such films could not be banned in the United States because of the U.S. Constitution's free-speech rights.

more open to possible circumscription than would be acceptable in the United States," she says.

Even some who promote free expression worry about the United States taking a leading role in its promotion, because of the risk of it being seen elsewhere as an American value being imposed from without.

"The problem is freedom of expression has come to be seen as either an American or Anglo-Saxon construct, whereas we would all like to see it as a universal principle," says Kampfner, the British journalist. "There is a danger that if this value is seen as proselytized primarily by the United States, it will reinforce those who are suspicious of it."

But it may be that America's staunch adherence to free speech makes the United States uniquely well-suited to promote and defend the idea.

"The United States values a free press and should promote those values abroad," says Robert Mahoney, deputy director of the Committee to Protect Journalists.

"No Western country wants to appear to be lecturing other countries to uphold its values, but it's not an American construct," he says. "We have a duty to remind them of that, and we expect international bodies like the U.N. and countries like the United Kingdom and the European Union to do the same thing."

During his first trip abroad as secretary of State, John Kerry in February defended free speech — including

CHRONOLOGY

1940s–1980s *New laws, international entities and court decisions expand free-speech rights.*

1946 French constitution upholds principle that "free communication of thought and of opinion is one of the most precious rights of man."

1948 United Nations adopts Universal Declaration of Human Rights, declaring "the right to freedom of opinion and expression" for all.

1952 U.S. Supreme Court extends First Amendment protection to movies.

1954 Congress effectively criminalizes the Communist Party.

1961 British jury allows Penguin to publish the novel *Lady Chatterly's* Lover, which had been on a list of obscene material.

1964 In landmark *New York Times v. Sullivan* decision, U.S. Supreme Court rules that public officials must prove "actual malice" on the part of journalists to sue for libel. . . . Free Speech Movement at University of California, Berkeley, insists that administrators allow campus protests.

1968 U.K. abolishes 400-year-old laws allowing for government censorship of theater performances.

1971 In the first instance of prior restraints on the press in U.S. history, a court blocks *The New York Times* from publishing the Pentagon Papers, but the Supreme Court OKs publication of the classified Vietnam War history.

1989 Iran's Islamic government issues a fatwa, or kill order, against *Satanic Verses* author Salman Rushdie, forcing him into hiding for years. . . . Supreme Court upholds the right to burn the U.S. flag in protest.

2000s *In response to terrorist attacks, many Western countries limit civil liberties.*

2000 At the first meeting of the post-Cold War Community of Democracies, 106 countries pledge to uphold democratic principles, including freedom of expression.

2005 George W. Bush administration ultimately fails in its year-long campaign to press *New York Times* not to publish a story about warrantless wiretaps.

2006 More than 200 people die in violent protests across the Muslim world after the Danish newspaper *Jyllands-Posten* publishes cartoons satirizing the Prophet Muhammad. . . . United Kingdom bans language intended "to stir up religious hatred." . . . In response to July 2005 terrorist bombings of bus and subway system that killed more than 50 people, U.K. enacts Prevention of Terrorism Act, which curtails speech in the name of security. . . . Crusading Russian journalist Anna Politkovskaya, known for her coverage of the Chechen conflict, is assassinated.

2010s *In an age of new media, both rich and developing countries restrict speech that may offend.*

2010 WikiLeaks publishes thousands of sensitive documents related to U.S. diplomatic efforts in Iraq, Afghanistan and elsewhere. . . . Google announces it is pulling out of China due to government censorship of its service.

2012 U.S. Supreme Court finds the Stolen Valor Act unconstitutional; the 2006 law made it a crime to falsely claim to have won military decorations. . . . Members of the Russian punk band Pussy Riot are convicted of hooliganism for protesting President Vladimir Putin's policies in a Moscow church. . . . "Innocence of Muslims," an anti-Muslim video posted on YouTube, triggers riots in several Middle Eastern and North African countries. . . . Twitter blocks German access to posts by a banned neo-Nazi party, its first bow to "country-withheld content" regulations. . . . Inquiry on press abuses in Britain spurred by telephone-hacking scandal by media outlets calls for greater regulation. . . . Egyptian court sentences to death in absentia Florida pastor Terry Jones, who had offended Muslims through Quran burnings and promotion of an anti-Muslim film. . . . . Former National Security Agency contractor Eric Snowden leaks documents showing agency's collection of U.S. citizens' personal phone and online data. . . .

2013 Egypt's military-backed government issues law essentially banning protests. . . . Three al Jazeera journalists arrested in Egypt, accused of broadcasting false news and belonging to Muslim brotherhood.

2015 Two militant jihadists kill 12 people at French satirical weekly *Charlie Hebdo* that published caricatures of Prophet Mohammed. . . . .Protestors demonstrate in Paris on behalf of publication. . . . Protests against publication take place in Chechnya. . . . Obama calls for freedom of speech and respect for religion. . . . Norway, Iceland abolish "blasphemy" laws. . . . Egyptian president enacts new law on counterterrorism that bars news that

contrast with government statements. . . . Twitter announces guidelines prohibiting abusive speech. . . . Obama signs into law measure allowing companies and government to share cyberthreat information.

2016 Facebook announces initiative to remove hate speech from its site, pledges to help Germany crack down on posts expressing dislike for foreigners and migrants. Google launches version of YouTube in Pakistan allowing government to censor material. . . . Russia threatens technology tax against Google, Facebook, Apple.

the "right to be stupid" — as a virtue "worth fighting for."[39]

It's important that individuals and groups in foreign countries take the lead in explaining free-speech rights, "so it's not seen as a Western concept," says Reidy, the Index on Censorship editor.

"Certain human rights are not Western," he says, "they're universal. That's the whole point of human rights."

BACKGROUND
Refusal to "*Revoco*"

The struggle for free speech has been a long story about testing limits. Many of the most famous moments in the development of free speech in the Western world involved notable figures such as the French philosopher Voltaire, the Biblical translator William Tyndale and the Italian astronomer Galileo, who were variously exiled, executed or forced to recant things they had said or written.

"Governments in all places in all times have succumbed to the impulse to exert control over speech and conscience," writes Rodney A. Smolla, president of Furman University.[40]

The first great flowering of democracy and free speech occurred 500 years before the birth of Christ in the Greek city-state of Athens. The city pioneered the idea of government by consent, allowing the people the freedom to choose their own rules.

"Free speech was an inseparable part of the new Athenian order," Robert Hargreaves, who was a British

broadcaster, writes in his 2002 book *The First Freedom*. "Never before had ordinary citizens been given the right to debate such vital matters as war and peace, public finance or crime and punishment."[41]

But although Athens embraced, off and on, the concept of government by consent, it did not yet accept the idea of individual free speech that might upset the prevailing order. Athens now may be remembered less for pioneering free speech than for trying and executing the great philosopher Socrates in 399 B.C., after he refused to recant his teachings.

Demanding that critics and heretics recant has been a persistent theme throughout history. After Martin Luther printed his *Ninety-Five Theses* in 1517, which criticized clerical abuses, Cardinal Thomas Cajetan, the papal legate in Rome, asked him to say *revoco*, or "I recant," and all would be well. Luther refused.

Cajetan wanted to turn Luther over to Rome on charges of heresy, but Frederick III, the elector of Saxony, allowed him to stay. Luther's works became bestsellers. Not only was he a celebrity, but his writings helped spark the Protestant Reformation.

Eventually, Pope Leo X and the Holy Roman Emperor Charles V also asked Luther to recant his writings. He argued that he was defending works about the teachings of Christ and therefore was not free to retract them. He offered this famous defense: "Here I stand; God help me; I can do no other."[42]

As a result, the pope excommunicated him, and the emperor condemned him as an outlaw.

Free Speech Can Be Deadly in Russia

"Many journalists end up dead, assaulted or threatened."

Aleksei A. Navalny expected to go to jail. In March 2013, a Russian court announced it would schedule a trial against Navalny, who was accused of embezzling from a timber company, even though the case was dismissed in 2012 for lack of evidence. Still, Navalny said, "Honestly, I am almost certain I am going to prison."[1]

That July – three months after he announced he would run for president – Navalny was sentenced to jailed for five years. As many as 10,000 protestors gathered in Moscow within hours, and the next morning Navalny was released.[2]

Many of Navalny's supporters believed his real crimes were organizing protests in Moscow in 2011 and 2012, blogging and running a nonprofit group that operates websites that allow citizens to report incidents of government corruption.

Navalny is not the only activist that has come under pressure from Russia's government. Since Vladimir Putin returned to the presidency in May 2012, new restrictions have been imposed on Internet content, and fines of up to $32,000 have been imposed for participating in protests deemed illegal.

International nonprofit groups such as Amnesty International, Human Rights Watch and Transparency International have been ordered to register as foreign agents. All have refused, and their offices recently have been raided by government investigators.

In 2013, Dmitry Gudkov, an opposition politician and one of only two members of the Russian parliament to support public protests such as those organized by Navalny, was accused of treason by some of his colleagues after he visited the United States. Gudkov's father was stripped of his seat in parliament the previous fall.

While cracking down on opposition voices, Putin's government has been able to rely on friendly state-run media coverage, including from Channel One, the nation's most widely watched television station. During his U.S. visit, Gudkov noted that Russian state-controlled media had accused him of treason and selling secrets.

And now Russia is threatening a technology tax on Google, Facebook, and Apple, threatening their presence there.

While some countries try to crack down on independent media outlets through intimidation, Russia for the most part controls communications directly, with the state or its friends owning most of the major newspapers and broadcasters.

Arch Puddington, vice president for research at Freedom House, a Washington-based watchdog group, says what he calls the "Putin model" is widely practiced. "They buy television stations and turn them into mouthpieces of the government," he says.

It's a case of, "If you can't beat them, buy them," says Anthony Mills, deputy director of the International Press Institute in Austria.

Russia is not alone. In some Central Asian and Latin American countries, government-owned media are commonly used for propaganda and to negate foreign criticism.

In Turkey, most of the media are controlled by a few private companies, which leads more to collusion than intimidation, says former Rep. Tom Perriello, D-Va. "In Turkey, you have less of the situation of people being shaken down [or threatened] if they print this story," he says. "Instead, many of the TV companies are doing con-

Controlling the Press

Luther's writings were spread thanks to the advent of the printing press, a new technology that governments sought to control. The Star Chamber of the British Parliament in 1586 strictly limited the number of master printers, apprentices and printing presses that could operate in London. All books were required to be licensed by the archbishop of Canterbury or the bishop of London.

A few decades later, members of Parliament won the ability to speak and vote without royal restraint. This led to a freer press, as London printers began publishing journals that were largely accounts of Parliament but also contained news. By 1645, the printers were putting out an average of 14 separate weekly titles.[43]

A year earlier, the English poet John Milton had published his *Aereopagitica*, remembered as one of the most

tracts with the government, so there's a financial interest in not wanting to irritate people in the . . . government."

In other countries, antagonism is the norm. According to Freedom House, Ecuadoran President Rafael Correa has called the press his "greatest political enemy," which he says is "ignorant," "mediocre," "primitive," "bloodthirsty" and "deceitful."[3]

"Ecuador under its president of the last five years, Rafael Correa, has become one of the world's leading oppressors of **free speech**," Peter Hartcher, international editor for *The Sydney Morning Herald*, wrote in 2012. "Correa has appropriated, closed and intimidated many media outlets critical of his government. He has sued journalists for crippling damages."

Analysts say the Venezuelan government tries to own or control nearly all media, while vilifying and jailing independent journalists.

And in Russia, government harassment of independent voices is common. Only a few independent outlets operate, such as *Novaya Gazeta*, a newspaper co-owned by former Soviet President Mikhail Gorbachev, but they aren't widely read or heard except by law enforcement agencies that often arrest, beat and — according to watchdog groups — even kill journalists.

The 2006 killing of Anna Politkovskaya, a *Novaya Gazeta* reporter noted for her coverage of the Chechen conflict, drew international attention, although no one has been convicted of her murder. "Russia is among the most dangerous countries in which to be a journalist," says Rajan

Russian activist Aleksei Navalny, a leading critic of President Vladimir Putin, addresses an anti-Putin rally in St. Petersburg on Feb. 12, 2012.

OLGA MALTSEVA/AFP/Getty Images

Menon, a political scientist at City College of New York. "Many journalists end up dead, assaulted or threatened for looking into hot-button issues, especially corruption."

In some countries, state-owned media criticize their own governments, says Robert Mahoney, deputy director of the Committee to Protect Journalists, citing the example of the BBC. But when nearly all media are owned by a few individuals or companies, it's not "good in the long term for a diverse and vibrant **free** press," he says.

Nor is it good when journalists fear they might be killed for digging into stories. In Russia, for instance, journalists are routinely killed with impunity. "There are 17 cases where journalists were killed in the last dozen years or so," Mahoney says, "and there have been no prosecutions."

— *Alan Greenblatt*

[1] Andrew E. Kramer, "With Trial Suddenly Looming, Russian Activist Expects the Worst," *The New York Times*, March 28, 2013, p. A4, www.nytimes.com/2013/03/28/world/europe/with-case- reopened-the-russian-activist-aleksei-navalny-expects-the-worst.html.

[2] "Russian protest leader Alexei Navalny jailed for corruption," *The Guardian*, July 18, 2013, http://www.bbc.com/news/world-europe-23352688; Masha Gessen, "Alexey Navalny's Very Strange For of Freedom," *The New Yorker*, Jan. 15, 2016, http://www.newyorker.com/news/news-desk/alexey-navalnys-very-strange-form-of-freedom.

[3] "Freedom of the Press 2011: Ecuador," Freedom House, Sept. 1, 2011, www.freedomhouse.org/report/freedom-press/2011/ecuador.

eloquent pleas for a free press ever penned. "Truth is strong next to the Almighty, she needs no policies, no stratagems nor licensing to make her victorious," Milton wrote in the treatise. "Give her but room, and do not bind her."

Although it grew out of ongoing debates about press licensing and limiting free speech, the *Aereopagitica* had little influence in its day. The press remained heavily

regulated both in the United Kingdom and in its American colonies.

In 1734, a German-born printer in New York named John Peter Zenger published criticism of royalist Gov. William Cosby, calling him "a governor turned rogue" who was undermining the colony's laws. At Zenger's trial the following year, attorney Andrew Hamilton argued that the judge and jury should not separately consider

China Opens Up – But Just a Crack

Journalists' and dissenters' activities are still monitored.

It's been decades now since China opened up to the West. But it's still not completely open, especially with regard to freedom of speech and the press.

In recent years, angered by coverage it viewed as hostile, such as reports that the families of top government officials have enriched themselves while the officials have been in power, China has denied entry visas to reporters from media organizations such as *The New York Times*, Al-Jazeera English and Reuters.

In October 2012, it blocked access within China to *The Times'* website, and later Chinese hackers broke into email accounts belonging to reporters from *The Times* and *The Wall Street Journal*, possibly to determine the sources of stories critical of government officials.

China has long maintained a "Great Firewall," blocking its citizens from accessing critical content from foreign sources. But the Chinese government is also at pains to block internal criticism from its own citizens and media, as well.

In any given year, China typically ranks in the world's top two or three countries in terms of how many journalists it imprisons.[1]

"There's a certain level of very localized dissent allowed, but it can never be expressed directly at the regime," says Padraig Reidy, news editor for Index on Censorship, a free-speech advocacy group.

"You can say a local official is corrupt — maybe," Reidy says. "But you can't say the party is corrupt. That's the end of you."

Besides tracking journalists' activities, China's government also monitors activists' online postings.

Computer scientist Dan Wallach of Rice University and several colleagues in 2013 released details of a study that found that China could be employing more than 4,000 censors to monitor the 70,000 posts per minute uploaded to Weibo, the Chinese version of Twitter.[2]

The censors tend to track known activists and use automated programs to hunt for forbidden phrases. "Certain words you know are never going to get out of the gate," Wallach says. "Falun Gong" — a spiritual practice China has sought to ban —"those three characters you can't utter on any Chinese website anywhere in the country."

Weibo users are "incredibly clever" at coming up with misspellings and neologisms to sneak past the censors, Wallach says. For instance, a colloquial phrase for China, the Celestial Temple, is sometimes rewritten as "celestial bastard," using similar-looking characters.

But once such usage becomes widespread, the censors are quick to catch on and such terms also are quickly eradicated from websites. "China is definitely the market leader in technical tools for clamping down on free expression," says British journalist John Kampfner.

Aside from imprisonment and hacking attacks, China uses self-censorship to suppress criticism of the state, says Robert Mahoney, deputy director of the New York-based Committee to Protect Journalists. Reporters and others constantly worry about what sort of statements could trigger a crackdown.

"With self-censoring, journalists tend to be more conservative," Mahoney says. Such sensitivity to what censors will think extends even to Hollywood movies. Given the

the questions of whether he had published the material and whether it was libelous, as was the practice at the time, but rather simply determine whether it could not be libel because it was true.

The jury's verdict of not guilty was considered an important precedent, but it would be 70 years before New York changed its libels laws so the question of truth could be entered into evidence.

William Blackstone, in his *Commentaries on the Laws of England* of 1769, laid the groundwork for the idea

that there should be no licensing or prior restraint of the press, but that publishers could still face punishment after publication. This formed the basis for the thinking of the American Founders, who remained skeptical about a completely free press.

"License of the press is no proof of liberty," John Adams wrote in his *Novanglus Letters* of 1774. "When a people are corrupted, the press may be made an engine to complete their ruin . . . and the freedom of the press, instead of promoting the cause of liberty, will but hasten its destruction."

growing importance of the Chinese film market, the country's censors now review scripts and inspect sets of movies filmed in China to make sure that nothing offends their sensibilities.

"There were points where we were shooting with a crew of 500 people," said Rob Cohen, director of "The Mummy: Tomb of the Dragon Emperor," which kicked off a recent wave of co-productions between Chinese companies and American studios. "I'm not sure who was who or what, but knowing the way the system works, it's completely clear that had we deviated from the script, it would not have gone unnoticed."[3]

The Academy Award-winning "Django Unchained" was initially cut to delete scenes of extreme violence, but censors blocked its scheduled April 2013 release due to shots of full-frontal nudity.

In addition to carefully inspecting Western content coming into the country, China is seeking to export its model for rigid media control to other countries. "It's fascinating to look at Chinese investment in Africa," says Anthony Mills, deputy director of the Austria-based International Press Institute. "They've bought into a variety of media outlets in Africa."

While China can't impose censorship in Africa, its control of media outlets there helps ensure favorable coverage. Beijing has promoted its image abroad through news-content deals with state-owned media in countries including Zimbabwe, Nigeria, Cuba, Malaysia and Turkey, according to the South African Institute of International Affairs. "Countries that need Chinese trade, aid and recognition, and those with tense relations with the U.S., are more likely to be influenced by China's soft power," the institute concluded in a report last year.[4]

"China has this model in which the economic welfare and the perceived welfare of the state as a whole trump individual freedoms," Mills says.

Some Western observers, such as Reidy, believe China eventually will have to become more open, because capitalist investment demands a free flow of information.

But others wonder whether China's more authoritarian approach represents a challenge to the transatlantic model that has been fairly dominant around the globe since World War II, with freedom of expression seen as essential to democracy and economic growth.

Already, says former Rep. Tom Perriello, D-Va., residents of countries such as Turkey complain less about individual freedoms while the economy is growing.

"If you actually get to a point where China is associated with economic prosperity more than Western countries are, then people look differently at democracy and human rights," he says. "I wish they didn't, but that's part of the fear, that we can't assume there's this natural march toward more liberalism."

— *Alan Greenblatt*

---

[1] Madeline Earp, "Disdain for Foreign Press Undercuts China's Global Ambition," Committee to Protect Journalists, March 11, 2013, www.cpj.org/2013/02/attacks-on-the-press-china-tightens-control.php

[2] "Computer Scientists Measure the Speed of Censorship on China's Twitter," *The Physics arXiv Blog*, March 6, 2013, www.technologyreview.com/view/512231/computer-scientists-measure-the-speed-of-censorship-on-chinas-twitter.

[3] Michael Cieply and Brooks Barnes, "To Get Movies Into China, Hollywood Gives Censors a Preview," *The New York Times*, Jan. 15, 2013, p. A1, www.nytimes.com/2013/01/15/business/media/in-hollywood-movies-for-china-bureaucrats-want-a-say.html.

[4] Yu-Shan Wu, "The Rise of China's State-Led Media Dynasty in Africa," South African Institute of International Affairs, June 2012, p. 11, www.saiia.org.za/images/stories/pubs/occasional_papers_above_100/saia_sop_%20117_wu_20120618.pdf.

As U.S. president, Adams signed the Alien and Sedition Acts, which led to multiple arrests and convictions of printers and publicists (all Republicans, or political opponents of Adams). The law was overturned under Thomas Jefferson, who had been skeptical about the need for unbridled press but embraced it in his second inaugural, stating that the press needed no other legal restraint than the truth.

The principle that there was a right to disseminate facts in a democracy was crystallized in British philosopher John Stuart Mill's *On Liberty* of 1859. "News, independently gathered and impartially conveyed, was seen to be an indispensable commodity in a society where the people ruled themselves," Mill wrote.

Expanding Rights

The U.S. Supreme Court seldom examined the question of free speech during the 19th century, but justices began to expand its sense in the 20th century.

During World War I, more than 1,900 Americans were prosecuted under the Espionage Act of 1917 and the Sedition Act of 1918, which banned printing, writing and uttering of statements deemed disloyal or abusive of the U.S. government.

One case led to the famous formulation of Justice Oliver Wendell Holmes. "The most stringent protection of free speech would not protect a man in falsely shouting 'fire' in a crowded theater and creating a panic," Holmes wrote in his dissent in *Schenck v. U.S.* in 1919. "The question in every case is whether the words used are used in such circumstances and are of such a nature to create a clear and present danger that they will bring about the substantive evils that Congress has a right to prevent."

Although fewer dissenters were prosecuted during World War II there were still dozens. "The Roosevelt administration investigated suspects for their 'un-American' associations and employed a variety of legal devices to harass the dissenters and suppress the dissent," writes historian Richard W. Steele.[44]

During the 1940s and '50s, Congress did what it could to ban Communist Party activities in the United States, but after World War II, the sense that free speech was an inalienable right took deep hold in the country and the courts. It was even included in Article 19 of the Universal Declaration of Human Rights, adopted by the United Nations in 1948, which says: "Everyone has the right to freedom of opinion and expression; this right includes freedom to hold opinions without interference and to seek, receive and impart information and ideas through any media and regardless of frontiers."[45]

A series of lectures by American free-speech advocate Alexander Meiklejohn published in 1948 was hugely influential as a defense of the notion that free speech and democracy are intertwined. "The phrase 'Congress shall make no law . . . abridging the freedom of speech,' is unqualified," Meiklejohn wrote. "It admits of no exceptions. . . . That prohibition holds good in war and peace, in danger as in security."[46]

In the 1960s, the U.S. Supreme Court protected racist speech, as well as speech by advocates of integration. "A decision protecting speech by a Ku Klux Klan member cited a decision that protected an African-American antiwar state legislator, and the case of the klansman was, in turn, cited [in 1989] to protect a radical who burned the American flag as a political protest," writes Wake Forest law professor Michael Kent Curtis.[47]

In 1964, the Supreme Court limited libel suits brought by public officials, finding that the First Amendment required "actual malice" — that is, knowledge that information published was false.[48] Seven years later, a lower court blocked *The New York Times* from publishing further portions of the Pentagon Papers, a government history of the Vietnam War — the first example in U.S. history of prior restraint.

The Supreme Court lifted the injunction. Justice Hugo Black wrote, "In revealing the workings of government that led to the Vietnam War, the newspapers nobly did precisely that which the Founders hoped and trusted they would do."[49]

After a long period of expansion, press freedoms and other civil liberties were challenged following the terrorist attacks of Sept. 11, 2001. Once again, free speech was seen as possibly undermining the government at a time when security concerns had become paramount. "Press freedoms are positively correlated with greater transnational terrorism," write University of Chicago law professor Posner and Harvard University law professor Adrian Vermeule. "Nations with a free press are more likely to be targets of such terrorism."[50]

For example, they cited a 2005 *New York Times* story on the so-called warrantless wiretapping program at the National Security Agency, which they argue alerted terrorists that the United States was monitoring communications the terrorists believed were secure.[51] The Bush administration made similar arguments to The Times, which held the story until after the 2004 presidential election.

Worried that the administration would seek a federal court injunction to block publication, *The Times* first published the story on its website. "In the new digital world of publishing, there were no printing presses to stop," notes Samuel Walker, a University of Nebraska law professor.[52]

Security vs. Privacy

On Feb. 28, 2013, Army Pfc. Bradley Manning, who leaked thousands of diplomatic, military and intelligence cables to WikiLeaks, pleaded guilty to 10 charges of illegally acquiring and transferring government secrets, agreeing to spend 20 years in prison. Manning pleaded not guilty, however, to 12 additional counts — including espionage — and faces a general court-martial in June 2013.

Manning's case made him a cause célèbre among some on the left who saw him as being unduly persecuted. A similar dynamic played out in memory of American online activist and pioneer Aaron Swartz, who committed suicide in January 2013 while facing charges that could carry a 35-year prison sentence in a case involving his downloading of copyrighted academic journals.

That March 2013, the entire editorial board of the Journal of Library Administration resigned over what one member described as "a crisis of conscience" over the 26-year-old Swartz's death.[53]

The librarians were concerned not only about the Swartz case but the larger issue of access to journal articles, feeling that publishers were becoming entirely too restrictive in their terms of use.

The tables turned a bit on the government in the summer of 2013. The Guardian published information provided by former analyst Eric Snowden, a contractor with Booz Allen Hamilton working at a National Security Agency facility in Hawaii, revealing the agency's program to collect data from wireless providers and Internet companies on domestic users.

Booz Allen Hamilton immediately fired Snowden and the U.S. Justice Department charged him with acts of espionage. But by that time he already had fled the country, ultimately ending up in Moscow where he is granted temporary asylum. Pentagon officials report serious damage had been done to military security by Snowden's leaks, while groups such as the American Civil Liberties Union protested the government's intrusion into citizen's privacy.[54]

Yet continued concerns about terrorist threats prompt Congress and the administration to seek legal avenues for sharing cyber information. In November 2014, a group calling itself the "Guardians of Peace" hacked into the computer system of Sony Pictures Entertainment and leaked information about employees and their families and demanded Sony pull its film "The Interview". The group threatened terrorist attacks at theaters that showed the film, which was a comedy about a plot to assassinate North Korean leader Kim Jong Un. North Korean denied U.S. allegations it was behind the attack.[55]

Spencer Platt/Getty Images

Ku Klux Klan members in Pulaski, Tenn. participate in a march honoring Nathan Bedford Forrest, a Confederate general who helped found the Klan, on July 11, 2009. The U.S. Supreme Court has ruled that even hate groups like the Klan have a constitutional right to express their racist views publicly.

CURRENT SITUATION
Government Secrets

The Department of Homeland Security is starting to share information with a limited number of companies under a new law, the Cybersecurity Information Sharing Act, known as CISA. But many cybersecurity experts, companies and free speech advocates question whether the new law erodes personal privacy more than it can actually protect citizens against terrorist attacks.[56]

CISA, which Congress included at the last minute in a massive catchall government funding bill that President Obama signed in December 2015, seeks to make it easier for companies to share cybersecurity information with federal agencies. Before including the measure, lawmakers tweaked the proposal to allow law enforcement to access such data whenever it detects a "specific threat."

Democratic Sen. Ron Wyden said it was a surveillance bill disguised as a cybersecurity protection measure. "Americans deserve policies that protect both their security and their liberty," he said. "This bill fails on both counts."[57]

Groups such as the American Library Association and a digital rights group called Fight for the Future, had called for the Obama administration to oppose the bill when the Senate initially took it up.

"Now is when we'll find out whether President Obama really cares about the Internet and freedom of

Is the Clean Power Plan good policy?

YES STEVEN BARNETT
Professor of Communications, University of Westminster, London, England

Written for *CQ Researcher*, April 2013

In an ideal world, a free press should not be constrained any more than free speech. Unfortunately, this is not an ideal world. Would-be terrorists seek to recruit supporters, grossly offensive material can reap huge financial rewards and some publications try to boost circulation and scoop competitors using immoral and even downright malicious methods.

Some methods, such as hacking into voicemails, are illegal in Britain. Others are not. Public outrage was sparked by atrocious behaviour that some British newspapers have sanctioned in the name of "journalism," such as splashing on the front page the private and intimate diaries of Kate McCann after the disappearance of her daughter Madeleine. Although Mrs. McCann begged the *News of the World* not to publish the diaries, the newspaper ignored her pleas. Such callous indifference to people's feelings had become institutionalized in some of Britain's best-selling newspapers.

What is required is not state control or statutory regulation. But the press must be held accountable for egregious abuses of its own privileged position within a democracy.

In the United Kingdom, Sir Brian Leveson, who chaired a judicial inquiry into press practices and ethics as a result of the phone-hacking scandal, recommended the moderate solution of voluntary self-regulation overseen by an autonomous body that would assess whether self-regulation was effective and independent. If so, news organizations choosing to belong would be entitled to financial incentives such as lower court costs and exemption from exemplary damages if sued. It is, I repeat, a voluntary incentive-based system, which is needed to protect ordinary people from amoral and sometimes vindictive practices that have no place in journalism.

Such proposals might feel uncomfortable in the land of the First Amendment, but it is exceptionally mild by European standards. In Finland, a Freedom of Expression Act mandates, among other things, that aggrieved parties have a right of reply or correction without undue delay. In Germany, newspapers are required to print corrections with the same prominence as the original report. Scandinavian countries have passed legislation on press ethics.

These countries are not rampant dictatorships. But they all, as will Britain, find a proper balance between unconstrained journalism and the rights of ordinary people not to have their misery peddled for corporate profit.

NO ANTHONY MILLS
Deputy Director, International Press Institute, Vienna, Austria

Written for *CQ Researcher*, April 2013

In any healthy democracy, the media play a watchdog role, holding elected officials accountable and serving the public interest by satisfying citizens' right to know what is being done in their name in the often not-so-transparent corridors of power. In the United States, for instance, the Watergate scandal was unearthed and covered, at not inconsiderable risk, by two young *Washington* Post reporters.

Not surprisingly, there are those in office for whom such media scrutiny is, to put it mildly, unwelcome. And, lo and behold, they become advocates for state regulation of the media. They may very well point to one or more examples of egregious, even criminal, journalist behavior as evidence of the need to exert greater control.

No one suggests that journalists are above the law. But when they engage in criminal behavior, they should be held accountable in criminal courts. The profession must not be overseen by the very elected officials whom it is supposed to hold to account. Surely, from the perspective of the politicians, that would be a conflict of interest.

The answer is self-regulation. That could be accomplished through independent regulatory bodies with the teeth to hold journalists ethically accountable or through ethical standards rigorously and systematically imposed by media outlets themselves as is the case in the United States, where the First Amendment right to freedom of the press is fiercely guarded.

Professional peers must lead by example.

In the absence of self-regulation, or where it is not effectively implemented, the path is easily paved for statutory regulation, whether direct, or roundabout, in form. The aftermath of the *News of the World* phone-hacking scandal in the U.K., and the ensuing inquiry by Lord Justice Leveson, have amply demonstrated this. The U.K. press is set to be bound by statutory legislation for the first time in hundreds of years. That cannot be healthy for democracy, and other countries tend to follow the lead of their democratic "peers."

So it is incumbent upon everyone in the profession to resist any efforts to impose statutory regulation of the press by those upon whom the press is supposed to be keeping its watchful eye. But it falls upon the press to ensure that the standards it embraces are of the highest order of professionalism and integrity. Anything less offers cannon fodder for those targeting a free media.

speech, or whether he's happy to roll over and allow technologically illiterate members of Congress break the Internet in the name of cybersecurity," said the group's campaign director, Evan Greer.[58]

Companies like Apple and Dropbox also opposed the measure. But the Obama administration already had indicated its support. White House spokesman Eric Schultz last summer released a statement that "cybersecurity is an important national security issue."

Information Explosion

The explosion of information on the Internet and in online databases has made legal concerns about free speech more complicated, says Randall Bezanson, a law professor at the University of Iowa. For most of U.S. history, such concerns turned largely on the question of whether the government had the power to censor speech. Now, he says, regulating speech involves the government not just quashing the speech of individuals but in protecting documents and databases — its own, and others — from disclosure.

The Obama administration has learned that lesson well, he says, and is doing its best to keep state secrets secret. "Eric Holder, attorney general under President Barack Obama, has prosecuted more government officials for alleged leaks under the World War I-era Espionage Act than all his predecessors combined," Bloomberg News reported in 2012.[59]

The administration was disturbed by the leak of thousands of diplomatic cables, which were published in 2010 by the whistleblower website Wiki-Leaks, founded by former Australian computer hacker Julian Assange.[60]

"The Julian Assange episode and those disclosures of pretty well unfiltered information, I think, scared people in government and raised a whole different specter of what could be done and what the consequences are, and that has probably triggered a more aggressive approach in the Justice Department," Bezanson says.

In general, Bezanson says, courts are becoming less accepting of the idea that "information wants to be free," as the Internet-era slogan has it. The courts are not only more supportive of copyright holders but seemingly more skeptical about free speech in general, with the Supreme Court in recent cases having curbed some of the free-speech rights it had afforded to students and hate groups in previous decisions.

"The doctrine of the First Amendment is going to be more forgiving of regulated speech," Bezanson says.

Regulating the Press?

In other countries, concern is growing that freedom of speech and of the press have been badly abused in recent years. A phone-hacking scandal involving *the News of the World*, a British tabloid, shocked the United Kingdom in 2011 and led to more than 30 arrests, as well as a high-profile inquiry chaired by Sir Brian Leveson, then Britain's senior appeals judge. Leveson's report, released in November, called for a new, independent body to replace the Press Complaints Commission, the news industry's self-regulating agency. The recommendations triggered difficult negotiations among leaders of the United Kingdom's coalition government, which eventually announced a compromise deal in 2013.

"While Lord Leveson was quite correct to call for a regulator with more muscle that can impose substantial fines for future misconduct, [Prime Minister] David Cameron pledged that he would resist the clamor for such measures to be backed by law," the *Yorkshire Post* editorialized. "Given that to do so would be to take the first step on the slippery slope toward censorship of the press, a weapon that has been employed by many a corrupt dictatorship around the globe, he was right to do so."[61]

The U.K. is not the only country that has been considering new media regulations. In March, Australia's government proposed tighter regulation of media ownership and a new media overseer with statutory authority. "Australians want the press to be as accountable as they want politicians, sports people and business people," said Stephen Conroy, Australia's communications minister.[62]

Media executives argued that the proposals were draconian and amounted to the government's revenge for hostile coverage. "For the first time in Australian history outside wartime, there will be political oversight over the conduct of journalism in this country," said Greg Hywood, the CEO of Fairfax Media.[63]

In response to such criticisms, Australia's government quickly withdrew the proposals but discussions continued.

Reporters Under Attack

Journalists, commentators, artists and writers are facing increasingly dangerous fates around the world, according to Reporters Without Borders. The group's 2015 World Press Freedom index states: "Beset by wars, the growing threat from non-state operatives, violence during demonstrations and the economic crisis, media freedom is in retreat on all five continents."[64] Kenneth Roth, the head of Human Rights Watch, wrote "The world has not seen this much tumult for a generation."

According to the Committee to Protect Journalists 199 journalists were jailed around the world in 2015, down slightly from 2014 when 221 were jailed. But the number of those killed increased — from 61 in 2014 to 71 the next year, including 49 that were murdered.[65]

The Committee reported that Syria and France were the "most deadly" countries for journalists. Of 69 journalists killed in 2015, 40 percent were killed by Islamic militant groups like Al-Qaeda and the Islamic State. [66]

The most high profile incident occurred in January 2015 when two militant jihadists killed 12 people at the French satirical publication *Charlie Hebdo* in response to the publication of caricatures of the Prophet Mohammed some said were offensive. Massive public demonstrations took over the streets of Paris is support of the publications, but a month later protests against the publication took place in Grozny, capital of Chechnya.

"You and I see how European journalists and politicians under false slogans about free speech and democracy proclaim the freedom to be vulgar, rude, and insult the religious feelings of hundreds of millions of believers," President Ramzan Kadyrov told the protestors.[67]

In January 2016, the documentary "Salafists" opened in five theaters in France and reportedly depicted bloody images of Islamist propaganda and its directors were accused of "flirting with advocating terrorism." Culture Minister Fleur Pellrin barred youth under 18 from seeing the firm, prompting a public debate about the film's threats versus whether the government was attacking freedom of expression.

Many eyes also are on Iran, where authorities in November 2015 arrested several local journalists. But in January it released *Washington Post* report Jason Rezaian – who had been imprisoned for 544 days on charges of espionage – in a prisoner swap with the U.S.[68]

Egypt also continues to be a dangerous place for journalists, particularly with increasing laws banning protests and allowing censorship. Three al Jazeera journalists were arrested in Egypt in December 2013 and a court two years later ruled they had broadcast false news, but they were subsequently released.[69]

Joel Simon, executive director of the Committee to Protect Journalists, says journalists are in more danger now because of technology. While the Internet allows news to flow into countries a bit more freely, it also is seen as a useful tool by violent groups to control information. "Journalists are seen as dispensable j– more useful as hostages or props in elaborately staged executive videos. In this context, identifying yourself as a journalist merely makes you a target," he wrote in *The Dallas News*.[70]

"I slightly fear it's going in the wrong direction in all of them," Kampfner says.

There have been other signs of hope for free-speech advocates. In 2014, for the first time in half a century, privately owned daily newspapers hit newsstands in Myanmar. *The Myanmar Times* announced the following year it would launch an English-language daily.[71]

And in Syria, new newspapers emerged to cover the civil war, countering bias from both government-controlled media and opposition-friendly satellite channels based in Qatar and Saudi Arabia.

Students Seek Safety

Meanwhile, college students across the U.S. are seeking to curtail speech they view derogatory or harmful. They request administrators impose restrictions on provocative or offensive texts assigned by professors or Halloween costumes they view as offensive, and try to bar journalists from reporting campus protests.

Yale University students in 2015, for example, loudly balked when lecturer Erika Christakis responded to a directive by the campus Intercultural Affairs Committee calling on students to avoid wearing costumes that could be viewed as offensive to others — such as those featuring headdresses or blackface. Christakis said students should be allowed to wear what they want. "Is there no room anymore for a child or young person to be a little obnoxious," she wrote in an e-mail, "a little bit inappropriate or provocative or, yes, offensive?"

Students complained to the University president about both Christakis and her husband Nicholas, who were dormitory masters. One student told Nicholas it was his "job" to create an intellectual space but also "a place of comfort and home." The University president defended Christakis, but that December she resigned her position as lecturer.[72]

Many universities in the U.S. have been pushed to create so-called safe spaces where students can avoid confrontations with other students. And it's happening on British campuses as well.[73]

Many professors and free speech advocates are baffled by the effort to crack down on speech, rather than push for more freedom as student protestors did in the 1960s. "It's been frustrating, watching the sort of speech [suppression] shift over from administrators to students," said Greg Lukianoff, author of "Unlearning Liberty: Campus Censorship and the End of American Debate" and president of the Foundation for Individual Rights in Education, which advocates for free speech on campuses. "Students should be aware that these tools are not always going to be on their side," he adds. "Make sure you imagine the [environment] you're creating." [74]

Morton Shapiro, president of Northwestern University, defended the idea of safe spaces, noting for example that African American students on campus have had their own student life center called the "Black House". He wrote in *The Washington Post*: ". . . students don't fully embrace uncomfortable learning unless they are themselves comfortable. Safe spaces provide that comfort. The irony, it seems, is that the best hope we have of creating an inclusive community is to first create spaces where members of each group feel safe."[75]

The debate continues among students, professors, administrators and free speech activists about the balance between protecting students from offensive speech and protecting First Amendment rights. [76]

OUTLOOK

Shame, Not Laws?

It's always impossible to predict the future, but it's especially difficult when discussing free speech, which is now inextricably bound up with constantly changing technologies.

"I don't know what's next," says Reidy, *the Index on Censorship* news editor. "None of us five years ago thought we would be spending our lives on Twitter." Still, Reidy says, the fact that so many people are conversing online makes them likely to equate blocking the Internet with more venerable forms of censorship, such as book burning.

"Within the next five years, you will have a lot of adults in the Western world who literally don't know what life is like without the Internet," he says. "That is bound to change attitudes and cultures."

Information technology is penetrating deeper into the developing world, says Kampfner, the British journalist and author. For instance, thanks to mobile technology African farmers can access more information they need about crop yields and prices. And with cell phones, everyone has better access to information on disasters.

However, "In terms of changing the political discourse, the jury is out," Kampfner says. "Every new technology, by its nature, is open to both use and abuse."

Activists wanting to use technology to spread information and governments trying to stop them play an ongoing "cat and mouse game," says Galperin, of the Electronic Frontier Foundation.

Given how easily commercial applications can track individuals' specific interests and movements online, it's not difficult to imagine that political speech will be tracked as well, Belarus-born writer and researcher Evgeny Morozov, a contributing editor at *The New Republic* and a columnist for *Slate*, contends in his 2011 book *The Net Delusion*. It's not the case, as some have argued, he says, that the need to keep the Internet open for commercial purposes will prevent regimes from stamping out other forms of online discourse.

"In the not so distant future, a banker perusing nothing but Reuters and *Financial Times*, and with other bankers as her online friends, would be left alone to do anything she wants, even browse Wikipedia pages about human-rights violations," he writes. "In contrast, a person of unknown occupation, who is occasionally reading *Financial Times* but is also connected to five well-known political activists through Facebook and who has written blog comments that included words like 'democracy' and 'freedom,' would only be allowed to visit government-run websites, or . . . to surf but be carefully monitored."[77]

In democratic nations, concerns about security and offending religious believers could lead to more restrictions — although not necessarily in terms of new laws, says Arch Puddington, vice president for research at Freedom House, but through shaming and "other informal methods" of disciplining unpopular ways of speaking.

"What you could have over the next 10 years in the U.S. and abroad is a distinction between rights and norms," says former Rep. Perriello, at the Center for American Progress Action Fund. "Having a legal right to say certain things does not actually mean one should say certain things."

Anthony Mills, the deputy director of the International Press Institute in Austria, suggests that the more things change, the more they will stay recognizably the same. "Unfortunately, in 10 years we'll still be having similar conversations about efforts by everyone from criminals to militants and government operatives to target the media and silence them," Mills says.

"But at the same time, . . . a variety of media platforms — of journalists and of media practitioners — will continue to defy that trend," he says. "I have no doubt that in the grand scheme of things, the truth will always come out. The dynamic of the flow of information is unstoppable."

Wallach, the Rice University computer scientist, is equally certain that despite all legal, political and technological ferment, the basic underlying tension between free expression and repressive tendencies will remain firmly in place.

"There will always be people with something to say and ways for them to say it," Wallach says. Likewise, "There will also always be people who want to stop them."

NOTES

1. https://www.hrw.org/news/2015/08/19/egypt-counterterrorism-law-erodes-basic-rights

2. Jonathan Turley, "Shut Up and Play Nice," *The Washington Post*, Oct. 14, 2012, p. B1, http://articles.washingtonpost.com/2012-10-12/opinions/35499274_1_free-speech-defeat-jihad-muslim-man.

3. For background, see Peter Katel, "Protecting Whistleblowers," *CQ Researcher*, March 31, 2006, pp. 265–288. Also see Jon Greenberg, "CNN's Tapper: Obama has used Espionage Act more than all previous administrations," Politifact, Jan. 10, 2014, http://tinyurl.com/mslflhg.

4. See Hugh Tomlinson, "The New UK Model of Press Regulation," The London School of Economics Media Policy Project, March 2014, http://tinyurl.com/zqyeqam.

5. "Memorandum to the European Union on Media Freedom in Hungary," Human Rights Watch, Feb. 16, 2012, www.hrw.org/node/105200.

6. For background, see Kenneth Jost, "Unrest in the Arab World," *CQ Researcher*, Feb. 1, 2013, pp. 105–132; and Roland Flamini, "Turmoil in the Arab World," CQ Global Researcher, May 3, 2011, pp. 209–236.

7. See Andrew Jacobs, "China Further Tightens Grip on the Internet," *The New York Times*, Jan. 29, 2015, http://tinyurl.com/nx8b84x; George Chen, et. al., "China's Great Firewall is Rising," Foreign Policy, Feb. 3, 2015, http://foreignpolicy.com/2015/02/03/china-great-firewall-is-rising-censorship-internet/

8. Tom Gjelten, "Shutdowns Counter the Idea of a World-Wide Web," NPR, Dec. 1, 2012, www.npr.org/2012/12/01/166286596/shutdowns-raise-issue-of-who-controls-the-internet.

9. Jessica Chasmar, "French Jewish Group Sues Twitter Over Racist, Anti-Semitic Tweets," *The Washington Times*, March 24, 2013, www.washingtontimes.com/news/2013/mar/24/french-jewish-group-sues-twitter-over-racist-anti-semitism.

10. Emily Bell, "Twitter tackles the free speech conundrum," *The Guardian*, Jan. 10, 2016, http://tinyurl.com/z7zj5yh.

11. Jean-Paul Marthoz, "Extremists Are Censoring the Story of Religion," Committee to Protect Journalists, Feb. 14, 2013, www.cpj.org/2013/02/attacks-on-the-press-journalism-and-religion.php. See also, Frank Greve, "Combat Journalism," *CQ Researcher*, April 12, 2013, pp. 329–352.

12. Chris York, "Pussy Riot Member Yekaterina Samutsevich Freed on Probation by Moscow Court," *The Huffington Post* UK, Oct. 10, 2012, www.huffingtonpost.co.uk/2012/10/10/pussy-riot-member-yekaterina-samutsevich-frees-probation-moscow-court_n_1953725.html.

13. Ethan Zuckerman, "The First Twitter Revolution?" *Foreign Policy*, Jan. 15, 2011, 5 / http://foreignpolicy.com/2011/01/15/the-first-twitter-revolution-2/

14. Thomas Fuller, "E-mails of Reporters in Myanmar Are Hacked," *The New York Times*, Feb. 10, 2013, www.nytimes.com/2013/02/11/world/asia/journalists-e-mail-accounts-targeted-in-myanmar.ht ml.

15. Yves Alexandre de Mountjoye, et al., "Unique in the Crowd: The Privacy Bounds of Human Mobility," *Nature*, March 25, 2013, www.nature.com/srep/2013/130325/srep01376/full/srep01376.html.

16. "UK surveillance powers explained," BBC News, Nov. 5, 2015, http://www.bbc.com/news/uk-34713435

17. Thomas Erdbrink, "Iran Blocks Way to Bypass Internet Filtering System," *The New York Times*, March 11, 2013, www.nytimes.com/2013/03/12/world/middleeast/iran-blocks-software-used-to-bypass-internet-filtering-system.html.

18. Andrew Jacobs, "China Further Tightens Grip on the Internet," *The New York Times*, Jan. 29, 2015, http://tinyurl.com/nx8b84x.

19. Andrew Griffin, "Facebook launches 'Initiative for Civil Courage Online' to delete racist and threatening posts," *The Independent*, Jan. 19, 2016, http://tinyurl.com/jz9g3rp.

20. Google Transparency Reports, Government requests to remove content (products affected by requests), https://www.google.com/transparencyreport/removals/government/?hl=en (accessed Feb. 17, 2015).

21. Andrew Higgins, "Danish Opponent of Islam Is Attacked, and Muslims Defend His Right to Speak," *The New York Times*, Feb. 28, 2013, p. A8, www.nytimes.com/2013/02/28/world/europe/lars-hedegaard-anti-islamic-provocateur-receives-support-from-danish-muslims.html.

22. Kenan Malik and Nada Shabout, "Should Religious or Cultural Sensibilities Ever Limit Free Expression?" *Index on Censorship*, March 25, 2013, www.indexoncensorship.org/2013/03/should- religious-or-cultural-sensibilities-ever-limit-free-expression/.

23. "Freedom of Thought 2012: A Global Report on Discrimination Against Humanists, Atheists and the Nonreligious," International Humanist and Ethical Union, Dec. 10, 2012, p. 11, http://iheu.org/newsite/wp-content/uploads/IHEU%20Freedom%20of%20Thought%202012.pdf.

24. Asim Tanveer, "Pakistani Man Accuses Ambassador to U.S. of Blasphemy," Reuters, Feb. 21, 2013, http://news.yahoo.com/pakistan-accuses-ambassador-u-blasphemy-124213305.html.

25. Huma Yusuf, "The Censors' Salon," *Latitude*, March 14, 2013, http://latitude.blogs.nytimes.com/2013/03/14/in-lahore-pakistan-the-censors-salon/.

26. Leslie Hook and Farhan Bokhari, "Pakistan lifts 3-year ban on YouTube," *The Financial Times*, Jan. 18, 2016, http://www.ft.com/cms/s/0/b878b146-be09-11e5-9fdb-87b8d15baec2.html#axzz40S3e4j2t.

27. See "Speech to the United Nations General Assembly —"Practical progress towards realizing those ideals in the world," Sept. 26, 2012, www.pm.gov.au/press-office/speech-united-nations-general-assembly-%E2%80%9Cpractical-progress-towards-realising-those-idea.

28. Turley, *op. cit.*

29. Aryeh Neier, "Freedom, Blasphemy and Violence," Project Syndicate, Sept. 16, 2012, www.project-syndicate.org/commentary/freedom–blasphemy--and-violence-by-aryeh-neier.

30. C. W. Nevius, "Free Speech Protects Offensive Ads on Muni," *The San Francisco Chronicle*, March 14, 2013, p. D1, www.sfgate.com/bayarea/nevius/article/Offensive-ads-on-Muni-protected- speech-4352829.php.

31. Martha Bellisle, The Associated Press, "Anti-Muslim group's ads won't run on Seattle=area buses," *Portland Press-Herald*, Aug. 12, 2015, http://tinyurl.com/gsxbk64.

32. Jonathan Stempel, "Judge orders NY transit agency to run 'Killing Jews' ad," Reuters, April 21, 2015, http://www.reuters.com/article/us-new-york-mta-ad-idUSKBN0NC1YS20150421.

33. Nicole Dungka, "MBTA bans all ads on political and social issues," *The Boston Globe*, Nov. 23, 2015, http://tinyurl.com/znsyrz2.

34. Martin Finucane and Nicole Dungca, "Supreme Court declines to hear case over ads on MBTA," *The Boston Globe*, Jan. 11, 2016, http://tinyurl.com/jnjhzz3.

35. Clinton's remarks are available at http://www.state.gov/secretary/20092013clinton/rm/2011/12/178511.htm.

36. Obama's remarks are available at www.whitehouse .gov/the-press-office/2012/09/25/remarks-president-un-general-assembly.

37. Anthea Butler, "Opposing View: Why 'Sam Bacile' Deserves Arrest," *USA Today*, Sept. 13, 2012, http:// usatoday30.usatoday.com/news/opinion/story/2012-09-12/Sam-Bacile-Anthea-Butler/ 57769732/1.

38. Eric Posner, "The World Doesn't Love the First Amendment," *Slate*, Sept. 25, 2012, www.slate.com/ articles/news_and_politics/jurisprudence/2012/09/ the_vile_anti_muslim_video_and_the_first_amend-ment_does_the_u_s_overvalue_free_speech_.single .html.

39. Eyder Peralta, "John Kerry to German Students: Americans Have 'Right to Be Stupid,'" NPR, Feb. 26, 2013, www.npr.org/blogs/thetwo-way/2013/ 02/26/172980860/john-kerry-to-german- students-americans-have-right-to-be-stupid.

40. Rodney A. Smolla, *Free Speech in an Open Society* (1992), p. 4.

41. Robert Hargreaves, *The First Freedom* (2002), p. 5.

42. *Ibid.*, p. 51.

43. *Ibid.*, p. 95.

44. Richard W. Steele, *Free Speech in the Good War* (1999), p. 1.

45. See "The Universal Declaration of Human Rights," United Nations, www.un.org/en/documents/udhr/ index.shtml#a19.

46. Alexander Meiklejohn, *Free Speech and Its Relation to Self-Government* (1948), p. 17.

47. Michael Kent Curtis, Free Speech, 'The People's Darling Privilege': Struggles for Freedom of Expression in American History (2000), p. 406.

48. David W. Rabban, Free Speech in Its Forgotten Years (1997), p. 372.

49. "Supreme Court, 6-3, Upholds Newspapers on Publication of Pentagon Report," *The New York Times*, July 1, 1971, www.nytimes.com/books/97/ 04/13/reviews/papers-final.html.

50. Eric A. Posner and Adrian Vermeule, *Terror in the Balance: Security, Liberty, and the Courts* (2007), p. 26.

51. James Risen and Eric Lichtblau, "Bush Lets U.S. Spy on Callers Without Courts," *The New York Times*,

Dec. 16, 2005, www.nytimes.com/2005/12/16/ politics/16program.html.

52. Samuel Walker, *Presidents and Civil Liberties From Wilson to Obama: A Story of Poor Custodians* (2012), p. 468.

53. Russell Brandom, "Entire Library Journal Editorial Board Resigns," *The Verge*, March 26, 2013, www .theverge.com/2013/3/26/4149752/library-journal-resigns-for-open-access-citing-aaron-swartz.

54. Matthew Cole and Mike Brunker, "Edward Snowden: A Timeline," NBC News, May 26, 2014, http://www.nbcnews.com/feature/edward-snowden-interview/edward-snowden-timeline-n114871.

55. Lori Grisham, "Timeline: North Korea and the Sony Pictures hack," *USA Today*, Jan. 5, 2015, http://www.usatoday.com/story/news/nation-now/2014/12/18/sony-hack-timeline-interview-north-korea/20601645/

56. John P. Mello Jr., "DHS Ready to Share Intelligence with Private Sector," TechNewsWorld, Feb. 18, 2016, http://www.technewsworld.com/story/83127.html.

57. Andy Greenberg, "Congress Slips CISA Into a Budget Bill That's Sure to Pass," *Wired*, Deember 16, 2015, http://www.wired.com/2015/12/congress-slips-cisa-into-omnibus-bill-thats-sure-to-pass/.

58. Rudy Takala, "Cyber bill set to pass as part of omnibus spending package," *Washington Examiner*, Dec. 14, 2015, http://www.washingtonexaminer.com/cyber-bill-set-to-pass-as-part-of-omnibus-spending-pack age/article/2578347.

59. Phil Mattingly and Hans Nichols, "Obama Pursuing Leakers Sends Warning to Whistle-Blowers," *Bloomberg News*, Oct. 17, 2012, www.bloomberg .com/news/2012-10-18/obama-pursuing-leakers-sends-warning-to-whistle-blowers.html.

60. For background, see Alex Kingsbury, "Government Secrecy," *CQ Researcher*, Feb. 11, 2011, pp. 121–144.

61. "A Vital Test for Democracy," *Yorkshire Press*, March 19, 2013, www.yorkshirepost.co.uk/news/debate/yp-comment/a-vital-test-for-our-democracy-1-5505331.

62. Sabra Lane, "Stephen Conroy Defends Media Change Package," Australian Broadcasting Company, March 13, 2013, www.abc.net.au/am/ content/2013/s3714163.htm.

63. Nick Bryant, "Storm Over Australia's Press Reform Proposals," BBC, March 19, 2013, www.bbc.co.uk/news/world-asia-21840076.

64. "World Press Freedom Index 2015: All Front," Reporters Without Borders, 2015, http://index.rsf.org/#!/presentation.

65. "2015 prison census: 199 journalists jailed worldwide," Committee to Protect Journalists, https://cpj.org/imprisoned/2015.php; "71 Journalists Killed in 2015/Motive Confirmed," Committee to Protect Journalists, https://cpj.org/killed/2015/ (both accessed Feb. 18, 2016)

66. "Syria, France most deadly countries for the press," Committee to Protect Journalists, Dec. 29, 2015, https://cpj.org/reports/2015/12/journalists-killed-syria-france-most-deadly-countries-for-the-press.php.

67. Andrew Roth, "In Retort to Paris, Chechens Denounce 'Permissiveness," *The New York Times*, Jan. 19, 2015, http://www.nytimes.com/2015/01/20/world/europe/chechens-march-to-protest-religious-caricatures.html.

68. "Washington Post reporter Jason Rezaian is free, Iran news outlet says," Committee to Protect Journalists, Jan. 16, 2016, https://cpj.org/2016/01/washington-post-reporter-jason-rezaian-is-free-ira.php.

69. Associated Press in Cairo, " Al-Jazeera journalists jailed for airing 'false news', Egyptian court ruling says," *The Guardian*, Sept. 6, 2015, http://www.theguardian.com/media/2015/sep/06/al-jazeera-journalists-jailed-for-airing-false-news-egyptian-court-ruling-says.

70. Joel Simon, "Joel Simon: Blame technology for the rise in violence against media," *The Dallas News*, Jan. 17, 2015, http://www.dallasnews.com/opinion/sunday-commentary/20150117-joel-simon-blame-technology-for-the-rise-in-violence-against-media.ece.

71. Aye Aye Win, "Privately Owned Daily Newspapers Return to Myanmar," The Associated Press, April 1, 2013, www.huffingtonpost.com/huff-wires/20130401/as-myanmar-new-newspapers/.

72. Anemona Hartocollis, "Yale Lecturer Resigns After Email on Halloween Costumes," *The New York Times*, Dec. 7, 2015, http://www.nytimes.com/2015/12/08/us/yale-lecturer-resigns-after-email-on-halloween-costumes.html?_r=0.

73. Andrew Anthony, "Is free speech in British universities under threat?" *The Guardian*, Jan. 24, 2016, http://www.theguardian.com/world/2016/jan/24/safe-spaces-universities-no-platform-free-speech-rhodes.

74. Susan Milligan, "From Megaphones to Muzzles," *U.S. News and World Report*, Sept. 25, 2015, http://tinyurl.com/hvsh94b.

75. Morton Shapiro, "I'm Northwestern's president. Here's why safe spaces for students are important," *The Washington Post*, Jan. 15, 2016, http://tinyurl.com/hn3wmc8.

76. For more information, see Sarah Glazer, "Free Speech on Campus," *CQ Researcher*, May 8, 2015, pp. 409-432.

77. Eugeny Morozov, *The Net Delusion* (2011), p. 97.

BIBLIOGRAPHY
Books

Ghonim, Wael, *Revolution 2.0: The Power of the People Is Greater Than the People in Power*, Houghton Mifflin Harcourt, 2012.
A Google employee who became a leader in using social media to organize protests against the government in Egypt during the so-called Arab Spring of 2011 writes a memoir about those tumultuous times.

Hargreaves, Robert, *The First Freedom: A History of Free Speech*, Sutton Publishing, 2002.
The late British broadcaster surveys the long history of speech, from Socrates to modern times, highlighting the personalities and legal cases that eventually led to greater liberties.

Lukianoff, Greg. *Unlearning Liberty: Campus Censorship and the End of American Debate*, 2014.
An attorney and president of the Foundation for Individual Rights in Education, a Philadelphia-based nonprofit that defends First Amendment rights at colleges and universities, looks at a history of censorship on campuses.

Ziek, Timothy, *The Cosmopolitan First Amendment: Protecting Transorder Expressive and Religious Liberties*, 2015.
A William and Mary Law School professor looks at the relationship of the First Amendment to the protection of

speech and religious liberties outside the U.S. and its influence in other countries.

Articles

Erdbrink, Thomas, "Iran Blocks Way to Bypass Internet Filtering System," *The New York Times*, **March 11, 2013, www.nytimes.com/2013/03/12/ world/middleeast/iran-blocks-softwareused-to-bypass-internet-filtering-system.html.**
Iran's Ministry of Information and Communications Technology has begun blocking the most popular software used by millions of Iranians to bypass the official Internet censoring system.

"Journalist: Egypt's Anti-Terror Law Restricts Freedom Of Expression," National Public Radio, Sept. 4, 2015.
Robert Siegel, host of NPR's All Things Considered, interviews Khaled Dawoud, deputy editor of Al Ahram weekly, about how a new anti-terrorism law in Egypt restricts the media. http://www.npr.org/2015/09/04/437597052/journalist-egypts-anti-terror-law-restricts-freedom-of-expression

Malik, Kenan, and Nada Shabout, "Should Religious or Cultural Sensibilities Ever Limit Free Expression?" *Index on Censorship*, **March 25, 2013, www.indexoncensorship.org/2013/03/should-religious-or-cultural-sensibilities-ever-limit-free-expression/.**
An Indian-born British broadcaster (Malik) and an Iraqi art historian debate whether even the most offensive and blasphemous speech should be protected.

Posner, Eric, "The World Doesn't Love the First Amendment," *Slate*, **Sept. 25, 2012, www.slate.com/ articles/news_and_politics/jurisprudence/2012/09/ the_vile_anti_muslim_video_and_the_first_amendment_does_the_u_s_overvalue_free_speech_.single.html.**
In the wake of violent protests across the globe triggered by an anti-Muslim video that was produced in the United States, a University of Chicago law professor argues that freedom of expression must give way at times to other values.

Reports and Studies

"Attacks on the Press: Journalism on the Front Lines," Committee to Protect Journalists, April 2015.
The latest edition of this annual report documents how more journalists are being imprisoned or killed around the world.

"The Freedom of Thought Report 2015: A global report on the rights, legal status and discrimination against humanists, atheists and the non-religious," International Humanist and Ethical Union, Dec. 11, 2015, http://freethoughtreport.com/2015/12/11/preface-to-2015-edition-by-rafida-bonya-ahmed/.
The latest global survey of laws regulating religious beliefs and expression.

Zhu, Tao, *et al.*, **"The Velocity of Censorship: High-Fidelity Detection of Microblog Post Deletions," March 4, 2013, http://arxiv.org/abs/1303.0597.**
A team of computer scientists examined the accounts of 3,500 users of Weibo, China's microblogging site, to see if it was being censored. The scientists found that thousands of Weibo employees were deleting forbidden phrases and characters.

For More Information

Access, P.O. Box 115, New York, NY 10113; 888-414-0100; www.accessnow.org. A digital-rights group, founded after protests against Iran's disputed 2009 presidential election.

Article 19, Free Word Centre, 60 Farringdon Rd., London, United Kingdom, EC1R 3GA; +44 20 7324 2500; www.article19.org. A group named for a section of the Universal Declaration of Human Rights that designs laws and policies promoting freedom of expression.

Committee to Protect Journalists, 330 7th Ave., 11th Floor, New York, NY 10001; 212-465-1004; www.cpj.org.

Documents attacks on journalists; publishes its findings and works to promote press freedom.

Freedom House, 1301 Connecticut Ave., N.W., 6th Floor, Washington, DC 20036; 202-296-5101; www .freedomhouse.org. An independent watchdog group founded in 1941 that advocates greater political and civil liberties.

Index on Censorship, Free Word Centre, 60 Farringdon Rd., London, United Kingdom, EC1R 3GA; +44 20 7324 2522; www.indexoncensorship.org. Founded in 1972 to publish stories of communist dissidents in Eastern Europe; promotes global free speech through journalistic reports and advocacy.

International Press Institute, Spielgasse 2, A-1010, Vienna, Austria; +43 1 412 90 11; www.freemedia.at. A global network of media executives and journalists founded in 1950, dedicated to promoting and safeguarding press freedoms.

Reporters Committee for Freedom of the Press, 1101 Wilson Blvd., Suite 1100, Arlington, VA 22209; 703-807-2100; www.rcfp.org. Provides free legal advice and other resources to journalists on First Amendment issues.

13

Global Hunger

Tom Price

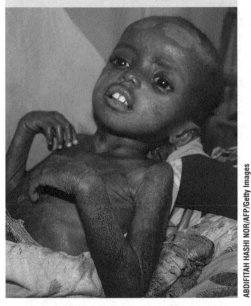

A severely malnourished girl convalesces at a hospital in Mogadishu, Somalia, on July 15, 2014. Food is scarce in the country, where civil war has been raging for years. Affluent countries sent some 5 million metric tons of food to the world's hungry in 2012, mostly for emergency relief. The United States donated the most — 44 percent of the total.

ABDIFITAH HASHI NOR/AFP/Getty Images

From *CQ Researcher*, August 8, 2014.

As radical Islamists overran the Iraqi city of Mosul in mid-June, taxi driver Abdel Hady, his wife and their six children began walking north toward the relatively peaceful autonomous region of Kurdistan, sleeping in the homes of generous strangers along the way.

When the Hadys arrived at the Garmava refugee camp three days later, workers were pitching tents and digging latrines to prepare for some of the 300,000 or more Iraqis who had fled combat zones the previous week alone, joining 250,000 Syrians already in Kurdish territory.

More than 2.5 million Syrians have fled that country's bloody civil war to neighboring Kurdistan, Turkey, Jordan and Lebanon, and the Iraqi conflict is expected to produce 1.5 million more refugees, straining local resources and draining the budgets of United Nations (U.N.) relief agencies and humanitarian organizations.[1] Feeding the Syrian refugees alone costs $38 million to $40 million a week, dramatically demonstrating how warfare contributes to global hunger.[2]

But such conflicts represent only a fraction of the food shortages that today leave 842 million people around the world undernourished. That figure is down from just over 1 billion in 1992, due to new agricultural technology that has enabled global food supplies to outstrip population growth. The number of hungry people worldwide dropped by 26 million — 3 percent — in 2013 alone, according to the U.N. Food and Agriculture Organization (FAO).[3] The FAO defines hunger, or undernourishment, as "not having enough food for an active and healthy life" or not being able to meet "dietary energy requirements."[4]

Hunger Concentrated in Sub-Saharan Africa, Southeast Asia

Seven African countries, Timor Leste in Southeast Asia and Haiti in the Caribbean have the world's highest concentrations of hunger, or daily undernourishment.* Twenty-one other countries — including 14 African nations, Iraq, North Korea and Guatemala — have "high" rates of undernourishment, with 25 percent to 35 percent of their population classified as hungry.

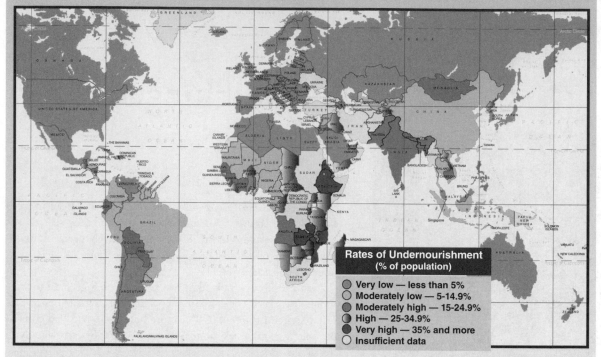

Rates of Undernourishment
(% of population)

- Very low — less than 5%
- Moderately low — 5-14.9%
- Moderately high — 15-24.9%
- High — 25-34.9%
- Very high — 35% and more
- Insufficient data

* Undernourishment is defined as not having enough calories (energy) to meet minimum physiological needs for an active life. It is a less visible form of hunger than starvation, which the World Food Programme calls acute hunger.

Source: "Hunger Map 2013," World Food Programme, United Nations, http://tinyurl.com/plddrmr

Still, 12 percent of the Earth's population does not get enough to eat. Most of the hungry are in the developing world, and 70 percent are small farmers or agricultural laborers who can't grow sufficient food to feed their families or sell to others.[5] The problem is severest in sub-Saharan Africa, where one in four goes hungry, but that is down from one in three in the early '90s.[6]

Experts worry that over the long term, expanding middle classes in rapidly developing countries such as China and India will raise demand for more expensive foods that overtax the environment, further boosting food prices. And climate change and modern industrial agricultural practices threaten future agricultural production and the environment in a variety of ways, scientists say.

Currently, hunger kills nearly 3.1 million children under 5 each year — 45 percent of all deaths in that age range. One-sixth of the children in developing countries — 100 million — are underweight.[7] Hunger also helps to truncate adults' lives. Life expectancy in Africa is 58, for instance, compared with 67 in Southeast Asia, 68 in the Eastern Mediterranean and 79 in the United States.[8]

Paradoxically, the Earth produces more food than its inhabitants need, but the food is unevenly distributed. In the United States and other affluent countries, more people are overweight or obese than hungry — the result of eating too much high-calorie food and getting insufficient exercise. Obesity also is growing in rapidly developing countries such as China, where childhood obesity rose from 1.5 percent of the child population in 1989 to 6.9 percent of boys and 2.8 percent of girls last year.[9]

"One billion people in the world don't have enough food, while one billion people eat too much," said World Wildlife Fund Senior Vice President Jason Clay.[10]

Experts say hunger has a number of causes, including war, poverty, population growth, poor farming practices, government corruption, ineffective food distribution, inclement weather, climate change and waste. "Short-term hunger usually is due to natural disaster or war," says Christopher Barrett, director of the School of Applied Economics and Management at Cornell University, who researches hunger and poverty. "Chronic hunger is related to chronic poverty."

Due to inadequate technology and resources, for instance, Africa's agricultural productivity is less than half the world average and is rising at half the rate of the continent's population growth.[11]

Some anti-hunger activists say affluent nations also add to the world hunger problem. Government subsidies to growers in wealthy nations can depress world commodity prices, they say, reducing the earnings of small-scale farmers in developing nations. Promoting plant-based biofuel also drives up world food prices, making it more expensive for the poor. Consuming meat- and dairy-rich diets increases the cost of food by diverting food and land to feeding and raising animals. In addition, critics say certain aspects of the donor countries' aid policies exacerbate hunger, such as a U.S. provision requiring food aid to be shipped on U.S.-flagged vessels, which are often more expensive than other ships.

United States and U.N. Are Largest Food Donors

The United States delivered nearly 2.2 million metric tons of food aid in 2012, more than twice the combined amount of the next three largest donors — Japan, Brazil and Canada. The United Nations and European Commission, the largest international government organizations, together provided more than 700,000 metric tons.

Largest Food Donors, Countries, 2012		Largest Food Donors, International Organizations, 2012	
Country	Total Food Aid (in metric tons)	Type of Organization	Total Food Aid (in metric tons)
United States	2,195,285	United Nations	565,796
Japan	406,585	European Commission	137,002
Brazil	334,294	Others	86,192
Canada	293,293	International Government	60,075
China	243,381	Nongovernmental	40,443
Germany	168,486	Private	28,003
Australia	72,817		
Russia	61,606		
United Kingdom	59,876		
Sweden	47,343		

Source: "Table 6, Food Aid Deliveries in 2012 by Donor and Category (Mt — Cereals In Grain Equivalent)," Food Aid Flows 2012 Report Annex Tables, World Food Programme, United Nations, p. 16, http://tinyurl.com/llklkap

About a third of the world's food is wasted, the FAO estimates.[12] "In the undeveloped world, the waste happens before the food gets to people," said North Dakota farmer Roger Johnson, president of the National Farmers Union. "The food rots" because of lack of roads and proper storage facilities. In the developed world, he said, waste is due to "the staggering amount of food that's thrown out after it gets to our plates."

Food production and distribution are hampered in many countries by prolonged conflict and political instability, such as in Nepal, incomplete land reform, as in Tajikistan, and population growth and extreme poverty in countries like Uganda, according to the FAO.[13] Erratic rainfall and more frequent droughts have exacerbated hunger in the Sahel, the arid region just south of the Sahara Desert where 20 million people have inconsistent access to food and 5 million children face acute malnutrition, according to the U.S. Agency for International Development (USAID).[14]

Countries that are winning the war against hunger have governments that are consistently committed to "long-term rural development and poverty reducing plans," says the FAO. For instance, in Bangladesh, Ghana and Nicaragua, hunger has been cut in half in the last two decades through economic growth and freer trade, the agency said. Ghana and Nicaragua also have enjoyed political stability and high world prices for their exports.[15]

Speaking to a gathering of African diplomats in 2010, Johnnie Carson, then U.S. assistant secretary of State for African affairs, said that "our ability to achieve our shared long-term goals of democracy, stability and prosperity on the continent depends entirely on the integrity and effectiveness of African leadership."[16]

Most food aid responds to emergencies, rather than chronic hunger. Affluent countries sent just over 5 million metric tons of food to the hungry in 2012, 70 percent of which was for emergency relief. The biggest donor, the United States, contributed 2.2 million tons — 44 percent of the total, and more than four times as much as the next-biggest donor, Japan, which gave 407,000 tons.[17]

The United States will spend about $3.5 billion on international food aid and agricultural development programs this year. The Food for Peace program receives almost $1.5 billion of that, used primarily to buy U.S. farmers' commodities, which are shipped abroad as emergency relief. Another $600 million provides cash for such emergency relief activities as giving food vouchers to individuals and purchasing food near where it is consumed.

The Obama administration's Feed the Future initiative — which supports development programs led by farmers and local, regional and national governments in the developing world — gets about $1.1 billion. The rest supports child and school feeding activities, increased agricultural productivity and expanded trade in agricultural products.

Almost all of the U.S. emergency relief is distributed by the U.N.'s World Food Programme; non-emergency relief is supplied by nongovernmental organizations. A small amount is distributed directly by the United States, such as when the military responds to natural disasters.[18]

Back at the Garmava refugee camp, a Mosul police officer named Taha and his wife Shahla (who declined to give their last names to a reporter) faced a key danger posed by inadequate nutrition: Shahla was about to give birth.[19] "The people who are especially vulnerable to hunger are those in the first 1,000 days — from the beginning of pregnancy to age 2," says Richard Leach, president and CEO of the World Food Program USA, an independent nonprofit that supports the U.N.'s World Food Programme through fundraising and advocacy in the United States. If mothers and children don't receive adequate nutrition then, he says, the children "won't develop intellectually or physically to the degree that they could have."

Maternal undernourishment followed by inadequate childhood nutrition causes stunting — abnormally short growth. Stunting affected 160 million children in the developing world — 28 percent — in 2011, down from 45 percent in 1990.[20]

Children's health is affected by the quality of the food they eat as well as the quantity. Not consuming enough Vitamin A impairs growth, increases vulnerability to infection and is the leading cause of childhood blindness. Iron deficiency impedes children's intellectual development and women's chances of successful pregnancy.[21]

As government officials, relief workers, advocates and scholars debate the best ways to attack hunger, here are some of the questions they are addressing:

Are developed countries' aid policies making hunger worse?

Anti-hunger activists cheered when Congress in 2012 adopted a modest reform to U.S. international food-aid programs by lowering a requirement that 75 percent of food be shipped on U.S.-flagged vessels. By this spring, the cheers had morphed into complaints, as the House moved to repeal the reform.

That legislation — which cleared the House April 1 and awaits Senate consideration — illustrates activists' contention that developed countries' aid policies and lifestyles make hunger worse or lessen the effectiveness of food-aid programs.[22]

The critics especially cite U.S. aid policies that rely heavily on purchasing food from American farmers rather than using cash to acquire food near where it will be consumed. Most of the purchased food is given to the hungry, usually through the World Food Programme. But in some cases, commodities may be "monetized" — or sold on the market and the proceeds used for developmental activities. Because of the cost of purchasing commodities in the United States and shipping them overseas, critics say it would be more efficient in both cases to buy food near where it's consumed and to allocate cash to pay for development programs.

Even the 2012 shipping change had fallen far short of activists' desires. It still required that half of U.S. food aid be transported on the more-expensive U.S.-flagged ships, costing $75 million more per year than if the shipping were open to global competition, according to Cornell's Barrett and Erin C. Lentz, assistant professor of international relations at Bucknell University.[23]

Authors of the House legislation repealing the change — Reps. Duncan Hunter, R-Calif., and Elijah Cummings, D-Md. — said requiring the food to be transported on U.S. ships supports a Merchant Marine that is "essential to sustaining our military."[24] But the Defense and Transportation departments told the House Foreign Affairs Committee that the preference is unnecessary.[25]

The requirement "forces a huge premium price on ocean shipping and generates windfall profits for a handful of shipping lines, most [of them] foreign owned" despite being U.S.-flagged, says Barrett, who has studied the matter in depth. Even without the shipping markup, locally bought food is often faster and cheaper to deliver, he says.

"For the same [aid] budget," says agricultural economics professor Michael Carter, "we can save millions more people." Carter, of the University of California-Davis, directs a research consortium funded by USAID.

But several nonprofits and companies that grow, process and ship the food defend existing commodities programs. In a letter to Congress during last year's debate on reauthorization of a major farm bill, several of them wrote: "Growing, manufacturing, bagging, shipping and transporting nutritious U.S. food creates jobs and economic activity here at home, provides support for our U.S. Merchant Marine, essential to our national defense sealift capability, and sustains a robust domestic constituency for these programs not easily replicated in alternative foreign aid programs."[26]

Rep. Jeff Duncan, R-S.C., asked: "How is wiring cash to someone in a developing country a good idea instead of giving them wholesome, nutritious commodities grown by hard-working Americans."[27]

As for the criticisms of monetization programs, a 2012 study commissioned by the Alliance for Global Food Security — a coalition of 14 relief and development organizations, some of which engage in monetization — found that properly managed monetization transactions can avoid pitfalls while providing benefits that cash-only support cannot.

Informa Economics — a Memphis-headquartered firm that conducts agriculture-related research — analyzed five monetization programs and found that they were designed not to compete with local production or disrupt commercial trade. Although the sales were made at fair-market value, the study concluded, the programs were able to offer the recipient countries other benefits, such as flexible payment terms. As a result, some recipients were able to make the purchases despite volatile exchange rates and avoid higher shipping costs associated with low-volume sales, the researchers said.[28]

The key is using "the right tool at the appropriate place," says Leach, of the World Food Program USA. "There are countries like Sudan that do not have access to food" and need to have it shipped in. "In Syria, it's much better to buy food regionally," because it's difficult to move commodities through a combat zone.

Shipping U.S. commodities also can make sense when responding to a nearby disaster in the Americas, Barrett says. And when the need is for foods fortified with vitamins and minerals, "you can start to enjoy the efficiency of modern American food processing."

Aside from advanced nations' aid policies, their agricultural subsidies, biofuel mandates and eating habits also can aggravate hunger, critics say.

Farm subsidy programs "tend to reduce worldwide commodity prices, hurting farmers in the developing world," said Daniel Sumner, an agricultural economics professor at the University of California-Davis and director of the University of California Agricultural Issues Center.[29]

Supporters of farm subsidies say they help stabilize U.S. agriculture production. Critics should "feel lucky we don't have runs on grocery stores," said Rep. Tim Walz, D.-Minn.[30]

And donating U.S.-grown commodities — or selling them at below-market prices — can also depress local crop prices, says Robert Rector, a senior research fellow at the Heritage Foundation, a conservative think tank in Washington. "You have to be careful not to undermine domestic production," Rector says. "Cheap and free food takes away from the [local] market, particularly if you're doing it consistently."

Critics say subsidies and mandates promoting biofuels such as corn-based ethanol — designed to reduce greenhouse gas emissions and lower American and European dependence on foreign oil — raise food prices and divert food to fuel production. Action Against Hunger, an international relief and development organization, said the amount of U.S. corn being converted into biofuels could feed 570 million people a year.[31]

Converting food to fuel "poses risks to ecosystems and biodiversity," said the U.N. Intergovernmental Panel on Climate Change, which previously supported biofuel production.[32]

Oxfam, an international relief and advocacy organization, has called for Europe and the United States to end their biofuel mandates and subsidies, which are projected to total between $9.2 billion and $11.5 billion in Europe in 2015, says Damon Vis-Dunbar, project and communications manager for the International Institute for Sustainable Development, a Canadian-based research organization with offices in the United States, Europe and China. The United States, which offered $6.6 billion in subsidies in 2010, cut them to around $1 billion in 2012.[33]

To meet Europe's biofuel demand, companies are planting land in developing countries that would be better used feeding the poor who live nearby, Oxfam said.[34]

Biofuels corporate executive Paul Beckwith argued that the ethanol mandate has stimulated important investment that has put the United States ahead of the world in getting "new advanced renewable energy into commercialization." Beckwith is CEO of Butamax Advanced Biofuels, a joint venture of BP and DuPont that develops biofuel manufacturing technology.[35]

The affluent world's appetite also taxes the environment and threatens the developing world's access to sufficient food, critics say. For instance, raising animals for consumption is far less efficient than using land to grow food plants — and that much-coveted steak is the least efficient of all.

Every 100 calories of grain fed to an animal produces only about 40 new calories of milk, 22 calories of eggs, 12 of chicken, 10 of pork or three of beef, according to Jonathan Foley, who is leaving his position as director of the University of Minnesota's Institute on the Environment on Aug. 15 to become executive director of the California Academy of Sciences.[36] By another reckoning, it takes about a pound of feed to produce a pound of farmed fish, but seven to make a pound of beef.[37]

Despite the relative efficiency of farmed fish, affluent diners' desire for wild-caught seafood — along with pollution and global warming — is depleting wild fish populations, which in turn threatens the livelihoods of poor fishermen who compete with sophisticated fleets from developed countries.

The International Programme on the State of the Ocean at Oxford University has declared the planet "at high risk of entering a phase of extinction of marine species unprecedented in human history."[38] For instance, overfishing — both legal and illegal — threatens the scalloped hammerhead shark, used in shark fin soup, a delicacy in many Asian countries.[39]

Is climate change making hunger worse?

Oxfam has called climate change "the single biggest threat to fighting hunger."[40]

Scientists have issued dire warnings about the threat global warming poses to humanity's ability to feed itself in the future, and they cite damage that's already occurring. The World Food Programme says climate change could wipe out two-thirds of Africa's arable land by 2025, boost food prices by 50 to 90 percent by 2030 and raise the risk of hunger by 10 to 20 percent by 2050.[41]

But when it comes to climate change, agriculture is both a victim and a villain. Farming is a major source of greenhouse gases — including methane, carbon dioxide and nitrous oxide — which scientists say are warming the planet. Agriculture emits more greenhouse gases than all forms of transportation combined. Fuel-burning farm machinery emits carbon dioxide. Cattle release large amounts of methane, fertilizer emits nitrous oxide and soil releases carbon dioxide (CO_2) when cultivated.[42]

Some say a warming planet and more atmospheric CO_2 will reduce hunger by improving agricultural productivity. "Plants love warmth and sunshine," says Dennis Avery, a senior fellow at the conservative Heartland and Hudson institutes and director of Hudson's Center for Global Food Issues. "Both animals and vegetation have a much greater tolerance for temperature changes than the [widely used scientific] models would have us believe."

Describing CO_2 as "like fertilizer for plants," which breathe it in like animals breathe oxygen, Avery says doubling atmospheric CO_2 concentrations would increase crop yields by about 35 percent.

Similarly, Andrei Illarionov, a senior fellow at the libertarian Cato Institute, points out that in warmer places "there is usually more precipitation than in drier areas, the cost of heating and volume of food required to sustain human life [are] lower, while vegetation and [ice-free] navigation periods are longer, and crops' yields are higher."[43]

Arguing that the Earth simply is in the warm period of a routine climate cycle, Avery says the greater threat to food production will occur during the next Ice Age.

Other climate-change skeptics contend that proposed responses to global warming, such as switching to biofuels production, can threaten food supplies.

Scientists agree that CO_2 by itself could increase plant yields, but most say the damage to food done by greenhouse gases will outweigh the benefits. For instance, two recent studies found that higher CO_2 levels diminish plants' nutritional value and resistance to pests.[44]

More broadly, scientists warn that rising temperatures, more drought, and more violent weather will lead to diminished agricultural yields, particularly in warmer regions where many of the poor live.

This past May was the hottest on record, according to the National Oceanic and Atmospheric Administration (NOAA).[45] The first decade of this century was the hottest in recorded history, and temperatures are even higher so far this decade, according to the University Corporation for Atmospheric Research, a consortium based in Boulder, Colo., that manages the National Center for Atmospheric Research.[46]

Already, according to the American Association for the Advancement of Science (AAAS), heat waves and extreme storms are becoming worse and more frequent. The Greenland and Antarctic ice sheets are melting more rapidly. The oceans are absorbing growing amounts of carbon dioxide, which makes them more acidic and degrades coral reefs where millions of marine species live.[47]

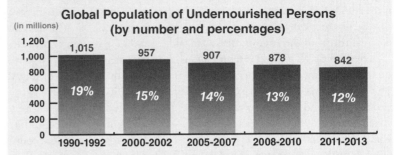

Global Hunger on the Decline

The number of undernourished people worldwide fell from more than 1 billion in 1992, one-fifth of the global population, to 842 million in 2013, or 12 percent.

Global Population of Undernourished Persons (by number and percentages) (in millions)

1990-1992	2000-2002	2005-2007	2008-2010	2011-2013
1,015	957	907	878	842
19%	15%	14%	13%	12%

Source: "Hunger Portal," U.N. Food and Agriculture Organization, undated, http://tinyurl.com/yz2bcrh

Meanwhile deserts are expanding. The growing Sahara Desert has been destroying crops and leaving farmers in West Africa without food.[48] To escape rising temperatures, plants and animals are migrating toward the poles, up mountainsides and deeper into the sea. Droughts this year devastated crops in Brazil's southeast and in California, which grows nearly half of America's fruits, vegetables and nuts.[49] Global wheat and corn productivity is declining.[50]

"We're facing the specter of reduced yields in some of the key crops that feed humanity," said Rajendra Pachauri, chairman of the U.N.'s climate change panel. The panel's report warned that altered ocean chemistry could cause fish extinctions, and changes in climate could threaten apple orchards in Washington, cherry orchards in California and coffee crops in Central and South America, often tended by subsistence farmers who depend on their coffee crops for survival.[51]

Are genetically modified crops needed to end hunger?

A group of farmers and activists this spring protested at the office of Philippine Agriculture Secretary Proceso Alcala, calling on him to block tests of so-called "golden rice," a genetically modified grain designed to combat vitamin A deficiency in the developing world. Last year, about 400 protesters tore down fences surrounding a golden rice test field and ripped the plants from the ground.

"There are not enough studies to ensure the safety of golden rice to humans," Chito Medina, national coordinator of the Filipino activist group known by its acronym MASIPAG, said in explaining the protests. "To plant the genetically engineered rice, or the golden rice, is a real threat to the environment," he said.[52]

The Philippine protesters represent just one of numerous campaigns worldwide opposing genetically modified organisms (GMOs). Scientists make genetically modified (GM) plants and animals by adding genes that introduce specific traits — such as pest resistance — to the organism. Opponents fear GMO plants could harm humans, animals or the environment. They paint GMOs as part of a plot by Western agribusiness to control farming in the developing world.

So far, their actions have produced mixed results: GMOs are common in the United States, rare in Europe and subject to heated debate in the developing world.

Golden rice was created in 1999 by Ingo Potrykus of the Swiss Federal Institute of Technology and Peter Beyer of the University of Freiburg in Germany. They inserted genes from a daffodil and a bacterium into rice to enable it to generate beta-carotene, which the human body converts into vitamin A. Later, beta-carotene production was boosted by replacing the daffodil gene with one from corn.

The Philippines-based nonprofit International Rice Research Institute, which is developing the rice, said field trials there met beta-carotene goals but produced a lower yield than varieties currently in use. The institute is continuing research focused on yield.[53]

Proponents say GM foods are safe and essential to ease hunger and meet the demands of a growing world population, particularly as developing countries' become more affluent and demand more and higher-quality food. GM crops, they say, increase yields, survive with less fertilizer and pesticides and can be more nutritious. Scientists are working on drought-tolerant corn, sweet potatoes with high beta-carotene content, bacteria-resistant bananas, cassava varieties that resist viruses and contain added beta-carotene and other nutrients, and corn that requires less fertilizer.

GM plants grow on more than half of U.S. farmland, represent nearly all of America's soybeans and 70 percent of its corn and are common in Canada.[54] However, European countries effectively ban GMOs, with some exceptions. Some GMO animal feed can be imported, for example, and Spain, Portugal, the Czech Republic, Romania and Slovakia grow some genetically modified crops.[55]

More than half the acreage planted in GM crops last year was in developing countries, 87 percent of that in Brazil, Argentina, India, China and South Africa. Only three other African countries — Sudan, Egypt and Burkina Faso — grow GM crops, partly due to fear among farmers in other African countries that GM crops can't be sold in Europe.[56]

Some countries refuse to accept GMOs as food aid, says Steve Taravella, the World Food Programme's senior spokesman in the United States. And some donor nations prohibit their aid money from being used to purchase GM food, Taravella adds.

Richard Roberts — a Nobel laureate for genetic research and chief scientific officer for a company that makes genetic-research supplies — called opposition to GM crops a "crime against humanity," because the foods are needed to feed the hungry.[57]

Michael Purugganan, a professor of genomics and biology and dean for science at New York University, lamented the "misinformation" circulated by GM opponents. "The genes they inserted to make the vitamin [in golden rice] are not some weird manufactured material but are also found in squash, carrots and melons," he said.[58]

The AAAS has noted that the World Health Organization, the American Medical Association, the U.S. National Academy of Sciences, the British Royal Society and "every other respected organization that has examined the evidence" has concluded that eating GM plants is no riskier than eating plants bred with traditional farming technology.[59]

Opponents, however, contend that there are better ways to feed the hungry. "Most GMOs are not used to solve hunger" but to increase the profitability of industrial farming, says Greenpeace USA researcher Mark Floegel. "We have [other] technologies that subsistence farmers could use to make their lives better."

Paul Johnston and Dave Santillo, scientists in Greenpeace International's Science Unit, argued that history proves the need for caution in using GMOs. Citing the ill effects of "one-time 'wonder chemicals,' such as

PCBs and many pesticides," they contended that "new problems continue to emerge from chemicals put into widespread use without the drawbacks having been fully investigated." Thus, they said, "If you are in doubt about the consequences of what you intend to do, then don't do it."[60]

Others take a more nuanced approach. GMO technology can be used "for good or bad," says Walter Willett, chair of Harvard University's Department of Nutrition. GMOs used in the United States probably don't pose health threats, he says, but they also probably don't produce a significantly higher yield. Noting the need to increase global food production, he adds, "I wouldn't take them off the table."

Oxfam is "agnostic about GMOs," says Gawain Kripke, Oxfam America's policy director. Most GM products brought to market so far primarily benefit industrial farming, he notes, but he finds attempts to enrich plants' nutrients "pretty interesting."

Similarly, World Food Program USA's Leach says, "We will accept food from a country if that country would use that food to feed its own population, and we will take that food into any country that will accept it."

Farmers in Burkina Faso in West Africa have found that GM cotton "cuts pesticide and labor costs," the University of California's Carter says. That shows that "small-scale farmers can potentially make good use of at least some of these technologies," he adds.

However, in the United States insects have developed resistance to GM cotton, which initially allowed farmers to use less pesticide. So pesticide use is rising, according to Charles Benbrook, research professor at Washington State University's Center for Sustaining Agriculture and Natural Resources. Similarly, corn engineered to tolerate Monsanto's Roundup herbicide requires increasing amounts of the product to kill weeds that have developed resistance, he said.[61]

BACKGROUND

Early Famines

History records serious famine in every part of the world. Egyptian stone carvers chronicled lengthy droughts and famines in the third millennium B.C. They also portrayed the first recorded hunger-relief efforts — by the Egyptian upper class.

In *Famine: A Short History*, Irish economist Cormac Ó Gráda identifies multiple causes of hunger, including too much or too little rain, extreme temperatures, conflict, overpopulation, poverty, ideology and autocratic governments. Often the causes converged, as when conflict coincided with poor harvests, or drought struck an impoverished community. Famine most frequently hit the poor and seldom occurred in democracies.

The Old Testament book of Nehemiah, likely written in the fifth century B.C., describes overpopulation compelling the poor to sell their children because there was not enough food. The Punic Wars triggered famine in Rome in the first century B.C. Heavy rains and low temperatures brought famine to Europe in the early 14th century A.D. Authoritarian communist government policies turned poor harvests into mass starvation in the Soviet Union and China in the 20th century and continue to do so in North Korea.[62]

Ó Gráda, an economics professor at University College Dublin, chronicles famines throughout history, including in Turkey (499-501), Bengal (1176), Japan (1229-32), Mexico (1454), Africa (often) and, of course, in Ireland, during the potato famine in the 1840s and '50s, one of the best known.[63]

Potato blight struck Ireland's potatoes — the primary sustenance of half the population — in 1845. The fungus-like micro-organism, carried to Ireland from Mexico, devastated the crop and led to the deaths of more than 750,000 Irish over the next decade. Two million people fled to England, Canada or the United States.[64] During the latter part of the century, 50 million people died in famines in India, China, Korea, Brazil, Russia, Ethiopia and Sudan.[65]

Ireland's Great Hunger marked the beginning of the end of peacetime famine in Europe, except for Russia. The last natural famine in Western Europe was in Finland in 1867-68.[66]

Previously, societies had responded to hunger with personal and religious philanthropy. Some governments imposed price controls, distributed food and subsidized migration to places without food shortages. In the 19th and 20th centuries nongovernment relief organizations emerged, as did major advances in agricultural technology.[67]

In the United States, the 1862 Morrill Act funded state colleges and universities focused on agriculture and mechanical arts. The U.S. government also established the Cooperative State Research, Education and Extension Service to disseminate agricultural research findings.[68] In 1883, the Department of Agriculture began research on boosting agricultural production.[69] And, in 1905, German chemist Fritz Haber enabled a gigantic leap in agricultural yield by extracting nitrogen from air, which permitted the manufacture of nitrogen-based synthetic fertilizer.[70]

Advances in transportation, storage, medicine and the understanding of nutrition as well as the spread of democracy also helped end peacetime famine in developed countries. In the developing world, hunger was lessened and dealt with more quickly because of the growth of relief organizations, creation of inexpensive nutrient-dense foods that could be stored and transported easily and the expansion of communication technology that enabled news of food emergencies to spread rapidly.

Residents of affluent countries were eating more, including more expensive food. Per capita annual meat consumption in Germany, for instance, rose from less than 44 pounds before 1820 to almost 115 pounds by the early 20th century. In 1800 a typical European consumed 2,000 calories a day, which rose to 3,000 calories by the early 20th century.

In the mid-20th century, nearly 60 percent of the world's population lived in countries with an average daily diet of less than 2,200 calories. By the mid-'80s, only 10 percent did.[71]

Manmade Famine

Some of the most notorious 20th-century famines were substantially caused by humans.

In 1932-33, for instance, an estimated 6 million to 8 million people died — many of starvation — during Russian dictator Josef Stalin's violent push to collectivize agriculture and turn the Soviet Union into an industrial power. Beginning in 1929, small peasant farms were forced into collectives of up to 247,000 acres. Many peasants resisted, and the government cracked down brutally. As farm production fell by 40 percent, the state seized and exported grain to raise funds for industrial equipment, leaving peasants without enough to eat.[72]

Mao Tse-tung pressed the same disastrous policies on Communist China 25 years later. Between 1958 and 1962, 36 million starved to death.[73]

In the late 1960s, between 500,000 and 2 million people — many of them children — died of starvation during civil war in Nigeria. Warfare disrupted food supplies, and the Nigerian government blocked relief shipments into the breakaway region of Biafra.[74]

In the early 1980s, several factors converged to create severe famine in Ethiopia. The country was struggling to recover from drought-caused famine in the 1970s when another drought hit. Poor farming techniques worsened the effects, leading to deforestation, soil erosion and expanding deserts. Civil war — between Ethiopia's Marxist dictatorship and rebels in the north — compounded the suffering.

The government tried to keep news of the starvation from the world. But after the BBC televised images of the devastation, relief supplies flowed into the country. The government then blocked shipments to rebel-controlled areas, and diverted food from starving Ethiopians to the army. An estimated 1 million people died in 1984-85.[75]

Relief Efforts

The United States led relief efforts in Ethiopia, just as it had around the world since early in the century, especially after World War II.[76] The United Nations, created after that war, also facilitated international relief programs.

The U.N. established the FAO in 1945 and the International Children's Emergency Fund (UNICEF) in 1946. It added the World Food Programme in 1961, the U.N. Development Programme in 1966 and the U.N. Population Fund in 1969.[77] The World Bank got into the act in 1973, when bank President Robert McNamara set a goal of reducing malnutrition and poverty in the developing world by making loans for agricultural and rural development.[78]

In 1954, the United States institutionalized its relief efforts by creating the Food for Peace program, under which Congress authorized the purchase of surplus commodities from American farmers for resale at low prices overseas. The process was designed to help both U.S. farmers and the hungry abroad. It also provided the basis for a later debate about whether shipping commodities across the ocean was the best way to aid the hungry. Over the years, the program's emphasis shifted from sales, which essentially ceased during the 1990s, to donations.

CHRONOLOGY

1845-1984 *As technology and anti-hunger organizations fight famine, wars and other human actions become leading causes of hunger.*

1845 Potato blight causes Irish famine that kills 750,000 and sends millions of refugees to England, Canada and United States.

1862 U.S. government begins to support agricultural research and education.

1868 End of Finnish famine marks last in heart of Europe.

1905 German chemist Fritz Haber "fixes" nitrogen from air, enabling manufacture of modern fertilizer.

1929 Soviet Union begins forcing farmers into collectives while pushing industrial development, leading to collapse of agricultural production and 6 to 8 million deaths, many from starvation.

1944 American biologist Norman Borlaug begins research that leads to "Green Revolution" of high-yield farming.

1945 U.N. establishes Food and Agriculture Organization (FAO).

1953 American biochemist James Watson and British biophysicist Francis Crick describe the structure of DNA, enabling eventual creation of genetically modified organisms.

1954 Congress authorizes purchase of surplus commodities for resale at low prices overseas to feed the hungry.

1958 Communist China copies Soviet Union's collectivism/industrialization efforts; 36 million starve.

1961 U.N. creates World Food Programme to distribute food to the hungry.

1967 Secessionist war in Nigeria's Biafra state leads to 500,000 to 2 million starvation deaths.

1973 Scientists create first genetically engineered organism; World Bank begins to address hunger.

1984 Drought, poor farming practices and civil war cause famine that kills 1 million Ethiopians.

1994-2014 *New agricultural technologies incite controversy; anti-hunger organizations focus on sustainability.*

1994 Food and Drug Administration approves sale of genetically modified (GM) food.

2000 Genes from genetically engineered StarLink corn, approved only for animal feed, are found in taco shells after farmers sell the corn for human consumption.

2002 GM crops in United States produce 4 billion pounds more food and fiber with less pesticide per acre than conventional plants, raise farm income by $1.5 billion.

2006 To help protect wildlife habitat, World Wildlife Fund works with food companies to promote efficient farming practices.

2007 Overuse of Green Revolution techniques in India have made Punjab state's agriculture "unsustainable and nonprofitable," according to local officials. World Food Programme, with support from the Bill & Melinda Gates and Howard Buffett foundations, begins teaching better agricultural practices to poor farmers and buying their crops for use in relief deliveries.

2009 Obama administration launches Feed the Future program that seeks leadership from developing countries and taps private-sector expertise of nonprofit and profit-making organizations to promote agricultural development.

2011 Study finds high-tech sensors can increase crop yields while reducing fuel consumption and fertilizer and pesticide overuse.

2012 Farmers raise more fish than beef for the first time.

2013 FAO counts 842 million hungry people worldwide — 26 million fewer than in 2012.

2014 Climate-change threat to food production underscored by University Corporation for Atmospheric Research report that this decade is on track to being hottest ever recorded.

Videographer Farmers Promote Best Practices

Locally produced videos have credibility.

The scene — played out thousands of times across rural India — led one journalist to liken poor farmers to the late Indian filmmaker Satyajit Ray.[1] After a crash course in filmmaking, farmers set up tripods and use small, battery-powered, digital cameras to record interviews with fellow farmers about their best agricultural practices. They then edit their work to eight- to 10-minute presentations.

Finally, with a tiny, battery-powered projector and perhaps a sheet stretched between trees, they show the videos to other indigenous farmers at bus stops, temples, schools, street corners or local government offices — anywhere they find farmers with time on their hands and an interest in learning how to grow more food at less cost in environmentally friendly ways. Sometimes government workers attend the meetings and distribute materials needed to implement the suggested practices.[2]

The program is organized and supported by Digital Green, the brainchild of Indian-American Rikin Gandhi, who got the idea about a decade ago while researching technology for emerging markets at Microsoft Research India.

Traditional government agricultural extension programs, provided via broadcast or print media, don't reach many small-scale farmers, many of whom are illiterate. So Gandhi decided to combine the high technology of making videos with low-tech means of distributing them to far-flung rural communities. The equipment is small enough to fit into a backpack for transport by bicycle or on foot.[3]

Gandhi figured farmers would be more likely to listen to their peers. So, while the information comes from experts, farmers tell about their own experiences using the new technologies. Having locals produce the videos adds to the films' credibility, Gandhi said, and enables the films to be shot in the local languages.

"Farmers listen to farmers," says Jason Clay, senior vice president at the World Wildlife Fund, "They listen to their neighbors and to people who speak their language." Worldwide, farmers speak about 6,000 different languages, he says.

When the videos are shot by farmers, Gandhi said, other farmers "instantly connect with it."[4] "The first questions farmers often ask when they see these videos are, 'What is the name of the farmer in the video?' and 'Which village is he or she from?' " he said.[5]

Farmers adopt the new techniques about 45 percent of the time, compared to a 33 percent rate for traditional agricultural extension programs in India, according to Digital Green. Microsoft Research India also found that the program spent $3.70 to get a single farmer to adopt a new practice, while traditional approaches cost $38.[6]

One farmer who adopted a new technique after attending a Digital Green presentation was Chaitan Gadaba, from Putpandi in eastern India, who learned how to grow okra with minimal irrigation. He had been cultivating rice on a portion of his land, and leaving the rest fallow for lack of water. After watching the video, he began planting all of his property.[7]

Similarly, farmers in Karnataka in western India learned to use the azolla fern as cattle fodder to increase milk yields. Originally shot in the Kannada language, the video was later produced in Hindi for farmers in Madhya Pradesh, some 600 miles away, where the practice became popular as well, Gandhi said.[8]

The postwar era also fostered scientific and technological advances that led to an unprecedented increase in agricultural productivity. In 1944, American biologist Norman Borlaug went to Mexico to work in a Rockefeller Foundation-funded program that launched what became the "Green Revolution" of high-yield farming.[79] In 1953, American biochemist James Watson and British biophysicist Francis Crick described the double-helix structure of DNA, which paved the way for mapping the genetic code and creating genetically modified organisms.[80] Both advances later faced criticisms that they may do more harm than good.

Borlaug, who won the 1970 Nobel Peace Prize, focused on using conventional breeding processes to develop disease-resistant and high-yield wheat varieties.[81] The advances were accompanied by development of chemical fertilizers and pesticides, improved irrigation techniques and increased use of mechanized equipment. Agricultural productivity soared.

Launched in 2006, Digital Green had reached 20 villages by 2008. By 2009 it had spun off as an independent nonprofit.[9] Since then, the organization has produced more than 2,800 videos in over 20 languages and shown them to more than 330,000 farmers in 3,000 villages. It operates in eight Indian states and in Ethiopia, Ghana, Mozambique and Tanzania.[10] Gandhi wants to reach 10,000 villages by next year.[11] The videos are available at www.digitalgreen.org.

A case study by the OneWorld Foundation India called Digital Green "a viable solution to the major problems afflicting government agricultural extension programs," which require a "huge number of staff" and "usually restrict their interactions to the richer, more enterprising farmers within a village."[12]

Gawain Kripke, policy director at Oxfam America, the U.S. affiliate of the international relief and advocacy organization, says Digital Green adopts a key concept in agricultural development: Education should be embraced, directed and delivered by farmers themselves.

"You don't just arrive with new seeds and say try this," Kripke explains. "You invite them to ask questions and request support for what they're trying to do. You can't come to grow maize if they want to grow mangos."

— *Tom Price*

Courtesy Digital Green

Farmers in the central Indian state of Madhya Pradesh, one of the country's most undeveloped regions, shoot a video on chemical treatment of paddy seeds being grown in a nursery, to be shown to other farmers interested in environmentally friendly, lower-cost farming methods.

[1] Rajiv Rao, "Aspiring astronaut helps farmers," *Business Standard* (India), Aug. 9, 2011, http://tinyurl.com/l5cqevt.

[2] *Ibid.*; "Case Study: Digital Green," Governance Knowledge Centre, Department of Administrative Reforms and Public Grievances, Ministry of Personnel, Public Grievances and Pensions, Government of India, June 2011, http://tinyurl.com/qayfl8p.

[3] David Bornstein, "Where YouTube Meets the Farm," *The New York Times*, April 3, 2013, http://tinyurl.com/ozbjohp.

[4] M. J. Prabu, "Video clippings educate on methods practised elseware," *The Hindu*, Feb. 17, 2011, http://tinyurl.com/qchfubr.

[5] "Tech-based Farming Advice Should Stay People-Centred," *SciDev. Net* (London), Nov. 20, 2013, http://tinyurl.com/obp2u4a.

[6] Bornstein, *op. cit.*

[7] "Latest technology helps ryots get good yield," *The Hindu*, Aug. 4, 2011, http://is.gd/Tmi1Yq.

[8] Geeta Padmanabhan, "When farmers turn filmmakers," *The Hindu*, Sept. 18, 2013, http://tinyurl.com/o9uh6so.

[9] Rao, *op. cit.*; Priyanka Golikeri, "MIT alumnus chucks space dreams for terra firma," *DNA India*, March 24, 2011, http://tinyurl.com/lmmp8hn; "Ashoka Innovators For The Public: Rikin Gandhi," Ashoka, http://tinyurl.com/kxhlwlr.

[10] "An Innovative Platform for Rural Development," *Digital Green*, http://tinyurl.com/pzqv99k.

[11] Padmanabhan, *op. cit.*

[12] "Case Study: Digital Green," *op. cit.*

Mexico became self-sufficient in wheat during the 1950s, with yields increasing sixfold between 1950 and 1970.[82] In India, wheat yields tripled between the mid-'60s and mid-'90s.[83]

Overall, the Green Revolution has saved up to 1 billion people from starvation, according to former U.S. Agriculture Secretary Dan Glickman and former U.N. World Food Programme Executive Director Catherine Bertini.[84]

Genetic Engineering

It took 41 years for Watson and Crick's DNA breakthrough to bring genetically engineered food to market. Scientists created the first genetically engineered organism, a bacterium, in 1973. Calgene — a California-based company that is now a subsidiary of Monsanto — patented the genetically modified FlavrSavr tomato in 1989, but it didn't get Food and Drug Administration approval for sale until 1994. Two years later, Monsanto introduced Roundup

Freezing Food's Footprint to Save Wildlife

"The biggest threat to biodiversity is agricultural sprawl."

A few years ago, the World Wildlife Fund (WWF) took a look around the globe and determined that one of the biggest threats to wildlife is habitat loss, and the biggest threat to wildlife habitat is the human appetite.

Tigers no longer live in areas of Malaysia and Sumatra that have been converted to oil palm plantations, for instance. And oil palm cultivation has driven the Sumatran rhino from parts of Malaysia, Sumatra and Borneo.[1]

Overall, the fund says, habitat loss is a major hazard for 85 percent of species on the International Union for Conservation of Nature's list of threatened and endangered species. During the 1990s, more than 230 million acres of forests — 2.4 percent of the world's total — were cut down, almost 70 percent for conversion to agriculture.[2] Between 1960 and 2000, the globe's cultivated land grew by 13 percent.[3] And conservationists worry that demand for farmland will soar in the future.

Earth's population — currently 7 billion — is expected to grow to 9 billion or more by the middle of this century, notes Jason Clay, the organization's senior vice president for market transformation. And as economic growth creates larger middle classes in places like China and India, those populations will consume greater amounts of food, especially more animal protein. Thus, by mid-century individuals may require twice as much food as they do now — counting what they consume and the food consumed by the animals they eat, Clay says.

Without greatly improved productivity and more environmentally friendly farming techniques, "the biggest threat to biodiversity becomes agricultural sprawl," Clay says. "Wildlife need homes, too."

So the WWF set out to "freeze the footprint of food," as Clay puts it, by promoting more efficient agricultural practices: producing more crops on existing cropland, thus halting the conversion of natural habitat to farmland.

The fund's goal is to improve the efficiency of all food producers — from the largest conglomerate to the smallest subsistence farmer — so they use less land, water, fertilizer and pesticides. The organization decided to focus first on companies that produce or trade in 15 commodities whose cultivation poses the biggest threat to wildlife habitat, including soy, sugar, palm oil, beef and farmed salmon.

"We needed to find the business case for change," Clay says, a case he says can be found in the value of intangible assets such as a company's reputation. "Killing that last population of orangutans can affect your corporate value," he says. "So companies see this as a huge risk."

WWF negotiators also argued that producing more food on the same land — or in the same water — was good for the bottom line.

Currently, with support from the Mars food corporation, the WWF also is working with the Beijing Genomic Institute to map the genomes of Africa's most important food crops, such as yams, plantains and cassava. The findings will be released in the public domain, so plant breeders can use the information to improve African crops.

"The goal is to produce better materials" so farmers can "double, triple or quadruple productivity" in areas where hunger is most common, Clay says.

Ready soybeans, which could survive when the fields were sprayed with the company's Roundup weed killer.

By 2002, U.S. farmers were producing 4 billion pounds more food and fiber per acre with GM crops than with conventional plants, reducing pesticide use by 46 million pounds and raising farm income by $1.5 billion, according to the National Center for Food and Agricultural Policy, a Washington-based research and education institution.[85]

Farmers also got an unintentional boost from the 1973 Arab oil embargo. As the embargo pushed up the cost of oil-based fertilizer, pesticides and fuel, governments turned to plant-based ethanol as an alternative fuel. In 1975, Brazil required that ethanol from sugarcane be blended with gasoline. The United States exempted ethanol from gasoline taxes in 1978.[86]

In 2007, the United States required that an increasing amount of ethanol be blended with gasoline — from

The information can be used to improve plants either through genetic engineering or traditional breeding. Breeders can identify plants with favorable genetic traits, then use traditional techniques to reproduce them.

The fund also has worked on food-related issues with such industry giants as Wal-Mart, Coca-Cola, General Mills and Kellogg. Now it is focusing on trade associations in order to have a broader, faster impact, Clay says. "Working with companies one by one is not fast enough," he says.

Among other things, the WWF has encouraged industries to have their practices evaluated by independent certification organizations. For example, 15 salmon-farming companies, which represent 70 percent of global production, have committed to having all of their practices meet third-party standards for minimizing environmental damage by 2020, Clay says.

Members of the Consumer Goods Forum — a 400-member international trade association of manufacturers, retailers and service providers whose business lines range from food to beer to laundry supplies — have agreed to stop contributing to deforestation in their production and acquisition of beef, soy, paper and palm-oil products, he says. The fund also is helping palm-oil processors enable their small-scale suppliers to implement environment-friendly practices, he says.

WWF's market transformation program has become "a bit of a model for others, including Oxfam," says Oxfam America Policy Director Gawain Kripke. "We launched a campaign a couple years ago — called Behind the Brands — that's modeled on what WWF has done, but with a slightly different focus."

Oxfam rates how companies treat land, water, climate, women, farmers and workers and then asks its supporters to contact the companies demanding improvement. "We're actually having constructive engagement with these companies," Kripke says. "They've done stuff we think is really positive in the last couple of years."

Forest habitats for endangered Sumatran tigers have been lost to conversion to massive oil palm plantations in Malaysia and Indonesia, leading environmentalists to call "agricultural sprawl" the biggest threat to the planet's biodiversity.

Coca-Cola, for instance, raised its score for how fairly it treats land issues from 1, the lowest, in 2013 to 7, the highest, this year by requiring its sugar suppliers to respect the property rights of small-scale farmers, who often have their land seized by larger organizations, Oxfam reported.[4]

— *Tom Price*

[1] "Palm oil & biodiversity loss," World Wildlife Fund, http://tinyurl .com/oce8a9t.

[2] "Impact of habitat loss on species," World Wildlife Fund, http:// tinyurl.com/pgv3ota. For background, see Reed Karaim, "Vanishing Biodiversity," *CQ Researcher*, Nov. 6, 2012, pp. 497-520.

[3] Hugh Turral, "Climate change, water and food security," U.N. Food and Agriculture Organization, 2011, p. 31, http://tinyurl.com/nlh3q5b.

[4] "Race to the top: One year of looking Behind the Brands," Oxfam International, Feb. 26, 2014, http://tinyurl.com/acxglfh. For background, see Jina Moore, "Resolving Land Disputes," *CQ Researcher*, Sept. 11, 2011, pp. 421-446.

9 billion gallons in 2008 to 36 billion by 2022. Last year, the Environmental Protection Agency, which implements the law, required fuel producers to use 14 billion gallons of corn-based ethanol and 2.75 billion from nonfood sources, such as wood or inedible parts of the corn plant.

The United States, Brazil and later European countries were aiming to reduce dependence on foreign oil and cut carbon pollution caused by burning fossil fuels. By 2011, ethanol production was consuming 40 percent of the U.S. corn crop, which rose to 44 percent last year, according to Sen. Dianne Feinstein, D-Calif. Critics began bemoaning the unintended consequences of ethanol use: higher food prices and disappointing environmental benefits.[87]

Unintended Consequences

Genetic engineering and the Green Revolution produced other unintended consequences.

Many people's fears of GM crops were heightened in 2000 when genes from genetically modified StarLink corn — approved only for use in animal feed — were found in taco shells. Some farmers admitted selling the corn for human consumption.[88] The same year, Roundup-resistant weeds were found in Delaware. Three years later, bollworms resistant to GM cotton were discovered in the South.[89]

The modern agriculture spawned by the Green Revolution — including large, industrialized farms that replant the same crops in the same places year after year — has overused chemicals, drained aquifers, depleted soil, threatened wildlife and biodiversity, spewed greenhouse gases and created its own pesticide-resistant crops.

Even small-scale farmers in India have discovered the Green Revolution's downside. Beginning in the 1960s, high-yield seeds, fertilizer, pesticides and irrigation multiplied productivity in Punjab and made the state the breadbasket of a nation that had transformed itself from a land of starvation to a food exporter. Over the decades, however, Punjab's farmers depleted the soil, created pesticide-resistant insects and weeds and polluted the water sources with chemicals. In 2007, the Punjab State Council for Science and Technology reported that "the most stunning example of the Green Revolution in India . . . has become unsustainable and non-profitable."[90]

Pat Mooney, executive director of the ETC Group, an Ottawa-based organization that studies how technologies affect the poor, says the Green Revolution "deserves credit for having produced a lot more wheat and rice and maize. Some people might otherwise not have been fed." But, he adds, "it became a one-size-fits-all model. In the long term it caused a lot of damage and ended up focusing on yields beyond nutrition."

A review of academic literature conducted by Barrett of Cornell and others found that the Green Revolution led to some poor people consuming a calorie-rich but nutrition-poor diet. "From the 1970s to the mid-1990s, the price of staple foods [such as rice and wheat] decreased relative to the price of micronutrient rich foods [such as vegetables] in much of Asia," they wrote. As a result, the poor were eating more grain and fewer vegetables, they said.[91]

Barrett also notes other Green Revolution shortcomings. "In initially making water available essentially for free to farmers, it pretty much guarantees they will overuse water," he says. He also notes the overuse of chemicals.

But, he adds, "The Green Revolution had an amazing effect. It increased per capita calorie availability. It drove down food prices. There's no better way to fight hunger than to bring down the price of the food, and the Green Revolution achieved that more than anything before or since."

The Green Revolution was much less successful in Africa, where countries lacked good roads or railways to transport food to market or to distribute high-yield seeds, fertilizers and pesticides. African governments also did not offer farmers the support provided by Asian governments, such as credit, training and subsidies.[92] And since independence, many African countries have suffered from government corruption, authoritarianism, anti-free market ideologies and strife, U.S. Assistant Secretary of State for African Affairs Carson lamented in 2010.

"Mismanagement, embezzlement of state revenues and centralized approaches to economic management precipitated economic decline and the deterioration of infrastructure and government services," Carson said. However, since the 1990s, he said, a growing number of African countries have "liberalized their economies, embraced market reforms and adopted pro-business policies."[93]

CURRENT SITUATION
Sustainable Food

The Senate Environment and Public Works Committee is considering a proposal to repeal the mandate that results in nearly half of America's corn crop being burned as motor fuel. Supporters of the legislation say the mandate diverts food to fuel and drives up food prices.

Cosponsored by liberal California Democrat Feinstein, and conservative Oklahoma Republican Sen. Tom Coburn, the measure would eliminate the requirement that an increasing amount of corn-based ethanol be blended into the nation's gasoline. However, it would continue a mandate for burning so-called advanced biofuels, which are made from inedible vegetation.

Feinstein said she still supports shifting to low-carbon fuels, but opposes the corn mandate because it raises the cost of food and damages the environment. Coburn called for letting "market forces, rather than political and parochial forces, determine how to diversify fuel supplies."[94]

The bill fits into a larger movement that emphasizes sustainable food production that uses environmentally friendly agriculture and boosts the resiliency of small-scale farmers in the developing world when they face drought and other challenges, says Leach of World Food Program USA. The efforts include providing drought- and pest-resistant seeds, teaching more effective farming techniques and combining relief with development projects.

The most effective attacks on hunger and its effects, Cornell's Barrett says, are providing health care for children and women of childbearing age, educating children and investing in boosting poor farmers' agricultural productivity.

The Obama administration, U.N. agencies and private relief organizations are adopting policies based on the theory that increasing small farmers' productivity while protecting the environment can lift them out of poverty while reducing hunger and boosting the local economy.

"Half of hungry people globally are small-scale farmers," Leach says. "We can take them out of hunger by creating economic opportunity."

For six years the U.N. World Food Programme has been teaching developing-world farmers better techniques, helping to organize them into associations to store and distribute food more efficiently and providing access to credit. The agency then purchases their crops to provide food relief for the hungry.

The goal is to "get them producing the quantity and quality they need to feed themselves, then to sell to the World Food Programme and then to graduate to selling to the marketplace," Leach explains.

Feed the Future

The Obama administration's efforts to push a similar approach in U.S. hunger programs have had a "transformative impact on the whole international community," Leach says.

Similarly, Oxfam's Kripke describes Obama as "a real leader across the world in pushing agriculture development as a priority." Unfortunately, he adds, "many other donors haven't really been following very effectively."

Called Feed the Future, the U.S. approach assumes that anti-hunger and antipoverty programs are most effective when embraced and led by developing world farmers and their local, regional and national governments.

It also seeks to tap expertise of both nonprofit and profit-making private organizations.

The administration, for instance, has asked the Agriculture Department and college agriculture schools to research technologies to enable small farmers to increase productivity. In addition, the New Alliance for Food Security and Nutrition, launched in 2012 by the Group of Eight leading industrial nations,* now includes 10 African countries and more than 160 companies that have pledged to invest more than $15 billion in African agriculture.

Carter, the UC-Davis researcher, credits the administration for targeting assistance to the specific needs of various farmer groups, such as by conducting research into the most effective and affordable farming techniques for a small geographic area. "It's one thing to move to the frontier of what's technologically possible," he says, "and it's another to put resources into situations where farmers can exploit what's available."

Barrett cites increased funding for agriculture research as key to the program. Overall, according to Barrett, the $1.1-billion Feed the Future program is "a step in the right direction, but is severely underfunded."

"We should be spending more for preventative action than for curative treatment," he says, suggesting that "$10 billion is in the neighborhood of what's needed."

Cornell's Barrett is also optimistic about a trend in which relief agencies acquire food from local and regional sources rather than shipping commodities from donor countries. In the United States, the 2014 farm bill took modest steps in that direction by increasing the amount of aid that can be provided in cash instead of commodities or that can be used to purchase food near where it's consumed.

Corporations also are pitching in. Wal-Mart, for instance, helps farmers in Mexico and Central America follow more sustainable practices and improve their post-harvest food handling, where much waste occurs. The Keurig Green Mountain coffee company helps coffee growers in Mexico, Central America and Africa diversify their crops to combat seasonal hunger.[95]

---

* The eight were France, Germany, Italy, Japan, the United Kingdom, Canada, Russia and the United States. Russia was expelled after its seized Crimea this year.

Should hunger programs ban genetically modified food?

YES — Éric Darier, Ph.D.
Food for Life Campaigner, Greenpeace International

Written for *CQ Researcher*, August 2014

The biotech industry has been exploiting food crises to promote genetically modified (GM) crops, claiming they can solve world hunger. People experiencing hunger should have decent solutions, not be used to promote controversial technologies. Even in emergency situations, desperate people should have the right to choose what they eat.

Greenpeace opposes the deliberate release of GM organisms into the environment. They can multiply and cross-breed and pose a threat of irreversible damage to biodiversity and ecosystems. Furthermore, we don't know if GM crops are safe to eat, especially over the long term. Therefore, with regard to GM foods, it is urgent that we apply the "precautionary principle," which could be summarized as "in case of doubt, leave it out."

Genetic modification makes crops prone to unexpected effects. Evaluating food safety requires looking for such effects, which is extremely difficult, if not impossible, as reflected in the ongoing controversy surrounding the assessment of the safety of GM crops.

U.S. food aid containing GM grains has been used to provide famine relief. Greenpeace is most concerned about the potential uncontrolled environmental spread of GM organisms into the affected countries. Notably, the United States has not joined 167 other countries in ratifying the U.N. Cartagena Protocol on Biosafety, a treaty regulating the movement of GM organisms among nations.

Millions of people around the world suffer from food shortages, high food prices and hunger, due to several factors: industrial farming, bad harvests, inadequate access to food due to poverty and inequality, rising oil prices, changing consumption patterns, commodities speculation and the rush to produce unsustainable biofuels.

Instead, ecological farming enables and encourages communities to produce enough food to feed themselves while fostering sustainable farming and healthy food.

There are many ecological alternatives to GM crops. The U.N. agriculture assessment known as IAASTD recommended policies that would lead to scaling up ecological agriculture. More recently, the report of the U.N. special rapporteur on the right to food urged governments to "move away from business as usual" and to tackle the systemic failure of the current food system.

Let people choose which ecological agriculture solutions best allow them to feed themselves while protecting nature. GM crops are part of the problem, not the solution.

NO — Dennis T. Avery
Environmental Economist and Senior Fellow, Heartland Institute; Co-author, Unstoppable: Global Warming Every 1,500 Years

Written for *CQ Researcher*, August 2014

GM crops produce more food during good years and have the potential to resist drought and disease more effectively than traditional crops. They are ideal for famines and emergencies.

Pessimists say we can't yet trust GM foods, but they've turned up no valid dangers. In fact, the European Commission in 2010 said GM is slightly safer than conventional crops because of the targeted research conducted on them.

Aside from hunger emergencies, GM is also critically important to meeting the enormous food challenge of the next 40 years. The world must roughly double its food output, quickly, in order to feed a larger, more affluent population. (After 2050, world population will begin a slow, steady decline as increasingly literate women live in cities where it is expensive to raise a child.)

Ideally, we will be able to double food output without plowing under wildlife habitat equal to the land area of South America — just to produce low-yield crops. The world's prime farmland is already under cultivation, so farmers must redouble per-acre yields on existing fields. More nitrogen fertilizer and herbicides can be used in Africa, but most of the world's farmland is already using today's high-tech inputs. That leaves a major food-supply gap that only higher-yield new technology — such as biotechnology — can fill.

The last time the world faced such a problem, during the Little Ice Age (1300-1850 AD), it was also solved with technology. Governments ordered farmers to rotate crops and livestock on the same land to maintain soil nitrogen. Better sailing ships brought Europe crops such as corn and potatoes from the New World and cold-tolerant turnips from China as a feed crop. Drought-tolerant New World corn was planted across China. Food production surged, averting famine — except in France, where people claimed potatoes were poisonous. Famine then brought on the French Revolution.

A California biotech researcher believes he has found a one-gene solution to a massive Third World food problem. The soil in about half of the world's tropical cropland is naturally saturated with toxic aluminum. Traditional crop plants struggle to survive in the toxic soils, but the researcher has devised a way to genetically modify plants to thrive on the same soils. However, the scientist is being discouraged due to public GM mistrust in wealthy, aid-donor countries.

Corporate involvement is doubly important, according to Clay of the World Wildlife Fund, because "when companies like Wal-Mart or McDonald's make commitments to sustainability, their supply chains follow suit."

Reversing Damage

Private organizations also are moving to overcome environmental damage caused by modern agriculture, which affects the Earth's future ability to feed itself.

Some advocates are looking to the sea as a source of food, because water covers 70 percent of the globe but provides less than 2 percent of the planet's food. They face significant obstacles, however. Many ocean areas have been overfished, and fish farms pose significant pollution challenges.[96]

Farmers raised more fish than beef for the first time in 2012, harvesting more than 70 million tons of seafood — 14 times what they produced in 1980. But, just as agriculture has destroyed wildlife habitat, depleted soil and polluted fresh water supplies on land, aquaculture has destroyed mangroves to create shrimp farms and released fertilizers, pesticides, antibiotics and fish waste into oceans.[97]

To avoid aquaculture's downsides, some farmers are raising fish in tanks on land; others are adopting environmentally friendly practices at sea.

In landlocked western Virginia, for instance, Blue Ridge Aquaculture has devised a land-based fish farming method that produces 12,000 pounds of antibiotic- and hormone-free tilapia each day. Company president Bill Martin describes his indoor fish farming process as having "as close to zero impact on the oceans as we can get."

Others are working to minimize the impact of their ocean-based fish farms. Off the coast of Panama, for instance, Open Blue raises hundreds of thousands of cobia in cages 60 feet below the Caribbean. Ocean currents flush the pens to provide the fish with clean water and to dilute waste. The farm does not use antibiotics, and researchers have not found waste outside the farm.

To the north, off Canada's British Columbia coast, University of Victoria researchers are raising sablefish (also called black cod) while keeping the Pacific Ocean clean. Down-current from the fish pens, baskets of shellfish eat the fish excretions. Sugar kelp grow next to the baskets and consume almost all of the remaining nitrates

and phosphorus. Eighty feet below, sea cucumbers ingest the waste that falls to the sea floor.[98]

Farmers who grow crops and livestock on land are deploying "precision-agriculture" technology to increase yields while decreasing environmental damage. Global Positioning System devices attached to farm equipment detect precise locations where water, fertilizer or pesticides are needed. Other machines drag sensors over and through soil to measure treatment needs.

Precise measurements enabled New Zealand farmer Hugh Wigley to cut his lime use by 40 percent, for instance. Wigley, who also supplies precision equipment to other farmers, says one client discovered he didn't need to spread any lime on land where he had been using about two tons per acre.[99]

A 2011 Agriculture Department study found that precision agriculture has enabled farmers to reduce the damage caused by runoff of fertilizers and pesticides, reduced fuel consumption and increased crop yields.[100]

OUTLOOK
Solvable Problem

While food production has been growing more quickly than consumption, experts worry that expanding middle classes in countries such as China and India will boost demand for more expensive foods that put a greater strain on the environment than cheaper foods. That could drive already-rising food prices higher, making it harder for the poorest of the poor to purchase enough to eat.

Fulfilling demand for meat — especially beef — will divert food to animal feed and put added pressure on the environment. In addition, climate change could disrupt the growth of crops and livestock. But technological advances promise to enable farmers to increase yields while protecting the environment. And many experts are optimistic that hunger not caused by conflict or natural disaster can be eliminated.

"Hunger is a solvable problem," Leach of World Food Program USA says. "We are smarter now in terms of understanding the causes of hunger and in having creative strategies to address hunger. And there's greater understanding by the private sector about how to enhance their businesses and at the same time have positive social impact."

Big remaining challenges include addressing climate change and creating "better mechanisms to prevent conflict," Leach adds.

Cornell's Barrett also expects the private sector to contribute to reducing hunger. Rising food prices are drawing more private investment into production, he says. And reducing agriculture's threat to the environment goes hand in hand with reducing farmers' costs, he says.

"As you develop products that are greener and lower-cost, farmers adopt them pretty quickly," Barrett explains. "They're doing a better job of dosing inorganic fertilizers precisely so we reduce inorganic runoff to waterways. People are figuring out better ways to control pests with natural predators and natural secretions from plants. And we're doing a much better job developing efficient machinery."

Unfortunately, these improvements are not occurring fast enough to meet expected future demand, he adds. Kripke, of Oxfam, agrees. As to whether poor farmers will benefit from increasing food demand, Kripke says, "It's possible. It's not inevitable."

Clay, of the World Wildlife Fund, worries that rising food prices — which may be good for farmers — will "leave people with less money in a real bad way." But he's hopeful today's young adults will tackle hunger because "they care a lot about [how their food is] produced and knowing that it's produced sustainably."

Mooney, of the ETC Group, contends that affluent eaters must change their habits, and relief organizations must teach the poor how to grow their own food and eat more healthily. "We've got to adapt our consumer habits to our planet and to our health needs, which means we need to reduce our meat and dairy consumption," he says.

Developed nations waste food because "you go to the grocery once a week and buy all sorts of stuff, and it spoils in the back of the refrigerator," Mooney says. Shoppers should visit the store more frequently and buy less on each trip, he says.

Large-scale farms will continue to produce a substantial amount of the world's food, Mooney says. But "that doesn't mean it has to be highly chemical farming." Small-scale farmers probably will adapt to climate change more easily than large agricultural corporations, if researchers focus on small-scale agriculture's needs, he says.

Avery of the Heartland and Hudson institutes predicts that large-scale, high-tech agriculture will not be replaced. "We need more food and more high-value food, and we have to think about tripling the yield of crops and livestock on the good land that we currently farm, because there's no more good land," he says.

Without continued technological advances — including with GMOs and chemicals —"we will have more famine, and there will be loss of wildlife habitat on a massive scale" as more land is allocated to farming, Avery says.

NOTES

1. Abigail Hauslohner, "U.N. agency raises disaster designation in Iraq as refugees flood into Kurdistan," *The Washington Post*, June 18, 2014, http://tinyurl.com/k7deo5v; Mac McClelland, "How to Build a Perfect Refugee Camp," *The New York Times*, Feb. 13, 2014, pp. MM-24, http://tinyurl.com/ljnvc3v.

2. Olivia Ward, "Canadian aid timely for starving children," *The Toronto Star*, May 30, 2014, p. A10, http://tinyurl.com/nrmc86w.

3. "The State of Food Insecurity in the World: The multiple dimensions of food security," Food and Agriculture Organization of the United Nations, 2013, http://tinyurl.com/njzqzjp.

4. *Ibid.*

5. "The State of Food Insecurity in the World 2013," Food and Agriculture Organization of the United Nations (executive summary), 2013, http://tinyurl.com/nq8npru; "Wake up before it is too late: Make agriculture truly sustainable now for food security in a changing climate," U.N. Conference on Trade and Development, September 2013, http://tinyurl.com/kly4c3r.

6. "The State of Food Insecurity in the World 2013," *op. cit.*

7. "Hunger Statistics," World Food Programme, http://tinyurl.com/lhjx45.

8. "World Health Statistics 2014 Part III: Global Health Indicators," World Health Organization, http://tinyurl.com/q5fgmmx.

9. Chris Otter, "Feast and Famine: The Global Food Crisis," *Origins: Current Events in Historical Perspective*, Ohio State University, Vol. 3, Issue 6, March 2010, http://tinyurl.com/l988h56. Also see "Table: Age-standardised regional and national

estimates of the prevalence of overweight and obesity combined and obesity alone for girls, boys, men, and women for 2013, for 188 countries and 21 GBD regions" in "Global, regional, and national prevalence of overweight and obesity in children and adults during 1980-2013," *The Lancet*, May 29, 2014, http://tinyurl.com/k8slkbu.

10. Jason Clay, "Freezing the Footprint of Food," World Wildlife Fund, Oct. 23, 2012, http://tinyurl.com/kohxm3k.

11. Andrew C. Revkin, "It's Time for Africa's Green Revolution, Focused on Corn," *The New York Times* (blog), April 10, 2014, http://tinyurl.com/kdn4kqx.

12. Brian Jones, "Wasting food can eat away the future," *Canberra Times*, April 5, 2014, p. B9, http://tinyurl.com/oyezt6e.

13. "The State of Food Insecurity in the World 2013," *op. cit.*; Mark Koba, "A hungry world: lots of food, in too few places," CNBC, July 22, 2013, http://tinyurl.com/n8trpyp.

14. Chris Thomas, "Improving nutrition, building resilience for families, societies," USAID, May 22, 2014, http://tinyurl.com/kfqwn9d.

15. "The State of Food Insecurity in the World 2013," *op. cit.*

16. Johnnie Carson, "Africa: Remarks at the African Diplomatic Corp's Celebration of Africa Day," U.S. State Department Documents and Publications, May 25, 2010, http://tinyurl.com/39o78ar.

17. "Food Aid Flows 2012 Report," World Food Programme, United Nations, December 2013, http://tinyurl.com/jwcl2tn.

18. Statistics from interview with Alan Jury, senior adviser to World Food Program USA.

19. Hauslohner, *op. cit.*

20. Miguel I. Gómez, *et al.*, "Post-green revolution food systems and the triple burden of malnutrition," Food Policy, October 2013, Vol. 42, pp. 129-138, http://tinyurl.com/ozugl6n.

21. *Ibid.*

22. "H.R. 4005 — Coast Guard and Maritime Transportation Act of 2014," Library of Congress, http://tinyurl.com/ozso9el.

23. Christopher B. Barrett and Erin C. Lentz, "Highway Robbery on the High Seas," *The Hill*, May 29, 2014, http://tinyurl.com/l9t7gp7.

24. Elijah E. Cummings and Duncan D. Hunter, "Food aid supports sea-lift abilities," *The Washington Post*, May 17, 2013, p. A16, http://tinyurl.com/ls4c9jd.

25. "Senator Coons introduces bill to reform and modernize America's food aid program," Office of Sen. Christopher Coons, June 3, 2014, http://tinyurl.com/lab8wf9.

26. Letter to Sens. Debbie Stabenow and Thad Cochran, wheatworld.org, March 21, 2013, http://tinyurl.com/nwav3dq.

27. Steve Baragona, "Congress Debates Limiting US Farmers' Role in Food Aid," Voice of America News, June 18, 2013, http://tinyurl.com/oswob8b.

28. "The Value of Food Aid Monetization: Benefits, Risks and Best Practices," *Informa Economics*, November 2012.

29. Daniel A. Sumner, "Picking on the Poor, How US Agricultural Policy Hurts the Developing World," AmericanBoondoggle.com, http://tinyurl.com/ko62jfk.

30. Tim Krohn, "Farm bill up against misperceptions, lawmakers say," *The* [Mankato, Minnesota] *Free Press*, Feb. 19, 2014, http://tinyurl.com/m5p9nyl.

30. *Ibid.*

31. James Phelan, "U.S. Food Aid: To Ship Food or Send Cash — the Obama Administration Weighs In," Action Against Hunger, April 9, 2013, http://tinyurl.com/mw3wpxo.

32. Dennis T. Avery, "Column: Biofuels have fallen out of fashion," *Orange County Register*, May 8, 2014, http://tinyurl.com/q5c2kgp.

33. "Direct federal financial Interventions and Subsidies in Energy in fiscal Year 2010," U.S. Energy Information Administration, Aug. 1, 2011, http://tinyurl.com/nvm97sz; Robert Pear, "After Three Decades, Tax Credit for Ethanol Expires," *The New York Times*, Jan. 1, 2012, http://tinyurl.com/a3ve67x.

34. Timothy Spence, "Europe Worsening Hunger Worldwide," Inter Press Service, May 31, 2011,

http://tinyurl.com/plzmtup. For background see Jina Moore, "Resolving Land Disputes," *CQ Researcher*, Sept. 6, 2011, pp. 421-446.

35. "National Journal Holds a Policy Summit on Biofuels Mandate," *Political Transcript Wire*, Oct. 9 2013, http://tinyurl.com/nctkqo4.

36. Jonathan Foley, "A Five-Step Plan to Feed the World," *National Geographic*, undated. http://tinyurl.com/l3b2jaw.

37. Joel K. Bourne, Jr., "How to Farm a Better Fish," *National Geographic*, June 2014, http://tinyurl.com/l5hbosw. For background, see Daniel McGlynn, "Whale Hunting," *CQ Researcher*, June 29, 2012, pp. 573-596.

38. Richard Black, "World's oceans in 'shocking' decline," BBC News, June 20, 2011, http://tinyurl.com/oqtyo9p. Also see Reid Wilson, "Fisheries at Risk as Oceans Acidify," *The Washington Post*, July 31, 2014, p. A3, http://tinyurl.com/pqwtvk7.

39. "The IUCN Red List of Threatened Species: *Sphyrna lewini*," International Union for Conservation of Nature, http://tinyurl.com/qexdyos.

40. "4 steps food companies can take to help stop climate change," Oxfam, May, 20, 2014, http://tinyurl.com/ow3ffrm.

41. "7 Facts About Climate Change And Hunger," World Food Programme, United Nations, Dec. 4, 2011, http://tinyurl.com/7zw9c4u.

42. Foley, *op. cit.*

43. Andrei Illarionov, "A Few Notes on Climate Change," The Cato Institute, Dec. 11, 2009, http://tinyurl.com/ourmqpg.

44. Eli Kintisch, "High CO2 Makes Crops Less Nutritious," *National Geographic*, May 7, 2014, http://tinyurl.com/p3ud8fc.

45. Terrell Johnson and Jon Erdman, "World's Hottest May Is Now May 2014: NOAA," The Weather Channel, June 23, 2014, http://tinyurl.com/kcnjgpn.

46. "How Much Has the Global Temperature Risen in the Last 100 Years?" The University Corporation for Atmospheric Research, http://tinyurl.com/a8gygt3.

47. Fiona Harvey, "Rate of ocean acidification due to carbon emissions is at highest for 300m years," *The Guardian*, Oct. 2, 2013, http://tinyurl.com/o55anz3.

48. Coral Davenport, "Climate Change Deemed Growing Security Threat by Military Researchers," *The New York Times*, May 13, 2014, http://tinyurl.com/q9jnvak.

49. Winnie Byanyima, "World 'woefully unprepared' for climate impacts on food," Oxfam International, March 25, 2014, http://tinyurl.com/oxwbatz.

50. Justin Gillis, "Panel's Warning on Climate Risk: Worst Is Yet to Come," *The New York Times*, March 31, 2014, http://tinyurl.com/mstxs6b.

51. Alex Renton, "How climate change will wipe out coffee crops — and farmers," *The* (London) *Observer*, March 29, 2014, http://tinyurl.com/pdgl6wb. Also see The Associated Press, "Cost of change," *The Denver Post*, April 1, 2014, p. A-14.

52. Rio N. Araja, "Golden rice entry blocked," *Manila Standard Today*, May 1, 2014, http://tinyurl.com/pvblyoh; Amy Harmon, "Golden Rice: Lifesaver?" *The New York Times*, Aug. 24, 2013, p. SR1, http://tinyurl.com/nvannmk.

53. "What is the status of the Golden Rice project coordinated by IRRI?" International Rice Research Institute, March 2014, http://tinyurl.com/la6moer.

54. Richard Roberts, "GMOs are a key tool to addressing global hunger," *The Boston Globe*, May 23, 2014, http://tinyurl.com/q5gespx. See also Reed Karaim, "Farm Subsidies," *CQ Global Researcher*, May 1, 2012, pp. 205-228.

55. Marjorie Olster, "Key points in the genetically modified food debate," The Associated Press, Aug. 2, 2013, http://tinyurl.com/mkuwj2b; "Beyond Promises: Top 10 Facts about Biotech/GM Crops in 2013," International Service for the Acquisition of Agri-biotech Applications, http://tinyurl.com/mjopzge. For background, see Jason McLure, "Genetically Modified Food," *CQ Researcher*, Aug. 31, 2012, pp. 717-740.

56. Sharon Schmickle, "Hungry African nation at center of a food debate," *The Washington Post*, Oct. 8, 2013, p. A10, http://tinyurl.com/k2wmkfl; "Beyond Promises: Top 10 Facts about Biotech/GM Crops in 2013," *op. cit.*

57. Roberts, *op. cit.*

58. Harmon, *op. cit.*

59. Ginger Pinholster, "AAAS Board of Directors: Legally Mandating GM Food Labels Could 'Mislead and Falsely Alarm Consumers,'" American Association for the Advancement of Science, Oct. 25, 2012, http://tinyurl.com/no6eyt9.

60. Paul Johnston and David Santillo, "Precaution is simply common sense," Greenpeace International, May 24, 2012, http://tinyurl.com/pgj29pa.

61. Carey Gillam, "Pesticide use ramping up as GMO crop technology backfires: study," Reuters, Oct 1, 2012, http://tinyurl.com/9etfaj5.

62. Cormac Ó Gráda, *Famine: A Short History* (2009), http://tinyurl.com/6slof8r. Also see Joohee Cho, "North Korean Prison Camp Atrocities Detailed in UN Report," ABC News, Feb. 17, 2014, http://tinyurl.com/o23wb4w.

63. Ó Gráda, *op. cit.*

64. "The Irish Potato Famine," *Digital History*, University of Houston, http://tinyurl.com/jwwnh96.

65. Otter, *op. cit.*

66. Ó Gráda, *op. cit.*

67. Robert Denning, "Review: Famine: A Short History," *Origins: Current Events in Historical Perspective*, Ohio State University, October 2009, http://tinyurl.com/pv26cvv.

68. For background, see Tom Price, "Science in America," *CQ Researcher*, Jan. 11, 2008, pp. 25-48.

69. See Jennifer Weeks, "Farm Policy," *CQ Researcher*, Aug. 10, 2012, pp. 693-716.

70. "Fritz Haber," Chemical Heritage Foundation, undated, http://tinyurl.com/m6b7w4w.

71. Otter, *op. cit.*

72. "Ukraine: The famine of 1932-33," *Encyclopaedia Britannica*, http://tinyurl.com/k4eumoo; David P. Lilly, "The Russian Famine of 1932-1933," The Center for Volga German Studies, Concordia University, http://tinyurl.com/k6mafp8.

73. Yang Jisheng, "China's Great Shame," *The New York Times*, Nov. 13, 2012, http://tinyurl.com/n7m3drb; Anne Applebaum, "When China Starved," *The Washington Post*, Aug. 12, 2008, http://tinyurl.com/l63626u.

74. "The Biafran War," Inventory of Conflict and Environment, American University, http://tinyurl.com/n5c235o.

75. Tony Hall with Tom Price, *Changing the Face of Hunger* (2006); "Ethiopian Famine 25th Anniversary — Questions and Answers," ONE, Oct. 23, 2009, http://tinyurl.com/m6akc5v.

76. Denning, *op. cit.*

77. See Tom Price, "Assessing the United Nations," *CQ Global Researcher*, March 20, 2012, pp. 129-152.

78. See Mary H. Cooper, "World Hunger," *CQ Researcher*, Oct. 25, 1991, pp. 801-824. Also see Marcia Clemmitt, "Global Food Crisis," *CQ Researcher*, June 27, 2008, pp. 553-576.

79. Tina Rosenberg, "A Green Revolution, This Time for Africa," *The New York Times*, April 9, 2014, http://tinyurl.com/kc6v4zf.

80. For background, see Jason McLure, "Genetically Modified Food," *CQ Researcher*, Aug. 31, 2012, pp. 717-740.

81. "Our History," International Maize and Wheat Improvement Center, http://tinyurl.com/q79dynr.

82. *Ibid.*

83. Rosenberg, *op. cit.*

84. Dan Glickman and Catherine Bertini, "Saving A Billion People from Starvation," *The Huffington Post*, Sept. 18, 2009, http://tinyurl.com/nkdjx8n.

85. McLure, *op. cit.*

86. For background, see Sarah Glazer, "Rising Food Prices" *CQ Global Researcher*, Oct. 18, 2011, pp. 499-524.

87. Charles Kenny, "Congress Wakes Up to the Bad News About Biofuels," *BloombergBusinessweek*, Jan. 6, 2014, http://tinyurl.com/pfmg6e8; "Feinstein, Coburn Introduce Bipartisan Bill to Eliminate Corn Ethanol," Office of Sen. Dianne Feinstein, Dec. 12, 2013, http://tinyurl.com/pal8nyz.

88. Andrew Pollack, "Altered Corn Surfaced Earlier," *The New York Times*, Sept. 4, 2001, http://tinyurl.com/qg5nu24.

89. McLure, *op. cit.*

90. Kenneth Weiss, "In India, agriculture's Green Revolution dries up," *Los Angeles Times*, July 22, 2012, http://tinyurl.com/luofrj2.

91. Miguel I. Gómez, *et al.*, *op. cit.*

92. Revkin, *op. cit.*

93. Carson, *op. cit.*

94. Office of Sen. Dianne Feinstein, *op. cit.*

95. Andrew C. Revkin, "A Coffee Seller Seeks to Cut Hunger Among Coffee Growers," *The New York Times*, Oct. 9, 2012, http://tinyurl.com/m8o4enb; "Food Security," Keurig Green Mountain, http://tinyurl.com/k5ln3r7.

96. Alan Ward, "Weighing Earth's Water from Space," National Aeronautics and Space Administration, Dec. 23, 2003, http://tinyurl.com/qxjjoqa.

97. Bourne, *op. cit.*

98. *Ibid.*

99. Tim Cronshaw, "Soil mapping technology a big step forward," *The* (Christchurch, New Zealand) *Press*, July 4, 2014, p. 15.

100. David Schimmelpfennig and Robert Ebel, "On the Doorstep of the Information Age: Recent Adoption of Precision Agriculture," U.S. Dept. of Agriculture Economic Research Service, August 2011, http://tinyurl.com/m8qan98.

BIBLIOGRAPHY
Selected Sources
Books

Buffett, Howard G., *40 Chances: Finding Hope in a Hungry World*, Simon & Schuster, 2013.
A philanthropist and son of billionaire investor Warren Buffett analyzes how the well-fed world should fight hunger and poverty.

Falcon, Walter, and Rosamond Naylor, eds., *Frontiers in Food Policy: Perspectives in Sub-Saharan Africa*, Stanford Center on Food Security and the Environment, 2014.
Experts at an agricultural development symposium address various aspects of hunger and rural poverty in the hungriest region on Earth.

Gratton, Lynda, *The Key: How Corporations Succeed by Solving the World's Toughest Problems*, McGraw-Hill, 2014.
A professor of management practice at London Business School argues that global problems such as hunger cannot be solved without help from major corporations and their executives.

Ó Gráda, Cormac, *Famine: A Short History*, Princeton University Press, 2009.
An economics professor at University College, Dublin, traces the history of hunger from ancient Egypt onward.

Thurow, Roger, *The Last Hunger Season: A Year in an African Farm Community on the Brink of Change*, Public Affairs, 2012.
A senior fellow for global agriculture and food policy at the Chicago Council on Global Affairs tells the stories of four small-scale farmers in western Kenya and concludes that relief and development organizations are headed in the right direction.

Articles

Barrett, Christopher B., and Erin C. Lentz, "Highway Robbery on the High Seas," *The Hill*, May 29, 2014, http://tinyurl.com/l9t7gp7.
The director of Cornell University's School of Applied Economics and Management (Barrett) and an assistant professor of international relations at Bucknell University lament that hungry people go unfed because Congress requires at least half of U.S. food aid to be shipped in U.S.-flagged vessels. The American vessels tend to be more expensive, so less food can be purchased when they are used.

Bourne, Joel K., Jr., "How to Farm a Better Fish," *National Geographic*, undated, http://tinyurl.com/l5hbosw.
A former senior editor for *National Geographic* explores environmentally friendly approaches to fish farming.

Otter, Chris, "Feast and Famine: The Global Food Crisis," *Origins: Current Events in Historical Perspective*, March 2010, http://tinyurl.com/l988h56.
An assistant professor of history at Ohio State University provides a historical perspective on the modern paradox of global hunger and widespread obesity.

Rosenberg, Tina, "When Food Isn't the Answer to Hunger," *The New York Times*, April 24, 2013, http://tinyurl.com/n7b7ndm.

Monetary aid can better solve hunger than food aid under certain circumstances.

Reports and Studies

"Case Study: Digital Green," Governance Knowledge Centre, Department of Administrative Reforms and Public Grievances, Ministry of Personnel, Public Grievances and Pensions, Government of India, June 2011, http://tinyurl.com/qayfl8p.
A case study prepared for the Indian government evaluates Digital Green, a nonprofit that uses information technology to educate poor farmers about agricultural practices.

"The State of Food Insecurity in the World 2013," U.N. Food and Agriculture Organization, Sept. 1, 2013, http://tinyurl.com/mbt7g5g.
An annual U.N. report says the world is approaching the U.N.'s 2015 hunger-reduction target, but achieving it would require "considerable and immediate additional efforts."

"Wake up before it is too late: Make agriculture truly sustainable now for food security in a changing climate,"

U.N. Conference on Trade and Development, September 2013, http://tinyurl.com/kly4c3r.
A U.N. agency report says farmers should grow a larger variety of crops and reduce fertilizer use, while food-aid organizations should support small-scale farmers and consumption of locally grown food.

"What is the status of the Golden Rice project coordinated by IRRI?" International Rice Research Institute, March 2014, http://tinyurl.com/la6moer.
A nonprofit explains the challenges of developing "golden rice," a genetically modified grain designed to combat blindness and other ailments due to Vitamin-A deficiency.

Schimmelpfennig, David, and Robert Ebel, "On the Doorstep of the Information Age: Recent Adoption of Precision Agriculture," Economic Research Service, U.S. Department of Agriculture, August 2011, http://tinyurl.com/m8qan98.
Government economists evaluate farmers' use of technology such as optical sensors and GPS systems to more accurately fertilize, protect and water their crops.

For More Information

Center for Global Food Issues, P.O. Box 202, Churchville, VA, 24421; 540-337-6354; www.cgfi.org. Project of the conservative Hudson Institute think tank that promotes free trade in agricultural products and contends that agricultural productivity is key to environmental conservation.

ETC Group, 180 Metcalfe St., Suite 206, Ottawa, ON K2P 1P5, Canada; 613-241-2267; www.etcgroup.org. Research and advocacy group that studies how new technologies, especially in agriculture, affect the poor.

Food and Agriculture Organization, Viale delle Terme di Caracalla, 00153 Rome, Italy; 39-06-57051; www.fao.org/home/en. U.N.'s chief agency for food and agriculture issues; compiles statistics and publishes reports on hunger.

Oxfam International, Second Floor, 228-240 Banbury Road, Oxford OX2 7BY, United Kingdom; 44-1865-339-100; www.oxfam.org. U.S. affiliate: **Oxfam America**, 226

Causeway St., Fifth Floor, Boston, MA 02114-2206; 800-776-9326; www.oxfamamerica.org. Global relief, development and advocacy organization.

World Food Programme, Via Cesare Giulio Viola 68,?Parco dei Medici, 00148 Rome, Italy; 39-06-65131; www.wfp.org. U.N. agency that is the world's largest anti-hunger organization, distributing 58 percent of the world's food aid in 2012.

World Food Program USA, 1725 I St., N.W., Suite 510, Washington, DC 20006; 202-627-3737; www.wfpusa.org. An independent nonprofit organization that supports the U.N.'s World Food Programme.

World Wildlife Fund, 1250 24th St., N.W., Washington, DC 20037; 202-293-4800; www.worldwildlife.org. Wildlife conservation organization that sees agricultural expansion as a threat to wildlife habitat.

14

Global Population Growth

Jennifer Weeks

A billboard in Kenya's capital, Nairobi, funded by the U.S.-based group Catholics For Choice, promotes the use of condoms. Official Catholic Church doctrine calls such modern birth control methods unacceptable because in the church's view, they amount to preventing life. But most Catholics in developed countries, and many in developing nations, support the use of contraceptives.

From *CQ Researcher*, January 16, 2015.

Public health groups and women's rights advocates in the Philippines celebrated last April when the nation's Supreme Court ruled that the government should provide free contraceptives for the poor.

In a nation where more than 80 percent of the population is Catholic, the church's strong opposition to all forms of "artificial" birth control had blocked efforts to pass family planning laws for more than 15 years.*[1] Contraceptives were legally available, but only to those who could pay for them, putting them out of reach for millions of Filipinos.

Then in 2012 President Benigno Aquino III signed a landmark bill requiring the government to provide free birth control for the poor and mandating sex education classes in public schools. Catholic leaders petitioned the Philippine Supreme Court to overturn the law, arguing that the law violated a provision in the nation's constitution protecting "the life of the unborn."[2] Philippine bishops contended that any form of birth control other than abstention amounted to preventing human life.[3]

But the court's decision last spring held that the law was constitutional. "A grateful nation salutes the majority of justices for their favorable ruling promoting reproductive health and giving impetus to sustainable human development," said legislator Edcel Lagman, the law's lead author.[4] (The law did not legalize abortion, which remains against the law in the Philippines.)

---

* The Catholic Church defines all birth control methods as artificial except for the so-called rhythm method, or abstaining from sex when a woman is ovulating and likely to conceive.

Global Population Projected to Be Older

As the world population expands over the next 85 years, it is expected to grow older, according to United Nations population experts. The proportion of the global population 65 or older is projected to rise from today's 8 percent to 22 percent by 2100. During the same period, the share of those under 25 will fall from 42 percent to 30 percent. Meanwhile, the share of people of childbearing age — 15-49 years old — will drop from 52 percent to 43 percent by 2100, helping to moderate population growth.

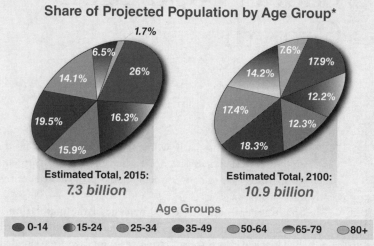

Share of Projected Population by Age Group*

Estimated Total, 2015: *7.3 billion*

Estimated Total, 2100: *10.9 billion*

Age Groups

● 0-14 ● 15-24 ● 25-34 ● 35-49 ● 50-64 ● 65-79 ● 80+

* Totals may not add to 100 percent because of rounding.

Source: "World Population Prospects: The 2012 Revision," United Nations Population Division, Department of Economic and Social Affairs, June 2013, http://tinyurl.com/p9vackr

the world's population would stop expanding this century, United Nations experts now call that scenario unlikely.

Last September U.N. and academic analysts projected that global population will rise from 7.2 billion now to 9.6 billion in 2050 and 10.9 billion in 2100, with virtually all of that growth expected to occur in the developing world.[7]

Rapid population growth slows development and makes it harder to raise the poor out of poverty. Governments in many fast-growing countries are straining to provide housing, sanitation, education and other services. A growing population also increases demands for land, water, energy and other natural resources. And studies show that fast population growth in low-income countries can promote wars, riots and other forms of instability.

People in the poorest, least-developed countries typically have large families for practical reasons: These countries usually lack welfare or social security programs for the elderly, so children are seen as sources of free labor and support for their parents as they age. And because many children die in infancy or in the first few years of life, often from preventable diseases, couples have large families to increase the chance that at least some of their children will reach adulthood.

As nations develop, these incentives change. Medical and public health improvements enable more children to reach adulthood, and parents eventually recognize that they do not need to have as many children. Birth rates decline from an average of six or seven children per woman to one or two.

Helping nations move through this shift, known as the demographic transition, is a central goal of international and national population policies. Reducing birth rates makes it easier for developing countries to provide

Development experts hope the law will help the Philippines curb population growth, which they see as critical to helping raise millions of Filipinos out of poverty. The country's population more than doubled in the past three decades, growing from 45 million to more than 100 million.[5] A quarter of the population lives below the poverty line, and one-fifth of children below age 5 are underweight. Millions of Filipinos lack access to basic sanitary facilities, such as clean drinking water and modern toilets.[6]

The Philippines is not unique. Population growth threatens to undercut economic progress in many developing countries, including large nations such as India and Nigeria and smaller ones, particularly in sub-Saharan Africa. Contrary to experts' predictions a decade ago that

health care and other services and frees up resources for infrastructure and other sectors that help generate jobs.

But some countries are moving through the demographic transition more slowly than others. In central, East and West Africa, women still average five to six live births during their childbearing years.[8]

"Only about 19 percent of women in the region are using effective contraception," says Elizabeth Leahy Madsen, senior technical adviser with Futures Group, a global health consulting firm in Washington, D.C. In contrast, 63 percent of women globally, and up to 75 percent in wealthy countries, use contraception.[9]

Worldwide, some 225 million women have unmet needs for contraception, according to the Alan Guttmacher Institute, a nonprofit in New York that conducts research and public education on reproductive health and rights.[10] That includes women who want to avoid pregnancy but are not using contraception.

Some are unable to obtain or afford it, but access is not the only obstacle. "Many women are worried about health impacts or side effects" says Leahy Madsen. "And women or their husbands may oppose family planning for religious or cultural reasons. People can have competing preferences: Women may not want to get pregnant and also not believe in using contraception."

Reducing poverty and promoting global economic development are important humanitarian goals. And over time these policies can help poor countries become potential trading partners. Thus, wealthy countries provide more than $1 billion yearly in direct aid and through the U.N. to support family planning in low- and middle-income countries.

Curbing population growth may also reduce violence and civil conflict. In a widely cited 2006 study, Norwegian political scientist Henrik Urdal found that risks of armed conflict, terrorism and riots or violent demonstrations

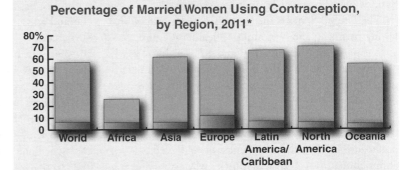

'Modern' Contraception Widely Used

Married women in Africa use what the United Nations calls "modern" contraception methods, such as birth control pills and intrauterine devices, less than women in most other regions. Traditional methods, such as timing sexual activity according to a woman's fertility cycle, are used by a minority of women in all regions.

Percentage of Married Women Using Contraception, by Region, 2011*

* Includes women in unions or regularly cohabiting with men in a marriage-like relationship.

** Modern methods include birth control pills, injections, implants, intrauterine devices, male and female condoms and spermicides. Traditional methods include rhythm, withdrawal and prolonged abstinence.

Source: "World Contraceptive Patterns 2013," United Nations Population Division, Department of Economic and Social Affairs, October 2013, http://tinyurl.com/mng2veq

were significantly higher in nations with a disproportionately young population — ages 15 to 24 — which is typical in fast-growing countries.[11] The centrist Center for Strategic and International Studies (CSIS) in Washington recently called rapid population growth a key factor threatening stability in many Middle East and North African countries.[12]

Environmentalists also raise concerns about whether the world can sustainably produce enough food to support nearly 11 billion people. "Food production has a bigger impact on the planet than any other single human activity when you add up water use, soil damage, loss of biodiversity and greenhouse gas emissions," says Jason Clay, a senior vice president with the World Wildlife Fund (WWF), a coalition of conservation groups that works in more than 100 countries.

In a 2014 report the WWF estimated that the number of mammals, birds, reptiles, amphibians and fish on

Earth declined by more than 50 percent between 1970 and 2010 due to effects of human activities, such as land degradation, overfishing, overharvesting and climate change.[13] "We are already living beyond the planet's carrying capacity," says Clay. "And we will need to provide for 30 percent more people by 2050 who consume nearly twice as much per capita." Consumption increases as nations develop and consumer income rises.

The United States is the largest single donor to global family planning and reproductive health programs, providing between $425 million and $715 million yearly over the past decade.[14] But domestic politics, particularly disagreements over abortion, frequently spur controversy over these efforts.

In 1984 President Ronald Reagan imposed the so-called Mexico City Policy, which denied U.S. aid to organizations abroad that provided or counseled patients about abortion — even in countries where abortion was legal. The policy, which Reagan announced at a population conference in Mexico City, has been suspended and reimposed repeatedly over the past 30 years, based on presidents' positions on abortion.

As health and development experts, national governments and advocacy groups weigh strategies for managing population growth, here are some issues they are considering:

Will population growth level off by 2100?

When U.N. experts projected last fall that world population would likely reach nearly 11 billion by 2100, the announcement sparked debate. The United Nations has issued biennial reports on world population prospects since the early 1950s, but since 2011 U.N. demographers have used a new method for calculating their projections, leading some experts to disagree with the findings.

Before 2011 the U.N. had projected global population growth only through 2050, but in 2011 it estimated that population would reach 10.1 billion by the end of the century. In 2013 it raised that estimate to 10.9 billion and repeated the figure in an article published by U.N. and academic specialists in 2014.[15]

Previously, the U.N.'s Population Division had integrated population and statistics experts' opinions about trends in birth and death rates into the forecast. Starting in 2011 the U.N. developed its own projections of fertility

trends, using data from around the world and probability to estimate which paths were more and less likely. The new models generated higher growth projections.

"We did thousands of simulations, country by country," says Patrick Gerland, a demographer with the U.N. Population Division. "For each country some futures are more likely than others. Our goal was to show a range of possibilities with upper and lower bounds." Gerland and his colleagues calculated that there was an 80 percent chance that world population would total between 9.6 billion and 12.3 billion in 2100. (The group's projection of 10.9 billion is roughly at the midpoint of this range.) The group estimated that there was only a 30 percent chance that world population growth would peak before 2100.[16]

But other forecasters reached different answers. Deutsche Bank global strategist Sanjeev Sanyal predicted in 2013 that world population would peak at 8.7 billion in about 2055 and decline to 8 billion by 2100. "This is obviously a radically different view of the world," Sanyal wrote, arguing that the U.N. was overestimating how long it would take for fertility rates to fall in developing countries such as Nigeria.[17]

Sanyal predicted that the global fertility rate would fall to the "replacement rate" — or about 2.1 children per woman — by 2025, some 50 years sooner than the U.N. projected.[18] The replacement rate is the level at which a couple has just enough children to replace themselves without increasing the global population. It is slightly above two to offset children who die in the first years of life.

However, Gerland argues that major demographic changes typically do not occur over large regions all at once. "Things don't happen in the same way at the same time everywhere," he says. "Our work with probabilities tries to factor in variations from country to country."

Population experts at the International Institute for Applied Systems Analysis (IIASA), a social science research center in Vienna, Austria, also say the U.N. estimates are too high. IIASA developed the probabilistic approach now used by the U.N., but the institute also considers additional factors.

Notably, IIASA experts say education is a key influence on fertility rates.[19] When countries expand access to education, fertility rates decline and women can play greater roles in the economy, making them less likely to want large families.[20]

Because educational opportunities are increasing in fast-growing countries, IIASA's most-likely scenario projects an 85 percent chance that world population will peak at 9.4 billion in around 2070 and decline to 9.0 billion by 2100.[21]

Many experts emphasize that long-term population projections are scenarios of possible outcomes and should not be taken literally. "When you project out to 2100, you're definitely stepping onto thin ice," says Carl Haub, a senior demographer at the nonprofit Population Reference Bureau, which conducts research and analysis on population issues in Washington. "The U.N., IIASA, and [other sources such as] the U.S. Census Bureau all have their own approaches, and most of us don't totally understand all the implications of differences between them."

Even when countries reduce fertility rates to replacement levels, he notes, their populations continue to increase for some time while a large cohort of young people — the first generation born after child mortality declines but while fertility rates are still high — passes through adulthood. Demographers call this pattern population momentum.

"You don't get steep reductions until members of that generation work through their childbearing years," Haub says. "I don't think world population can stop growing before 2100. But in the U.N.'s mid-range projection, you're only adding about 10 million people every year by then [compared to 80 million now], so you're making progress."

Can Earth support nearly 11 billion people?

For centuries observers have debated whether human population growth will use up Earth's resources. Today many environmental advocates warn that human activities are damaging land, forests, fisheries and other resources faster than they can recover. Skeptics counter that humans will find new ways to produce food and other necessities more efficiently or find technological substitutes for them.

Human activities increasingly impact the planet as the population grows, but other factors also play important roles. In the early 1970s two University of California professors, Paul Ehrlich (a biologist) and John Holdren (a physicist), developed an equation to describe human effects on the environment: $I = P \times A \times T$, where I stands for impacts, P for population, A for affluence (wealth), and T for technology.[22]

This formula recognized that as people become wealthier they consume more resources per capita. Technology can make the impacts worse if people demand resource-intensive goods, such as gas-guzzling cars or meat-centered diets. Or it can reduce humans' environmental footprint by making it possible to produce goods more efficiently.

Ehrlich and Holdren contended that humans were pushing up against fundamental ecological limits that could not be overcome through technological solutions.[23] But many critics argued then and now that scientific advances could offset scarcity.

"Yes, pockets of the world face famine — usually in regions with corrupt, despotic governments. But overall, the world hasn't outgrown its ability to feed itself," wrote American financial author and commentator Lara Hoffmans. "And while global population has grown, life expectancies keep increasing, quality of life keeps improving and per capita GDP keeps expanding."[24]

Feeding a growing population is a serious challenge. The U.N. Food and Agriculture Organization (FAO) in Rome has estimated that although world population is projected to grow by about one-third by 2050, feeding 9.6 billion people will require 70 percent more food, because people consume more meat as incomes rise, requiring more grain to feed livestock. Then-FAO Assistant Director-General Hafez Ghanem, now a scholar at the Brookings Institution think tank in Washington, has said the agency is "cautiously optimistic" that the challenge can be met, but only if nations boost agricultural investments and take steps to ensure that everyone has access to food.[25]

Ehrlich still contends that the depletion of Earth's resources will cause imminent disaster unless humans take radical action.[26] In 2013, he and his wife, biologist Anne Ehrlich, wrote that "for the first time, humanity's *global* civilization . . . is threatened with collapse by an array of environmental problems" that could be triggered by anything from nuclear war to conflict over "increasingly scarce necessities." To avoid this scenario, they called for cutting fossil fuel use and limiting population growth to 8.6 billion by 2050.[27]

The Ehrlichs cited work by the Global Footprint Network (GFN), a nonprofit based in Oakland, Calif.,

Bolivia is now promoting quinoa, a protein-rich grain that grows well in harsh climates, as one solution for growing global food needs. Agricultural specialists say continued population growth will exacerbate hunger problems if current food consumption rates and preferences, especially demand for meat, continue. Some experts call for overhauling the world's food system. Others advocate expanded use of genetically modified crops, but critics contend they are unsafe.

that annually measures the effects of human activity on the planet — including use of land, forests and fisheries and emissions of greenhouse gases, which cause global climate change — and compares them to the resources Earth can produce in a year. According to GFN, humans have been in "overshoot" since the early 1970s — using more resources than the planet can replace.

"We use more resources today than the Earth can regenerate, and we're adding more people every year," says GFN President Mathis Wackernagel. "You can see the impacts of overshoot in depleted places like Haiti, and also in events like the Arab Spring," which some analysts say was triggered in part by high youth unemployment and rising bread prices.

GFN calculates that most wealthy nations consume far more resources than they produce. For example, the group estimates that the United States uses nearly twice as many resources annually as it generates, and Japan consumes seven times what it produces.[28] Wackernagel does not predict that world resources will run out at a specific point. Rather, he says, scarcity already exists in many places, especially for the world's poor.

"More than 70 percent of the world's population lives in nations that are consuming more resources than they produce and are middle- or low-income countries," he says.[29] "How will they afford to import supplies from abroad when their local resources are depleted? We should be redesigning our lifestyles to consume fewer resources, but we keep building the old economy instead of rethinking it."

Some experts say that by drastically overhauling the global food system, food supplies could be doubled sustainably by 2050. A group led by Jonathan Foley, director of the Institute on the Environment at the University of Minnesota, proposes five steps: Stop expanding onto uncultivated land; grow more on existing farms, using both high-tech and organic methods; use fertilizer, pesticides and water more efficiently; reduce global meat consumption; and reduce food waste. (According to Foley's group, an estimated 25 percent of food calories and up to 50 percent of total food weight worldwide are lost or wasted before they reach consumers.)

"We already know what we have to do; we just need to figure out how to do it," Foley writes.[30]

The World Wildlife Fund advocates a similar plan, including specific steps such as using biotechnology to increase yields of major African food crops. "We need to focus on crops that are important there, like cowpeas and cassava, instead of growing more corn and shipping it there," says the WWF's Clay. "These crops are quite productive, but they haven't been targeted by modern science."

Some development experts and advocates contend that expanding the use of crops that have been genetically modified to increase their productivity and resistance to heat and drought should be a key strategy for feeding a growing world population. But critics argue that genetically modified organisms (GMOs) are unsafe for the environment and human health.[31] WWF's proposal for expanding food production includes marker-assisted breeding, an approach that does not involve transferring genetic material between species. *

* Marker-assisted breeding is a combination of traditional genetics and molecular biology. Scientists use molecular "markers" to find genes that are associated with a desired trait, such as heat resistance. Then they introduce that trait into new plant strains through selective breeding.

Foley is open to use of GMOs but asserts that they have not significantly increased world food production yet — mainly because biotechnology developers have focused on crops grown in developed countries, such as corn, rather than those eaten in the developing world, such as cassava. "While [GMO] technology itself might 'work,' it has so far been applied to the wrong parts of the food system to truly make a dent in global food security," he wrote.[32]

Clay sees progress occurring in many areas. "Two years ago, total aquaculture [fish farming] production surpassed total beef production worldwide," he says. Raising fish requires significantly less protein and causes fewer harmful environmental effects than producing beef, although some forms of aquaculture are more sustainable than others.[33]

"Major corporations are pledging to support sustainable production of commodities like palm oil," says Clay. "And we don't have to double production to get to our goal. We can do a lot by reducing waste. If we could eliminate food waste worldwide, we'd be halfway there."

Is family planning a universal human right?

Since 1994 international family planning policy has promoted a woman's right to choose whether and when to have children. At the global conference where this new agenda was approved, 179 nations adopted a goal of providing universal access to a full range of safe, reliable and legal family planning and reproductive health services.

But in 2012, the U.N. Population Fund (UNFPA) reported that the modern contraception needs of more than 220 million women worldwide were still unmet.

"This is inexcusable. Family planning is a *human right*. It must therefore be available to all who want it," wrote U.N. Under-Secretary-General and UNFPA Executive Director Babatunde Osotimehin. "It is high time we lived up to that commitment and made voluntary family planning available to all."[34] The report

Life Spans Lowest in Developing Countries

While life expectancy has risen worldwide in recent decades, it remains far lower in developing countries than in advanced ones. People born in Monaco can expect to live the longest — more than 89 years — while those born in Chad can expect to live only until age 49. Four of the five countries with the world's lowest life expectancies are in Africa.

Countries With Longest Estimated Life Expectancy at Birth, 2014		Countries With Shortest Estimated Life Expectancy at Birth, 2014	
Country	**Years**	**Country**	**Years**
Monaco	89.6	Swaziland	50.5
Macau	84.5	Afghanistan	50.5
Japan	84.5	Guinea-Bissau	49.9
Singapore	84.4	South Africa	49.6
San Marino	83.2	Chad	49.4

Source: "Country Comparison: Life Expectancy at Birth," *The World Factbook*, Central Intelligence Agency, updated Aug. 15, 2014, http://tinyurl.com/yrq7l8

marked the first time the UNFPA had explicitly called family planning a human right.[35]

Conservatives oppose this view, however. Calling family planning a human right represents "U.N. dominance over individual states' national sovereignty," Janice Shaw Crouse, a spokeswomen for the Concerned Women for American Legislative Action Committee, a conservative advocacy group in Washington that works to "protect and promote Biblical values among all citizens," argued in response to the UNFPA.[36] Such a usurpation of national sovereignty amounts to "modern-day colonialism," she said.[37]

Meanwhile, U.S. officials have been debating whether employers should be required to provide workers with health insurance that covers contraception at no cost — effectively declaring that all Americans should have free access to contraception. Catholic leaders and conservative legislators strongly oppose this policy.

"They don't have the authority under the First Amendment of the United States Constitution to tell someone in this country or some organization in this country what their religious beliefs are," said then-Senate

JAY DIRECTO/AFP/Getty Images

Women wait to receive family-planning advice at a health center in Manila, capital of the Philippines. The country's Supreme Court ruled last April that a law requiring the government to provide free birth control for the poor and mandating sex education in public schools was constitutional. Development experts hope the law will help the country — which is more than 80 percent Catholic — curb population growth, which they see as critical to raising millions of Filipinos out of poverty.

Minority Leader Mitch McConnell, a Republican from Kentucky, in 2013.[38] The Supreme Court ruled in the landmark *Hobby Lobby* case last June that some types of employers could be exempted under religious freedom laws from covering contraceptives through their employees' health plans.[39]

Advocates of family planning contend that it empowers poor women by letting them choose whether and when to have children. "Creating societies where people enjoy basic health, relative prosperity, fundamental equality, and access to contraceptives is the only way to secure a sustainable world," billionaire philanthropist Bill Gates wrote in his 2014 annual letter to supporters of the Bill & Melinda Gates Foundation. "We will build a better future for everyone by giving people the freedom and the power to build a better future for themselves and their families."[40]

The Catholic Church remains opposed to abortion and all forms of birth control other than "natural" family planning. In 2013 Pope Francis reaffirmed the church's position, stating that human life "is always sacred and inviolable, in any situation and at every stage of development. . . . It is not 'progressive' to try to resolve problems by eliminating a human life."[41]

Last April, the U.N. observer delegation from the Holy See (the government of the Catholic Church) said

a strong focus on universal reproductive rights seemed "to treat fertility and pregnancy as a disease which must either be prevented or managed via government or outside assistance. While this may well reflect the concerns of certain highly developed countries . . . it certainly skews the population and development realities for the most part of the developing countries of the world, for whom other issues take greater priority."[42]

Catholic leaders and organizations have traditionally supported action to help the world's poor and, more recently, to protect the environment, but do not advocate population-based strategies to achieve those goals. Instead, they contend, policies should focus on improving the lives of the poor and reducing consumption in wealthy nations.

"The global climate change debate cannot become just another opportunity for some groups — usually affluent advocates from the developed nations — to blame the problem on population growth in poor countries," the U.S. Conference of Catholic Bishops stated in 2001. "Development policies that seek to reduce poverty with an emphasis on improved education and social conditions for women are far more effective than usual population reduction programs and far more respectful of women's dignity."[43]

In practice, however, surveys show that most Catholics in developed countries and many in developing nations support the use of birth control.[44]

Critics argue that Catholic leaders and aid organizations that operate in developing countries retard progress toward reproductive health goals, such as providing wider access to contraception. "The Catholic hierarchy has lost the battle [on contraception] in the global North, but they are controlling it in the global South," says Jon O'Brien, president of Catholics for Choice, an advocacy group in Washington, D.C., that advocates for Catholics who support personal choice on sex and reproductive health issues.

For example, in Kenya, which is about one-quarter Catholic, Catholic leaders have urged women to boycott a tetanus vaccination campaign sponsored by the World Health Organization and the United Nations Children's Fund (UNICEF) because Kenyan bishops assert that the vaccine contains a hormone that suppresses fertility and is actually intended to sterilize women. The WHO, UNICEF and Kenya's health ministry all say the vaccine is safe, but the Kenyan parliament has asked for more testing in response to the bishops' claims.[45]

But O'Brien sees steps such as the Philippines' reproductive health law and Uruguay's passage of a 2012 law legalizing first-trimester abortions as signs that the Catholic Church's influence is starting to erode.[46] "Those were real steps forward to democracy and reproductive health, and they may inspire other politicians to legislate for the common good," he says.

Many other faith-based organizations also help deliver family planning and reproductive health services around the world. While some groups oppose abortion or specific contraceptive methods, most generally support the importance of access to a range of family planning options.

The United Methodist Church, for instance, states that family planning provides "priceless and countless" direct and indirect benefits, including smaller families, healthier mothers and children and reduced economic burdens on families.[47]

BACKGROUND

Malthus' Warning

In pre-industrial societies, survival — rather than rapid population growth — was a pressing concern. Families typically had large numbers of children, but many people died of infectious diseases such as cholera and measles.

It took more than 200,000 years for the world's human population to reach 1 billion, in 1804. At that time the Industrial Revolution was just beginning in England and spreading to the United States. New tools and techniques enabled farmers to produce larger quantities of food, while steam power made it possible to mass-produce textiles, machinery and many other goods.

English cleric Thomas Malthus viewed the growth that he saw in the early years of industrialization with alarm. In 1798 Malthus published his famous "Essay on the Principle of Population," in which he argued that human population growth would increase faster than food supplies and other essential resources, leading to "misery and vice," such as war, famine and disease.[48]

In the early 19th century, however, the idea that humans could ever become numerous enough to deplete Earth's resources would have seemed far-fetched. Thousands of people who moved from farms to cities found themselves living in overcrowded, squalid urban slums. But starting in the 1840s, public health movements in Europe and the United States began to address urban conditions, providing clean water, collecting garbage and eventually adopting regulations to reduce overcrowding in tenements. Over the next century, urban life gradually became healthier.

Life expectancy improved further as scientists developed the germ theory of disease. Before the 1860s little was known about what caused many kinds of sickness. Epidemics were attributed to many factors, including bad air, filth and personal sins. Cholera, a disease caused by contaminated water, killed thousands of people in London and New York between 1830 and 1860.[49]

In the 1860s French scientist Louis Pasteur showed that micro-organisms, which could be killed by heating, caused many kinds of food and drink to spoil. The heating process was named pasteurization in his honor.

Then, in 1876 German physician Robert Koch demonstrated that a certain bacterium caused a disease called anthrax in animals. Koch identified the bacterium that caused cholera in 1883. Other scientists used his methods to culture and identify agents that caused typhus, tetanus and plague, and later to develop antibiotics and vaccines against common infectious diseases.[50]

Growth in Developing Countries

Disease outbreaks continued to occur worldwide. One of the worst, a global flu pandemic in 1918-1919, killed an estimated 20 to 40 million people worldwide.[51] But by the 1940s, immunization, safer food-handling, better sanitation and clean drinking water had greatly reduced epidemics and early deaths in industrialized countries. The 1928 discovery of penicillin, one of the first antibiotics, which could kill many harmful bacteria, was also a critical development.[52]

However, in much of Africa and Asia — continents that had been colonized by European powers in the 19th century and exploited for labor and natural resources — most people were desperately poor and lived in pre-industrial conditions.

After World War II Britain, France, Belgium and other colonial powers withdrew from their overseas empires. Dozens of countries in Asia, Africa and the Pacific gained independence. Leaders at the United Nations, created in 1945 to promote international cooperation, sought to

CHRONOLOGY

1798-1928 *Industrialization boosts world population, and public health movements reduce deaths from diseases.*

1798 English cleric Thomas Malthus' *An Essay on the Principle of Population* warns about unlimited population growth.

1804 World population reaches 1 billion.

1848 England's Parliament passes the world's first modern, proactive, public-health law.

1876 German doctor Robert Koch demonstrates that *Bacillus anthracis* causes anthrax. Using Koch's methods, other scientists isolate bacteria that cause such diseases as typhus and plague.

1928 Alexander Fleming, a professor of bacteriology in London, discovers penicillin.

1946-1980 *Conservationists warn that population growth in developing countries could lead to famine.*

1946 United Nations creates Population Commission to research demographics and advise the U.N. on population trends and policies.

1960 International Rice Research Institute created to improve food yields in developing nations.

1968 Pope Paul VI issues an encyclical affirming the church's ban on all artificial birth control methods.

1972 The Club of Rome, an international think tank, publishes "The Limits to Growth," which projects that unregulated growth could lead to global economic collapse.

1973 Congress adopts the Helms Amendment, barring use of U.S. foreign aid for abortions.

1979 China announces a one-child-per-family policy to limit population.

1984-2000 *World leaders debate connections between population growth and development.*

1984 President Ronald Reagan announces the Mexico City Policy, barring federal funding for nongovernment organizations that provide or advise on abortion.

1993 President Bill Clinton waives the Mexico City Policy, stating that it undermines efforts to promote safe and effective family planning in developing countries.

1994 At an international conference in Cairo, Egypt, 179 countries adopt a 20-year action plan focusing on empowering women and meeting educational and health needs.

2000 At the United Nations, 189 nations endorse the Millennium Development Goals, a blueprint for ending poverty by 2015 that promotes gender equality, empowering women and improving maternal health.

2001-Present *Global population growth rate moderates, but total continues to climb.*

2001 President George W. Bush reinstates the Mexico City Policy and expands it to other programs.

2003 Bush commits $15 billion over five years to fight the global HIV/AIDS pandemic, averting an estimated 1.1 million deaths in Africa.

2008 President Barack Obama waives Mexico City Policy.

2009 Stanford University biologist Paul Ehrlich and his wife Anne reassert the central warning of his 1968 book, *The Population Bomb*, focusing on HIV/AIDS, rising food prices and disruption of agriculture due to climate change.

2011 World population reaches 7 billion.

2012 U.N. Population Division asserts that family planning is a human right.

2013 China eases one-child policy.

2014 U.N. demographers predict world population will reach 10.9 billion by 2100.

help these nations develop and raise their people out of poverty. In 1946 the U.N. created a Population Commission to carry out demographic studies and advise the organization on population policy.

Buoyed by a global postwar economic boom, incomes in many developing countries rose over the next several decades. U.N. agencies, the World Bank and other multilateral development institutions and programs such as the U.S. Peace Corps spent millions of dollars to reduce poverty, hunger and disease worldwide. World population, which had doubled from 1 billion to 2 billion between 1804 and 1927, took only 33 years to add a third billion (1960) and 14 years to add a fourth billion (1974).

Although this rapid growth meant that fewer people were dying young, many experts worried that population would outstrip food supplies. In 1960 the Ford and Rockefeller foundations partnered with the Philippine government to found the International Rice Research Institute (IRRI), an independent organization charged with developing higher-yielding strains of rice and new farming techniques. IRRI and other centers formed a network called the Consultative Group on International Agricultural Research (CGIAR), which spearheaded the Green Revolution — a campaign to develop strains of rice, wheat and corn that were high yielding, responsive to fertilizer and disease-resistant.

The initiatives, led by American biologist Norman Borlaug, increased yields of staple cereals in developing countries fourfold in the 1960s and '70s.[53]

But environmentalists warned that these new methods only worked when farmers used large quantities of water, synthetic fertilizers and chemical pesticides, which many farmers in poor areas could not afford.[54] And some scholars asserted that despite these tools, large-scale population growth would quickly exhaust Earth's resources, leading to catastrophe.

"In the 1970s and 1980s hundreds of millions of people will starve to death in spite of any crash programs embarked upon now," Stanford University biologist Paul Ehrlich predicted in his 1968 best-seller *The Population Bomb*. Ehrlich argued that the United States should lead by controlling its own population, "hopefully through changes in our value system, but by compulsion if voluntary methods fail."[55]

The book made Ehrlich a media star, but many critics — including conservative politicians and economists,

as well as some liberal scientists and advocates — argued that Ehrlich's predictions were exaggerated and alarmist. and did not sufficiently address social justice for the world's poor.[56]

In 1972 the Club of Rome, an international think tank, published another warning called *The Limits to Growth*, which used computer modeling to project how human activities would affect world resources. It concluded that if population growth and consumption continued on existing paths, a global economic collapse and millions of deaths could occur by 2030.[57]

Liberals embraced these predictions, but some prominent economists argued that societies would regulate pollution, and technological advances would lead to discovery of new resources.[58] They also criticized the Club of Rome's models. MIT economist Robert Solow, who later would win the Nobel Prize in economics, called them "worthless as science and as guides to public policy," arguing that they ignored normal ways in which markets responded to scarcity.[59]

Abortion Controversies

Although development experts viewed slowing population growth as a crucial step to reduce poverty, some powerful critics disagreed. In 1968 Pope Paul VI issued an encyclical that maintained the Catholic Church's ban on all forms of birth control short of abstention. A papal review commission had recommended lifting the ban, but the pope overrode the commission, fearing that changing direction would undermine the church's authority.[60]

Governments could help solve the population problem, the pope asserted, by "enacting laws which will assist families and by educating the people wisely."[61]

U.S. population policy became sharply politicized in 1980 with the election of President Ronald Reagan, who strongly opposed abortion. In 1984 Reagan announced a new policy at an international population conference in Mexico City. It required all foreign nongovernmental organizations (NGOs) that received funds from the U.S. Agency for International Development (USAID), which manages anti-poverty and development efforts abroad, to certify that they would not perform, support or actively promote abortion in other countries — even if it was legal there and the groups used non-U.S. funds to pay

Life Expectancy Varies Widely

"People in high-income countries have a much better chance of living longer."

Imagine that two babies are born on the same day — one in the tiny Mediterranean country of Monaco, bordering France, the other in the impoverished, desert nation of Chad in north-central Africa. The baby in Monaco can expect to live to nearly 90; the Chad baby, a bit beyond age 49.[1]

Life expectancy is the statistical average number of years a person can be expected to live, based on assumptions about death rates in a given time and place. It reflects how wealthy a population is and whether people have access to health care and basic services such as sanitation and clean water.

Many nations with long life expectancies are in Western Europe, Asia and North America. Compared with other areas of the globe, they have high income levels and strong social welfare programs ensuring at least basic services for most of their citizens.

Globally, life expectancy at birth is trending upward as nations develop their physical and social infrastructures and health conditions improve. Worldwide, a baby born in 1970 could be expected to live to about age 58; by 2013 that had risen to 71.[2]

But those averages mask many gaps. Women outlive men worldwide, typically by five or six years in developed countries and smaller margins in developing countries where maternal mortality is high. No one has definitively explained why women outlive men. Some experts believe women have inherent biological advantages, while others say men are more likely to engage in unhealthy behaviors such as smoking and drinking.[3]

Even larger gaps in life expectancy exist among nations. From 1970 through 2013 life expectancy at birth rose from 71 to 79 in the world's most developed countries. In the least developed nations it rose from 44 to 61.[4] "There is still a major rich-poor divide: People in high-income countries continue to have a much better chance of living longer than

people in low-income countries," said Margaret Chan, director-general of the World Health Organization.[5]

Gaps also exist within countries. In the United States, whites live about four years longer than African-Americans. Paradoxically, Hispanics live two to three years longer than whites, although their income and education levels average closer to those of blacks. Demographers believe low smoking rates, strong social networks and traditional diets may explain Hispanics' advantage.[6]

Differences even exist at the local level. Life expectancy in affluent St. Johns County in northeastern Florida is nearly 83 for women and 78 for men. But next door in less wealthy Putnam County, life expectancy is 78 for women and 71 for men. "It doesn't take a rocket scientist to figure this out," said Jeff Feller, chief executive of the WellFlorida Council, a regional nonprofit group that manages health programs in 16 Florida counties. "This [gap] is fueled by poor economics and a lack of access to health insurance and health coverage."[7]

Pandemics, wars and political upheaval can dramatically affect life expectancy. In Russia, death rates increased from the 1960s through the 1980s, bucking global trends, because the bureaucratic Soviet health care system failed to meet public needs.[8] Death rates spiked after the Soviet Union dissolved in 1991 and Russia plunged into an economic crisis. Already-steep alcohol abuse and smoking rates rose, and many Russians were unable to afford health care. Life expectancy for Russian men fell from 63 in 1990 to 58 in 2000.[9] Although it improved over the next decade, it still is significantly lower than in many neighboring countries. A Russian male born in 2013 can expect to live to age 65, compared to 71 in Bulgaria and Hungary and 73 in Poland.[10]

In South Africa, the HIV/AIDS pandemic reduced life expectancy in the early 2000s by an estimated 26 years.[11] The disease's effects were especially severe because President Thabo

for abortion-related activities. Congress in 1973 had already barred use of U.S. foreign aid funds to pay for abortions or coerce people into having abortions.[62]

Family planning advocates dubbed this policy the "Global Gag Rule" because organizations that received

U.S. aid could not even talk about abortion. They argued that it was harmful because it cut aid to hospitals and clinics in developing countries that performed other important services, such as providing contraceptives and educating people about HIV/AIDS.[63]

Mbeki (1999-2008) endorsed a widely discredited theory that HIV/AIDS is caused by poverty rather than a virus. Mbeki's government first rejected and later limited distribution of antiretroviral (ARV) drugs — a policy that Harvard University researchers estimated led to 330,000 deaths.[12]

After Mbeki left office, South Africa reversed its stance and developed the world's largest ARV program, with more than $3 billion in U.S. support from the President's Emergency Plan for AIDs Relief (PEPFAR), launched by President George W. Bush in 2003. Between 2008 and 2014, life expectancy in South Africa increased by nine years, from 52.2 to 61.2 years. (This life expectancy estimate is from the South African government and is markedly higher than the CIA estimate on p. 56.)[13]

Now, however, that progress could erode, as PEPFAR aid is redirected to poorer countries. But South Africa's health minister, Aaron Motsoaledi, predicted that his nation would remain committed to fighting HIV/AIDS. "From whatever angle you look at, it's cheaper to treat people early," he said. "The treasury minister understands that. It's becoming easy for him to agree."[14]

— *Jennifer Weeks*

A nurse from Indonesia cares for an elderly woman at a nursing home in Tokyo. In graying nations like Japan, foreigners are needed to make up for the shortage of younger workers.

TORU YAMANAKA/AFP/Getty Images

[1] "Country Comparison: Life Expectancy at Birth," *World Factbook* (2014), U.S. Central Intelligence Agency, http://tinyurl.com/yrq7l8.

[2] "2014 World Population Data Sheet," Population Reference Bureau, p. 13, http://tinyurl.com/mufdwk2.

[3] See Christopher Middleton, "Why Do Women Live Longer Than Men?" *Newsweek*, Aug. 1, 2014, http://tinyurl.com/p5suq8w, and Hallie Levine, "Five Reasons Women Live Longer Than Men," *Health*, Oct. 13, 2014, http://tinyurl.com/m6blksq.

[4] "2014 World Population Data Sheet," *op. cit.*

[5] "Life Expectancy Rising, But UN Report Shows 'Major' Rich-Poor Longevity Divide Persists," United Nations News Centre, May 15, 2014, http://tinyurl.com/p8odrmf.

[6] Paola Scommegna, "Exploring the Paradox of U.S. Hispanics' Longer Life Expectancy," Population Reference Bureau, July 2013, http://tinyurl.com/kkmv3qc.

[7] Michael A. Fletcher, "Research Ties Economic Inequality to Gap in Life Expectancy," *The Washington Post*, March 10, 2013, http://tinyurl.com/d86zbtz.

[8] Julie DaVanzo and David Adamson, "Russia's Demographic 'Crisis': How Real Is It?" *RAND Issue Paper 162* (1997), http://tinyurl.com/p2r8d45.

[9] Eugen Tomiuc, "Low Life Expectancy Continues to Plague Former Soviet Countries," Radio Free Europe/Radio Liberty, April 2, 2013, http://tinyurl.com/blhe5c7.

[10] "2014 World Population Data Sheet," *op. cit.*

[11] Chuks J. Mba, "Impact of HIV/AIDs Mortality on South Africa's Life Expectancy and Implications for the Elderly Population," *African Journal of Health Sciences*, vol. 14, no. 3-4 (July-December 2007), p. 201, http://tinyurl.com/l6gl6bl.

[12] Sarah Bosely, "Mbeki AIDS Policy 'Led To 330,000 Deaths,'" *The Guardian*, Nov. 26, 2008, http://tinyurl.com/q96w2r6.

[13] "HIV Drugs 'Boost South African Life Expectancy,'" BBC News, Aug. 1, 2014, http://tinyurl.com/kvkm7nf; Donald G. McNeil, "AIDS Progress in South Africa Is in Peril," *The New York Times*, Aug. 25, 2014, http://tinyurl.com/k35mjfz.

[14] *Ibid.*, *The New York Times.*

For example, when Nepal's government decided to legalize abortion under certain conditions in 2002, the Family Planning Association of Nepal — which had received U.S. aid for nearly 30 years — had to refuse further U.S. funding so it could inform Nepalese women about abortion. "Whatever we decide, the women of Nepal suffer," the group's director, Dr. Nirmal K. Bista, told the Senate Foreign Relations Committee in 2001. "Our colleagues all over the world face this same agonizing decision."[64]

Fertility Rates Remain High in Many Countries

High population growth can impede economic progress, experts say.

As nations develop, their living conditions improve, death rates fall and many people who once may have depended on their children's help for survival realize they no longer need a large family. Birth rates eventually decline and the population stabilizes.

That process, typical of industrializing countries, is known as the "demographic transition," and nations go through it it at different speeds. "A lot depends on whether national governments make population reductions a goal or pay no attention to the issue," says Carl Haub, a senior demographer at the nonprofit Population Reference Bureau in Washington, which carries out research and public education on population issues.

Since the 1960s many developing countries have completed this transition within several decades. For example, between 1970 and 2013 Vietnam, Iran, Bangladesh, Qatar, El Salvador and Mexico all reduced total fertility rates from more than six children per woman to 2.2 or fewer.[1] Many experts say reducing fertility rates is crucial for developing countries because money spent on housing, medical care and schools could instead be used to promote economic growth, such as by building factories, roads and ports and developing industries.

But today that transition has slowed or even stalled in many African nations. While most countries in northern and southern Africa have reduced fertility levels to 3.5 children or fewer, others in western, eastern and central Africa still average six children or more per woman. In Niger, South Sudan, Chad, the Central African Republic and the Democratic Republic of Congo — the continent's least developed nations — fertility rates increased between 1970 and 2013. Women in Nigeria, Africa's most populous country, still average 5.6 children each.[2]

"Sub-Saharan Africa is still following the classic demographic transition model, but it's taking a lot longer than other developing countries," says Haub. "One problem is that many African women still don't have a lot of say in their households. Their authority is quite a bit weaker than in other countries." Studies show that in societies where gender inequality and violence are prevalent, women have less access to birth control and control over their reproductive choices.

U.S. officials also sparred over the U.N. Population Fund (UNFPA), which some critics accused of supporting forced abortions in China as part of its programs there. China introduced a one-child limit per family in 1979 to reduce social and environmental pressures from rapid population growth. Reports soon emerged that some women in rural areas who refused to comply had been forced to have abortions or sterilizations.[65]

In 1985 Congress adopted the Kemp-Kasten Amendment, named after its sponsors Rep. Jack Kemp, R-N.Y., and Sen. Sen. Robert Kasten, R-Wis., which barred U.S. funding for any organizations that supported coercive family planning.[66] Between 1985 and 2008 the United States determined 15 times that UNFPA was violating this restriction and withheld U.S. contributions, which had averaged nearly $35 million yearly between 1981 and 1985.[67] All of these determinations occurred under Republican administrations except one in 1999 under Democratic President Bill Clinton (1993-2001). In that year, Congress denied the administration's funding request for UNFPA after the agency renewed programs that it had suspended in regions where coercive policies were alleged.[68]

During this time investigations by two NGOs and the U.S. State Department concluded that UNFPA was not supporting forced abortions or coercive family planning policies in China.[69] But a 2001 investigation by the Virginia-based Population Research Institute — a nonprofit that works to "expose the myth of overpopulation" — concluded that UNFPA funds were supporting coercive practices in the county visited by the report's authors.[70]

Presidents Clinton and Barack Obama (2008-current) both waived the Mexico City Policy and determined that UNFPA activities in China did not violate

Women's attitudes also can reinforce high fertility rates. "Unless your country has basic social services that guarantee your security in old age, you have very little incentive to limit how many children you have," says Françoise Girard, president of the New York-based International Women's Health Coalition, a nonprofit that works to advance reproductive health and rights for women and girls in developing countries.

"And if women don't believe they have other options," Girard continues, "they don't see a role for themselves outside the home. Many families in Africa still invest in boys and keep girls at home because they don't see girls as worth the investment. Twelve-year-old girls in Africa can see what's coming, and it's crushing to hear them dread their future."

But that situation is changing in many places, Girard emphasizes. As an example she points to her organization's affiliate in Nigeria, Action Health Inc.[3] "They have mentored tens of thousands of girls to think of themselves as full participants in society, stay in school, fight back against harassment and violence and aspire to be leaders," Girard says. "AHI also proposed a sexuality education program that was rolled out in all of Nigeria's public schools this year. They are reaching millions of Nigerian teenagers and teaching them what girls can hope for and how boys should relate to them."

Elizabeth Leahy Madsen, a senior technical adviser with the Washington, D.C., consulting firm Futures Group, emphasizes that conditions vary widely across sub-Saharan Africa. "There is runaway population growth, but also some really bright signs," she says. "In the 1980s and 1990s the rate of decline in fertility in Kenya was stalled, but new data show that contraceptive use there rose from 39 percent to 55 percent in just six years, which is a real success."

As a region, sub-Saharan Africa is making steady progress toward many of the Millennium Development Goals, a set of targets for reducing poverty worldwide adopted at the United Nations in 2000. The goals include expanding education and improving maternal and child health. But high population growth can impede progress. For example, net regional enrollment in primary schools rose from 60 percent in 2000 to 78 percent in 2012. But during that period the population of school-age children grew by 35 percent. Armed conflict and declining aid for basic education also helped to bar millions of African children from attending school.[4]

"Making progress on these issues involves more than just putting [contraceptive] products on the shelf or reducing their cost," says Leahy Madsen. "We also need to tackle deep-seated gender and cultural barriers and difficult conditions."

— *Jennifer Weeks*

---

[1] "2014 World Population Data Sheet," Population Reference Bureau, pp. 8-10, http://tinyurl.com/mufdwk2.

[2] *Ibid.*, pp. 7-8.

[3] For more information see "Bring Back Our Girls," Action Health Inc., http://tinyurl.com/35vxwce.

[4] "Steady Progress on Many Millennium Development Goals Continues in Sub-Saharan Africa," United Nations, July 7, 2014, http://tinyurl.com/lnadopz.

Kemp-Kasten, while stating concerns about coercive population control in China. "These excessively broad conditions . . . have undermined efforts to promote safe and effective voluntary family planning programs in foreign nations," Obama wrote in a memo waiving the Mexico City Policy.[71]

New Commitments

As abortion controversies roiled U.S. population policy, international thinking about population and development took a much broader turn. In 1994, delegates from 179 countries met at a conference in Cairo, Egypt, and endorsed an action plan that focused on improving health and expanding rights for people in developing countries, especially women, as a strategy for reducing population growth.

The Cairo action plan set five major goals to be achieved by 2015:

- Provide universal access to a full range of safe and reliable family planning methods and services;
- Reduce infant mortality rates to fewer than 35 infant deaths per 1,000 live births and child mortality to fewer than 45 deaths of children under age 5 per 1,000 live births;
- Close the gap in maternal mortality between developed and developing countries;
- Increase life expectancy at birth to 70 years or more; and
- Achieve universal primary education and increase secondary and higher education for women and girls.[72]

These targets helped pave the way for the Millennium Development Goals (MDGs), a set of targets for reducing poverty worldwide, adopted at the United Nations in 2000.[73] The MDGs also addressed education, gender

The Cat Survival Trust in Welwyn, England, shelters more than two dozen threatened cats, including puma, lynx, Scottish wildcats and this snow leopard. The World Wildlife Fund estimated in 2014 that the number of mammals, birds, reptiles, amphibians and fish on Earth declined by more than 50 percent between 1970 and 2010 due to the effects of human activities, such as land degradation, overfishing, overharvesting and climate change.

equality, child mortality and maternal health, along with other issues including poverty and environmental sustainability.

Over the following decade developing countries made significant progress toward these goals. But many women in the world's poorest nations still had trouble obtaining access to contraceptives and information about family planning. In 2012 the U.K. government and the Bill & Melinda Gates Foundation convened an international summit in London, where wealthy governments and NGOs vowed to provide access to these services for an additional 120 million women worldwide by 2020, a plan that would cost $4.3 billion.[74]

At the conference, participating governments, NGOs, foundations, research institutions and private organizations pledged $2.6 billion toward this goal. In 2013 (the most recent year for which data was available), donor governments alone provided $1.3 billion to support family planning in low-and middle-income countries — up nearly 20 percent over 2012.[75]

Advocates at the conference stressed what they saw as a need to offer many types of contraceptives and deliver them to hard-to-reach areas. "When you think about family planning from the perspective of the women who want to use it, everything changes," said Melinda Gates, who announced that the Gates Foundation would double

its investment in family planning to a total of more than $1 billion between 2012 and 2020.[76]

CURRENT SITUATION
Aging Populations

When wealthy industrialized nations think about population issues, they often worry that they are growing too slowly. In the United States, Canada, Europe, Japan, South Korea and Taiwan, couples today have two or fewer children on average. As a result, their populations will only grow if they admit large numbers of immigrants. Another worrisome factor is the rising average age in these countries.[77]

Some observers worry that population aging will have negative social effects. In "graying" nations a relatively small number of workers must generate enough wealth to pay for health care, housing and other costs for a large number of older citizens. In Japan, where women average 1.4 children each, local governments are already struggling to provide services for older citizens.

Many of those elderly residents live in rural areas, often continuing to farm well into their later years. "In the countryside . . . more and more elderly people will be unable to drive, making it difficult for them to buy food and other essentials or to receive medical care," *The Japan Times* commented in 2013.[78] The paper suggested moving elderly people closer to social services and providing incentives to attract more women and young people into the labor force to generate tax revenues to help pay for those services.

China is grappling with similar issues, on a much larger scale. The nation's one-child policy has produced a severe imbalance between workers and retirees. By 2040 more than one-fourth of China's population will be 65 or older.[79] And China is not as wealthy as countries like Japan or Norway, which have generous social programs for elderly citizens. China formally eased the one-child policy in 2013, but this step did not produce a quick baby boom, perhaps because many young Chinese adults are already struggling to care for aging parents.[80]

"Those who can't rely on their family to provide care may be dismayed to discover the appalling social provisions for the elderly," Chinese journalist Lijia Zhang wrote after putting her 86-year-old father into hospice care. Such facilities, according to Zhang, can only accommodate about 1.6 percent of China's elderly. "An all-out

AT ISSUE

Should the Mexico City Policy be reinstated?

YES

U.S. Rep. Chris Smith, R-N.J.

Written for *CQ Researcher*, January 2015

Someday future generations of Americans will look back and wonder why such a rich and seemingly enlightened society, so blessed and endowed with the capacity to protect and enhance human life, could have instead so aggressively promoted death to children by abortion both here and overseas.

Abortion is violence against children and women. It is extreme child abuse.

Because we have a duty to protect the weakest and most vulnerable, the Mexico City Policy should be reinstated. First announced by the Reagan administration at a 1984 U.N. Population Conference in Mexico City, the policy simply requires that foreign nongovernmental organizations agree, as a condition of their receipt of U.S. federal grant money for family-planning activities, to neither perform nor actively promote abortion as a method of family planning. The three exceptions are cases of rape, incest and when the life of the mother is in jeopardy. The policy does not reduce funding for family planning.

Today, American population-control funding has become a vehicle for exporting the violence of abortion abroad. The United States annually provides hundreds of millions of dollars to radically pro-abortion organizations committed to undermining pro-life cultures around the world. The most recent government funding bill appropriates not less than $575 million for so-called population control.

Pro-abortion groups that refuse to comply with the Mexico City Policy do so because they are so ideologically wed to abortion that they insist on promoting and performing the killing of unborn children rather than accepting U.S. aid.

As humanitarians and as policymakers, we must affirm, care for and tangibly assist both women and unborn children. We must increase access to maternal and prenatal care, especially nutrition during the first 1,000 days of life — from conception to the second birthday.

Best practices to radically reduce maternal mortality must be life affirming — protecting both the mother and the child in the womb. We have known for more than 60 years what actually saves women's lives: skilled birth attendants, treatment to stop hemorrhages, access to safe blood, emergency obstetric care, antibiotics, repair of fistulas, adequate nutrition and pre- and post-natal care.

Expanding these measures will reduce deaths and injury to both mothers and children. No one is expendable. No one's life is cheap. The humane way forward is to reinstate the Mexico City Policy and provide foreign aid that respects and assists both women and their unborn children.

NO

U.S. Rep. Nita Lowey, D-N.Y.

Written for *CQ Researcher*, January 2015

Freedom of speech is one of our most sacred tenets, and we enthusiastically promote it in foreign countries to advance the cause of democracy. The Mexico City Policy, however, runs contrary to this founding principle.

By forcing health providers to choose between receiving U.S. funding or providing comprehensive health care to their patients, the policy muzzles free speech, limits civil society's participation in government and interferes with the doctor-patient relationship. The deafening silence caused by this ill-conceived measure lends a more appropriate name: the Global Gag Rule.

In short, the Global Gag Rule severely weakens the effectiveness of U.S. foreign-assistance funding by limiting our ability to partner with capable organizations. Service providers have reported that the cycle of stopping and later restoring their U.S. funding leaves clinics, patients, doctors and whole communities uncertain about how best to plan for future initiatives and serve women in need.

Instead, we should make it easier — not harder — to equip communities abroad with the tools necessary to achieve a better life in their society.

There is no evidence that the Global Gag Rule has reduced the incidence of abortion globally. In fact, studies show the incidence of abortion decreases when women have increased access to family planning services and supplies, such as contraceptives.

The status of women is a good indicator of a country's overall social and economic health, and I have traveled the globe and seen this phenomenon firsthand. Women in every corner of the world deserve full and consistent access to family planning and reproductive health services. This empowers them to make choices that enable healthier and more economically stable families.

That is why I reintroduced H.R. 2738, the Global Democracy Promotion Act, to permanently repeal the Global Gag Rule. Nongovernmental organizations (NGOs) would never again have to choose between free speech or U.S. assistance, nor would NGOs be barred from U.S.-supported programs abroad solely because they provide legal health services — including counseling services — with their own, non-U.S. funds. This legislation would not impact in any way the longstanding restrictions that prohibit U.S. funding from being used to pay for abortion services overseas.

It is simply bad policy for the United States to stifle free speech and prevent NGOs from empowering women, strengthening communities and enabling prosperity abroad. Let us end this debate once and for all by finally, and permanently, repealing the Global Gag Rule.

war is needed. The government should build more affordable old people's homes; communities should build leisure centers and other facilities for the elderly and train community nurses to provide basic medical care."[81]

But some experts also see social benefits from aging populations. "Elderly people tend to generate fewer carbon emissions from activities like driving than younger people, so aging societies are greener," says Emilio Zagheni, an assistant professor of sociology at the University of Washington.

Moreover, Zagheni notes, people are becoming healthier in general, and are not needing major medical care until later in life. "That means they can be productive members of the labor force for a longer period," he says.

Leahy Madsen of Futures Group concurs. "Alarmism about aging in developed countries has been a bit over-blown," she says. "Aging countries generally have well-educated and wealthier populations. It's a fallacy to think that someone becomes a dependent overnight at 65."

Population aging can also stimulate the economy if older citizens have saved money in bank accounts and stocks for retirement. These funds act as investments that drive economic growth. "And researchers have found that older adults are just as likely to support their grown children as to be a financial burden on them," says Leahy Madsen. "Overall, it's much better to be an aging society than a fast-growing young society."

U.S. Politics

With Republican now controlling both houses of Congress, sparring between Congress and the Obama administration over population issues may increase.

Early in his first term, Obama waived the Mexico City Policy and authorized U.S. contributions to the U.N. Population Fund. Anti-abortion politicians oppose both positions.

Last year the House approved a funding bill for foreign operations that reinstated the Mexico City Policy and denied funding to UNFPA.[82] The Senate Appropriations Committee then approved an amendment, sponsored by Sen. Jeanne Shaheen, D-N.H., that would have repealed the policy permanently.[83] But the 2015 omnibus bill funding most federal programs, including foreign operations, eventually was approved without changing either policy.[84]

Family planning advocates say U.S. leadership on population issues is critical. "The United States is the largest single donor to family planning and reproductive health efforts, so it has a big role in setting agendas and framing issues," says Jen Kates, director of global health and HIV policy for the Kaiser Family Foundation, which conducts research and analysis on health issues.

For 2015 Congress approved $610 million for global family planning and reproductive health issues, including $35 million for UNFPA — the same levels as 2014.[85] In recent years the United States has provided about one-third of total world funding for these programs. Other major donors include the United Kingdom, the Netherlands, Sweden and Canada.[86]

Restoring abortion-related limits on U.S. family planning aid would be harmful, Kates contends. "The United States has more-restrictive policies than other donor governments," she says. "Other donors have to adjust to meet gaps that the United States does not fund and respond to fluctuations in U.S. funding levels."

Legislators who support abortion-related restrictions on foreign aid typically argue that U.S. policy should promote the inherent rights of everyone, including those of unborn children. Many focus on countries such as India and China where forced abortions and sterilizations are alleged to occur. Rep. Chris Smith, R-N.J., a senior member of the House Foreign Affairs Committee, has held multiple hearings on forced abortions abroad.

Chairing a 2013 hearing on "India's Missing Girls" (referring to female fetuses that are aborted because of a cultural preference for male children), Smith said, "By shining a light on what is happening in India, with its missing girls, we hope to move forward towards a world where every woman is valued and deeply respected because of her intrinsic dignity and where every child is welcome regardless of his or her sex."[87]

O'Brien of Catholics for Choice does not expect major shifts in U.S. family planning aid immediately but predicts that it will be an issue in the 2016 presidential election. O'Brien also expects the Supreme Court's 2014 *Hobby Lobby* ruling to influence U.S. foreign policy in this area.[88]

"The default position will be to increase funding for religious groups that discriminate," he predicts.

Beyond the MDGs

U.N. leaders and global development experts are final-izing new targets to succeed the 2000 Millennium Development Goals. The General Assembly will debate post-2015 goals this year and is expected to adopt a new set at a high-level summit in New York in September.

Sexual and reproductive health and rights were omitted from the original version of the Millennium Development Goals in 2000, although a target on increasing access to reproductive health was added in 2007, after several years of NGO lobbying.[89] Now advocates focusing on these issues say the MDGs have produced mixed results.

"Maternal mortality has been cut roughly in half since 2000, with big variations from country to country," says Françoise Girard, president of the New York-based International Women's Health Coalition, which works to protect women's and girls' reproductive health and rights in developing countries. "Girls' enrollment in primary schools has increased, but we don't know whether they actually stay in school or how much they learn. Women's political participation has increased significantly in countries that have set quotas."

Last month the U.N. published a special report that draws on consultations with numerous governments, NGOs and advocates for family planning and women's rights about post-2015 priorities.[90] The report emphasizes the need to protect human rights, including reproductive health and rights. It also calls for "zero tolerance of violence against or exploitation of women and girls," and for ending child, early and forced marriages.[91]

Expanding women's rights and opportunities beyond 2015 will help slow population growth, experts say. "Improving education, especially for girls, is a basic goal that all countries should be focusing on," says U.N. demographer Gerland. "Delaying marriage is a second goal that would complement improved education. All women should have a choice about when to marry. And they also should have a choice about when to have chil-dren and how many to have. The more those three conditions are met, the more progress we can expect toward moderating world population growth."

Comprehensive sex education should also be included on the post-2015 agenda, Girard says. The proposed post-2015 agenda includes a goal of ensuring "universal access to sexual and reproductive health care services" including information and education.[92]

The Holy See and nations including Afghanistan, Saudi Arabia, Chad, Ghana, Honduras, Libya and Yemen have objected to this provision, which they view as undercut-ting national laws against abortion or Sharia (Islamic law) or parents' rights and religious freedoms. For example, negotiators for Honduras stated that references to concepts such as sexual health and reproductive rights did not "include or contemplate abortion or termination of preg-nancy, nor accept them as a way for controlling fertility or regulating population."[93]

However, Girard argues that sex education is a key tool for promoting girls' equality and protecting their health. "We have a huge cohort of young people in the world, today, but we are doing very little to teach them about their bodies, or about how girls can control their bodies and avoid unwanted pregnancies and sexually transmitted diseases," she says. "That whole area is key and has not been addressed."

OUTLOOK
Bending the Curve

Although population growth rates remain high in many developing nations, experts say that scenarios of nearly 11 billion or more people on Earth are not inevitable.

"There are many possible futures," says the U.N.'s Gerland. "Extremely rapid change has occurred in coun-tries like Bangladesh and Iran over one generation. But that kind of progress requires support from national leaders and local leaders, and also from societies."

Iran reduced national fertility rates from 5.6 births per woman in 1985 to 2.0 in 2000 by providing free family planning services and contraceptives to married couples and encouraging couples to have small families.[94] Last year, however, it banned abortions, vasectomies and other forms of permanent sterilization after supreme religious leader Ayatollah Ali Khamenei called on couples to have more children.[95]

"National leaders in many sub-Saharan African countries need to perceive that population growth is a problem," says Haub of the Population Reference Bureau. "A lot of them still don't see it that way. Ghana, Kenya and Rwanda are leaders, but their total fertility rates are still at around four children per family, and other countries aren't doing as well."

Haub cites India, which is expected to surpass China as the world's most populous country by about 2030, as another key test case. India's total fertility rate is 2.4, but that number masks wide gaps between its wealthiest and poorest states. "State governments in India are very independent and have multiple political parties seeking power," says Haub. "There is also widespread corruption and graft, which is a general drag on government's ability to get things done, such as delivering supplies to medical clinics."

Wealthy nations also have important roles to play — for example, by following through on their commitments at the 2012 London Family Planning Summit, says Kates of the Kaiser Family Foundation.

The summit's $2.6 billion funding target "has tremendous health implications for women and girls," she says. "It will be very important to see whether [donor] commitments keep rising and we reach the goal."

Girard of the International Women's Health Coalition sees support for women's rights as another important way to moderate population growth. "Strong, autonomous women's movements in developing countries are key to progress on women's rights, equality and health," she says. "The underlying issue is how girls' lives are valued — whether they are fed and educated equally and given the opportunities for equal lives."

NOTES

1. "Philippine Top Court Approves Birth Control Law," *The National*, April 8, 2014, http://tinyurl.com/o8qjxfw; population and religion data from *World Factbook*, U.S. Central Intelligence Agency, 2014, http://tinyurl.com/2y58zo.

2. The 1987 Constitution of the Republic of the Philippines, Article II, Section 12, http://tinyurl.com/knnsc6m.

3. Floyd Whaley, "Bill to Expand Birth Control Is Approved in Philippines," *The New York Times*, Dec. 17, 2012, http://tinyurl.com/oyw9z6c.

4. "Philippine Top Court Approves Birth Control Law," *op. cit.*

5. "Amid Population Explosion, Birth Control Access Roils Philippines," PBS NewsHour, Aug. 24, 2014, http://tinyurl.com/k74nk2u.

6. *World Factbook, op. cit.*

7. Patrick Gerland, *et al.*, "World Population Stabilization Unlikely This Century," *Science*, vol. 346, issue 6206, Oct. 10, 2014, pp. 234-237.

8. "2014 World Population Data Sheet," Population Reference Bureau, pp. 7-8, http://tinyurl.com/mufdwk2, using total fertility rates by region for 2013.

9. "World Contraceptive Patterns 2013," United Nations Population Division, 2013, http://tinyurl.com/mng2veq. These numbers include women in relationships in which men use contraceptives.

10. Susheela Singh, Jacqueline E. Darroch and Lori S. Ashford, "Adding It Up: The Costs and Benefits of Investing in Sexual and Reproductive Health 2014," Alan Guttmacher Institute, 2014, http://tinyurl.com/q85ox9u.

11. Henrik Urdal, "A Clash of Generations? Youth Bulges and Political Violence," *International Studies Quarterly*, vol. 50, no. 3, September 2006, pp. 607-629.

12. Anthony H. Cordesman, "The Causes of Stability and Unrest in the Middle East and North Africa: An Analytic Survey," Center for Strategic and International Studies, Feb. 13, 2012, http://tinyurl.com/p6tkvnx. For background see Kenneth Jost, "Unrest in the Arab World," *CQ Researcher*, Feb. 1, 2013, pp. 105-132.

13. "Living Planet Report 2014," World Wildlife Fund, 2014, http://tinyurl.com/2dmoua4.

14. "The U.S. Government and International Family Planning and Reproductive Health," Kaiser Family Foundation, August 2014, p. 3, http://tinyurl.com/po6rywj.

15. Gerland, *et al., op. cit.*; "World Population Prospects: The 2012 Revision," U.N. Population Division, 2013, vol. 1, p. xv, http://tinyurl.com/o35dmkf; "World Population Prospects: The 2014 Revision," U.N. Population Division, 2011, vol. 1, p. xvi, http://tinyurl.com/o9vwv25.

16. Gerland, *et al., op. cit.*

17. James Pethokoukis, "The End of Global Population Growth May Be Almost Here — and a Lot Sooner Than the UN Thinks," AEIdeas (American Enterprise Institute), Sept. 13, 2013, http://tinyurl.com/oaurbo8.

18. James Saft, "Investing for Peak Population," Reuters, Sept. 11, 2013, http://tinyurl.com/pqru3l2.

19. Wolfgang Lutz, *et al.*, "9 Billion or 11 Billion? The Research Behind New Population Projections," Nexus, International Institute for Applied Systems Analysis, Sept. 23, 2014, http://tinyurl.com/o6c2foj.

20. For example, see remarks of IIASA World Population Program Director Wolfgang Lutz at Woodrow Wilson International Center for Scholars, Oct. 23, 2014, http://tinyurl.com/nawnq4g.

21. Lutz, *op. cit.*

22. Holdren is now President Obama's science adviser and director of the White House Office of Science and Technology Policy.

23. Paul Sabin, *The Bet: Paul Ehrlich, Julian Simon, and Our Gamble Over Earth's Future* (2013), pp. 96-99.

24. Lara Hoffmans, "7 Billion Reasons Malthus Was Wrong," *Forbes*, Oct. 31, 2011, http://tinyurl.com/pb7e7pd.

25. "2050: A Third More Mouths to Feed," U.N. Food and Agriculture Organization, Sept. 23, 2009, http://tinyurl.com/l4rhwq.

26. Paul R. Ehrlich, *The Population Bomb* (1968), p. xi.

27. Paul R. Ehrlich and Anne H. Ehrlich, "Can a Collapse of Global Civilization Be Avoided?" Proceedings B of the Royal Society, Jan. 9, 2013, http://tinyurl.com/bgg7d3h.

28. "Earth Overshoot Day 2014," Global Footprint Network, updated Sept. 4, 2014, http://tinyurl.com/oca83u.

29. For 2015 The World Bank classifies nations with a gross national income (GNI) of $1,045 or less as low-income, and those with GNIs between $1,046 and $12,746 as middle-income. "Country and Lending Groups," World Bank, http://tinyurl.com/ocnfn72.

30. Jonathan Foley, "A Five-Step Plan to Feed the World," *National Geographic*, May 2014, http://tinyurl.com/l4c8xky. For the analysis supporting these steps see Jonathan A. Foley, *et al.*, "Solutions for a Cultivated Planet," *Nature*, vol. 478, Oct. 20, 2011, pp. 337-342.

31. For background see Jason McLure, "Genetically Modified Food," *CQ Researcher*, Aug, 30, 2012, pp. 717-740.

32. Jonathan Foley, "GMOs, Silver Bullets, and the Trap of Reductionist Thinking," *Ensia*, Feb. 25, 2014, http://tinyurl.com/q8r5x7j.

33. For background see Jennifer Weeks, "Fish Farming," *CQ Researcher*, July 27, 2007, pp. 625-648.

34. Margaret Greene, Shareen Joshi and Omar Robles, "By Choice, Not by Chance: Family Planning, Human Rights and Development," U.N. Population Fund, Nov. 14, 2012, p. iii, http://tinyurl.com/n3957ym.

35. "UN Calls Contraception Access a 'Universal Human Right,'" CBS News, Nov. 14, 2012, http://tinyurl.com/n8s29xw.

36. For more information see http://tinyurl.com/l7au95k.

37. Janice Shaw Crouse, "U.N. Declares Contraception Basic Human Right," *The Washington Times*, Nov. 22, 2012, http://tinyurl.com/m9fwybc.

38. Leigh Ann Caldwell, "McConnell: Contraceptive Issue 'Will Not Go Away,'" CBS News, Feb. 12, 2012, http://tinyurl.com/k6zrpoe.

39. *Burwell v. Hobby Lobby Stores Inc.*, decided June 30, 2014, http://tinyurl.com/pmk6tvd. For background see Kenneth Jost, "Religion and Law," *CQ Researcher*, Nov. 7, 2014, pp. 937-960.

40. Bill Gates, "2014 Gates Annual Letter," http://tinyurl.com/jvqoknt.

41. Evangelii Gaudium, Nov. 24, 2013, sections 213 and 214, http://tinyurl.com/mvreyv4.

42. "Statement by Permanent Observer Mission of the Holy See to the United Nations," Commission on Population and Development, New York, April 10, 2014, http://tinyurl.com/l3xzjho.

43. "Global Climate Change: A Plea for Dialogue, Prudence and the Common Good," U.S. Conference of Catholic Bishops, June 15, 2001, http://tinyurl.com/3smna5c.

44. "Keeping Facts Straight on 98% of Catholic Women," *PolitiFact.com*, Feb. 17, 2012, http://tinyurl.com/k3w2gdg; Michelle Boorstein and Peyton M. Craighill, "Pope Francis Faces Church Divided Over Doctrine, Global Poll of Catholics Finds," *The Washington Post*, Feb. 9, 2014, http://tinyurl.com/np33994.

45. Abby Olheiser, "The Tense Standoff Between Catholic Bishops and the Kenyan Government

Over Tetanus Vaccines," *The Washington Post*, Nov. 14, 2014, http://tinyurl.com/mr9q6jd.

46. "Uruguay Legalises Abortion," BBC News, Oct. 17, 2012, http://tinyurl.com/nuvh8pw.

47. "Maternal Health: The Church's Role," United Methodist Church, adopted 2012, http://tinyurl.com/m83svfr. See also Sneha Barot, "A Common Cause: Faith-Based Organizations and Promoting Access to Family Planning in the Developing World," *Guttmacher Policy Review*, Fall 2013, http://tinyurl.com/me3ushk.

48. Thomas Malthus, "An Essay on the Principle of Population," http://tinyurl.com/lplkp22.

49. "Cholera," Virtual New York, http://tinyurl.com/mx6572s; "Cholera in Westminster," Cholera and the Thames, http://tinyurl.com/poeazzn.

50. "Germ Theory," Science Museum (London), http://tinyurl.com/3ugoknr.

51. "The Influenze Pandemic of 1918," Stanford University, http://tinyurl.com/lsnvyka.

52. "Discovery and Development of Penicillin," American Chemical Society, 1999, http://tinyurl.com/njbv2zs.

53. For details see Gordon Conway, *One Billion Hungry: Can We Feed the World?* (2012), pp. 42-50.

54. Bernhard Glaeser, *The Green Revolution Revisited: Critique and Alternatives* (2013), pp. 1-2.

55. Ehrlich, *op. cit.*, pp. xi-xii.

56. Sabin, *op. cit.*, pp. 20-61.

57. Donella H. Meadows, *et al.*, *The Limits to Growth: A Report for the Club of Rome's Project on the Predicament of Mankind* (1972), http://tinyurl.com/lnfl46c.

58. Leonard Silk, "Predicament of Mankind," *The New York Times*, April 12, 1972.

59. Quoted in Sabin, *op. cit.*, p. 91.

60. Gerald Slevin, "New Birth Control Commission Papers Reveal Vatican's Hand," *National Catholic Reporter*, March 23, 2011, http://tinyurl.com/p9954r3; Elaine Tyler May, "How the Catholic Church Almost Came to Accept Birth Control — in the 1960s," *The Washington Post*, Feb. 24, 2012, http://tinyurl.com/ohza39l.

61. "Encyclical Letter Humanae Vitae of the Supreme Pontiff Paul VI," (1968), section 23, http://tinyurl.com/9km3.

62. Luisa Blanchfield, "Abortion and Family Planning-Related Provisions in U.S. Foreign Assistance Law and Policy," Congressional Research Service, Jan. 31, 2014, pp. 3-4, http://tinyurl.com/os4zfpk.

63. For examples see "Access Denied: U.S. Restrictions on International Family Planning," Population Action International, 2005, http://tinyurl.com/lutzfsp.

64. "Mexico City Policy: Effects of Restrictions on International Family Planning Funding," hearing before the Committee on Foreign Relations, U.S. Senate, July 19, 2001, http://tinyurl.com/k76kfdl.

65. Susan Scutti, "One-Child Policy Is One Big Problem for China," *Newsweek*, Jan. 23, 2014, http://tinyurl.com/lyerwel.

66. "Kemp-Kasten Amendment Legislative History," U.S. Agency for international Development, http://tinyurl.com/ogt6l9t.

67. Luisa Blanchfield, "The U.N. Population Fund: Background and the U.S. Funding Debate," Congressional Research Service, July 24, 2008, http://tinyurl.com/noammyw (funding levels on p. 8).

68. "Funding Timeline," Friends of UNFPA, http://tinyurl.com/oz3srp9.

69. Blanchfield, *op. cit.*, pp. 18-19.

70. "Coercive Population Control in China," Population Research Institute, http://tinyurl.com/obj4c3t. For information about the Population Research Institute, see http://tinyurl.com/kgyd8nl.

71. "Mexico City Policy — Voluntary Population Planning," Memorandum for the Secretary of State, Jan. 23, 2009, http://tinyurl.com/kq36hb.

72. Lori S. Ashford, "What Was Cairo? The Promise and Reality of ICPD," Population Reference Bureau, September 2004, http://tinyurl.com/o4hc7y5.

73. Details at http://tinyurl.com/catlk.

74. "London Summit on Family Planning," Family Planning 2020, p. 4, http://tinyurl.com/qhv3afw.

75. "Donor Government Assistance for Family Planning in 2013," Henry Kaiser Family Foundation, November 2014, p. 1, http://tinyurl.com/ovjd5hp.

76. "Melinda French Gates remarks at London Summit on Family Planning," July 11, 2012, http://tinyurl.com/ocdajm2.

77. "2014 World Population Data Sheet," *op. cit.*, pp. 8, 10-11. For background see Brian Beary, "European Unrest," *CQ Researcher*, Jan. 9, 2015, pp 25-48.

78. "Japan's Depopulation Time Bomb," *Japan Times*, April 17, 2013, http://tinyurl.com/qhx52mu.

79. Alex Coblin, "China's Approaching Storm," American Enterprise Institute, Oct. 28, 2013, http://tinyurl.com/mek2c2u.

80. Katie Holliday, "China To Ease 1-Child Rule Further, But Do People Care?" CNBC, Oct. 21, 2014, http://tinyurl.com/nr568je.

81. Lijia Zhang, "The Everyday Challenges of China's Ageing Population Demand Attention," *South China Morning Post*, Oct. 27, 2014, http://tinyurl.com/lcgpvm7.

82. "Appropriations Committee Releases Fiscal Year 2015 State and Foreign Operations Appropriations Bill," House Committee on Appropriations, June 16, 2014, http://tinyurl.com/kqancqh.

83. "Appropriations Committee Approves Bipartisan Shaheen Amendment Protecting Women's Health Care," Office of Sen. Jeanne Shaheen, June 19, 2014, http://tinyurl.com/pzmwcpx.

84. "How Family Planning Fared in the Cromnibus," Population Action International, Dec. 11, 2014, http://tinyurl.com/pxyjcfu.

85. *Ibid.*

86. "Donor Government Assistance for Family Planning in 2013," Kaiser Family Foundation, November 2014, pp. 1-2, http://tinyurl.com/ovjd5hp.

87. Chairman Smith's Opening Statement, "India's Missing Girls," House Foreign Affairs Committee, Sept. 10, 2013, http://tinyurl.com/k7zb2zq. For background, see Robert Kiener, "Gendercide Crisis," *CQ Global Researcher*, Oct. 4, 2011, pp. 473-498.

88. Jost, "Religion and Law," *op. cit.*

89. "Making Reproductive Rights and Sexual and Reproductive Health a Reality for All," U.N. Population Fund, 2008, p. 7, http://tinyurl.com/qerex2j.

90. "The Road to Dignity by 2030: Ending Poverty, Transforming All Lives, and Protecting the Planet," United Nations, 2014, http://tinyurl.com/ke8wkw8.

91. *Ibid.*, pp. 20-21, 23-24.

92. Francoise Girard, "Sexual and Reproductive Health and Rights and the Post-2015 Agenda: What's Next?" International Women's Health Coalition, Nov. 5, 2014, http://tinyurl.com/lyzyegv.

93. "Addendum to Report of the Open Working Group on Sustainable Development Goals," NGOs Beyond 2014, Dec. 16, 2014, http://tinyurl.com/mk6ovjc.

94. Farzaneh Roudi-Fahimi, "Iran's Family Planning Program: Responding to a Nation's Needs," Population Reference Bureau, 2002, pp. 1-3, http://tinyurl.com/n2aeeof.

95. Jason Rezaian, "Iran's Baby Shortage Leads to a Plan to Ban Permanent Contraception," *The Washington Post*, June 25, 2014, http://tinyurl.com/lyo7mm5.

BIBLIOGRAPHY
Selected Sources
Books

Conway, Gordon, *One Billion Hungry: Can We Feed the World?* Cornell University Press, 2012.
The former president of the Rockefeller Foundation, an expert on global food needs, sets out an agenda for feeding a growing world population sustainably.

Sabin, Paul, *The Bet: Paul Ehrlich, Julian Simon, and Our Gamble Over Earth's Future*, Yale University Press, 2013.
A Yale University history professor describes biologist Paul Ehrlich's debate with economist Julian Simon about how humans affect Earth's resources and shows what each scholar got right and wrong.

Taylor, Paul, *The Next America: Boomers, Millennials, and the Looming Generational Showdown*, Public Affairs, 2014.

Drawing on Pew Research Center data, the center's executive vice president explores the effects of racial, social and economic shifts occurring in the United States.

Weisman, Alan, *Countdown: Our Last, Best Hope for a Future on Earth?* Little, Brown, 2013.

An award-winning journalist travels to more than 20 countries to assess how many people the planet can support and what limits people are willing to accept.

Articles

"The Dividend Is Delayed," *The Economist*, March 8, 2014, http://tinyurl.com/pj5kmyx.

Fertility rates in many African countries are falling more slowly than many demographers expected, preventing those nations from catching up economically with more developed nations.

Burkitt, Laurie, "China's Changed One-Child Policy Doesn't Give Baby Boost," *The Wall Street Journal*, Nov. 7, 2014, http://tinyurl.com/l5xmetb.

One year after China relaxed its one-child-per-family policy, slightly more than 800,000 couples have applied to have a second child, well short of the 2 million births officials had hoped would offset the nation's aging population.

Dimick, Dennis, "As World's Population Booms, Will Its Resources Be Enough for Us?" *National Geographic.com*, Sept. 20, 2014, http://tinyurl.com/pf3j8c8.

Population growth is stressing Earth's resources, but over-consumption and waste are equally harmful, *National Geographic*'s environment editor contends.

Gerland, Patrick, *et al.*, "World Population Stabilization Unlikely This Century," *Science*, Oct. 10, 2014, pp. 234-237, http://tinyurl.com/m6vlqxs.

Demographers from the United Nations and several universities project that the world's population is unlikely to stop growing in this century, contrary to earlier estimates, and is likely to rise to between 9.6 billion and 12.3 billion by 2100.

Keating, Joshua, "Did Russia Really Boost Its Birthrate by Promising New Mothers Prize Money and Refrigerators?" *Slate*, Oct. 13, 2014, http://tinyurl.com/l5475df.

Russia's population has been growing slowly since 2009, after years of contraction following the breakup of the Soviet Union. The main drivers are immigration and modest gains in life expectancy, not government incentives for couples to have more children.

Kluge, Fanny, *et al.*, "The Advantages of Demographic Change after the Wave: Fewer and Older, but Healthier, Greener, and More Productive?" PLoS One, September 2014, http://tinyurl.com/kn42cpg.

Population aging in developed countries may have unexpected positive effects, including longer life expectancy and reduced stress on natural resources.

Reports and Studies

"Housing America's Older Adults: Meeting the Needs of an Aging Population," Joint Center for Housing Studies, Harvard University, 2014, http://tinyurl.com/ny2f39h.

The number of Americans aged 50 or older is projected to grow 20 percent by 2030, to 132 million, but the United States does not have enough affordable and accessible housing to meet older adults' needs.

"The Millennium Development Goals Report 2014," United Nations, http://tinyurl.com/pfz4kn9.

The U.N.'s latest report on progress toward the Millennium Development Goals says that despite progress, more action is needed, especially on improving maternal health and reducing child mortality from preventable diseases.

Cordesman, Anthony H., Chloe Coughlin-Schulte and Nicholas S. Yarosh, "The Underlying Causes of the Crises and Upheavals in the Middle East and North Africa: An Analytic Survey," Center for Strategic and International Studies, 4th edition, Aug. 21, 2013, http://tinyurl.com/mu7fcmq.

A Washington, D.C., think tank finds that rapid population growth is worsening economic and social pressures that threaten the stability of many Middle East and North African countries.

For More Information

Catholics for Choice, 1436 U St., N.W., Suite 301, Washington, DC 20009; 202-986-6093; www.catholics forchoice.org. Advocates for Catholics who support personal choice on sex and reproductive health issues.

Global Footprint Network, 312 Clay St., Suite 300, Oakland, CA 94607; 510-839-8879; www.footprintnet work.org. Measures the environmental effects of human behavior, based on consumption of natural resources.

Henry J. Kaiser Family Foundation, 2400 Sand Hill Rd., Menlo Park, CA 94025; 650-854-9400; www.kff.org. Seeks to increase public understanding of national health issues and the U.S. role in global health policy.

International Women's Health Coalition, 333 Seventh Ave., Sixth Floor, New York, NY 10001; 212-979-8500; www.iwhc.org. Works to advance reproductive health and rights of women and young people in developing countries.

Population Reference Bureau, 1875 Connecticut Ave., N.W., Suite 520, Washington DC 20009; 800-877-9881; www.prb.org. Educates key audiences around the world about population, health and the environment.

United Nations Population Division, 2 United Nations Plaza, Room DC2-1950, New York, NY 10017; 212-963-3179; www.un.org/en/development/desa/population/. Produces demographic estimates and projections for all countries and advises governments on population and development issues.

United States Conference of Catholic Bishops, 3211 Fourth St., N.E., Washington, DC 20017; 202-541-3000; www.usccb.org. An assembly of Catholic Church leaders in the United States.

World Wildlife Fund, 1250 24th St., N.W., Washington, DC 20037; 202-293-4800; www.wwf.org. Network of international conservation groups in 100 countries.

15

Emerging Infectious Diseases

Marcia Clemmitt

Live chickens are sold at a market in Yen Bai Province in northern Vietnam. Infected poultry can cause bird (avian) flu, which has led to hundreds of deaths worldwide in the last decade. Some experts say bird flu has the potential to become a lethal pandemic because humans' immune systems have not been exposed to bird flu viruses and thus have no immunity to it.

From *CQ Researcher*, February 13, 2015.

The scenes were heart-rending: In villages and cities throughout West Africa, families mourned loved ones suddenly struck down by a mysterious disease against which local health officials had little defense.

Previously seen only in Central Africa, Ebola emerged for the first time in the far western part of the continent, killing nearly 9,000 people. The deaths occurred mainly in Guinea, Liberia and Sierra Leone, where poverty is rife and the health care infrastructure is weak or nonexistent. The disease also made it to Spain, Great Britain and the United States.[1]

Ebola wasn't the only unusual infectious disease to make headlines in the past year. In December, scientists at the U.S. Centers for Disease Control and Prevention (CDC) finally identified a "fast-moving and severe" illness that had killed a Kansas farmer last summer. The mysterious virus, likely transmitted by ticks, had never surfaced in the United States before even though it was known in Asia, Africa and Eastern Europe.[2]

Also in 2014, an unusually high number of American children came down with a severe respiratory virus, Enterovirus D68, which previously had infected only a handful of Americans every year since first being spotted in California in 1962. Worse, more than 50 children, some of whom tested positive for virus, were stricken with a mysterious polio-type paralysis, a symptom not commonly associated with Enterovirus D68 and similar pathogens.

Public health experts refer to illnesses that have never been seen before or that reappear in new places or with new severity as "emerging infectious diseases." " 'Emerging' means different things to different people, but it encompasses meanings like 'new,' 'changing,'

Deadliest Emerging Diseases: HIV and Swine Flu

HIV/AIDS has killed 39 million people globally since its identification in 1981. More than 284,500 people have died from H1N1 Influenza, or swine flu, since 2009. Ebola has killed 10,533 worldwide since emerging in Central Africa in 1976.

Emerging Disease	Description	Year Identified	Cases*	Deaths*
Human Immunodeficiency Virus/Acquired Immune Deficiency Syndrome (HIV/AIDS)	Attacks immune system's T cells; spread through body fluids	1981	78 million	39 million
H1N1 (2009) Influenza ("swine flu")	Fever; transmitted by pigs or humans	2009	unknown	>284,500
Ebola virus	Hemorrhagic fever; spread via body fluids	1976	24,796	10,533
Severe Acute Respiratory Syndrome (SARS)	Fever, shortness of breath; transmitted by close contact with infected people	2003	8,096	774
H5N1 Influenza ("bird flu")	Conjunctivitis, flu, respiratory illness; spread by recent contact with sick or dead poultry	1997	668	393
Variant Creutzfeldt-Jakob disease (vCJD or "mad cow")	Dementia, pronounced psychiatric/behavioral symptoms, painful sensitivity to touch, neurologic signs; spread by eating contaminated cattle products	1996	229	229
Middle East Respiratory Syndrome (MERS)	Acute respiratory illness; spread by close contact with infected persons	2012	699	209
Chikungunya (CHIKV)	Fever and joint pain; transmitted by mosquitoes and at birth	1952	>1,135,000	176
H7N9 Influenza ("bird flu")	Severe pneumonia requiring medical attention; spread by exposure to infected poultry	2013	453	175
Enterovirus D68 (EV-D68)	Mild to severe respiratory illness, muscle aches; spread through infected person's respiratory secretions	1962	1,116	11
Acute Flaccid Myelitis	Sudden limb weakness in children, spinal cord inflammation, paralysis; cause and transmission method unknown	2014	111	N/A

The numbers of cases and deaths are as of Dec. 5, 2014, except for Acute Flaccid Myelitis (as of January 2015) and H5N1 Influenza (2003-Dec. 5, 2014).

Sources: "CDC A-Z Index," Centers for Disease Control and Prevention, January 2015, http://tinyurl.com/6m9aw6; "The U.S. Government and Global Emerging Infectious Disease Preparedness and Response," The Kaiser Family Foundation, Dec. 8, 2014, http://tinyurl.com/krho3gb; Ebola data updated from http://tinyurl.com/nrzolre

'evolving,' " says James Nataro, a professor of pediatrics specializing in diarrheal diseases at the University of Virginia School of Medicine.

A half century after health experts thought antibiotics and vaccines had nearly conquered deadly infectious illnesses, emerging contagious diseases are on the rise. Experts attribute the emergence and spread of infectious disease to a number of factors, including environmental change, population growth, industrialized farming, wildlife habitat destruction, persistent poverty, poor health infrastructure, fast worldwide travel and globalization.

What's more, scientists warn that overuse of antibiotics is rapidly robbing them of their power to quell bacterial infections. At the same time, some people in developed countries are refusing vaccination for diseases once thought largely eliminated but cropping up again, such as measles.[3]

The odds of encountering a previously unknown disease have been rising over time, says Peter Daszak, president of New York City-based EcoHealth Alliance, an international scientific group studying interconnections among wildlife, ecosystems and human health. "The number of emerging diseases is rising even if you include the fact that more people are looking for them." About five entirely new infectious human diseases emerge each year, with perhaps three of the five typically coming from insects and other animals, such as ticks or poultry, Daszak says.

The emergence of new diseases would have shocked medical experts 50 years ago, when many considered the age of infectious disease essentially over. With antibiotics shutting down bacterial infections and vaccines conquering previously devastating viral illnesses such as smallpox, many believed pathogenic — disease-causing — organisms had been eradicated. Although infectious diseases — those caused by microorganisms — still regularly ran out of control in the poorest countries, infection largely was seen as a problem of the past in the industrialized world.

But that view has changed, especially since the 1980s, when the HIV/AIDS epidemic took the United States and other industrialized nations by surprise. AIDS has killed 39 million people worldwide since 1981.[4]

When Ebola emerged last year, the world's "political and scientific establishments were caught off guard —

Ebola Survival Rate Has Improved

Although the number of Ebola cases has soared since 2011, the death rate from the virus has fallen sharply — from 72 percent during the 1976-99 period when Ebola first emerged to 40 percent in 2011-15. Experts attribute the rise in survival to better community outreach and early care of infected individuals.

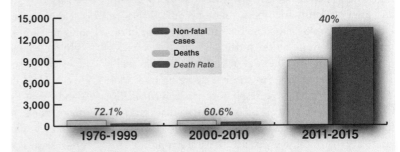

Total Ebola Cases, Deaths and Death Rate, 1976-2015*

Legend: Non-fatal cases, Deaths, Death Rate

1976-1999: 72.1%
2000-2010: 60.6%
2011-2015: 40%

* 2015 cases updated as of Feb. 4.

Source: "Outbreaks Chronology: Ebola Virus Disease," Centers for Disease Control and Prevention, updated Feb. 4, 2015, http://tinyurl.com/nrzolre

partly due to arrogance" — and did little until the epidemic was out of control because they underestimated its potential effects, says Ronald Corley, a microbiology professor at the Boston University School of Medicine and director of its National Emerging Infectious Diseases Laboratories. Diseases spread differently, depending on population density, but experts apparently overlooked that well-known phenomenon. Ebola had previously appeared only in rural areas, but in 2014 it turned up in urban areas, where it spread rapidly.

By the beginning of 2015, however, the epidemic was turning a corner, says John Drake, an associate professor in the University of Georgia's Odum School of Ecology, in Athens. With help from other countries and from nongovernmental groups such as the physicians aid organization Doctors Without Borders, the three heavily affected countries had expanded their health care capacity so infected patients could be isolated.

And in Liberia, "there's been a tremendous response by the communities, with people putting aside local burial traditions — which had contributed to the infection's spread — to allow Red Cross burial teams to come in," says Drake. People also followed public-health workers' advice to practice "social distancing" — limiting contact with others to prevent unwitting transmission.

African countries affected by Ebola will continue to see severe consequences, says Jamie Childs, a senior research scientist in epidemiology at the Yale University School of Medicine. "Obviously it hurt their economies incredibly. You're already seeing starvation — farmers can't put crops in the field," he says. "There are huge numbers of orphans," and without families to care for and anchor family members, many become displaced. Displaced people "can contribute to more spread of disease" when they are on the move.

Meanwhile, public-health experts are keeping an eye on a large number of other worrisome emerging infections, including the Middle East Respiratory Syndrome (MERS); Chagas disease, a parasitic blood infection that can cause severe heart problems; and the mosquito-borne West Nile virus, which can cause severe neurological symptoms.

Serious diseases also are emerging in wild and domestic animals, and these, too, can cause problems for humans by jeopardizing the food supply or wiping out certain species, such as bats, which pollinate plants and eat some insect pests. White-nose syndrome, a fatal disease of hibernating bats, is spreading across the United States; a fungal disease is killing off entire populations of frogs and salamanders; and a respiratory and a diarrheal disease quickly spread through U.S. hog farms last year.

Some disease-causing microorganisms — notably *E.coli* bacteria and the influenza virus — mutate so fast they are considered always emerging, since new strains can appear overnight with heightened abilities to infect and spread. Tuberculosis and, in East Africa's island nation of Madagascar, bubonic plague — the legendary Black Death of the Middle Ages — are re-emerging in forms that resist antibiotics.[5]

But while emerging diseases are plentiful, experts generally agree that most are also controllable if public-health efforts such as sanitation and local disease surveillance, are effective. For example, New York City's "strong, well-resourced" public-health system performed well during a 2009-2010 pandemic* caused by a novel

---

* A pandemic occurs when a disease occurs at unusually high rates in many places. An epidemic is a disease occurring at an unusually high rate in one area.

swine-flu virus, a disease that can very easily get out of control, says Lily Hoffman, an associate professor of sociology at City College of New York. Using its long-established local disease-surveillance system, the city based its flu-control plan on timely local data. Public-health workers' intimate knowledge of the city's various ethnic communities helped them successfully promote disease-containment measures such as social distancing, she says.

Resources to sustain such disease-preventing measures are slim in many places, however.

In the United States support for public-health agencies varies widely, says Laura Kahn, a research scholar in science and global security at Princeton University's Woodrow Wilson School of Public and International Affairs. For example, each of more than 100 municipalities in New Jersey has its own public-health office, and some are so tiny that a disease outbreak can leave them understaffed and struggling, Kahn says.

Meanwhile, in the developing world, fast-growing slums don't even have basic sanitation, let alone public-health offices, says Childs. "One of the biggest worries is the problem of growing slums in cities worldwide, where people live very close together, with no clean water or sanitation or a health infrastructure at all," he says. "That's where disease can spread fastest."[6]

But while many public-health experts and liberal politicians call for boosting funding for dealing with emerging infections, many conservatives argue that public-health agencies have expanded their purview too far beyond infectious-disease control and that a return to traditional priorities could reduce the perceived resource shortage.

The Centers for Disease Control and Prevention (CDC), for example, has spent money "on things that have little or nothing to do with the agency's mission of protecting Americans from health threats," said Michael Tanner, a senior fellow at the Cato Institute, a libertarian think tank in Washington, citing studies on gun violence and campaigns urging Americans to exercise more or to breastfeed.[7]

The CDC says its public-health role is broader than just fighting infectious diseases. It is also responsible for improving health, lowering health-care costs and helping to prevent all leading causes of illness, injury, disability and death, the agency says. That includes helping states implement car child-safety seat legislation and encouraging schools to serve healthier lunches, according to the agency.[8]

As policymakers, scientists and the public consider how best to control emerging diseases, here are some questions being asked:

Could an unstoppable global pandemic emerge?

Few potential catastrophes haunt public-health experts as persistently as global pandemics. The Black Death (or bubonic plague), a bacterial disease that rampaged through Asia and Europe in the 14th century, may have killed a third of Europe's population — 20 million — and up to 200 million people worldwide. The viral Spanish flu pandemic of 1918 and 1919 may have killed 50 million.[9]

But disease watchers say a devastating global pandemic is less likely today, in part because of improved disease surveillance. At the same time, they note, microorganisms can change quickly and unpredictably, making the possibility of an out-of-control pandemic impossible to discount.

The flu is the most worrisome infectious agent, in part because the virus occurs in seemingly endless varieties, disease experts say.

Flu is a so-called RNA virus, whose genetic material consists of the nucleic acid RNA rather than DNA, as in some other viruses.* Unlike DNA, RNA has no self-correcting mechanism for the tiny errors — or mutations — that inevitably happen when genetic code is copied during reproduction, so it can quickly develop new traits, including lethal ones.[10]

Moreover, if two influenza viruses infect the same animal, they can swap whole sections of their RNA, says Robert Belshe, a professor of infectious diseases and immunology at the St. Louis University School of Medicine. Most of these changes "don't help the virus. But once in a while one does," he says. For instance, some flu viruses are "airborne and transmissible from human to human" as well as being transmissible "before you're feeling ill, so it can be transmitted in busy places like airports," says Yale's Childs.

---

* DNA and RNA are two types of large molecules that encode genetic information for use in reproduction and protein synthesis.

Nevertheless, scientists note some reasons to hope that pandemic worst-case scenarios won't materialize.

For one thing, many deaths in the 1918-1919 pandemic were due to secondary bacterial infections that took advantage of flu patients' weakened state, says Andrew Noymer, an associate professor of population health and disease prevention at the University of California, Irvine. "There's a lot less co-infection nowadays with other pathogens in the lungs," Noymer says. "The human-built environment is a cleaner place."

A flu virus similar to the 1918 version would cause many fewer deaths today, wrote Anthony Fauci, director of the National Institute of Allergy and Infectious Diseases, and David Morens, Fauci's senior scientific adviser. "Public health is much more advanced, with better prevention knowledge, good influenza surveillance, more trained personnel at all levels, established prevention programs featuring annual vaccination with up-to-date influenza and pneumococcal vaccines, . . . a national and international prevention infrastructure," and antiviral medicines.[11]

Today's known pathogens are highly unlikely to cause a severe pandemic, said Ontario-based science writer and educator Jason Tetro. To trigger a pandemic, a pathogen must cause a fairly high mortality, be transmissible from human to human and infect people quickly enough to make it difficult for health systems to nip it in the bud. Even today's known pathogens that meet those criteria are unlikely to cause a global catastrophe, said Tetro.

"For example, almost everyone believes that Ebola virus would make a great pandemic," he wrote. But while Ebola is lethal, human-to-human transmission requires very close contact — greatly limiting its ability to spread. And for now, at least, the various types of flu that are transmissible between humans are not lethal enough to cause mass destruction.[12]

Nevertheless, disease experts don't rule out the possibility of a global disease catastrophe.

The flu-virus types that have circulated among humans for decades have grown much less deadly over the years. But the H7 and H9 bird flus, which thus far have been detected in only a tiny handful of people, could conceivably be lethal to humans, whose immune systems have not been exposed to them, says Noymer. "And there are other diseases that could go global," he

Thirteen-year-old Billy Sticklen, who developed polio-like paralysis last summer during an outbreak of the respiratory virus Enterovirus D68, works with a therapist at Children's Mercy Hospital in Kansas City, Mo. More than 50 children, some of whom tested positive for the virus, were stricken with the mysterious paralysis, a symptom not commonly associated with Enterovirus D68 and similar pathogens.

says, such as Middle East Respiratory Syndrome, or MERS, a serious illness first reported in humans in 2012.

"The world is full of surprises. We're going to see more infections emerge," says Childs, of Yale. "We haven't seen the devastation of 1918 and 1919 again. But we're going to see it."

"If it's a living pathogen, it'll be unpredictable," says the University of Virginia's Nataro. "Change among living organisms is inevitable. When we think we know, that is when we get into trouble."

According to Lawrence Madoff, director of immunization and epidemiology for the Massachusetts Department of Public Health and a professor of infectious diseases at the University of Massachusetts Medical School, "The threat [of devastating global pandemics] isn't over." Disaster movies about unstoppable plagues "are dramatized and they play to fears, but there is every reason to think that there will be more bad disease outbreaks," he says.

It's true that countries today are "in better shape than Europe at the time of the plague," he points out. "There's clean food and water, sewage systems. But the possibility still exists. We're always just a mutation away from the next one."

Is the U.S. health care system prepared to handle emerging infectious diseases?

The United States has one of the world's most advanced systems for coping with emerging disease, including a strong surveillance system. Many warn, however, that gaps in the system remain, including inconsistently followed infectious-disease guidelines and too little attention paid to diseases that may pass from animals to humans.

"We have in this country and a lot of developed countries really good disease surveillance systems," says Madoff, of the Massachusetts Department of Public Health. "They could always be stronger, but in general they're pretty robust, pretty extensive and they monitor lots of types of disease."

Scientific understanding of where infectious diseases come from and how they spread also continues to advance, Madoff says. "We have a better understanding of what drives outbreaks," which makes emerging disease easier to spot and contain.

Nevertheless, even in the relatively well-prepared United States, substantial gaps remain, analysts say. The true front lines for diagnosis and care in infectious-disease outbreaks are not public-health agencies but the thousands of hospitals and medical facilities whose day-to-day work has little relation to epidemic disease.

That lack of daily practice in infectious-disease care could be disastrous, said Judy Stone, a Maryland physician specializing in infectious diseases. Stone described a hospital in her area with high-tech equipment designed to help with infection control. It has "neither stethoscopes nor other dedicated equipment for the isolation rooms. So nurses and docs gown up to go in the room of a patient with a 'superbug' but take their stethoscopes into the room and then go on to other patients," without necessarily remembering to clean the stethoscopes, Stone said.[13]

Some call the lack of universal health coverage an emerging-disease liability that is virtually unique to the United States. Having "a huge cadre of uninsured people is a national security threat," Princeton's Kahn argues.

Kahn is among many observers who speculate that a lack of health insurance may have played a role in the death of Thomas Eric Duncan, a Liberian man visiting Texas who has been one of only two people to die of Ebola in the United States during the recent outbreak.[14]

"When it comes to contagious diseases, we automatically shoot ourselves in the foot by not having universal insurance, especially since that's combined with having most hospitals being proprietary" and thus dependent on making money from every patient they treat, Kahn says.

The Dallas hospital that initially released, then later treated, Duncan denies that his uninsured status caused staff to take his first visit lightly. But Kahn is not convinced.[15]

"An uninsured poor black man gets sent back into the community with a bottle of antibiotics," despite having informed hospital staff that he had just returned from Liberia, a country heavily affected by Ebola, says Kahn. "It's not a stretch to think they looked at him and said, 'Well, he can't pay.' That's in effect sending him out to infect others. So what happens when an emerging infectious disease sends many uninsured people to ERs?"

One of the most glaring gaps in U.S. preparedness is the lack of attention to infectious disease in animals. Between three-fifths and three-quarters of emerging human diseases are thought to have crossed over from animals. In addition, both wild and domestic animals are at risk from infections inadvertently imported from other countries, posing dangers to the food supply and to the environment, scientists say.

The only U.S. government agency with authority over animal-disease matters is the Department of Agriculture, which is charged only with "making sure meat is healthy enough to eat," says Kahn.

In addition, while some animals — such as dogs, cats and turtles — must undergo testing for certain diseases before they are imported, trade in many wildlife species is virtually unregulated when it comes to disease, and the lack of regulation has known consequences, says Reid Harris, a professor of biology at James Madison University, in Harrisonburg, Va. Importation of amphibians such as frogs for the pet trade and for laboratory use is now understood to be behind a massive decades-long amphibian die-off, attributed to a fungal

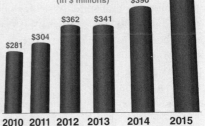

Federal Funds for Emerging Diseases Rise

Of the more than $6 billion budgeted for the Centers for Disease Control and Prevention this fiscal year, the office responsible for fighting emerging infectious and zoonotic (animal-origin) diseases will receive $405 million — up 44 percent since 2010.

Funding for the National Center for Emerging and Zoonotic Infectious Diseases, 2010-15

(in $ millions)

2010	2011	2012	2013	2014	2015
$281	$304	$362	$341	$390	$405

Source: "Emerging and Zoonotic Infectious Diseases," Centers for Disease Control and Prevention, updated March 7, 2014, http://tinyurl.com/ojzdylm; 2015 budget updated from http://tinyurl.com/ou8cuqk

disease, Harris says. Humans "were responsible for spreading the fungus around by importation," he says. Many imported animals "don't have to be tested [for diseases they might be carrying], which we'd like to get changed."[16]

In the last two years, two pig diseases formerly seen only in Europe and China, porcine epidemic diarrhea and porcine coronavirus, emerged in the Midwest and then nationwide, says Juergen Richt, a professor of diagnostic medicine and pathobiology at the Kansas State University College of Veterinary Medicine. The diarrheal disease infected U.S. animals that had never been exposed to the virus, wiping out entire generations of young pigs. "There are now farms where there are 5,000 sows and no piglets," Richt says. "People believe it came in feed that was made in China, sprayed with dried pigs' blood to add protein, and exported all over the world.

"There are many sources today through which viruses can slip in," he continues. "We've got to plug these holes, change our rules. My idea is — don't feed pigs pig protein." Strengthening protections against emerging diseases in domestic animals would pay off, Richt says. "A million dollars spent on mitigation can save $10 million."

Do public health programs need more money to deal with emerging diseases?

Many public-health experts say their field faces special challenges in garnering funding and political support because its successes — health crises that are prevented — are largely invisible. Some public-policy analysts, however, point out that much of today's funding goes not toward infectious-disease work but to less traditional public-health priorities such as chronic disease and accident prevention.

Many public-health agencies have faced inconsistent or dwindling funding over the past decade, especially at state and local levels, public-health advocates say.

A week after the Sept. 11, 2001, terrorist attacks, anthrax-laced letters began arriving at media outlets and politicians' offices. Fears of bioterror boosted federal public-health funding. But since 2006 the CDC budget has remained fairly flat when adjusted for inflation, according to the Trust for America's Health, a Washington, D.C.-based public-health advocacy group, and the Robert Wood Johnson Foundation in Princeton, N.J.

In addition, funding for the CDC's Public Health Emergency Preparedness grant program for state, local, territorial and tribal health agencies fell from nearly $1 billion in fiscal 2006 to $640 million in fiscal 2014. Meanwhile, funding for the center's Hospital Preparedness Program (HPP) dropped by more than half from fiscal 2004 to fiscal 2014. The HPP helps hospitals bolster their emergency preparedness and develops regional coalitions to maximize so-called surge capacity for responding to large events such as epidemics.[17]

From 2008 through 2012, budgets were cut at least once for public-health agencies in 48 states, three U.S. territories and the District of Columbia, according to the Association of State and Territorial Health Officials (ASTHO). Cuts in fiscal 2013, for example, averaged 3 percent. In addition, 50,600 state and local public health employees had their jobs cut in 2008-2012, according to the association.[18]

"We're losing a lot of gray-haired professionals with extraordinary experience who aren't being replaced" at public-health agencies, said Robert Kadlec, a Virginia-based biodefense and public-health consultant and former director of biodefense preparedness for Republican President George W. Bush. "Emergency supplemental funds get you through a short period of time but do very little for the next outbreak. . . . [I]f we don't continuously support the development of medical countermeasures and training for public health workers on the latest devices and machines, when an emergency occurs, we'll be hopelessly behind."[19]

Skimping on infectious-disease preparedness is pennywise and pound foolish, says Daszak, of EcoHealth Alliance, because pandemics "have a disproportionate effect on the economy." For instance, SARS — severe acute respiratory syndrome — broke out in China's Guangdong province near Hong Kong in late 2002. It killed only about 800 people but cost the affected economies between $10 billion and $20 billion, including losses to businesses that closed temporarily or moved.[20]

The United States and other wealthy countries should put more resources into helping poor countries develop their capacities for dealing with infectious diseases, many experts say. "I hope Ebola makes clear that if you don't spend in the country where the disease is present, it's much easier for the disease to come to you," says Kansas State's Richt.

In addition, says Yale's Childs, funding is far less useful when it is sporadically boosted in response to certain momentary priorities rather than being provided over the long term so an agency can disburse funds according to what ongoing science suggests is most important in preparing for future outbreaks.

"Too much funding is reactive," Childs says. When he was a CDC branch chief for zoonoses — diseases that can transfer from animals to humans — "there were only two branches that didn't get specific mandates for congressional funding — ours and influenza," likely the most serious infectious-disease issues over the long haul. "Mandates were coming in for chronic fatigue, all kinds of things" that were far less urgent, he says.

Many conservative analysts argue, however, that refocusing public-health efforts and disease research on traditional priorities such as emerging-disease control and vaccine development is the key to ensuring sufficient resources.

At the CDC, for example, funding "tripled from 2001 to 2010, with big spikes in spending after the 2001 anthrax attacks and then again after the 2005 avian flu scare," said David Harsanyi, editor of the conservative web magazine *The Federalist*. Much of the 2001-2010

A worker wears a mask while tending a camel at a farm near Riyadh, the capital of Saudi Arabia. Camels are thought to be a source of Middle East Respiratory Syndrome (MERS), but the disease can also be transmitted from human to human via close contact with an infected person. The acute illness has killed more than 200 people since first being identified in humans in 2012.

funding boost was frittered away on lesser priorities, such as a museum and "a massive staff," said Harsanyi. "If there is a money crunch, perhaps the CDC needs to rethink its scope."[21]

The CDC argues that communication and education through initiatives such as its museum are important to the agency's public-health mission. The museum educates middle and high school students, as well as the general public, about "the value of prevention-based public health," the agency says.[22]

Disease-related research funds at the National Institutes of Health (NIH) also have gone to non-priority items, said Veronique de Rugy, a senior research fellow at George Mason University's market-oriented Mercatus Center think tank. NIH funding levels "are actually higher than historical norms," she said. However, "much of NIH's budget goes to projects that have nothing to do with researching vaccines," such as public-health initiatives aimed at disease control through behavioral change, including developing more pleasurable condoms.[23]

But when it comes to controlling infectious diseases, health agencies must look beyond vaccine development to behavioral change, argued NIH's Fauci. For AIDS prevention to succeed, for example, "those who are already infected or at risk of infection must faithfully practice recommended treatment and/or prevention strategies,

including . . . using a condom every time they have sex; and, for those who inject drugs, always using a clean needle and syringe."[24]

BACKGROUND
Ancient Infections

The history of infectious disease is a story of endlessly repeated struggles for survival between humans and certain small organisms — such as bacteria, viruses and fungi — that can live and reproduce inside human bodies. In recent years, science has learned much more about those struggles, including the conditions under which infections most likely emerge.

Most microorganisms that live on or inside humans are harmless or useful (bacteria in the gut, for instance, digests food and fights infection). A small number, though, are both pathogenic — disease causing — and capable of spreading through a population, either transmitted directly by sexual contact, for example, or carried by so-called disease vectors, such as mosquitoes.[25]

The infectious-disease story is a shifting panorama. Throughout history, many never-before-seen diseases have emerged. Some quickly disappeared; others persisted as threats to human life — such as smallpox — or as simple annoyances, such as the common cold.

Two factors drive the constant change.

One is the speed with which microbes evolve. Because bacteria and viruses reproduce very quickly, a microorganism can evolve rapidly — in a matter of days, in some cases — to develop new abilities that make it a successful pathogen. For instance, a microbe might develop the ability to exploit a particular molecular mechanism in a human host in order to reproduce, damaging human cells in the process. Or it may gain the ability to be transmitted through a sneeze, thus improving its descendants' chances of survival while facilitating the spread of illness.

Human change also drives disease emergence. For instance, changes in living patterns, from urbanization to the invention of sewage systems, have been major forces in the emergence — or disappearance — of disease, scholars say. Over the past several decades, researchers have learned much more about these connections.

"Looking at diseases of the past can help us understand how certain kinds of diseases behave," thus improving our knowledge of similar modern diseases, says Bruce Rothschild,

FAYEZ NURELDINE/AFP/Getty Images

CHRONOLOGY

1900s-1930s *Viral diseases kill millions as scientists seek answers.*

1905 Polio found to be contagious.

1918 Pandemic H1N1 flu kills 50 million people.

1933 Influenza virus isolated.

1937 West Nile virus first isolated in Uganda.

1940s-1960s *Antibiotic drugs are introduced; bacteria develop resistance.*

1942 Penicillin comes into wide use.

1953 American scientist Jonas Salk develops polio vaccine.

1957 In the 20th century's second flu pandemic, "Asian flu" kills around 1 million people. . . . West Nile virus causes severe neurological symptoms among nursing home residents in Israel.

1959 First reports made of Bolivian hemorrhagic fever.

1968 "Hong Kong" flu pandemic begins, killing around 1 million people.

1969 Lassa hemorrhagic fever emerges in Nigeria.

1970s-1980s *Global awareness of emerging infectious diseases grows.*

1976 Lyme disease first reported in Old Lyme, Conn. . . . Ebola first reported, in Democratic Republic of the Congo (then Zaire) and Sudan. . . . U.S. plans to vaccinate millions against a "swine flu" outbreak; program is canceled when the outbreak is less serious than expected and some people report severe vaccine side effects.

1981 An aggressive form of Kaposi's sarcoma tumor among gay men in New York City and high rates of pneumonia among gay men in Los Angeles alert health officials to emergence of HIV/AIDS. By early 2015, the disease will have killed 39 million worldwide.

1986 "Mad cow" disease emerges in the United Kingdom.

1990s-Present *Globalization speeds spread of emerging infections.*

1997 H5N1 flu first appears in humans, in Hong Kong.

1999 West Nile virus is first reported in Western Hemisphere, among birds and humans in New York City.

2002 SARS, severe acute respiratory syndrome, spreads from China to Toronto, killing 800 people and costing affected economies up to $20 billion.

2005 World Health Organization announces that as of 2007, countries may no longer limit disease reporting to a specific list of infections but must report "all diseases of global significance."

2006 First H5N1 human influenza is seen outside of Southeast Asia, mostly in the Middle East.

2007 An H7 bird flu causes mild illness among humans in Canada and the Netherlands.

2009 H1N1 "swine flu" pandemic kills from 150,000 to as many as 500,000 people.

2012 First human cases of Middle East Respiratory Syndrome reported. . . . State and local public-health agencies have cut 50,600 jobs since a steep recession began in 2008.

2014 Ebola emerges in West Africa as well as Spain, the United Kingdom and the United States, eventually killing nearly 9,000 people. . . . More cases of the severe respiratory virus Enterovirus D68 are reported across the U.S. than in any year since 1962, when it first appeared in California. . . . Two pig diseases formerly seen only in Europe, Africa and China, one respiratory and one diarrheal, emerge in Iowa and then across the country.

2015 Measles cases are confirmed in 17 states and the District of Columbia and are linked to December visitors to Disneyland; measles has been re-emerging as some families refuse to vaccinate children.

a professor of medicine and biological anthropology at the University of Kansas, in Lawrence. Researchers examine skeletons or mummies for clues about diseases' physical effects and for traces of microbial DNA that reveal ancient diseases' evolutionary relationship to current diseases, he says. To determine how diseases spread, researchers examine historical artifacts, such as books and public records.

Based on these studies, scholars point to a few historical turning points that likely ushered in eras of especially high infectious-disease emergence.

One occurred between 10,000 and 15,000 years ago, when humans abandoned a nomadic life of hunting and gathering and switched to a communal existence of planting crops and domesticating animals. Most researchers agree that the new, larger, more densely populated and interconnected communities were far more conducive to the emergence and spread of infectious disease. To keep from depleting food supplies, nomadic groups that lived by foraging had to remain small and keep their distance from others, so diseases could not easily spread.

Farm life also brought humans into close, constant contact with animals, likely leading to the first zoonoses, or animal diseases transmissible to humans. "Many pathogens now endemic* in humans appear to have evolved from an ancestor that moved into our populations at around the time we first domesticated animals," wrote Daszak, of EcoHealth Alliance. Measles, for example, is closely related to hoofed livestock diseases such as rinderpest.[26]

After humans began farming, many new infectious diseases emerged, including some with high child-mortality rates, such as smallpox, and some that remain common today, such as malaria.

Later, "global transportation networks, exploration, conquest and trade" enabled diseases endemic in one region to spread, blossoming into epidemics elsewhere as new populations without immunity were exposed to them, wrote Daszak. For example, the Black Death — or plague — spread from Asia to Europe in the 14th century, and the conquistadors — Spanish and Portuguese conquerors of the Americas in the 15th and 16th centuries — brought smallpox.[27]

Infection and Modernity

In the 18th century, the Industrial Revolution in Europe changed living patterns again, this time in ways that diminished the threat of infections.

Standards of living gradually rose for people in wealthier nations such as the United States, bringing sanitation and clean water, sturdy housing less likely to be invaded by disease-carrying rodents and bugs, and education that increased awareness of hygiene, including among doctors, who began washing their hands before delivering babies, for example.

Although the worldwide death toll from infections remained high, in industrializing countries infectious-disease mortality dropped sharply. Lifespans lengthened and ills such as cancer and heart disease replaced infection as the main drivers of sickness and death.

Eventually, a key medical innovation — vaccines — also contributed to the progress, says Belshe, of Saint Louis University. Vaccination works by injecting a human or animal with some form or part of a microbe that will acquaint the body with a disease-causing microorganism but not cause illness. The immune system then learns to counter the organism when it's encountered again.

The first true vaccine was administered against smallpox, in England in 1796, and others followed. In 1953, for example, American scientist Jonas Salk developed a vaccine against polio, a devastating crippler of children.

Despite the vaccines and clean water, however, some infectious diseases remained effective killers. In 1918, an emerging, vicious form of influenza led to one of history's deadliest pandemics. A third or more of the world's population may have been infected, including people in the remotest regions. With a mortality rate of about 2.5 percent, far higher than the usual rate for flu, the pandemic is thought to have killed at least 50 million people, including 675,000 in the United States.[28]

Scientists scrambled to find the cause, but viruses were too small to be seen with existing microscopes. Beginning in the 1930s, researchers turned up more clues, isolating similar influenza viruses from humans and pigs. Decades

---

* An endemic disease is one that is regularly found at similar levels among people or animals in a region.

* Flu viruses are differentiated according to which types of two specific proteins — dubbed H and N proteins — they have on their outer shells.

Genome Studies Hold Keys to Diseases' Origins

Scientists generate new ideas about vaccines, treatments and diagnoses.

New lab technologies and techniques, plus an ever-growing body of knowledge, have revolutionized the study of microorganisms over the past 15 years. As a result, scientists have gained new insights into how microbes become pathogenic and new ideas about devising vaccines and treatments.

In the past, genome analysis was slow and expensive, so researchers analyzed only disease-causing microorganisms, says Jonathan Eisen, a professor of evolutionary microbiology at the University of California, Davis. "Now we can look at everything, and that's useful because we can know everything in a [microbial] community," including microorganisms that live together and interact in a particular ecosystem such as the human stomach.

Microorganisms can evolve and develop new abilities quickly, and bacteria can pick up new traits by "swapping" some genes with other nearby bacteria. So analyzing the community of microbes that exists alongside, say, a hospital-acquired infection can reveal where the infectious organism got the genes that have turned it into a problem, Eisen says.

"Did they come from the human biome?" he asks, referring to the community of microorganisms that normally live on and in a human body and all other living organisms. Or did they come "from some animals we eat?" By answering such questions, genomics will provide insight into the most dangerous problems of emerging diseases, Eisen says.

Scientists' growing knowledge of the functions and interactions of microbial communities may provide new treatment and prevention strategies. For instance, studying microbial interactions has been an active area of the research on the fungal disease chytridiomycosis, which has been killing off amphibians and even driving some species to extinction in Australia and North and South America and elsewhere for more than 20 years, says Reid Harris, a professor of biology at James Madison University in Harrisonburg, Va.

Like other creatures, frogs and salamanders have interacting communities of microbes on their skin. Substances produced by some of those microbes seem to be a "protective factor" against the disease-causing fungus, which humans apparently introduced to North

of research followed, continuing today, with few conclusive answers. The 1918 flu was a so-called H1N1* flu. It is the genetic ancestor of most other flus that have circulated among humans since — having outcompeted previously circulating flu viruses.

Shortly before the 1918 outbreak, the virus may have made its first leap to humans from animals — likely pigs or birds. The secrets of its lethality remain largely unknown, though many victims died of pre-existing conditions, such as tuberculosis.

Declaring Victory

By the mid-20th-century many medical scientists believed the threat of infectious disease might soon be over, largely due to the invention of antibiotics.

At least by the late 19th century, scientists understood that many microorganisms in soil and elsewhere were in a deadly competition for resources and space. The early 20th century saw discovery of several classes of microbes that exuded substances that killed certain other organisms. The most famous — a mold called Penicillium notatum — was found in 1928. In 1942 it became the mass-producible antibiotic drug penicillin.[29]

Through the 1970s, numerous new antibiotic molecules derived from microorganisms came to market.

In fact, Australian virologist and Nobel Prize winner Sir Macfarlane Burnet predicted in 1962 that the era would be "one of the most important social revolutions in history, the virtual elimination of the infectious diseases as a significant factor in social life."[30]

America by importing animals, mostly from Africa and Asia, for labs and the pet trade, Harris says. He says protective microbes could possibly be added to the skins of animals that lack them.

Understanding species' natural microbiomes eventually could yield health benefits for animals and people, says Eisen, by signaling what health problems they face. For example, some infectious diseases are all but undetectable in their early stages, he says. When HIV "first infects someone, things happen to the [body's] biology, but then the virus goes dormant for years," Eisen says. "People who've had Ebola for a fexw days don't have major symptoms."

It's now clear, however, that when someone gets an infection, changes occur in their microbial community, "probably because the immune system ramps up," Eisen says. Understanding these microbial changes would allow for early detection of disease — a skill that would benefit not only humans but other living species. "Plants and animals can't describe their symptoms or tell someone when they aren't feeling just right," says Eisen. "I can easily imagine a chicken farm surveying chickens' microbial biomes" as part of regular health screenings.

Vaccines and, especially, therapies to treat viral illnesses (which antibiotics do not affect) remain few and far between. But new understandings of how viruses work are sparking new ideas, scientists say. The flu virus' ability to evolve literally overnight leaves scientists scrambling each year to produce a vaccine effective against its latest incarnation.

However, researchers now wonder if they can concoct a vaccine that would work for all flus.

Vaccinations inject humans or animals with something that will acquaint their immune systems with a disease-causing microbe — thus teaching them how to combat the agent if it's encountered again — without making them ill, says Robert Belshe, a vaccine expert and professor of infectious diseases and immunology at the St. Louis University School of Medicine. To produce a universal flu vaccine requires examining proteins that are shared by all flu strains. One candidate under study, Belshe says, is a "very tiny component" of influenza viruses' outer layer called the M2 ion channel protein, which regulates electricity flow across the virus and is involved in viral replication.

Some new treatments may also be on the horizon, says David P. Clark, a professor of microbiology at Southern Illinois University in Carbondale.

"Viruses mutate to avoid being destroyed by the immune system," and so-called RNA viruses, such as the flu and Ebola, mutate at an extremely high rate, Clark says. "Viruses are sort of teetering on the edge. If they don't mutate, they'll be zapped by the immune system, but if they mutate too far they'll lose their ability to function.

"Now there is a drug that pushes the mutation rate to the point that it makes the virus go extinct," he says. "That could be applicable to all RNA viruses."

— *Marcia Clemmitt*

Macfarlane was far from alone in his belief. With infections on the wane, the United States and other industrialized countries began shifting public-health efforts toward combating so-called chronic "diseases of civilization," such as cancer and heart disease.[31]

Overlooked in the brief period of rejoicing, however, were two disturbing facts.

First, each new antibiotic began losing its power as soon as it came into use. Widespread antibiotic use puts strong evolutionary pressure on bacteria populations to produce drug-resistant offspring, and bacterias' ability to evolve rapidly to adopt new traits did the rest. As soon as penicillin entered the market, some strains of *Staph* bacteria began producing enzymes that deactivated it, and by 1950 half were resistant to the drug.[32] Each

new antibiotic met the same fate. Moreover, though new drugs were developed, their active substances were variations of fewer than two dozen core molecules, making it easy for pathogens to evolve to circumvent them.[33]

Second, infectious diseases continued to emerge, mostly in developing countries.

In 1964, two young doctors from the National Institutes of Health completed a two-year quest to identify and tame a horrifying contagion emerging in a remote region of Bolivia, in west-central South America. Found to be viral — and thus untreatable with antibiotics — it caused intense neurological symptoms including seizures, severe hemorrhaging and, often, death. Named after the river near the original outbreak, the Machupo virus eventually was halted by trapping small rodents that were the infection's source.[34]

Data Collection Crucial to Fighting Emerging Ills

Mathematical modelers inch toward predicting epidemics' course.

Lesson one in fighting infectious disease is to keep your eyes open: You never know when a pathogen might be gaining on you.

In public health parlance, that's called "surveillance" — continual, systematic collection and analysis of information that holds clues to a population's health. Today, efforts are underway to expand data collection, and scientists are increasingly using disease data to model, or project, how outbreaks will spread. Yet the obstacles to developing accurate models are formidable.

The Chinese learned "the hardest way" that surveillance is vital, says James Nataro, a specialist in pediatric diarrheal diseases at the University of Virginia School of Medicine. "They have the most diseases — followed by Africa — but they didn't invest in surveillance. They got caught by SARS," the severe acute respiratory syndrome that sickened 5,327 people and killed 349 in China in 2002 and 2003.[1]

Spotting emerging diseases is challenging because, early on, many are hard to distinguish from other illnesses. For example, SARS likely spread beyond China because a physician acted on the usually accurate assumption that community-acquired pneumonia-type illnesses aren't easily transmitted.[2]

With concern over pandemics growing, governments and international groups want to strengthen surveillance. The U.S. Centers for Disease Control and Prevention works with several countries and the United Nations' health arm, the World Health Organization, to establish a global network of regional disease-detection centers. Ten centers now operate or are in development.[3]

Even with large-scale infrastructure in place, however, data gathering remains hard. When outbreaks begin, the salient facts are visible only at the individual and neighborhood level. And in most poor countries, clinics, health practitioners and local public-health offices that traditionally discover such information are few.

That's why more informal surveillance networks are expanding, says Lawrence Madoff, director of immunization and epidemiology for the Massachusetts Department of Public Health.

Madoff is an editor of ProMED-mail, one of an international group of Internet-based systems through which infectious-disease specialists gather, screen and publish online infection-related reports from multiple sources. ProMED, a project of the Brookline, Mass.-based International Society for Infectious Diseases, has put "a lot of effort" into establishing regional networks in Africa and Southeast Asia, where participants can monitor "rumors, Twitter [and] local news reports." In the age of wireless communications, such decentralized networks "can be put in place more quickly than public health systems," Madoff says. Similar projects include Google Flu Trends, HealthMap and Flu Near You.[4]

"There are lots of attempts to control information," of course, many made "for very good reasons," Madoff notes. "If a country says they have a cholera problem, then trade in shellfish will suffer, tourism will suffer." Nevertheless, "we want information to flow freely. You might not think that an ER doctor in Toronto needs to know about SARS, but you'd be wrong." SARS' spread to Canada and killed 43 of the 251 people infected.[5]

Other diseases also emerged. In 1967, a group of German pharmaceutical-industry workers contracted Marburg virus, a hemorrhagic fever, after being accidentally exposed to tissue from infected African monkeys. Seven workers died. In 1969, another hemorrhagic ailment, Lassa fever, was identified in Nigeria. In 1976, the first Ebola virus cases were reported, in a rural area of the Democratic Republic of the Congo (then called Zaire).

Global Health

Was a new era opening that would be rife with emerging diseases? Some experts began to think so. Moreover, patterns seen in previous eras of disease emergence were repeating themselves.

Like measles, which may have come from hoofed stock, and plague, which had been carried by rats, many emerging diseases were crossing over from animals. The Marburg

Increasingly, scientists use data to predict a disease's course. Computerized mathematical models simulate real-life outbreaks and incorporate current data to project an epidemic's next development.

Models start out as conceptual, not data-based, explains John Drake, an associate professor at the University of Georgia's Odum School of Ecology in Athens. Model-building requires, among other things, "as good an understanding as possible of disease transmission, routes of transmission [and] how individuals contact each other," he says. Scientists construct dozens of models simulating possible interactions of these variables, then check data from past events "to see which models are backed up and which [can be] ruled out."

The more that's known of a disease, the better the model. Because influenza has been around awhile, models of the 2009 flu pandemic produced very accurate projections, such as predicting the pandemic's November peak three months in advance, says Alessandro Vespignani, a professor of physics at Northeastern University in Boston.

Emerging diseases such as Ebola pose bigger challenges. For Ebola, researchers know little about people's mobility in and beyond their communities, yet understanding mobility patterns is crucial to predicting how the infection will spread, Vespignani says.

Because diseases are so fluid, the ability to predict their course is time-limited, for now anyway. "Models that try to tell what will happen in six months? That would be very hard," says Vespignani. "Projecting what will happen in the next few weeks is more realistic."

But more ambitious goals are on the horizon.

Drake and colleagues envision developing models that can predict which diseases are close to emerging. Although the work is "all theory," he says they think such a model is possible because scientists are closer to figuring out the threshold at which an outbreak can occur — an epidemiological tipping point. "There are ways to measure the distance a disease is from the tipping point," based on patterns seen in diseases that were nearly eliminated before re-emerging and those that crossed from wildlife to humans, Drake says.

Models have much to offer policymakers, Vespignani says. "People want to know where and when they're going to see new cases" so they can deploy staff and supplies and create contingency plans for peak periods.

But scientists have much work to do before public health policymakers accept models' projections, Vespignani says. The situation is akin to weather modeling, which policymakers do trust, he says: "a portfolio of models," all validated, but incorporating slightly different assumptions. That's necessary because "if all the models use the same data, then they risk all going wrong if one part of the data is wrong."

"Building such a coalition of modelers will take time. But there is much more communication going on between the various [health] agencies and modelers today," Vespignani says. "I envision this in the future — 10 to 15 years down the road."

— *Marcia Clemmitt*

[1] "Summary of probable SARS cases with onset of illness from 1 November 2002 to 31 July 2003," World Health Organization, April 21, 2004, http://tinyurl.com/pwj9h6a.

[2] Stephen S. Morse, "Emerging Infections: Condemned to Repeat?" in *Microbial Evolution and Co-Adaptation: A Tribute to the Life and Scientific Legacies of Joshua Lederberg* (2009), pp. 195-207.

[3] "Global Disease Detection," Centers for Disease Control and Prevention, December 2013, http://tinyurl.com/pecybwn; "Global Disease Detection: Regional Centers," Centers for Disease Control and Prevention, Dec. 20, 2012, http://tinyurl.com/qz9x9pv.

[4] ProMED-mail, http://tinyurl.com/3p472v; "Google Flu Trends — United States," Google.org, http://tinyurl.com/yzgedl6; "HealthMap: Global Health, Local Information," HealthMap, http://tinyurl.com/dzlylf; and "Flu Near You" Do you have it in you?" HealthMap, http://tinyurl.com/npqdxfg.

[5] "Summary of probable SARS cases," *op. cit.*

virus came from monkeys; Lassa fever from a rodent. About 60 percent of all human infectious diseases and as many as 75 percent of those emerging in the current era are zoonoses, says Daszak, of EcoHealth Alliance.[35]

That's not surprising, Daszak says. Every animal species, including humans, has particular viruses that are endemic to it, while other viruses take various species as hosts. Considering the approximately 50,000 vertebrate species alone, "if we estimate that each . . . carries 20 endemic, unknown viruses (almost certainly a gross underestimate), then there is a global diversity of 1 million viruses."[36]

Also, as in past eras, changes in human living patterns, especially those that involved changing the natural environment, contributed to disease emergence. For example, deforestation had disrupted the habitat of the rodent that carries the Machupo virus, which took up residence in local homes and spread the deadly illness in Bolivia.[37]

Most new diseases emerged in developing countries where, as in the past, shoddy housing, poor nutrition and lack of sanitation encouraged disease to spread. For some time, the new outbreaks drew little notice elsewhere.

The rapid spread of HIV/AIDS in the 1980s changed that. While a few HIV infections likely occurred before 1970, the pandemic is thought to have begun — unnoticed — in Africa around the mid-1970s. By 1980 and 1981, though, it had already appeared on at least five continents — North and South America, Europe, Asia and Australia — and infected at least 100,000 people.

Speed of travel, economic globalization and, for many, rising standards of living that sparked dramatic increases in travel and transport helped to establish the new era in emerging infectious disease: one in which disease anywhere could easily become disease everywhere.[38]

"It used to take a long time to get around the world, but now you can do it, if you make all your connections, in 24 to 48 hours," said Stephen Morse, a professor of epidemiology at Columbia University's Mailman School of Public Health. "If you do not make all your connections, as happens to most of us, then you spend time in a usually crowded airport, where you have even more opportunity to infect others."[39]

CURRENT SITUATION
Public-Health Priorities

In 2015, policymakers will continue to debate emerging-disease funding priorities as well as strategic matters, such as how much to invest in vaccines.

In September 2014, Ebola fears spurred Congress to provide $30 million in emergency funds for the CDC to fight the illness.[40]

The support paid off, said President Obama in his 2015 State of the Union address on Jan. 20. "In West Africa, our troops, our scientists, our doctors, our nurses and health care workers are rolling back Ebola — saving countless lives and stopping the spread of disease," Obama said.[41]

In December, the lame-duck Congress included a small increase over previous-year funding for the CDC in its omnibus fiscal 2015 spending bill, funding the agency at $6.9 billion, 0.3 percent more than last year.

The legislation includes $5.4 billion in emergency funds for continuing international and domestic initiatives to combat the Ebola outbreak. The CDC's Emerging and Zoonotic Infectious Diseases (EZID) program received a 3.8 percent boost of $15 million — to $405 million — with $30 million of that directed to the Advanced Molecular Detection and Response to Infectious Disease Outbreaks program, which combines genome sequencing with advanced computing to speed up identification and study of pathogens.[42]

In the long run, though, Republicans and Democrats view the role of public-health agencies differently, making an upcoming tussle over fiscal 2016 funds likely.

Many Democrats are calling for more long-term money to strengthen domestic and international infectious-disease surveillance and improve living standards to help quell disease emergence in poor countries. "The world needs to use this lesson [of Ebola] to build a more effective global effort to prevent the spread of future pandemics, invest in smart development and eradicate extreme poverty," Obama said.[43]

But many Republicans say the CDC wouldn't need more funds if it focused its work correctly. Out of $3 billion in preventive-health funding the agency received under the Affordable Care Act, only $180 million went to disease research, wrote Eric Boehm, a writer for the conservative news site *Watchdog.org*. The rest funded "less productive" activities such as "convincing Americans to make smart choices . . . — essentially taxpayer-funded advertising telling you to put down that giant soda and eat more salad."[44]

As the 2014 Ebola crisis winds down, scrutiny of the world's response has triggered calls for reforms, especially by the World Health Organization (WHO), the U.N. agency charged with advising and supporting governments in public-health emergencies. Many public-health experts caution, however, that the quality of WHO's work depends in large measure on whether nations sustain a strong commitment to international public-health activities.

"For many years we've been able to manage medium, small-sized [disease] outbreaks," said WHO Director General Margaret Chan on Jan. 25. "But the Ebola outbreak was a mega-crisis, and it overwhelmed the capacity of WHO." It was too slow to respond to the outbreak, which underscored the need for "urgent change" at the agency, she said.[45]

Should CDC funding be raised to fight emerging diseases?

YES
Stephen Calderwood, MD
President, Infectious Diseases Society of America

Written for *CQ Researcher*, February 2015

Combating emerging infectious disease demands increased funding from the Centers for Disease Control and Prevention (CDC). Responding to infectious disease threats demands a sustained and forward-looking investment in public health. Threats that emerged over the past few years, such as H1N1 pandemic influenza, Middle East Respiratory Syndrome and Enterovirus D68, remind us that widespread outbreaks are not a relic of the past. And the ongoing Ebola outbreak illustrates that deadly pathogens respect no borders.

As an infectious disease physician, I witness the incredible toll that infectious agents take on patients and their families. We cannot afford to be unprepared for emerging and re-emerging infectious threats. We also must address the threats that have been with us for decades, such as antibiotic-resistant bacteria — the "ticking time bombs" of U.S. public health. At the same time, HIV/AIDS, tuberculosis and hepatitis C continue to strain our health care system, leaving many people undiagnosed or lacking access to treatment. Without greater efforts to prevent and treat these diseases, the magnitude of the problem may outstrip our ability to respond.

Rather than resorting to emergency funding every time a new infectious disease threat emerges, we must invest in a more stable manner that allows long-term planning to provide a better system to detect and respond to these threats.

The CDC leads national infectious disease surveillance and administers and coordinates preparedness and response efforts, with state and local public health departments, hospitals and communities. When a crisis like Ebola or pandemic influenza erupts, we count on the CDC to respond. Despite this, the agency's total funding was reduced nearly $600 million under across-the-board fiscal 2013 cuts and has remained flat relative to fiscal 2010 — diminishing funds available for state and local health systems as well.

New initiatives are needed to build the public-health infrastructure. For example, the CDC's Detect and Protect Against Antibiotic Resistance initiative would build surveillance infrastructure to reduce the burden of drug-resistant bacteria and preserve the effectiveness of antibiotics integral to the continued success of modern medicine. It's a great example of how we could make a public-health investment now that would save lives and taxpayer dollars in the near future, but Congress deleted it from the CDC's fiscal 2015 spending.

A stably financed and sustainable public-health infrastructure is our strongest asset in securing Americans against microbial threats.

NO
Michael D. Tanner
Senior Fellow, Cato Institute

Written for *CQ Researcher*, February 2015

Nearly everyone, regardless of political ideology, agrees that protecting the public health is a legitimate function of government. A large part of that responsibility is protecting Americans from infectious disease, a task made all the more difficult by the emergence of new threats like Ebola or Enterovirus D68, a respiratory virus that sickened children around the country in 2014.

Yet, that doesn't mean we should fall into the knee-jerk Washington trap of believing that every new challenge requires more taxpayer money.

While it is true that spending for the federal Centers for Disease Control and Prevention (CDC) has dipped ever so slightly since 2011, those cuts followed years of massive increases. Overall, since 2000, CDC outlays have almost doubled, from $3.5 billion to $6.8 billion (in 2014 constant dollars). It's not that the CDC hasn't had money, it's that the money has been spent on things that have little or nothing to do with protecting Americans from infectious disease.

Over the last decade, in fact, the CDC has spent much of its time — and money — studying such peripheral issues as seatbelt use, infant car seat safety and obesity. Rather than standing on the front lines against infectious disease, the CDC has transformed itself into a major player in the nanny state.

These may or may not be worthy topics, but this focus makes it somewhat harder for Democrats to turn around and blame budget cutting for a lack of attention to the things that the CDC is actually supposed to do — such as protect us from contagious diseases.

To understand just how misplaced the agency's priorities have been, one need look no further than the CDC's Prevention and Public Health Fund, which was included in Obamacare. The fund has received some $3 billion over the past five years from a dedicated stream of mandatory funding, yet only a little more than 6 percent of that went toward epidemiology, lab capacity or programs to fight infectious diseases. The rest has become a giant slush fund that has been used for everything from installing streetlights and improving sidewalks to promoting breastfeeding.

No doubt the CDC would like to have more funding. Find me a government agency that wouldn't. But we should never forget that that money comes from hardworking taxpayers. Before the CDC demands more of that money, perhaps it should rethink its current priorities. To govern, after all, means to choose.

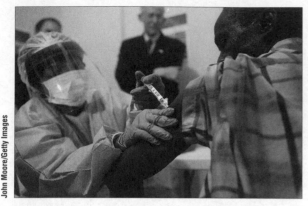

John Moore/Getty Images

A nurse vaccinates a man in Monrovia, the capital of Liberia, as part of an Ebola vaccine study being conducted, by Liberian health officials and the U.S. National Institutes of Health. At least 3,700 Liberians have died from Ebola. In January senior health officials from 34 countries agreed to establish a quick-response fund for dangerous infectious disease outbreaks and a reserve international public-health workforce for emergency deployment.

Many agree with Chan. The Ebola outbreak "was the Hurricane Katrina" of the organization, "its moment of failure," observed an NPR report on Feb. 6. The WHO initially downplayed the outbreak's potential for harm, then wasted more time urging the affected nations to take more responsibility for handling the crisis, according to NPR.[46]

On Jan. 25, WHO's board, made up of senior health officials from 34 countries, agreed to implement reforms, including creating a quick-response fund for dangerous outbreaks and establishing a reserve international public-health workforce for fast deployment to emergencies.[47]

Some observers point out, however, that such plans are easier made than accomplished.

For one thing, international organizations are rife with politics, which often impede action, say many observers. One reason for the WHO's slow response to Ebola, for example, "was because their African regional office isn't staffed with the most capable people but with political appointees," said Ebola discoverer Peter Piot, director of the London School of Hygiene & Tropical Medicine. Furthermore, he said, "the [WHO] headquarters in Geneva suffered large budget cuts that had been agreed to by member states. The department for hemorrhagic fevers, [which include Ebola] and the

one responsible for the management of epidemic emergences were hit hard."[48]

The cuts occurred after the 2008 global financial crisis, and left the WHO with a two-year budget of around $4 billion, *New York Times* correspondent Sheri Fink told NPR. As a comparison, the CDC budget is around $6 billion for one year, Fink noted. Today, only 20 percent of the WHO's funding comes from dues paid by member nations, while 80 percent comes from voluntary donations from governments and private individuals and groups.

"I was amazed to learn" that in 2013 the Bill & Melinda Gates Foundation gave more "than any single country," said Fink.[49]

Fink said voluntary contributions, public and private, often are directed to specific projects, and "wouldn't be immediately shiftable into, say, an Ebola outbreak."[50] Public and private donors have pledged almost $3 billion to the WHO and other public and private public-health groups to address the Ebola outbreak, but the agencies have received only about $1 billion of that total so far.[51]

Control Strategies

Meeting the challenge of emerging disease requires crafting the best control strategies. Every disease is different, however, so focusing exclusively on vaccine development, for example, is not as simple as it may appear.

In the case of Ebola, some analysts argue that public-health officials wrongly promoted disease-control approaches over development of a preventive vaccine.

As the 2014 Ebola outbreak's early months made clear, disease-containment efforts that "prioritize manpower over technology" — such as tracking infected patients' contacts and isolating infected people — were inadequate, wrote Scott Gottlieb, a resident fellow at the free market-oriented American Enterprise Institute, and Tevi Troy, president of the American Health Policy Institute, a think tank studying issues important to employers who provide health coverage. Meanwhile, at least two vaccines in fairly advanced development stages were not aggressively pushed ahead by governments as the top priorities for Ebola, they said.[52]

"The U.S. dropped the ball on advancing a number of promising Ebola drugs and vaccines," they wrote. Funding had been sparse, and regulators questioned the ethics of conducting placebo trials in regions where the disease was active.[53] The severity of the 2014 outbreak, however, made clear that U.S. and European pharmaceutical regulators should "collaborate full time with companies on developing Ebola drugs," they said.[54]

For more than a century vaccines have played vital roles in quelling infectious disease, and they will do so in the future, says Belshe, of Saint Louis University School of Medicine. For "smallpox, measles, Hepatitis A, we've had tremendous effect with vaccines, either eliminating a disease or being on the cusp of doing so."

Nevertheless, he and others say, vaccines are seldom a simple solution. Manufacturers are reluctant to spend money on a vaccine if they are not sure they will recoup their investment, says Kansas State's Richt. In 2010, when Ebola apparently threatened only Africa, Ames, Iowa-based NewLink Genetics bought the rights to an Ebola vaccine from its developer, the government-owned Public Health Agency of Canada, for $200,000. "That tells you the value of a vaccine when it's only needed in Africa," says Richt.[55]

But by November 2014, after several Ebola-infected travelers from West Africa showed up in the United States and Europe during the massive Ebola outbreak, NewLink sold the rights to Kenilworth, N.J.-based pharmaceutical giant Merck & Co. Inc. for $50 million.

"It's easy to sell the vaccine idea" to the public and to Congress, says EcoHealth Alliance's Daszak. But relying on a vaccine, which can cost $10 billion to produce, for all potentially threatening viruses would not "be cost-effective," he says.

Moreover, "there's a long, long time between perceiving the need for a vaccine and making that vaccine," says Madoff, of the Massachusetts Department of Public Health. "And some diseases are very serious but very rare. Do you make a vaccine for those?"

Even when most agree that a vaccine is needed — as in the case of the H5 bird-flu viruses, which have strong pandemic potential — producing enough vaccine on time could be a huge challenge, says Belshe. For example, research-trial vaccines for bird flu didn't stimulate enough immune response until people had received two strong doses, which would make it very hard to manufacture enough, he says. (Last year, Belshe and colleagues found that people mounted an immune response after only one vaccine dose if they had received a different vaccine for an older form of H5 flu virus a year earlier.)[56]

Behavioral approaches help control Ebola, which is relatively difficult to catch since human-to-human transmission occurs only if one comes into direct contact with fluids emitted by an infected person, such as blood or mucus, says Daszak. The Democratic Republic of the Congo, which had its first Ebola outbreak in 1976, had another in 2014. But the virus was identified within three days of being diagnosed, "and they quickly got it under control," he says.

Like many emerging diseases, Ebola enters the human population when people come into close contact with or eat infected animals. To combat its emergence in humans, Congo "has programs to educate hunters" about which animals may be dangerous, says Daszak. "People can learn a rule like, 'You don't need to stop eating bushmeat, but never eat a primate,' " for example.

Hoffman, of City College of New York, points out that developing a successful vaccine is just the first step. (Case in point: the re-emergence of measles in the United States despite the existence of a highly effective vaccine.) "What cures is not a vaccine but vaccination," she says. "You have to get people vaccinated," a multifaceted challenge that demands, among other things, ties with a community and cultural understanding, she says. "In public policy, the need for those things is often forgotten."

OUTLOOK
Learning to Cope

Just 50 years ago, medical scientists declared the age of infectious illness nearly at an end. Now scientists say future policymakers will — and must — consider the links to emerging infectious disease in everything from chronic illnesses to deforestation.

Emerging diseases will just keep coming, says Boston University's Corley. Possibly on tap this summer, for example — an East Coast outbreak of the mosquito-borne fever and joint-pain illness Chikungunya, now active in Africa and Asia. "You can't spray enough poison," says Corley. "You have to figure out how to stop mosquitoes from spreading it."

The realities of emerging infections will require science to reorder some research priorities, says Childs of Yale. In particular, meticulous, hands-on observational study of nature has largely been displaced by high-tech research in genetics. Medical entomology — the study of disease-carrying insects — "has disappeared from most universities," and along with it centuries of hard-won, vital knowledge, he says. That knowledge will be needed again, but the scholarly infrastructure for producing and transmitting it to new generations may have to be rebuilt from scratch. "When we talk to Africans about malaria, they say, 'We need medical entomologists.' But where are they? Already, no one's around to train new ones."

American medicine's decades-long near-sole focus on "diseases of civilization" such as cancer and diabetes also will need to be rethought, public-health experts say. Increasingly, medicine will ask whether pathogens are playing an unnoticed role in health conditions.

"Over the next 10 years," it will become imperative to consider the threat of emerging infectious disease in policy and business decisions related to environmental change, says Daszak, of EcoHealth Alliance. Striking a balance between what people want to do and what they must do to head off threats will be a tricky balancing act, he says. "You can't do things that keep economies from growing."

In places such as the Southeast Asian island nation of Borneo, rainforest deforestation proceeds apace as new palm oil plantations are established, and the tree cutting "opens up an area to new diseases," Daszak says. One strategy could be to allow companies to establish plantations only if they also establish local clinics equipped to deal with emerging infections, he says.

"We're at a point where emerging diseases are not weird things that creep out of the jungle. They're often a product of our economic success," says Daszak. "We have to accept that and take steps that insure against those risks."

NOTES

1. "Ebola Virus Disease," World Health Organization, September 2014, http://tinyurl.com/p9729bn; "Ebola Situation Report," World Health Organization, Feb. 4, 2015, http://tinyurl.com/o3rxvo9. A handful of cases also appeared in the United States and Europe, after people infected in Africa traveled there. In those countries, though, health officials rapidly contained the disease, and few people died.

2. Denise Grady, "Mysterious Virus That Killed a Farmer in Kansas Is Identified," *The New York Times*, Dec. 23, 2014, http://tinyurl.com/lj6ufk7.

3. For background, see Todd C. Frankel, "Forget 'anti-vaxxers.' The Disney measles outbreak could change the minds of an even more crucial group," *The Washington Post*, Jan. 26, 2015, http://tinyurl.com/pmttat6.

4. "CDC A-Z Index," U.S. Centers for Disease Control and Prevention, January 2015, http://tinyurl.com/6m9aw6.

5. Kent Sepkowitz, "Bubonic Plague Is Back (But It Never Really Left)" *The Daily Beast*, Nov. 27, 2014, http://tinyurl.com/pj4ektn.

6. For background, see Jennifer Weeks, "Rapid Urbanization," *CQ Researcher*, April 1, 2009, pp. 91-118.

7. Michael D. Tanner, "Budget Cuts and Ebola," Cato Institute, Oct. 15, 2014, http://tinyurl.com/nfvsh44.

8. "CDC 2009-2012 Accomplishments" ("Save Lives and Protect People; Support Public Health In Your Community"), Centers for Disease Control and Prevention, http://tinyurl.com/kg69tcq.

9. For background, see "De-Coding the Black Death," BBC News, Oct. 3, 2001, http://tinyurl.com/pzpx62a; "Black Death," History, http://tinyurl.com/bk3z46l; Stephen S. Morse, "Emerging Infections: Condemned to Repeat?" in *Microbial Evolution and Co-Adaptation: A Tribute to the Life and Scientific Legacies of Joshua Lederberg: Workshop Summary* (2009), http://tinyurl.com/mnyruon.

10. For background, see Covering Pandemic Flu, "The Science," Nieman Foundation, http://tinyurl.com/nhegxqm; and "What Is a Virus?" *Encyclopedia of Life*, http://eol.org/info/458.

11. "Review of 1918 Pandemic Flu Studies Offers More Questions than Answers," National Institute of Allergy and Infectious Diseases, news release, Feb. 28, 2007, http://tinyurl.com/kxernzg; and David M. Morens and Anthony S. Fauci, "The 1918 influenza pandemic: Insights for the 21st century," *The Journal of Infectious Diseases*, April 1, 2007, pp. 1018-1028.

12. Robert Richardson and Jason Tetro, "Pandemics — How likely are we to see a major pandemic?" *Offgrid Survival*, http://tinyurl.com/lvx4b7c.

13. Judy Stone, "Ebola in the U.S. — Politics and Public Health Don't Mix," *Scientific American* (blog), Oct. 6, 2014, http://tinyurl.com/mskmooe.

14. The other fatality was Martin Salia, a surgeon who lived part time in Maryland and part time in his native Sierra Leone. Salia was flown for treatment from Sierra Leone to Omaha, Neb., where he died Nov. 17, 2014. Abby Phillip and Emily Wax-Thibodeaux, " 'Critical Threshold': The failed race to save the life of Ebola-stricken doctor Martin Salia," *The Washington Post*, Nov. 17, 2014, http://tinyurl.com/kxrt3y6.

15. For background, see Walt Zwirko, "Hospital will pay Duncan's medical bills, set up charity," *USA Today*, Nov. 12, 2014, http://tinyurl.com/m4rcfrb.

16. For background, see Karen R. Lips and Joseph R. Mendelson III, "Stopping the Next Amphibian Apocalypse," *The New York Times*, Nov. 14, 2014, http://tinyurl.com/knkehpv.

17. "Outbreaks: Protecting Americans From Infectious Diseases 2014," Trust for America's Health/Robert Wood Johnson Foundation, December 2014, p. 46, http://tinyurl.com/n5opyhn.

18. "Budget Cuts Continue to Affect the Health of Americans," Association of State and Territorial Health Officials, October 2013, http://tinyurl.com/lps4rjq.

19. Quoted in "Outbreaks: Protecting Americans From Infectious Diseases 2014," *op. cit.*, p. 6.

20. Jamison Pike, *et al.*, "Economic optimization of a global strategy to address the pandemic threat," *PNAS*, Nov. 17, 2014, http://tinyurl.com/pbtssja.

21. David Harsanyi, "The CDC Doesn't Have a Funding Problem, It Has a Mission Creep Problem," *The Federalist*, Oct. 3, 2014, http://tinyurl.com/mc2wp7z.

22. "About the David J. Sencer CDC Museum," U.S. Centers for Disease Control and Prevention, http://tinyurl.com/l3rbcft.

23. Veronique de Rugy, "Surprise! Surprise! Obama's Ebola response political not responsible," *The Roanoke* [Va.] *Times*, Nov. 13, 2014, http://tinyurl.com/klk45qm.

24. "NIH Research: Dr. Anthony S. Fauci: 'An AIDS-free generation is closer than we might think,' " *NIH Medline Plus*, Fall 2013, http://tinyurl.com/kuhzukd.

25. For background, see "Introduction to Pathogens," from *Molecular Biology of the Cell* (2002), http://tinyurl.com/pna35tn; Ron Barrett and George Armelagos, *An Unnatural History of Emerging Infections* (2013); Lisa A. Beltz, *Emerging Infectious Diseases: A Guide to Diseases, Causative Agents, and Surveillance* (2011).

26. Peter Daszak, "Can We Predict Future Trends in Disease Emergence?" in *Microbial Evolution and Co-Adaptation* (2009), p. 252.

27. *Ibid.*, p. 253.

28. For background, see "The Influenza Pandemic of 1918," *Human Virology at Stanford*, February 2005, http://tinyurl.com/qgjfvte; Welling Oei and Hiroshi Nishiura, "The Relationship between Tuberculosis and Influenza Death During the Influenza (H1N1) Pandemic from 1918-1919," *Computational and Mathematical Methods in Medicine*, 2012, http://tinyurl.com/plvx3y5; Jeffrey K. Taubenberger and David M. Morens, "1918 Influenza: The Mother of All Pandemics," *Emerging Infectious Diseases*, January 2006, pp. 15-22, http://tinyurl.com/otanpy6; Mark Joseph Stern, "The Worst Pandemic in History," *Slate*, Dec. 26, 2012, http://tinyurl.com/cz7ano5; Andrew Noymer, "The 1918 influenza pandemic hastened the decline of tuberculosis in the United States: An age, period, cohort analysis," *Vaccine*, 2011, pp. B38-B41; "Interview: Jeffrey Taubenberger," "Influenza 1918," "American Experience," PBS, 1998, http://tinyurl.com/oom6nyz.

29. Howard Markel, "The Real Story Behind Penicillin," *The Rundown* blog, PBS NewsHour, Sept. 27, 2013, http://tinyurl.com/ohucqbu; Rustam I. Aminov, "A Brief History of the Antibiotic Era: Lessons Learned and Challenges for the Future," *Frontiers in Microbiology*, Dec. 8, 2010, http://tinyurl.com/pb44ynz; "A Brief Overview of Classes of Antibiotics," *Compound Interest*, Sept. 8, 2014.

30. Quoted in Gerald B. Pier, "On the Greatly Exaggerated Reports of the Death of Infectious Diseases," letter to the editor, *Clinical Infectious Diseases*, Oct. 15, 2008, p. 1113, http://tinyurl.com/oe6gy2n.

31. Barrett and Armelagos, *op. cit.*, Kindle edition, Loc. 138.

32. David M. Livermore, "Antibiotic resistance in staphylococci," *International Journal of Antimicrobial Agents*, November 2000, http://tinyurl.com/olame2p; Tony Mazzulli, "Methicillin Resistant Staphylococcus Aureus (MRSA), Canadian Antimicrobial Resistance Alliance, http://tinyurl.com/pfefobe.

33. Barrett and Armelagos, *op. cit.*, Loc. 148; "List of Antibiotics," *eMed Expert*, http://tinyurl.com/knoopr7.

34. For background, see Garrett, *op. cit.*

35. For background, see Mark Woolhouse and Eleanor Gaunt, "Ecological Origins of Novel Human Pathogens," in *Microbial Evolution and Co-Adaptation*, *op. cit.*

36. Daszak, "Can We Predict Future Trends," *op. cit.*, p. 261.

37. Garrett, *op. cit.*

38. Jonathan M. Mann, "AIDS: A worldwide pandemic," in Michael S. Gottlieb, *et al.*, eds., *Current Topics in AIDS*, Vol. 2 (1989).

39. Morse, *op. cit.*, p. 206.

40. Brett Norman, "Ebola highlights CDC fund crunch," *Politico*, Oct. 2, 2014, http://tinyurl.com/kakytas.

41. "Transcript: President Obama's State of the Union Address," NPR, Jan. 20, 2015, http://tinyurl.com/l5mczdb.

42. "Fiscal Year 2015 Brings Stagnant Funding for ID, HIV," *IDSA News*, December 2014, http://tinyurl.com/ou8cuqk; Mandi, "5 ways the omnibus spending bill impacts public health," *Public Health Newswire*, American Public Health Association, Dec. 16, 2014, http://tinyurl.com/ntdo9dn; H.R. 83, House Amendment to Senate Amendment, Dec. 11, 2014, U.S. Government Printing Office, http://tinyurl.com/km3cans.

43. "Transcript: President Obama's State of the Union . . .," *op. cit.*; Norman, *op. cit.*

44. Eric Boehm, "Updated: after wasting tax dollars, officials at CDC, NIH claim budget cuts hurt Ebola preparedness," Watchdog.org, Oct. 15, 2014, http://tinyurl.com/lxptx92.

45. Quoted in Simeon Bennett and Jason Gale, "Ebola Spurs WHO Plan for Health Reserves After Missteps," *Bloomberg Business*, Jan. 25, 2015, http://tinyurl.com/lk9znn4.

46. Jason Beaubien, "Critics Say Ebola Crisis Was WHO's Big Failure. Will Reform Follow?" NPR, Feb. 6, 2015, http://tinyurl.com/m7nagy7.

47. Bennett and Gale, *op. cit.*

48. Quoted in Rafaela von Bredow and Veronika Hackenbroch, "Interview with Ebola Discoverer Peter Piot: 'It Is What People Call a Perfect Storm,'" *Spiegel Online International*, Sept. 26, 2014, http://tinyurl.com/ojhpbl5.

49. Melissa Block, "Budget Cuts Hobble the World Health Organization's Ebola Response," NPR, Sept. 4, 2014, http://tinyurl.com/n3b9lns.

50. *Ibid.*

51. Sarah Kollmorgen, "Donors Pledged Nearly $3 Billion to the Ebola Crisis, But Have Paid Only $1 Billion," *The New Republic*, Feb. 3, 2015, http://tinyurl.com/krmv8se.

52. Scott Gottlieb and Tevi Troy, "Stopping Ebola Before it Turns Into a Pandemic," *The Wall Street Journal*, Oct. 3, 2014, http://tinyurl.com/kdz36ce.

53. For background, see "Experimental Drugs and the Ethics of Fighting Ebola," Room for Debate, *The New York Times*, Dec. 1, 2014, http://tinyurl.com/m78opgx.

54. Gottlieb and Troy, *op. cit.*

55. For background, see Mark Terry, "Merck & Co., NewLink Genetics in Secret Talks on Producing Ebola Vaccine," Biospace.com, Nov. 21, 2014, http://tinyurl.com/mtgdgxq; Ransdell Pierson, "Merck buys rights to NewLink's experimental Ebola vaccine," Reuters, Nov. 24, 2014, http://tinyurl.com/k7h53ek.

56. Robert B. Belshe, *et al.*, "Immunogenicity of Avian Influenza A/Anhui/01/2005(H5N1) Vaccine With MF59 Adjuvant: A Randomized Clinical Trial," *JAMA*, Oct. 8, 2014, pp. 1420-1428, http://tinyurl.com/lh28ydo; "JAMA Findings Reveal Vaccine Approach to Fight Pandemic Bird Flu," press release, Saint Louis University, Oct. 7, 2014, http://tinyurl.com/muq8pkj.

BIBLIOGRAPHY
Selected Sources
Books

Microbial Evolution and Co-Adaptation: A Tribute to the Life and Scientific Legacies of Joshua Lederberg, **Institute of Medicine Forum on Microbial Threats workshop, National Academies Press, 2009, http://tinyurl.com/q8gywel.**
Leading scholars who helped spearhead the resurgence of interest in infectious disease contribute papers on the evolution of pathogenic microbes and other topics.

Barrett, Ron, and George J. Armelagos, *An Unnatural History of Emerging Infections*, **Oxford University Press, 2013.**
An associate professor of anthropology at Macalester College (Barrett) and a former Emory University anthropology professor who died in 2014 (Armelagos) present a history of emerging infectious diseases, starting with the pre-agricultural era.

Webber, Roger, *Communicable Diseases: A Global Perspective*, **4th ed., CABI, 2012.**
A tropical-disease epidemiologist describes the general principles governing infectious diseases and provides detailed descriptions of today's emerging and endemic human pathogens.

Articles

Gavrilles, Beth, "For monarch butterflies, loss of migration means more disease," Phys.org, Jan. 16, 2015, http://tinyurl.com/q86bxpa.
Butterflies that have stopped migrating because of habitat loss are developing more diseases.

Gholipour, Bahar, "What 11 Billion People Mean for Disease Outbreaks," *LiveScience*, **Nov. 25, 2013, http://tinyurl.com/puq8tez.**
Population growth and increased travel and transport have changed the emerging-disease picture over the past several decades and will continue to do so.

Llanos, Miguel, "Killer Virus Takes Emotional Toll on Pig Farmers," NBC News, April 28, 2014, http://tinyurl.com/o8nczp8.

Porcine Epidemic Diarrhea virus — which is fatal for newborn pigs — arrived in the United States from China in 2013 and within a year had spread to 30 states.

O'Connor, Anahad, "Enterovirus 68: What Experts Are Learning," Well blog, *The New York Times*, **Oct. 2, 2014, http://tinyurl.com/pkmyhu3.**
A new strain of a familiar respiratory virus is more severe than older strains.

Resnick, Brian, "How Veterinarians Prevent Animals From Spreading Disease to Humans," *The Atlantic*, **Nov. 29, 2014, http://tinyurl.com/qzs7utc.**
Because many pathogens can infect both animals and humans, closer cooperation between the medical and veterinary communities can help identify and combat emerging infectious diseases.

Reports and Studies

"Mapping of poverty and likely zoonoses hotspots," report to U.K. Department for International Development, International Livestock Research Institute, July 2, 2012, http://tinyurl.com/lbo7bln.
A combination of rural poverty and heavy reliance on livestock farming puts some countries at particularly high risk for emerging-disease outbreaks, according to a nonprofit international research group on food-supply issues.

"Outbreaks: 2014 – Protecting Americans From Infectious Diseases," Trust for America's Health/ Robert Wood Johnson Foundation, December 2014, http://tinyurl.com/peeyxvy.
Two nonprofit organizations involved in public-health issues describe current infectious-disease threats to the United States and evaluate state and federal disease preparedness and responses.

Alexander, K.A., *et al.*, **"What Factors Might Have Led to the Emergence of Ebola in West Africa?" PLOS Blogs, Nov. 11, 2014, http://tinyurl.com/q92gtqa.**
The 2014 Ebola outbreak in West Africa was the deadliest and longest on record, and the reasons for the disease's appearance in countries in which it had never been seen before remain unclear. War, population growth, poverty and poor health infrastructure played roles, however.

Daszak, Peter, Andrew A. Cunningham, and Alex D. Hyatt, "Emerging Infectious Diseases of Wildlife — Threats to Biodiversity and Human Health," *Science*, Jan. 21, 2000, pp. 443-449.
Ecologists describe the discovery of multiple new pathogens in wildlife and the threats they may pose to biodiversity and to the health of humans and domestic animals.

Pike, Jamison, *et al.*, "Economic optimization of a global strategy to address the pandemic threat," *PNAS*, Nov. 17, 2014, http://tinyurl.com/pudx783.
Economists and ecologists argue that efforts aimed at preventing spillover of wildlife diseases into human and domestic-animal populations would substantially decrease the risk of pandemics and save billions of dollars in pandemic-related economic losses.

For More Information

Division of Global Health Protection, Centers for Disease Control and Prevention, 1600 Clifton Rd., Atlanta, GA 30329-4027; 800-2323-4636; www.cdc.gov/globalhealth/healthprotection/default.htm. Federal office that works with international partners to improve global surveillance of, and response to, infectious diseases.

Doctors Without Borders (Medicins Sans Frontieres), 333 7th Ave., New York, NY 10001-5004; 212-679-6800; www.doctorswithoutborders.org. Nonprofit volunteer medical group that assists with medical crises in low-income countries and provides information on global health issues, including infectious disease.

EcoHealth Alliance, 460 W. 34th St., 17th Floor, New York, NY 10001-2320; 212-380-4460. Nonprofit scientific organization that conducts research and sponsors international projects related to the prevention of emerging-disease outbreaks and the conservation of biodiversity.

Infectious Diseases Society of America, 1300 Wilson Blvd., Suite 300, Arlington, VA 22209; 703-299-0200. Professional membership organization for physicians, scientists and other professionals who specialize in infectious disease.

National Center for Zoonotic and Emerging Infectious Diseases, Centers for Disease Control and Prevention, 1600 Clifton Rd., Atlanta, GA 30329-4027; 800-2323-4636; www.cdc.gov/ncezid. Federal center that sponsors research and develops public policy on emerging and zoonotic infectious diseases.

PREDICT, School of Veterinary Medicine, University of California, Davis, 1 Shields Ave., Davis, CA 95616; www.vetmed.ucdavis.edu/ohi/predict. Federally sponsored research network studying ways to detect and limit spread of emerging human and animal infectious disease.

ProMED-mail, 9 Babcock St., Unit 3, Brookline, MA 02446; 617-277-0551; www.promedmail.org. Internet-based reporting system that collects and disseminates information from multiple sources about emerging infectious diseases around the world.

World Health Organization, Avenue Appia 20, 1211 Geneva 27, Switzerland; + 41 22 791 21 11; www.who.int/en. U.N. agency that helps shape global health policy and research agenda and provides technical assistance to countries on health matters.

16 Protecting the Oceans

Jennifer Weeks

Fishermen harvest sea scallops off the coast of western France on Nov. 16, 2011. Scientists widely agree that the world's fisheries and ocean ecosystems have been heavily damaged by overfishing, as well as by climate change, pollution, coastal development and heavy ship traffic. Off the New England coast, tight regulations have helped revive a failing scallop fishery.

From *CQ Researcher*, October 17, 2014.

Maine's nickname is "The Pine Tree State," but many of the tourists who pump more than $7 billion into the state's economy every year come for something else: lobster.[1] Eighty percent of all lobster sold in the United States is caught in Maine, where most fishermen still haul traps by hand.

An elected council of fishermen manages the state's lobster fishery through a system of geographic zones and catch limits. In 2013 the fishery was certified as sustainable by the London-based Marine Stewardship Council, a nonprofit that recognizes fisheries that do not over-harvest fish stocks or damage the environment.[2]

But lobster producers are seeing ominous signs in their traps, such as lobsters with mottled, diseased shells, which scientists say are caused by increased ocean acidity due to climate change. Others increasingly are finding black sea bass, native to warmer waters farther south, along with lobsters. The bass, which are shifting northward because climate change is warming ocean waters, prey on baby shellfish and could damage lobster stocks.[3]

Climate change is the newest stress on the world's fisheries and ocean ecosystems, already heavily damaged by overfishing, pollution, coastal development and heavy ship traffic. According to the United Nations Food and Agriculture Organization (FAO), 29 percent of global wild fish stocks are overfished (being caught faster than they can reproduce), and more than 60 percent are being fished near or at their maximum sustainable production levels.[4]

Human activities also are severely damaging coral reefs, mangrove forests and coastal marshes — seaside areas that shelter juvenile fish and shellfish and help to buffer against storms, erosion

Coral Bleaching, Dead Zones Are Spreading

The Florida Reef and Australia's Great Barrier Reef are among hundreds of coral reefs damaged by severe bleaching, caused by rising ocean temperatures. Additionally, dead zones, where nutrient pollution has depleted oxygen levels so much that life cannot survive, have formed in the Gulf of Mexico, U.S. Atlantic Coast and Mediterranean Sea.

Source: Dead zones mapped by Robert Simmon and Jesse Allen, based on data by Robert Diaz, Virginia Institute of Marine Science, "Aquatic Dead Zones," National Aeronautics and Space Administration, July 17, 2010, http://tinyurl.com/2e87q8y; ReefBase Global Database, accessed Oct. 9, 2014, http://tinyurl.com/ysdfaf. Map by Lewis Agrell.

● Dead Zones
● Reef Degradation

and flooding. And many forms of pollution, such as plastic waste, toxic chemicals and nutrients from farms and urban runoff, are reducing water quality and killing fish and shellfish.[5]

"We humans have this idea that the Earth . . . [is] so vast and so resilient it doesn't matter what we do to it. This is especially true of the ocean, where impacts are less obvious than for terrestrial systems," writes oceanographer Sylvia Earle, former chief scientist at the National Oceanic and Atmospheric Administration (NOAA) and a National Geographic explorer-in-residence.[6]

But in her view, the oceans are ailing. Some fisheries have shrunk by 90 percent in recent decades, and even plankton — microscopic organisms that form the base of ocean food chains — are declining.[7] Plankton produce about half of Earth's oxygen supply through photosynthesis.

"If you think the ocean isn't important, imagine life on Earth without it," Earle warns. "Mars comes to mind. No blue, no green. No ocean, no life-support system."[8]

Healthy oceans provide humans with a wide range of benefits. Besides serving as habitats for thousands of marine species and absorbing carbon dioxide from the atmosphere, oceans help to regulate Earth's weather and climate, and provide millions of jobs in the tourism, recreation, fishing and shipping industries.

And of course, oceans provide food, as U.S. Secretary of State John Kerry pointed out at an international conference on ocean conservation in Washington, D.C., on June 16. "Protecting our ocean is . . . a great necessity for global food security, given that more than 3 billion people — 50 percent of the people on this planet — in every corner of the world depend on fish as a source of protein," he said. "The connection between a healthy ocean and life itself cannot be overstated."[9]

A 2012 study by a group of economists estimated that if ocean stresses continue to grow at their current pace, the world would lose ecological services (such as carbon storage, biodiversity and food production) worth nearly $2 trillion annually by the year 2100. Rapid action to address climate change, they calculated, could cut those losses by two-thirds, to about $612 billion per year by 2100.[10]

While the oceans still perform many functions well, such as supporting subsistence-scale fishing, they are impaired in other areas, such as absorbing carbon dioxide. The Ocean Health Index — a scorecard developed by aquariums, conservation groups and academic scientists — rates the health of marine ecosystems by the functions they perform. Currently, the index rates oceans worldwide at 67 on a 100-point scale.

Daniel Schrag, a professor of geology and environmental science and engineering at Harvard University, says that although many human activities are degrading the oceans, overfishing has caused the worst damage so far. "We don't understand perfectly how warming or acidification will affect the oceans, but we know that overfishing has already caused huge stress to marine ecosystems," he says.

When fish are harvested faster than they can reproduce, stocks decline and may even collapse — or fall to 10 percent of their maximum previous level.[11] And even if fishing stops, fisheries do not automatically recover. After heavy fishing drove cod stocks to near-zero in the North Atlantic's historic Grand Banks, Canada imposed a moratorium on cod fishing in the area in 1992, but cod still have not returned in large numbers.[12]

Managers have preserved or rebuilt some fisheries by counting fish populations accurately, setting strict catch limits and banning gear and practices that damage undersea habitat, such as bottom trawling (dragging large nets across the ocean floor).[13] This approach is known as science-based management because it relies on detailed information about the condition of ecosystems and fish stocks.

Conservationists also support the creation of marine reserves — areas where fishing and other activities are limited or barred. Last month President Obama expanded the Pacific Remote Islands Marine National Monument, an 87,000-square-mile sanctuary around

Grading the Oceans' Health

The Ocean Health Index rates the world's oceans according to how sustainably they are delivering benefits. The least sustainable ocean functions were tourism and recreation and providing food and non-food products such as aquarium fish and seashells. Small-scale fishing and providing biodiversity received the highest scores. Overall, oceans worldwide received a 67 rating in 2014 on a 100-point scale. Scientists at conservation groups, aquariums and universities created the index using data from coastal nations.

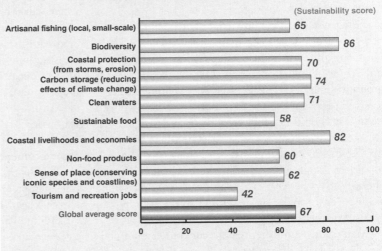

Global Ocean Health Index, 2014

(Sustainability score)

Artisanal fishing (local, small-scale)	65
Biodiversity	86
Coastal protection (from storms, erosion)	70
Carbon storage (reducing effects of climate change)	74
Clean waters	71
Sustainable food	58
Coastal livelihoods and economies	82
Non-food products	60
Sense of place (conserving iconic species and coastlines)	62
Tourism and recreation jobs	42
Global average score	67

Source: Ocean Health Index, http://tinyurl.com/ngvlb8c

U.S.-controlled islands in the central Pacific, established in 2009 by President George W. Bush. Obama used his power under the Antiquities Act to broaden the monument to nearly 500,000 square miles, barring all commercial fishing in what his proclamation described as a "highly pristine deep sea and open ocean ecosystem with unique biodiversity."[14]

But many fishermen argue that creating such reserves harms both fishermen and consumers. "When you close a resource, you lose it. We still have to feed people," said Hawaiian fisherman Makani Christensen at a public forum in Honolulu in August.[15]

Fishermen often acknowledge that catch limits and other control policies can help preserve fish stocks. In New England, a thriving scallop fishery has developed on Georges Bank, a once-rich zone that was closed for groundfishing in the 1990s after stocks plummeted.

"Ten years ago I would have never even believed we'd be in this condition," said New Bedford, Mass., scallop fisherman Eric Hansen, who estimated that he earned up to $40,000 on a single 10-day fishing trip. The scallop fishery is tightly regulated: Fishermen can only spend about 90 days per year at sea, and can only fish specific scallop beds, leaving others closed so the scallops can grow to market size.[16]

Many American fishermen accept conservation policies as necessary to preserve or restore fish stocks, but they want a role in applying those policies. When Ben Hartig, chair of the South Atlantic Fishery Management Council, first became involved with the council some 40 years ago, "fishermen were not . . . open and cooperative with researchers," he writes. But when NOAA began assessing overfished red snapper stocks in the Gulf of Mexico in 2009, Hartig says, fishermen understood that "better data leads to better assessments." Fishermen began working with federal regulators to tag and count red snapper to assess whether the fish were becoming more abundant.[17]

However, some fishermen are skeptical about government management of fisheries. "I don't understand why the fishermen are being vilified," said Ricardo DeRosa, a purse seine fisherman from American Samoa who opposed the Obama administration's decision to expand the Pacific Islands marine reserve. "I love the environment as well. We're not miners. We're not big oil companies. We're fishermen. We're feeding people."[18]

Environmental advocates cheered Obama's decision to expand the reserve, but have criticized other administration decisions on ocean issues. In July the Interior Department announced that it would allow energy companies to conduct offshore seismic testing along the Atlantic Coast from Delaware to Florida to look for oil and gas deposits.[19]

Currently, the United States allows offshore drilling only in the western and central Gulf of Mexico and in certain waters off the coast of Alaska. But Interior could open Atlantic waters in its next offshore leasing plan, which will run from 2017 through 2022.

Environmental groups say seismic testing, in which engineers fire compressed-air guns underwater and measure how the loud noises they produce reverberate off the ocean floor, harms marine life. An Interior Department review concluded that the tests would have minor to moderate effects on marine animals and sea turtles.[20]

Officials in mid-Atlantic and northern states and Florida contend that drilling poses an unacceptable risk of oil spills that could damage fisheries and coastlines. But energy companies and many officials in Virginia, North Carolina, South Carolina and Georgia say expanding offshore drilling will increase energy supplies and generate jobs.

As scientists, government leaders and activists debate how to protect and restore the oceans, here are some issues they are considering:

Do marine reserves work?

Along with catch limits and controls on fishing gear, many conservationists contend that creating marine reserves can effectively conserve ocean health. Also known as sanctuaries, protected areas and marine wildlife refuges, marine reserves are areas where fishing and other human activities are limited or banned in order to protect important species or their habitat.

"Marine reserves protect ocean ecosystems against the impacts of overfishing," says Andrea Kavanagh, director of the Southern Ocean Sanctuaries Campaign for the Pew Charitable Trusts, a nonprofit advocacy group that works on issues including ocean conservation. "They also improve ocean life beyond their boundaries, because larvae drift out and repopulate areas outside of reserve borders."

More than 6,700 marine protected areas have been created in 168 countries worldwide, but they encompass less than 2 percent of the oceans.[21] And limits on fishing vary among these areas.

For example, the Pacific island nation of Kiribati established the Phoenix Islands Protected Area around its islands in 2006 and expanded it in 2008 to nearly 165,000 square miles — about the size of California. But initially Kiribati banned commercial fishing in only 3 percent of the reserve, leaving the rest open to industrial tuna fishing. In June, however, Kiribati's president, Anote Tong, announced that it would end commercial fishing across the entire reserve.[22]

Tong made his announcement on June 16 at the State Department conference in Washington on the state of the world's oceans, organized by Kerry.[23] At the same meeting leaders from Palau, the Cook Islands and the Bahamas pledged to expand existing marine reserves or create new ones, and Obama announced his plans to expand the Pacific Remote Islands monument.[24]

But, Kerry said in September, marine protected areas "won't matter if no one's monitoring them. And the kind of enforcement that we're going to need is going to take training; it's going to take resources."[25] Without monitoring, illegal fishing practices often continue long after they are banned.

For example, driftnets — large nets rigged with floats on top and weights on their lower edge so that they drift in the oceans like curtains — ensnare whatever swims into them, including many untargeted species such as whales, dolphins and seals. The U.N. banned driftnets in 1992, and the International Commission for the Conservation of Atlantic Tunas, which regulates the Atlantic tuna fishery, followed in 2003, but some French, Italian and Moroccan fishing boats continue to use them illegally.[26]

New technologies, such as sonar buoys and low-cost listening devices known as hydrophones, may help regulators, fishermen and conservation groups detect illegal fishing in large marine reserves. The United States is also working to persuade nations to sign the Port State Measures Agreement, which requires members to keep illegally caught fish out of their markets. The U.S. Senate ratified the agreement last April.[27]

According to scientists, many marine reserves are ineffective. Last February a team of scientists from more than a dozen countries published a study analyzing 87 marine protected areas in 40 countries. Effective reserves, they found, had five key features: They did not allow any fishing and were more than 10 years old, larger than 100 square kilometers (about 39 square miles), isolated from other areas by deep water or sand and well enforced. Almost 60 percent of the reserves in the study had only one or two of these features, and were "not ecologically distinguishable" from fished areas.[28]

Relatively few marine protected areas ban all types of fishing and other commercial activities, which Kavanagh says is necessary to make them work. "We contend that less than 1 percent of the ocean is protected, because we only count marine reserves that don't allow fishing," she says.

Conservation groups want nations with interests in Antarctica to establish a system of marine reserves in the surrounding oceans, home to thousands of seabirds, penguins, seals and minke whales. Antarctica is governed under the Antarctic Treaty, whose members pledge to use the region only for scientific research. The Commission for Conservation of Antarctic Marine Living Resources, an international organization established in 1982, has sought to create marine reserves in the Ross Sea and Eastern Antarctica to prevent overfishing of what many observers call the world's last unspoiled ocean. But Russia, China and Ukraine have blocked attempts to impose fishing limits.[29]

"Clearly, the conservation message just isn't getting across," said Clive Evans, an associate professor of biology at New Zealand's University of Auckland, after commission members failed for a third time last November to agree on a proposal for protected areas in the Antarctic.[30]

Should governments limit nutrient pollution?

One of the most widespread and damaging effects of ocean pollution is a condition called hypoxia (lack of oxygen), which occurs when excess nitrogen and phosphorus — nutrients essential for animal and plant growth — wash into bays and coastal waters. The main sources of such nutrients are excess fertilizer and animal waste from farmlands, urban stormwater runoff, discharges from sewer and septic systems and burning of fossil fuel, which emits nitrogen.

In lakes, bays and ocean waters near the shore, these nutrients stimulate huge "blooms" of plankton, which die and decompose. As bacteria break down the plankton,

A man tries to rescue a dolphin that washed ashore in Sinop, northern Turkey, on Sept. 12, 2014. Although the U.N. in 1992 banned drift nets, which kill many dolphins, whales and seals each year, some fishing fleets still use the devices. In the United States, researchers are studying the possible role oil spills may have played in the strandings and die-offs of dozens of dolphins since the 2010 Deepwater Horizon oil rig disaster in the Gulf of Mexico.

they consume so much dissolved oxygen from the surrounding water that it cannot support life.

More than 500 dead zones exist in offshore waters around the world, covering 250,000 square kilometers (96,000 square miles). The number of such areas has doubled every 10 years since the 1960s, rising along with world population.[31]

Environmentalists and many scientists say the only effective way to shrink dead zones is to set firm limits on nutrient pollution. As a model they cite the Chesapeake Bay, where dead zones form in summer, reducing habitat for aquatic grasses and once-abundant oysters, blue crabs and fish.[32] In 2010 the Environmental Protection Agency (EPA) imposed a Total Maximum Daily Load (TMDL) for nutrient pollution from for six surrounding states whose waters drain into the bay.

The plan, often referred to as a "pollution diet," limits the quantities of nitrogen and phosphorus that can flow into the bay each year and requires states to create pollution controls to help meet those targets. The plan regulates pollution being dumped from pipes or other identifiable sources and from broad areas, such as runoff from farms.[33] The nonprofit Chesapeake Bay Foundation, which has worked to reverse pollution in the bay since 1967, calls the plan "the Chesapeake Bay's best, and perhaps last, chance for real restoration."[34]

According to the EPA, states around the bay are making progress, but more cuts are needed to reduce pollutants to specific levels outlined in the plan by 2017 and 2025.[35]

But the American Farm Bureau Federation, the nation's largest agricultural lobby, is suing to block the plan. Twenty-one states outside of the Chesapeake Bay watershed, stretching from Florida to Alaska, support the Farm Bureau, arguing that the EPA does not have legal authority to set binding nutrient pollution limits for states and that complying with such plans would be costly for states and businesses. A Pennsylvania court ruled for the EPA in 2013, but the Farm Bureau is appealing the decision.[36]

The case "has far-reaching implications" for other states, the intervening states asserted in a recent legal brief. "If this TMDL is left to stand, other watersheds, including the Mississippi River Basin (which spans 31 states from Canada to the Gulf Coast), could be next."[37]

Environmentalists want the EPA to set nutrient limits for the Mississippi River Basin to reduce a huge dead zone that forms in the Gulf of Mexico every summer. Although it fluctuates from year to year, over the past 30 years the dead zone has covered an average of roughly 13,650 square kilometers (5,300 square miles) — larger than the entire Chesapeake Bay.[38] The agency is working with states in the area to develop effective limits on nutrient pollution but has not proposed regional nutrient pollution limits.

"The Chesapeake Bay agreement is unique," says Ellen Gilinsky, a senior policy adviser at the EPA and former director of water programs for the state of Virginia. "States recognized that the bay was in bad shape and came up with voluntary strategies to reduce nutrient pollution. It was hard to meet their targets, so they asked EPA to write a multi-state TMDL plan." Furthermore, Gilinsky notes, the Mississippi basin is a much larger area, and agriculture is the main source of nutrients there. In contrast, stormwater and wastewater play larger roles in the Chesapeake. "We have a task force of 12 states and five federal agencies, but it will take time to develop reduction frameworks for such a big area," says Gilinsky.

In Europe, recent international efforts have reduced nutrient levels in the Black Sea, which was ravaged during the Soviet era by nutrient pollution carried down the Danube River from Eastern European farms and sewage discharges.[39] After the Soviet Union dissolved in 1991 and former East Bloc countries joined the European Union (EU), the United Nations and World Bank encouraged more than $3.5 billion of investments in regional programs to clean up the Danube and the Black Sea. The programs included wastewater treatment upgrades in former East Bloc countries and education campaigns for farmers. In addition, the EU adopted limits on nitrate pollution from agriculture.[40] Today Black Sea nutrient levels have fallen, algae blooms are less frequent and stocks of plankton and small fish are beginning to increase.[41]

"The European Union has standards that apply across all states, including very strong limits on manure application" to fields, said Nancy Rabalais, executive director of the Louisiana Universities Marine Consortium, who has studied the Gulf of Mexico dead zone extensively. "Nitrogen and phosphorus levels in the Black Sea have been dramatically reduced." Such approaches could also be effective in the Mississippi River Basin, she said.

"We know that the majority of nutrients [in the Gulf] come from big agribusiness," Rabalais said. "What we're missing is the social and political will to reduce nutrient pollution."[42]

Can coral reefs survive climate change?

Coral reefs are among the oceans' most biologically and economically important ecosystems. Although they cover only about one-tenth of 1 percent of the ocean floor, they serve as shelters or feeding grounds for more than 4,000 species of fish, plus other organisms such as sponges, worms and algae.[43]

Fish Harvest Soars

The quantity of fish produced from the world's oceans rose 62 percent between 1980 and 2012, to 104.4 million metric tons.* Scientists say overfishing threatens the health of the seas.

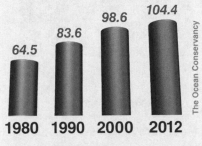

Ocean Fish Production, 1980-2012
(in millions of metric tons)

The Ocean Conservancy

* A metric ton equals 1.1 tons.

Source: "Overview: Major Trends and Issues," Food and Agriculture Organization, United Nations, 2014, p. xxii, http://tinyurl.com/lzftwbs

Scientists have developed anti-cancer and antiviral drugs based on substances produced by coral reef species and are researching other products.[44]

Reefs also serve as physical barriers that protect shorelines against storm surges and flooding. According to one estimate, coral reefs provide ecological services (including recreation, fishing, and biodiversity) worth up to $30 billion yearly.[45]

Worldwide, about 30 million people depend on coral reefs for their livelihoods or live on coral atolls. Another 500 million get some benefits from coral reefs, including income from fishing and tourism.[46]

Since the 1990s climate change studies have shown that the world's oceans are warming and becoming more acidic.[47] Acidification occurs when the oceans absorb carbon dioxide (CO_2), the most common greenhouse gas that comes from human activities. This process also reduces levels of calcium carbonate minerals in the water, used by corals, shellfish and other marine organisms to make their shells and skeletons.[48]

Many scientists and environmentalists argue that unless national governments act soon to reduce the greenhouse gas emissions that drive climate change,* the warmer, more acidic ocean waters could kill many of the world's coral reefs by the end of this century. But others contend that the most important stresses on reefs are local threats, especially overfishing and pollution.

Researchers are using climate models to estimate how corals will be affected if warming continues on its current path. A 2013 study projected that ocean waters

---

* The most prevalent planet-warming greenhouse gases are carbon dioxide, methane and nitrous oxide.

What Is Coral Reef Bleaching?

Rising ocean temperatures can cause "bleaching" of coral. When temperatures rise, corals expel tiny algae that live within their tissues and provide the corals with food — and their vivid colors. When the algae are insert image expelled, the corals begin to starve and turn white.

Coral reefs — shallow undersea ridges made of rock, sand and colonies of coral and other marine life that form an interdependent ecosystem — can recover from occasional bleaching. But repeated episodes can weaken or kill corals. Bleaching has killed portions of Australia's Great Barrier Reef and the Florida Reef, the largest living coral reef in the continental United States at nearly 150 miles long and about 4 miles wide, located along the Atlantic side of the Florida Keys.

Healthy corals are animals that live close together in colonies of thousands of polyps that produce a calcium carbonate skeleton resembling rock. They have a symbiotic relationship with the algae, called zooxanthellae, which live in the soft tissue of the coral polyps and use sunlight to produce food through photosynthesis. The zooxanthellae provide the corals with food, and the corals provide the algae with shelter and nutrients.

When water temperatures rise, corals expel the zooxanthellae and begin to die. Corals can heal if temperatures return to normal levels, but bleaching can affect corals' ability to reproduce and fight off disease.

When warm temperatures persist for more than eight weeks, coral reefs begin to die. If they survive, reefs damaged by bleaching may need decades to recover.

Source: "Coral bleaching," Great Barrier Reef Marine Park Authority, undated, http://tinyurl.com/knacyuq; "What is coral bleaching?" National Oceanic and Atmospheric Administration, U.S. Department of Commerce, updated March 5, 2014, http://tinyurl.com/bqm66yu; "Welcome to Corals," National Oceanic and Atmospheric Administration, U.S. Department of Commerce, Jan. 26, 2005, http://tinyurl.com/l8jl2jz

would be warm enough to create bleaching conditions yearly for 74 percent of the world's reefs by 2045, and for all corals by 2056.[49] Bleaching occurs when water temperatures rise: coral polyps expel tiny algae that live within their tissues and provide part of the corals' food supply. The algae give corals their color, so when they are expelled reefs turn white. Reefs can recover from bleaching, but these episodes weaken corals, and can eventually kill them.

"When bleaching happens frequently, corals will be compromised after the first year," says Andrea Grottoli, a biogeochemist at Ohio State University.

Another recent study calculated that if global carbon emissions were not reduced, ocean water would be more acidic by 2100 than at any time in the pre-industrial era.[50] "We can't say with 100 percent certainty that all shallow-water coral reefs will die, but it is a pretty good bet," said Katharine Ricke, a postdoctoral fellow in global ecology at the Carnegie Institution in Washington, D.C., and co-author of the study.[51]

But other experts say the damage to coral reefs caused by humans now is more urgent than the longer-range harm that could be caused by climate change. "Corals are already under huge stress from overfishing," says Harvard's Schrag. "Acidification sounds scary, but overfishing and pollution are destroying reefs already. If we care about reefs, we should address those issues."

In July the Global Coral Reef Monitoring Network published a study showing that the total coral area in 90 reefs in 34 Caribbean countries had declined by more than 50 percent since 1970. However, in countries such as Bermuda and Bonaire, where governments had strictly limited fishing, coastal development and tourism, much less coral had been lost than in countries that had not regulated such threats. Moreover, the healthier reefs were less seriously damaged by hurricanes and bleaching episodes than reefs degraded by overfishing and water pollution, the study found.[52]

The report highlighted the importance of parrotfish and other plant-eating species that "graze" on reefs, eating seaweed and large algae that otherwise can smother coral. Overfishing removes those species. Pollution — including sewage discharges, farm runoff and sediments from dredging and construction — clouds coastal waters, blocking the sunlight that corals need to grow.

These dangers are at issue in Australia, where activists are fighting plans to expand a coal port near the 1,400-mile Great Barrier Reef. Under public pressure, the government recently reversed its decision to allow dredged mud and rock from the port expansion to be dumped into the ocean next to the reef. Instead, the material will be deposited on land.

But critics say other port activities, including ship traffic and dust blowing into the ocean from huge piles of coal at the harbor, will directly threaten the reef, which has lost half of its coral cover in the past 30 years. And burning more coal over the long term will make oceans warmer and more acidic, further damaging the reef.[53]

"We need to stop all forms of overfishing, establish large and effectively enforced marine protected areas and impose strict regulations on coastal development and pollution, while . . . working to reduce fossil fuel emissions driving climate change," marine biologist Jeremy Jackson, lead author of the report on Caribbean reefs, wrote in *The New York Times*. "It's not either/or. It's all of the above."[54]

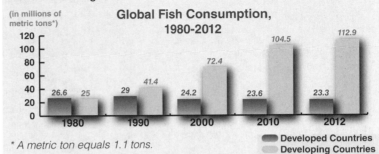

Developing Nations Drive Seafood Consumption

Fish consumption — from both ocean and inland sources — declined slightly in developed countries between 1980 and 2012 but more than quadrupled in developing nations, which consumed 83 percent of the world's fish caught in 2012.

Global Fish Consumption, 1980-2012 (in millions of metric tons*)

Year	Developed Countries	Developing Countries
1980	26.6	25
1990	29	41.4
2000	24.2	72.4
2010	23.6	104.5
2012	23.3	112.9

*A metric ton equals 1.1 tons.

Source: "Overview: Major Trends and Issues," Food and Agriculture Organization, United Nations, 2014, p. xxiii, ttp://tinyurl.com/lzftwbs

BACKGROUND
Industrial Fishing

Humans have relied on the oceans throughout history as sources of food and as routes for travel and trade. Before the industrial era, the impacts humans had on the oceans were local and relatively small. But starting in the 19th century, science and technology made it possible for humans to explore the oceans more widely — and to exploit them on ever-larger scales.

Whaling illustrates this trend. For thousands of years communities have hunted whales, which were abundant until a commercial whaling industry developed in the 19th century. In the 1860s Norwegian whalers introduced steam-powered boats equipped with deck cannons and harpoons that exploded on impact, enabling ships to range farther and kill whales more quickly and efficiently.[55]

Over the ensuing decades, steamships grew larger and more powerful. In 1904 10 Canadian whaling vessels operating from Newfoundland and Labrador killed 1,275 whales. But that rate could not be sustained: The harvest fell to 892 whales in 1905 and fewer than 500 in 1906. By 1916, with annual catch levels down to 100, the fishery temporarily shut down. It revived several times during the following decades, but the annual catch exceeded 500 only five times in more than 50 years.[56]

CHRONOLOGY

1900s-1950s *As fishing industry grows and becomes more industrialized, fish stocks decline.*

1905 First steam-powered trawler launched in Massachusetts.

1930 Inventor Clarence Birdseye begins selling quick-frozen seafood.

1946 Fifteen nations sign International Convention for the Regulation of Whaling.

1956 First container ship sails from Newark, N.J., to Houston.

1959 Twelve nations sign the Antarctic Treaty, agreeing to protect the region for peaceful scientific research.

1960s-1970s *Environmentalists in U.S. and Europe press for stronger water pollution controls and regulation of fishing and whaling.*

1964 Woods Hole Oceanographic Institution commissions *Alvin*, a submersible for deep ocean exploration.

1972 Congress passes Clean Water Act, Marine Mammal Protection Act and Coastal Zone Management Act.

1973 Fifteen nations adopt International Convention for the Prevention of Pollution from Ships. The treaty enters into force in 1983 and is later expanded to cover other pollution from ships, including sewage, garbage and air emissions.

1974 Louisiana State University scientists identify large dead zone in the Gulf of Mexico, caused by Mississippi River nutrient pollution.

1976 Congress passes Magnuson-Stevens Act, excluding foreign fishing within a 200-mile exclusive economic zone.

1977 Scientists discover unexpected life forms around hydrothermal vents on the ocean floor.

1980s-1990s *Nations protect some fisheries, but others remain under pressure. Overfishing and development cause widespread damage to Caribbean coral reefs.*

1980 Concerned about unregulated krill fishing, 25 nations adopt the Convention for the Conservation of Antarctic Marine Living Resources, pledging to manage fish in the region sustainably.

1981 United Nations designates Australia's Great Barrier Reef as a World Heritage Site in recognition of its natural beauty and ecological importance.

1982 Convention on the Law of the Sea becomes first international treaty to regulate navigation, territorial limits and uses of marine resources in international waters.

1992 Canada shuts its cod fishery after over-harvesting decimates stocks.

1999 Marine Stewardship Council launches eco-labeling program for sustainable seafood.

2000s-Present *Scientists predict that climate change will drastically alter ocean life. Science-based catch limits improve some yields.*

2003 British scientists report that Caribbean corals have declined 80 percent over three decades.

2006 Congress amends Magnuson-Stevens Act to require science-based catch limits in all U.S. fisheries.

2010 *Deepwater Horizon* spill releases nearly 210 million gallons of oil into the Gulf of Mexico. . . . Census of Marine Life estimates the number of known marine species at 250,000.

2013 Scientists project that climate change could cause oceans to warm by up to 2 degrees Celsius (3.6 degrees Fahrenheit) by 2100 and weaken Atlantic Ocean circulation patterns, potentially altering global weather patterns.

2014 Obama administration allows seismic testing to map potential oil and gas reserves from Delaware to Florida. . . . U.S. adds 20 corals to Endangered Species List. . . . State Department hosts the latest in a string of international summits on the world's oceans; Secretary of State John Kerry urges world leaders to commit themselves to protecting oceans.

Up to the mid-20th century, most nations only claimed control over territorial water extending three nautical miles out from their coasts.[57] But since major fishing grounds lay in international waters, fishing nations competed intensely to exploit them. Engine power enabled ships to pull "otter trawls" — huge nets, held open by floats and anchored by rollers that are dragged across the ocean floor. Between the 1890s and 1920s motorized ships with otter trawls, which could haul in catches up to six times larger than sail-powered ships, became standard for European and U.S. fishing fleets.[58]

Another breakthrough came in 1925, when inventor Clarence Birdseye, founder of the General Seafoods Co. in Gloucester, Mass., developed a technique called flash-freezing, which preserved foods quickly without forming large ice crystals that ruined flavors and textures. The combination of flash-freezing and machines for filleting fish launched the frozen seafood industry. By the 1940s shipbuilders were producing "factory ships" that could process and freeze huge catches while still at sea.[59]

As bigger ships pulled in more fish, yields began to decline. In one striking case, the sardine fishery off Monterey, Calif., collapsed: Catches fell from 250,000 tons in 1941 to 26,000 tons in 1946 and 49 tons in 1953.[60]

Early Conservation

Environmental groups in the 1960s and '70s protested widespread pollution and wasteful consumption. In the United States, an offshore oil well blowout near Santa Barbara, Calif., in 1969 helped catalyze protests that led to the first Earth Day in April 1970. Congress enacted a string of environmental laws, including the Clean Water Act, the Marine Mammal Protection Act and the Coastal Zone Management Act.

At the time the global shipping industry was growing quickly, thanks to the development of container shipping in the mid-1950s. Standard-size containers could be moved seamlessly and efficiently among trucks, trains and ships, streamlining cargo handling. Specialized container ports developed in cities such as Hong Kong, Rotterdam and Los Angeles, while other, smaller ports fell into disuse.

As global shipping traffic expanded, 15 nations adopted the International Convention for Prevention of Pollution from Ships, known as MARPOL, in 1973. The treaty initially covered pollution from oil, chemicals, sewage and garbage and would later be expanded to cover other pollution sources, such as air pollution from ships.

By the mid-1970s it was becoming clear that "factory ships" were depleting many valuable fish stocks worldwide. In 1976 Congress enacted the Magnuson-Stevens Act, which laid claim to an Exclusive Economic Zone extending 200 miles from U.S. coastlines. It also created a system of regional fishery management councils, charged with preventing overfishing. However, it did not require the councils to set catch limits or use scientific methods to determine how many fish could be harvested sustainably. As a result, many U.S. fisheries were depleted over the following decades, including New England cod and yellowtail flounder, Gulf of Mexico red snapper and Pacific Coast swordfish.[61]

Ocean science also grew rapidly in the 1960s and '70s. In 1964 the Woods Hole Oceanographic Institution in Massachusetts commissioned *Alvin*, the first manned submersible vehicle developed for underwater exploration. Woods Hole scientists and other researchers used submersibles to explore deep waters, photograph the sea floor and collect rock samples.

A major breakthrough came in 1977, when researchers found hydrothermal vents between Ecuador and the Galapagos Islands, where seawater flowed down through cracks in the Earth's crust, was heated by hot magma in the planet's interior and then flowed upward back into the ocean. Around the vents scientists found previously unknown life forms, including huge clams, mussels and tube worms that fed on bacteria in the hot fluids pouring out of the vents.

"Isn't the deep ocean supposed to be like a desert?" one scientist asked a colleague. "Well, there's all these animals down here."[62]

Sounding Alarms

In 1980 international action to protect marine resources gained momentum when 25 nations signed the Convention for the Conservation of Antarctic Marine Living Resources. Antarctica was already governed as an international scientific preserve under the 1959 Antarctic Treaty, but Soviet and Japanese fishing fleets were harvesting krill (small shrimp-like creatures, used mainly for bait and fish feed) in the Southern Ocean, and other nations feared that this important fishery would be depleted. (Krill is the key prey species for many animals in the Antarctic, including

Scientists Still Measuring Effects of BP Oil Spill

Dire predictions during the spill may have been too pessimistic.

Four years after the *Deepwater Horizon* oil spill released nearly 210 million gallons of crude into the Gulf of Mexico, government agencies are still measuring how the spill affected Gulf Coast ecosystems.

Under the Oil Pollution Act governing federal responses to oil spills, federal and state agencies and Native American tribes must conduct a Natural Resource Damage Assessment (NRDA). The process, likely to last into 2015, requires many scientific studies to measure how the spill affected Gulf natural resources, from corals and deepwater organisms to marine mammals, seagrass beds and shorelines. The results will serve as a basis for a federal lawsuit under the Clean Water Act against oil company BP and other parties responsible for the spill and will be used to develop a Gulf restoration plan.

Few results have been released so far, and those that have provide only small pieces of a larger puzzle.[1] For example, one study found severe reductions in the number and diversity of organisms such as worms and tiny invertebrates living on the deep ocean floor within 9.3 square miles around the BP wellhead.[2] "The tremendous biodiversity of [tiny invertebrates] in the deep-sea area of the Gulf of Mexico we studied has been reduced dramatically," said Jeffrey Baguley, a University of Nevada biologist and co-author of the study.[3]

Another NRDA study, conducted in a laboratory, suggested that oil exposure may have harmed the Gulf's mahi-mahi-fishery by reducing juveniles' ability to find food and avoid prey.[4]

Scientists are also studying whether the oil spill exacerbated an ongoing die-off of dolphins in the Gulf. In February 2010 — two months before the *Deepwater Horizon* spill — the National Oceanic and Atmospheric Administration (NOAA) began receiving reports that unusual numbers of dolphins were stranding themselves on the shores of the northern Gulf of Mexico and in Lake Pontchartrain, immediately north of New Orleans.[5] Between Feb. 1 and April 20, 2010, the date of the spill, there were 114 such strandings recorded. Another 121 dolphins stranded between the oil spill and early November that year. Since then dolphins have been stranding at a higher rate — more than 1,000 in the past four years.[6]

NOAA is investigating whether the spill contributed to the higher rate of strandings or whether it is caused by other factors, such as bacterial infections found in a handful of dolphins. But large marine vertebrates "are very hard to assess," said Lori Schwacke, a senior NOAA scientist, "because they are long-lived and legally protected." The Marine Mammal Protection Act bars pursuing or otherwise disturbing marine mammals in the wild.

NOAA also is studying the health of dolphin groups that live near shore, especially in Louisiana's Barataria Bay, which was heavily oiled during the spill. Early data published in 2011 found significant health issues in the dolphins. For example, some had lung diseases, and others were underweight. But pending results from more recent studies suggest improvement in dolphin health in the area, Schwacke said.[7]

---

seals, whales, seabirds, fish and squid.) The treaty set international catch limits for krill, which initially were well above actual catch levels because few countries had the equipment to work in the difficult conditions of the Southern Ocean.[63]

Another important step toward international regulation came in 1982, when the United Nations adopted the U.N. Convention on the Law of the Sea (UNCLOS), the first international treaty to regulate navigation, territorial limits

and the development of marine resources in international waters. The United States and many other industrialized nations objected to provisions that restricted deep sea-bed mining. After UNCLOS was amended in 1994 to address these criticisms, most industrialized countries signed it, including Japan, Germany, Italy, the United Kingdom, China and Russia. However, the United States continued to reject the agreement, which conservatives argued gave too much power to international organizations.[64]

Until all the NRDA results are released, scientists and environmentalists will continue to debate the environmental impact of the spill. Some say dire predictions during the spill may have been too pessimistic. "There was a lot of damage to the Louisiana and Mississippi coastlines," says Jorge Brenner, associate director of marine science for the Texas chapter of The Nature Conservancy, an international conservation group. "But we have not seen a big decline in fisheries or devastation of critical habitats yet."

Like many environmental advocates, Brenner points out that the Gulf had suffered heavy damage from human activities before the BP spill. "The coastal environment has been deteriorating for a long time," he says. "Hardly any areas are pristine. You have to go to a coral reef several miles offshore to see intact zones."

For example, Louisiana's coastal marshes have been disappearing for decades because levees prevent the Mississippi River from spilling over and adding new sediments to build up the delta area. In addition, oil and gas companies have cut canals and installed pipelines throughout the marshes, which lets in salt water, killing freshwater marsh plants and causing erosion.[8]

BP already has paid $1 billion for early restoration projects along the Gulf Coast, such as rebuilding coastal marshes and restoring damaged beaches. Eventually, planners expect the NRDA process to yield more money in criminal penalties against BP and others.

"The question is whether we will seize that opportunity to fix the root problems that are degrading the Gulf, instead of just making quick fixes," says Brenner. "That's a political and social decision."

— *Jennifer Weeks*

---

[1] Ed Crooks, "Deepwater Horizon: Cleaning Up," *The Financial Times*, April 20, 2014, http://tinyurl.com/kbsr7p4.

Petty Officer 3rd Class Tom Atkeson/MCT/MCT via Getty Images

Fire boats battle a blaze on the Deepwater Horizon oil rig in the Gulf of Mexico on April 21, 2010, near New Orleans. Eleven crew members died in the disaster, which released 210 million gallons of oil into the Gulf.

[2] Paul A. Montagna, *et al.*, "Deep-Sea Benthic Footprint of the Deepwater Horizon Blowout," *PLoS One*, August 2013 (updated April 21, 2014), http://tinyurl.com/ke436lm.

[3] "Deep Sea Ecosystem May Take Decades to Recover from Deepwater Horizon Spill," *ScienceDaily*, Sept. 25, 2013, http://tinyurl.com/n24utv3.

[4] "Deepwater Horizon Crude Oil Impairs Swimming Performance of Juvenile Mahi-Mahi," *ScienceDaily*, June 11, 2014, http://tinyurl.com/lolxz9t.

[5] Lake Pontchartrain has brackish water (mixed salt and fresh water) and is connected to Mississippi Sound by two tidal passes that allow dolphins to enter the lake. For background, see Thomas J. Billitteri, "Offshore Drilling," *CQ Researcher*, June 25, 2010, pp. 553-580.

[6] "2010-2014 Cetacean Unusual Mortality Event in Northern Gulf of Mexico," *NOAA Fisheries*, updated Sept. 30, 2014, http://tinyurl.com/msbq4px.

[7] Comments were made at Society of Environmental Journalists conference, New Orleans, La., Sept. 6, 2014.

[8] See Nathaniel Rich, "The Most Ambitious Environmental Lawsuit Ever," *The New York Times Magazine*, Oct. 5, 2014, http://tinyurl.com/p4awbx8.

By the mid-1990s it was clear that many important global fisheries were under severe pressure. Canada's once-abundant North Atlantic cod fishery declined so sharply that the government closed it in 1992, hoping stocks would rebound. Two years later the New England Fishery Management Council closed 9,600 square kilometers (3,700 square miles) of fishing grounds on Georges Bank, a submerged plateau 70 miles off the Massachusetts coast, because the cod, haddock and yellowtail flounder stocks were dwindling.[65]

Uncertain Outlook

Steep declines in Atlantic cod and other historically abundant fish stocks prompted scientists to look more broadly at how humans were affecting the oceans. In 2003 two fisheries experts at Canada's Dalhousie University calculated that populations of large fish — such as tuna, swordfish, marlin, halibut and flounder — had fallen by 90 percent since 1950.

Great Whites Returning to Cape Cod

Crowds are coming to see the sharks, not to hunt them.

Curious tourists have been flocking to Chatham, Mass., a Cape Cod fishing village, to catch a glimpse of one of the world's most feared predators: the notorious great white shark, among the world's largest shark species and one of the few known to attack humans.

Experts say a burgeoning population of gray seals on rocks, islands and sandbars around the Cape, boosted by a decades-long conservation effort, has attracted great whites, which prey on the seals. Shark sightings off the coast of the Cape rose from four in 2004 to 21 in 2012.[1]

"Gray seals are big and have lots of blubber," says Greg Skomal, a senior fisheries biologist with the Massachusetts Department of Fish and Game and head of the state's shark research program. "So they are the main species that sharks target" in this area, he says. "We expected that we'd see more sharks as seal numbers climbed."

The northeastern United States had robust seal populations for centuries, "until we started hunting them in the 1700s and 1800s," Skomal explains. But since the Marine Mammal Protection Act was adopted in 1972, their numbers have risen, and "they are recolonizing areas where they used to live," he says.

Today fishermen routinely see thousands of seals along the eastern coast of Cape Cod. Last year federal scientists estimated that about 16,000 seals lived around the Cape and the neighboring islands of Nantucket and Martha's Vineyard.[2] No firm population count exists for great white sharks in the area because they range widely, often migrating in the winter from New England to South Carolina or Florida.[3]

The great whites have fascinated — and frightened — beachgoers, swimmers and boaters, especially after the 1975 thriller "Jaws" portrayed a New England town terrorized by a great white shark that kills several people and attacks a boat carrying shark hunters. In 2012 a great white bit a swimmer on the leg in the first confirmed shark attack on a human at the Cape since 1936. Beaches along the Massachusetts coast have been closed several times since 2012 after sharks were spotted offshore.[4]

Nonetheless, many tourists in Cape Cod today are excited by the chance to see sharks, not to hunt them. "In Chatham now, [if] you yell 'shark!' in the middle of town, people come running to the beach, not away from it," said Kevin McLain, executive director of the town's restored movie theater, which shows "Jaws" twice daily in the summer.[5]

"I give a lot of public talks about shark research, and no one is coming up to me and complaining about the return of sharks to the Cape," says Skomal. Increased sightings also have aided researchers, who placed tags and transmitters on 34 great whites between 2009 and 2012. The devices are providing data about the sharks' feeding patterns, preferred habitat and migration routes along the Atlantic Coast.[6]

"[I]ndustrial fishing has scoured the global ocean. There is no blue frontier left," said fisheries biologist Ransom Myers, lead author of the study.[66]

Another study that year reported that coral reefs across the Caribbean had shrunk by an average of 80 percent over the past three decades. The authors did not find convincing evidence that climate change had caused reefs to die back. Rather, they concluded, some combination of natural factors (such a storms and disease) as well as human activities such as overfishing and pollution were the most likely causes.[67]

Two expert commissions — one mandated by Congress, the other privately funded — issued reports in 2003 and 2004 underlining the message that the world's oceans were under heavy stress.[68] In response Congress revised the Magnuson-Stevens Act to require regional fishery management councils to establish annual catch limits, based on recommendations from scientific advisers. By 2012 two dozen important U.S. fisheries were rebounding, including Gulf of Mexico red snapper, New England yellowtail flounder and Pacific coho salmon.[69]

Other problems persisted, however, not the least of which were the dead zones that formed in the Gulf of Mexico and Chesapeake Bay every summer, as well as in many smaller water bodies. In the Chesapeake, states made some progress reducing nutrient pollution from

In Skomal's view, public education is helping to show that while sharks are powerful predators, in fact many shark species are threatened or endangered, due mainly to commercial fishing. Millions of sharks are killed every year, often for shark fin soup, a delicacy in Asia. "There are negative feelings toward the seals, but not much toward sharks. We have much better communication about sharks today, and it's changing attitudes," says Skomal.

Many Cape Cod fishermen dislike the seals because they prey on fish, including popular types such as cod, whose stocks are already declining.[7] Some have called for controlled hunts, known as culling, to reduce the seal population. But that would require Congress to amend the Marine Mammal Protection Act, a step environmental advocates and scientists say is unlikely.

"Most of the fishermen who want culling grew up during a time when there were no seals around, and they see culling as a way to get back to that time," says Skomal. "But that would require killing massive numbers of animals, and there's no way that Congress would allow that kind of action, or that the public would tolerate it."

— *Jennifer Weeks*

A great white shark swims off the Massachusetts coast, near Chatham. Sightings of great whites, which are attracted to Cape Cod by a growing gray seal population, rose from four in 2004 to 21 in 2012.

Wendy Maeda/The Boston Globe via Getty Images

[1] Paul Starobin, "The Seal Problem," *Boston Magazine*, July 2013, http://tinyurl.com/pxf693x.

[2] *Ibid.*

[3] "White Shark Research," Massachusetts Office of Energy and Environmental Affairs, (undated), http://tinyurl.com/qdsjsog.

[4] Matthew DeLuca, "Shark sighting Shuts Down Cape Cod Beach as Summer Heats Up," NBC News, June 11, 2013, http://tinyurl.com/nyye6tm; Conor Berry, "Massachusetts DCR: Shark Sightings Close South Coast Beaches in Westport and Dartmouth," *MassLive.com*, Aug. 8, 2013, http://tinyurl.com/nqhoqas.

[5] Katharine Q. Seelye, "They're Going to Need a Bigger Gift Shop," *The New York Times*, July 27, 2014, http://tinyurl.com/qdg7ce2.

[6] "White Shark Research," *op. cit.*

[7] Patrick Whittle, "As Gray Seal Populations Boom, So Do Conflicts, As Residents Decry Those They Once Protected," The Associated Press, July 20, 2014 (updated Sept. 19, 2014), http://tinyurl.com/ox8mh4f; Alana Semuels, "Cape Cod's Namesake Fish Population Rapidly Disappearing," *Los Angeles Times*, Aug. 30, 2014, http://tinyurl.com/kjo36c6.

sources such as wastewater treatment plants, but struggled to curb nutrient runoff from farms. Finally, in 2010 states around the bay asked the EPA to write a Total Maximum Daily Load plan for the bay's entire watershed by 2025, covering some 64,000 square miles. The plan mandated that by 2025 each state reduce the amount of nitrogen it released into the bay by 25 percent and the amount of phosphorus by 24 percent.[70]

President Barack Obama, who campaigned as an advocate for the environment, has taken a number of steps to protect ocean resources. As recommended by the national ocean commissions in 2003-2004, Obama set up a National Ocean Council at the White House and issued a national ocean policy, designed to reduce bureaucratic conflicts among the many federal agencies with overlapping responsibilities for ocean issues.[71]

During his first term, Obama also pressed Congress to pass national limits on greenhouse gas emissions to slow global climate change. After that effort failed, his administration worked to cut U.S. emissions through measures that did not require congressional approval, such as setting carbon dioxide emission limits for coal-fired power plants.[72]

But some of Obama's other actions have angered ocean advocates, particularly his April 2010 proposal to expand offshore drilling in federal waters as part of a broad energy

Fresh tuna is sold in General Santos, the southernmost city in the Philippines, on May 21, 2014. Fisheries experts at Canada's Dalhousie University calculated in 2003 that populations of large fish — such as tuna, swordfish, marlin and halibut — had fallen by 90 percent since 1950 because of industrial-scale fishing. President Obama recently expanded the 87,000-square-mile Pacific Remote Islands Marine National Monument to nearly 500,000 square miles, barring all commercial fishing in the area.

and climate change strategy. "It turns out, by the way, that oil rigs today generally don't cause spills. They are technologically very advanced," Obama said on April 2.[73] Less than a month later, a blowout and fire on the *Deepwater Horizon* drilling rig killed 11 crew members and spilled nearly 210 million gallons of oil into the Gulf of Mexico.

After the *Deepwater Horizon* spill, the Obama administration stepped up Interior Department oversight of offshore energy production. But conservation advocates were dismayed when the new agency, renamed the Bureau of Ocean Energy Management, Regulation and Enforcement, allowed Shell to carry out exploratory drilling in waters off Alaska's Arctic coast — a much more challenging location than the heavily developed Gulf of Mexico. Shell ran into operating problems, including weather delays and a drilling rig that ran aground in late 2012 — proving, critics said, that oil companies were not ready to operate in the harsh Arctic environment.[74]

CURRENT SITUATION
Climate Change

Several major reports warn that climate change is already altering conditions in the oceans, and that those effects will intensify in the coming decades.

The Intergovernmental Panel on Climate Change (IPCC) released its fifth major assessment of climate change science in 2013 and 2014. It found that worldwide, the upper 75 meters (250 feet) of the ocean warmed by about 0.11 degrees Celsius (0.2 degrees Fahrenheit) per decade from 1971 through 2010.[75] By the end of this century, the report projected that the ocean would warm by an additional 0.6 degrees Celsius (1 degree Fahrenheit) and that heat would penetrate to the deep levels of the ocean and weaken the Atlantic Meridional Overturning Circulation (AMOC), a major current that carries warm water northward and cold water southward.[76] Weakening the AMOC could alter weather and climate patterns, possibly causing some cooling over Europe, although this effect would probably be offset by further warming of Earth's atmosphere.[77]

This year the U.S. Global Change Research Program released a report showing that surface waters are 30 percent more acidic now than they were before the industrial era, and are acidifying roughly 50 times faster than at any time in history. As a result, within the next 50 years shellfish, corals and other marine organisms that form shells will become stressed due to acidification in large areas of the Pacific Coast, the Bering Sea and the western Arctic Ocean.[78]

"We expect the surface of the ocean to warm faster than the deeper water, but we don't know yet how quickly those layers will mix," says Harvard's Schrag. Ocean mixing happens when winds blow across the ocean, pushing surface water away, and colder water rises up in its place. This process brings nutrients to the surface, "fertilizing" plankton, which are the base of ocean food chains.[79]

Much will depend on how rapidly oceans warm, according to Schrag. For comparison, he points to an episode called the Paleocene-Eocene Thermal Maximum, which occurred about 55 million years ago when unknown factors triggered the release of massive quantities of carbon into the ocean and atmosphere over a period of several thousand years.[80]

"We think CO_2 levels roughly tripled and global temperatures rose by about 6 degrees Celsius, which is comparable to what could happen in the next couple of centuries," says Schrag. "A lot of organisms flourished during that time, but that doesn't mean climate change will be good for biodiversity. Warming is happening much faster today, so life has less time to adapt. And

AT ISSUE

Should the United States open new areas to offshore drilling?

YES — Andy Radford
Senior Policy Adviser, American Petroleum Institute

Excerpted from remarks to the press on June 13, 2014

NO — Gov. Deval Patrick
D-Massachusetts

Excerpted from comments to the Department of Interior on the 2017-2022 Outer Continental Shelf Oil and Gas Leasing Program, Aug. 20, 2014

The United States has a long and successful history of producing oil and natural gas offshore, but the federal government has largely chosen to restrict activity to the western and central Gulf of Mexico and select areas in Alaska. These restrictions keep 87 percent of federal offshore waters locked away — along with the potential to develop the vast energy resources they contain.

The Interior Department will soon begin . . . developing the government's next five year plan for offshore lease sales, which will take effect in 2017. Decisions made now, . . . will have impacts well into the future.

Knowing this, the department should thoroughly analyze the resource-rich areas of interest throughout the entire U.S. Outer Continental Shelf and draft an expansive leasing plan that maintains current leasing areas and seeks to unlock new areas that are currently off-limits, such as the Atlantic and the eastern Gulf of Mexico.

. . . Including these areas in the next leasing plan would send a signal to the markets and to the world that America's oil and natural gas renaissance is here to stay.

Accessing this bounty is also safer now than ever before. In the last four years, the oil and natural gas industry has worked both independently and with regulators to enhance the safety of offshore operations. As the co-chairs of the [National Commission on the BP Deepwater Horizon Oil Spill and Offshore Drilling] recently said, offshore development is safer today because industry and the government have enhanced spill prevention, containment and response, revised existing standards and regulations and created new ones and worked hard to foster a strong industry safety culture.

The Center for Offshore Safety in Houston continues to work with companies and the regulators to ingrain safety culture even more deeply into day-to-day operations. And if an incident does occur, state-of-the-art well containment technology can now be rapidly deployed from strategically placed locations.

. . . America's oil and natural gas renaissance has nurtured our economy with good jobs, affordable energy and stable prices, but if we want these benefits to last for the long term, we cannot afford to make short-sighted decisions about our energy future.

The U.S. has an unprecedented opportunity to be the global leader in energy for decades to come, but [that] will take leadership and foresight from those in government who hold the key to accessing our offshore energy reserves.

Put simply: the search for and extraction of additional fossil fuels off our coast is inconsistent with Massachusetts' and the Northeast region's policy directions, our binding commitments to greenhouse gas reductions and our leadership in addressing climate change. . . .

Since 2009, my administration has been working closely with [the Bureau of Ocean Energy Management] . . . on the planning, siting and analysis of offshore wind in two areas south of Martha's Vineyard. . . . The National Renewable Energy Laboratory estimates that these areas have the potential to generate more than 5,000 megawatts of clean, renewable wind energy — enough . . . to power the majority of homes in Massachusetts. . . . Our focus is on continuing this nation-leading work, and any potential exploration or development plans for oil and gas will present a significant distraction and curtail progress for an emerging offshore wind industry at a time when the U.S. is far behind many other nations.

Finally, . . . the waters of the Outer Continental Shelf off Massachusetts contain rich natural resources and important marine ecosystems and habitats that warrant strong protections. The potential impacts from oil and gas development and the calamitous effects of spills cannot justify the risk of moving forward with this industrial activity in the North Atlantic. The scallop and groundfish fisheries . . . around Georges Bank are regarded as the most commercially important fisheries on the Atlantic coast and are critically important to the economies and social fabric of many coastal communities. The scallop fishery off Georges Bank has contributed several billion dollars to the Massachusetts and northeast regional economy in the last decade. . . .

Some of these fish stocks are under great stress. . . . Further impact to the fishery would be devastating to an industry which has already seen enormous cutbacks resulting from federal catch limitations intended to rebuild the fishery. These ocean waters also contain critically important habitat for endangered whales, sea turtles and marine birds.

In summary, Massachusetts does not consider the exploration or extraction of oil and gas off our coast as necessary for the Commonwealth's, the Northeast region's or the nation's energy future or in the best interest of the same. Instead, we need to be focusing our energies and efforts and committing national leadership to a sustainable energy future.

Sanjit Das/Bloomberg via Getty Images

Fishing nets dry atop boats in Puducherry, India, on July 19, 2014. Rising global population, notably in India and China, will put additional stress on ocean fish stocks. At the State Department's "Our Ocean" conference last June, the United States and other nations pledged new efforts to protect the oceans, including ending overfishing by 2020, reducing nutrient pollution by 20 percent by 2025 and cutting carbon emissions to reduce ocean acidification.

when ice disappears, organisms adapted to living on it have no place to go."

New Discoveries

Researchers continue to discover new ocean life forms. From 2000 through 2010, more than 2,700 scientists from 80 nations participated in the Census of Marine Life, which sought to measure the abundance and diversity of marine life. They estimated that the ocean contains nearly 250,000 known species (up from 230,000 before the census), including 1,200 identified during the census. Microbes accounted for 90 percent of the total mass of life in the ocean — the equivalent of 35 elephants for each person on Earth.[81]

Many questions about basic aspects of ocean life have yet to be answered, especially for species living in deep waters far from coasts. Earlier this year an international team published a study that combined acoustic data from a research ship with computer modeling to estimate how many fish live in the mesopelagic zone, between 200 and 1,000 meters deep (656 to 3,280 feet) — an area sometimes called the sea's twilight zone because very little sunlight penetrates to that depth. Previously, scientists thought that about a billion tons of small fish lived in this zone. But the new study calculated that about 10 times as many fish live there, making mesopelagic fish the most abundant vertebrates on Earth.[82]

"We know embarrassingly little about these zones," says Simon Thorrold, a senior scientist at the Woods Hole Oceanographic Institution. "We are a long way from understanding how the open ocean functions, especially where most marine life spends a lot of time in deep water. It's critical to understand food webs and how large predators move through those areas, so we can develop effective conservation strategies."

Thorrold and other Woods Hole scientists attach pop-up tags to large open-ocean species such as sharks and devil rays to track their movements. Eventually, the tags pop loose, float to the surface and transmit data to the scientists via satellites. Recently they have found a previously unknown site where whale sharks gather in the Red Sea and documented that devil rays in the North Atlantic dive to depths of nearly two kilometers (1.2 miles), presumably to feed.

"There's not much point in creating a conservation strategy that focuses on one geographic area if the species has a much larger range," Thorrald says.

New Pledges

At the State Department's "Our Ocean" conference last June, the United States and other countries announced initiatives and partnerships to protect ocean resources, valued at a total of more than $1.8 billion. Notably:

- The United States announced a new program to improve seafood transparency and traceability, enabling consumers to verify how their seafood is raised or harvested;
- Norway pledged to spend $150 million to improve global fisheries management;
- Togo announced a new agreement with the governments of Benin, Ghana and Nigeria to combat illegal fishing in West African waters;
- The Global Environment Facility, an independent international agency, committed $460 million for programs to protect marine biodiversity and improve management of fisheries and coastal resources; and
- The U.S. Agency for International Development said it would provide more than $170 million for marine conservation, sustainable fisheries, coastal adaptation to climate change and controls on illegal fishing in developing countries.[83]

The conference set new ocean conservation goals, including ending overfishing of all marine stocks by 2020; reducing total nutrient pollution in marine areas by 20 percent by 2025 to reduce dead zones and harmful algal blooms; cutting carbon emissions to slow ocean acidification; and conserving at least 10 percent of coastal and marine areas as marine reserves by 2020.[84]

"[T]here is nothing that we're looking at that doesn't have a solution — acidification, nitrate overload, dead zones," said Secretary of State Kerry. "We have to change the politics . . . and start to make the decisions that put the money into enforcement, into science, into all the things that can actually save the oceans."[85]

Chile agreed to host a follow-on conference in 2015.

OUTLOOK

Tipping Points?

As scientists produce increasingly detailed assessments of climate change, some studies are starting to discuss the possibility that continued warming could push Earth's climate to "tipping points," in which ecosystems or parts of Earth's intricate climate system are radically altered or runaway damage occurs. In the oceans, those potential tipping points include widespread collapses of coral reefs or abrupt changes in ocean circulation patterns.

Such changes could cause severe harm, such as loss of important food sources for millions of people or abrupt warming or cooling in heavily populated areas. And instead of taking place over centuries, these changes might occur within much shorter time frames, making it very difficult for societies to adapt to them.[86]

Ocean experts say there is still time to prevent human actions from irreparably damaging the oceans — if societies act now. "We haven't lost a wild ocean yet, but we're getting close," says the Woods Hole Oceanographic Institution's Thorrold. "We need to conserve enough open ocean environments to sustain important populations of large apex predators like sharks and rays. The next 20 years will determine what the ocean looks like in 100 years." Eliminating apex predators — those at the top of the food chain — allows other species to multiply and potentially unbalance ecosystems.[87]

The EPA's Gilinsky is optimistic that nutrient pollution can be curbed. "I think we're going to make great strides in the next decade, because the public, local governments,

agriculture and industry are paying attention," she says. "They know what the important sources are and are looking for ways to reduce them. We have the techniques."

However, she notes, the problem will not disappear. "More development will mean more runoff and more water treatments plants, so it's a balance between pollution control and population growth," she says. According to some projections, world population (which until recently was expected to level off between 2050 and 2100 at roughly 9 billion people) could continue to grow through 2100 to 11 billion people or more.[88]

Similarly, Harvard's Schrag emphasizes that oceans are resilient. "The oceans have an amazing way of recovering when we reduce our impacts," he says. "In some ways, it's harder to eradicate life in oceans because things move around. Migration is easier [in the oceans], so for certain species there is more potential for adaptation than on land."

At the same time, Schrag does not minimize the effects of climate change. "Fish are migrating to higher latitudes. For example, Long Island's lobster fishery has already collapsed," he says. "Ocean warming has already been dramatic, and it's going to get a lot warmer before it's done."

NOTES

1. Greg Dugal, "Maine's Tourism Economy: The Numbers Don't Lie," *The Working Waterfront*, June 18, 2014, http://tinyurl.com/lxotl4n.

2. "Lobster Management in Maine," Maine Lobster Marketing Collaborative, (undated), http://tinyurl.com/kfhlfv3; Bill Trotter, "International Council Certifies Maine Lobster Fishery as Sustainable," *Bangor Daily News*, March 10, 2013, http://tinyurl.com/kpzb3ve. For information on the Marine Stewardship Council, see www.msc.org/.

3. David Abel, "In Maine, Scientists See Signs of Climate Change," *The Boston Globe*, Sept. 21, 2014, http://tinyurl.com/k22qyat.

4. "Report Highlights Growing Role of Fish in Feeding the World," U.N. Food and Agriculture Organization, May 19, 2014, http://tinyurl.com/l2vd896.

5. For background see Robert Kiener, "Plastic Pollution," *CQ Global Researcher*, July 2010, pp. 157-184; and Fiona Harvey, "Pollution Triples Mercury Levels in Ocean Surface Waters, Study

Finds," *The Guardian*, Aug. 6, 2014, http://tinyurl .com/q8ru2dx.

6. Sylvia Earle, " 'Mission Blue' Warning: The Ocean Is Not Too Big to Fail," *The Daily Beast*, Aug. 15, 2014, http://tinyurl.com/k49ovxz.

7. Steve Connor, "The Dead Sea: Global Warming Blamed for 40 Percent Decline in the Ocean's Phytoplankton," *The Independent*, July 29, 2010, http://tinyurl.com/2frjttp; "Has Climate Change Caused a Drop-Off in a Food Source Crucial to Ocean Creatures?" The Associated Press, Nov. 25, 2013, http://tinyurl.com/mekb8on.

8. Earle, *op. cit.*

9. "Welcoming Remarks at Our Ocean Conference, U.S. Department of State, June 16, 2014, http:// tinyurl.com/k5oz77y.

10. Kevin Noone, Rashid Sumalia and Robert J. Diaz, eds., "Valuing the Ocean," Stockholm Environment Institute, 2012, pp. 9-11, http://tinyurl.com/p4y57pn.

11. Kevin M. Bailey, "An Empty Donut Hole: The Great Collapse of a North American Fishery," *Ecology and Society*, vol. 16, 2011, http://tinyurl.com/om9s7vy.

12. Aaron Beswick, "Cod Aren't Coming Back — Yet," *The Chronicle Herald* (Nova Scotia), April 26, 2013, http://tinyurl.com/ns2h758.

13. John Waldman, "How Norway and Russia Made a Cod Fishery Live and Thrive," *Yale Environment 360*, Sept. 18, 2014, http://tinyurl.com/pjsg7vs; "The Law That's Saving American Fisheries," Pew Charitable Trusts and the Ocean Conservancy (2013), http://tinyurl.com/oaqagr9.

14. Juliet Eilperin, "Obama to Create World's Largest Protected Marine Reserve in Pacific Ocean," *The Washington Post*, Sept. 25, 2014, http://tinyurl.com/ qdoqjvf.

15. "Opposition Mounts to Obama's Proposed Pacific Monument Expansion at Honolulu Town hall Listening Session," Western Pacific Regional Fishery Management Council, Aug. 25, 2014, http:// tinyurl.com/pql6ahh.

16. John Dyer, "Scallops Giving New Bedford Fishermen a Welcome Break," *The Boston Globe*, Dec. 1, 2013, http://tinyurl.com/qcl266h.

17. "South Atlantic Update," South Atlantic Fishery Management Council, Summer 2014, p. 2, http:// safmc.net/sites/default/files/newsletter/pdf/ Summer2014SAUpdateFinal.pdf.

18. "Opposition Mounts," *op. cit.*

19. Jennifer A. Dlouhy, "Seismic Rift: Obama Splits With Environmentalists on Atlantic Oil Exploration," *The Houston Chronicle*, July 18, 2014, http://tinyurl.com/o9jhg7u.

20. Helen Scales, "Atlantic Seismic Tests for Oil: Marine Animals at Risk?" *National Geographic News*, Feb. 28, 2014, http://tinyurl.com/jvvcm63.

21. "Marine Protected Areas," *National Geographic*, http://tinyurl.com/6mwcjlm.

22. Brian Clark Howard, "Pacific Nation Bans Fishing in One of World's Largest Marine Parks," *National Geographic News*, June 16, 2014, http://tinyurl.com/ mvfofsb.

23. For information see http://tinyurl.com/n9y2rdf.

24. Brian Clark Howard, "Several nations Announce Massive Marine Reserves in the Pacific," *National Geographic News*, June 17, 2014, http://tinyurl .com/myo53ha.

25. "Kerry on Sustainable Fishing, Marine Protected Areas," U.S. Department of State, Sept. 25, 2014, http://tinyurl.com/qx5g6od.

26. "Oceana Says EU Should Act Against True 'Walls of Death,' " *Oceana*, May 14, 2014, http://tinyurl. com/m2sdb95; "Illegal Driftnet Fishing Returns to Morocco," *World Fishing & Aquaculture*, June 18, 2014, http://tinyurl.com/nwtxdbe.

27. Brian Clark Howard, "For the U.S., A New Challenge: Keeping Poachers Out of Newly Expanded Marine Reserve in the Pacific," *National Geographic News*, Sept. 25, 2014, http://tinyurl.com/q7rc5b2.

28. Graham J. Edgar, *et al.*, "Global conservation Outcomes Depend on Marine Protected Areas with Five Key Features," *Nature*, Feb. 13, 2014, pp. 216-220, http://tinyurl.com/pdul93l.

29. Daniel Cressey, "Disappointment as Antarctic Protection Bid Fails," *Nature*, Nov. 1, 2012, http:// tinyurl.com/crvlc7y; "Antarctic Marine Reserves: Russia and China Block Plans," BBC News, Nov. 1, 2013, http://tinyurl.com/q78qdse.

30. "Antarctic Marine Reserve Bid Fails — Experts Respond," Science Media Centre (New Zealand), Nov. 1, 2013, http://tinyurl.com/m5tafmj.

31. "Ocean Hypoxia — 'Dead Zones,' " *Issue Brief*, United Nations Development Programme, May 2013, http://tinyurl.com/llvgsne.

32. "DeadZone Shows Bay's Pollution Problems," *The Virginian-Pilot*, Sept. 3, 2014, http://tinyurl.com/nqq9vlz.

33. "Chesapeake Bay Total Maximum Daily Load," *Fact Sheet*, Environmental Protection Agency, undated, http://tinyurl.com/ppotq4l.

34. "What is the Chesapeake Clean Water Blueprint?" Chesapeake Bay Foundation, http://tinyurl.com/pvovn6e.

35. Tim Wheeler, "EPA Finds Progress, Shortfalls in Bay Cleanup Efforts," *The Baltimore Sun*, June 27, 2014, http://tinyurl.com/qy7a347.

36. *American Farm Bureau Federation, et al., v. United States Environmental Protection Agency*, U.S. District Court for the Middle District of Pennsylvania, Sept. 13, 2013, http://tinyurl.com/p29bnh3.

37. *Amicus curiae brief, American Farm Bureau Federation vs. Environmental Protection Agency*, U.S. court of Appeals for the Third Circuit, Feb. 3, 2014, p. 1, http://tinyurl.com/mntfhss.

38. "What is hypoxia?" Louisiana Universities Marine Consortium, http://tinyurl.com/pvcj6tx.

39. For background see Colin Woodard, "Oceans in Crisis," *CQ Global Researcher*, October 2007, pp. 244-245.

40. "The Danube-Black Sea Cleanup Story," International Commission for Protection of the Danube River, January 2007, http://tinyurl.com/k272ram; "Joint Effort helps Restore Danube River and Black Sea Ecosystems," United Nations Development Programme, March 21, 2011, http://tinyurl.com/lkz66ro.

41. "The Black Sea Environment," Commission on the Protection of the Black Sea Against Pollution, http://tinyurl.com/ljmtgmp.

42. Comments at Society of Environmental Journalists conference, New Orleans, La., Sept. 5, 2014.

43. "Importance of Coral Reefs," National Oceanic and Atmospheric Administration, last updated March 25, 2008, http://tinyurl.com/crw39dy.

44. Andrew W. Bruckner, "Life-Saving Products From Coral Reefs," *Issues in Science and Technology*, Nov. 27, 2013, http://tinyurl.com/pafu7nc.

45. "Value of Coral Reef Ecosystems, National Oceanic and Atmospheric Administration, last updated May 13, 2011, http://tinyurl.com/mtz9fvg.

46. "How Many People Are Dependent on Coral Reefs?" National Oceanic and Atmospheric Administration, last updated May 13, 2011, http://tinyurl.com/pjsr6yg.

47. For background see Jennifer Weeks, "Climate Change," *CQ Researcher*, June 14, 2013, pp. 521-544.

48. "What is Ocean Acidification?" National Oceanic and Atmospheric Administration, http://tinyurl.com/3vrws5h.

49. "New Maps Depict Potential Worldwide Coral Bleaching by 2056," *ScienceDaily*, Feb. 25, 2013, http://tinyurl.com/ab5hcnd.

50. Katharine L. Ricke, *et al.*, "Risks to Coral Reefs from Ocean Carbonate Chemistry Changes in Recent Earth System Model Projections," *Environmental Research Letters*, 2013, http://tinyurl.com/oa2bynj.

51. "Major Changes Needed for Coral Reef Survival," Carnegie Institution, June 8, 2013, http://tinyurl.com/q2knvaa.

52. Jeremy Jackson, *et al.*, eds., "Status and Trends of Caribbean Coral Reefs: 1970-2012," Global Coral Reef Monitoring Network, 2014, http://tinyurl.com/kq262py.

53. Tim Flannery, "The Great Barrier Reef and the Coal Mine That Could Kill It," *The Guardian*, Aug. 1, 2014, http://tinyurl.com/p66uuw9; Rob Taylor, "Australia Rethinks Great Barrier Reef Dredging Plan," *The Wall Street Journal*, Sept. 2, 2014, http://tinyurl.com/pfvo5k2.

54. Jeremy Jackson and Ayana Elizabeth Johnson, "We Can Save the Caribbean's Coral Reefs," *The New York Times*, Sept. 18, 2014, http://tinyurl.com/keretqo.

55. "'Modern' Whaling, 1861-1987 — An Overview," New Bedford Whaling Museum, http://tinyurl.com/752c8hj.

56. "Commercial Whaling in Newfoundland and Labrador in the 20th Century," Newfoundland and Labrador Heritage, http://tinyurl.com/mucbmcd.

57. "History of the Maritime Zones Under International Law," National Oceanic and Atmospheric Administration, Office of Coast Survey, http://tinyurl.com/lasbf5x.

58. Mark Kurlansky, *Cod: A Biography of the Fish That Changed the World* (1997), pp. 131-132.

59. *Ibid.*, p. 139.

60. Stephen R. Palumbi and Carolyn Sotka, *The Death and Life of Monterey Bay* (2010), pp. 165, 180. Research decades later showed that Pacific waters cooled in the 1940s, driving sardine stocks southward, but overfishing was also a major cause of the collapse.

61. "The Law That's Saving American Fisheries: The Magnuson-Stevens Fishery Conservation and Management Act," Pew Charitable Trusts and Ocean Conservancy, 2013, p. 12, http://tinyurl.com/oaqagr9.

62. "The Discovery of Hydrothermal Vents," Woods Hole Oceanographic Institution, 2002, http://tinyurl.com/ocllokx.

63. Stephen Nicol, Jacqueline Foster and So Kawaguchi, "The fishery for Antarctic Krill — Recent Developments," *Fish and Fisheries*, 2011, pp. 1-2, http://tinyurl.com/qhdjx69.

64. For background see Jennifer Weeks, "Future of the Arctic," *CQ Researcher*, Sept. 20, 2013, pp. 794-795.

65. John H. Cushman, Jr., "Commercial-Fishing Halt Is Urged for Georges Bank," *The New York Times*, Oct. 27, 1994, http://tinyurl.com/6p4wr5d.

66. "Big-Fish Stocks Fall 90 Percent Since 1950, Study Says," *National Geographic News*, May 15, 2003, http://tinyurl.com/tlok.

67. Toby A. Gardner, *et al.*, "Long-Tem Region-Wide Declines in Caribbean Corals," *Science*, Aug. 15, 2003, pp. 958-960.

68. America's Living Oceans: Charting a Course for Sea Change, Pew Oceans Commission, 2003, http:// tinyurl.com/onep8df; "An Ocean Blueprint for the 21st Century," U.S. Commission on Ocean Policy, 2004, http://tinyurl.com/qjj6eeo.

69. "The Law That's Saving American Fisheries," *op. cit.*, pp. 20-21.

70. "EPA Establishes Landmark Chesapeake Bay 'Pollution Diet,' " U.S. Environmental Protection Agency, Dec. 29, 2010, http://tinyurl.com/l898ywb.

71. Juliet Eilperin, "National Ocean Policy Sparks Partisan Fight," *The Washington Post*, Oct. 28, 2012, http://tinyurl.com/peajx7f.

72. For details see Christina L. Lyons, "Climate Change," "Hot Topic," *CQ Researcher*, June 27, 2014.

73. "Remarks by the President in a Discussion on Jobs and the Economy in Charlotte, North Carolina," The White House, April 2, 2010, http://tinyurl.com/ybqa56c.

74. See Weeks, "Future of the Arctic," *op. cit.*, pp. 789-812.

75. "Climate Change 2013: The Physical Science Basis, Summary for Policymakers, Intergovernmental Panel on Climate Change," 2013, p. 8, http://tinyurl.com/l8w5g5l.

76. *Ibid.*, p. 24.

77. Fiona Harvey, "Climate Change Likely to Turn U.K.'s Weather More Extreme," *The Guardian*, Sept. 27, 2013, http://tinyurl.com/q4t76uk. For background see "Atlantic Meridional Overturning Circulation," *Encyclopedia of Earth*, http://tinyurl.com/nbsucxz.

78. "Climate Change Impacts in the United States," U.S. Global Change Research Program, 2014, pp. 48-49, http://tinyurl.com/nsboa5l.

79. "Ocean Facts: Upwelling," National Oceanic and Atmospheric Administration, revised Jan. 11, 2013, http://tinyurl.com/cjxoz2s.

80. For background see "Global Warming 55 Million Years Ago — Wyoming," Smithsonian Museum of Natural History, http://tinyurl.com/qaznbzg.

81. "Summary of the First Census of Marine Life," 2010, p. 2, http://tinyurl.com/5to32o5.

82. Xabier Irigoen, *et al.*, "Large Mesopelagic Fish Biomass and Trophic Efficiency in the Open Ocean," *Nature Communications*, Feb. 7, 2014,

http://tinyurl.com/pvt6mx9; Douglas Main, "There are 10 Times More Fish in the Sea Than We Thought," *Popular Science*, March 5, 2014, http://tinyurl.com/mule4lc.

83. "Our Ocean Initiatives," U.S. Department of State, June 17, 2014, http://tinyurl.com/pynkyf5.

84. "Our Ocean Action Plan: Sustainable Fisheries," U.S. Department of State, June 17, 2014, http://tinyurl.com/ofdwp2b.

85. "Opening the Next Steps Panel of Our Ocean Conference," U.S. Department of State, June 17, 2014, http://tinyurl.com/osneexb.

86. See "Abrupt Impacts of Climate Change: Anticipating Surprises," National Research Council, 2013, pp. 13-14.

87. "Loss of Top Animal Predators Has Massive Ecological Effects," *ScienceDaily*, July 14, 2011, http://tinyurl.com/3wd985j.

88. Robert Kunzig, "A World With 11 Billion People?" *National Geographic News*, Sept. 18, 2014, http://tinyurl.com/qbwosyw.

BIBLIOGRAPHY
Selected Sources
Books

Beatley, Timothy, *Blue Urbanism: Exploring Connections between Cities and Oceans*, Island Press, 2014.
The chair of the University of Virginia's Department of Urban and Environmental Planning argues that coastal cities have paid too little attention to oceans and should do more to engage residents with the marine world.

Greenberg, Paul, *American Catch: The Fight for Our Local Seafood*, Penguin Press, 2014.
An award-winning author explains why more than 90 percent of the seafood Americans eat is imported and examines three U.S. products: New York oysters, Louisiana brown shrimp and Alaskan sockeye salmon.

McCalman, Iain, *The Reef: A Passionate History: The Great Barrier Reef From Captain Cook to Climate Change*, Scientific American/Farrar, Strauss and Giroux, 2014.

A historian and explorer chronicles 20 humans' encounters with Australia's Great Barrier Reef over more than 200 years and explains how climate change threatens the reef today.

Weller, John, *The Last Ocean: Antarctica's Ross Sea Project: Saving the Most Pristine Ecosystem on Earth*, Rizzoli, 2013.
Written and illustrated by photographer Weller, this book argues that Antarctica's Ross Sea should be declared a marine protected area to shield it from overfishing.

Articles

Abel, David, "Gulf of Maine's Cod Stock Falling, Study Says," *The Boston Globe*, Aug. 2, 2014, http://tinyurl.com/lsbc5fe.
Federal regulators estimate that northern New England's once-abundant cod fishery has fallen to 3 or 4 percent of the number of fish required to sustain a healthy population.

Dropkin, Alex, "The Gulf's Red Snapper Fishery Makes a Comeback," *The Texas Observer*, Sept. 24, 2014, http://tinyurl.com/nth5f7q.
The Gulf of Mexico's once-depleted red snapper fishery is rebounding, thanks to individual quotas that let fishermen decide when to catch their share of the harvest.

Gillis, Justin, "In the Ocean, Clues to Change," *The New York Times*, Aug. 11, 2014, http://tinyurl.com/q83asey.
Scientists believe an apparent pause in global warming may have occurred because more heat is being absorbed by the deep oceans.

Helvarg, David, "California's New Parks under the Sea," *Alert Diver*, Summer 2014, http://tinyurl.com/kdodh5u.
California has designated 16 percent of its 1,100-mile coastline as marine reserves, but not without more than a decade of controversy.

Sayre, Katherine, "BP Carries Most Blame for Gulf of Mexico Oil Spill, Judge Rules," *NOLA.com/The Times-Picayune*, Sept. 4, 2014, http://tinyurl.com/mgxagm4.
A federal judge ruled that oil company BP's role in the 2010 Gulf of Mexico oil spill demonstrated "gross

negligence." The holding could quadruple BP's penalty under the Clean Water Act for each barrel of oil it released into the Gulf.

Seelye, Katharine Q., "They're Going to Need a Bigger Gift Shop," *The New York Times*, July 27, 2014, http://tinyurl.com/n8f9pcu.
Great white sharks have returned to Cape Cod, Mass., and visitors are flocking to see the sharks rather than to hunt them.

Welch, Craig, and Steve Ringman, "Sea Change: The Pacific's Perilous Turn," *Seattle Times*, 2013, http://tinyurl.com/loe9gu6.
An award-winning multimedia series chronicles how acidification is affecting corals, shellfish and other Pacific Ocean life forms.

Studies and Reports

"Climate Change 2014: Impacts, Adaptation, and Vulnerability," Intergovernmental Panel on Climate Change, 2014, http://tinyurl.com/nxk7lab.
The fifth report to governments by a scientific panel finds that climate change will have far-reaching effects on the world's coastal areas (chapter 5) and oceans (chapter 6), including warmer and more acidic ocean waters, more rapid growth of dead zones and increased coastal flooding.

Jackson, Jeremy, *et al.*, eds, "Status and Trends of Caribbean Coral Reefs: 1970-2012," Global Coral Reef Monitoring Network, 2014, http://tinyurl.com/kq262py.
A detailed study of Caribbean coral reefs finds that tourism and overfishing are responsible for much of the damage suffered in recent decades, and that protecting reefs against these stresses could make them more resistant to climate change.

Perez, Michelle, Sara Walker and Cy Jones, "Nutrient Trading in the MRB: A Feasibility Study for Using Large-Scale Intrastate Nutrient Trading in the Mississippi River Basin to Help Address Hypoxia in the Gulf of Mexico," World Resources Institute, 2013, http://tinyurl.com/mpf73g2.
An analysis by a Washington, D.C., think tank concludes that trading nutrient-reduction credits would be a cost-effective way to reduce the Gulf of Mexico dead zone.

For More Information

American Petroleum Institute, 1220 L St., N.W., Washington, DC 20005; 202-682-8000; www.api.org. Trade association representing the oil and gas industry on issues including offshore energy production.

National Oceanic and Atmospheric Administration, 1401 Constitution Ave., N.W., Washington, DC 20230; 202-482-6090; www.noaa.gov. An agency of the Department of Commerce that manages fisheries and is the lead U.S. agency for research on ocean and coastal issues.

Nature Conservancy, 4245 N. Fairfax Drive, Suite 100, Arlington, VA 22203; 703-841-5300; www.nature.org. Environmental advocacy group that works in the United States and more than 35 countries to protect habitats, including coral reefs.

Pew Charitable Trusts, One Commerce Square, 2005 Market St., Suite 2800, Philadelphia, PA 19103; 215-575-9050; www.pewtrusts.org. Nonprofit organization that conducts research and advocacy on a range of issues, including ocean conservation.

U.S. Environmental Protection Agency, Office of Water, 1200 Pennsylvania Ave., N.W., Washington, DC 20460; 202-272-0167; www2.epa.gov/aboutepa/about-office-water. Federal agency that regulates water quality, including nutrient pollution and other issues affecting oceans, coasts and estuaries.

Woods Hole Oceanographic Institution, 266 Woods Hole Rd., Woods Hole, MA 02543; 508-289-2252; www.whoi.edu. Renowned center for ocean science and exploration, founded in 1930; works to advance understanding of oceans and their interaction with other Earth systems.